G000295064

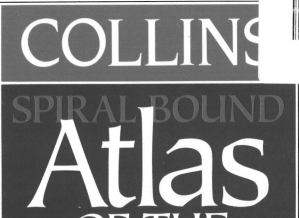

COLLINS

SPIRAL BOUND

Atlas
OF THE
WORLD

HarperCollins*Publishers*

Collins *Spiral Bound* Atlas of the World
First published 1993 by
HarperCollins*Publishers*
77-85 Fulham Palace Road
Hammersmith
London W6 8JB

Maps © HarperCollins*Publishers* and Collins-Longman Atlases
Illustrated section and statistics © HarperCollins*Publishers*

Produced by HarperCollins, Hong Kong

The contents of this edition of the Collins *Spiral Bound* Atlas of the World
are believed to be correct at the time of printing. Nevertheless,
the publishers can accept no responsibility for errors, or for omissions,
or for changes in detail given.

ISBN 0 00 448076 7

Foreword

This latest addition to the series of Collins World Atlases is derived from the popular Collins Paperback Atlas of the World and presents a comprehensive set of world maps accompanied by essential geographical data in a convenient and easy-to-use format.

WORLD DATA

This section presents, using an amalgamation of maps, diagrams and statistics, a clear picture of both the political and physical world. Nations of the World contains data on every independent country: population, area, form of government, capital city, languages and currency. This is supplemented by maps depicting such world themes as population growth and life expectancy. Comparisons in the size of continents, oceans, lakes and islands are illustrated in the section on the physical world which also includes details of mountain heights and river lengths. A world map showing World Time Zones concludes this section.

WORLD ATLAS

Map coverage extends to every part of the world in a balanced scheme that avoids any individual country or regional bias. Map areas are chosen to reflect the social, economic, cultural or historic importance of a particular region. Generous map overlaps are included to maintain continuity. Each of the continents is treated systematically in a subsection of its own. As an additional aid, a small key map is incorporated into the top margin of each single or double page map.

Map measurements give preference to the metric system. All spot heights and ocean depths are shown in metres and the relief and submarine layer delineation is based on metric contour levels. However, all linear scalebar and height reference column figures are given in metric and imperial equivalents. A full explanation of symbols used on the maps precedes the world atlas section.

Map place names have been selected in accordance with maintaining legibility at a given scale and at the same time striking an appropriate balance between natural and man-made features. Name forms have been standardized according to the widely accepted principle, now well established in international reference atlases, of including place names and geographical terms in the local language of the country in question. In the case of non-Roman scripts (e.g. Arabic), transliteration and transcription have either been based on the rules recommended by the United States Board on Geographical Names, or as in the case of the adopted Pinyin transcription of Chinese names, a system officially proposed by the country concerned. The diacritical signs used in each language or transliteration have been retained on all the maps and throughout the index. However the English language reader's requirements have also been recognised in that the names of all countries, oceans, major seas and land features as well as familiar alternative name versions of important towns are presented in English.

WORLD INDEX

Preceding the index is a comprehensive glossary which explains most of the foreign language and geographical terms which are to be found incorporated in the place names on the maps and in the index. The index lists alphabetically all individual place names to be found on the maps, which total about 20,000.

CONTENTS

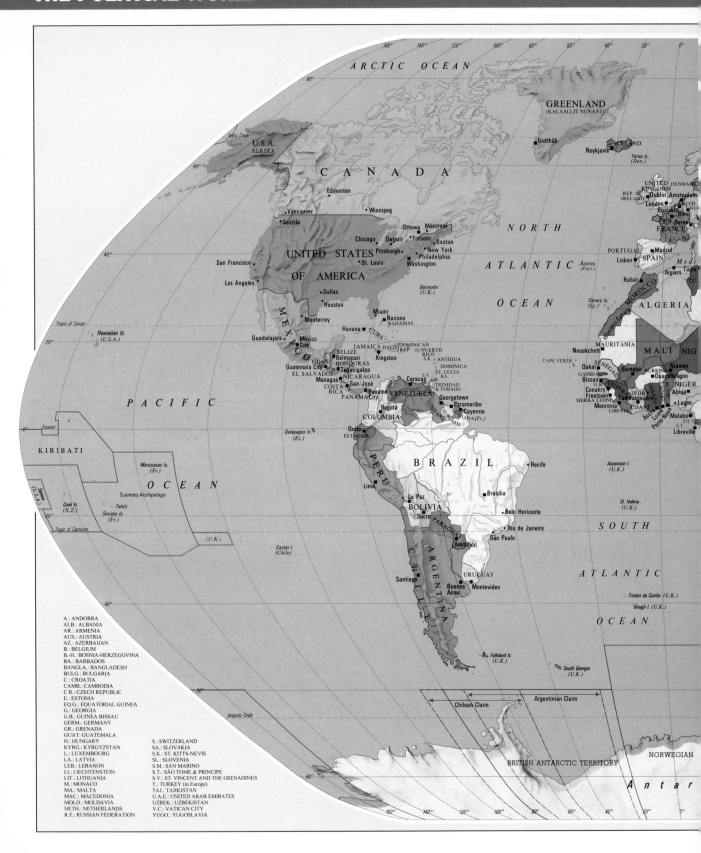

ARCTIC OCEAN

GREENLAND
(KALAALLIT NUNAAT)

Godthåb

ICELAND
Reykjavik

Faroe Is.
(Den.)

C A N A D A

Edmonton

Vancouver
Seattle
Winnipeg

Ottawa Montreal
Chicago Detroit Toronto Boston
Pittsburgh New York
San Francisco
UNITED STATES Washington Philadelphia
OF AMERICA St. Louis

Los Angeles

Dallas
Houston

Miami
Monterrey Nassau
BAHAMAS
Havana CUBA

Hawaiian Is.
(U.S.A.)

Guadalajara Mexico
City
BELIZE JAMAICA HAITI DOMINICAN
GUAT. Belmopan Kingston REP. PUERTO
HONDURAS RICO
Guatemala City Tegucigalpa S.K. ANTIGUA
EL SALVADOR DOMINICA
NICARAGUA ST. LUCIA
Managua B.A.
San José Caracas GR. TRINIDAD
COSTA & TOBAGO
RICA PANAMA City VENEZUELA
PANAMA Georgetown
Bogotá Paramaribo
COLOMBIA Cayenne
GUIANA (Fr.)

Quito
ECUADOR
Galapagos Is.
(Ec.)

P A C I F I C

KIRIBATI

Marquesas Is.
(Fr.)

O C E A N
Tuamotu Archipelago
Tahiti
Cook Is. Society Is.
(N.Z.) (Fr.)

Samoa
(U.S.A.)

PERU B R A Z I L
Lima Recife

La Paz Brasília
BOLIVIA Belo Horizonte
Sucre
Rio de Janeiro
São Paulo
Asunción

Santiago Buenos URUGUAY
Aires Montevideo

Easter I.
(Chile)

N O R T H

A T L A N T I C

O C E A N

Bermuda
(U.K.)

Azores
(Port.)

Canary Is.
(Sp.)

Ascension I.
(U.K.)

St. Helena
(U.K.)

S O U T H

A T L A N T I C

O C E A N

Tristan da Cunha (U.K.)
Gough I. (U.K.)

Falkland Is.
(U.K.)

South Georgia
(U.K.)

UNITED DENMARK
KINGDOM
REP. OF Dublin Amsterdam
IRELAND London NETH.
Brussels Bonn
Paris Berne
FRANCE

PORTUGAL Madrid
Lisbon SPAIN Med
Algiers Tunis

Rabat MOROCCO ALGERIA

Nouakchott MAURITANIA MALI NIG

CAPE VERDE Dakar SENEGAL Bamako BURKINA Niamey
GAMBIA Ouagadougou NIGER Abuja
Bissau GUINEA IVORY Lagos
Conakry Yamoussoukro COAST Malabo
Freetown
SIERRA LEONE Monrovia Accra Porto Novo EQ.
LIBERIA S.T.
Libreville

Argentinian Claim
Chilean Claim

Antarctic Circle

BRITISH ANTARCTIC TERRITORY NORWEGIAN

Antar

Abbreviations key:

A.: ANDORRA
ALB.: ALBANIA
AR.: ARMENIA
AUS.: AUSTRIA
AZ.: AZERBAIJAN
B.: BELGIUM
B.-H.: BOSNIA-HERZEGOVINA
BA.: BARBADOS
BANGLA.: BANGLADESH
BULG.: BULGARIA
C.: CROATIA
CAMB.: CAMBODIA
C.R.: CZECH REPUBLIC
E.: ESTONIA
EQ.G.: EQUATORIAL GUINEA
G.: GEORGIA
G.B.: GUINEA BISSAU
GERM.: GERMANY
GR.: GRENADA
GUAT: GUATEMALA
H.: HUNGARY
KYRG.: KYRGYZSTAN
L.: LUXEMBOURG
LA.: LATVIA
LEB.: LEBANON
LI.: LIECHTENSTEIN
LIT.: LITHUANIA
M.: MONACO
MA.: MALTA
MAC.: MACEDONIA
MOLD.: MOLDAVIA
NETH.: NETHERLANDS
R.F.: RUSSIAN FEDERATION

S.: SWITZERLAND
SA.: SLOVAKIA
S.K.: ST. KITTS-NEVIS
SL.: SLOVENIA
S.M.: SAN MARINO
S.T.: SÃO TOME & PRINCIPE
S.V.: ST. VINCENT AND THE GRENADINES
T.: TURKEY (in Europe)
TAJ.: TAJIKISTAN
U.A.E.: UNITED ARAB EMIRATES
UZBEK.: UZBEKISTAN
V.C.: VATICAN CITY
YUGO.: YUGOSLAVIA

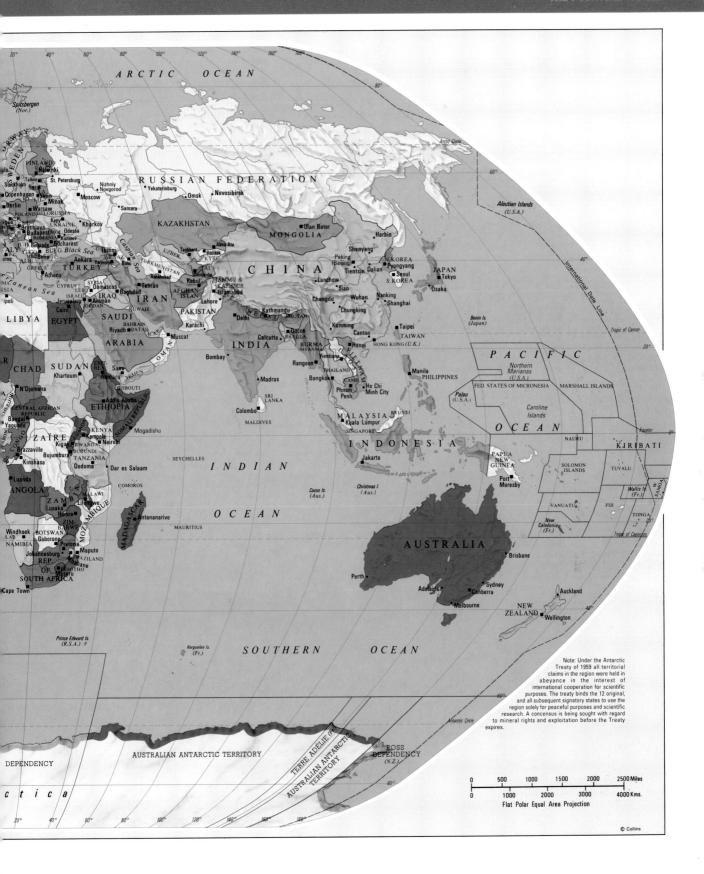

ARCTIC OCEAN

Spitsbergen (Nor.)

RUSSIAN FEDERATION

Arctic Circle

SWEDEN
FINLAND
Helsinki
Oslo
Tallinn
Riga
St. Petersburg
Nizhniy Novgorod
Yekaterinburg
Omsk
Novosibirsk
Aleutian Islands (U.S.A.)
Stockholm
Copenhagen
Vilnius
Minsk
Moscow
Berlin
Warsaw
Samara
POLAND
BELORUSSIA
Kiev
UKRAINE
Kharkov
KAZAKHSTAN
Ulan Bator
MONGOLIA
Harbin
Bratislava
Budapest
Kishinev
Odessa
Alma-Ata
Tashkent
Bishkek
Shenyang
N.KOREA
Pyongyang
JAPAN
ITALY
YUGO
Belgrade
BULG
Black Sea
Tbilisi
UZBEK
KYRG
Peking (Beijing)
Tientsin
Dalian
Seoul
S.KOREA
Tokyo
Rome
ALB
Sofia
Ankara
Yerevan
Baku
TURKMENISTAN
CHINA
Lanchow
Osaka
GREECE
Athens
TURKEY
SYRIA
Damascus
Ashkhabad
Kabul
TAJI
JAMMU & KASHMIR
Sian
Nanking
Shanghai
CYPRUS
LEB
ISRAEL
IRAQ
Baghdad
Tehran
AFGHAN-ISTAN
Islamabad
Chengdu
Wuhan
Jerusalem
JORDAN
Amman
KUWAIT
PAKISTAN
Lahore
NEPAL
Kathmandu
Chungking
Nanking
Bonin Is. (Japan)
Tropic of Cancer
LIBYA
EGYPT
SAUDI
BAHRAIN
QATAR
Riyadh
U.A.E.
Muscat
OMAN
Karachi
Delhi
BHUTAN
Kunming
Canton
Taipei
TAIWAN
ARABIA
Calcutta
BANGLA
Dacca
HONG KONG (U.K.)
PACIFIC
CHAD
SUDAN
ERIT-REA
YEMEN
INDIA
BURMA
MYANMAR
Hanoi
VIETNAM
Northern Marianas (U.S.A.)
Khartoum
Asmara
Sana
Bombay
Rangoon
Vientiane
Manila
PHILIPPINES
MARSHALL ISLANDS
N'Djamena
DJIBOUTI
Madras
THAILAND
LAOS
Bangkok
CAMB
Ho Chi Minh City
FED. STATES OF MICRONESIA
CENTRAL AFRICAN REPUBLIC
ETHIOPIA
SOMALI REPUBLIC
SRI LANKA
Phnom Penh
Palau (U.S.A.)
Bangui
CAMEROON
Addis Ababa
Colombo
MALDIVES
BRUNEI
Caroline Islands
Yaounde
KENYA
Mogadishu
MALAYSIA
Kuala Lumpur
OCEAN
CONGO
ZAIRE
UGANDA
Kampala
Nairobi
SINGAPORE
Equator
KIRIBATI
Brazzaville
Kigali
RWANDA
BURUNDI
SEYCHELLES
INDONESIA
NAURU
Kinshasa
Bujumbura
TANZANIA
Dodoma
Dar es Salaam
Jakarta
PAPUA NEW GUINEA
SOLOMON ISLANDS
TUVALU
Luanda
INDIAN
Port Moresby
ANGOLA
ZAMBIA
MALAWI
COMOROS
Cocos Is. (Aus.)
Christmas I. (Aus.)
Wallis Is. (Fr.)
W. SAMOA
Lusaka
Lilongwe
OCEAN
Horare
ZIM-
BABWE
MADAGASCAR
Antananarivo
VANUATU
FIJI
TONGA
Windhoek
BOTSWANA
MOZAMBIQUE
MAURITIUS
New Caledonia (Fr.)
Tropic of Capricorn
NAMIBIA
Gaborone
Pretoria
SWAZILAND
AUSTRALIA
Johannesburg
Maputo
Mbabane
REP. OF
SOUTH AFRICA
LESOTHO
Maseru
Brisbane
Cape Town
Perth
Adelaide
Sydney
Canberra
Auckland
Melbourne
NEW ZEALAND
Wellington

International Date Line

Prince Edward Is. (R.S.A.)
Kerguelen Is. (Fr.)
SOUTHERN OCEAN

Note: Under the Antarctic Treaty of 1959 all territorial claims in the region were held in abeyance in the interest of international cooperation for scientific purposes. The treaty binds the 12 original, and all subsequent signatory states to use the region solely for peaceful purposes and scientific research. A concensus is being sought with regard to mineral rights and exploitation before the Treaty expires.

Antarctic Circle

DEPENDENCY
AUSTRALIAN ANTARCTIC TERRITORY
TERRE ADELIE (Fr.)
AUSTRALIAN ANTARCTIC TERRITORY
ROSS DEPENDENCY (N.Z.)

ctica

	0	500	1000	1500	2000	2500 Miles
	0	1000	2000	3000	4000 Kms.	

Flat Polar Equal Area Projection

© Collins

NATIONS OF THE WORLD

COUNTRY	FORM OF GOVERNMENT	CAPITAL CITY	MAIN LANGUAGES	CURRENCY	AREA miles²	km²	POPULATION
AFGHANISTAN	republic	Kābol	Pushtu,Dari	afghani	251,824	652,225	16,120,000
ALBANIA	republic	Tiranë	Albanian	lek	11,100	28,750	3,250,000
ALGERIA	republic	Alger (Algiers)	Arabic	dinar	919,593	2,381,745	25,012,000
ANDORRA	principality	Andorra	Catalan	French franc,Spanish peseta	180	465	52,000
ANGOLA	republic	Luanda	Portuguese	kwanza	481,351	1,246,700	10,020,000
ANTIGUA & BARBUDA	constitutional monarchy	St John's	English	East Caribbean dollar	171	442	77,000
ARGENTINA	federal republic	Buenos Aires	Spanish	austral	1,072,515	2,777,815	32,322,000
ARMENIA	republic	Yerevan	Armenian,Russian	rouble	11,506	29,800	3,324,000
AUSTRALIA	monarchy (federal)	Canberra	English	dollar	2,966,139	7,682,300	17,086,000
AUSTRIA	federal republic	Wien (Vienna)	German	schilling	32,376	83,855	7,712,000
AZERBAIJAN	republic	Baku	Azerbaijani,Russian	rouble	33,436	86,600	7,153,000
BAHAMAS	constitutional monarchy	Nassau	English	dollar	5353	13,865	253,000
BAHRAIN	emirate	Al Manāmah	Arabic	dinar	255	661	503,000
BANGLADESH	republic	Dhaka	Bengali	taka	55,598	144,000	115,594,000
BARBADOS	constitutional monarchy	Bridgetown	English	dollar	166	430	255,000
BELGIUM	constitutional monarchy	Bruxelles (Brussels) Brussel	French,Dutch,German	franc	11,784	30,520	9,845,000
BELIZE	constitutional monarchy	Belmopan	English	dollar	8867	22,965	188,000
BELORUSSIA (BELARUS)	republic	Minsk	Belorussian	rouble	80,309	208,000	10,278,000
BENIN	republic	Porto-Novo	French	CFA franc	43,483	112,620	4,736,000
BHUTAN	constitutional monarchy	Thimbu	Dzongkha	Indian rupee,ngultrum	18,000	46,620	1,517,000
BOLIVIA	republic	La Paz / Sucre	Spanish,Aymara	boliviano	424,160	1,098,575	7,400,000
BOSNIA-HERZEGOVINA	republic	Sarajevo	Serbo-Croat	dinar	19,741	51,130	4,200,000
BOTSWANA	republic	Gaborone	English,Tswana	pula	231,804	600,372	1,291,000
BRAZIL	federal republic	Brasília	Portuguese	cruzeiro	3,286,473	8,511,965	150,368,000
BRUNEI	sultanate	Bandar Seri Begawan	Malay	dollar	2226	5,765	266,000
BULGARIA	people's republic	Sofiya (Sofia)	Bulgarian	lev	42,822	110,910	8,980,000
BURKINA	republic	Ouagadougou	French	CFA franc	105,869	274,200	9,001,000
BURMA (MYANMA)	military regime	Yangon (Rangoon)	Burmese	kyat	261,788	678,030	41,675,000
BURUNDI	republic	Bujumbura	French,Kirundi	franc	10,747	27,834	5,458,000
CAMBODIA	republic	Phnom Penh	Cambodian,Khmer	riel	69,884	181,000	8,246,000
CAMEROON	republic	Yaoundé	French,English	CFA franc	183,591	475,500	11,834,000
CANADA	monarchy (federal)	Ottawa	English,French	dollar	3,831,037	9,922,385	26,603,000
CAPE VERDE	republic	Praia	Portuguese,Creole	escudo	1558	4,035	370,000
CENTRAL AFRICAN REPUBLIC	republic	Bangui	French,Sango	CFA franc	241,303	624,975	3,039,000
CHAD	republic	N'Djamena	French,Arabic	CFA franc	495,753	1,284,000	5,679,000
CHILE	republic	Santiago	Spanish	peso	290,203	751,625	13,173,000
CHINA	people's republic	Beijing (Peking)	Mandarin	yuan	3,698,456	9,579,000	1,139,060,000
COLOMBIA	republic	Bogotá	Spanish	peso	439,736	1,138,915	32,987,000
COMOROS	federal republic	Moroni	Comoran,Arabic,French	CFA franc	718	1,860	551,000
CONGO	republic	Brazzaville	French	CFA franc	132,046	342,000	2,271,000
COSTA RICA	republic	San José	Spanish	colon	19,653	50,900	2,994,000
CROATIA	republic	Zagreb	Serbo-Croat	Dinar	21,830	56,540	4,600,000
CUBA	people's republic	La Habana (Havana)	Spanish	peso	44,218	114,525	10,609,000
CYPRUS	republic	Levkosía (Nicosia)	Greek	pound	3571	9,250	702,000
CZECH REPUBLIC	federal republic	Praha (Prague)	Czech	koruna	30,448	78,864	10,300,000
DENMARK	constitutional monarchy	Köbenhavn (Copenhagen)	Danish	krone	16,631	43,075	5,140,000
DJIBOUTI	republic	Djibouti	French,Somali,Afar	franc	8880	23,000	409,000
DOMINICA	republic	Roseau	English,French	East Caribbean dollar	290	751	83,000
DOMINICAN REPUBLIC	republic	Santo Domingo	Spanish	peso	18,703	48,440	7,170,000

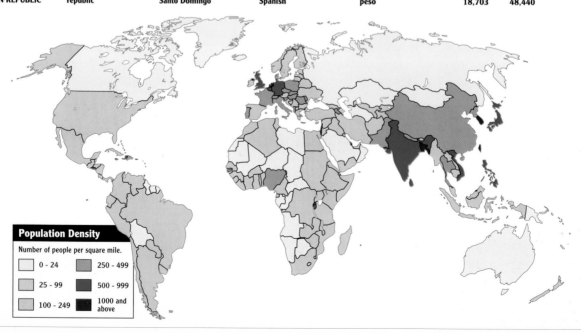

Population Density

Number of people per square mile.

- 0 – 24
- 25 – 99
- 100 – 249
- 250 – 499
- 500 – 999
- 1000 and above

COUNTRY	FORM OF GOVERNMENT	CAPITAL CITY	MAIN LANGUAGES	CURRENCY	AREA miles²	km²	POPULATION
CUADOR	republic	Quito	Spanish	sucre	178,176	461,475	10,782,000
GYPT	republic	Al Qāhirah (Cairo)	Arabic	pound	386,197	1,000,250	53,153,000
L SALVADOR	republic	San Salvador	Spanish	colón	8261	21,395	5,252,000
QUATORIAL GUINEA	republic	Malabo	Spanish	CFA franc	10,830	28,050	348,000
RITREA	republic	Asmera (Asmara)	Tigrinya, Arabic	birr	45,405	117,600	2,853,000
STONIA	republic	Tallinn	Estonian, Russian	kroon	17,413	45,100	1,583,000
THIOPIA	people's republic	Ādīs Ābeba (Addis Ababa)	Amharic	birr	349,490	905,450	47,921,000
EDERATED STATES OF MICRONESIA	federal republic	Palikir on Pohnpei	English, Kosrean, Yapese, Pohnpeian, Trukese	US dollar	271	702	99,000
IJI	republic	Suva	English, Fiji, Hindustani	dollar	7077	18,330	765,000
INLAND	republic	Helsinki	Finnish, Swedish	markka	130,127	337,030	4,986,000
RANCE	republic	Paris	French	franc	210,025	543,965	56,440,000
ABON	republic	Libreville	French	CFA franc	103,346	267,665	1,172,000
AMBIA	republic	Banjul	English	dalasi	4127	10,690	861,000
EORGIA	republic	Tbilisi	Georgian, Russian	rouble	26,911	69,700	5,464,000
ERMANY	federal republic	Berlin, Bonn	German	mark	138,173	357,868	79,479,000
HANA	military regime	Accra	English	cedi	92,010	238,305	15,028,000
REECE	republic	Athinai (Athens)	Greek	drachma	50,959	131,985	10,123,000
RENADA	constitutional monarchy	St George's	English	East Caribbean dollar	133	345	85,000
UATEMALA	republic	Guatemala	Spanish	quetzal	42,042	108,890	9,197,000
UINEA	military regime	Conakry	French	franc	98,400	254,855	5,756,000
UINEA-BISSAU	republic	Bissau	Portuguese	peso	13,948	36,125	965,000
UYANA	republic	Georgetown	English	dollar	83,000	214,970	796,000
AITI	republic	Port-au-Prince	French, Creole	gourde	10,714	27,750	6,486,000
ONDURAS	republic	Tegucigalpa	Spanish	lempira	43,276	112,085	5,105,000
UNGARY	republic	Budapest	Magyar	forint	35,919	93,030	10,553,000
CELAND	republic	Reykjavík	Icelandic	króna	39,699	102,820	255,000
NDIA	republic	New Delhi	Hindi, English	rupee	1,222,714	3,166,830	843,931,000
NDONESIA	republic	Jakarta	Bahasa Indonesia	rupiah	741,098	1,919,445	179,300,000
RAN	Islamic republic	Tehrān	Persian	rial	636,293	1,648,000	54,608,000
RAQ	republic	Baghdād	Arabic, Kurdish	dinar	169,284	438,445	18,920,000
RELAND, REPUBLIC OF	republic	Dublin	English, Irish	punt	26,600	68,895	3,503,000
SRAEL	republic	Yerushalayim (Jerusalem)	Hebrew	shekel	8019	20,770	4,659,000
TALY	republic	Roma (Rome)	Italian	lira	116,311	301,245	57,662,000
VORY COAST (CÔTE D'IVOIRE)	republic	Yamoussoukro	French	CFA franc	124,504	322,465	11,998,000
AMAICA	constitutional monarchy	Kingston	English	dollar	4411	11,425	2,420,000
APAN	monarchy	Tōkyō	Japanese	yen	142,741	369,700	123,537,000
ORDAN	monarchy	Ammān	Arabic	dinar	37,066	96,000	4,010,000
AZAKHSTAN	republic	Alma-Ata	Kazakh, Russian	rouble	1,049,151	2,717,300	16,742,000
ENYA	republic	Nairobi	Kiswahili, English	shilling	224,959	582,645	24,032,000
IRGHIZIA (KYRGYZSTAN)	republic	Bishkek	Kirghiz, Russian	rouble	76,641	198,500	4,394,000
IRIBATI	republic	Bairiki on Tarawa Atoll	English, Gilbertese, I-Kiribati	Australian dollar	264	684	66,000
UWAIT	emirate	Al Kuwayt (Kuwait)	Arabic	dinar	9375	24,280	2,143,000
AOS	people's republic	Vientiane (Viangchan)	Lao	new kip	91,400	236,725	4,139,000
ATVIA	republic	Rīga	Latvian, Russian	Latvian rouble	24,595	63,700	2,686,000
EBANON	republic	Bayrūt (Beirut)	Arabic	pound	4015	10,400	2,701,000
ESOTHO	monarchy	Maseru	English, Sesotho	maluti	11,716	30,345	1,774,000
IBERIA	republic	Monrovia	English	dollar	43,000	111,370	2,607,000
IBYA	socialist state	Tarābulus (Tripoli)	Arabic	dinar	679,359	1,759,540	4,545,000

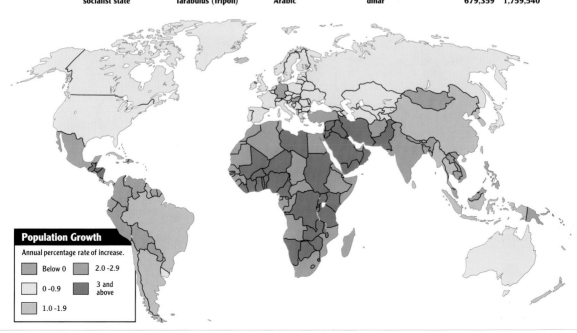

Population Growth

Annual percentage rate of increase.

- Below 0
- 0 - 0.9
- 1.0 - 1.9
- 2.0 - 2.9
- 3 and above

COUNTRY	FORM OF GOVERNMENT	CAPITAL CITY	MAIN LANGUAGES	CURRENCY	AREA miles²	km²	POPULATION
LIECHTENSTEIN	constitutional monarchy	Vaduz	German	Swiss franc	62	160	29,000
LITHUANIA	**republic**	**Vilnius**	**Lithuanian**	**Litas**	**25,174**	**65,200**	**3,731,000**
LUXEMBOURG	constitutional monarchy	Luxembourg	Letzeburgish,French,German	franc	998	2,585	381,000
MADAGASCAR	**republic**	**Antananarivo**	**Malagasy,French**	**Malagasy franc**	**229,413**	**594,180**	**11,197,000**
MALAWI	republic	Lilongwe	English,Chichewa	Kwacha	36,324	94,080	8,289,000
MALAYSIA	**constitutional monarchy**	**Kuala Lumpur**	**Bahasa Malay**	**ringgit**	**128,558**	**332,965**	**17,861,000**
MALDIVES	republic	Malé	Divehi	rufiyaa	115	298	215,000
MALI	**republic**	**Bamako**	**French,Bambara**	**CFA franc**	**478,819**	**1,240,140**	**8,156,000**
MALTA	republic	Valletta	Maltese,English	pound	122	316	354,000
MARSHALL ISLANDS	**republic**	**Dalap-Uliga-Darrit**	**Marshallese,English**	**US dollar**	**70**	**181**	**40,000**
MAURITANIA	republic	Nouakchott	Arabic,French	ouguiya	397,954	1,030,700	2,025,000
MAURITIUS	**constitutional monarchy**	**Port Louis**	**English,Creole**	**rupee**	**720**	**1,865**	**1,075,000**
MEXICO	federal republic	Ciudad de México,(Mexico City)	Spanish	peso	761,600	1,972,545	86,154,000
MOLDAVIA (MOLDOVA)	**republic**	**Kishinev**	**Romanian,Russian**	**rouble**	**13,012**	**33,700**	**4,368,000**
MONACO	constitutional monarchy	Monaco	French	French franc	1	2	29,000
MONGOLIA	**republic**	**Ulaanbaatar (Ulan Bator)**	**Khalka Mongol**	**tugrik**	**604,247**	**1,565,000**	**2,190,000**
MOROCCO	monarchy	Rabat	Arabic	dirham	172,413	446,550	25,061,000
MOZAMBIQUE	**republic**	**Maputo**	**Portuguese**	**metical**	**302,994**	**784,755**	**15,656,000**
NAMIBIA	republic	Windhoek	Afrikaans,English	Namibian dollar	318,261	824,295	1,781,000
NAURU	**republic**	**Yaren**	**Nauruan,English**	**Australian dollar**	**8**	**21**	**10,000**
NEPAL	monarchy	Kathmandu	Nepali	rupee	54,600	141,415	18,916,000
NETHERLANDS	**constitutional monarchy**	**Amsterdam**	**Dutch**	**guilder**	**15,892**	**41,160**	**14,935,000**
NEW ZEALAND	constitutional monarchy	Wellington	English,Maori	dollar	102,375	265,150	3,346,000
NICARAGUA	**republic**	**Managua**	**Spanish**	**córdoba**	**57,143**	**148,000**	**3,871,000**
NIGER	republic	Niamey	French	CFA Franc	458,073	1,186,410	7,732,000
NIGERIA	**federal republic**	**Abuja**	**English**	**naira**	**356,699**	**923,850**	**88,500,000**
NORTH KOREA	people's republic	Pyŏngyang	Korean	won	47,224	122,310	21,773,000
NORWAY	**constitutional monarchy**	**Oslo**	**Norwegian**	**krone**	**125,056**	**323,895**	**4,242,000**
OMAN	sultanate	Masqaṭ (Muscat)	Arabic	rial	105,000	271,950	1,502,000
PAKISTAN	**federal Islamic republic**	**Islāmābād**	**Urdu,Punjabi,English**	**rupee**	**310,402**	**803,940**	**112,049,000**
PANAMA	republic	Panamá City	Spanish	balboa	30,315	78,515	2,418,000
PAPUA NEW GUINEA	**constitutional monarchy**	**Port Moresby**	**English,Pidgin,Motu**	**kina**	**178,703**	**462,840**	**3,699,000**
PARAGUAY	republic	Asunción	Spanish,Guarani	guaraní	157,046	406,750	4,277,000
PERU	**republic**	**Lima**	**Spanish,Quechua**	**sol**	**496,222**	**1,285,215**	**21,550,000**
PHILIPPINES	republic	Manila	Pilipino,English	peso	115,830	300,000	61,480,000
POLAND	**republic**	**Warszawa (Warsaw)**	**Polish**	**zloty**	**120,728**	**312,685**	**38,180,000**
PORTUGAL	republic	Lisboa (Lisbon)	Portuguese	escudo	34,340	88,940	10,525,000
QATAR	**emirate**	**Ad Dawḥaḥ (Doha)**	**Arabic**	**riyal**	**4415**	**11,435**	**486,000**
ROMANIA	republic	Bucureşti (Bucharest)	Romanian	leu	91,699	237,500	23,200,000
RUSSIAN FEDERATION	**republic**	**Moskva (Moscow)**	**Russian**	**rouble**	**6,593,822**	**17,078,000**	**148,263,000**
RWANDA	republic	Kigali	Kinyarwanda,French	franc	10,166	26,330	7,181,000
ST KITTS-NEVIS	**constitutional monarchy**	**Basseterre**	**English**	**East Caribbean dollar**	**101**	**261**	**44,000**
ST LUCIA	constitutional monarchy	Castries	English,French	East Caribbean dollar	238	616	151,000
ST VINCENT & THE GRENADINES	**constitutional monarchy**	**Kingstown**	**English**	**East Caribbean dollar**	**150**	**389**	**116,000**
SAN MARINO	republic	San Marino	Italian	Italian lira	24	61	24,000
SÃO TOMÉ & PRÍNCIPE	**republic**	**São Tomé**	**Portuguese,Creole**	**dobra**	**372**	**964**	**121,000**
SAUDI ARABIA	monarchy	Ar Riyāḍ (Riyadh)	Arabic	riyal	926,988	2,400,900	14,870,000
SENEGAL	**republic**	**Dakar**	**French**	**CFA franc**	**75,954**	**196,720**	**7,327,000**

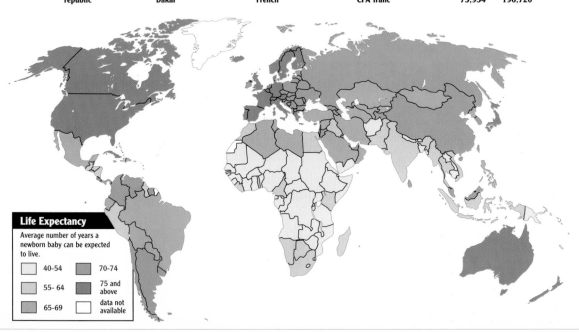

Life Expectancy

Average number of years a newborn baby can be expected to live.

- 40-54
- 55- 64
- 65-69
- 70-74
- 75 and above
- data not available

COUNTRY	FORM OF GOVERNMENT	CAPITAL CITY	MAIN LANGUAGES	CURRENCY	AREA miles²	km²	POPULATION
SEYCHELLES	republic	Victoria	English,French,Creole	rupee	156	404	67,000
SIERRA LEONE	**republic**	**Freetown**	**English**	**leone**	**27,925**	**72,325**	**4,151,000**
SINGAPORE	republic	Singapore	Bahasa Malay,English, Chinese,Tamil	dollar	238	616	3,003,000
SLOVAKIA	**republic**	**Bratislava**	**Slovak**	**koruna**	**18,933**	**49,035**	**5,300,000**
SLOVENIA	republic	Ljubljana	Slovene	dinar	7819	20,250	1,900,000
SOLOMON ISLANDS	**constitutional monarchy**	**Honiara**	**English**	**dollar**	**11,502**	**29,790**	**321,000**
SOMALI REPUBLIC	republic	Muqdisho (Mogadishu)	Arabic,Somali,Italian,English	shilling	243,243	630,000	7,497,000
SOUTH AFRICA, REPUBLIC OF	**republic**	**Cape Town (Kaapstad) / Pretoria**	**Afrikaans,English**	**rand**	**457,461**	**1,184,825**	**35,282,000**
SOUTH KOREA	republic	Sŏul (Seoul)	Korean	won	38,010	98,445	42,793,000
SPAIN	**constitutional monarchy**	**Madrid**	**Spanish**	**peseta**	**194,934**	**504,880**	**38,959,000**
SRI LANKA	republic	Colombo	Sinhala,Tamil	Rupee	25,332	65,610	16,993,000
SUDAN	**military regime**	**Al Kharṭūm (Khartoum)**	**Arabic**	**pound**	**967,496**	**2,505,815**	**25,204,000**
SURINAM	republic	Paramaribo	Dutch,English	guilder	53,251	163,820	422,000
SWAZILAND	**monarchy**	**Mbabane**	**English,Siswati**	**lilangeni**	**6705**	**17,365**	**768,000**
SWEDEN	constitutional monarchy	Stockholm	Swedish	krona	173,664	449,790	8,559,000
SWITZERLAND	**federal republic**	**Bern (Berne)**	**German,French, Italian,Romansh**	**franc**	**15,940**	**41,285**	**6,712,000**
SYRIA	republic	Dimashq (Damascus)	Arabic	pound	71,691	185,680	12,116,000
TAIWAN	**republic**	**Taipei**	**Mandarin**	**dollar**	**13,896**	**35,990**	**20,300,000**
TAJIKISTAN	republic	Dushanbe	Tajik,Russian	rouble	55,251	143,100	5,303,000
TANZANIA	**republic**	**Dodoma**	**Kiswahili,English**	**shilling**	**362,842**	**939,760**	**25,635,000**
THAILAND	monarchy	Bangkok (Krung Thep)	Thai	baht	198,456	514,000	57,196,000
TOGO	**republic**	**Lomé**	**French**	**CFA franc**	**21,925**	**56,785**	**3,531,000**
TONGA	constitutional monarchy	Nuku'alofa	English,Tongan	pa'anga	270	699	95,000
TRINIDAD AND TOBAGO	**republic**	**Port of Spain**	**English**	**dollar**	**1981**	**5,130**	**1,227,000**
TUNISIA	republic	Tunis	Arabic	dinar	63,378	164,150	8,180,000
TURKEY	**republic**	**Ankara**	**Turkish**	**lira**	**300,946**	**779,450**	**56,098,000**
TURKMENISTAN	republic	Ashkhabad	Turkmenian	rouble	188,456	488,100	3,670,000
TUVALU	**constitutional monarchy**	**Funafuti**	**English,Tuvaluan**	**Australian dollar**	**10**	**25**	**10,000**
UGANDA	republic	Kampala	Kiswahili,English	shilling	91,344	236,580	18,795,000
UKRAINE	**republic**	**Kiev**	**Ukrainian,Russian**	**rouble**	**233,089**	**603,700**	**51,857,000**
UNITED ARAB EMIRATES	federation of emirates	Abū Ẓaby (Abu Dhabi)	Arabic	dirham	29,015	75,150	1,589,000
UNITED KINGDOM	**constitutional monarchy**	**London**	**English**	**pound**	**94,500**	**244,755**	**57,411,000**
UNITED STATES OF AMERICA	federal republic	Washington	English	dollar	3,615,108	9,363,130	249,975,000
URUGUAY	**republic**	**Montevideo**	**Spanish**	**peso**	**72,172**	**186,925**	**3,096,000**
UZBEKISTAN	republic	Tashkent	Uzbek,Russian	rouble	172,741	447,400	20,531,000
VANUATU	**republic**	**Vila**	**English,French,Bislama**	**vatu**	**5701**	**14,765**	**147,000**
VATICAN CITY	ecclesiastical state	Vatican City	Italian	lira	0.5	1	1000
VENEZUELA	**federal republic**	**Caracas**	**Spanish**	**bolívar**	**352,141**	**912,045**	**19,735,000**
VIETNAM	people's socialist republic	Hanoi	Vietnamese	dong	127,245	329,565	66,200,000
WESTERN SAMOA	**constitutional monarchy**	**Apia**	**Samoan,English**	**tala**	**1097**	**2,840**	**164,000**
YEMEN	republic	San'a	Arabic	rial,dinar	203,850	527,969	11,282,000
YUGOSLAVIA	**federal republic**	**Beograd (Belgrade)**	**Serbo-Croat, Macedonian,Albanian**	**dinar**	**49,376**	**127,885**	**10,000,000**
ZAÏRE	republic	Kinshasa	French,Lingala	zaïre	905,564	2,345,410	35,562,000
ZAMBIA	**republic**	**Lusaka**	**English**	**kwacha**	**290,585**	**752,615**	**7,818,000**
ZIMBABWE	republic	Harare	English	dollar	150,699	390,310	9,369,000

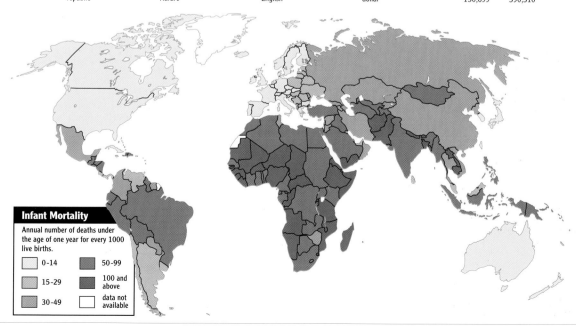

Infant Mortality

Annual number of deaths under the age of one year for every 1000 live births.

- 0-14
- 15-29
- 30-49
- 50-99
- 100 and above
- data not available

Population	City	Country
2,168,000	**Abidjan**	**Ivory Coast**
1,891,000	Ādis Ābeba (Addis Ababa)	Ethiopia
3,297,655	**Ahmadābād**	**India**
3,033,000	Alger (Algiers)	Algeria
1,947,000	**Al Kharţūm (Khartoum)**	**Sudan**
15,000,000	Al Qāhirah (Cairo)	Egypt
1,151,300	**Alma-Ata**	**Kazakhstan**
1,297,100	Ammān	Jordan
1,061,766	**Amsterdam**	**Netherlands**
2,559,471	Ankara	Turkey
1,370,000	**Anshan**	**China**
1,500,000	Ar Riyāḍ (Riyadh)	Saudi Arabia
3,096,000	**Athinai (Athens)**	**Greece**
2,834,000	Atlanta	USA
935,085	**Auckland**	**New Zealand**
4,044,000	Baghdād	Iraq
1,780,000	**Baku**	**Azerbaijan**
2,382,000	Baltimore	USA
2,535,000	**Bandung**	**Indonesia**
4,993,000	Bangalore	India
5,876,000	**Bangkok (Krung Thep)**	**Thailand**
1,653,175	Barcelona	Spain
1,500,000	**Bayrūt (Beirut)**	**Lebanon**
10,819,407	Beijing (Peking)	China
2,103,330	**Belo Horizonte**	**Brazil**
3,420,600	Berlin	Germany
1,554,826	**Beograd (Belgrade)**	**Yugoslavia**
2,312,700	Birmingham	UK
4,851,000	**Bogotá**	**Colombia**

Population	City	Country
12,571,720	Bombay	India
2,871,000	**Boston**	**USA**
1,841,028	Brasília	Brazil
960,324	**Bruxelles (Brussels)**	**Belgium**
2,325,037	Bucureşti (Bucharest)	Romania
2,018,035	**Budapest**	**Hungary**
12,200,000	Buenos Aires	Argentina
10,916,272	**Calcutta**	**India**
310,000	Canberra	Australia
2,310,000	**Cape Town (Kaapstad)**	**South Africa**
4,092,000	Caracas	Venezuela
3,210,000	**Casablanca**	**Morocco**
2,214,000	Changchun	China
1,362,000	**Changsha**	**China**
1,148,000	Chelyabinsk	Russian Federation
3,004,000	**Chengdu**	**China**
6,070,000	Chicago	USA
3,151,000	**Chongqing**	**China**
2,543,000	Dalian	China
3,885,000	**Dallas - Fort Worth**	**USA**
1,657,000	Dar es Salaam	Tanzania
8,375,000	**Delhi**	**India**
4,382,000	Detroit	USA
2,651,000	**Dimashq (Damascus)**	**Syria**
6,646,000	Dhaka	Bangladesh
926,000	**Dublin**	**Republic of Ireland**
2,712,500	Essen - Dortmund	Germany
1,420,000	**Fushun**	**China**
375,957	Genève (Geneva)	Switzerland

Population	City	Country
2,846,720	**Guadalajara**	**Mexico**
3,671,000	Guangzhou (Canton)	China
1,640,000	**Hamburg**	**Germany**
1,412,000	Hangzhou	China
3,056,146	**Hanoi**	**Vietnam**
2,966,000	Harbin	China
3,924,435	**Ho Chi Minh (Saigon)**	**Vietnam**
5,950,000	Hong Kong	UK colony
3,711,000	**Houston**	**USA**
4,280,261	Hyderābād	India
6,620,241	**Istanbul**	**Turkey**
9,253,000	Jakarta	Indonesia
1,800,000	**Jiddah (Jedda)**	**Saudi Arabia**
1,327,000	Jilin	China
2,415,000	**Jinan**	**China**
1,714,000	Johannesburg	South Africa
1,300,000	**Kābol**	**Afghanistan**
7,702,000	Karāchi	Pakistan
2,616,000	**Kiyev (Kiev)**	**Ukraine**
3,505,000	Kinshasa	Zaire
1,336,855	**Köbenhavn (Copenhagen)**	**Denmark**
1,711,00	Kuala Lumpur	Malaysia
5,689,000	**Lagos**	**Nigeria**
2,099,000	La Habana (Havana)	Cuba
4,092,000	**Lahore**	**Pakistan**
6,404,500	Lima	Peru
1,603,000	**Lisboa (Lisbon)**	**Portugal**
9,131,000	London	UK

Economic Groups

- Colombo Plan
- Organisation for Economic Co-operation and Development (OECD)
- Organisation for Petroleum Exporting Countries (OPEC)
- North American Free Trade Area (NAFTA)
- Latin American Integration Assoc. (ALADI)
- Caribbean Community (CARICOM)
- Central American Common Market (CACM)
- Economic Community of West African States (ECOWAS)
- Economic Community of Central African States (CEEAC)
- South African Development Co-ordination Conference (SADCC)
- Association of South-East Asian Nations (ASEAN)
- Not a member of any of the organisations shown on the map
- European Community (EC)
- European Free Trade Association (EFTA)
- European Economic Area (EEA)

Note:- Countries represented by colour stripes are those which belong to more than one of the Economic Groups shown on the map.

Population	City	Country	Population	City	Country	Population	City	Country
,274,000	Los Angeles	USA	2,057,000	Pittsburg	USA	2,383,000	Surabaya	Indonesia
5,361,468	Madras	India	1,254,642	Pôrto Alegre	Brazil	3,656,900	Sydney	Australia
,984,576	Madrid	Spain	1,212,000	Praha (Prague)	Czech Republic	2,228,834	Taegu	South Korea
2,561,600	Manchester	UK	3,797,566	Pusan	South Korea	2,719,659	Taipei	Taiwan
1,475,000	Manila-Quezon City	Philippines	2,230,000	Pyŏngyang	North Korea	2,199,000	Taiyuan	China
1,585,000	Medellín	Colombia	645,000	Quebec	Canada	484,400	Tallinn	Estonia
,081,000	Melbourne	Australia	2,040,000	Qingdao	China	1,500,000	Tarābulus (Tripoli)	Libya
8,748,000	Mexico City	Mexico	1,387,887	Quito	Ecuador	2,094,000	Tashkent	Uzbekistan
,937,000	Miami	USA	1,472,000	Rabat	Morocco	1,280,000	Tbilisi	Georgia
2,464,000	Minneapolis-St Paul	USA	1,335,684	Recife	Brazil	6,773,000	Tehrän	Iran
,637,000	Minsk	Belorussia	915,000	Riga	Latvia	1,029,700	Tel Aviv	Israel
2,521,697	Monterrey	Mexico	5,487,346	Rio de Janeiro	Brazil	9,371,000	Tianjin	China
,197,000	Montevideo	Uruguay	3,784,000	Roma (Rome)	Italy	11,935,700	Tôkyô	Japan
3,127,000	Montreal	Canada	1,481,000	Sacramento	USA	3,893,000	Toronto	Canada
,000,000	Moskva (Moscow)	Russian Federation	2,075,392	Salvador	Brazil	1,603,000	Vancouver	Canada
1,219,600	München (Munich)	Germany	2,498,000	San Diego	USA	593,000	Vilnius	Lithuania
,160,000	Nagoya	Japan	5,185,000	San Francisco	USA	1,655,700	Warszawa (Warsaw)	Poland
1,503,000	Nairobi	Kenya	1,390,000	San Juan	Puerto Rico	3,924,000	Washington DC	USA
,415,000	Nanchang	China	4,734,000	Santiago	Chile	324,792	Wellington	New Zealand
2,265,000	Nanjing	China	2,203,000	Santo Domingo	Dominican Rep.	1,533,176	Wien (Vienna)	Austria
,139,000	New York	USA	9,700,111	São Paulo	Brazil	652,000	Winnipeg	Canada
1,443,000	Novosibirsk	Russian Federation	13,341,896	Shanghai	China	2,859,000	Xian	China
,106,000	Odessa	Ukraine	4,763,000	Shenyang	China	3,295,000	Yangon (Rangoon)	Burma (Myanmar)
8,520,000	Osaka - Kobe	Japan	2,763,000	Singapore	Singapore	1,202,000	Yerevan	Armenia
461,644	Oslo	Norway	1,190,000	Sofiya (Sofia)	Bulgaria	508,000	Yerushalayim (Jerusalem)	Israel
921,000	Ottawa	Canada	10,979,000	Sôul (Seoul)	South Korea			
,063,384	Paris	France	2,444,000	St Louis	USA	3,250,000	Yokohama	Japan
4,857,000	Philadelphia	USA	5,035,000	St Petersburg	Russian Federation	703,799	Zagreb	Croatia
,122,000	Phoenix	USA	1,654,511	Stockholm	Sweden	2,430,000	Zibo	China

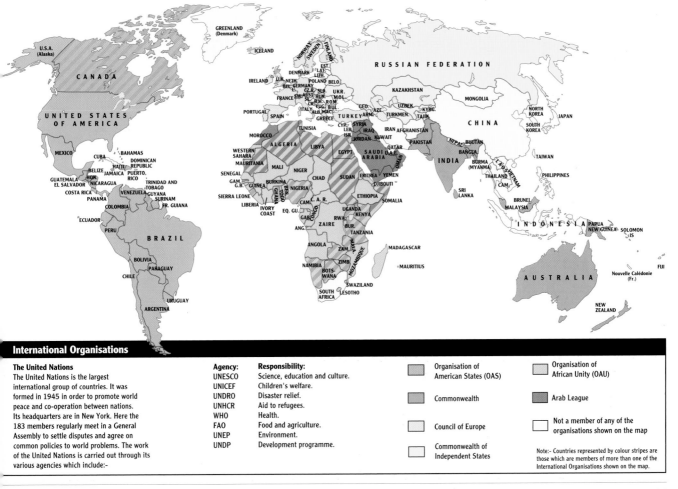

International Organisations

The United Nations
The United Nations is the largest international group of countries. It was formed in 1945 in order to promote world peace and co-operation between nations. Its headquarters are in New York. Here the 183 members regularly meet in a General Assembly to settle disputes and agree on common policies to world problems. The work of the United Nations is carried out through its various agencies which include:-

Agency:	Responsibility:
UNESCO	Science, education and culture.
UNICEF	Children's welfare.
UNDRO	Disaster relief.
UNHCR	Aid to refugees.
WHO	Health.
FAO	Food and agriculture.
UNEP	Environment.
UNDP	Development programme.

Organisation of American States (OAS)

Commonwealth

Council of Europe

Commonwealth of Independent States

Organisation of African Unity (OAU)

Arab League

Not a member of any of the organisations shown on the map

Note:- Countries represented by colour stripes are those which are members of more than one of the International Organisations shown on the map.

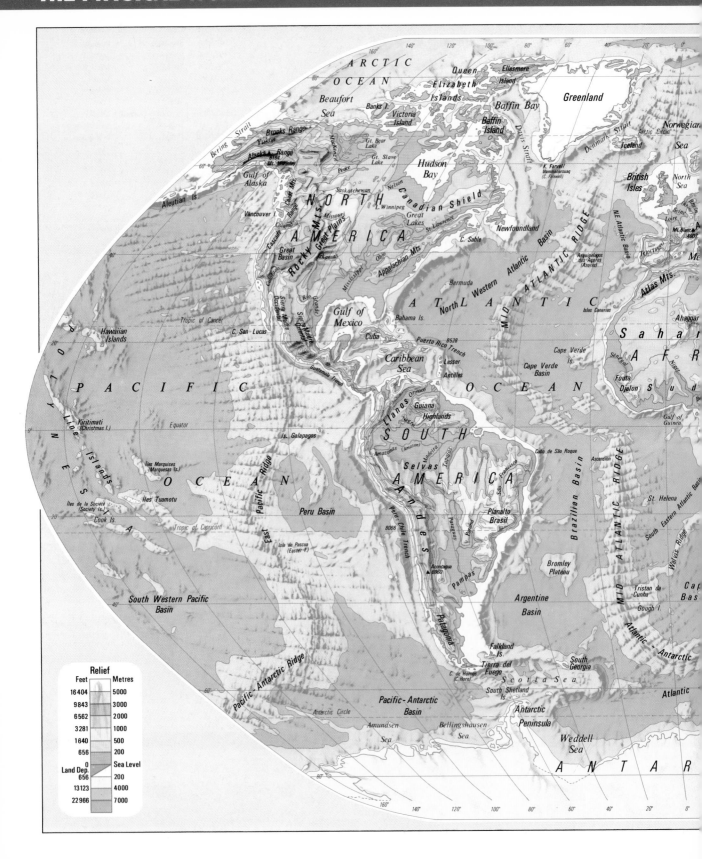

Relief

Feet		Metres
16 404		5000
9843		3000
6562		2000
3281		1000
1640		500
656		200
0		Sea Level
Land Dep.		
656		200
13 123		4000
22 966		7000

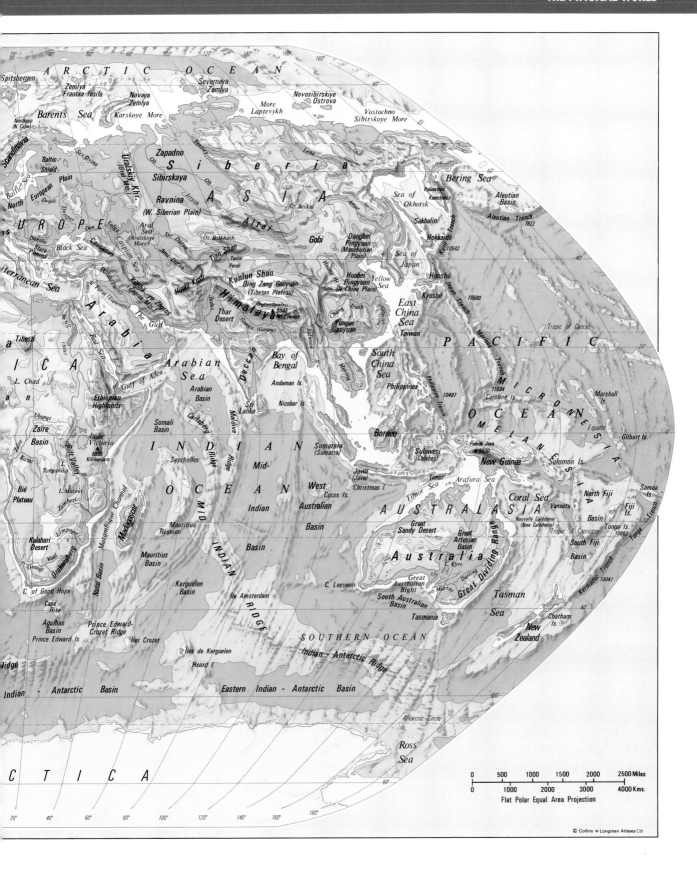

Continents and Oceans

Land area $\square$ = 1,000,000 square kms
386,000 square miles

Water area $\square$ = 1,000,000 square kms
386,000 square miles

EARTH'S DIMENSIONS		
Superficial area	196,936,679 miles²	510,066,000 km²
Land surface	57,268,725 miles²	148,326,000 km²
Water surface	139,667,953 miles²	361,740,000 km²
Equatorial circumference	24,902 miles	40,075 km
Meridional circumference	24,859 miles	40,007 km
Volume	259,902x10⁶ miles³	1,083,230x10⁶ km³
Mass	5.882x10²¹ tons	5.976x10²¹ tonnes

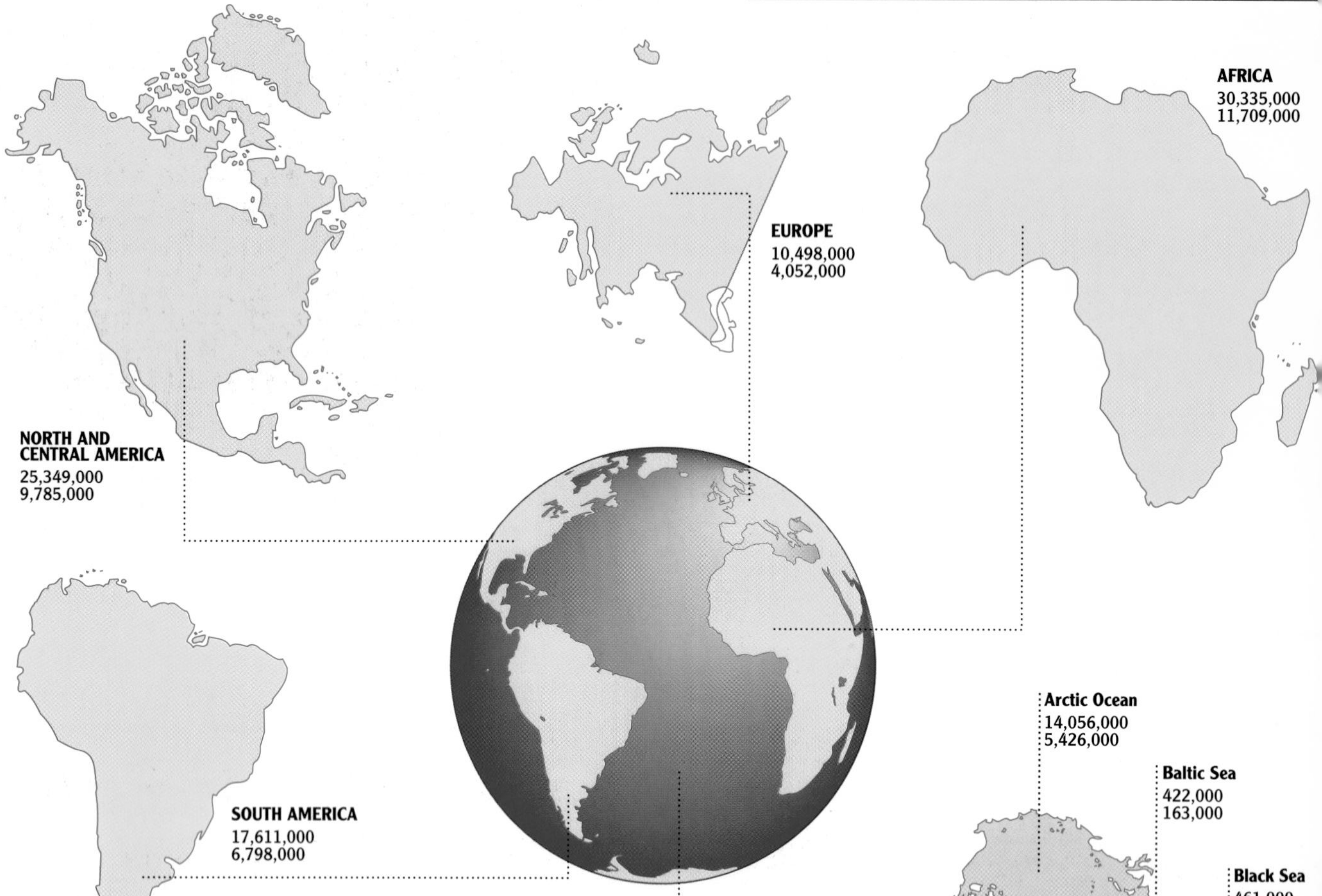

AFRICA
30,335,000
11,709,000

EUROPE
10,498,000
4,052,000

NORTH AND CENTRAL AMERICA
25,349,000
9,785,000

SOUTH AMERICA
17,611,000
6,798,000

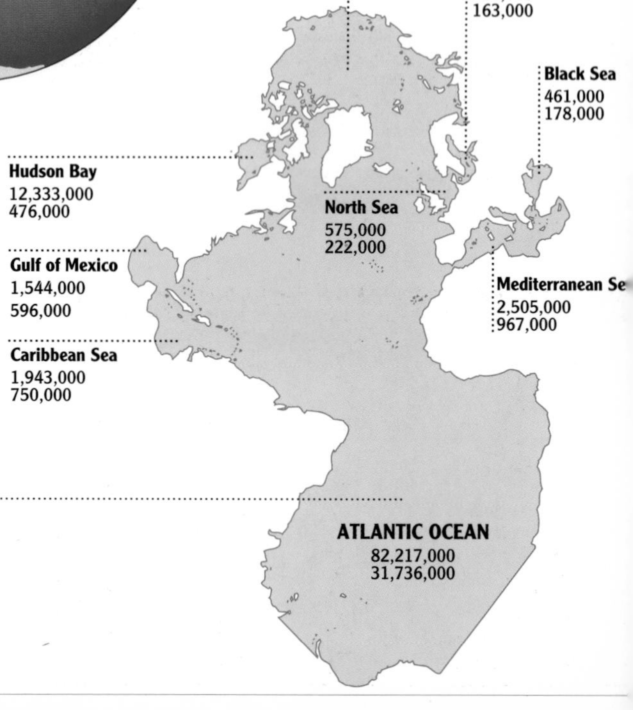

Arctic Ocean
14,056,000
5,426,000

Baltic Sea
422,000
163,000

Black Sea
461,000
178,000

Hudson Bay
12,333,000
476,000

North Sea
575,000
222,000

Gulf of Mexico
1,544,000
596,000

Mediterranean Se
2,505,000
967,000

Caribbean Sea
1,943,000
750,000

ATLANTIC OCEAN
82,217,000
31,736,000

RIVER LENGTHS		
An Nīl (Nile); Africa	4,160 miles	6,695 km
Amazonas; (Amazon); South America	4,048 miles	6,516 km
Chang Jiang (Yangtze); Asia	3,964 miles	6,380 km
Mississippi-Missouri; North America	3,740 miles	6,020 km
Ob-Irtysh; Asia	3,461 miles	5,570 km
Huang He (Hwang Ho); Asia	3,395 miles	5,464 km
Zaïre; Africa	2,900 miles	4,667 km
Mekong; Asia	2,749 miles	4,425 km
Amur; Asia	2,744 miles	4,416 km
Lena; Asia	2,734 miles	4,400 km
Mackenzie; North America	2,640 miles	4,250 km
Yenisey; Asia	2,541 miles	4,090 km
Niger; Africa	2,504 miles	4,030 km
Murray-Darling; Australia	2,330 miles	3,750 km
Volga; Europe	2,291 miles	3,688 km

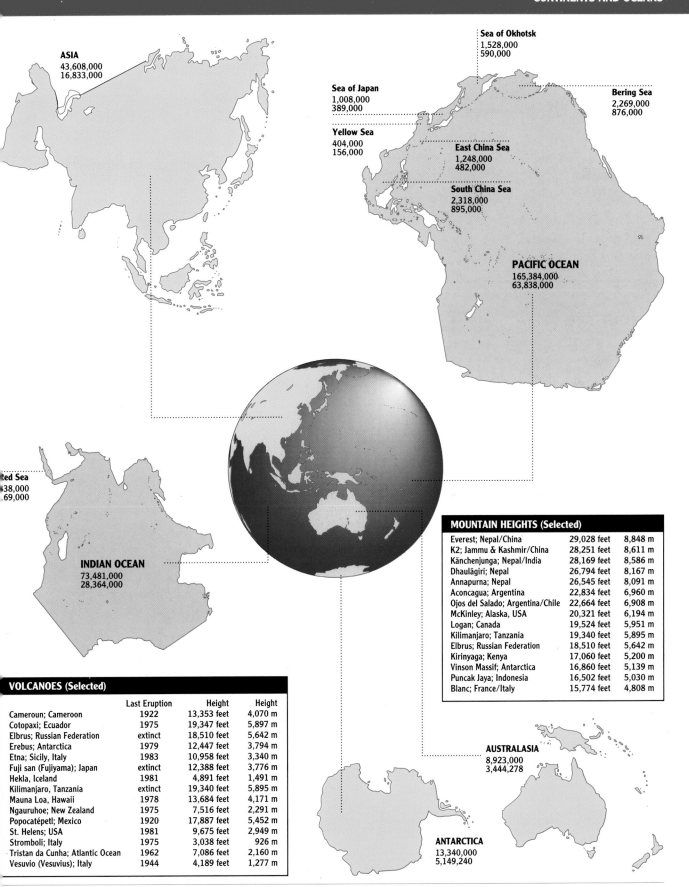

ASIA
43,608,000
16,833,000

Sea of Okhotsk
1,528,000
590,000

Sea of Japan
1,008,000
389,000

Bering Sea
2,269,000
876,000

Yellow Sea
404,000
156,000

East China Sea
1,248,000
482,000

South China Sea
2,318,000
895,000

PACIFIC OCEAN
165,384,000
63,838,000

Red Sea
438,000
169,000

INDIAN OCEAN
73,481,000
28,364,000

MOUNTAIN HEIGHTS (Selected)

Everest; Nepal/China	29,028 feet	8,848 m
K2; Jammu & Kashmir/China	28,251 feet	8,611 m
Kānchenjunga; Nepal/India	28,169 feet	8,586 m
Dhaulāgiri; Nepal	26,794 feet	8,167 m
Annapurna; Nepal	26,545 feet	8,091 m
Aconcagua; Argentina	22,834 feet	6,960 m
Ojos del Salado; Argentina/Chile	22,664 feet	6,908 m
McKinley; Alaska, USA	20,321 feet	6,194 m
Logan; Canada	19,524 feet	5,951 m
Kilimanjaro; Tanzania	19,340 feet	5,895 m
Elbrus; Russian Federation	18,510 feet	5,642 m
Kirinyaga; Kenya	17,060 feet	5,200 m
Vinson Massif; Antarctica	16,860 feet	5,139 m
Puncak Jaya; Indonesia	16,502 feet	5,030 m
Blanc; France/Italy	15,774 feet	4,808 m

VOLCANOES (Selected)

	Last Eruption	Height	Height
Cameroun; Cameroon	1922	13,353 feet	4,070 m
Cotopaxi; Ecuador	1975	19,347 feet	5,897 m
Elbrus; Russian Federation	extinct	18,510 feet	5,642 m
Erebus; Antarctica	1979	12,447 feet	3,794 m
Etna; Sicily, Italy	1983	10,958 feet	3,340 m
Fuji san (Fujiyama); Japan	extinct	12,388 feet	3,776 m
Hekla, Iceland	1981	4,891 feet	1,491 m
Kilimanjaro, Tanzania	extinct	19,340 feet	5,895 m
Mauna Loa, Hawaii	1978	13,684 feet	4,171 m
Ngauruhoe; New Zealand	1975	7,516 feet	2,291 m
Popocatépetl; Mexico	1920	17,887 feet	5,452 m
St. Helens; USA	1981	9,675 feet	2,949 m
Stromboli; Italy	1975	3,038 feet	926 m
Tristan da Cunha; Atlantic Ocean	1962	7,086 feet	2,160 m
Vesuvio (Vesuvius); Italy	1944	4,189 feet	1,277 m

AUSTRALASIA
8,923,000
3,444,278

ANTARCTICA
13,340,000
5,149,240

Islands and Inland Waters

Land area ☐ = 10,000 square kms
3,860 square miles

Inland water surface area ☐ = 1,000 square kms
386 square miles
Deepest point 229 metres
751 feet

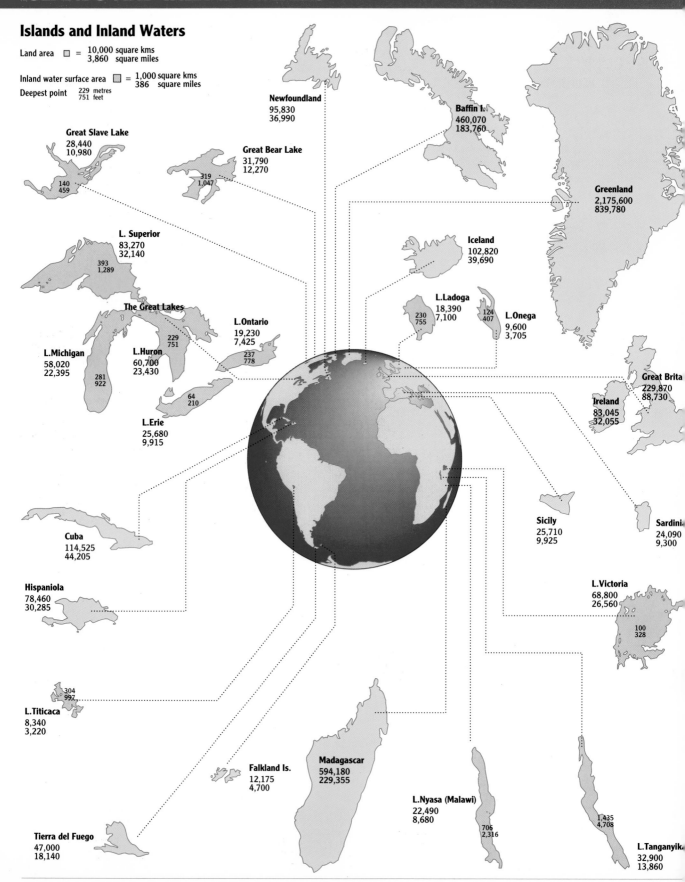

Newfoundland
95,830
36,990

Baffin I.
460,070
183,760

Greenland
2,175,600
839,780

Great Slave Lake
28,440
10,980
140
459

Great Bear Lake
31,790
12,270
319
1,047

L. Superior
83,270
32,140
393
1,289

The Great Lakes

Iceland
102,820
39,690

L.Ladoga
18,390
7,100
230
755

L.Onega
9,600
3,705
124
407

L.Ontario
19,230
7,425
229
751

L.Michigan
58,020
22,395
281
922

L.Huron
60,700
23,430
237
778

Great Brita
229,870
88,730

Ireland
83,045
32,055

L.Erie
25,680
9,915
64
210

Cuba
114,525
44,205

Sicily
25,710
9,925

Sardini
24,090
9,300

Hispaniola
78,460
30,285

L.Victoria
68,800
26,560
100
328

L.Titicaca
8,340
3,220
304
997

Falkland Is.
12,175
4,700

Madagascar
594,180
229,355

L.Nyasa (Malawi)
22,490
8,680
706
2,316

L.Tanganyika
32,900
13,860
1,435
4,708

Tierra del Fuego
47,000
18,140

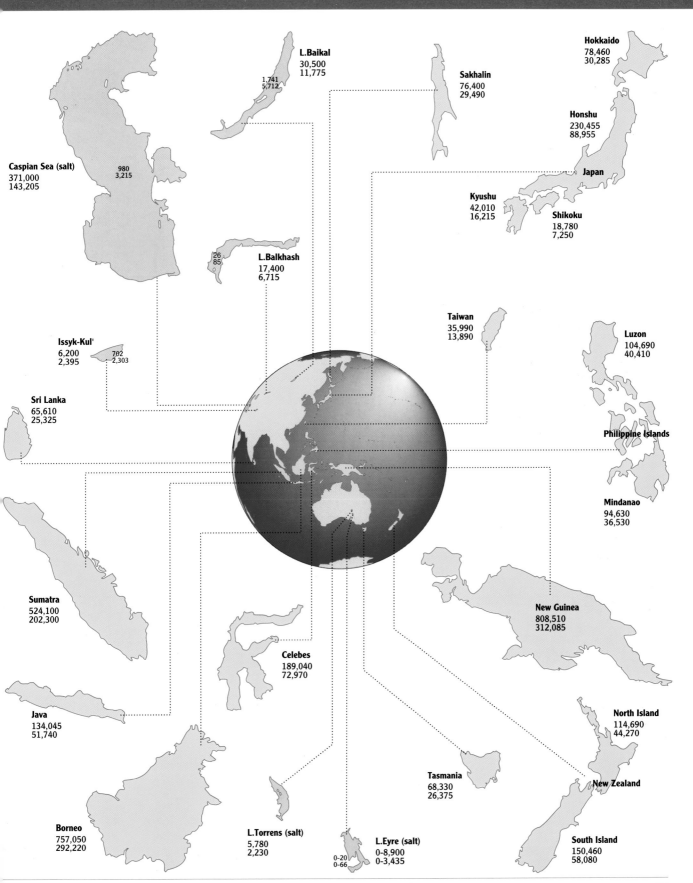

Hokkaido
78,460
30,285

L.Baikal
30,500
11,775

1,741
5,712

Sakhalin
76,400
29,490

Honshu
230,455
88,955

Japan

Caspian Sea (salt)
371,000
143,205

980
3,215

Kyushu
42,010
16,215

Shikoku
18,780
7,250

26
85

L.Balkhash
17,400
6,715

Taiwan
35,990
13,890

Luzon
104,690
40,410

Issyk-Kul'
6,200
2,395

702
2,303

Philippine Islands

Sri Lanka
65,610
25,325

Mindanao
94,630
36,530

Sumatra
524,100
202,300

Celebes
189,040
72,970

New Guinea
808,510
312,085

Java
134,045
51,740

North Island
114,690
44,270

Tasmania
68,330
26,375

New Zealand

Borneo
757,050
292,220

L.Torrens (salt)
5,780
2,230

0-20
0-66

L.Eyre (salt)
0-8,900
0-3,435

South Island
150,460
58,080

WORLD TIME ZONES

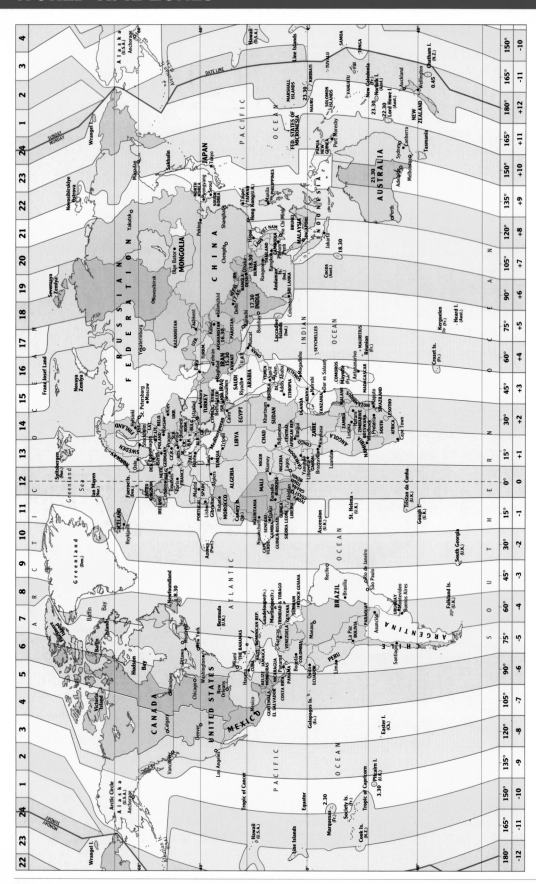

Zone Times (given in bold figures at the top of the map) are the Standard Times kept on land and sea compared with 12 hours (noon) Greenwich Mean Time. Daylight Saving Time (normally one hour in advance of local Standard Time), which is observed by certain countries for part of the year, is not shown on the map.

WORLD ATLAS

SYMBOLS

Relief

		Relief	
		Feet	Metres
⬯	Land contour	16404	5000
▲ 8848	Spot height (metres)	9843	3000
		6562	2000
⋈	Pass	3281	1000
▭	Permanent ice cap	1640	500
		656	200
		0	Sea Level
		Land Dep.	
		656	200

Hydrography

		13123	4000
⬯	Submarine contour	22966	7000
▼11034	Ocean depth (metres)		
(217)	Lake level (metres)		
∼∼∼	Reef		
∼∼	River		
∼∼∼	Intermittent river		
∼∼	Falls		
∼∼	Dam		
∼∼	Gorge		
⊥⊥⊥⊥	Canal		
⬭	Lake/Reservoir		
⬭	Intermittent lake		
∼∼	Marsh/Swamp		

Communications

─Tunnel─	Main railway
⊕	Main airport
- - - -	Track

Road representation varies with the scale category.

═══	Principal road	} Large scale
───	Other main road	
───	Principal road	} Medium scale
───	Other main road	
───	Principal road	Small scale

Administration

───	International boundary
- - -	Undefined/Disputed international boundary
-·-·-	Internal division : First order
-··-··-	Internal division : Second order
⊠ ◉ ◎ ⊡ ◻ ▪	National capitals

Settlement

Each settlement is given a town stamp according to its relative importance and scale category.

		Large Scale	Medium Scale	Small Scale
⊠		Major City	Major City	Major City
◉		City	City	City
◎		Large Town	Large Town	Large Town
⊙		Town	Town	Town
○		Small Town	Small Town	–
•		Village	–	–
⬟		Urban area (Large scale only)		

The size of type used for each settlement is graded to correspond with the appropriate town stamp.

Other features

∴	Ancient monument
⌣	Oasis
⬭	National Park
▲	Oil field
△	Gas field
-∘-∘-	Oil/Gas pipeline

Lettering

Various styles of lettering are used-each one representing a different type of feature.

ALPS	Physical feature	KENYA	Country name
Red Sea	Hydrographic feature	IOWA	Internal division
Paris	Settlement name	*(Fr.)*	Territorial administration

© Collins

EUROPE

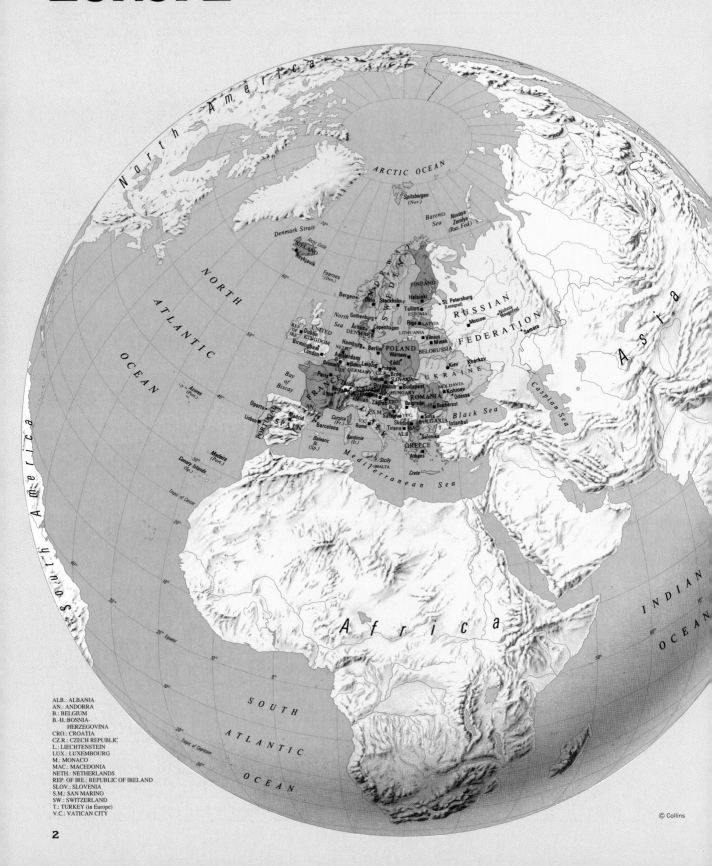

ALB.: ALBANIA
AN.: ANDORRA
B.: BELGIUM
B.-H.: BOSNIA-
    HERZEGOVINA
CRO.: CROATIA
CZ.R.: CZECH REPUBLIC
L.: LIECHTENSTEIN
LUX.: LUXEMBOURG
M.: MONACO
MAC.: MACEDONIA
NETH.: NETHERLANDS
REP. OF IRE.: REPUBLIC OF IRELAND
SLOV.: SLOVENIA
S.M.: SAN MARINO
SW.: SWITZERLAND
T.: TURKEY (in Europe)
V.C.: VATICAN CITY

© Collins

2

BRITISH ISLES

ATLANTIC

OCEAN

1788

NORWAY

Bergen
Haugesund
Karmøy
Stavanger
Egersund
Kristiansand
Lindesnes Mandal

Sotra
Stord

Oslo

Skien
Risør
Arendal

Skagerrak

DENMARK

Esbjerg
Ringkøbing
Holstebro
Silkeborg
Viborg

159

Orkney Islands
Kirkwall
Cape Wrath
Thurso
Pentland Firth
Wick

Shetland Islands
Lerwick

Clair

Magnus
Tern Murchison
Thistle
Cormorant Statfjord
Dunlin Brent Gullfaks
Hutton
Heather Ninian
Columba

Troll
Oseberg
Hild Brage
Odin
Frigg N.E.
Frigg E.
Frigg

Bruce
Beryl
Heimdal
Crawford
Balder
Brae
Gudrun
S. Brae
Dagny
Thelma
Sleipner
Piper
Tartan Balmoral
Maureen
143 Andrew
Claymore

Stromway
Lewis
Outer Hebrides
Skye
Inverness
Moray Firth
Elgin
Peterhead
Aberdeen

NORTH

SEA

Esmond Forbes
Gordon

Auk
Argyll
Fulmar
Duncan

Albuskjell
Josephine Tor
Ekofisk
Eldfisk
Valhall

Roar Adda
Tyra
Germ Ruth
Anne Dan

Nordfriessche Inseln

Hüsum

SCOTLAND
Aviemore
Spey
Ben Nevis
Mull Oban
Lomond Stirling
Perth
Dundee
Kirkcaldy
Firth of Forth
Edinburgh
Dunfermline
Berwick-upon-Tweed
Glasgow
Motherwell Galashiels
Ayr
Southern Uplands Tweed
Dumfries
Hexham

Buchan Glenn
Montrose
Lomond Ula
Cod
Gannet

1633

Inner Hebrides
Firth of Lorn
Jura Islay
Arran
Firth of Clyde
North Channel
Malin Hd.
Londonderry
Lough Neagh
NORTHERN IRELAND
Belfast
Armagh
Dundalk

Donegal Bay
Achill Island
Westport
Lough Mask
REPUBLIC OF IRELAND
Athlone
Mullingar
Galway
Galway Bay
Lough Derg
Limerick
Shannon
Tralee
Killarney
Carrauntoohil 1041
Cork
Kinsale Head
Cape Clear

Stranraer
Larne
Solway Firth
Workington
Carlisle
UNITED
KINGDOM
Newcastle upon Tyne
Sunderland
Middlesbrough
Darlington
Scarborough
Isle of Man
Barrow-in-Furness
Morecambe Lancaster
Blackpool
Preston
Southport Blackburn
Bradford Leeds
Huddersfield
Bolton Manchester
Liverpool
Stockport
Chester Stoke-on-Trent
Crewe
Derby Nottingham
Snowdon
Shrewsbury
Mansfield
Lincoln
Grimsby
Kingston upon Hull
The Wash

West Sole Ann
Viking
Indefatigable
Amethyst
Valiant
Dotty
Leman Scram
Bank
Hewett
Rough

Placid
Leeuwarden
Noordwinning
Den Helder
Groningen
Assen
Emden
Oldenburg
Delmenhorst

Ostfriesische Inseln
Wilhelmshaven
Emmerhaven
Cuxhaven
Bremerhaven

NETHERLANDS
Amsterdam
Haarlem
Hilversum
's Gravenhage
(The Hague)
Rotterdam
Dordrecht
Breda

Lingen
Nordhorn
Rheine
Osnabrück
Münster

GERMANY
Duisburg
Essen
Dortmund
Düsseldorf
Köln
Siegen
Aachen Bonn

IRISH
SEA

Anglesey
Holyhead
Cardigan Bay
Aberystwyth
WALES
113

Caernarfon
Snowdonia
Dolgellau
Cader Idris
Shrewsbury
Birmingham
Coventry
Worcester
ENGLAND
Northampton
Bedford
Cambridge
King's Lynn
Leicester
Norwich
Great Yarmouth

Valiant
Sean
Noordwinning
Helder Helm

Waddenzee

's-Hertogenbosch
Eindhoven
Antwerpen
BELGIUM
Bruxelles
Brussel

Krefeld
Mönchen-Gladbach
Verviers

Wexford
Waterford
St. George's Channel
Fishguard
Cardigan

Swansea
Newport
Cardiff
Cotswold Hills
Gloucester
Cheltenham
Oxford Luton
Swindon
Reading
Bristol
Bath
Bristol Channel
Exmoor
Taunton
Barnstaple
Exeter
Dartmoor

Stratford
Banbury
Aylesbury
Stevenage
Watford
LONDON
Woking
Basingstoke
Guildford
Crawley
Southampton
Portsmouth Brighton
Isle of Wight

Ipswich
Harwich
Colchester
Chelmsford
Southend-on-Sea
Margate
Maidstone Dover
Canterbury
Folkestone
Ostende
Dunkerque
Calais
Boulogne

's Gravenhage
(The Hague)

Open
1993

Strait of Dover

Berck

Aachen
Bonn

753

Antwerpen
Roubaix
Lille
Tournai
Douai
Arras
Mons
Valenciennes
Charleroi
Namur
LUXEMBOURG

Celtic
Truro
Penzance
Land's End
Isles of Scilly
Plymouth
Torquay
Weymouth
Bournemouth

Sea

English *Channel*

Dieppe
Abbeville
Somme
Amiens
St. Quentin
Sedan
Charleville-
Mézières

Verdun
Thionville
Metz

Luxembourg
Saarbrücken
Forbach
Sarreguemines

10°

C. de la Hague
Cherbourg
Guernsey
Channel Islands
Jersey
122

Le Havre
Bolbec
Rouen

Beauvais
Creil
Compiègne
Soissons
Laon
Reims
Épernay
Châlons-sur-Marne

Nancy
Strasbourg

Bayeux
Caen
Lisieux
Golfe de St. Malo
Granville
Flers
Argentan
Evreux
Dreux

Chartres
Versailles
Paris
Fontainebleau
Melun
Meaux
Marne

Vitry
Troyes
St. Dizier
Chaumont
Épinal

I. d'Ouessant
Brest
Morlaix
St. Brieuc
Dinan
St. Malo
Douarnenez
Quimper
Vitré Laval
Rennes
FRANCE
Le Mans
Alençon
Châteaudun
Orléans
Auxerre

Mulhouse
Belfort

Relief

Feet	Metres
16 404	5000
9843	3000
6562	2000
3281	1000
1640	500
656	200
0	Sea Level
Land Dep.	
656	200
13123	4000
22966	7000

Lorient
Vannes
Belle Île
St. Nazaire
Nantes
Cholet

Châteaubriant
Angers
Trélazé
Saumur
Tours
Blois
Vierzon
Bourges
Montargis
Gien

Chalon-sur-Saône
Dijon
Besançon
Neuchâtel

La Roche-sur-Yon
Cholet
Parthenay
Niort
Poitiers
Châtellerault
Châteauroux
Moulins
Montluçon

Nevers
Le Creusot
Montceau-
les-Mines
Mâcon

Genève
Lausanne
Bern
Biel

0   50   100   150 Miles
0   50 100 150 200 250 Kms.

Conic Projection

© Collins ○ Longman Atlases Cbii

3

ENGLAND AND WALES

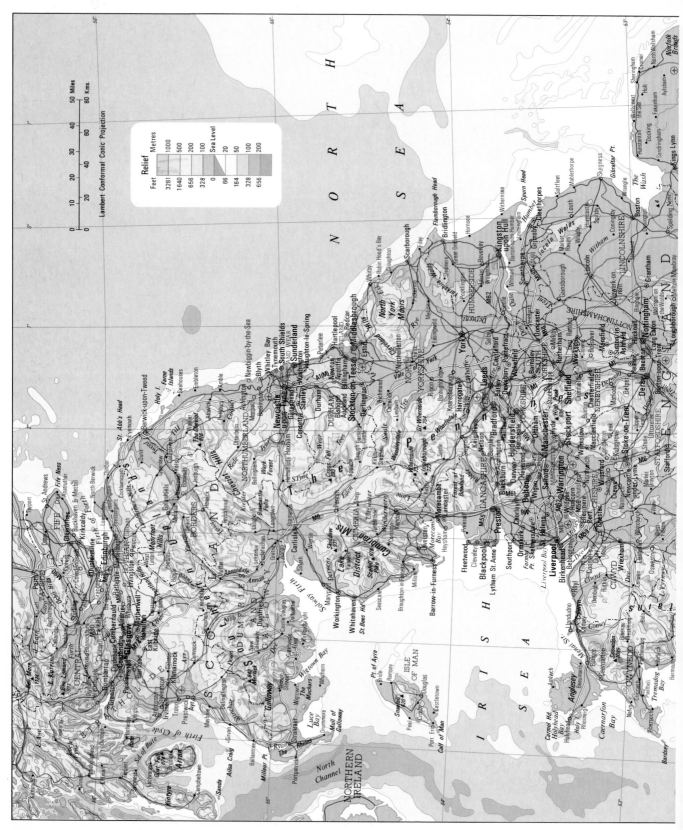

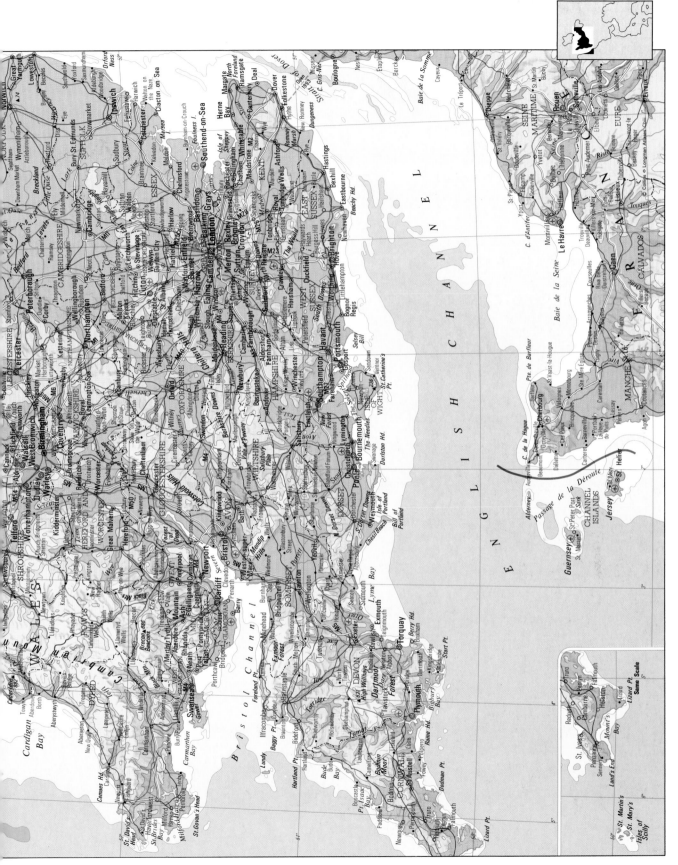

SCOTLAND

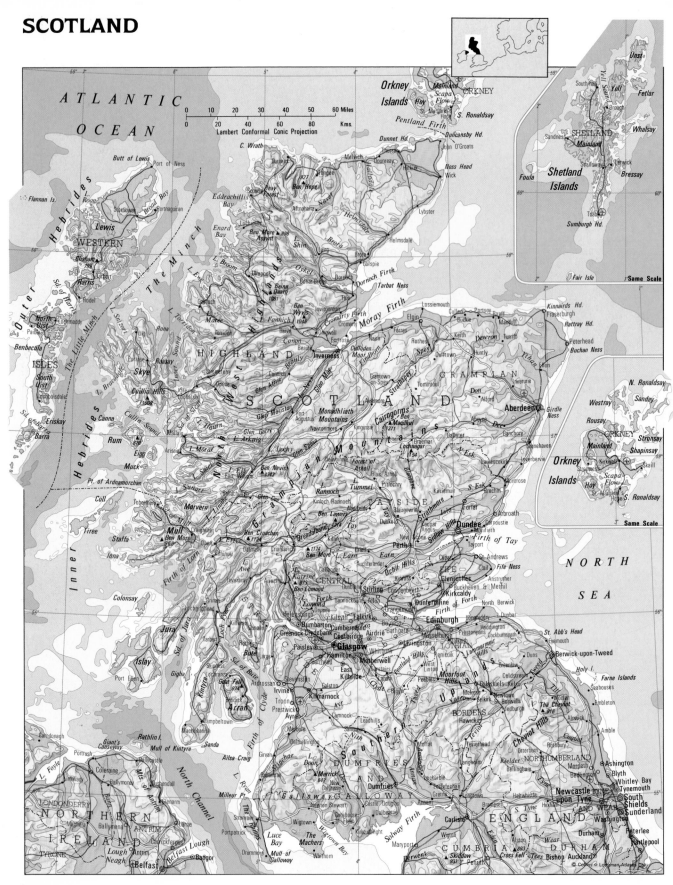

IRELAND

THE LOW COUNTRIES

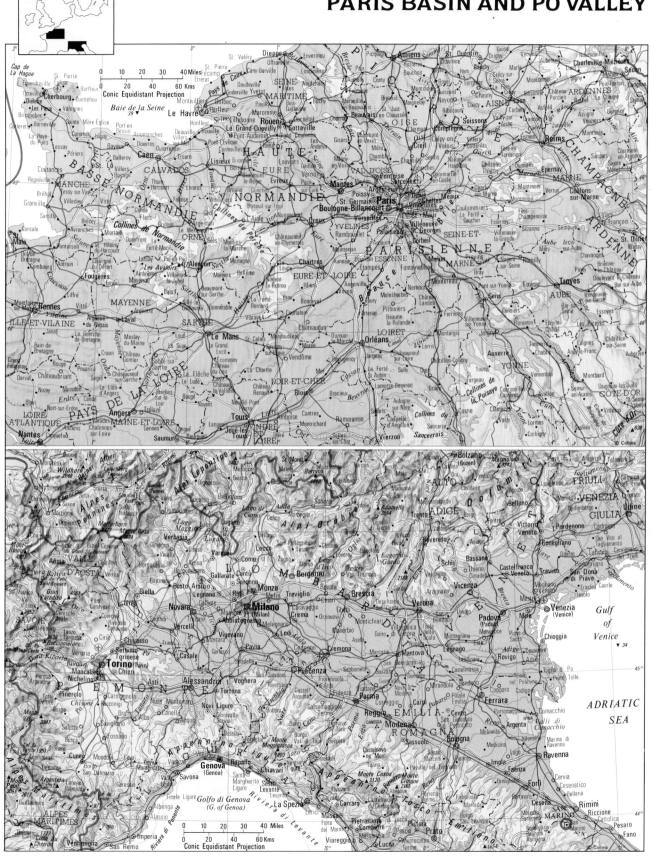

SPAIN AND PORTUGAL

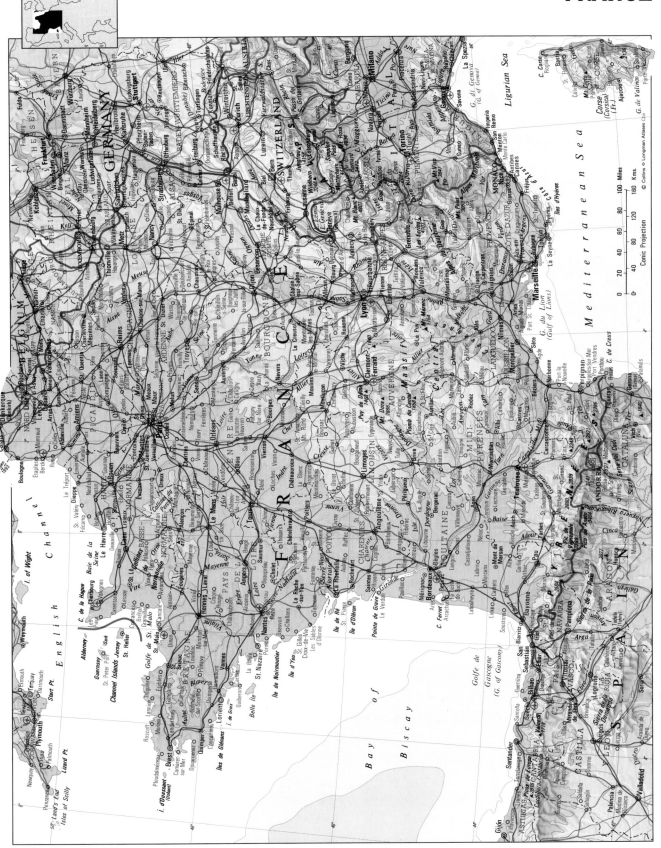

ITALY AND THE BALKANS

13

CENTRAL EUROPE

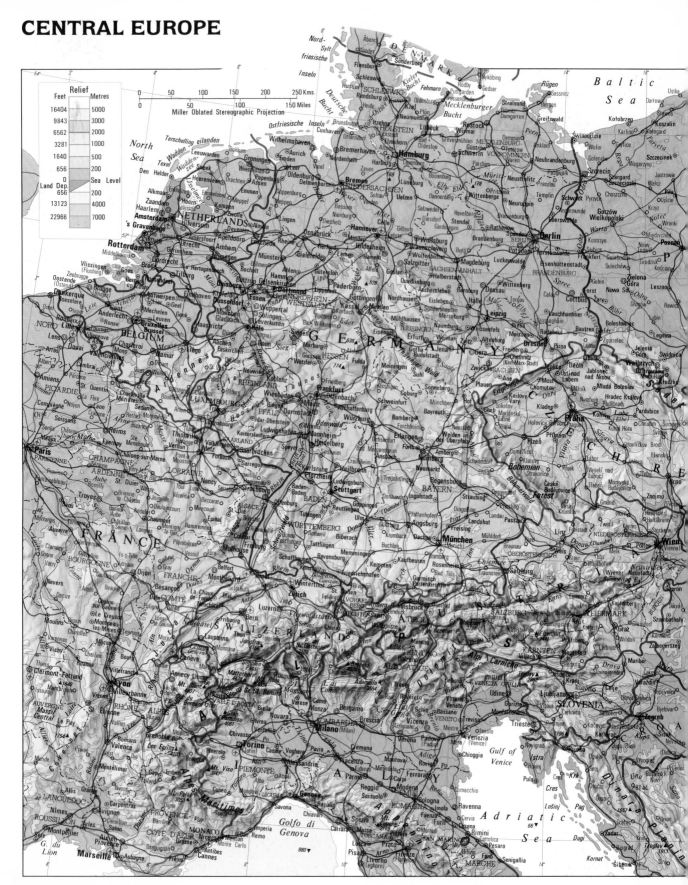

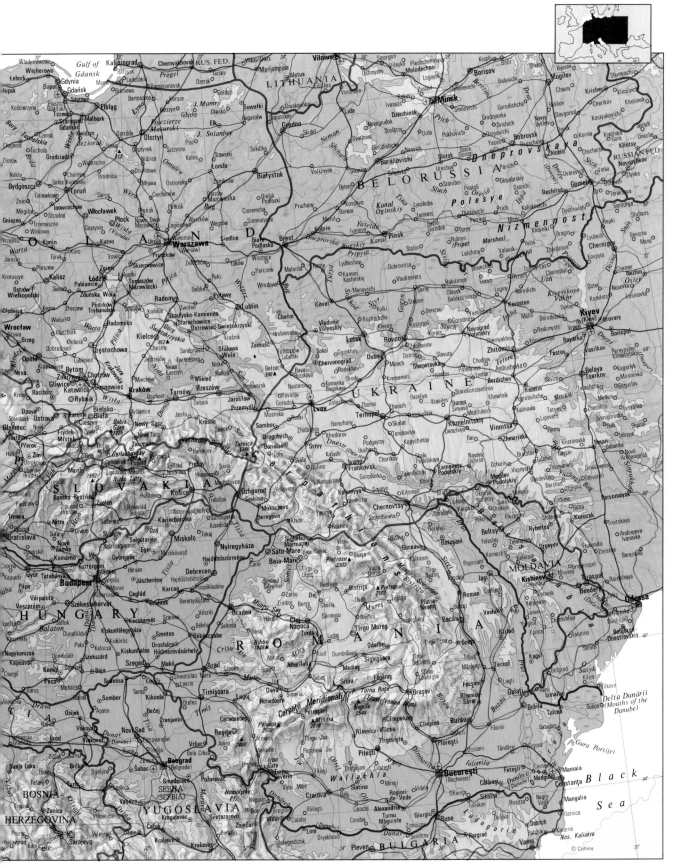

15

SCANDINAVIA AND BALTIC LANDS

ICELAND
on the same scale

© Collins

FAROE IS.
(Denmark)
on the same scale

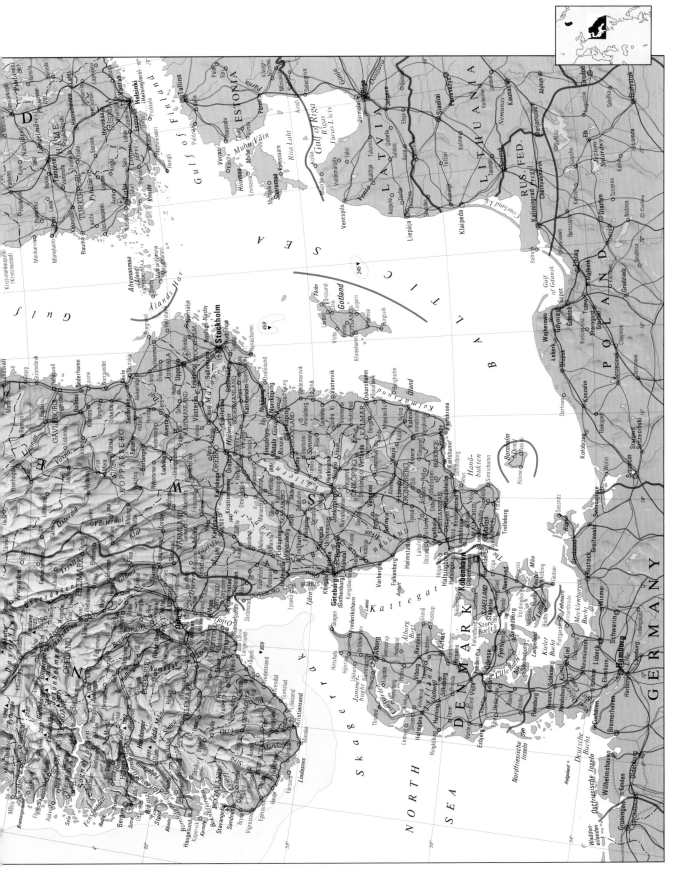

RUSSIAN FEDERATION, WEST & UKRAINE

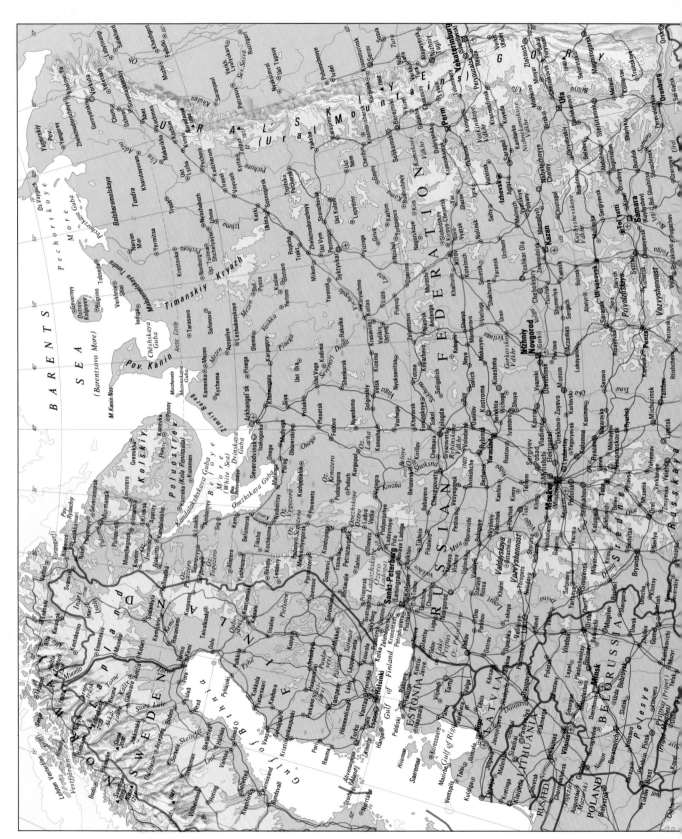

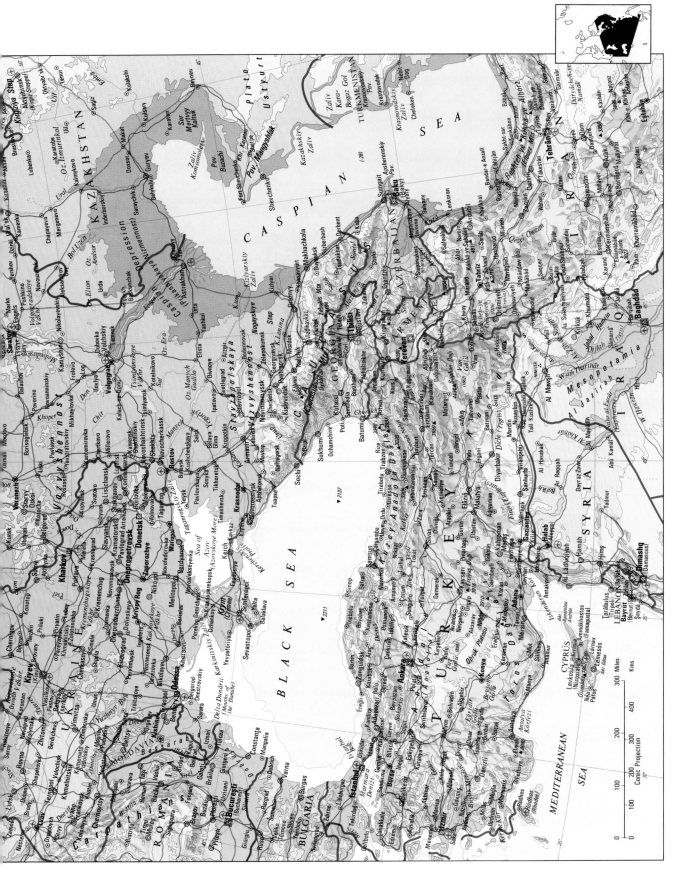

19

NORTH
ASIA

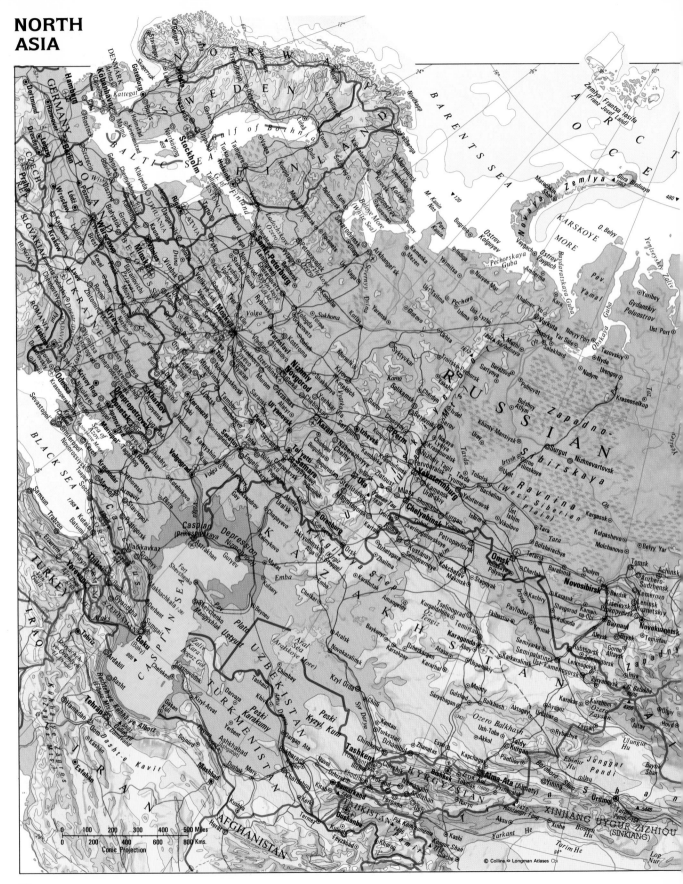

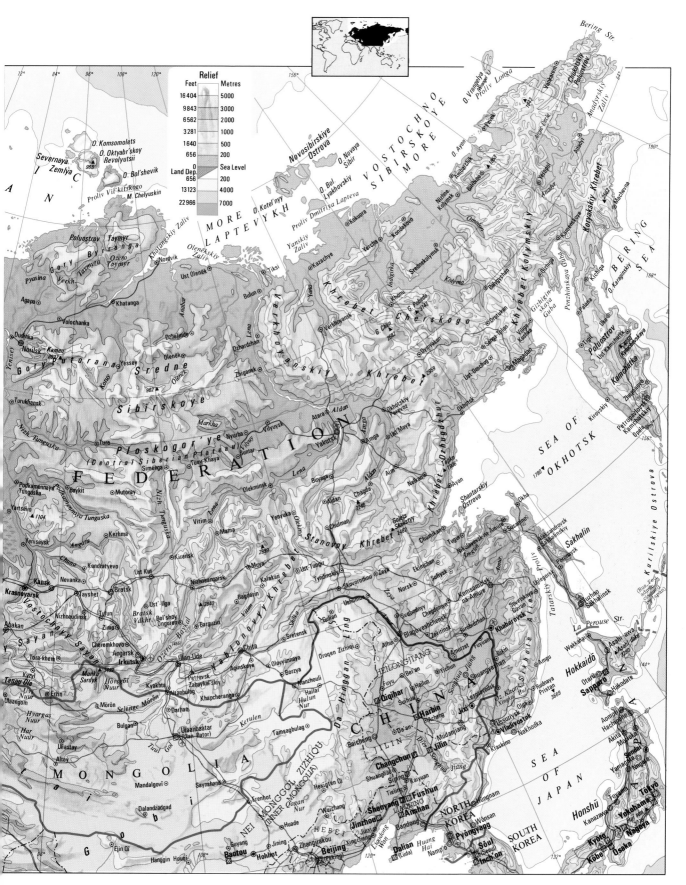

Relief

Feet	Metres
16 404	5000
9843	3000
6562	2000
3281	1000
1640	500
656	200
	Sea Level
Land Dep.	
656	200
13 123	4000
22 966	7000

Bering Str.

O. Komsomolets
O. Oktyabr'skoy
Revolyutsii
O. Bol'shevik
Proliv Vil'kitskogo
M. Chelyuskin

Severnaya
Zemlya

A R C T I C   O C E A N

Novosibirskiye Ostrova

O. Novaya Sibir
O. Bol. Lyakhovskiy
O. Kotel'nyy

MORE LAPTEVYKH

VOSTOCHNO SIBIRSKOYE MORE

Chukotskiy Poluostrov

BERING SEA

Poluostrov Taymyr
Gory Byrranga
Ozero Taymyr

Khatangskiy Zaliv
Olenekskiy Zaliv
Yanskiy Zaliv
Proliv Dmitriya Lapteva

Tiksi
Khatanga
Nordvik
Ust Olenek
Bulun

Khrebet Cherskogo

Khrebet Kolymskiy

Koryakskiy Khrebet

Kamchatka
Poluostrov Kamchatka
Petropavlovsk-Kamchatskiy

SEA OF OKHOTSK

Gory Putorana
Srednesibirskoye Ploskogor'ye
(Central Siberian Plateau)

R U S S I A N   F E D E R A T I O N

Sakhalin

Kurilskiye Ostrova

Stanovoy Khrebet

Khabarovsk

Vladivostok

Hokkaidō
Sapporo

SEA OF JAPAN

Honshū

MONGOLIA

Ulaanbaatar (Ulan Bator)

C H I N A

HEILONGJIANG

Qiqihar
Harbin
Jilin
Changchun
JILIN
Mudanjiang

Shenyang Fushun
Anshan
LIAONING
Jinzhou

Baotou
Hohhot
NEI MONGGOL ZIZHIQU (INNER MONGOLIA)
HEBEI
Beijing
Tianjin

Dalian (Luda)
Huang Hai

NORTH KOREA
Pyŏngyang

SOUTH KOREA
Sŏul (Seoul)
Inch'ŏn

Tōkyō
Yokohama
Nagoya
Kyōto
Kōbe Osaka

21

ASIA

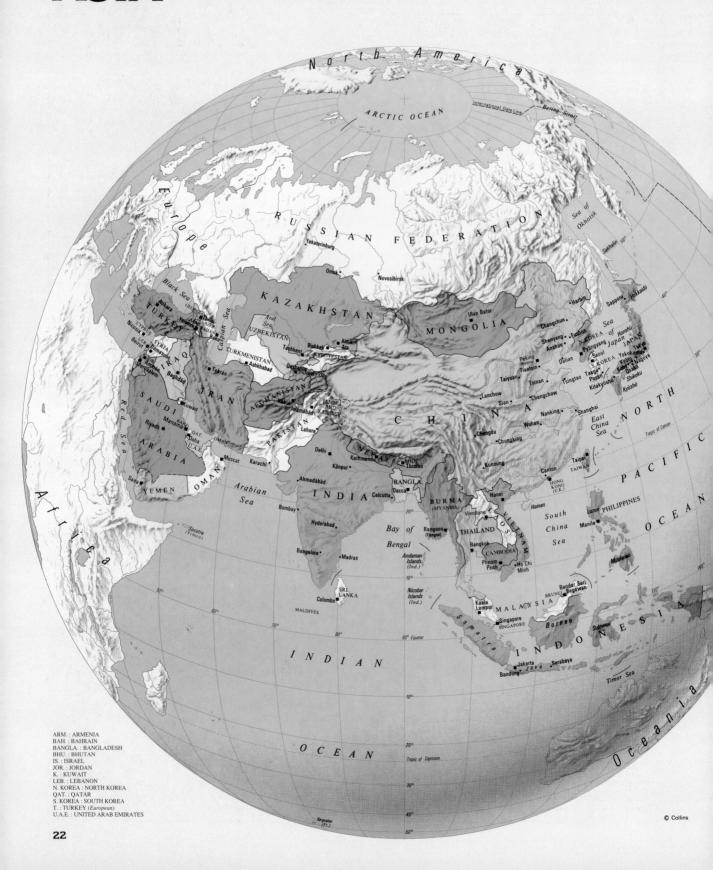

North America

ARCTIC OCEAN

International Date Line

Bering Strait

Europe

RUSSIAN FEDERATION

Sea of Okhotsk

Yekaterinburg

Omsk

Novosibirsk

Sakhalin

KAZAKHSTAN

MONGOLIA

Ulan Bator

Harbin

Sapporo

Hokkaidō

Black Sea

Ankara

GEORGIA

Aral Sea

Caspian Sea

UZBEKISTAN

Tashkent

Bishkek

Alma Ata

KYRGYZSTAN

Changchun

Fushun

N.KOREA

Sea of Japan

JAPAN

TURKEY

Nicosia

CYPRUS

Yerevan

ARM.

AZER.

Shenyang

Anshan

Pyongyang

Kyoto

Nagoya

S.KOREA

Seoul

Yokohama

Tokyo

SYRIA

Damascus

TURKMENISTAN

Ashkhabad

Dushanbe

TAJIKISTAN

Peking (Beijing)

Dalian

Pusan

Ōsaka

Kōbe

Beirut

LEB.

Baghdad

Tehrān

AFGHANISTAN

Taiyuan

Tientsin

Tsingtao

Taegu

Kitakyūshū

Shikoku

Amman

JERUSALEM

IRAQ

IRAN

JAMMU AND KASHMIR

Lanchow

Tsinan

Kyūshū

IS.

JOR.

SAUDI

Kuwait

K.

Islāmābād

Sian

Chengchow

Nanking

Shanghai

Riyadh

Manama

BAH.

QAT.

Doha

U.A.E.

OMAN

PAKISTAN

Lahore

CHINA

Chengdu

Wuhan

East China Sea

NORTH

ARABIA

Red Sea

Muscat

Karachi

Delhi

Kānpur

NEPAL

Kathmandu

Chungking

Kunming

Canton

Shanghai

Tropic of Cancer

Sana

YEMEN

OMAN

Arabian Sea

Ahmadābād

Islāmābād

Lahore

BHU.

Thimbu

Taipei

TAIWAN

PACIFIC

Africa

Socotra (Yemen)

Bombay

INDIA

Calcutta

BANGLA.

Dacca

Hanoi

HONG KONG (U.K.)

Hainan

South China Sea

Luzon

PHILIPPINES

OCEAN

Hyderabad

Bay of Bengal

Rangoon (Yangon)

BURMA (MYANMA)

Vientiane

VIETNAM

Manila

Mindanao

Bangalore

Madras

Andaman Islands (Ind.)

THAILAND

Bangkok

CAMBODIA

Phnom Penh

Ho Chi Minh

SRI LANKA

Colombo

Nicobar Islands (Ind.)

Bandar Seri Begawan

BRUNEI

MALDIVES

Equator

Kuala Lumpur

MALAYSIA

Borneo

Sulawesi

INDONESIA

Oceania

Sumatra

Singapore

SINGAPORE

INDIAN

Jakarta

Java

Surabaya

Bandung

Timor Sea

OCEAN

Tropic of Capricorn

Kerguelen (Fr.)

© Collins

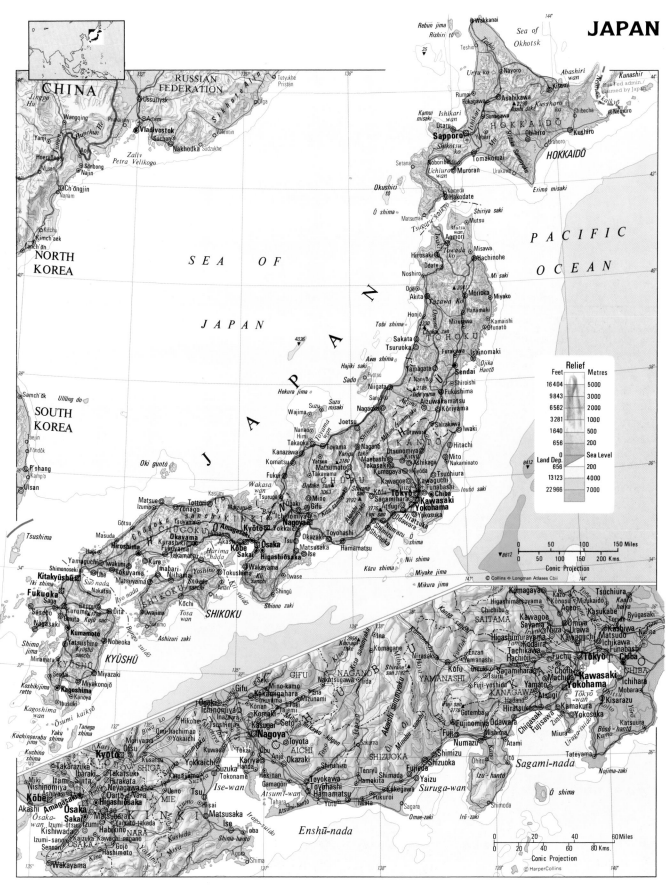

JAPAN

Rebun jima
Rishiri tō
Wakkanai
Sea of Okhotsk

RUSSIAN FEDERATION

CHINA

Teshio

Uruy ko
Abashiri wan
Kunashir
Rus Fed admin./ claimed by Japan

Ussuriysk
Rumoi
Nayoro
Kitami
Memuro Kaikyō

Artem
Fukagawa
Asahikawa
▲2290
Shibecha

Vladivostok
Otaru
Asahi dake
Kussharo ko

Nakhodka
Kamui misaki
Ishikari wan
Sapporo
Sunagawa
Obihiro
Kushiro

Suchan
Shikotsu ko
HOKKAIDŌ
Mt Hidaka Sammyaku
Urahoro
HOKKAIDŌ

Ch'ŏngjin
Noboribetsu
Tomakomai

NORTH KOREA
Uchiura wan
Muroran
Urakawa
Erimo misaki

Okushiri tō
Kameda
Hakodate
Shiriya saki

PACIFIC OCEAN

Ō shima
Matsumae
Tsugaru kaikyō
Mutsu
Mutsu wan

Samch'ŏk
Aomori
Misawa

SOUTH KOREA
Hirosaki
Towada ko
Hachinohe

Ōdate
Mi saki

Noshiro
Morioka
Miyako

Oga
Akita
Tazawa ko
Hanamaki
Kamaishi

Honjō
Mizusawa
Ōfunato

Tobi shima
Sakata
Ishinomaki

Awa shima
Tsuruoka
Furukawa

Hajiki saki
Yamagata
Sendai
Shiroishi

Sado
Niigata
Nan'yō
Fukushima

Hekura jima
Sanjō
Aizuwakamatsu
Kōriyama

Wajima
Nagaoka
Shirakawa
Iwaki

Nanao
Joetsu
Utsunomiya
Hitachi

Takaoka
Toyama
Nagano
Maebashi
Kiryū
Mito

Kanazawa
Matsumoto
Takasaki
Kumagaya
Ashikaga
Nakaminato

Komatsu
Takayama
Tsuchiura

Fukui
Mino
Kawagoe
Kawaguchi

Matsue
Tottori
Gifu
Tōkyō
Chiba

Izumo
Yonago
Ichinomiya
Nagoya
Yokohama
Kawasaki

Masuda
Matsue
Kyōto
Ōsaka
Hiratsuka

Hiroshima
Okayama
Kōbe
Sakai
Higashiōsaka

Yamaguchi
Fukuyama
Akashi
Matsusaka
Ise
Wakayama

Kitakyūshū
Imabari
Matsuyama
Tokushima

Fukuoka
Saga
Kōchi
SHIKOKU

Nagasaki
Ōita

Kumamoto
Nobeoka

KYŪSHŪ
Miyazaki

Kagoshima

Inset (southern Honshū detail)

PACIFIC OCEAN

Tōkyō
Kawasaki
Yokohama
KANAGAWA

Nagoya
AICHI

Kyōto

Ōsaka
Kōbe
KINKI

Wakayama

Sagami-nada

Enshū-nada

Conic Projection
© HarperCollins

23

EAST ASIA

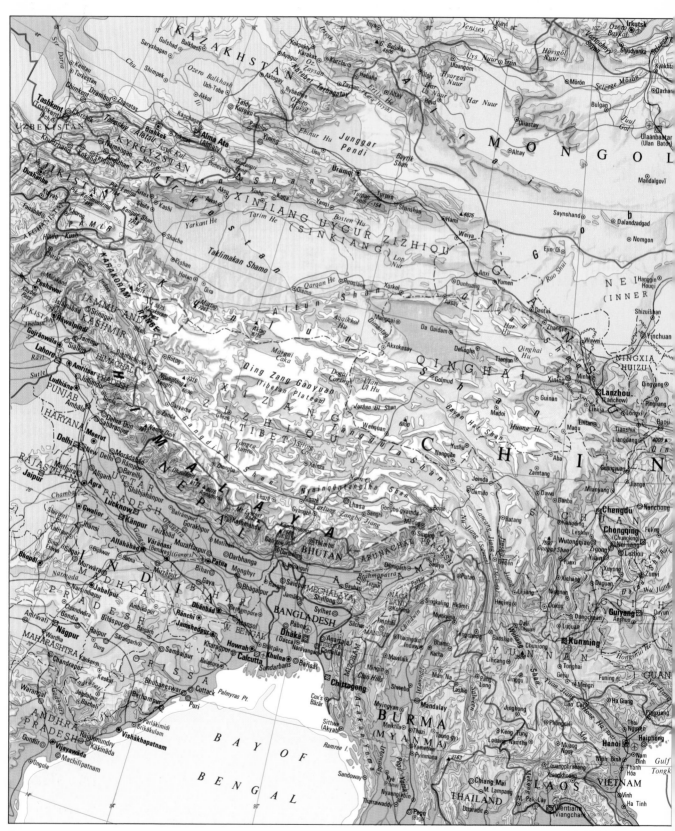

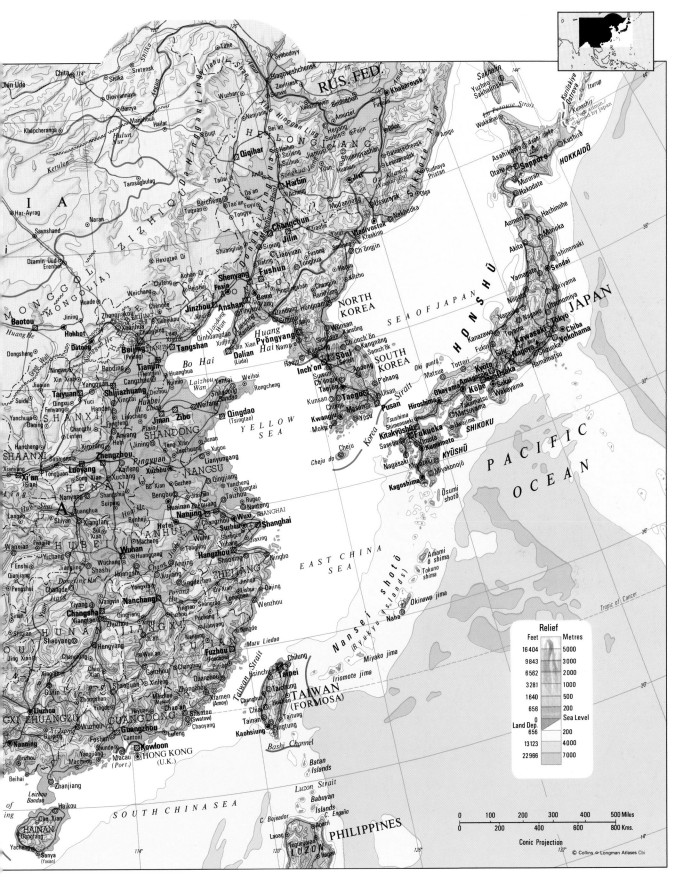

RUS. FED.

HEILONGJIANG

JILIN

MONGGOL (MONGOLIA)

NEI MONGOL ZIZHIQU

NORTH KOREA

SOUTH KOREA

SEA OF JAPAN

HOKKAIDŌ

HONSHŪ

JAPAN

SHIKOKU

KYŪSHŪ

PACIFIC OCEAN

SHANXI

SHAANXI

HENAN

HUBEI

ANHUI

HUNAN

JIANGXI

ZHEJIANG

JIANGSU

SHANDONG

FUJIAN

GUANGDONG

GXI ZHUANGZU

HAINAN

YELLOW SEA

Bo Hai

EAST CHINA SEA

Nansei shotō (Ryukyu Islands)

TAIWAN (FORMOSA)

SOUTH CHINA SEA

PHILIPPINES

LUZON

Tropic of Cancer

Batan Islands

Babuyan Islands

Luzon Strait

Bashi Channel

Relief		
Feet		Metres
16 404		5000
9843		3000
6562		2000
3281		1000
1640		500
656		200
0		Sea Level
Land Dep.		
656		200
13 123		4000
22 966		7000

0   100   200   300   400   500 Miles
0   200   400   600   800 Kms.

Conic Projection

© Collins · Longman Atlases Cbi

SOUTHEAST ASIA

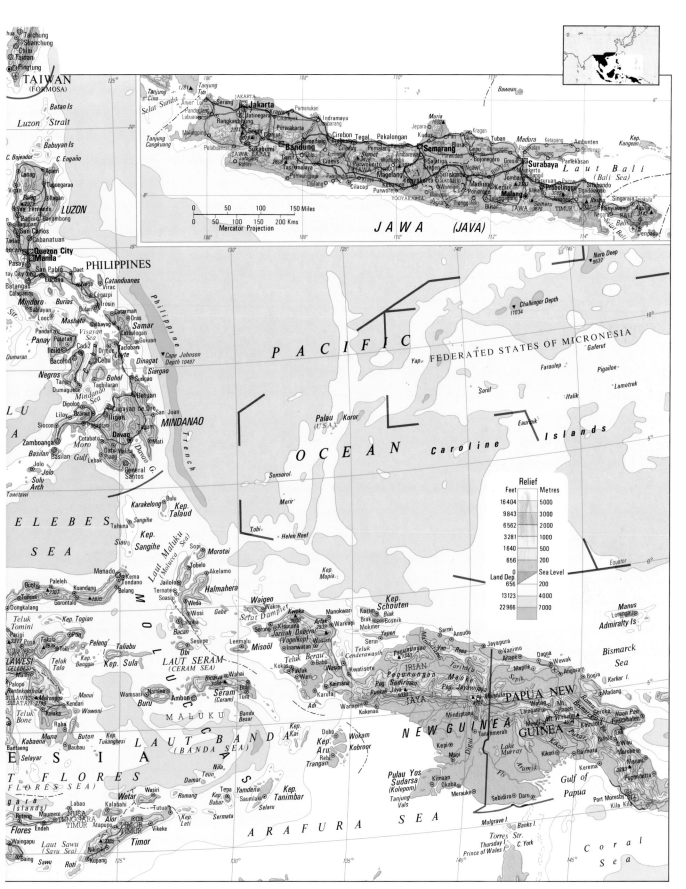

TAIWAN
(FORMOSA)

hua • Taichung
• Shanchung
Chiai
Tainan
• Pingtung

Batan Is

Luzon Strait

Babuyan Is

C. Bojeador
C. Engaño
Aparri
Laoag • Tuguegarao
Vigan
Ilagan
Puwg 2929
San Fernando LUZON
Baguio Bayombong
San Carlos
Cabanatuan
Tarlac
oncan
Quezon City
Pasay Manila PHILIPPINES
tay City San Pablo • Daet
San Pablo Naga • Catanduanes
Batangas Lucena Virac
Calapan Legazpi
Mindoro Burias Irosin
Sablayan Looc Catarman
Pandan Oras
Panay Masbate Catbalogan
Roxas Calbayog Samar
Iloilo Cadiz Ormoc Guiuan
Bacolod Cebu Leyte
Negros Siargao
Tanjay Bohol Tagbilaran
Dumaguete Betuan
Dipolog Cagayan de Oro
Liloy Oroma San Juan
Siocon Iligan Tagum
Zamboanga Pagadian MINDANAO
Basilan Cotabato Davao
Moro Datu Malita
Basilan Gulf Lebak Piang
Jolo General G.
Jolo Santos Mati
Sulu
Arch

Tawitawi

ELEBES

SEA

JAKARTA
Jakarta
Serang Krawang Pamanukan
Anyer Lor Jatinegara Cikampek Indramayu
Pandeglang Cibinong Cirebon Tegal Pekalongan
Labuan Bogor Sumedang Cilacap Pemalang
Malingping Rangkasbitung Purwakarta
Tanjung Sukabumi BANDUNG
Cangkuang Garut Ciledug Semarang
Pelabuanratu JAWA BARAT Tasikmalaya
Ciamis JAWA TENGAH
Cilacap Purwokerto
Purworejo YOGYAKARTA
YOGYAKARTA Surakarta

Muria 1602

Jepara Kudus Rembang Tuban Madura Ketapang
Demak Pati Blora Bojonegoro Gresik Bangkalan
Salatiga Ngawi Surabaya Pamekasan
Magelang Yogyakarta Madiun Jombang Pasuruan Probolinggo
Wonosari Ponorogo Malang
Blitar Kediri Semeru 3676 Raung
Trenggalek JAWA TIMUR

Laut Bali
(Bali Sea)

Singaraja Tejakula
Bali

50 100 150 Miles
50 100 150 200 Kms
Mercator Projection

JAWA (JAVA)

PACIFIC

Challenger Depth
11034

Nero Deep
9637

FEDERATED STATES OF MICRONESIA

Yap Gaferut

Faraulep Pigailoe

Sorol Ifalik Lamotrek

OCEAN Caroline Islands

Palau Koror
(U.S.A.) Eauripik

Cape Johnson
Depth 10497

Sonsorol

Merir

Tobi
Helen Reef

Kep.
Talaud

Bulu
Karakelong

Tahuna
Kep.
Sangihe
Siau

Sangihe

Laut Maluku (Molucca Sea)

Sopi
Morotai

Tobelo
Akelamo

Manado Kema
Tondano Jailolo
Belang Halmahera
Buol Paleleh Kuandang Weda
Tomini Gorontalo Soasiu Wosi
Dongkalang Belang Labuha
Teluk
Tomini Kep. Togian
Parigi
Poso Fokala Kep. Sula Peleng Taliabu
LAWESI Poto Toli Bacan
(CELEBES) Kep. Banggai Sesepe
Teluk Teluk Misoöl
Tolo Banggai
Kep. Sula

LAUT SERAM
(CERAM SEA)

Waigeo Wakre
Selat Dampier Kwoka
Sorong Klamono Artak 2939
Jazirah Doberai
(Vogelkop) Wasian
Lenmalu
Bacan

Manui Wamsasi Namlea
Kendari Wowoni Ambon Seram (Ceram)
Kolaka Buru Banda
Teluk Raha MALUKU Besar
Bone Muna Buton LAUT BANDA
Kabaena (BANDA SEA)
Bantaeng Tukangbesi
ESIA Selayar

Kep.
Mapia

Kep.
Schouten
Korim Biak
Manokwari Biak Bosnik
Warkopi Mokmer
Yapen
Teluk Serui
Cenderawasih Yan

Sarmi

Pk.
Peguningan 1340

Pk. Sudirman
IRIAN
JAYA
Peg. Sudirman
Puncak Jaya 5030
Pk. Mandala
Merauke

Ansudu

Jayapura

Vanimo
Aitape Dagua Wewak
Mapik Angoram
Bogia
Sepik Karkar I.
Madang

Mt. Hagen
Mendi 4694
Pk. Wilhelm

PAPUA NEW
GUINEA
NEW GUINEA

Manus
Lorengau
Admiralty Is

Bismarck
Sea

Saroka Huon Pen.
Kainantu Finschhafen
Lae

Bufolo
Marobe

MOLU

Teluk Berau
Kokas Babo
Fakfak Wasior
Weri

Kaimana
Karufa

Wanapiri
Kenenau

Mimika
Tanahmerah

Mindiptana

Kepi
Mapi

Digul
Lake
Murray

Kikori Baimoru

Kerema

Pupondetta
3993

Gulf of
Papua

Port Moresby
Kila Kila

FLORES
(FLORES SEA)

gara
Islands

NUSA
TENGGARA

Flores

Wetar Alor
Kalabahi Wasiri Romang Tepa
Atapupu Dili
TIMUR Tutuala
TIMUR
Vikeke Vikeke
Timor

Kupang
Roti

Baing
Sawu

Laut Sawu
(Savu Sea)

Nikimli 1005

Yamdena
Kep.
Babar
Saumlaki
Selaru

Kep.
Leti
Sermata

Pulau Yos
Sudarsa
(Kolepom)
Kimaan
Okaba

Tanjung
Vals

Sebidiro Daru

Mulgrave I.
Torres Str.
Thursday I.
Prince of Wales C. York

ARAFURA SEA

Dobo
Wokam
Kep.
Aru
Rebi
Trangan

Coral
Sea

Relief
Feet Metres
16 404 5000
9843 3000
6562 2000
3281 1000
1640 500
656 200
0 Sea Level
Land Dep.
656 200
13 123 4000
22 966 7000

27

SOUTH ASIA

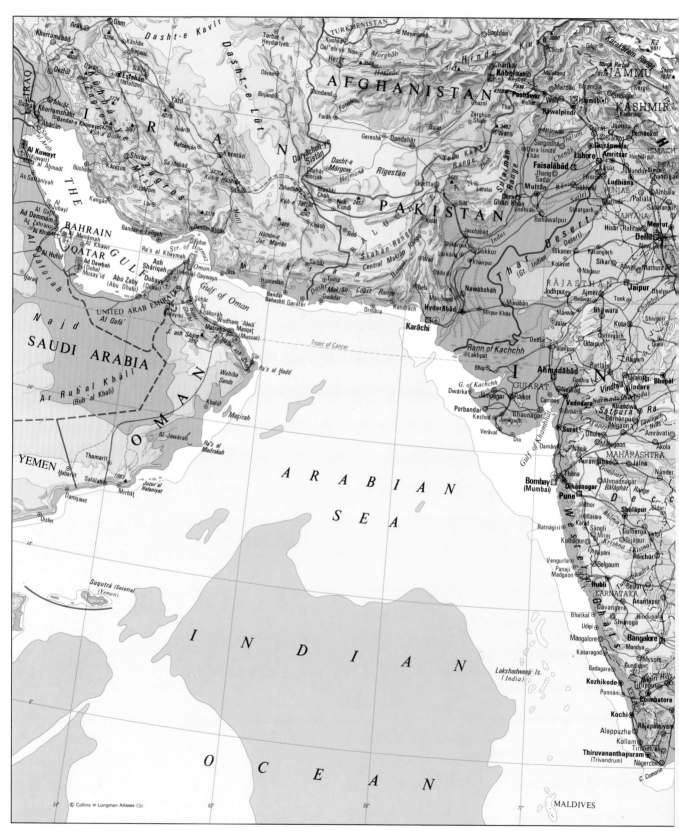

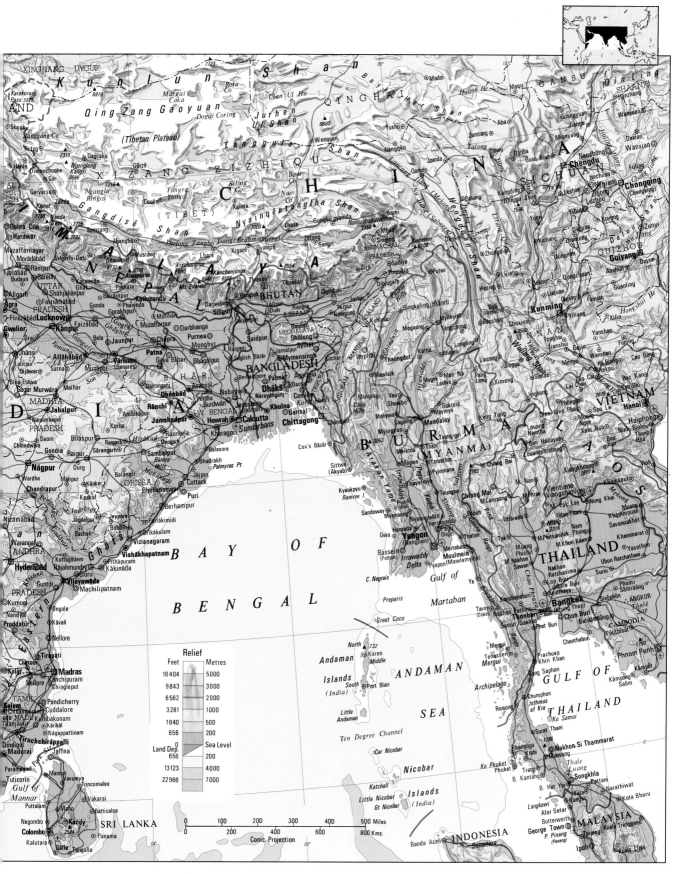

SOUTHWEST ASIA

THE LEVANT

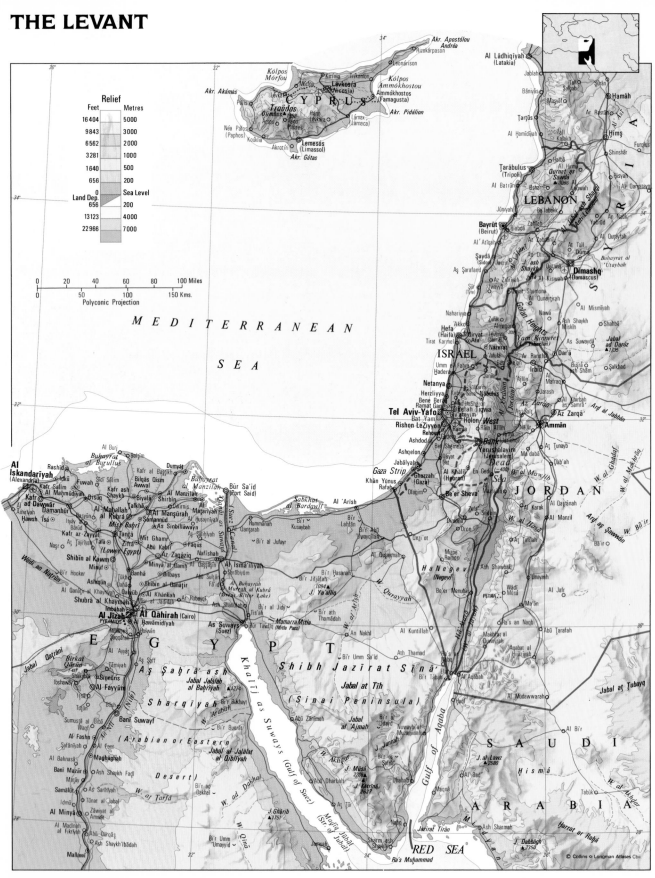

AFRICA

BUR.: BURUNDI
G.B.: GUINEA BISSAU
LES.: LESOTHO
MAL.: MALAWI
R.S.A.: REPUBLIC OF SOUTH AFRICA
RW.: RWANDA
S.L.: SIERRA LEONE
SW.: SWAZILAND

© Collins

NORTHERN AFRICA

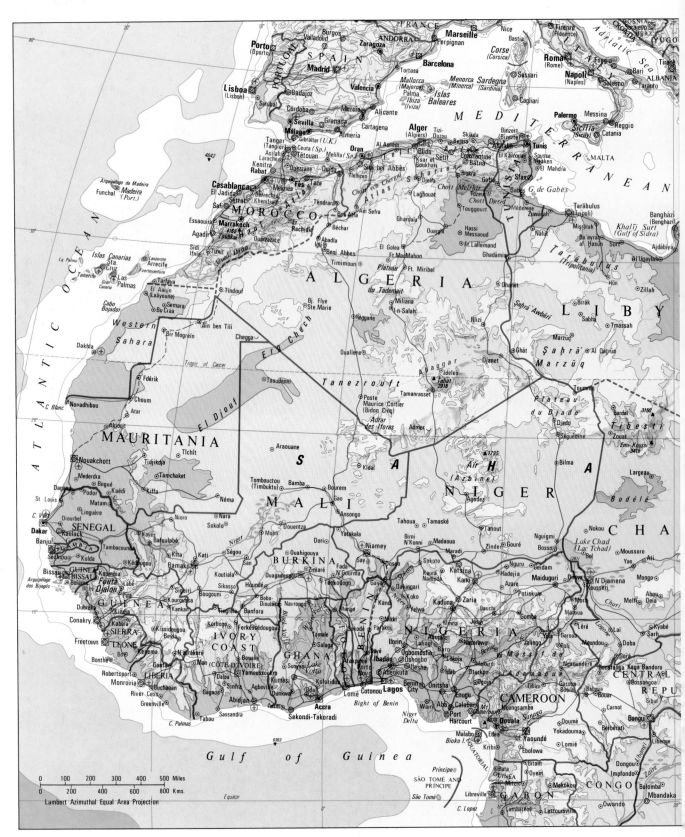

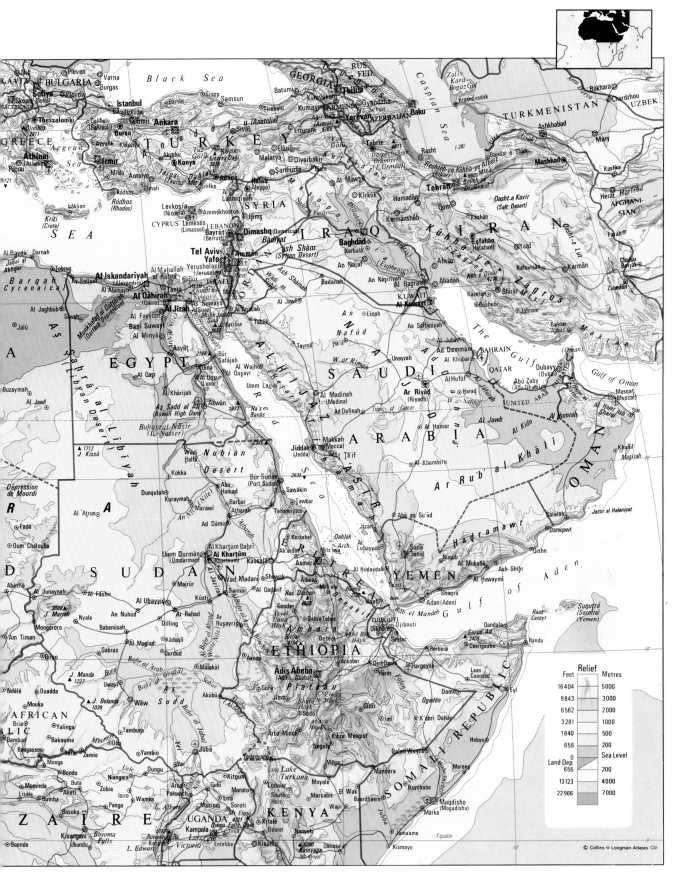

CENTRAL AND SOUTHERN AFRICA

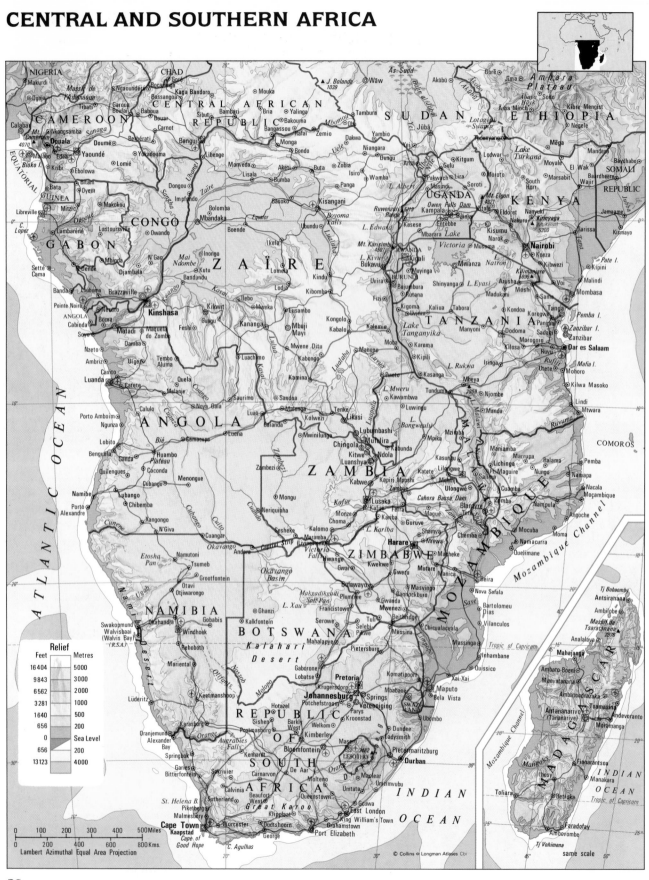

WEST AFRICA – EAST

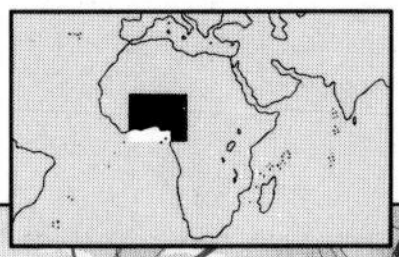

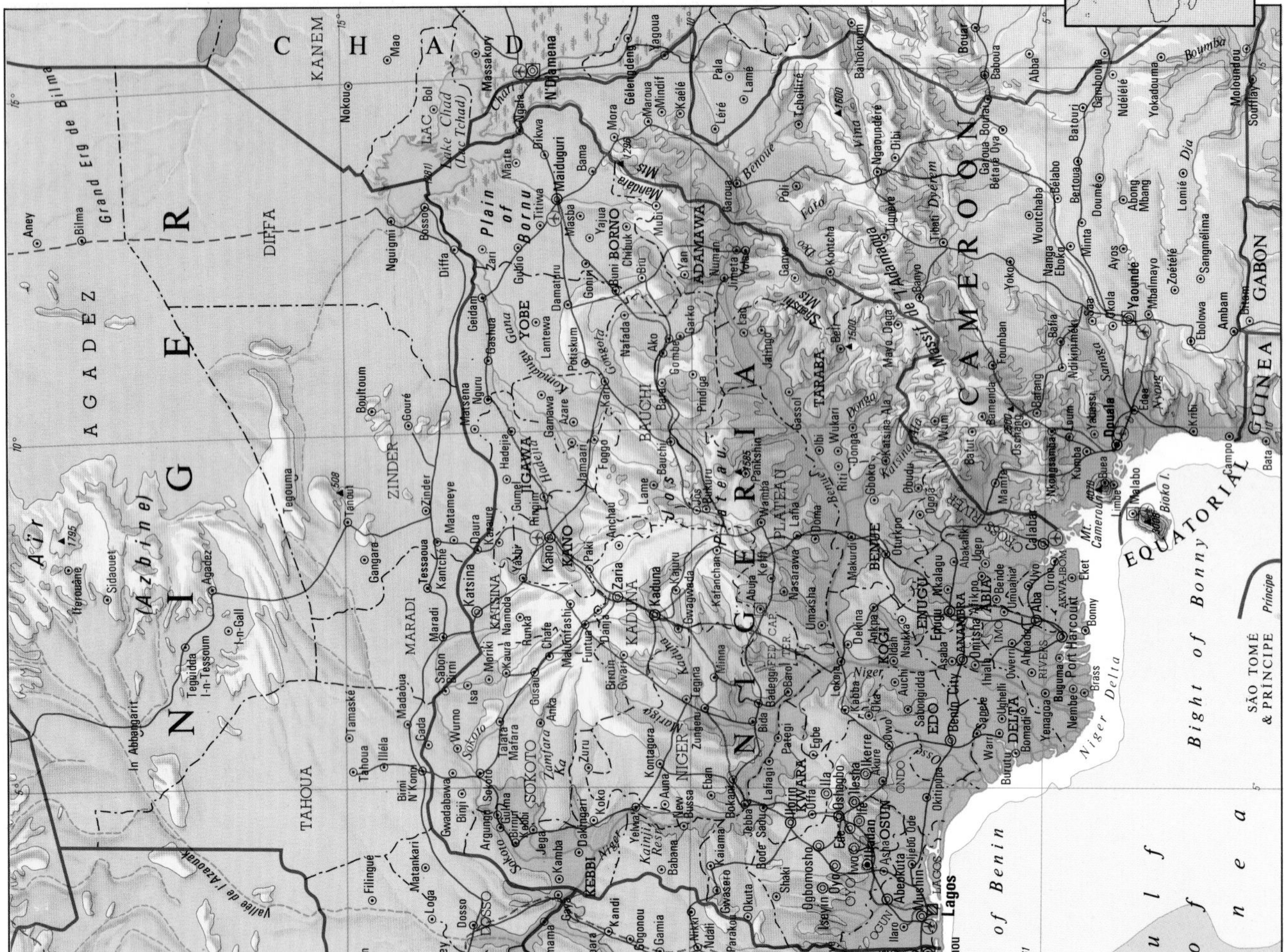

SOUTH AFRICA

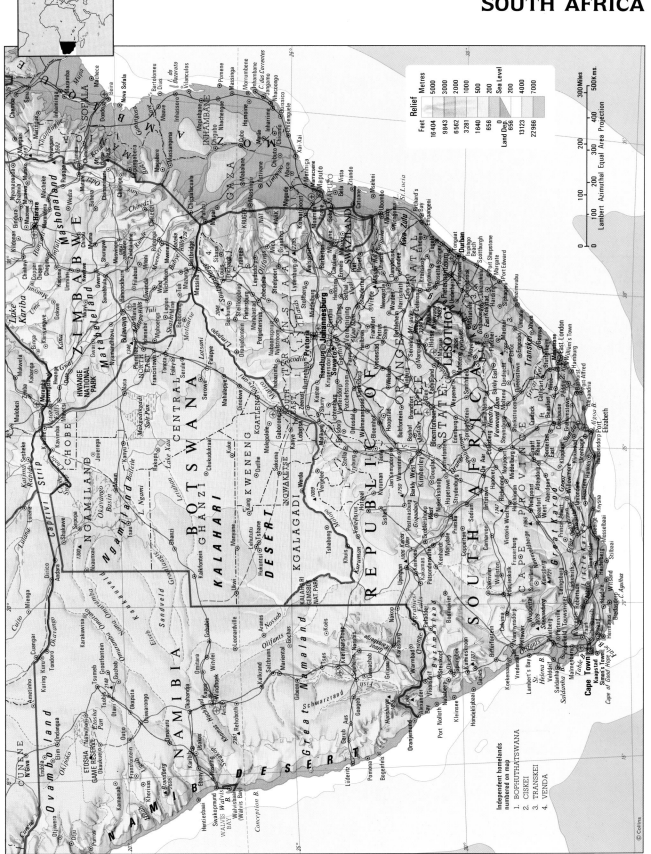

OCEANIA

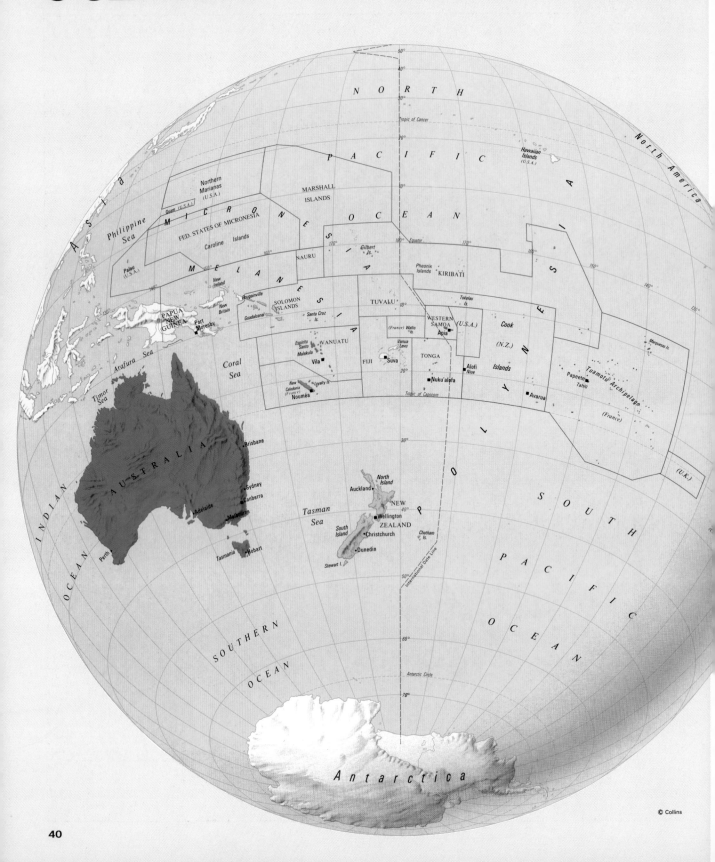

ASIA

NORTH

PACIFIC

OCEAN

North America

Tropic of Cancer

Hawaiian Islands
(U.S.A.)

Northern Marianas
(U.S.A.)

MARSHALL
ISLANDS

MICRONESIA

Guam (U.S.A.)

Philippine Sea

FED. STATES OF MICRONESIA

Caroline Islands

NAURU

Gilbert Is.

Pheonix Islands

KIRIBATI

Equator

Palau
(U.S.A.)

MELANESIA

New Ireland

Bougainville

New Britain

SOLOMON ISLANDS

Santa Cruz Is.

TUVALU

Tokelau Is.

WESTERN SAMOA

(U.S.A.)

Cook

Islands

(N.Z.)

Marquesas Is.

PAPUA NEW GUINEA

Port Moresby

Guadalcanal

(France) Wallis Is.

Apia

MICRONESIA

POLYNESIA

Arafura Sea

Coral Sea

Espiritu Santo

VANUATU

Malekula

Vanua Levu

FIJI

Suva

TONGA

Alofi
Niue

Tuamotu Archipelago

Papeete
Tahiti

Timor Sea

Vila

New Caledonia
(France)

Loyalty Is.

Nuku'alofa

Avarua

Tropic of Capricorn

(France)

Nouméa

AUSTRALIA

Brisbane

Sydney

Canberra

Adelaide

Melbourne

Perth

North Island

Auckland

NEW

ZEALAND

Wellington

(U.K.)

SOUTH

PACIFIC

OCEAN

INDIAN

OCEAN

Tasmania

Hobart

Tasman Sea

South Island

Christchurch

Chatham Is.

POLYNESIA

Dunedin

Stewart I.

International Date Line

SOUTHERN

OCEAN

Antarctic Circle

Antarctica

© Collins

40

AUSTRALIA

INDONESIA

Selat Makasar · Mamuju · Majene · Rantekombola 3455 · Kendari · Ujung Pandang · Watampone · Buton · Takalar · Baubau · Selayar

Kep Sula · Misool · Namlea · Buru · Ambon · Seram (Ceram) Bula · 3055 · Fakfak · Wasian · Serui · Wasior · Sarmi · Aitape · Wewak · Admiralty Is. · New Hanover · New Ireland · Bismarck Sea

LAUT BANDA (BANDA SEA) · 7440 · Kep. Kai · Kep. Aru · 4520 · Kep. Tanimbar

PAPUA NEW GUINEA · Pegunungan Maoke · Puncak Jaya 5030 · Kokenau · Mt. Hagen · Mendi · Mt. Wilhelm 4694 · Goroka · Madang · Hoskins · New Britain · Lae · Finschhafen · Solomon Sea · Wau · Kikori · Mt. Victoria 4073 · Popondetta · Owen Stanley Range

LAUT FLORES (FLORES SEA) · Lombok · Raba · Ruteng · Maumere · Flores · Ende · Alor · Dili · Kep. Leti · Wetar · ARAFURA SEA · Pulau Yos Sudarso (Kolepom) · Digul · Fly · Tandjung Vals · Merauke · Daru · Gulf of Papua · Port Moresby

Sumbawa · Sumba · Waingapu · Baing · Timor · Nikiniki · Kupang · Roti · Torres Strait

TIMOR SEA · Melville I. · Bathurst I. · Darwin · Bamaga · C. York · C. Grenville · CORAL SEA · Weipa · Cape York Peninsula · C. Melville 4520

Melville I. · Coburg Pen. · Wessel Is. · C. Wessel · C. Arnhem · Gulf of Carpentaria · Coen · Great

C. Londonderry · Joseph Bonaparte Gulf · Batchelor · Pine Creek · Arnhem Land · Groote Eylandt · Cooktown · Laura · Barrier

Bonaparte Archipelago · Wyndham · Katherine · Roper · Mataranka · Vanderlin I. · Wellesley Is. · Normanton · Cairns 1611 · Reef

C. Lévêque · King Leopold Range · Kununurra · Victoria River Downs · Daly Waters · Borroloola · Mitchell · Croydon · Innisfail · Ingham

Broome · Derby · Kimberley Plateau · Hall's Creek · Gordon Downs · Tennant Creek · Barkly Tableland · Camooweal · Burketown · Georgetown · Forsayth · Townsville · Home Hill · Bowen

Fitzroy Crossing · Hatches Creek · Avon Downs · Kajabbi · Hughenden · Pentland · Charters Towers · Proserpine · Mackay · C. Townshend

Eighty Mile Beach · Lagrange · Great Sandy Desert · South Esk Tablelands · **NORTHERN TERRITORY** · Urandangi · Austral Downs · Mount Isa · Cloncurry · Duchess · Dajarra · Winton · Blair Athol · Sarina

Port Hedland · Goldsworthy · Marble Bar · Nullagine · Percival Lakes · L. Mackay · Mt. Ziel 1511 · Alice Springs · Boulia · Longreach · Barcaldine · Emerald · Rockhampton · Gladstone

Barrow I. · Dampier · Newman · L. Disappointment · Gibson Desert · Macdonnell Ranges · Simpson Desert · Bedourie · **QUEENSLAND** · Springsure · Monto · Bundaberg

Onslow · Hamersley Range · Tom Price · L. Hopkins · Petermann Ranges · L. Amadeus · Birdsville · Windorah · Yaraka · Blackall · Gracemere Monto

Exmouth · Barlee Range · Tomkinson Ranges · Musgrave Ranges · Great Artesian Basin · Augathella · Mitchell · Maryborough · Gympie

L. MacLeod · Carnarvon · Gascoyne · L. Carnegie · Oodnadatta · Warrina · L. Eyre · Cooper Creek · Grey Range · Quilpie · Charleville · Roma · Dalby · Kingaroy · **Brisbane**

WESTERN AUSTRALIA · Meekatharra · Nannine · Cue · Mount Magnet · Leonora · Laverton · Great Victoria Desert · Coober Pedy · **SOUTH AUSTRALIA** · Tibooburra · Cunnamulla · St. George · Dirranbandi · Goondiwindi · Toowoomba · Warwick · Tenterfield · Lismore

Northampton · L. Barlee · Malcolm · L. Frome · Darling · Bourke · Walgett · Moree · Glen Innes · Casino · Coff's Harbour · Grafton

Geraldton · Mullewa · L. Moore · Kalgoorlie · Zanthus · Rawlinna · Leigh Creek · L. Torrens · Wilcannia · Cobar · Nyngan · Narrabri · Armidale 1433 · Kempsey

Dongara · Coolgardie · Nullarbor Plain · Oodnadatta · Tarcoola · Woomera · **NEW SOUTH WALES** · Nyngan · Dubbo · Tamworth · Taree

Moora · Southern Cross · Norseman · Penong · L. Gairdner · Peterborough · Broken Hill · Ivanhoe · Hay · Parkes · Bathurst · Singleton · Newcastle

Perth · Northam · York · Brookton · Newdegate · Esperance · Ceduna · Kimba · Eyre Pen. · Port Augusta · Port Pirie · Radium Hill · Balranald · Griffith · Orange · Cessnock · Maitland

Fremantle · Pinjarra · Narrogin · Hopetoun · Eyre Pen. · Whyalla · Port Pirie · Katina · Murray · Mildura · Lachlan · Wagga Wagga · Bathurst · **Sydney** · Wollongong

Bunbury · Kojonup · Mount Barker · Port Lincoln · Spencer Gulf · **Adelaide** · Pinnaroo · Ouyen · Kerang · Murrumbidgee · Albury · Mt. Kosciusko 2228 · Canberra · AUST. CAP. TER.

Busselton · Augusta · C. Leeuwin · Pemberton · Denmark · Albany · Kangaroo I. · Murray Bridge · Bordertown · Horsham · Bendigo · Shepparton · Wangaratta · **VICTORIA** · Great · Snowy Mts. · Bega · **TASMAN SEA**

GREAT AUSTRALIAN BIGHT · Naracoorte · Mount Gambier · Hamilton · Geelong · **Melbourne** · Morwell · Sale · Bairnsdale · C. Howe

Portland · Warrnambool · Wilson's Promontory · King I. · Bass Strait · Flinders I.

SOUTHERN OCEAN · 5670 · 5635 · Smithton · Burnie · Devonport · Launceston · Queenstown · Mt. Ossa 1617 · **TASMANIA** · New Norfolk · **Hobart** · South East C.

```
0    100  200  300  400  500 Miles
0      200    400    600   800 Kms.
Lambert Azimuthal Equal Area Projection
```

© Collins · Longman Atlases Cbi

WESTERN AUSTRALIA

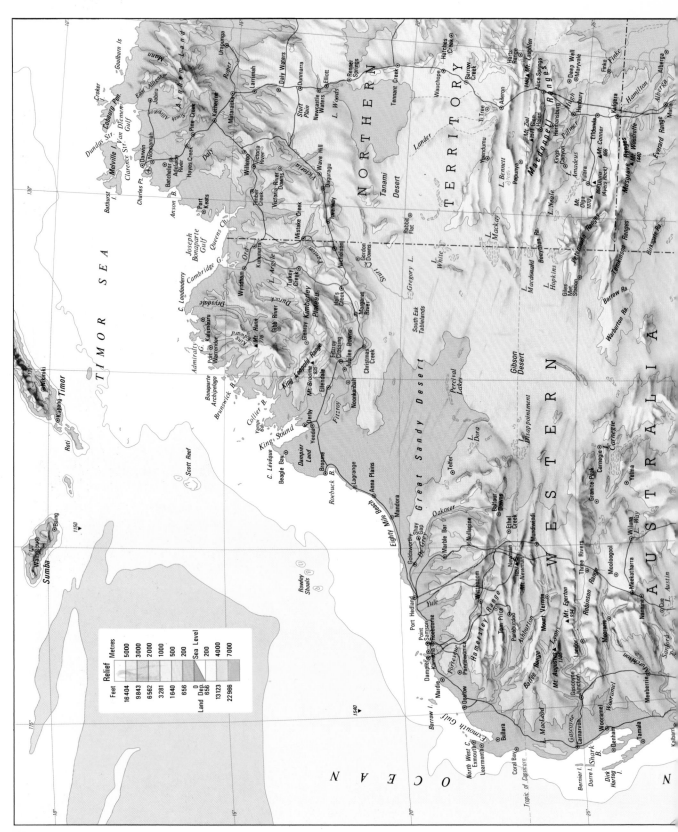

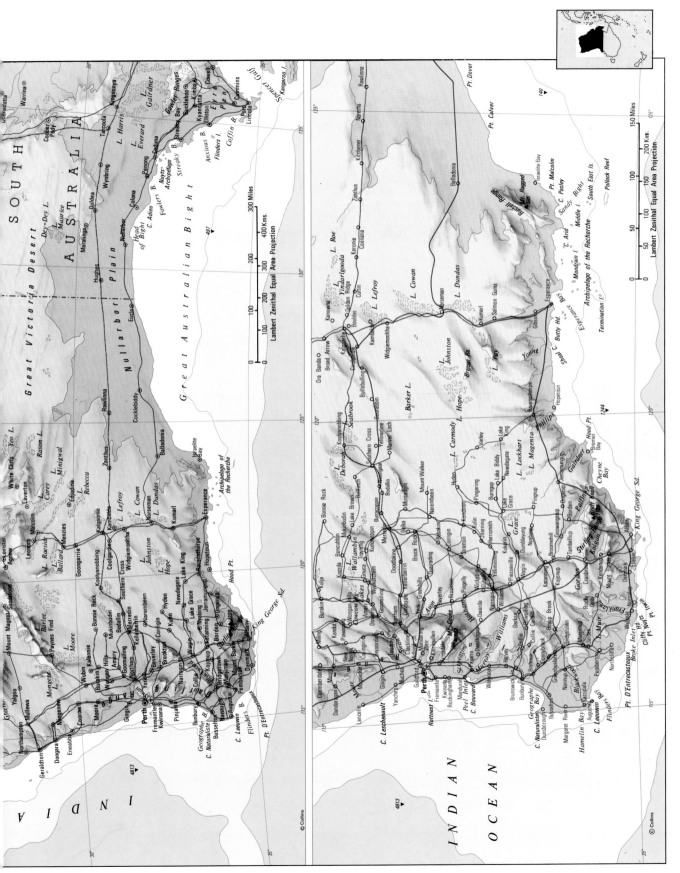

EASTERN AUSTRALIA

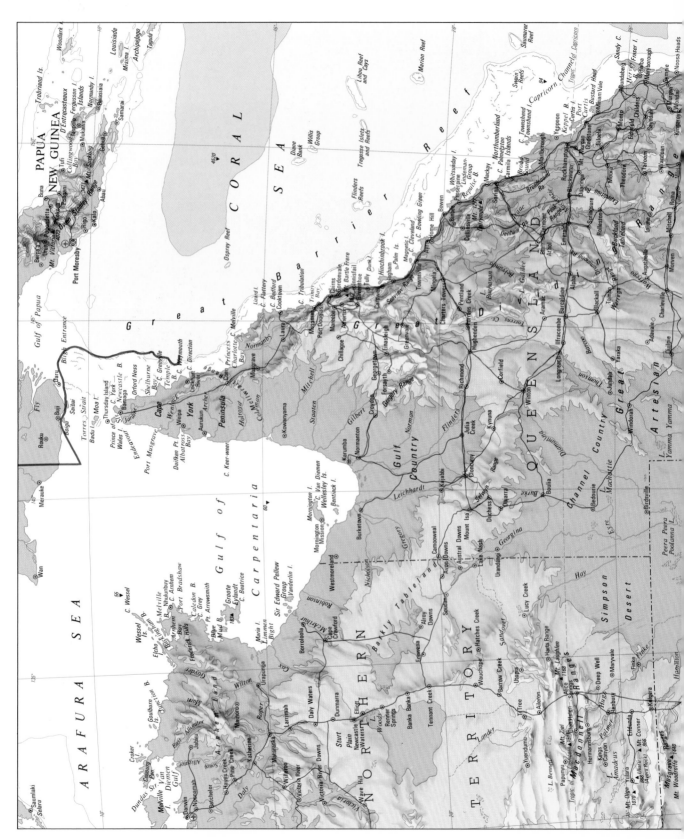

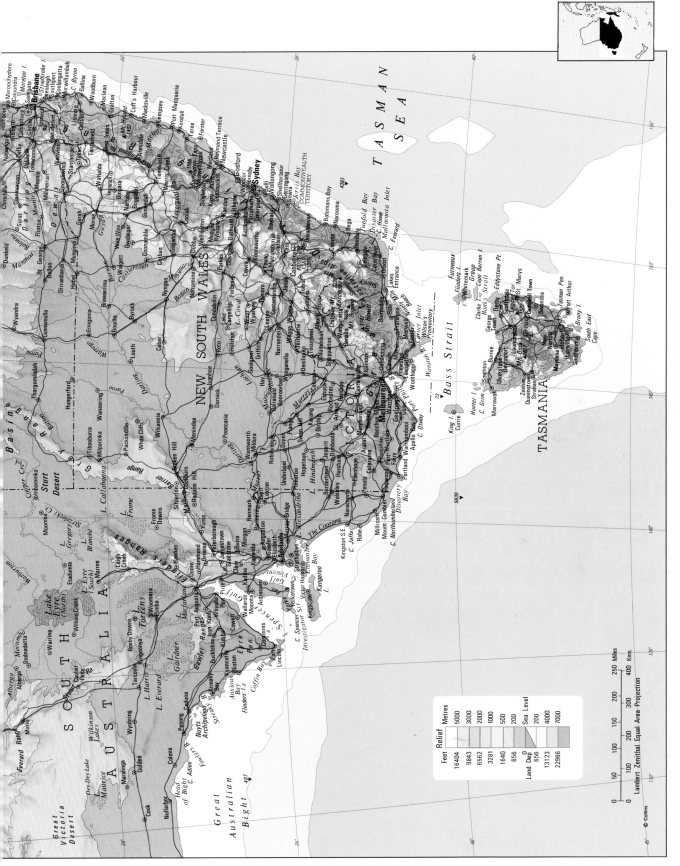

SOUTHEAST AUSTRALIA

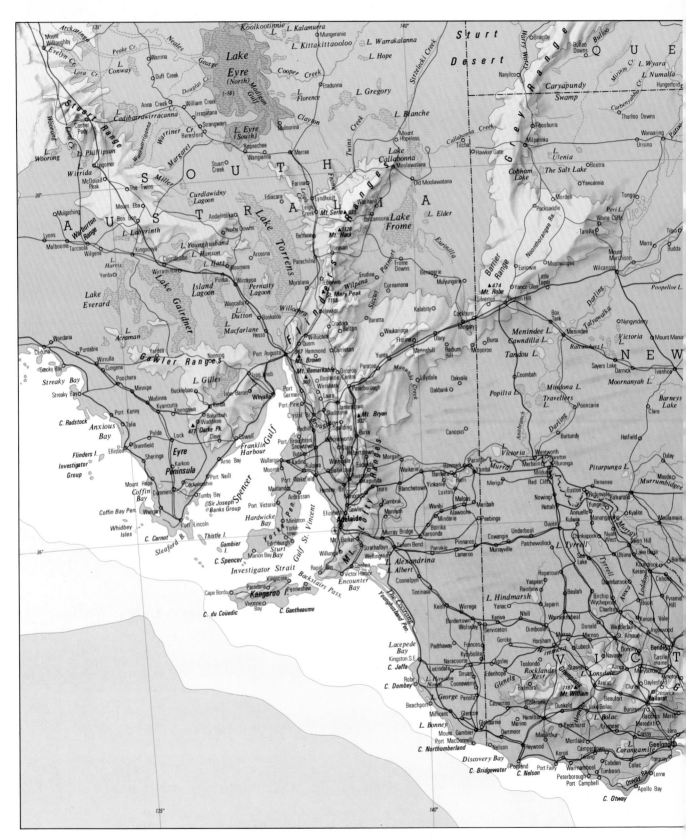

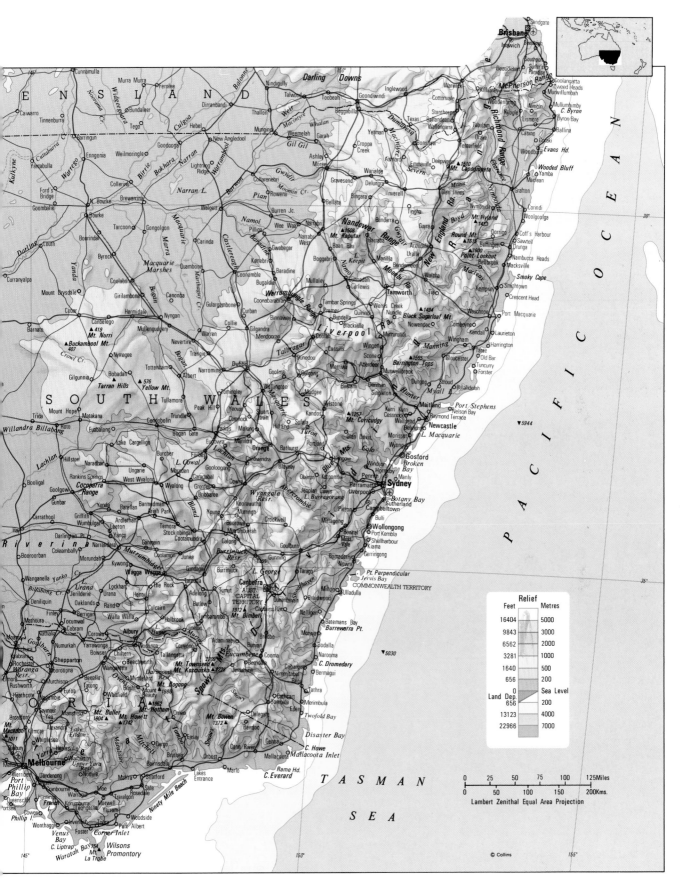

NEW ZEALAND

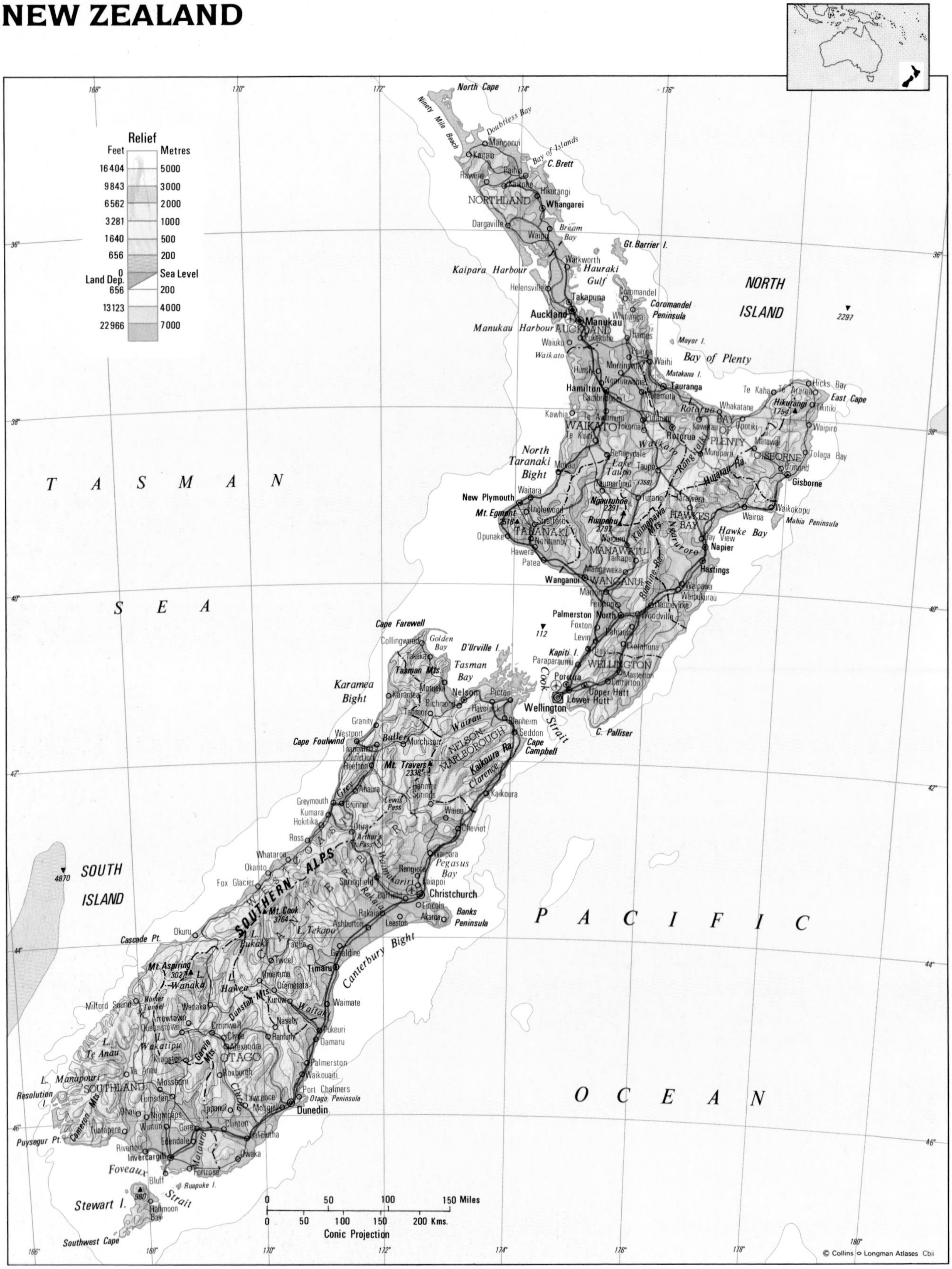

Relief

Feet	Metres
16 404	5000
9843	3000
6562	2000
3281	1000
1640	500
656	200
0	Sea Level
Land Dep.	
656	200
13123	4000
22966	7000

NORTH ISLAND

North Cape
Ninety Mile Beach
Doubtless Bay
Mangonui
Kaitaia
C. Brett
Paihia
Bay of Islands
Rawene
Kaikohe
Hikurangi
NORTHLAND
Whangarei
Dargaville
Waipu
Bream Bay
Gt. Barrier I.
Kaipara Harbour
Warkworth
Hauraki Gulf
Helensville
Coromandel
Takapuna
Coromandel Peninsula
Auckland
Manukau
AUCKLAND
Thames
Manukau Harbour
Mayor I.
Waiuku
Waihi
Bay of Plenty
Waikato
Huntly
Morrinsville
Tauranga
Matakana I.
Ngaruawahia
Te Kaha
Hicks Bay
Hamilton
Cambridge
Rotorua
Te Aroha
Whakatane
Opotiki
Te Araroa
East Cape
Kawhia
WAIKATO
Tokoroa
Hikurangi 1754
Tikitiki
Te Kuiti
Rotorua
BAY OF PLENTY
Waipiro
Murupara
GISBORNE
Tolaga Bay
North Taranaki Bight
Lake Taupo
Rongo Kuri
Gisborne
Waitara
Ngauruhoe 2291
Kaimanawa Mts
Waikokopu
New Plymouth
Inglewood
Tutira
Tarawera
Mahia Peninsula
Mt. Egmont 2516
Stratford
Ruapehu 2797
HAWKES BAY
Wairoa
Opunake
Eltham
Taihape
Bay View
Napier
TARANAKI
Normanby
MANAWATU
Waipukurau
Hawera
Waipawa
Patea
Taihape
Hastings
Wanganui
WANGANUI
Marton
Waipukurau
Feilding
Dannevirke
Palmerston North
Woodville
Foxton
Levin
Cape Farewell
Collingwood
Golden Bay
D'Urville I.
112
Kapiti I.
Paraparaumu
Otaki
Takaka
Tasman Mts
Tasman Bay
Otaki
Pahiatua
Karamea Bight
Karamea
Nelson
Picton
Porirua
WELLINGTON
Masterton
Richmond
Havelock
Lower Hutt
Upper Hutt
Wellington
Granity
Blenheim
Seddon
C. Palliser
Westport
Murchison
NELSON
Cape Campbell
Cape Foulwind
Buller
MARLBOROUGH
Cook Strait
Reefton
Mt. Travers 2338
Kaikoura Ra
Greymouth
Hanmer Springs
Clarence
Kumara
Lewis Pass
Waiau
Kaikoura
Hokitika
Brunner
Ross
Otira
Arthur's Pass
Cheviot
Whataroa
Waipara
Pegasus Bay
Okarito
Rangiora
Fox Glacier
Springfield
Kaiapoi
Christchurch
SOUTH ISLAND
4870
Darfield
Lincoln
Rakaia
Akaroa
Banks Peninsula
Mt. Cook 3764
Leeston
Ashburton
SOUTHERN ALPS
L. Tekapo
Geraldine
Cascade Pt.
Okuru
Canterbury Bight
Pukaki
Fairlie
Timaru
Mt. Aspiring 3027
L. Wanaka
Twizel
Mt. Tarawera
Omarama
Waimate
Hawea
Cromwell
Kurow
Queenstown Mts
Milford Sound
Homer Tunnel
Wanaka
Oamaru
Arrowtown
Naseby
Palmerston
Queenstown
Ranfurly
Wakatipu
Alexandra
L. Te Anau
Roxburgh
Waikouaiti
Port Chalmers
L. Manapouri
Nightcaps
Lawrence
Otago Peninsula
SOUTHLAND
Milton
Dunedin
Resolution I.
Lumsden
OTAGO
Winton
Gore
Balclutha
Puysegur Pt.
Riverton
Edendale
Invercargill
Foveaux Strait
Bluff
Ruapuke I.
Stewart I.
Halfmoon Bay
Southwest Cape

TASMAN SEA

PACIFIC OCEAN

2297

0 50 100 150 Miles
0 50 100 150 200 Kms.
Conic Projection

© Collins ● Longman Atlases Cbii

NORTH AMERICA

Asia

Europe

Africa

ARCTIC OCEAN

Bering Strait

Ellesmere I.

GREENLAND
(KALAALLIT NUNAAT)

Denmark Strait

Arctic Circle

Parry Islands

Baffin
Bay

Victoria
Island

Baffin Island

Godthåb/
Nuuk

ALASKA
U.S.

Anchorage

Hudson
Bay

Newfoundland

C A N A D A

Edmonton

50°

Seattle

Vancouver

Winnipeg

Québec

Montreal
Ottawa

Toronto
Hamilton

Boston

NORTH

Portland

U N I T E D   S T A T E S

Milwaukee
Chicago
Detroit
Cleveland
Pittsburgh

Buffalo
Paterson
Newark
New York

40°

San Francisco

O F

Denver

Indianapolis
Cincinnati

Baltimore
Washington

Philadelphia

NORTH

N
O
R
T
H

San José

A M E R I C A

Kansas City

St. Louis

ATLANTIC

Honolulu
Hawaiian
Islands
(U.S.A.)

Los Angeles
San Diego

San Bernardino

30°

Atlanta

Bermuda
(U.K.)

20°

OCEAN

Tijuana

Dallas

I. de
Guadalupe
(Mex.)

Tropic of Cancer

Houston

New Orleans

Miami

BAHAMAS

OCEAN

P A C I F I C

20°

Monterrey

Gulf of
Mexico

Havana

CUBA

Santiago
de Cuba

PUERTO   ST. KITTS-NEVIS
RICO   San   ANTIGUA
HAITI DOM. Juan   GUADELOUPE
Port- Santo   DOMINICA (Fr.)
au-   Domingo   ST. LUCIA
Prince   ST. V. AND G.   BARBADOS
                   Martinique
                   (Neth.)   GRENADA

40°

Guadalajara

León

M
E
X
I
C
O

Leh

Is. de
Revilla Gigedo
(Mex.)

JAMAICA
Kingston

Caribbean   Sea

OCEAN

10°

Belmopan
BELIZE

Guatemala
GUA.
San Salvador
SAL.

HONDURAS
Tegucigalpa
NICARAGUA

Panama
PANAMA CITY

Managua

COSTA RICA

San José

S O U T H

Equator

10°

S
o
u
t
h

P A C I F I C

20°

Tropic of Capricorn

A
m
e
r
i
c
a

30°

30°

OCEAN

160°

140°

120°

110°

100°

90°

80°

© Collins

CANADA AND ALASKA

Relief

Feet	Metres
16 404	5000
9843	3000
6562	2000
3281	1000
1640	500
656	200
0	Sea Level
Land Dep.	
656	200
13 123	4000
22 966	7000

0 100 200 300 400 500 Miles
0 100 200 300 400 500 600 700 800 Kms.

Bonne Projection

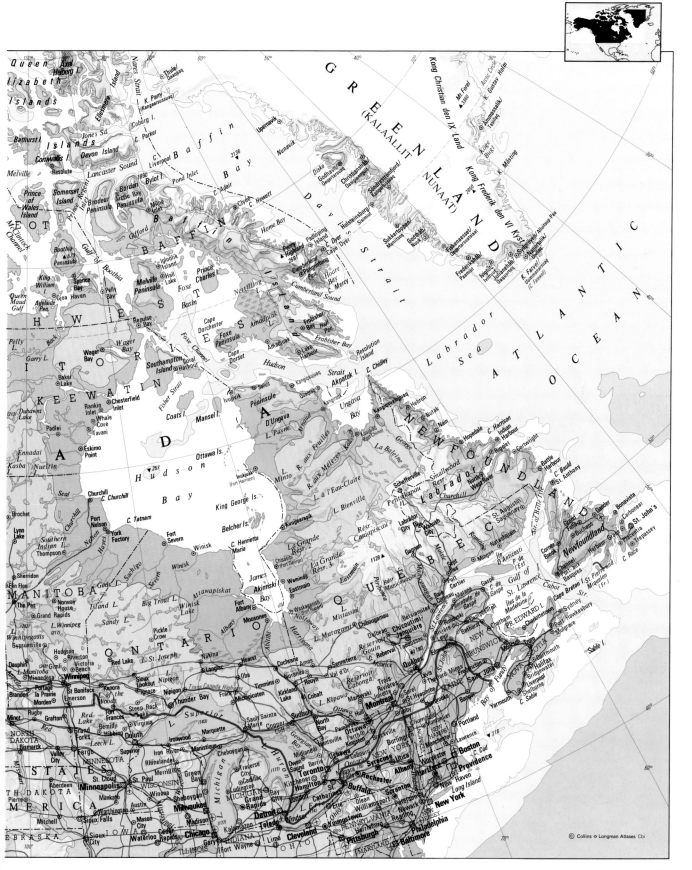

UNITED STATES

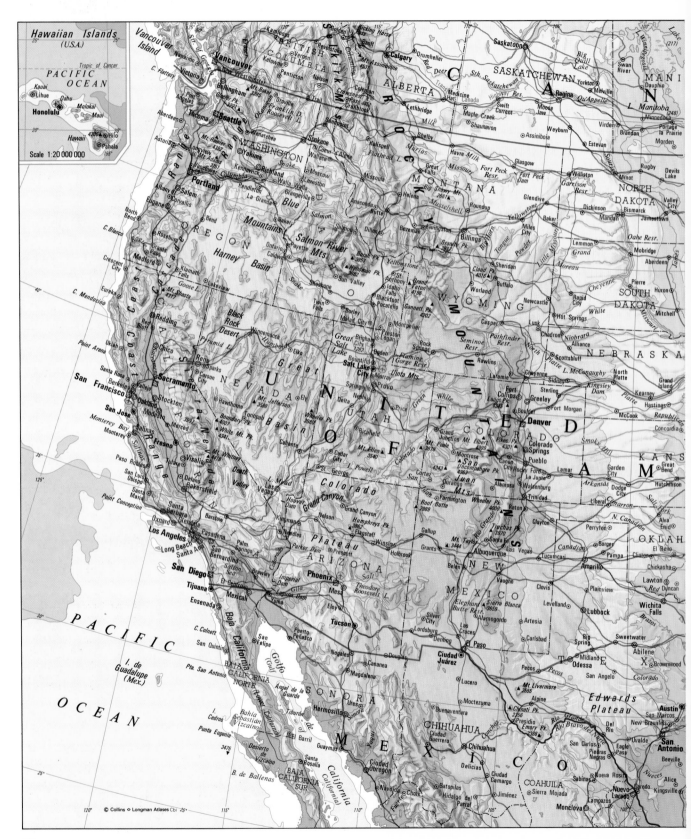

Hawaiian Islands
(U.S.A.)

PACIFIC
OCEAN

Scale 1:20 000 000

© Collins ◦ Longman Atlases Cbi

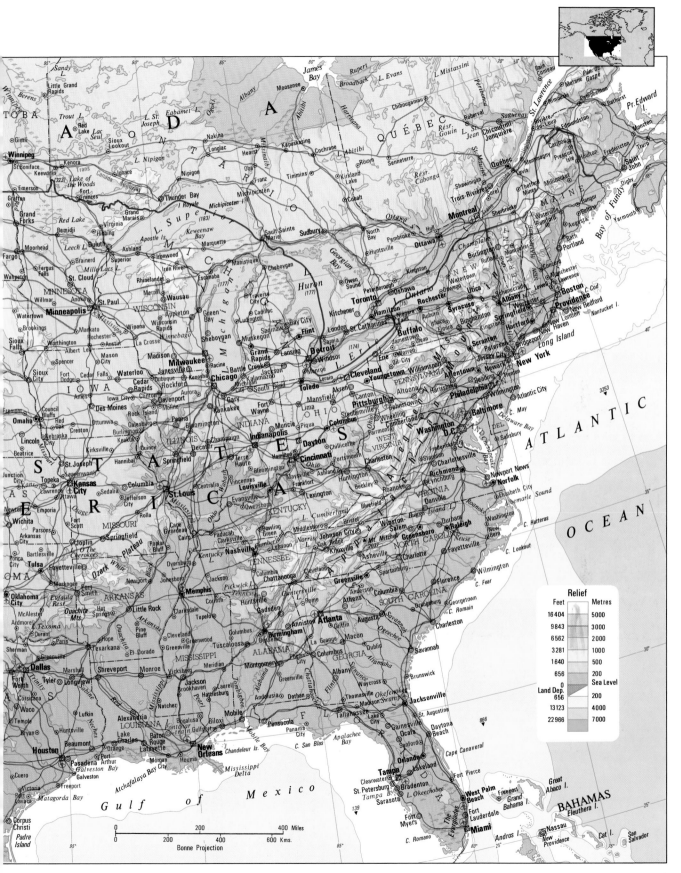

WESTERN UNITED STATES

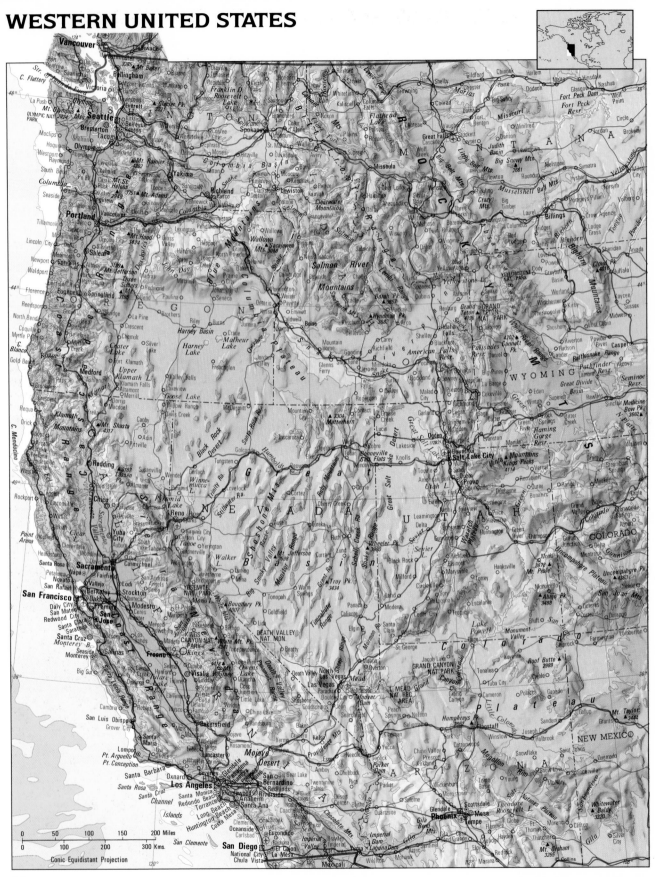

NORTHEAST U.S.A. – SOUTH CENTRAL CANADA

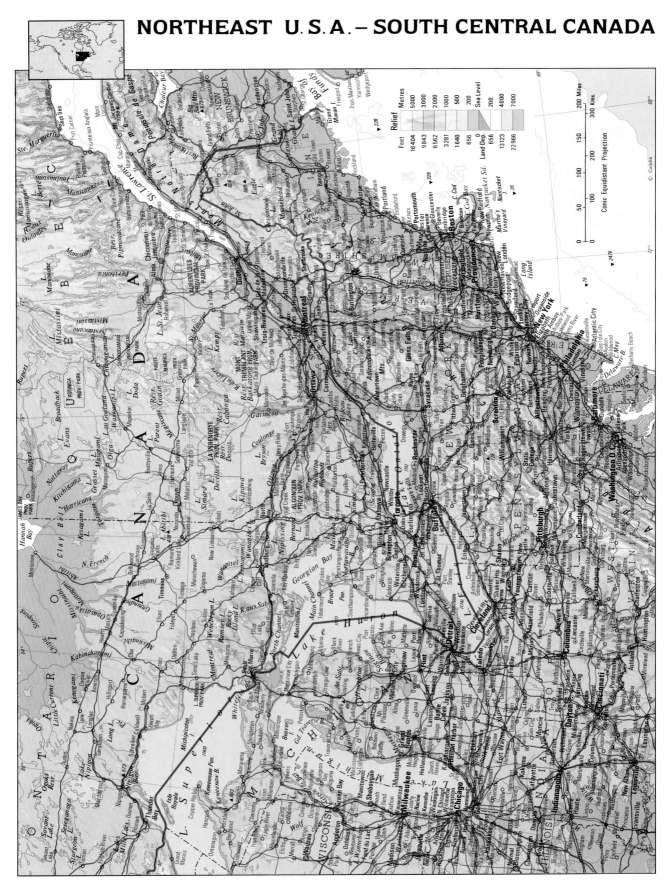

CENTRAL AMERICA AND THE CARIBBEAN

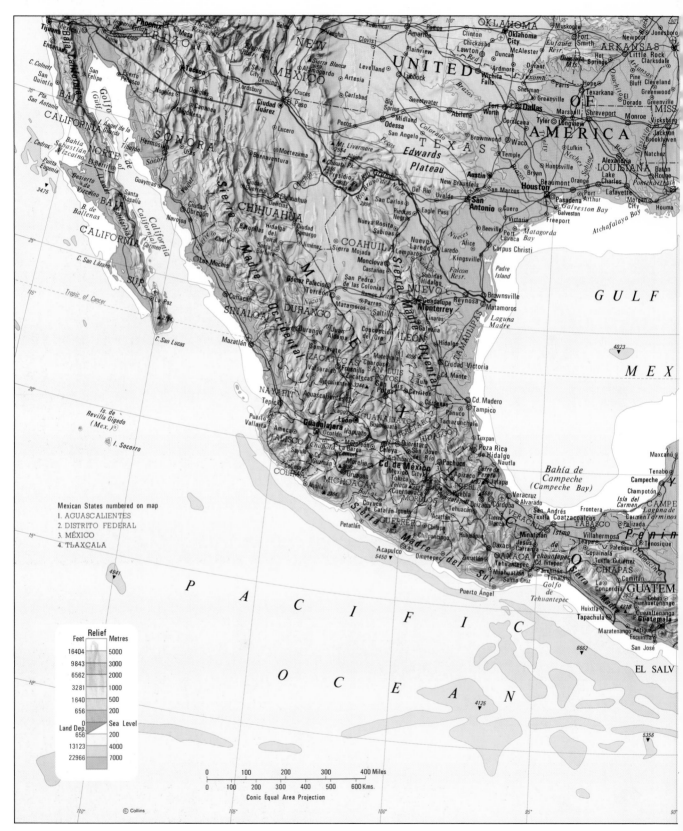

Mexican States numbered on map
1. AGUASCALIENTES
2. DISTRITO FEDERAL
3. MÉXICO
4. TLAXCALA

Relief		
Feet		Metres
16404		5000
9843		3000
6562		2000
3281		1000
1640		500
656		200
0		Sea Level
Land Dep.		
656		200
13123		4000
22966		7000

```
0        100      200      300      400 Miles
0    100   200   300   400   500   600 Kms.
        Conic Equal Area Projection
```

© Collins

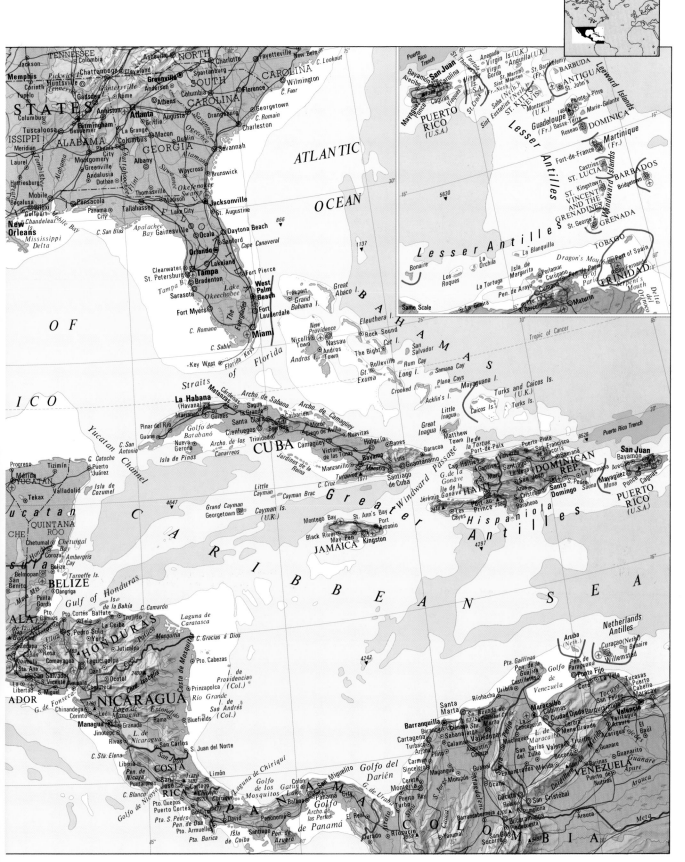

UNITED STATES

TENNESSEE
Jackson
Memphis
Corinth
Tupelo
Pickwick L.
Chattanooga
Cleveland
Asheville
NORTH
Charlotte
C. Lookout
Fayetteville New Bern
Huntsville
Gadsden
Guntersville
Rome
Greenville
SOUTH
CAROLINA
Columbia
Wilmington
C. Fear
MISSISSIPPI
Tuscaloosa
Columbus
Birmingham
Bessemer
Phenix City
Anniston
Atlanta
Griffin
Athens
Orangeburg
Georgetown
Meridian
ALABAMA
Montgomery
GEORGIA
Macon
Columbus
La Grange
Dublin
Augusta
Charleston
C. Romain
Laurel
Greenville
Andalusia
Dothan
Albany
Waycross
Brunswick
ATLANTIC
Hattiesburg
Mobile
Bogalusa
Biloxi
Gulfport
Pensacola
Panama City
Dothan
Thomasville
Madison
Tallahassee
Lake City
Okefenokee
Swamp
Savannah
Altamaha
OCEAN
New
Orleans
Chandeleur
Is.
Mississippi
Delta
C. San Blas
Apalachee
Bay
Gainesville
Jacksonville
St. Augustine
FLORIDA
866
30°
Apalachee
Bay
Gainesville
Ocala
Sanford
Daytona Beach
OF
Clearwater
St. Petersburg
Tampa
Bradenton
Lakeland
Orlando
Cape Canaveral
1137
Tampa Bay
Sarasota
Lake
Okeechobee
Fort Pierce
West
Palm
Beach
Freeport
Grand
Bahama I.
Great
Abaco I.
BAHAMAS
MEXICO
Fort Myers
The
Everglades
Fort
Lauderdale
Eleuthera I.
25°
C. Romano
New
Providence
Nicoll's
Town
Nassau
Rock Sound
Cat I.
Miami
C. Sable
Andros
Town
Andros
The Bight
San
Salvador
Tropic of Cancer
Key West
Florida Keys
Straits
Rolleville
Rum Cay
ICO
of Florida
Gt.
Exuma
Long I.
Samana Cay
Plana Cays
Mayaguana I.
Cárdenas
Matanzas
Crooked I.
Acklin's I.
Turks and Caicos Is.
(U.K.)
La Habana
(Havana)
Archo. de Sabana
Archo. de Camaguey
Caicos Is.
Turks Is.
Pinar del Río
Güines
Sagua
la Grande
Caibarién
Santa Clara
Puerto Rico Trench
8528
Guane
Golfo de
Batabanó
Cienfuegos
Sancti
Spíritus
Ciego de Ávila
Morón
Nuevitas
Holguín
Banes
Baracoa
Cap-Haïtien
Puerto Plata
San Francisco
de Macorís
Samaná
Nueva
Gerona
Archo. de
los
Canarreos
Trinidad
CUBA
Camagüey
Victoria
de las Tunas
Bayamo
S. Luís
Île de
la Tortue
Port-de-Paix
Valverde
La Vega
DOMINICAN
REP.
San Juan
Bayamón
Isla de Pinos
Jardines de
la Reina
Manzanillo
Turquino
1974
Maestra
Guantánamo
Santiago
de Cuba
Windward
Passage
G. de la
Gonâve
Gonaïves
Santiago
La Romana
Mayaguez
Ponce
Caguas
Little
Cayman
Cayman Brac
C. Cruz
Greater
Île de la
Gonâve
HAÏTI
Jérémie
Santo
Domingo
San Pedro
Saona
PUERTO
RICO
(U.S.A.)
Grand Cayman
Georgetown
Cayman Is.
(U.K.)
Montego Bay
St. Ann's Bay
Port
Antonio
Port-au-
Prince
Les
Cayes
Barahona
Hispaniola
Antilles
4297
Black River
May Pen
Kingston
JAMAICA
C A R I B B E A N   S E A
Chetumal
Chetumal
Bay
Ambergris
Cay
Corozal
Belize
Turneffe Is.
BELIZE
QUINTANA
ROO
Belmopan
Dangriga
Punta
Gorda
Gulf of Honduras
Isla
de la Bahía
C. Camarón
Laguna de
Caratasca
Netherlands
Antilles
Aruba
(Neth.)
Curaçao (Neth.)
Willemstad
San Benito
Maya Mts.
Pto.
Barrios
S. Pedro Sula
Yoro
Mosquitia
C. Gracias á Dios
Pta. Gallinas
Pen. de
La Guajira
Golfo de
Paraguaná
Punto Fijo
HONDURAS
Tegucigalpa
Juticalpa
Pto. Cabezas
Golfo
de
Venezuela
La Vela
Coro
San Felipe
Tucacas
Puerto
Cabello
Maracay
EL SALVADOR
San Salvador
Danlí
Ocotal
Prinzapolca
I. de
Providencia
(Col.)
Ríohacha
Uribia
Maracaibo
Cabimas
Ciudad Ojeda
Barquisimeto
Valencia
San Miguel
Comayagua
NICARAGUA
Río Grande
I. de
San Andrés
(Col.)
Santa
Marta
Nevada de
Sta. Marta
Valera
VENEZUELA
G. de Fonseca
León
Lago de
Managua
Estero
Bluefields
Barranquilla
Cartagena
Sabanalarga
Barinas
Managua
Granada
L. de
Nicaragua
San Carlos
S. Juan del Norte
Turbaco
COLOMBIA
NICARAGUA
Liberia
Pen. de
Nicoya
San
José
Limón
Laguna de Chiriquí
Golfo
de los
Mosquitos
Colón
PANAMA
Golfo del
Darién
G. de Urabá
Montería
Cúcuta
San Cristóbal
COSTA RICA
Puntarenas
Cartago
David
Penonomé
Panamá
Lake
Gatún
El Real
Arauca
Golfo de Nicoya
Pta. Burica
Isla de Coiba
Pen. de
Azuero
Santiago
Jurado
COLOMBIA

ATLANTIC OCEAN

Puerto
Rico
Trench
San Juan
Bayamón
Ponce
Caguas
Mayagüez
Arecibo
PUERTO
RICO
(U.S.A.)
Anegada
Virgin Is. (U.K.)
Anguilla (U.K.)
St. Barthélemy
(Fr.)
BARBUDA
ANTIGUA
St. John's
Virgin
Gorda
St. Thomas
St. Croix
Sint Maarten
(Neth.)
Saba
(Neth.)
Sint Eustatius (Neth.)
ST. KITTS
NEVIS
(U.K.)
Montserrat
Leeward Islands
Pointe-à-Pitre
Marie-Galante
Guadeloupe
(Fr.) Basse-Terre
Roseau
DOMINICA
1484
Lesser
Antilles
Fort-de-France
Martinique
(Fr.)
Castries
ST. LUCIA
Windward Islands
BARBADOS
ST.
VINCENT
AND THE
GRENADINES
Kingstown
Bridgetown
St. George's
GRENADA
5630
La Blanquilla
TOBAGO
Port of Spain
Bonaire
Los
Roques
La
Orchila
Isla de
Margarita
Dragon's Mouths
Pen. de Paria
Porlamar
Carúpano
San Fernando
TRINIDAD
Same Scale
La Tortuga
Pen. de Araya
Cumaná
Barcelona
Maturín
Delta
del
Orinoco

57

SOUTH AMERICA

North America

NORTH ATLANTIC OCEAN

40°

30°

Tropic of Cancer

20°

Caribbean Sea

Barranquilla

Maracaibo   Caracas   TRINIDAD AND TOBAGO

VENEZUELA   Georgetown   Paramaribo   Cayenne

Medellín   Bogotá   GUYANA   SURINAM   GUIANA (Fr.)

COLOMBIA   10°

Cali

Quito   Belém   Equator

ECUADOR   30°

Guayaquil   Fortaleza

Galapagos Is. (Ec.)   90°   B R A Z I L   20°

100°   Recife   10°

Lima   PERU   Salvador

110°   La Paz   Brasília

BOLIVIA   Belo Horizonte

Sucre   10°

120°   PARAGUAY   Rio de Janeiro

SOUTH   São Paulo   Santo André   20°

Asunción   Curitiba   SOUTH

San Félix (Chile)   Tropic of Capricorn

San Ambrosio   ATLANTIC

Córdoba   Pôrto Alegre   30°

Islas Juan Fernández (Chile)   URUGUAY

Valparaíso   Rosario   40°

PACIFIC   Santiago   Buenos Aires   Montevideo

La Plata   OCEAN

140°   ARGENTINA

CHILE   40°

OCEAN

Falkland Is. (U.K.)   50°

Tierra del Fuego   South Georgia (U.K.)

60°

Antarctic Circle

70°

International Date Line

A n t a r c t i c a

© Collins

58

TOCANTINS

Planalto do Mato Grosso

Planalto BAHIA Brasil

MATO GROSSO

GOIÁS

BRAZIL

SANTA CRUZ

BOLIVIA

Bañados de Izozog (Izozog Marshes)

MATO GROSSO DO SUL

MINAS GERAIS

Goiânia

Brasília

DISTRITO FEDERAL

Belo Horizonte

ESPÍRITO SANTO

Vitória

SÃO PAULO

PARAGUAY

PARANÁ

São Paulo

Rio de Janeiro

Niterói

Campos

Santos

FORMOSA

CHACO

Asunción

MISIONES

SANTA CATARINA

Curitiba

Joinville

Blumenau

Florianópolis

ARGENTINA

CORRIENTES

SANTA FE

ENTRE RIOS

RIO GRANDE DO SUL

Pôrto Alegre

Novo Hamburgo

Passo Fundo

Caxias do Sul

Rio Grande

URUGUAY

Montevideo

CÓRDOBA

Rosario

BUENOS AIRES

Buenos Aires

La Plata

PAMPA

Mar del Plata

Bahía Blanca

Relief

Feet		Metres
16404		5000
9843		3000
6562		2000
3281		1000
1640		500
656		200
0		Sea Level
Land Dep.		
656		200
13123		4000

0 100 200 300 400 Miles
0 100 200 300 400 500 600 Kms.

Lambert Azimuthal Equal Area Projection

MINAS GERAIS

Belo Horizonte

Divinópolis

Franca

SÃO PAULO

Araraquara

São Carlos

Rio Claro

Limeira

Piracicaba

Americana

Campinas

São Paulo

Santo André

São Caetano do Sul

São Vicente

Santos

RIO DE JANEIRO

Rio de Janeiro

Niterói

Petrópolis

Nova Friburgo

Volta Redonda

Barra Mansa

Juiz de Fora

Barbacena

Campos

0 40 80 Miles
0 40 80 120 Kms.

© Collins

© Collins © Longman Atlases Cbi

59

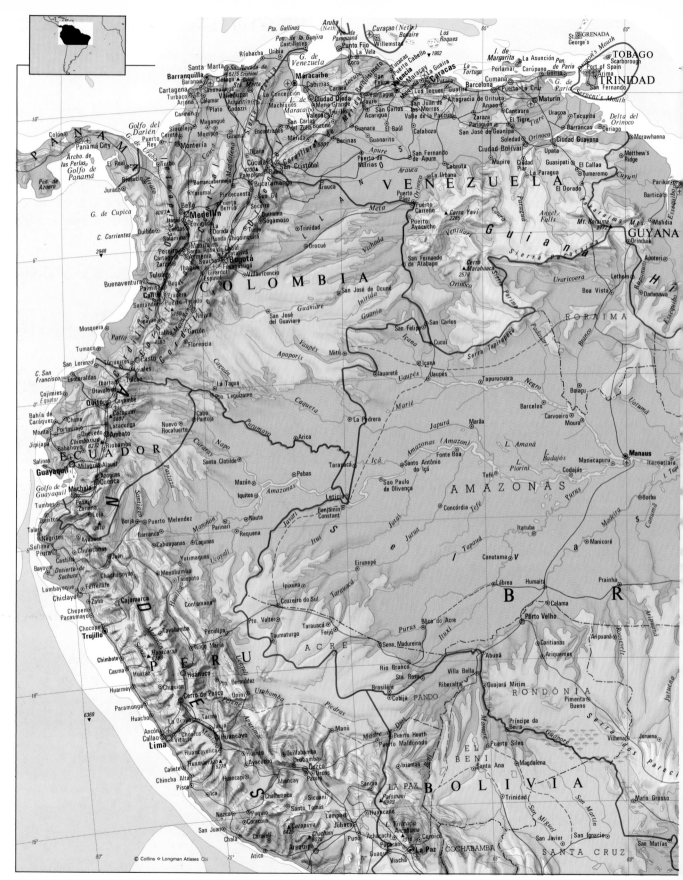

60

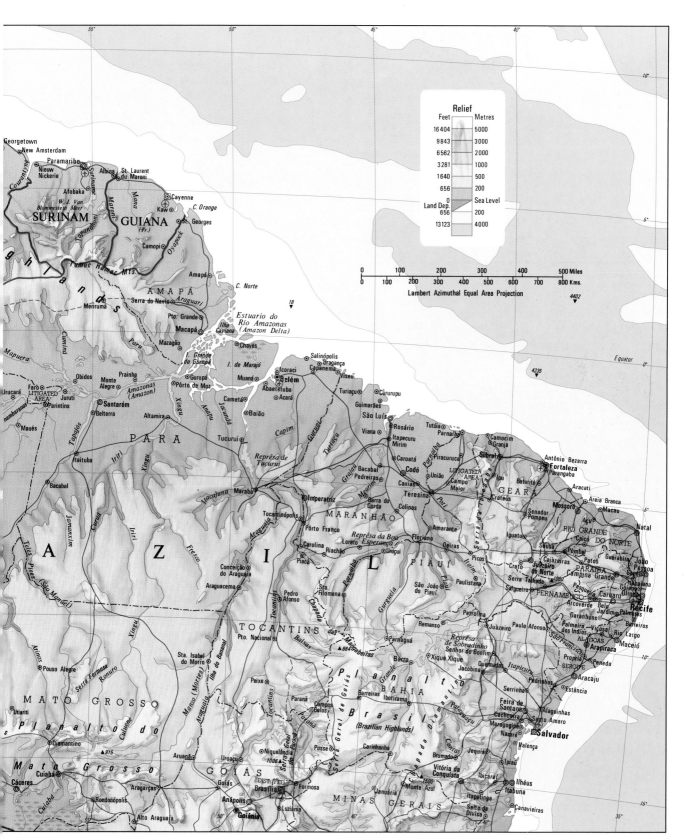

Relief

Feet	Metres
16 404	5000
9843	3000
6562	2000
3281	1000
1640	500
656	200
0	Sea Level
Land Dep.	
656	200
13 123	4000

0   100   200   300   400   500 Miles
0   100   200   300   400   500   600   700   800 Kms.
Lambert Azimuthal Equal Area Projection

SOUTH AMERICA — SOUTH

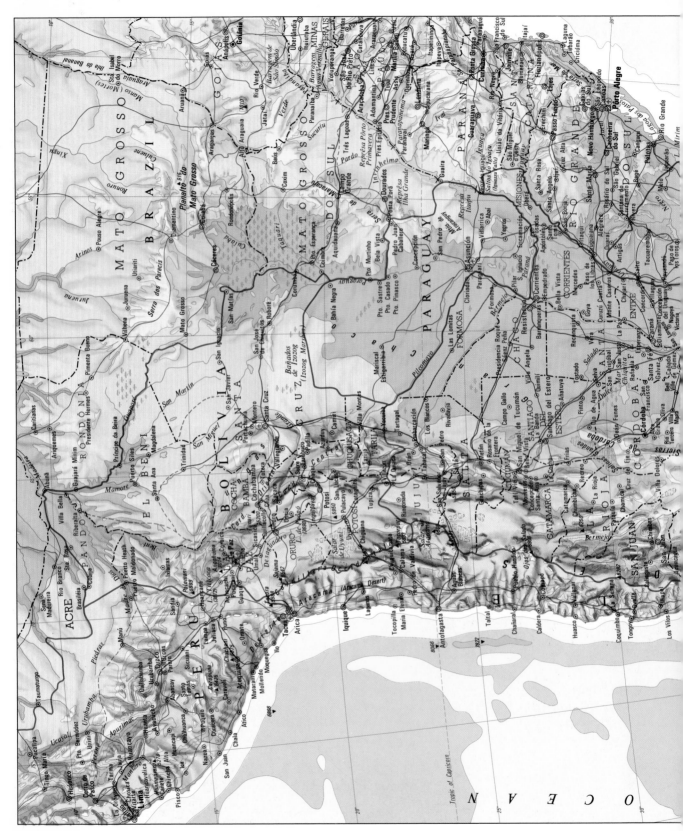

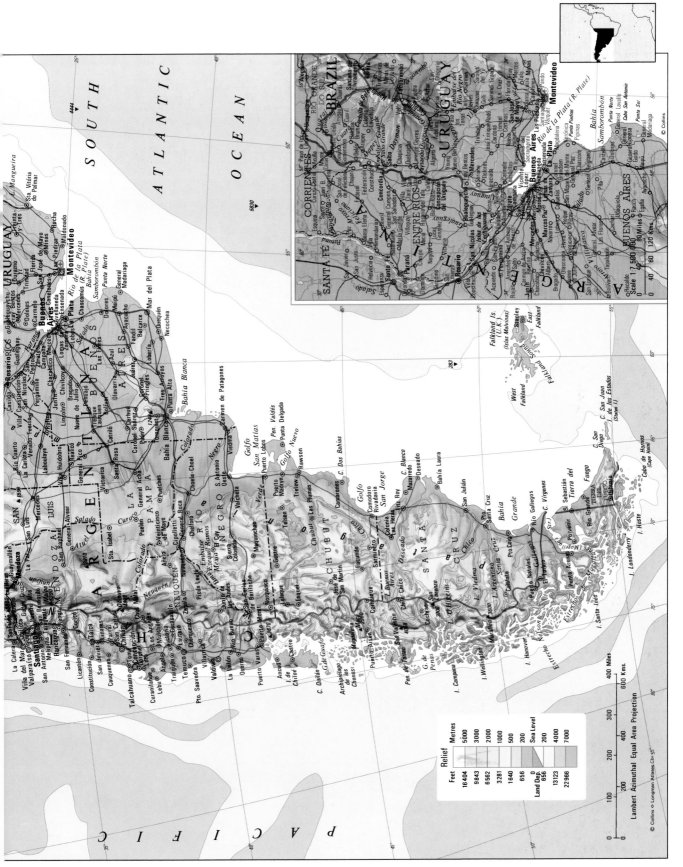

S O U T H

A T L A N T I C

O C E A N

URUGUAY

Montevideo

Buenos Aires

Río de la Plata (R. Plate)

A R G E N T I N A

B U E N O S   A I R E S

L A   P A M P A

M E N D O Z A

C H I L E

SAN LUIS

Santiago

N E U Q U É N

R Í O   N E G R O

C H U B U T

S A N T A   C R U Z

Golfo San Matías

Golfo San Jorge

Pen. Valdés

TIERRA DEL FUEGO

Cabo de Hornos (Cape Horn)

Estrecho de Magallanes

Falkland Is. (Islas Malvinas) (U.K.)

West Falkland

East Falkland

Stanley

Falkland Sound

P A C I F I C

O C E A N

BRAZIL

RIO GRANDE DO SUL

CORRIENTES

ENTRE RÍOS

SANTA FÉ

Buenos Aires

La Plata

Rosario

Paraná

Santa Fé

Montevideo

URUGUAY

A R G E N T I N A

Río de la Plata (R. Plate)

Bahía Samborombón

Scale 1:7 500 000

0   40   80   120 Kms.

© Collins

Relief		
Feet	Metres	
16404	5000	
9843	3000	
6562	2000	
3281	1000	
1640	500	
656	200	
	Sea Level	
	0	
Land Dep.	200	
656		
13123	4000	
22966	7000	

400 Miles

600 Kms.

Lambert Azimuthal Equal Area Projection

© Collins © Longman Atlases

POLAR REGIONS

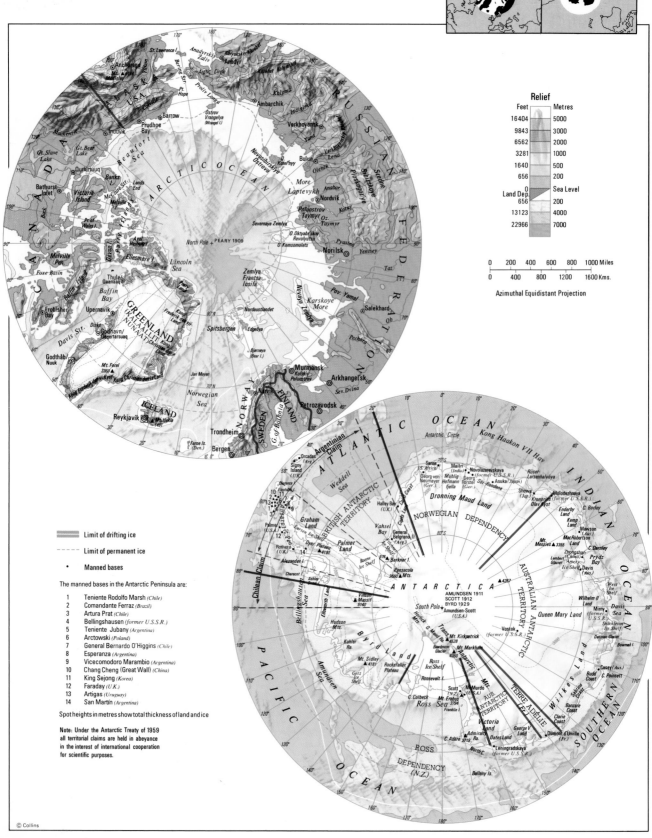

Relief

Feet		Metres
16404		5000
9843		3000
6562		2000
3281		1000
1640		500
656		200
0		Sea Level
Land Dep.		
656		200
13123		4000
22966		7000

0   200   400   600   800   1000 Miles

0   400   800   1200   1600 Kms.

Azimuthal Equidistant Projection

Limit of drifting ice

Limit of permanent ice

• Manned bases

The manned bases in the Antarctic Peninsula are:

1   Teniente Rodolfo Marsh *(Chile)*
2   Comandante Ferraz *(Brazil)*
3   Artura Prat *(Chile)*
4   Bellingshausen *(former U.S.S.R.)*
5   Teniente Jubany *(Argentina)*
6   Arctowski *(Poland)*
7   General Bernardo O'Higgins *(Chile)*
8   Esperanza *(Argentina)*
9   Vicecomodoro Marambio *(Argentina)*
10 Chang Cheng (Great Wall) *(China)*
11 King Sejong *(Korea)*
12 Faraday *(U.K.)*
13 Artigas *(Uruguay)*
14 San Martín *(Argentina)*

Spot heights in metres show total thickness of land and ice

Note: Under the Antarctic Treaty of 1959
all territorial claims are held in abeyance
in the interest of international cooperation
for scientific purposes.

© Collins

INDEX

INTERNATIONAL GLOSSARY

The Glossary of Geographical Terms lists in alphabetical order a selection of foreign language names and geographical terms, inclusive of any abbreviations, which are found in the names on the maps and in the index. The terms occur either as separate words (e.g. côte which means coast) or as parts of compound words (e.g. - oog in Langeoog which means island). A term preceded by a hyphen usually appears as an ending of a name on the map (e.g. - vesi in Puulavesi; - holm in Bornholm). Each term is followed by its language which is identified by abbreviations in brackets. A complete list of the language abbreviations used in the glossary is found below.

LANGUAGE ABBREVIATIONS

Afr.	Afrikaans	Fin.	Finnish	Man.	Manchurian
Alb.	Albanian	Fr.	French	Mon.	Mongolian
Ar.	Arabic	Gae.	Gaelic	Nor.	Norwegian
Ba.	Baluchi	Ger.	German	Per.	Persian
Ber.	Berber	Gr.	Greek	Pol.	Polish
Blg.	Bulgarian	Heb.	Hebrew	Port.	Portugese
Bur.	Burmese	Hin.	Hindi	Rom.	Romanian
Cat.	Catalan	I.-C.	Indo-Chinese	Rus.	Russian
Cbd.	Cambodian	Ice.	Icelandic	S.-C.	Serbo-Croat
Ch.	Chinese	It.	Italian	Sp.	Spanish
Cz.	Czech	Jap.	Japanese	Swe.	Swedish
Dan.	Danish	Kor.	Korean	Th.	Thai (Siamese)
Dut.	Dutch	Lao.	Laotian	Tur.	Turkish
Est.	Estonian	Lat.	Latvian	Ur.	Urdu
Eth.	Ethiopian	Ma.	Malagasy	Viet.	Vietnamese
Fae.	Faeroese	Mal.	Malay		

GLOSSARY OF GEOGRAPHICAL TERMS

A

āb (Per.)	water
ada (Tur.)	island
adrar (Ber., Ar.)	mountain region
ákra, akrotírion (Gr.)	cape
alb (Rom.)	white
alin (Man., Mon.)	mountain range
alpes (Fr.)	alps
alpi (It.)	alps
alt/a/o (It., Sp., Port.)	high
-an (Swe.)	river
ao (Ch., Th.)	bay, gulf
arquipélago (Port.)	archipelago
-ås, -åsen (Swe.)	hills

B

bāb (Ar.)	gate
backe (Swe.)	hill
bādiya/t (Ar.)	desert
baelt (Dan.)	strait
b., bahía (Sp.)	bay
baḥr (Ar.)	great river/lake
baía (Port.)	bay
b., baie (Fr.)	bay
ban (Hin., Ur.)	forest
ban (I.-C.)	village
bañados (Sp.)	marshes

bandao (Ch.)	peninsula
bassin (Fr.)	basin
baṭḥa (Ar.)	plain
beloyy (Rus.)	white
ben, beinn (Gae.)	mountain
bereg (Rus.)	shore
berg/en (Ger., Swe.)	mountain/s
biq'at (Heb.)	valley
birkat (Ar.)	lake
bog., bogazi (Tur.)	strait
bois (Fr.)	woods
bol.,bol'shaya (Rus.)	big
bory (Pol.)	forest
bredning (Dan.)	bay
brú (Ice.)	bridge
bucht (Ger.)	bay
bugt (Dan.)	bay
buḥayrat (Ar.)	lake
bukt/en (Nor., Swe.)	bay
burnu (Tur.)	cape
busen (Ger.)	bay
büyük (Tur.)	big

C

c., cabo (Sp., Port.)	cape
campo (Sp.)	field
c., cap (Fr.)	cape
capo (It.)	cape

causse (Fr.)	upland
cerro (Sp.)	mountain
chaco (Sp.)	jungle region
chaîne (Fr.)	chain
chapada (Port.)	hills
chott (Ar.)	salt lake
cime (Fr.)	summit
co (Ch.)	lake
co (Viet.)	mountain
col (Fr.)	pass
colline/s (Fr.)	hill/s
con (Viet.)	islands
cordillera (Sp.)	mountain range
costa (Sp.)	coast
côte (Fr.)	coast

D

d., daği, dağlari (Tur.)	mountain, mountain range
dake (Jap.)	peak
dal/en (Nor., Swe.)	valley
danau (Mal.)	lake
daqq (Per.)	salt flat
darya (Rus.)	river
daryācheh (Per.)	lake
dasht (Per.)	desert
denizi (Tur.)	sea
desierto (Sp.)	desert

détroit *(Fr.)*	strait
dhiórix *(Gr.)*	canal
dian *(Ch.)*	lake
-dijk *(Dut.)*	dyke
ding *(Ch.)*	mountain
do *(Kor.)*	island

E

eiland/en *(Afr., Dut.)*	island/s
embalse *(Sp.)*	reservoir
'emeq *(Heb.)*	valley
erg *(Ar.)*	sand desert
estrecho *(Sp.)*	strait
estuario *(Sp.)*	estuary
étang *(Fr.)*	pond

F

feng *(Ch.)*	peak
firth *(Gae.)*	strait
fjället *(Swe.)*	mountain
fjell *(Nor.)*	mountain
fj., fjorden *(Dan., Nor., Swe.)*	fjord
fjördhur *(Fae., Ice.)*	fjord
flói *(Ice.)*	bay
fonn *(Nor.)*	glacier

G

gau *(Ger.)*	district
gave *(Fr.)*	orrent
gebirge *(Ger.)*	mountains
ghubbat *(Ar.)*	bay
gji *(Alb.)*	bay
gobi *(Mon.)*	desert
gol *(Mon.)*	river
g., golfe *(Fr.)*	gulf
g., golfo *(Sp., It.)*	gulf
gölö *(Tur.)*	lake
golyam *(Blg.)*	great
g., gora/y *(Rus.)*	mountain/s
gorje *(S.C.)*	mountain range
gross *(Ger.)*	great
guba *(Rus.)*	bay
guntō *(Jap.)*	island group
guoyuan *(Ch.)*	plateau
gura *(Rom.)*	mouth

H

hai *(Ch.)*	sea
haixia *(Ch.)*	strait

ḥajar *(Ar.)*	mountain range
halvö *(Dan.)*	peninsula
halvöya *(Nor.)*	peninsula
hāmūn *(Per.)*	plain
hantō *(Jap.)*	peninsula
har *(Heb.)*	mountain range
hauteurs *(Fr.)*	hills
hav *(Dan., Nor., Swe.)*	sea
hawr *(Ar.)*	lake
hāyk' *(Eth.)*	lake
he *(Ch.)*	river
heiya *(Jap.)*	plain
hoch *(Ger.)*	high
hohe *(Ger.)*	height
höj *(Dan.)*	high, height
-holm *(Dan.)*	island
holt *(Nor.)*	wood
hory *(Cz.)*	mountain
hu *(Ch.)*	lake
-huk *(Swe.)*	cape

I

Î., Îs., Île/s *(Fr.)*	island/s
ilha/s *(Port.)*	island/s
insel/n *(Ger.)*	island/s
i., is., isla/s *(Sp.)*	island/s
isola/e *(It.)*	island/s
istmo *(Sp.)*	isthmus
iztochni *(Blg.)*	eastern

J

j., jabal *(Ar., Per.)*	mountain
jarvi *(Fin.)*	lake
jaure *(Swe.)*	lake
jawb *(Ar.)*	basin, waterhole
jazā'ir *(Ar.)*	island
jezero *(S.-C., Cz.)*	lake
jezioro *(Pol.)*	lake
jiang *(Ch.)*	river
jima *(Jap.)*	island
jökulen *(Nor.)*	glacier
jökull *(Ice.)*	glacier
jūras līcis *(Lat.)*	gulf, bay

K

kaikyō *(Jap.)*	strait
kaise *(Swe.)*	mountain range
kamm *(Ger.)*	ridge
k., kanal *(Ger., Pol., Rus., S.-C., Swe.)*	canal
kap *(Ger.)*	cape

kapp *(Nor.)*	cape
kep *(Alb.)*	cape
kep., kepulauan *(Mal.)*	archipelago
khalīj *(Ar., Per.)*	gulf, bay
khazzān *(Ar.)*	dam
khr., khrebet *(Rus.)*	mountain range
kladenets *(Blg.)*	well
klong *(Th.)*	canal, creek
ko *(Jap.)*	lake, bay
ko *(Th.)*	island
-kogen *(Jap.)*	plateau
koh *(Per.)*	mountains
kílpos *(Gr.)*	gulf
kör., körfezi *(Tur.)*	gulf, bay
kou *(Ch.)*	estuary
kryazh *(Rus.)*	ridge
kūh/ha *(Per.)*	mountain/s
kul *(Rus.)*	lake
kuppe *(Ger.)*	hilltop
kyst *(Dan.)*	coast

L

lac *(Fr.)*	lake
lacul *(Rom.)*	lake
l., lago *(It. Sp.)*	lake
lagoa *(Port.)*	lagoon
laguna *(Sp.)*	lagoon, lake
laut *(Mal.)*	north, sea
liedao *(Ch.)*	islands
liehtao *(Ch.)*	islands
l., límni *(Gr.)*	lake
ling *(Ch.)*	mountain range
llanos *(Sp.)*	plains
l., loch *(Gae.)*	lake
lora *(Ba.)*	stream
l., lough *(Gae.)*	lake
lule *(Swe.)*	eastern

M

maa *(Est., Fin.)*	land
mae *(Th.)*	river
mar/e *(It., Port., Sp.)*	sea
marsch *(Ger.)*	marsh
meer *(Afr., Dut.)*	lake, sea
mer *(Fr.)*	sea
mifraẕ *(Heb.)*	bay
misaki *(Jap.)*	cape
mont *(Fr.)*	mountain
montagne *(Fr.)*	mountain
mont/e/i *(It., Port., Sp.)*	mountain/s
moor *(Ger.)*	swamp, moor

more *(Rus.)*	sea
mörön *(Mon.)*	river
mui *(Viet.)*	point
mull *(Gae.)*	headland
munkhafaḍ *(Ar.)*	depression
munti/i *(Rom.)*	mountain/s
m., mys *(Rus.)*	cape

N

nada *(Jap.)*	sea, bay
nafūd *(Ar.)*	sandy desert
najd *(Ar.)*	pass
nam *(I.-C., Kor.)*	southern
nes *(Ice., Nor.)*	promontory
ness *(Gae.)*	promontory
nevada *(Sp.)*	snow-capped mountains
ngoc *(Viet)*	mountain
nísoi *(Gr.)*	islands
nizh., nizhne, nizhniy *(Rus.)*	lower
nizmennost' *(Rus.)*	depression
nord *(Dan., Fr., Ger., Nor., Swe.)*	northern
nur *(Ch.)*	lake, salt lake
nusa *(mal.)*	island
nuur *(Mon.)*	lake

O

occidental *(Sp.)*	western
odde *(Dan., Nor.)*	headland
ojo/s *(Sp.)*	spring/s
oki *(Jap.)*	bay
-oog *(Ger.)*	island
óros, óri *(Gr.)*	mountain, mountains
oriental/e *(Sp.)*	eastern
ort *(Ger.)*	settlement
o., os., ostrov/a *(Rus.)*	island/s
ost *(Ger.)*	east
oued *(Ar.)*	dry river bed
öy, öya *(Nor.)*	island
oz., ozero *(Rus.)*	lake

P

pampa/s *(Sp.)*	plain/s
parbat *(Ur.)*	mountain
passo *(It.)*	pass
peg., pegunungan *(Mal.)*	mountain range
pélagos *(Gr.)*	sea
pelleg *(Alb.)*	bay
peña *(Sp.)*	cliff
pendi *(Ch.)*	depression
péninsule *(Fr.)*	peninsula

pertuis *(Fr.)*	strait
peski *(Rus.)*	sand
phanom *(I.-C., Th.)*	mountain
phou *(Lao.)*	mountain
phu *(Th.)*	mountain
pic *(Fr.)*	peak
pico *(Sp.)*	peak
pik *(Rus.)*	peak
pingyuan *(Ch.)*	plain
plaine *(Fr.)*	plain
plana *(Sp.)*	plain
planalto *(Port.)*	plateau
pl., planina *(Blg., S.-C.)*	mountain range
plato *(Afr., Blg., Rus.)*	plateau
platosu *(Tur.)*	plateau
platte *(Ger.)*	plateau, plain
playa *(Sp.)*	beach
ploskogor'ye *(Rus.)*	plateau
pohorie *(Cz.)*	mountain range
pointe *(Fr.)*	promontory
pojezierze *(Pol.)*	lakeland
poleseye *(Rus.)*	area of marsh
polje *(S.-C.)*	plain, basin
pov., poluostrov *(Rus.)*	peninsula
porthmós *(Gr.)*	strait
porţi *(Rom.)*	entrance
portillo *(Sp.)*	gap
prliv *(Rus.)*	strait
puig *(Cat.)*	peak
pulau *(Mal.)*	island
pta., punta *(It., Sp.)*	point
puy *(Fr.)*	peak

Q

qā' *(Ar.)*	salt flat
qanāt *(Ar., Per.)*	canal
qolleh *(Per.)*	mountain
qu *(Ch.)*	canal, stream
qūr *(Ar.)*	buttes, ridge

R

ramlat *(Ar.)*	dunes
rann *(Hin.)*	swampy region
ras, ra's, rās *(Per., Ar.)*	cape
ravnina *(Rus.)*	plain
reprêsa *(Port.)*	reservoir
reshteh *(Per.)*	mountain range
retto *(Jap.)*	island group
ria, ría *(Port., Sp.)*	mouth of river
rijeka *(S.-C.)*	river
r., rio, río *(Port., Sp.)*	river

riviera *(It.)*	coast, river
r., riviàre *(Fr.)*	river
rocca *(It.)*	rock
rücken *(Ger.)*	ridge
rūd *(Per.)*	river

S

sable/s *(Fr.)*	sand/s
sadd *(Ar.)*	dam
sāgar *(Hin., Ur.)*	lake
ṣaḥrā *(Ar.)*	desert
ṣa'īd *(Ar.)*	highland
saki *(Jap.)*	cape
salar *(Sp.)*	salt flat
salina/s *(Sp.)*	salt marsh
sammyaku *(Jap.)*	mountain range
san *(Jap., Kor.)*	mountain
-sanchi *(Jap.)*	mountains
see *(Ger.)*	lake
seenplatte *(Ger.)*	lakeland
selat *(Mal.)*	strait
selatan *(Mal.)*	southern
selkä *(Fin.)*	ridge
selseleh *(Per.)*	mountain range
selva *(Sp.)*	forest
serra *(Port.)*	mountain range
serranía *(Sp.)*	ridge
sev., severo, severnyy *(Rus.)*	north
sha'īb *(Ar.)*	ravine, wadi
shamo *(Ch.)*	desert
shan *(Ch.)*	mountain
shankou *(Ch.)*	mountain pass
shaṭṭ *(Ar.)*	large river
shibh jazīrat *(Ar.)*	peninsula
shima *(Jap.)*	island
shotō *(Jap.)*	island group
shui *(Ch.)*	river
sa., sierra *(Sp.)*	mountain range
-sjon *(Swe.)*	lake
skog *(Nor., Swe.)*	forest
skov *(Dan.)*	forest
slieve *(Gae.)*	mountain
sor *(Rus.)*	salt flat
sör *(Nor.)*	southern
spitze *(Ger.)*	peak
sredne *(Rus.)*	central
step *(Rus.)*	steppe
stora *(Fae.)*	large
strath *(Gae.)*	valley
stretto *(It.)*	strait
suidō *(Jap.)*	strait
Şummān *(Ar.)*	escarpment

sund *(Dan., Ger., Ice., Nor., Swe.)*	sound
svart *(Nor., Swe.)*	black

T

take *(Jap.)*	peak
tall *(Ar.)*	mountain
tanjona *(Ma.)*	cape
tanjung *(Mal.)*	cape
tau *(Rus.)*	mountain
teluk *(Mal.)*	bay
testa *(It.)*	head
thale *(Th.)*	lagoon, sea
tierra *(Sp.)*	land, territory
tind *(Nor.)*	sharp peak
tō *(Jap.)*	island, eastern
tônlé *(Cbd.)*	lake
träsk *(Swe.)*	marsh
tunturi *(Fin.)*	treeless mountain

U

'urūq *(Ar.)*	dunes
utara *(Mal.)*	northern
uul *(mon., Rus.)*	mountain range

V

väin *(Est.)*	strait
val *(Fr., It.)*	valley
vand *(Dan.)*	water
vatn *(Ice., Nor.)*	lake
vatnet *(Nor.)*	lake
vatten *(Swe.)*	lake
veld *(Afr.)*	field
veliki *(S.-C.)*	large
verkh., verkhne, verkhniy *(Rus.)*	upper
-vesi *(Fin.)*	lake
vest, vester *(Dan., Nor.)*	west
vidda *(Nor.)*	plateau
-viken *(Nor., Swe.)*	gulf, bay
vdkhr., vodokhranilishche *(Rus.)*	reservoir
volcán *(Sp.)*	volcano
vostochno, vostochnyy *(Rus.)*	eastern
vozvyshennost *(Rus.)*	uplands
vrata *(Blg.)*	gate
vrh *(S.-C.)*	peak

W

wāhāt *(Ar.)*	oasis
wald *(Ger.)*	forest
wan *(Ch., Jap.)*	bay

Y

yam *(Heb.)*	sea
yama *(Jap.)*	mountain
yanchi *(Ch.)*	salt lake
yarimadasi *(Tur.)*	peninsula
yazovir *(Blg.)*	dam
yoma *(Bur.)*	mountain range
yumco *(Ch.)*	lake
yunhe *(Ch.)*	canal
yuzhnyy *(Rus.)*	south

Z

zaki *(Jap.)*	cape, peninsula
zaliv *(Rus.)*	bay
zan *(Jap.)*	mountain range
zangbo *(Ch.)*	stream, river
zapadno, zapadnyy *(Rus.)*	western
zatoka *(Pol.)*	bay
zemlya *(Rus.)*	land
zhou *(Ch.)*	island
zuid *(Dut.)*	south

INTRODUCTION AND ABBREVIATIONS

The index includes an alphabetical list of all names appearing on the maps in the World Atlas section. Each entry indicates the country or region of the world in which the name is located. This is followed by a page reference and finally the name's location on the map, given by latitude and longitude co-ordinates. Most features are indexed to the largest scale map on which they appear, however when the name applies to countries or other extensive features it is generally indexed to the map on which it appears in its entirety. Areal features are generally indexed using co-ordinates which indicate the centre of the feature. The latitude and longitude indicated for a point feature gives the location of the point on the map. In the case of rivers the mouth or confluence is always taken as the point of reference.

Names in the index are generally in the local language and where a conventional English version exists, this is cross referenced to the entry in the local language. Names of features which extend across the boundaries of more than one country are usually named in English if no single official name exists. Names in languages not written in the Roman alphabet have been transliterated using the official system of the country if one exists, e.g. Pinyin system for China, otherwise the systems recognised by the United States Board on Geographical Names have been used.

Names abbreviated on the maps are given in full in the Index. Abbreviations are used for both geographical terms and administrative names in the Index. All abbreviations used in the Index are given in the following list.

ABBREVIATIONS OF GEOGRAPHICAL TERMS

b., B.	bay, Bay
c., C.	cape, Cape
d.	internal division e.g country, region, state
des.	desert
est.	estuary
f.	physical feature e.g. valley, plain, geographic district or region
g., G.	gulf, Gulf
i.,I., is., Is.	island, Island, islands, Islands
l., L.	lake, Lake
mtn., Mtn.	mountain, Mountain
mts., Mts.	mountains, Mountains
pen,. Pen.	peninsula, Peninsula
Pt.	Point
r.	river
reser., Resr.	reservoir, Reservoir
Sd.	Sound
str., Str.	strait, Strait

ABBREVIATIONS OF COUNTRY / ADMINISTRATIVE NAMES

Afghan.	Afghanistan
A.H. Prov.	Alpes de Haut Provence
Ala.	Alabama
Alas.	Alaska
Alta.	Alberta
Ariz.	Arizona
Ark.	Arkansas
Baja Calif.	Baja California
Baja Calif. Sur	Baja California Sur
Bangla.	Bangladesh
B.C.	British Columbia
Bos.-Her.	Bosnia-Herzegovina
B.-Würt	Baden-Württemberg
Calif.	California
C.A.R.	Central African Republic
Char. Mar.	Charente Maritime
Colo.	Colorado
Conn.	Connecticut
C.P.	Cape Province
D.C.	District of Columbia
Del.	Delaware
Dom. Rep.	Dominican Republic
Equat. Guinea	Equatorial Guinea
Eth.	Ethiopia
Fla.	Florida
Ga.	Georgia
Guang. Zhuang	Guangxi Zhuangzu
H.-Gar.	Haute Garonne
Himachal P.	Himachal Pradesh
H. Zaïre	Haut Zaïre
Ill.	Illinois
Ind.	Indiana
Kans.	Kansas
K. Occidental	Kasai Occidental
K. Oriental	Kasai Oriental
Ky.	Kentucky
La.	Louisiana
Liech.	Liechtenstein
Lux.	Luxembourg

Madhya P.	Madhya Pradesh
Man.	Manitoba
Mass.	Massachusetts
Md.	Maryland
Mich.	Michigan
Minn.	Minnesota
Miss.	Mississippi
Mo.	Missouri
Mont.	Montana
M.-Pyr.	Midi-Pyrénées
N.B.	New Brunswick
N.C.	North Carolina
N. Dak.	North Dakota
Nebr.	Nebraska
Neth.	Netherlands
Nev.	Nevada
Nfld.	Newfoundland
N.H.	New Hampshire
N. Ireland	Northern Ireland
N.J.	New Jersey
N. Korea	North Korea
N. Mex	New Mexico
Nschn.	Niedersachsen
N.S.W.	New South Wales
N. Trönd.	North Tröndelag
N.T.	Northern Territory
N.-Westfalen	Nordrhein-Westfalen
N.W.T.	Northwest Territories
N.Y.	New York State
O.F.S.	Orange Free State
Okla.	Oklahoma
Ont.	Ontario
Oreg.	Oregon
P.E.I.	Prince Edward Island
Penn.	Pennsylvania
Phil.	Philippines
P.N.G.	Papua New Guinea
Poit.-Char.	Poitou-Charente
Pyr. Or.	Pyrénées Orientales
Qld.	Queensland
Que.	Québec
Raj.	Rājasthān
Rep. of Ire.	Republic of Ireland
Rhein.-Pfalz	Rheinland-Pfalz
R.I.	Rhode Island
R.S.A.	Republic of South Africa
Russian Fed.	Russian Federation

S.A.	South Australia
Sask.	Saskatchewan
S.C.	South Carolina
Sch.-Hol.	Schleswig-Holstein
S. Dak.	South Dakota
S. Korea	South Korea
S. Mar.	Seine Maritime
Sogn og Fj.	Sogn og Fjordane
Somali Rep.	Somali Republic
Switz.	Switzerland
Tas.	Tasmania
Tenn.	Tennessee
Tex.	Texas
T.G.	Tarn-et-Garonne
Trans.	Transvaal
U.A.E.	United Arab Emirates
U.K.	United Kingdom
U.S.A.	United States of America
Uttar P.	Uttar Pradesh
Va.	Virginia
Vic.	Victoria
Vt.	Vermont
W.A.	Western Australia
Wash.	Washington
W. Bengal	West Bengal
Wisc.	Wisconsin
W. Sahara	Western Sahara
W. Va.	West Virginia
Wyo.	Wyoming
Xin. Uygur	Xinjiang Uygur Zizhiqu
Yugo.	Yugoslavia

A

Aachen Germany **8** 50.46N 6.06E
Aalsmeer Neth. **8** 52.17N 4.46E
Aalst Belgium **8** 50.57N 4.03E
Äänekoski Finland **16** 62.36N 25.44E
Aarau Switz. **14** 47.24N 8.04E
Aardenburg Neth. **8** 51.16N 3.26E
Aare *r.* Switz. **14** 47.37N 8.13E
Aarschot Belgium **8** 50.59N 4.50E
Aba China **29** 32.55N101.42E
Aba Nigeria **38** 5.06N 7.21E
Abā as Su'ūd Saudi Arabia **35** 17.28N 44.06E
Ābādān Iran **31** 30.21N 48.15E
Abadan, Jazīreh-ye *i.* Iran **31** 30.10N 48.30E
Ābādeh Iran **31** 31.10N 52.40E
Abadla Algeria **34** 31.01N 2.45W
Abaetetuba Brazil **61** 1.45S 48.54W
Abaí Paraguay **62** 26.01S 55.57W
Abajo Peak *mtn.* U.S.A. **54** 37.51N109.28W
Abakaliki Nigeria **38** 6.17N 8.04E
Abakan Russian Fed. **21** 53.43N 91.25E
Abancay Peru **62** 13.35S 72.55W
Abau P.N.G. **44** 10.10S148.40E
Abay Kazakhstan **20** 49.40N 72.47E
Ābaya Hāyk' *l.* Ethiopia **35** 6.20N 38.00E
Abayḑ, Al Baḩr al *r.* Sudan **35** 15.45N 32.25E
Abba C.A.R. **38** 5.20N 15.11E
Abbeville France **11** 50.06N 1.51E
Abbiategrasso Italy **9** 45.24N 8.54E
Abbotsbury U.K. **5** 50.40N 2.36W
Abdulino Russian Fed. **18** 53.42N 53.40E
Abéché Chad **35** 13.49N 20.49E
Abengourou Ivory Coast **38** 6.42N 3.27W
Åbenrå Denmark **17** 55.02N 9.26E
Abeokuta Nigeria **38** 7.10N 3.26E
Aberayron U.K. **5** 52.15N 4.16W
Abercrombie *r.* Australia **47** 33.50S149.10E
Aberdare U.K. **5** 51.43N 3.27W
Aberdare Range *mts.* Kenya **37** 0.20S 36.40E
Aberdeen Australia **47** 32.10S150.54E
Aberdeen R.S.A. **39** 32.28S 24.03E
Aberdeen U.K. **6** 57.08N 2.07W
Aberdeen Md. U.S.A. **55** 39.30N 76.10W
Aberdeen Ohio U.S.A. **55** 38.39N 83.46W
Aberdeen S. Dak. U.S.A. **52** 45.28N 98.30W
Aberdeen Wash. U.S.A. **54** 46.59N123.50W
Aberdovey U.K. **5** 52.33N 4.03W
Aberfeldy U.K. **6** 56.37N 3.54W
Abergavenny U.K. **5** 51.49N 3.01W
Abersoch U.K. **4** 52.50N 4.31W
Aberystwyth U.K. **5** 52.25N 4.06W
Abetone Italy **9** 44.08N 10.40E
Abez Russian Fed. **18** 66.33N 61.51E
Abhar Iran **31** 36.09N 49.13E
Ābhē Bid Hāyk' *l.* Ethiopia **35** 11.06N 41.50E
Abia *d.* Nigeria **38** 5.45N 7.40E
Abidjan Ivory Coast **38** 5.19N 4.01W
Abilene Tex. U.S.A. **52** 32.27N 99.45W
Abingdon U.K. **5** 51.40N 1.17W
Abisko Sweden **16** 68.20N 18.51E
Abitibi *r.* Canada **55** 51.03N 80.55W
Abitibi, L. Canada **55** 48.42N 79.45W
Abnūb Egypt **30** 27.16N 31.09E
Åbo *see* Turku Finland **17**
Abomey Benin **38** 7.14N 2.00E
Abong Mbang Cameroon **38** 3.59N 13.12E
Abou Deïa Chad **34** 11.20N 19.20E
Aboyne U.K. **6** 57.05N 2.48W
Abrantes Portugal **10** 39.28N 8.12W
Abrud Romania **15** 46.17N 23.04E
Abruzzi *d.* Italy **12** 42.05N 13.45E
Absaroka Range *mts.* U.S.A. **54** 44.45N109.50W
Abu Dhabi *see* Abū Z̧aby U.A.E. **31**
Abū Dharbah Egypt **32** 28.29N 33.20E
Abū Ḩamad Sudan **35** 19.32N 33.20E
Abuja Nigeria **38** 9.12N 7.11E
Abū Kabīr Egypt **32** 30.44N 31.40E
Abū Kamāl Syria **30** 34.27N 40.55E
Abū Madd, Ra's *c.* Saudi Arabia **30** 24.50N 37.07E
Abunã Brazil **60** 9.41S 65.20W
Abū Qurqāş Egypt **32** 27.56N 30.50E
Abū Sulţān Egypt **32** 30.25N 32.19E
Abū Sunbul Egypt **30** 22.18N 31.40E
Abū Ţarafah Jordan **32** 30.00N 35.56E
Abū Tīj Egypt **30** 27.06N 31.17E
Abū Z̧aby U.A.E. **31** 24.27N 54.23E
Abū Zanīmah Egypt **32** 29.03N 33.06E
Åby Sweden **17** 58.40N 16.11E
Acámbaro Mexico **56** 20.01N101.42W
Acapulco Mexico **56** 16.51N 99.56W
Acará Brazil **61** 1.57S 48.11W
Acarigua Venezuela **60** 9.35N 69.12W
Acatlán Mexico **56** 18.12N 98.02W
Accra Ghana **38** 5.33N 0.15W
Accrington U.K. **4** 53.46N 2.22W
Aceh *d.* Indonesia **26** 4.00N 97.30E
Acevedo Argentina **63** 33.46S 60.27W
Achacachi Bolivia **62** 16.03S 68.43W
Achar Uruguay **63** 32.25S 56.10W
Acheng China **25** 45.32N126.59E
Achill I. Rep. of Ire. **7** 53.57N 10.00W
Achinsk Russian Fed. **20** 56.10N 90.10E
Acklin's I. Bahamas **57** 22.30N 74.10W
Aconcagua *mtn.* Argentina **62** 32.39S 70.00W
A Coruña *see* La Coruña Spain **10**
Acqui Italy **9** 44.41N 8.28E
Acraman, L. Australia **46** 32.02S135.26E
Acre *d.* Brazil **60** 8.50S 71.30W
Açu Brazil **61** 5.35S 36.57W
Acuña Argentina **63** 29.54S 57.57W
Adair, C. Canada **51** 71.24N 71.13W
Adamantina Brazil **59** 21.42S 51.04W
Adamaoua, Massif de l' *mts.* Cameroon / Nigeria **38** 7.05N 12.00E
Adamawa *d.* Nigeria **38** 9.55N 12.30E
Adamello *mtn.* Italy **9** 46.10N 10.35E
Adaminaby Australia **47** 36.04S148.42E
Adamintina Brazil **62** 21.42S 51.04W
Adams N.Y. U.S.A. **55** 43.49N 76.01W
Adams, Mt. U.S.A. **54** 46.12N121.28W
'Adan Yemen **35** 12.50N 45.00E
Adana Turkey **30** 37.00N 35.19E
Adapazari Turkey **30** 40.45N 30.23E
Adare, C. Antarctica **64** 71.30S171.00E
Adavale Australia **44** 25.55S144.36E
Adda *r.* Italy **9** 45.08N 9.55E
Aḑ Ḑab'ah Egypt **30** 31.02N 28.26E
Ad Dafīnah Saudi Arabia **30** 23.18N 41.58E
Ad Dahnā' *des.* Saudi Arabia **31** 26.00N 47.00E
Ad Dāmir Sudan **35** 17.37N 33.59E
Ad Dammām Saudi Arabia **31** 26.23N 50.08E
Ad Dawādimī Saudi Arabia **31** 24.29N 44.23E
Ad Dawḩah Qatar **31** 25.15N 51.34E
Aḑ Ḑiffah *f.* Africa **30** 30.45N 26.00E
Ad Dilam Saudi Arabia **31** 23.59N 47.10E
Ad Dīmās Syria **32** 33.35N 36.05E
Addis Ababa *see* Ādīs Ābeba Ethiopia **35**
Ad Dīwānīyah Iraq **31** 31.59N 44.57E
Adelaide Australia **46** 34.56S138.36E
Adelaide Pen. Canada **51** 68.09N 97.45W
Adelaide River *town* Australia **42** 13.14S131.06E
Adelong Australia **47** 35.21S148.04E
Aden *see* 'Adan Yemen **35**
Aden, G. of Indian Oc. **35** 13.00N 50.00E
Adendorp R.S.A. **39** 32.18S 24.31E
Adi *i.* Indonesia **27** 4.10S133.10E
Adieu, C. Australia **43** 31.59S132.09E
Adige *r.* Italy **9** 45.10N 12.20E
Adilang Uganda **37** 2.44N 33.28E
Adin U.S.A. **54** 41.12N120.57W
Adirondack Mts. U.S.A. **55** 44.00N 74.00W
Ādīs Ābeba Ethiopia **35** 9.03N 38.42E
Adiyaman Turkey **30** 37.46N 38.15E
Adjud Romania **15** 46.04N 27.11E
Admer *well* Algeria **34** 20.23N 5.27E
Admiralty G. Australia **42** 14.20S125.50E
Admiralty Is. P.N.G. **27** 2.30S147.20E
Admiralty Range *mts.* Antarctica **64** 72.00S164.00E
Adour *r.* France **11** 43.28N 1.35W
Adra Spain **10** 36.43N 3.03W
Adrano Italy **12** 37.39N 14.49E
Adrar des Iforas *mts.* Algeria / Mali **34** 20.00N 2.30E
Adria Italy **9** 45.03N 12.03E
Adrian Mich. U.S.A. **55** 41.55N 84.01W
Adriatic Sea Med. Sea **12** 42.30N 16.00E
Ādwa Ethiopia **35** 14.12N 38.56E
Adzopé Ivory Coast **38** 6.07N 3.49W
Adzva *r.* Russian Fed **18** 66.30N 59.30E
Aegean Sea Med. Sea **13** 39.00N 25.00E
Afghanistan Asia **28** 34.00N 65.30E
'Afīf Saudi Arabia **30** 23.53N 42.59E
Afikpo Nigeria **38** 5.53N 7.55E
Afjord Norway **16** 63.57N 10.12E
Afmadow Somali Rep. **37** 0.27N 42.05E
Afobaka Surinam **61** 5.00N 55.05W
Afognak I. U.S.A. **50** 58.15N152.30W
Afonso Cláudio Brazil **59** 20.05S 41.06W
Afsluitdijk *f.* Neth. **8** 53.04N 5.11E
'Afula Israel **32** 32.36N 35.17E
Afyon Turkey **30** 38.46N 30.32E
Agadez Niger **38** 17.00N 7.56E
Agadez *d.* Niger **38** 19.25N 11.00E
Agadir Morocco **34** 30.26N 9.36W
Agapa Russian Fed. **21** 71.29N 86.16E
Agartala India **29** 23.49N 91.15E
Agboville Ivory Coast **38** 5.55N 4.15W
Agde France **11** 43.19N 3.28E
Agen France **11** 44.12N 0.38E
Ageo Japan **23** 35.58N139.36E
Agger *r.* Germany **8** 50.45N 7.06E
Aghada Rep. of Ire. **7** 51.50N 8.13W
Aginskoye Russian Fed. **21** 51.10N114.32E
Agnew Australia **43** 28.01S120.30E
Ago Japan **23** 34.17N136.48E
Agordo Italy **9** 46.17N 12.02E
Āgra India **29** 27.09N 78.00E
Agra *r.* Spain **10** 42.12N 1.43W
Agraciada Uruguay **63** 33.48S 58.15W
Agreda Spain **10** 41.51N 1.55W
Agri *r.* Italy **13** 40.13N 16.45E
Ağri Turkey **30** 39.44N 43.04E
Ağri Dagi *mtn.* Turkey **31** 39.45N 44.15E
Agrigento Italy **12** 37.19N 13.36E
Agropoli Italy **12** 40.21N 15.00E
Agryz Russian Fed. **18** 56.30N 53.00E
Aguas Blancas Chile **62** 24.13S 69.50W
Aguascalientes Mexico **56** 21.51N102.18W
Aguascalientes *d.* Mexico **56** 22.00N102.00W
Agudos Brazil **59** 22.27S 49.03W
Águeda *r.* Spain **10** 41.00N 6.56W
Aguelhok Mali **38** 19.28N 0.52E
Aguilar de Campóo Spain **10** 42.47N 4.15W
Aguilas Spain **10** 37.25N 1.35W
Agulhas, C. R.S.A. **39** 34.50S 20.00E
Agulhas Negras *mtn.* Brazil **59** 22.20S 44.43W
Ahaggar *mts.* Algeria **34** 24.00N 5.50E
Ahar Iran **31** 38.25N 47.07E
Ahaura New Zealand **48** 42.21S171.33E
Ahaus Germany **8** 52.04N 7.01E
Ahklun Mts. U.S.A. **50** 59.15N161.00W
Ahlen Germany **8** 51.47N 7.52E
Ahmadābād India **28** 23.03N 72.40E
Aḩmadī Iran **31** 27.56N 56.42E
Ahmadnagar India **28** 19.08N 74.48E
Ahoada Nigeria **38** 5.06N 6.39E
Ahr *r.* Germany **8** 50.34N 7.16E
Ahram Iran **31** 28.52N 51.16E
Aḩsā', Wāḩat al *oasis* Saudi Arabia **31** 25.37N 49.40E
Ähtäri Finland **16** 62.34N 24.06E
Åhus Sweden **17** 55.55N 14.17E
Ahvāz Iran **31** 31.17N 48.44E
Ahvenanmaa *d.* Finland **17** 60.15N 20.00E
Ahvenanmaa *is.* Finland **17** 60.15N 20.00E
Aichi *d.* Japan **23** 35.02N137.15E
Aigle Switz. **9** 46.19N 6.58E
Aigues-Mortes France **11** 43.34N 4.11E
Aileron Australia **44** 22.38S133.20E
Ailette *r.* France **8** 49.35N 3.09E
Ailsa Craig *i.* U.K. **6** 55.15N 5.07W
Aim Russian Fed. **21** 58.50N134.15E
Aimorés Brazil **59** 19.30S 41.04W
Ain *r.* France **11** 45.47N 5.12E
Ainaži Estonia **17** 57.52N 24.21E
Aïn ben Tili Mauritania **34** 26.00N 9.32W
Aïn Sefra Algeria **34** 32.45N 0.35W
Aïr *mts.* Niger **38** 18.30N 8.30E
Airdrie U.K. **6** 55.52N 3.59W
Aire France **11** 43.39N 0.15W
Aire *r.* France **9** 49.19N 4.49E
Aire *r.* U.K. **4** 53.42N 0.54W
Aisne *d.* France **9** 49.30N 3.30E
Aisne *r.* France **9** 49.27N 2.51E
Aitape P.N.G. **27** 3.10S142.17E
Aiud Romania **15** 46.19N 23.44E
Aix-en-Provence France **11** 43.31N 5.27E
Aix-les-Bains France **11** 45.42N 5.55E
Aíyina *i.* Greece **13** 37.43N 23.30E
Aíyion Greece **13** 38.15N 22.05E
Aizpute Latvia **17** 56.43N 21.38E
Ajaccio France **11** 41.55N 8.43E
Ajdābiyā Libya **34** 30.48N 20.15E
'Ajlūn Jordan **32** 32.20N 35.45E
'Ajmah, Jabal al *f.* Egypt **32** 29.12N 33.58E
'Ajmān U.A.E. **31** 25.23N 55.26E
Ajmer India **28** 26.29N 74.40E
Akaishi sammyaku *mts.* Japan **23** 35.20N138.10E
Akámas, Akrotírion *c.* Cyprus **32** 35.06N 32.17E
Akaroa New Zealand **48** 43.50S172.59E
Akashi Japan **23** 34.38N134.59E
Akbulak Russian Fed. **19** 51.00N 55.40E
Akelamo Indonesia **27** 1.35N129.40E
Akershus *d.* Norway **17** 60.00N 11.10E
Aketi Zaïre **36** 2.46N 23.51E
Akhaltsikhe Georgia **30** 41.37N 42.59E
Akhḑar, Al Jabal al *mts.* Libya **35** 32.10N 22.00E
Akhḑar, Al Jabal al *mts.* Oman **31** 23.10N 57.25E
Akhḑar, Wādī *r.* Egypt **32** 28.42N 33.41E
Akhḑar, Wādī al *r.* Saudi Arabia **32** 28.30N 36.48E
Akhelóös Greece **13** 38.20N 21.04E
Akhisar Turkey **13** 38.54N 27.49E
Akhmīm Egypt **30** 26.34N 31.44E
Akhtyrka Ukraine **19** 50.19N 34.54E
Akimiski I. Canada **51** 53.00N 81.20W
Akita Japan **25** 39.44N140.05E
Akjoujt Mauritania **34** 19.44N 14.26W
Akkajaure *l.* Sweden **16** 67.40N 17.30E
'Akko Israel **32** 32.55N 35.04E
Akkol Kazakhstan **24** 45.04N 75.39E
Aklavik Canada **50** 68.12N135.00W
Ako Nigeria **38** 10.19N 10.48E
Ākobo *r.* Ethiopia **35** 8.30N 33.15E
Akola India **28** 20.44N 77.00E
Āk'ordat Eritrea **35** 15.35N 37.55E
Akpatok I. Canada **51** 60.30N 68.30W
Akranes Iceland **16** 64.19N 22.05W
Akron Ohio U.S.A. **55** 41.04N 81.31W
Akrotíri Cyprus **32** 34.36N 32.57E
Aksaray Turkey **30** 38.22N 34.02E
Aksarka Russian Fed. **20** 66.31N 67.50E
Aksay China **24** 39.28N 94.15E
Aksay Kazakhstan **19** 51.24N 52.11E
Akşehir Turkey **30** 38.22N 31.24E
Aksu China **24** 42.10N 80.00E
Aktag *mtn.* China **24** 36.45N 84.40E
Aktogay Kazakhstan **24** 46.59N 79.42E
Aktyubinsk Kazakhstan **19** 50.16N 57.13E
Akūbū Sudan **36** 7.47N 33.01E
Akūbū *r. see* Ākobo *r.* Sudan **36**
Akure Nigeria **38** 7.14N 5.08E
Akureyri Iceland **16** 65.41N 18.04W
Akuse Ghana **38** 6.04N 0.12E
Akwa-Ibom *d.* Nigeria **38** 4.45N 7.50E
Akxokesay China **24** 36.48N 91.06E
Akyab *see* Sittwe Burma **29**
Ål Norway **17** 60.38N 8.34E
Alabama *d.* U.S.A. **53** 33.00N 87.00W
Alabama *r.* U.S.A. **53** 31.05N 87.55W
Ālādāgh, Kūh-e *mts.* Iran **31** 37.15N 57.30E
Alagoas *d.* Brazil **61** 9.30S 37.00W
Alagoinhas Brazil **61** 12.09S 38.21W
Alagón Spain **10** 41.46N 1.12W
Alakol, Ozero *l.* Kazakhstan **24** 46.00N 81.40E
Alakurtti Russian Fed. **18** 67.00N 30.23E
Al 'Alamayn Egypt **30** 30.49N 28.57E
Al 'Amārah Iraq **31** 31.52N 47.50E
Al Āmirīyah Egypt **32** 31.01N 29.48E
Alamogordo U.S.A. **52** 32.54N105.57W
Alamosa U.S.A. **52** 37.28N105.52W
Åland *is. see* Ahvenanmaa *is.* Finland **17**
Ålands Hav *sea* Finland **17** 60.00N 19.30E
Alanya Turkey **30** 36.32N 32.02E
Alapayevsk Russian Fed. **18** 57.55N 61.42E
Alappuzha India **28** 9.30N 76.22E
Al 'Aqabah Jordan **32** 29.32N 35.00E
Al 'Aramah *f.* Saudi Arabia **31** 25.30N 46.30E
Alarcón, Embalse de *resr.* Spain **10** 39.36N 2.10W
Al 'Arīsh Egypt **32** 31.08N 33.48E
Alaşehir Turkey **13** 38.22N 28.29E
Alaska *d.* U.S.A. **50** 65.00N153.00W
Alaska, G. of U.S.A. **50** 58.45N145.00W
Alaska Pen. U.S.A. **50** 56.00N160.00W
Alaska Range *mts.* U.S.A. **50** 62.10N152.00W
Alassio Italy **9** 44.00N 8.10E
Al 'Atīqah Lebanon **32** 33.42N 35.27E
Al 'Aţrun Sudan **35** 18.11N 26.36E
Alatyr Russian Fed. **18** 54.51N 46.35E
Alausí Ecuador **60** 2.00S 78.50W
Alavus Finland **16** 62.35N 23.37E
Alawoona Australia **46** 34.44S140.33E
Al 'Ayyāţ Egypt **32** 29.37N 31.15E
Alazani *r.* Georgia **31** 41.06N 46.40E
Alba Italy **9** 44.42N 8.02E
Albacete Spain **10** 39.00N 1.52W
Al Bad' Saudi Arabia **32** 28.29N 35.02E
Al Badārī Egypt **30** 26.59N 31.25E
Al Bahnasā Egypt **32** 28.32N 30.39E
Alba-Iulia Romania **15** 46.04N 23.33E
Albania Europe **13** 41.00N 20.00E
Albany Australia **43** 34.57S117.54E
Albany *r.* Canada **51** 52.10N 82.00W
Albany Ga. U.S.A. **53** 31.37N 84.10W
Albany N.Y. U.S.A. **55** 42.39N 73.45W
Albany Oreg. U.S.A. **54** 44.38N123.06W
Al Başrah Iraq **31** 30.33N 47.50E
Al Bāţinah *f.* Oman **31** 24.25N 56.50E
Albatross B. Australia **44** 12.45S141.43E
Al Batrūn Lebanon **32** 34.16N 35.40E
Al Bawīţī Egypt **30** 28.21N 25.52E
Al Bayḑā' Libya **35** 32.50N 21.50E
Albemarle Sd. U.S.A. **53** 36.10N 76.00W
Albenga Italy **9** 44.03N 8.13E
Alberche *r.* Spain **10** 40.00N 4.45W
Alberga Australia **45** 27.12S135.28E
Alberga *r.* Australia **45** 27.12S135.28E
Albert Australia **47** 32.21S147.33E
Albert France **8** 50.02N 2.38E
Albert, L. Australia **46** 35.38S139.17E
Albert, L. Uganda / Zaïre **37** 1.45N 31.00E
Alberta *d.* Canada **50** 55.00N115.00W
Alberti Argentina **63** 35.01S 60.16W
Albertirsa Hungary **15** 47.15N 19.38E
Albert Kanaal *canal* Belgium **8** 51.00N 5.15E
Albert Lea U.S.A. **53** 43.38N 93.16W
Albert Nile *r.* Uganda **37** 3.30N 32.00E
Albi France **11** 43.56N 2.08E
Albina Surinam **61** 5.30N 54.03W
Albino Italy **9** 45.46N 9.47E
Albion Mich. U.S.A. **55** 42.14N 84.45W
Albion Penn. U.S.A. **55** 41.53N 80.22W
Al Bi'r Saudi Arabia **32** 28.52N 36.15E
Alborán, Isla de *i.* Spain **10** 35.55N 3.10W
Ålborg Denmark **17** 57.03N 9.56E
Ålborg Bugt *b.* Denmark **17** 56.45N 10.30E
Alborz, Reshteh-ye Kūhhā-ye *mts.* Iran **31** 36.00N 52.30E
Albuquerque U.S.A. **52** 35.05N106.40W
Al Buraymī U.A.E. **31** 24.15N 55.45E
Al Burj Egypt **32** 31.35N 30.59E
Alburquerque Spain **10** 39.13N 6.59W
Albury Australia **47** 36.03S146.53E
Alby Sweden **16** 62.30N 15.25E
Alcácer do Sal Portugal **10** 38.22N 8.30W
Alcalá de Chisvert Spain **10** 40.19N 0.13E
Alcalá de Henares Spain **10** 40.28N 3.22W
Alcalá la Real Spain **10** 37.28N 3.55W
Alcamo Italy **12** 37.59N 12.58E
Alcañiz Spain **10** 41.03N 0.09W
Alcántara, Embalse de *resr.* Spain **10** 39.45N 6.25W
Alcaudete Spain **10** 37.35N 4.05W
Alcázar de San Juan Spain **10** 39.24N 3.12W
Alcira Spain **10** 39.10N 0.27W
Alcobaça Portugal **10** 39.33N 8.59W
Alcova U.S.A. **54** 42.35N106.34W
Alcoy Spain **10** 38.42N 0.29W
Alcubierre, Sierra de *mts.* Spain **10** 41.40N 0.20W
Alcudia Spain **10** 39.51N 3.09E
Aldan Russian Fed. **21** 58.44N125.22E
Aldan *r.* Russian Fed. **21** 63.30N130.00E
Aldeburgh U.K. **5** 52.09N 1.35E
Alderney *i.* U.K. **5** 49.42N 2.11W
Aldershot U.K. **5** 51.15N 0.47W
Aldridge U.K. **5** 52.36N 1.55W
Alegre Brazil **59** 20.44S 41.30W
Alegrete Brazil **63** 29.46S 55.46W
Aleksandrov Gay Russian Fed. **19** 50.08N 48.34E
Aleksandrovsk Sakhalinskiy Russian Fed. **21** 50.55N142.12E
Além Paraíba Brazil **59** 21.49S 42.36W
Alençon France **9** 48.25N 0.05E
Aleppo *see* Ḩalab Syria **30**
Aléria France **11** 42.05N 9.30E
Alès France **11** 44.08N 4.05E
Alessandria Italy **9** 44.54N 8.37E
Ålesund Norway **16** 62.28N 6.11E
Aleutian Range *mts.* U.S.A. **50** 58.00N156.00W
Alexander Archipelago *is.* U.S.A. **50** 56.30N134.30W
Alexander Bay *town* R.S.A. **39** 28.36S 16.26E
Alexander I. Antarctica **64** 72.00S 70.00W
Alexandra Australia **47** 37.12S145.14E
Alexandra New Zealand **48** 45.14S169.26E
Alexandria B.C. Canada **50** 52.38N122.27W
Alexandria Ont. Canada **55** 45.18N 74.39W
Alexandria *see* Al Iskandarīyah Egypt **32**
Alexandria Romania **15** 43.58N 25.20E
Alexandria R.S.A. **39** 33.39S 26.24E
Alexandria La. U.S.A. **53** 31.19N 92.29W
Alexandria Va. U.S.A. **55** 38.48N 77.03W
Alexandrina, L. Australia **46** 35.26S139.10E
Alexandroúpolis Greece **13** 40.50N 25.53E
Aleysk Russian Fed. **20** 52.32N 82.45E
Al Fant Egypt **32** 28.46N 30.53E
Alfaro Spain **10** 42.11N 1.45W
Al Fāshir Sudan **35** 13.37N 25.22E
Al Fashn Egypt **32** 28.49N 30.54E
Al Fāw Iraq **31** 29.57N 48.30E
Al Fayyūm Egypt **32** 29.19N 30.50E
Alfeld Germany **14** 51.59N 9.50E
Alfenas Brazil **59** 21.28S 45.48W
Alfiós *r.* Greece **13** 37.37N 21.27E
Alfonsine Italy **9** 44.30N 12.03E
Alford U.K. **6** 57.14N 2.42W
Al Fujayrah U.A.E. **31** 25.10N 56.20E
Alga Kazakhstan **20** 49.49N 57.16E
Ålgård Norway **17** 58.46N 5.51E
Algeciras Spain **10** 36.08N 5.27W
Algemesí Spain **10** 39.11N 0.27W
Alger Algeria **34** 36.50N 3.00E
Algeria Africa **34** 28.00N 2.00E
Al Ghayl Saudi Arabia **31** 22.36N 46.19E
Alghero Italy **12** 40.33N 8.20E
Al Ghurdaqah Egypt **30** 27.14N 33.50E
Algiers *see* Alger Algeria **34**
Algoa B. R.S.A. **39** 33.50S 26.00E
Algonquin Prov. Park Canada **55** 45.27N 78.26W
Algorta Uruguay **63** 32.25S 57.23W
Al Ḩajar al Gharbī *mts.* Oman **31** 24.00N 56.30E
Al Ḩajar ash Sharqī *mts.* Oman **31** 22.45N 58.45E
Alhama Spain **10** 37.51N 1.25W
Al Ḩamād *des.* Saudi Arabia **30** 31.45N 39.00E
Al Ḩamar Saudi Arabia **31** 22.26N 46.12E
Alhambra U.S.A. **54** 34.06N118.08W
Al Ḩamīdīyah Syria **32** 34.43N 35.56E
Al Ḩanākīyah Saudi Arabia **30** 24.53N 40.30E
Al Ḩarīq Saudi Arabia **31** 23.37N 46.31E
Al Ḩasakah Syria **30** 36.29N 40.45E
Al Ḩawāmidīyah Egypt **32** 29.54N 31.15E
Al Ḩayz Egypt **30** 28.02N 28.39E
Al Ḩijāz *f.* Saudi Arabia **30** 26.00N 37.30E
Al Ḩillah Iraq **31** 32.28N 44.29E
Al Ḩillah Saudi Arabia **31** 23.30N 46.51E
Al Hirmil Lebanon **32** 34.25N 36.23E
Al Ḩudaydah Yemen **35** 14.50N 42.58E
Al Hufūf Saudi Arabia **31** 25.20N 49.34E
Al Ḩumrah *des.* U.A.E. **31** 22.45N 55.10E
Al Ḩusaynīyah Egypt **32** 30.52N 31.55E
Al Ḩuwaymī Yemen **35** 14.05N 47.44E
Alīābād, Kūh-e *mtn.* Iran **31** 34.09N 50.48E
Aliákmon *r.* Greece **13** 40.30N 22.38E
Alicante Spain **10** 38.21N 0.29W
Alice R.S.A. **39** 32.47S 26.49E
Alice U.S.A. **52** 27.45N 98.06W
Alice Springs *town* Australia **44** 23.42S133.52E
Alīgarh India **29** 27.54N 78.04E
Alīgūdarz Iran **31** 33.25N 49.38E
'Alījūq, Kūh-e *mtn.* Iran **31** 31.27N 51.43E
Alingsås Sweden **17** 57.56N 12.31E
Alīpur Duār India **29** 26.29N 89.44E
Aliquippa U.S.A. **55** 40.38N 80.16W
Al Iskandarīyah Egypt **32** 31.13N 29.55E
Al Ismā'īlīyah Egypt **32** 30.36N 32.15E
Aliwal North R.S.A. **39** 30.41S 26.41E
Al Jafr Jordan **32** 30.16N 36.11E
Al Jāfūrah *des.* Saudi Arabia **31** 24.40N 50.20E
Al Jaghbūb Libya **35** 29.42N 24.38E
Al Jahrah Kuwait **31** 29.20N 47.41E
Al Jawārah Oman **28** 18.55N 57.17E
Al Jawb *f.* Saudi Arabia **31** 23.00N 50.00E
Al Jawf Libya **35** 24.09N 23.19E
Al Jawf Saudi Arabia **30** 29.49N 39.52E
Al Jazirah *f.* Iraq **30** 35.00N 41.00E
Al Jazīrah *f.* Sudan **35** 14.30N 33.00E
Al Jifārah Saudi Arabia **31** 23.59N 45.11E
Al Jīzah Egypt **32** 30.01N 31.12E
Al Jubayl Saudi Arabia **31** 27.59N 49.40E
Al Junaynah Sudan **35** 13.27N 22.30E
Aljustrel Portugal **10** 37.55N 8.10W
Al Karak Jordan **32** 31.11N 35.42E
Al Khābūr *r.* Syria **30** 35.07N 40.30E
Al Khābūrah Oman **31** 23.58N 57.10E
Al Khalīl Jordan **32** 31.32N 35.06E
Al Khamāsīn Saudi Arabia **35** 20.29N 44.49E
Al Khānkah Egypt **32** 30.12N 31.21E
Al Khārijah Egypt **30** 25.26N 30.33E
Al Kharţūm Sudan **35** 15.33N 32.35E
Al Kharţūm Baḩrī Sudan **35** 15.39N 32.34E
Al Khawr Qatar **31** 25.39N 51.32E
Al Khirbah as Samrā' Jordan **32** 32.11N 36.10E
Al Khubar Saudi Arabia **31** 26.18N 50.06E
Al Khufayfīyah Saudi Arabia **31** 24.55N 44.42E
Al Khunn Saudi Arabia **31** 23.18N 49.15E
Al Kidn *des.* Saudi Arabia **35** 22.30N 54.00E
Al Kiswah Syria **32** 33.21N 36.14E
Alkmaar Neth. **8** 52.37N 4.44E
Al Kuntillah Egypt **32** 30.00N 34.41E
Al Kūt Iraq **31** 32.30N 45.51E
Al Kuwayt Kuwait **31** 29.20N 48.00E
Al Labwah Lebanon **32** 34.11N 36.21E
Al Lādhiqīyah Syria **32** 35.31N 35.47E
Allāhābād India **29** 25.57N 81.50E
Allakaket U.S.A. **50** 66.30N152.45W
Allanche France **11** 45.14N 2.56E
'Allāqī, Wādī al *r.* Egypt **30** 22.55N 33.02E
Allegheny *r.* U.S.A. **55** 40.27N 80.00W
Allegheny Mts. U.S.A. **53** 38.30N 80.00W
Allen, Lough Rep. of Ire. **7** 54.07N 8.04W
Allentown U.S.A. **55** 40.37N 75.30W
Aller *r.* Germany **14** 52.57N 9.11E
Alliance Nebr. U.S.A. **52** 42.06N102.52W
Allier *r.* France **11** 46.58N 3.04E
Al Līţānī *r.* Lebanon **32** 33.22N 35.14E
Alloa U.K. **6** 56.07N 3.49W
Allos France **11** 44.14N 6.38E
Al Luḩayyah Yemen **35** 15.43N 42.42E
Alluitsup-Paa *see* Sydpröven Greenland **51**
Alma Canada **55** 48.32N 71.40W
Alma Mich. U.S.A. **55** 43.23N 84.40W
Al Ma'ānīyah *well* Iraq **30** 30.44N 43.00E
Alma-Ata Kazakhstan **24** 43.19N 76.55E
Almadén Spain **10** 38.47N 4.50W
Al Madīnah Saudi Arabia **30** 24.30N 39.35E
Al Madīnah al Fikrīyah Egypt **32** 27.56N 30.49E
Al Mafraq Jordan **32** 32.20N 36.12E
Al Maghrah *well* Egypt **30** 30.14N 28.56E
Almagor Israel **32** 32.55N 35.36E
Al Maḩallah al Kubrá Egypt **32** 30.59N 31.12E
Al Maḩārīq Egypt **30** 25.37N 30.39E
Al Maḩmūdīyah Egypt **32** 31.10N 30.30E
Al Majma'ah Saudi Arabia **31** 25.52N 45.25E
Al Manāmah Bahrain **31** 26.12N 50.36E
Almanor U.S.A. **54** 40.15N121.08W
Almansa Spain **10** 38.52N 1.06W

Al Manshāh Egypt 30 26.28N 31.48E
Al Manşūrah Egypt 32 31.03N 31.23E
Al Manzil Jordan 32 31.03N 36.01E
Al Manzilah Egypt 32 31.10N 31.56E
Almanzor, Pico de mtn. Spain 10 40.20N 5.22W
Almanzora r. Spain 10 37.16N 1.49W
Al Maţarīyah Egypt 32 31.12N 32.02E
Almaty see Alma Ata Kazakhstan 24
Al Mawşil Iraq 30 36.21N 43.08E
Al Mayādīn Syria 30 35.01N 40.28E
Almazán Spain 10 41.29N 2.31W
Al Mazra'ah Jordan 32 31.16N 35.31E
Almeirim Portugal 10 39.12N 8.37W
Almelo Neth. 8 52.21N 6.40E
Almendralejo Spain 10 38.41N 6.26W
Almería Spain 10 36.50N 2.26W
Älmhult Sweden 17 56.33N 14.08E
Al Midhnab Saudi Arabia 31 25.52N 44.15E
Al Miḩrāḑ des. Saudi Arabia 31 20.00N 52.30E
Al Minyā Egypt 32 28.06N 30.45E
Al Mismīyah Syria 32 33.08N 36.24E
Almonte Spain 10 37.16N 6.31W
Al Mudawwarah Jordan 32 29.20N 36.00E
Al Muglad Sudan 35 11.01N 27.50E
Al Muḩarraq Bahrain 31 26.16N 50.38E
Al Mukallā Yemen 35 14.34N 49.09E
Almuñécar Spain 10 36.44N 3.41W
Al Muwayh Saudi Arabia 30 22.41N 41.37E
Alnwick U.K. 4 55.25N 1.41W
Alofi Niue 40 19.03S169.55W
Alónnisos i. Greece 13 39.08N 23.50E
Alor i. Indonesia 27 8.20S124.30E
Alor Setar Malaysia 26 6.06N100.23E
Alozero Russian Fed. 18 65.02N 31.10E
Alpena U.S.A. 55 45.04N 83.27W
Alpes Maritimes mts. France 11 44.07N 7.08E
Alpha Australia 44 23.39S146.38E
Alphen Neth. 8 52.08N 4.40E
Alpine U.S.A. 52 30.22N103.40W
Alps mts. Europe 11 46.00N 7.30E
Al Qaḑārif Sudan 35 14.02N 35.24E
Al Qafā' des. U.A.E. 31 23.30N 53.30E
Al Qāhirah Egypt 32 30.03N 31.15E
Al Qā'īyah Saudi Arabia 30 24.18N 43.30E
Al Qā'īyah well Saudi Arabia 31 26.27N 45.35E
Al Qalībah Saudi Arabia 30 28.24N 37.42E
Al Qanāţir al Khayrīyah Egypt 32 30.12N 31.08E
Al Qanţarah Egypt 32 30.52N 32.20E
Al Qaryatayn Syria 32 34.13N 37.13E
Al Qaşr Egypt 30 25.43N 28.54E
Al Qaşşāşīn Egypt 32 30.34N 31.56E
Al Qaţīf Saudi Arabia 31 26.31N 50.00E
Al Qaţrānah Jordan 32 31.15N 36.03E
Al Qaţrūn Libya 34 24.55N 14.38E
Al Qayşūmah Saudi Arabia 31 28.20N 46.07E
Al Qunayţirah Syria 32 33.08N 35.49E
Al Qurnah Iraq 31 31.00N 47.26E
Al Quşaymah Egypt 32 30.40N 34.22E
Al Quşayr Egypt 30 26.06N 34.17E
Al Qūşīyah Egypt 30 27.26N 30.49E
Al Quţayfah Syria 32 33.44N 36.36E
Alroy Downs town Australia 44 19.18S136.04E
Als i. Denmark 17 54.59N 9.55E
Alsace d. France 11 48.25N 7.40E
Alsask Canada 50 51.23N109.59W
Alsasua Spain 10 42.54N 2.10W
Ålsborg d. Sweden 17 58.00N 12.20E
Alsfeld Germany 14 50.45N 9.16E
Alsten i. Norway 16 65.55N 12.35E
Alston U.K. 6 54.48N 2.26W
Alta Norway 16 70.00N 23.15E
Alta r. Norway 16 69.50N 23.30E
Altafjorden est. Norway 16 70.10N 23.00E
Alta Gracia Argentina 62 31.40S 64.26W
Altagracia de Orituco Venezuela 60 9.54N 66.24W
Altai mts. Mongolia 24 46.30N 93.30E
Altamaha r. U.S.A. 53 31.15N 81.23W
Altamira Brazil 61 3.12S 52.12W
Altamont Oreg. U.S.A. 54 42.12N121.44W
Altamura Italy 13 40.50N 16.32E
Altay China 24 47.48N 88.07E
Altay Mongolia 24 46.20N 97.00E
Altea Spain 10 38.37N 0.03W
Altenburg Germany 14 50.59N 12.27E
Altenkirchen Germany 8 50.41N 7.40E
Altnaharra U.K. 6 58.16N 4.26W
Alto Araguaia Brazil 61 17.19S 53.10W
Alto Molocue Mozambique 37 15.38S 37.42E
Alton U.K. 5 51.08N 0.59W
Altona Germany 14 53.32N 9.56E
Altoona U.S.A. 55 40.30N 78.24W
Altun Shan mts. China 24 38.10N 87.50E
Al Ubayyiḑ Sudan 35 13.11N 30.10E
Al 'Ulá Saudi Arabia 30 26.39N 37.58E
Al' Uqaylah Libya 34 30.15N 19.12E
Al Uqşur Egypt 30 25.41N 32.24E
Al Urduun r. Asia 32 31.47N 35.31E
Al 'Uwaynah well Saudi Arabia 31 26.46N 48.13E
Al 'Uyūn Saudi Arabia 31 26.32N 43.41E
Alva U.S.A. 52 36.48N 98.40W
Alvarado Mexico 56 18.49N 95.46W
Älvdalen Sweden 17 61.14N 14.02E
Alvesta Sweden 17 56.54N 14.33E
Älvho Sweden 17 61.30N 14.46E
Älvkarleby Sweden 17 60.34N 17.27E
Älvsbyn Sweden 16 65.39N 20.59E
Al Wajh Saudi Arabia 30 26.16N 36.28E
Al Wakrah Qatar 31 25.09N 51.36E
Alwar India 28 27.32N 76.35E
Al Yamāmah Saudi Arabia 31 24.11N 47.21E
Alyaty Azerbaijan 31 39.59N 49.20E
Alytus Lithuania 15 54.24N 24.03E
Alzette r. Lux. 8 49.52N 6.07E
Amadeus, L. Australia 42 24.50S130.45E
Amadjuak Canada 51 64.00N 72.50W
Amadjuak L. Canada 51 65.00N 71.00W
Amagasaki Japan 23 34.43N135.25E
Åmål Sweden 17 59.03N 12.42E
Amaliás Greece 13 37.48N 21.21E
Amami ō shima i. Japan 25 28.20N129.30E
Amamula Zaïre 37 0.17S 27.49E
Amanā, L. Brazil 60 2.35S 64.40W
Amangeldy Kazakhstan 20 50.12N 65.11E
Amapá Brazil 61 2.00N 50.50W
Amapá d. Brazil 61 2.00N 52.00W
Amarante Brazil 61 6.14S 42.51W
Amareleja Portugal 10 38.12N 7.13W
Amares Portugal 10 41.38N 8.21W
Amarillo U.S.A. 52 35.14N101.50W
Amaro, Monte mtn. Italy 12 42.06N 14.04E
Amasya Turkey 30 40.37N 35.50E
Amazon r. see Amazonas r. Brazil 61
Amazonas d. Brazil 60 4.50S 64.00W
Amazonas r. Brazil 61 2.00S 52.00W
Amazonas, Estuario do Rio f. Brazil 61 0.00 50.30W
Amazon Delta see Amazonas, Estuario do Rio f. Brazil 61
Ambāla India 28 30.19N 76.49E
Ambam Cameroon 38 2.25N 11.16E
Ambarchik Russian Fed. 21 69.39N162.27E
Ambarnyy Russian Fed. 18 65.59N 33.53E
Ambato Ecuador 60 1.18S 78.36W
Ambato-Boeni Madagascar 36 16.28S 46.43E
Ambatondrazaka Madagascar 36 17.50S 48.25E
Amberg Germany 14 49.27N 11.52E
Ambergris Cay i. Belize 57 18.00N 87.58W
Ambikāpur India 29 23.07N 83.12E
Ambilobe Madagascar 36 13.12S 49.04E
Amble U.K. 4 55.20N 1.34W
Ambleside U.K. 4 54.26N 2.58W
Amboise France 9 47.25N 1.00E
Ambon Indonesia 27 4.50S128.10E
Ambovombe Madagascar 36 25.11S 46.05E
Amboy U.S.A. 54 34.33N115.44W
Ambrières France 9 48.24N 0.38W
Ambriz Angola 36 7.54S 13.12E
Amderma Russian Fed. 20 69.44N 61.35E
Ameca Mexico 56 20.33N104.02W
Ameland i. Neth. 8 53.28N 5.48E
Americana Brazil 59 22.44S 47.19W
American Falls Resr. U.S.A. 54 43.00N113.00W
American Fork U.S.A. 54 40.23N111.48W
Amersfoort Neth. 8 52.10N 5.23E
Amery Australia 43 31.09S117.05E
Ames U.S.A. 53 42.02N 93.39W
Ameson Canada 55 49.49N 84.34W
Ametinho Angola 39 17.20S 17.20E
Amga Russian Fed. 21 60.51N131.59E
Amga r. Russian Fed. 21 62.40N135.20E
Amgu Russian Fed. 25 45.48N137.36E
Amgun r. Russian Fed. 21 53.10N139.47E
Amhara Plateau f. Ethiopia 35 10.00N 37.00E
Amiata mtn. Italy 12 42.53N 11.37E
Amiens France 9 49.54N 2.18E
Åmli Norway 17 58.47N 8.30E
Amlwch U.K. 4 53.24N 4.21W
'Ammān Jordan 32 31.57N 35.56E
Ammanford U.K. 5 51.48N 4.00W
Ammassalik Greenland 51 65.40N 38.00W
Ammókhostos Cyprus 32 35.07N 33.57E
Ammókhostou, Kólpos b. Cyprus 32 35.12N 34.05E
Āmol Iran 31 36.26N 52.24E
Amorgós i. Greece 13 36.50N 25.55E
Amos Canada 55 48.34N 78.07W
Amoy see Xiamen China 25
Ampala Honduras 57 13.16N 87.39W
Amparo Brazil 59 22.44S 46.44W
Ampezzo Italy 9 46.25N 12.48E
Ampotaka Madagascar 36 25.03S 44.41E
Amqui Canada 55 48.28N 67.27W
Amrāvati India 28 20.58N 77.50E
Amritsar India 28 31.35N 74.56E
Amstelveen Neth. 8 52.18N 4.51E
Amsterdam Neth. 8 52.22N 4.54E
Amsterdam N.Y. U.S.A. 55 42.57N 74.11W
Am Timan Chad 35 11.02N 20.17E
Amu Darya r. Uzbekistan 20 43.50N 59.00E
Amundsen G. Canada 50 70.30N122.00W
Amundsen Sea Antarctica 64 72.00S120.00W
Amuntai Indonesia 26 2.24S115.14E
Amur r. Russian Fed. 21 53.17N140.00E
Amurzet Russian Fed. 25 47.50N131.05E
Anabar r. Russian Fed. 21 72.40N113.30E
Anabranch r. Australia 46 34.08S141.46E
Anaco Venezuela 60 9.27N 64.28W
Anaconda U.S.A. 54 46.08N112.57W
Anadolu f. Turkey 30 38.00N 35.00E
Anadyr Russian Fed. 21 64.40N177.32E
Anadyr r. Russian Fed. 21 65.00N176.00E
Anadyrskiy Zaliv g. Russian Fed. 21 64.30N177.50W
Anáfi i. Greece 13 36.21N 25.50E
Anaheim U.S.A. 54 33.51N117.57W
Analalava Madagascar 36 14.38S 47.45E
Anambas, Kepulauan is. Indonesia 26 3.00N106.10E
Anambra d. Nigeria 38 6.20N 7.25E
Anamur Turkey 30 36.06N 32.49E
Anantapur India 28 14.41N 77.36E
Anápolis Brazil 61 16.19S 48.58W
Anapú r. Brazil 61 1.53S 50.53W
Anār Iran 31 30.54N 55.18E
Anārak Iran 31 33.20N 53.42E
Anatolia f. see Anadolu f. Turkey 30
Anatone U.S.A. 54 46.08N117.09W
Añatuya Argentina 62 28.26S 62.48W
Ancenis France 9 47.21N 1.10W
Anchau Nigeria 38 11.00N 8.23E
Anchorage U.S.A. 50 61.10N150.00W
Ancohuma mtn. Bolivia 62 16.05S 68.36W
Ancón Peru 60 11.50S 77.10W
Ancona Italy 12 43.37N 13.33E
Ancuabe Mozambique 37 13.00S 39.50E
Ancud Chile 63 41.05S 73.50W
Ancy-le-Franc France 9 47.46N 4.10E
Anda China 25 46.25N125.20E
Andalsnes Norway 16 62.33N 7.43E
Andalucía d. Spain 10 37.36N 4.30W
Andalusia U.S.A. 53 31.20N 86.30W
Andaman Is. India 29 12.00N 93.00E
Andaman Sea Indian Oc. 29 11.15N 95.30E
Andamooka Australia 46 30.27S137.12E
Andanga Russian Fed. 18 59.11N 45.44E
Andara Namibia 39 18.04S 21.26E
Andelot France 11 48.15N 5.18E
Andenes Norway 16 69.18N 16.10E
Andenne Belgium 8 50.29N 5.04E
Anderlecht Belgium 8 50.51N 4.18E
Andernach Germany 8 50.25N 7.24E
Anderson r. Canada 50 69.45N129.00W
Anderson Ind. U.S.A. 55 40.05N 85.41W
Anderson S.C. U.S.A. 53 34.30N 82.39W
Andes mts. S. America 63 32.40S 70.00W
Andevoranto Madagascar 36 18.57S 49.06E
Andfjorden est. Norway 16 68.55N 16.00E
Andhra Pradesh d. India 29 17.00N 79.00E
Andikíthira i. Greece 13 35.52N 23.18E
Andizhan Uzbekistan 24 40.48N 72.23E
Andong S. Korea 25 36.37N128.44E
Andorra town Andorra 11 42.30N 1.31E
Andorra Europe 11 42.30N 1.32E
Andover U.K. 5 51.13N 1.29W
Andöy i. Norway 16 69.05N 15.40E
Andreyevo-Ivanovka Ukraine 15 47.28N 30.29E
Andria Italy 12 41.13N 16.18E
Ándros Greece 13 37.50N 24.57E
Ándros i. Greece 13 37.50N 24.50E
Andros I. Bahamas 57 24.30N 78.00W
Andros Town Bahamas 57 24.43N 77.47W
Andrushevka Ukraine 15 50.00N 28.59E
Andújar Spain 10 38.02N 4.03W
Anefis I-n-Darane Mali 38 17.57N 0.35E
Anegada i. B.V.Is. 57 18.46N 64.24W
Aného Togo 38 6.17N 1.40E
Añelo Argentina 63 38.20S 68.45W
Aneto, Pico de mtn. Spain 10 42.40N 0.19E
Aney Niger 38 19.24N 12.56E
Angara r. Russian Fed. 21 58.00N 93.00E
Angarsk Russian Fed. 21 52.31N103.55E
Angaston Australia 45 34.30S139.03E
Angatuba Brazil 59 23.27S 48.25W
Ånge Sweden 16 62.31N 15.40E
Ángel de la Guarda, Isla i. Mexico 56 29.20N113.25W
Angel Falls f. Venezuela 60 5.55N 62.30W
Ängelholm Sweden 17 56.15N 12.50E
Angels Camp U.S.A. 54 38.04N120.32W
Ångerman r. Sweden 16 63.00N 17.43E
Angermünde Germany 14 53.01N 14.00E
Angers France 9 47.29N 0.32W
Angerville France 9 48.19N 2.00E
Ångesån r. Sweden 16 66.22N 22.58E
Angkor ruins Cambodia 26 13.26N103.50E
Anglesey i. U.K. 4 53.16N 4.25W
Angoche Mozambique 37 16.10S 39.57E
Angol Chile 63 37.48S 72.43W
Angola Africa 36 12.00S 18.00E
Angola Ind. U.S.A. 55 41.38N 85.01W
Angola N.Y. U.S.A. 55 42.39N 79.02W
Angoram P.N.G. 27 4.04S144.04E
Angoulême France 11 45.40N 0.10E
Angra dos Reis Brazil 59 22.59S 44.17W
Anguilla i. Leeward Is. 57 18.14N 63.05W
Angumu Zaïre 37 0.10S 27.38E
Anholt i. Denmark 17 56.42N 11.34E
Anholt Germany 8 51.51N 6.26E
Anhui d. China 25 31.30N116.45E
Aniak U.S.A. 50 61.32N159.40W
Anina Romania 15 45.05N 21.51E
Anjō Japan 23 34.57N137.05E
Anjouan i. Comoros 37 12.12S 44.28E
Anju N. Korea 25 39.36N125.42E
Anka Nigeria 38 12.06N 5.56E
Ankara Turkey 30 39.55N 32.50E
Anklam Germany 14 53.51N 13.41E
Ankober Ethiopia 35 9.32N 39.43E
Ankpa Nigeria 38 7.26N 7.38E
Annaba Algeria 34 36.55N 7.47E
An Nabk Syria 32 34.02N 36.43E
Anna Creek town Australia 46 28.50S136.07E
An Nafūd des. Saudi Arabia 30 28.40N 41.30E
An Najaf Iraq 31 31.59N 44.19E
An Nakhl Egypt 32 29.55N 33.45E
Annam Highlands see Annamitique, Chaîne mts. Laos / Vietnam 26
Annamitique, Chaîne mts. Laos / Vietnam 26 17.40N105.30E
Annan U.K. 6 54.59N 3.16W
Annan r. U.K. 6 54.58N 3.16W
Annandale f. U.K. 6 55.12N 3.25W
Anna Plains Australia 42 19.18S121.34E
Annapolis U.S.A. 55 38.59N 76.30W
Annapurna mtn. Nepal 29 28.34N 83.50E
An Naqirah well Saudi Arabia 31 27.53N 48.15E
Ann Arbor U.S.A. 55 42.18N 83.43W
An Nāşirīyah Iraq 31 31.04N 46.16E
Annecy France 11 45.54N 6.07E
Anniston U.S.A. 53 33.38N 85.50W
Annonay France 11 45.15N 4.40E
Annuello Australia 46 34.52S142.54E
An Nuhūd Sudan 35 12.41N 28.28E
Anoka U.S.A. 53 45.11N 93.20W
Anqing China 25 30.20N116.50E
Ansbach Germany 14 49.18N 10.36E
Anshan China 25 41.05N122.58E
Anshun China 29 26.02N105.57E
Anson B. Australia 42 13.10S130.00E
Ansongo Mali 38 15.40N 0.30E
Anstruther U.K. 6 56.14N 2.42W
Ansudu Indonesia 27 2.11S139.22E
Antakya Turkey 30 36.12N 36.10E
Antalya Turkey 30 36.53N 30.42E
Antalya Körfezi g. Turkey 30 36.38N 31.00E
Antananarivo Madagascar 36 18.55S 47.31E
Antarctica 64
Antas Brazil 61 10.20S 38.20W
Antequera Spain 10 37.01N 4.34W
Antibes France 11 43.35N 7.07E
Anticosti, Île d' i. Canada 51 49.20N 63.00W
Antifer, Cap d' c. France 9 49.41N 0.10E
Antigua Guatemala 56 14.33N 90.42W
Antigua i. Leeward Is. 57 17.09N 61.49W
Anti-Lebanon mts. see Sharqī, Al Jabal ash mts. Lebanon 32
Antofagasta Chile 62 23.39S 70.24W
Antônio Bezerra Brazil 61 3.44S 38.35W
Antônio Carlos Brazil 59 21.18S 43.48W
Antrain France 9 48.28N 1.30W
Antrim U.K. 7 54.43N 6.14W
Antrim d. U.K. 7 54.58N 6.20W
Antrim, Mts. of U.K. 7 55.00N 6.10W
Antsiranana Madagascar 36 12.16S 49.17E
Anttis Sweden 16 67.16N 22.52E
Antwerp see Antwerpen Belgium 8
Antwerpen Belgium 8 51.13N 4.25E
Antwerpen d. Belgium 8 51.16N 4.45E
Anvik U.S.A. 50 62.38N160.20W
Anxi Gansu China 24 40.32N 95.57E
Anxious B. Australia 46 33.25S134.35E
Anyama Ivory Coast 38 5.30N 4.03W
Anyang China 25 36.04N114.20E
Anzhero-Sudzhensk Russian Fed. 20 56.10N 86.10E
Anzio Italy 12 41.27N 12.37E
Aohan Qi China 25 42.23N119.59E
Aomori Japan 25 40.50N140.43E
Aosta Italy 9 45.43N 7.19E
Apalachee B. U.S.A. 53 29.30N 84.00W
Apaporis r. Colombia 60 1.40S 69.20W
Aparri Phil. 27 18.22N121.40E
Apatin Yugo. 13 45.40N 18.59E
Apatity Russian Fed. 18 67.32N 33.21E
Apeldoorn Neth. 8 52.13N 5.57E
Apia W. Samoa 40 13.48S171.45W
Apizaco Mexico 56 19.25N 98.09W
Apollo Bay town Australia 46 38.45S143.40E
Apostle Is. U.S.A. 53 47.00N 90.30W
Apóstoles Argentina 62 27.55S 55.45W
Apostólou Andréa, Akrotírion c. Cyprus 32 35.40N 34.35E
Apoteri Guyana 60 4.02N 58.32W
Appalachian Mts. U.S.A. 53 39.30N 78.00W
Appennino mts. Italy 12 42.00N 13.30E
Appennino Ligure mts. Italy 9 44.30N 9.00E
Appennino Tosco-Emiliano mts. Italy 9 44.05N 11.00E
Appiano Italy 9 46.28N 11.15E
Appingedam Neth. 8 53.18N 6.52E
Appleby U.K. 4 54.35N 2.29W
Appleton U.S.A. 53 44.17N 88.24W
Apsheronsk Russian Fed. 19 44.26N 39.45E
Apsheronskiy Poluostrov pen. Azerbaijan 31 40.28N 50.00E
Apsley Australia 46 36.58S141.08E
Apsley Canada 55 44.45N 78.06W
Apucarana Brazil 59 23.34S 51.28W
Apure r. Venezuela 60 7.40N 66.30W
Apurimac r. Peru 60 10.43S 73.55W
Aqaba, G. of Asia 32 28.45N 34.45E
Aqabat al Ḩijāzīyah Jordan 32 29.40N 35.55E
'Aqdā Iran 31 32.25N 33.38E
Aqqikkol Hu l. China 24 35.44N 81.34E
Aquidauana Brazil 62 20.27S 55.45W
Aquila Mexico 56 18.30N103.50W
Aquitaine d. France 11 44.40N 0.00
'Arab, Baḩr al r. Sudan 35 9.02N 29.28E
Arabābād Iran 31 33.02N 57.41E
'Arabah, Wādī r. Egypt 32 29.07N 32.40E
Arabian Sea Asia 28 16.00N 65.00E
Araç Turkey 30 41.14N 33.20E
Aracaju Brazil 61 10.54S 37.07W
Aracanguy, Montañas de mts. Paraguay 62 24.00S 55.50W
Aracati Brazil 61 4.32S 37.45W
Araçatuba Brazil 59 21.12S 50.24W
Arad Romania 15 46.12N 21.19E
Arafura Sea Austa. 44 9.00S133.00E
Aragarças Brazil 61 15.55S 52.12W
Aragats mtn. Armenia 31 40.32N 44.11E
Aragón d. Spain 10 41.25N 1.00W
Aragón r. Spain 10 42.20N 1.45W
Araguacema Brazil 61 8.50S 49.34W
Araguaia r. Brazil 61 5.20S 48.30W
Araguari Brazil 59 18.38S 48.13W
Araguari r. Brazil 61 1.15N 50.05W
Arāk Iran 31 34.06N 49.44E
Arakan Yoma mts. Burma 29 20.00N 94.00E
Araks r. Azerbaijan 31 40.00N 48.28E
Aral Sea sea Asia 20 45.00N 60.00E
Aralsk Kazakhstan 20 46.56N 61.43E
Aralskoye More see Aral Sea sea Asia 20
Aralsor, Ozero l. Kazakhstan 19 49.00N 48.40E
Aramac Australia 44 22.59S145.14E
Aramia r. P.N.G. 27 8.00S143.20E
Aranda de Duero Spain 10 41.40N 3.41W
Aran I. Rep. of Ire. 7 53.07N 9.38W
Aran Is. Rep. of Ire. 7 53.07N 9.38W
Aranjuez Spain 10 40.02N 3.37W
Aranos Namibia 39 24.09S 19.09E
Araouane Mali 38 18.53N 3.31W
Arapey Uruguay 63 30.58S 57.30W
Arapey Grande r. Uruguay 63 30.55S 57.49W
Arapiraca Brazil 61 9.45S 36.40W
Arapkir Turkey 30 39.03N 38.29E
'Ar'ar, Wādī r. Iraq 30 32.00N 42.30E
Araraquara Brazil 59 21.46S 48.08W
Araras Brazil 59 22.20S 47.23W
Ararat Australia 46 37.20S143.00E
Ararat mtn. see Agri Daği mtn. Turkey 31
Aras r. see Araks r. Turkey 30
Arauca Colombia 60 7.04N 70.41W
Arauca r. Venezuela 60 7.05N 70.45W
Araure Venezuela 60 9.36N 69.15W
Araxá Brazil 59 19.37S 46.50W
Araxes r. Iran see Araks r. Iran 31
Ārba Minch' Ethiopia 35 6.02N 37.40E
Arbatax Italy 12 39.56N 9.41E
Arboga Sweden 17 59.24N 15.50E
Arbroath U.K. 6 56.34N 2.35W
Arcachon France 11 44.40N 1.11W
Arcata U.S.A. 54 40.52N124.05W
Archer r. Australia 44 13.28S141.41E
Archers Post Kenya 37 0.42N 37.40E
Arcis-sur-Aube France 9 48.32N 4.08E
Arckaringa r. Australia 46 27.56S134.45E
Arco Italy 9 45.55N 10.53E
Arco U.S.A. 54 43.38N113.18W
Arcoona Australia 46 31.06S137.19E
Arcos Brazil 59 20.12S 45.30W
Arcos Spain 10 36.45N 5.45W
Arcoverde Brazil 61 8.23S 37.00W
Arctic Bay town Canada 51 73.05N 85.20W
Arctic Ocean 64
Arctic Red r. Canada 50 67.26N133.48W
Arctic Red River town Canada 50 67.27N133.46W
Arda r. Greece 13 41.39N 26.30E
Ardabīl Iran 31 38.15N 48.18E
Ardahan Turkey 30 41.08N 42.41E
Årdalstangen Norway 17 61.14N 7.43E
Ardara Rep. of Ire. 7 54.46N 8.25W
Ard aş Şawwān f. Jordan 32 30.45N 37.15E
Ardèche r. France 11 44.31N 4.40E
Ardennes mts. Belgium 8 50.10N 5.30E
Ardennes d. France 9 49.40N 4.40E
Ardennes, Canal des France 9 49.26N 4.02E
Ardestān Iran 31 33.22N 52.25E
Ardfert Rep. of Ire. 7 52.20N 9.48W
Ardila r. Portugal 10 38.10N 7.30W
Ardlethan Australia 47 34.20S146.53E
Ardmore Rep. of Ire. 7 51.58N 7.43W
Ardmore Okla. U.S.A. 53 34.11N 97.08W
Ardnamurchan, Pt. of U.K. 6 56.44N 6.14W
Ardrossan Australia 46 34.25S137.55E
Ardrossan U.K. 6 55.38N 4.49W
Ards Pen. U.K. 7 54.30N 5.30W
Åre Sweden 16 63.25N 13.05E
Arecibo Puerto Rico 57 18.29N 66.44W
Areia Branca Brazil 61 4.56S 37.07W
Arena, Pt. U.S.A. 52 38.58N123.44W
Arendal Norway 17 58.27N 8.48E
Arequipa Peru 60 16.25S 71.32W
Arès France 11 44.47N 1.08W
Arévalo Spain 10 41.03N 4.43W
Arezzo Italy 12 43.27N 11.52E
Arfak mtn. Indonesia 27 1.30S133.50E
Arganda Spain 10 40.19N 3.26W
Argelès-sur-Mer France 11 42.33N 3.01E
Argens r. France 11 43.10N 6.45E
Argenta Italy 9 44.37N 11.50E
Argentan France 9 48.45N 0.01W
Argentera Italy 9 44.24N 6.57E
Argentera mtn. Italy 9 44.10N 7.18E
Argenteuil France 9 48.57N 2.15E
Argentina S. America 63 36.00S 63.00W
Argentino, L. Argentina 63 50.15S 72.25W
Argenton France 11 46.36N 1.30E
Argentré France 9 48.05N 0.39W
Argentré du Plessis France 9 48.03N 1.08W
Argeş r. Romania 13 44.13N 26.22E
Árgos Greece 13 37.37N 22.45E
Argostólion Greece 13 38.10N 20.30E
Arguello, Pt. U.S.A. 54 34.35N120.39W
Argun r. Russian Fed. 25 53.30N121.48E
Argungu Nigeria 38 12.45N 4.35E
Århus Denmark 17 56.09N 10.13E
Ariah Park town Australia 47 34.20S147.10E
Ariano Italy 12 41.04N 15.00E
Ariano nel Polesine Italy 9 44.56N 12.07E
Aribinda Burkina 38 14.17N 0.52W
Arica Chile 62 18.29S 70.20W
Arica Colombia 60 2.07S 71.46W
Arid, C. Australia 43 33.58S123.05E
Arieş r. Romania 15 46.26N 23.59E
Arīḩā Al Quds Jordan 32 31.51N 35.27E
Arima Trinidad 60 10.38N 61.17W
Arinos r. Brazil 61 10.20S 57.35W
Aripuanã Brazil 60 9.10S 60.38W
Aripuanã r. Brazil 60 5.05S 60.30W
Ariquemes Brazil 60 9.56S 63.04W
Aris Namibia 39 22.48S 17.10E
Arisaig U.K. 6 56.55N 5.51W
'Arīsh, Wādī al r. Egypt 32 31.09N 33.49E
Ariza Spain 10 41.19N 2.03W
Arizona d. U.S.A. 52 34.00N112.00W
Årjäng Sweden 17 59.23N 12.08E
Arjeplog Sweden 16 66.00N 17.58E
Arjona Colombia 60 10.14N 75.22W
Arkaig, Loch U.K. 6 56.58N 5.08W
Arkansas d. U.S.A. 53 35.00N 92.00W
Arkansas r. U.S.A. 53 33.50N 91.00W
Arkansas City U.S.A. 53 37.03N 97.02W
Arkhangel'sk Russian Fed. 18 64.32N 41.10E
Árki i. Greece 13 37.22N 26.45E
Arklow Rep. of Ire. 7 52.47N 6.10W
Arkville U.S.A. 55 42.09N 74.37W
Arlberg Pass Austria 14 47.00N 10.05E
Arles France 11 43.41N 4.38E
Arlington Oreg. U.S.A. 54 45.16N120.13W
Arlington Va. U.S.A. 55 38.52N 77.05W
Arlon Belgium 8 49.41N 5.49E
Armadale Australia 43 32.10S115.57E
Armagh U.K. 7 54.21N 6.41W
Armagh d. U.K. 7 54.16N 6.35W
Armançon r. France 9 47.57N 3.30E
Armavir Russian Fed. 19 44.59N 41.10E
Armenia Colombia 60 4.32N 75.40W
Armenia Europe 31 40.00N 45.00E
Armenia f. Iran / Turkey / Armenia 31 40.00N 44.30E
Armeniş Romania 15 45.12N 22.19E
Armentières France 8 50.41N 2.53E

Ballybay Rep. of Ire. 7 54.08N 6.56W
Ballycastle U.K. 7 55.12N 6.15W
Ballyclare U.K. 7 54.45N 6.00W
Ballyconnell Rep. of Ire. 7 54.06N 7.37W
Ballydehob Rep. of Ire. 7 51.34N 9.28W
Ballydonegan Rep. of Ire. 7 51.38N 10.04W
Ballygar Rep. of Ire. 7 53.32N 8.20W
Ballygawley U.K. 7 54.28N 7.03W
Ballykelly U.K. 7 55.03N 7.00W
Ballymena U.K. 7 54.52N 6.17W
Ballymoney U.K. 7 55.04N 6.31W
Ballyquintin Pt. U.K. 7 54.40N 5.30W
Ballyragget Rep. of Ire. 7 52.47N 7.21W
Ballyshannon Rep. of Ire. 7 54.30N 8.11W
Ballyvaughan Rep. of Ire. 7 53.06N 9.09W
Ballyvourney Rep. of Ire. 7 51.57N 9.10W
Balmoral Australia 46 37.17S141.50E
Balonne r. Australia 47 28.30S148.20E
Balrāmpur India 29 27.26N 82.11E
Balranald Australia 46 34.37S143.37E
Balş Romania 15 44.21N 24.06E
Balsas r. Brazil 61 9.00S 48.10W
Balsas r. Mexico 56 18.10N102.05W
Balta Ukraine 15 47.58N 29.39E
Baltanás Spain 10 41.56N 4.15W
Baltasar Brum Uruguay 63 30.44S 57.19W
Baltic Sea Europe 17 57.00N 20.00E
Balṭîm Egypt 32 31.34N 31.05E
Baltimore Md. U.S.A. 55 39.17N 76.37W
Baltiysk Russian Fed. 17 54.39N 19.55E
Baluchistan f. Pakistan 28 28.00N 66.00E
Balumbah Australia 46 33.16S136.14E
Balygychan Russian Fed. 21 63.55N154.12E
Balykshi Kazakhstan 19 47.04N 51.55E
Bām Iran 31 29.07N 58.20E
Bama Nigeria 38 11.35N 13.40E
Bamaga Australia 44 10.52S142.23E
Bamako Mali 34 12.40N 7.59W
Bamba Kenya 37 3.33S 39.32E
Bamba Mali 38 17.05N 1.23W
Bambari C.A.R. 36 5.40N 20.37E
Bamberg Germany 14 49.54N 10.53E
Bambuí Brazil 59 20.01S 45.59W
Bam Co l. China 29 31.30N 91.10E
Bamenda Cameroon 38 5.55N 10.09E
Bampton Devon U.K. 5 51.00N 3.29W
Bampūr Iran 31 27.13N 60.29E
Bampūr r. Iran 31 27.18N 59.02E
Bāmra Hills India 29 21.30N 84.30E
Banagher Rep. of Ire. 7 53.12N 8.00W
Bananal, Ilha do f. Brazil 61 11.30S 50.15W
Banās, Ra's c. Egypt 30 23.54N 35.48E
Ban Ban Laos 29 19.38N103.34E
Banbridge U.K. 7 54.21N 6.17W
Banbury U.K. 5 52.04N 1.21W
Banchory U.K. 6 57.03N 2.30W
Bancroft Canada 55 45.03N 77.51W
Banda Gabon 36 3.47S 11.04E
Banda, Laut sea Indonesia 27 5.00S128.00E
Banda Aceh Indonesia 26 5.35N 95.20E
Banda Besar i. Indonesia 27 4.30S129.55E
Bandama r. Ivory Coast 38 5.10N 4.59W
Bandar 'Abbās Iran 31 27.10N 56.15E
Bandar Beheshtī Iran 31 25.17N 60.41E
Bandar-e Anzalī Iran 31 37.26N 49.29E
Bandar-e Deylam Iran 31 30.05N 50.11E
Bandar-e Khomeynī Iran 31 30.26N 49.03E
Bandar-e Lengeh Iran 31 26.34N 54.53E
Bandar-e Rīg Iran 31 29.30N 50.40E
Bandar-e Torkeman Iran 31 36.55N 54.05E
Bandar Seri Begawan Brunei 26 4.56N114.58E
Banda Sea see Banda, Laut sea Indonesia 27
Bandawe Malaŵi 37 11.57S 34.11E
Bandeira mtn. Brazil 59 20.25S 41.45W
Bandiagara Mali 38 14.12N 3.29W
Bandirma Turkey 13 40.22N 28.00E
Bandon Rep. of Ire. 7 51.45N 8.45W
Bandon r. Rep. of Ire. 7 51.43N 8.38W
Bandundu Zaïre 36 3.20S 17.24E
Bandung Indonesia 26 6.57S107.34E
Banes Cuba 57 20.59N 75.24W
Banff Canada 50 51.10N115.34W
Banff U.K. 6 57.40N 2.31W
Banfora Burkina 38 10.36N 4.45W
Bangalore India 28 12.58N 77.35E
Bangassou C.A.R. 35 4.41N 22.48E
Banggai, Kepulauan is. Indonesia 27 1.30S123.10E
Banggi i. Malaysia 26 7.17N117.12E
Banggong Co l. China 29 33.45N 79.15E
Banghāzī Libya 34 32.07N 20.05E
Bangka i. Indonesia 26 2.20S106.10E
Bangkok Thailand 29 13.45N100.35E
Bangladesh Asia 29 24.00N 90.00E
Bangor Rep. of Ire. 7 54.09N 9.44W
Bangor U.K. 4 53.13N 4.09W
Bangor U.K. 7 54.40N 5.41W
Bangor Maine U.S.A. 55 44.49N 68.47W
Bang Saphan Thailand 29 11.14N 99.31E
Bangui C.A.R. 36 4.23N 18.37E
Bangweulu, L. Zambia 37 11.15S 29.45E
Banhā Egypt 32 30.28N 31.11E
Ban Hat Yai Thailand 26 7.00N100.28E
Ban Houayxay Laos 29 20.21N100.26E
Bani r. Mali 38 14.30N 4.15W
Banikoara Benin 38 11.21N 2.25E
Banī Mazār Egypt 32 28.29N 30.48E
Banī Suwayf Egypt 32 29.05N 31.05E
Bāniyās Syria 32 35.09N 35.58E
Banja Luka Bosnia-Herzegovina 13 44.47N 17.10E
Banjarmasin Indonesia 26 3.22S114.36E
Banjul Gambia 34 13.28N 16.39W
Banka Banka Australia 44 18.48S134.01E
Ban Kantang Thailand 29 7.25N 99.30E
Bankasse Mali 38 14.01N 3.29W
Banks I. N.W.T. Canada 50 73.00N122.00W
Banks Pen. New Zealand 48 43.45S173.10E
Banks Str. Australia 45 40.37S148.07E
Ban-m'drack Vietnam 26 12.42N108.47E
Bann r. U.K. 7 55.10N 6.46W
Bannockburn U.K. 6 56.06N 3.55W
Bannockburn Zimbabwe 39 20.16S 29.51E
Banská Bystrica Slovakia 15 48.44N 19.07E
Bantaeng Indonesia 26 5.32S119.58E
Banté Benin 38 8.26N 1.54E
Bantry Rep. of Ire. 7 51.41N 9.27W
Bantry B. Rep. of Ire. 7 51.40N 9.40W
Banyak, Kepulauan is. Indonesia 26 2.15N 97.10E
Banyo Cameroon 38 6.47N 11.50E
Banyuwangi Indonesia 26 8.12S114.22E
Banzare Coast f. Antarctica 64 66.30S125.00E
Baoding China 25 38.54N115.26E
Baoji China 24 34.23N107.16E
Baoshan China 29 25.07N 99.08E
Baotou China 25 40.38N109.59E
Bapaume France 8 50.07N 2.51E
Ba'qūbah Iraq 31 33.45N 44.38E
Bar Albania 13 42.05N 19.06E
Bar Ukraine 15 49.05N 27.40E
Bara Nigeria 38 10.24N 10.43E
Baraawe Somali Rep. 37 1.02N 44.02E
Barabinsk Russian Fed. 20 55.20N 78.18E
Baracoa Cuba 57 20.23N 74.31W
Baradero Argentina 63 33.50S 59.30W
Baradine Australia 47 30.56S149.05E
Baradine r. Australia 47 30.17S148.27E
Barahona Dom. Rep. 57 18.13N 71.07W
Baraka Zaïre 37 4.09S 29.05E
Bārāmūla Jammu & Kashmir 28 34.12N 74.21E
Baranoa Colombia 60 10.50N 74.55W
Baranof I. U.S.A. 50 57.05N135.00W
Baranovichi Belorussia 15 53.09N 26.00E
Baratta Australia 46 32.01S139.10E
Barbacena Brazil 59 21.13S 43.47W
Barbados Lesser Antilles 57 13.20N 59.40W
Barbar Sudan 35 18.01N 33.59E
Barbastro Spain 10 42.02N 0.07E
Barberton R.S.A. 39 25.46S 31.02E
Barbezieux France 11 45.28N 0.09W
Barbuda i. Leeward Is. 57 17.41N 61.48W
Barcaldine Australia 44 23.31S145.15E
Barcellona Italy 12 38.10N 15.13E
Barcelona Spain 10 41.25N 2.10E
Barcelona Venezuela 60 10.08N 64.43W
Barcelos Brazil 60 0.59S 62.58W
Barcoo r. Australia 44 25.30S142.50E
Barcs Hungary 15 45.58N 17.28E
Barcs Hungary 15 45.58N 17.28E
Bardai Chad 34 21.21N 16.56E
Bardejov Slovakia 15 49.18N 21.16E
Bardi Italy 9 44.38N 9.44E
Bardsey i. U.K. 4 52.45N 4.48W
Bardu Norway 16 68.54N 18.20E
Bardufoss Norway 16 69.00N 18.30E
Bareilly India 29 28.20N 79.24E
Barellan Australia 47 34.17S146.34E
Barentsovo More see Barents Sea Arctic Oc. 18
Barents Sea Arctic Oc. 18 73.00N 40.00E
Barfleur France 9 49.40N 1.15W
Barge Italy 9 44.43N 7.20E
Barguzin Russian Fed. 21 53.40N109.35E
Barham Australia 46 35.37S144.10E
Bari Italy 13 41.08N 16.52E
Baricho Kenya 37 3.07S 39.47E
Barīm i. Yemen 35 12.40N 43.24E
Barinas Venezuela 60 8.36N 70.15W
Bariri Brazil 59 22.04S 48.41W
Bârîs Egypt 30 24.40N 30.36E
Barisāl Bangla. 29 22.41N 90.20E
Barisan, Pegunungan mts. Indonesia 26 3.30S102.30E
Barito r. Indonesia 26 3.35S114.35E
Barker L. Australia 43 31.45S120.05E
Barking U.K. 5 51.32N 0.05E
Barkly East R.S.A. 39 30.58S 27.33E
Barkly Tableland f. Australia 44 19.00S136.40E
Barkly West R.S.A. 39 28.32S 24.29E
Bar-le-Duc France 11 48.46N 5.10E
Barlee, L. Australia 43 29.30S119.30E
Barlee Range mts. Australia 42 23.40S116.00E
Barletta Italy 12 41.20N 16.15E
Barmedman Australia 47 34.08S147.25E
Barmera Australia 46 34.15S140.31E
Barm Fīrūz, Kūh-e mtn. Iran 31 30.21N 52.00E
Barmouth U.K. 4 52.44N 4.03W
Barnard Castle town U.K. 4 54.33N 1.55W
Barnato Australia 47 31.38S144.59E
Barnaul Russian Fed. 20 53.21N 83.15E
Barnet U.K. 5 51.39N 0.11W
Barneveld Neth. 8 52.10N 5.39E
Barneville France 9 49.23N 1.45W
Barneys L. Australia 46 33.16S144.13E
Barnsley U.K. 4 53.33N 1.29W
Barnstaple U.K. 5 51.05N 4.03W
Baro Nigeria 38 8.37N 6.19E
Barqah f. Libya 35 31.00N 22.10E
Barquisimeto Venezuela 60 10.03N 69.18W
Barra Brazil 61 11.06S 43.15W
Barra i. U.K. 6 56.59N 7.28W
Barra, Sd. of U.K. 6 57.04N 7.20W
Barraba Australia 47 30.24S152.36E
Barra do Corda Brazil 61 5.30S 45.15W
Barra do Piraí Brazil 59 22.28S 43.49W
Barragem Agua Vermelha resr Brazil 59 19.50S 50.00W
Barragem de Sáo Simão resr Brazil 59 18.35S 50.00W
Barra Mansa Brazil 59 22.35S 44.12W
Barranca Peru 60 4.50S 76.40W
Barrancabermeja Colombia 60 7.06N 73.54W
Barrancas Venezuela 60 8.45N 62.13W
Barrancos Portugal 10 38.10N 7.01W
Barranqueras Argentina 59 27.30S 58.55W
Barranquilla Colombia 60 11.10N 74.50W
Barraute Canada 55 48.26N 77.39W
Barre U.S.A. 55 44.12N 72.30W
Barreiras Brazil 61 12.09S 44.58W
Barreiro Portugal 10 38.40N 9.05W
Barreiros Brazil 61 8.49S 35.12W
Barrême France 14 43.57N 6.22E
Barretos Brazil 59 20.37S 48.38W
Barrhead U.K. 6 55.47N 4.24W
Barrie Canada 55 44.24N 79.40W
Barrier Range mts. Australia 46 31.25S141.25E
Barrington Tops mts. Australia 47 32.30S151.28E
Barringun Australia 47 29.01S145.43E
Barron U.S.A. 54 48.44N120.43W
Barrow r. Rep. of Ire. 7 52.17N 7.00W
Barrow U.S.A. 50 71.16N156.50W
Barrow Creek town Australia 44 21.32S133.53E
Barrow I. Australia 42 21.40S115.27E
Barrow-in-Furness U.K. 4 54.08N 3.15W
Barrow Range mts. Australia 42 26.04S127.28E
Barry U.K. 5 51.23N 3.19W
Barstow U.S.A. 54 34.54N117.01W
Bar-sur-Aube France 9 48.14N 4.43E
Bar-sur-Seine France 9 48.07N 4.22E
Bartica Guyana 60 6.24N 58.38W
Bartin Turkey 30 41.37N 32.20E
Bartle Frere, Mt. Australia 44 17.23S145.49E
Bartlesville U.S.A. 53 36.44N 95.59W
Bartolomeu Dias Mozambique 39 21.10S 35.09E
Barton-upon-Humber U.K. 4 53.41N 0.27W
Bartoszyce Poland 15 54.16N 20.49E
Barwon r. Australia 47 30.00S148.05E
Barysh Russian Fed. 18 53.40N 47.09E
Basavilbaso Argentina 63 32.20S 58.52W
Basel Switz. 14 47.33N 7.36E
Bashi Channel Phil. / Taiwan 25 21.40N121.20E
Basilan Phil. 27 6.40N121.59E
Basilan i. Phil. 27 6.40N122.10E
Basildon U.K. 5 51.34N 0.25E
Basilicata d. Italy 12 40.30N 16.20E
Basin U.S.A. 54 44.23N108.02W
Basingstoke U.K. 5 51.15N 1.05W
Baskatong, Résr. Canada 55 46.48N 75.50W
Basoko Zaïre 36 1.20N 23.36E
Bassano Canada 50 50.47N112.28W
Bassano Italy 9 45.46N 11.44E
Bassari Togo 38 9.12N 0.18E
Bassein Burma 29 16.45N 94.30E
Basse Normandie d. France 9 49.00N 0.00
Basse-Terre Guadeloupe 57 16.00N 61.43W
Bass Str. Australia 45 39.45S146.00E
Bassum Germany 14 52.51N 8.43E
Båstad Sweden 17 56.26N 12.51E
Bastak Iran 31 27.15N 54.26E
Bastelica France 11 42.00N 9.03E
Bastia France 11 42.41N 9.26E
Bastogne Belgium 8 50.00N 5.43E
Basyūn Egypt 32 30.57N 30.49E
Bata Equat. Guinea 38 1.51N 9.49E
Batabanó, Golfo de g. Cuba 57 23.15N 82.30W
Batalha Portugal 10 39.39N 8.50W
Batang China 29 30.02N 99.01E
Batangas Phil. 27 13.46N121.01E
Batan Is. Phil. 27 20.50N121.55E
Bátaszék Hungary 15 46.12N 18.44E
Batatais Brazil 59 20.54S 47.37W
Bataysk Russian Fed. 19 47.09N 39.46E
Batchelor Australia 44 13.04S131.01E
Bătdâmbâng Cambodia 26 13.06N103.13E
Batemans Bay town Australia 47 35.55S150.09E
Bath Canada 55 46.30N 67.36W
Bath U.K. 5 51.22N 2.22W
Bath Maine U.S.A. 55 43.55N 69.49W
Bath N.Y. U.S.A. 55 42.20N 77.19W
Baṭḥā, Wādī al r. Oman 31 20.01N 59.39E
Bathgate U.K. 6 55.44N 3.38W
Bathurst Australia 47 33.27S149.35E
Bathurst Canada 55 47.37N 65.40W
Bathurst R.S.A. 39 33.30S 26.48E
Bathurst, C. Canada 50 70.30N128.00W
Bathurst I. Australia 42 11.45S130.15E
Bathurst I. Canada 51 76.00N100.00W
Bathurst Inlet town Canada 50 66.48N108.00W
Batié Burkina 38 9.42N 2.53W
Batina Croatia 15 45.51N 18.51E
Batley U.K. 4 53.43N 1.38W
Batlow Australia 47 35.32S148.10E
Batman Turkey 30 37.52N 41.07E
Batna Algeria 34 35.34N 6.11E
Baton Rouge U.S.A. 53 30.30N 91.10W
Batopilas Mexico 56 27.00N107.45W
Batouri Cameroon 38 4.26N 14.27E
Batticaloa Sri Lanka 29 7.43N 81.42E
Battle U.K. 5 50.55N 0.30E
Battle Creek town U.S.A. 55 42.20N 85.11W
Battle Harbour Canada 51 52.16N 55.36W
Batu, Kepulauan is. Indonesia 26 0.30S 98.20E
Batumi Georgia 30 41.37N 41.36E
Batu Pahat Malaysia 26 1.50N102.48E
Baturaja Indonesia 26 4.10S104.10E
Baturité Brazil 61 4.20S 38.53W
Bat Yam Israel 32 32.01N 34.45E
Baubau Indonesia 27 5.30S122.37E
Bauchi Nigeria 38 10.16N 9.50E
Bauchi d. Nigeria 38 10.40N 10.00E
Baugé France 9 47.33N 0.06W
Bauld, C. Canada 51 51.30N 55.45W
Bauru Brazil 59 22.19S 49.07W
Baús Brazil 59 18.19S 53.10W
Bauska Latvia 17 56.24N 24.14E
Bautzen Germany 14 51.11N 14.29E
Bavay France 8 50.18N 3.48E
Bawean i. Indonesia 26 5.50S112.35E
Bawku Ghana 38 11.05N 0.13W
Bayamo Cuba 57 20.23N 76.39W
Bayamón Puerto Rico 57 18.24N 66.10W
Bayan Har Shan mts. China 24 34.00N 97.20E
Bayburt Turkey 30 40.15N 40.16E
Bay City Mich. U.S.A. 55 43.35N 83.52W
Baydaratskaya Guba b. Russian Fed. 20 70.00N 66.00E
Baydhabo Somali Rep. 37 3.08N 43.34E
Bayern d. Germany 14 48.30N 11.30E
Bayeux France 9 49.16N 0.42W
Baykal, Ozero l. Russian Fed. 24 53.30N100.00E
Baykit Russian Fed. 21 61.45N 96.22E
Baykonyr Kazakhstan 20 47.50N 66.03E
Bay of Plenty d. New Zealand 48 38.00S177.10E
Bayombong Phil. 27 16.27N121.10E
Bayonne France 11 43.30N 1.28W
Bayovar Peru 60 5.50S 81.03W
Bayreuth Germany 14 49.56N 11.35E
Bayrūt Lebanon 32 33.52N 35.30E
Baytik Shan mts. China 24 45.15N 90.50E
Bay View New Zealand 48 39.26S176.52E
Baza Spain 10 37.30N 2.45W
Baza, Sierra de mts. Spain 10 37.15N 2.45W
Bazaliya Ukraine 15 49.42N 26.29E
Bazaruto, Ilha do i. Mozambique 39 21.40S 35.28E
Bazas France 11 44.26N 0.13W
Bazmān Iran 31 27.48N 60.12E
Bazmān, Kūh-e mtn. Iran 31 28.06N 60.00E
Beachport Australia 46 37.29S140.01E
Beachy Head U.K. 5 50.43N 0.15E
Beagle Bay Australia 42 16.58S122.40E
Bear I. see Bjørnøya i. Arctic Oc. 64
Bear L. U.S.A. 54 42.00N111.20W
Beatrice U.S.A. 53 40.17N 96.45W
Beatrice, C. Australia 44 14.15S136.59E
Beatty U.S.A. 54 36.54N116.46W
Beattyville Canada 55 48.53N 77.10W
Beauce f. France 9 48.22N 1.50E
Beaudesert Australia 47 27.58S153.01E
Beaufort Australia 46 37.28S143.28E
Beaufort Sea N. America 50 72.00N141.00W
Beaufort West R.S.A. 39 32.20S 22.34E
Beaugency France 9 47.47N 1.38E
Beauly U.K. 6 57.29N 4.29W
Beauly r. U.K. 6 57.29N 4.25W
Beaumaris U.K. 4 53.16N 4.07W
Beaumetz-lès-Loges France 8 50.15N 2.36E
Beaumont Belgium 8 50.14N 4.16E
Beaumont Tex. U.S.A. 53 30.04N 94.06W
Beaumont-le-Roger France 9 49.05N 0.47E
Beaumont-sur-Sarthe France 9 48.13N 0.07E
Beaune France 11 47.02N 4.50E
Beaune-la-Rolande France 9 48.04N 2.26E
Beaupréau France 11 47.12N 0.59W
Beauvais France 9 49.26N 2.05E
Beauval Canada 50 55.09N107.35W
Beauvoir France 11 46.55N 2.01W
Beaver Alaska U.S.A. 50 66.22N147.24W
Beaver I. U.S.A. 55 45.42N 85.28W
Beāwar India 28 26.02N 74.20E
Bebedouro Brazil 59 20.54S 48.31W
Bebington U.K. 4 53.23N 3.01W
Beccles U.K. 5 52.27N 1.33E
Bečej Yugo. 15 45.37N 20.03E
Béchar Algeria 34 31.35N 2.17W
Beckley U.S.A. 53 37.46N 81.12W
Beckum Germany 8 51.45N 8.02E
Beclean Romania 15 47.11N 24.10E
Bédarieux France 11 43.35N 3.10E
Bedford U.K. 5 52.08N 0.29W
Bedford U.S.A. 55 38.51N 86.30W
Bedford, C. Australia 44 15.14S145.21E
Bedford Levels f. U.K. 5 52.35N 0.08W
Bedfordshire d. U.K. 5 52.04N 0.28W
Bedlington U.K. 4 55.08N 1.34W
Bedourie Australia 44 24.21S139.28E
Beech Grove U.S.A. 55 39.42N 86.06W
Beechworth Australia 47 36.23S146.42E
Beenleigh Australia 47 27.43S153.09E
Be'er Menuha Israel 32 30.19N 35.08E
Be'er Sheva' Israel 32 31.15N 34.47E
Beerta Neth. 8 53.12N 7.07E
Beeston U.K. 4 52.55N 1.11W
Beeville U.S.A. 52 28.25N 97.47W
Beg, Lough U.K. 7 54.47N 6.29W
Bega Australia 47 36.41S149.50E
Bègles France 11 44.48N 0.32W
Begna r. Norway 17 60.32N 10.00E
Behbehān Iran 31 30.35N 50.17E
Bei'an China 25 48.17N126.33E
Beihai China 25 21.29N109.10E
Beijing China 25 39.55N116.25E
Beijing Shi d. China 25 40.15N116.30E
Beilen Neth. 8 52.51N 6.31E
Beinn Dearg mtn. U.K. 6 57.47N 4.55W
Beipa'a P.N.G. 44 8.30S146.35E
Beira Mozambique 39 19.49S 34.52E
Beirut see Bayrūt Lebanon 32
Beitbridge Zimbabwe 39 22.10S 30.01E
Beiuş Romania 15 46.40N 22.21E
Beja Portugal 10 38.01N 7.52W
Bejaïa Algeria 34 36.45N 5.05E
Béjar Spain 10 40.24N 5.45W
Bejestān Iran 31 34.32N 58.08E
Bejoording Australia 43 31.22S116.30E
Békés Hungary 15 46.46N 21.08E
Békéscsaba Hungary 15 46.41N 21.06E
Bela India 29 25.55N 82.00E
Bela Pakistan 28 26.12N 66.20E
Bélabo Cameroon 38 5.00N 13.20E
Bela Crkva Yugo. 15 44.54N 21.26E
Bel Air U.S.A. 55 39.32N 76.21W
Belalcázar Spain 10 38.35N 5.10W
Belang Indonesia 27 0.58N124.56E
Bela Vista Brazil 62 22.05S 56.22W
Bela Vista Mozambique 39 26.20S 32.41E
Belaya r. Russian Fed. 20 55.40N 52.30E
Belaya Glina Russian Fed. 19 46.04N 40.54E
Belaya Tserkov Ukraine 15 49.49N 30.10E
Belcher Is. Canada 51 56.00N 79.00W
Belcoo U.K. 7 54.18N 7.53W
Belebey Russian Fed. 18 54.05N 54.07E
Beled Weyne Somali Rep. 35 4.47N 45.12E
Belém Brazil 61 1.27S 48.29W
Belem Mozambique 37 14.11S 35.59E
Belén Uruguay 63 30.47S 57.47W
Belen U.S.A. 52 34.40N106.46W
Belén, Cuchilla de mts. Uruguay 63 30.49S 56.28W
Belev Russian Fed. 18 53.50N 36.08E
Belfast U.K. 7 54.36N 5.57W
Belfast Maine U.S.A. 55 44.27N 69.01W
Belfast Lough U.K. 7 54.42N 5.45W
Belfort France 11 47.38N 6.52E
Belfry U.S.A. 54 45.09N109.01W
Belgaum India 28 15.54N 74.36E
Belgium Europe 8 51.00N 4.30E
Belgorod Russian Fed. 19 50.38N 36.36E
Belgorod-Dnestrovskiy Ukraine 15 46.10N 30.19E
Belgrade see Beograd Yugo. 15
Beli Nigeria 38 7.53N 10.59E
Belitung i. Indonesia 26 3.00S108.00E
Belize Belize 57 17.29N 88.20W
Belize C. America 57 17.00N 88.30W
Belka Australia 43 31.45S118.09E
Bellac France 11 46.07N 1.04E
Bella Coola Canada 50 52.22N126.46W
Bellagio Italy 9 45.59N 9.15E
Bellaria Italy 9 44.09N 12.28E
Bellary India 28 15.11N 76.54E
Bellata Australia 47 29.55S149.50E
Bella Unión Uruguay 63 30.15S 57.35W
Bella Vista Corrientes Argentina 62 28.30S 59.00W
Bella Vista Tucuman Argentina 62 27.02S 65.19W
Bellbrook Australia 47 30.48S152.30E
Bellefontaine U.S.A. 55 40.22N 83.45W
Belle Île France 11 47.20N 3.10W
Belle Isle, Str. of Canada 51 51.35N 56.30W
Bellême France 9 48.22N 0.34E
Belleville Canada 55 44.10N 77.23W
Bellevue Idaho U.S.A. 54 43.28N114.16W
Bellevue Penn. U.S.A. 55 40.32N 80.08W
Bellevue Wash. U.S.A. 54 47.37N122.12W
Bellingen Australia 47 30.28S152.43E
Bellingham U.K. 4 55.09N 2.15W
Bellingham U.S.A. 54 48.46N122.29W
Bellingshausen Sea Antarctica 64 70.00S 88.00W
Bellinzona Switz. 9 46.11N 9.02E
Bello Colombia 60 6.20N 75.41W
Belluno Italy 9 46.09N 12.13E
Bell Ville Argentina 63 32.35S 62.41W
Bélmez Spain 10 38.17N 5.17W
Belmont Australia 47 33.02S151.40E
Belmopan Belize 57 17.25N 88.46W
Belmullet Rep. of Ire. 7 54.14N 10.00W
Belogradchik Bulgaria 15 43.38N 22.41E
Belo Horizonte Brazil 59 19.45S 43.54W
Belo Jardim Brazil 61 8.22S 36.22W
Belokorovichi Ukraine 15 51.04N 28.00E
Belomorsk Russian Fed. 18 64.34N 34.45E
Beloretsk Russian Fed. 18 53.59N 58.20E
Belorussia Europe 15 53.30N 28.00E
Beloye More sea Russian Fed. 18 65.30N 38.00E
Beloye Ozero l. Russian Fed. 18 60.12N 37.45E
Belozersk Russian Fed. 18 60.00N 37.49E
Belper U.K. 4 53.02N 1.29W
Beltana Australia 46 30.40S138.27E
Belterra Brazil 61 2.38S 54.57W
Belton Australia 46 32.12S138.45E
Beltsy Moldavia 15 47.45N 27.59E
Belukha, Gora mtn. Russian Fed. 24 49.48N 86.40E
Belyando r. Australia 44 21.38S146.50E
Belyayevka Ukraine 15 46.30N 30.12E
Belynichi Belorussia 15 54.00N 29.42E
Belyy, Ostrov Russian Fed. 20 73.10N 70.45E
Belyy Yar Russian Fed. 20 58.28N 85.03E
Bełżec Poland 15 50.24N 23.26E
Bemidji U.S.A. 53 47.29N 94.52W
Benagerie Australia 46 31.30S140.21E
Benalla Australia 47 36.35S145.58E
Benanee Australia 46 34.32S142.56E
Benares see Vārānasi India 29
Benavente Spain 10 42.00N 5.40W
Benbecula i. U.K. 6 57.26N 7.18W
Ben Cruachan mtn. U.K. 6 56.26N 5.18W
Bencubbin Australia 43 30.48S117.52E
Bend U.S.A. 54 44.03N121.19W
Bende Nigeria 38 5.34N 7.37E
Bendemeer Australia 47 30.52S151.10E
Bendery Moldavia 15 46.50N 29.29E
Bendigo Australia 46 36.48S144.21E
Bendoc Australia 47 37.10S148.55E
Benedorf Germany 8 50.26N 7.34E
Bénéna Mali 38 13.09N 4.17W
Benešov Czech Republic 14 49.45N 14.22E
Benevento Italy 12 41.07N 14.46E
Bengal, B. of Indian Oc. 29 17.00N 89.00E
Bengbu China 25 32.56N117.27E
Benghazi see Banghāzī Libya 34
Bengkulu Indonesia 26 3.46S102.16E
Benguela Angola 36 12.34S 13.24E
Ben Hope mtn. U.K. 6 58.24N 4.36W
Beni r. Bolivia 62 10.23S 65.24W
Beni Zaïre 37 0.29N 29.27E
Beni Abbes Algeria 34 30.08N 2.10W
Benicarló Spain 10 40.25N 0.25E
Benidorm Spain 10 38.33N 0.09W
Benin Africa 38 9.00N 2.30E
Benin, Bight of Africa 38 5.30N 3.00E
Benin City Nigeria 38 6.19N 5.41E
Benjamin Constant Brazil 60 4.22S 70.02W
Ben Lawers mtn. U.K. 6 56.33N 4.14W
Ben Lomond mtn. U.K. 6 56.12N 4.38W
Ben Macdhui mtn. U.K. 6 57.04N 3.40W
Ben More mtn. Central U.K. 6 56.23N 4.31W
Ben More mtn. Strath. U.K. 6 56.26N 6.02W
Ben More Assynt mtn. U.K. 6 58.07N 4.52W
Bennett Canada 50 59.49N135.01W
Bennett, L. Australia 44 22.50S131.01E

Ben Nevis mtn. U.K. 6 56.48N 5.00W
Benneydale New Zealand 48 38.31S175.21E
Benoni R.S.A. 39 26.12S 28.18E
Bénoué r. Cameroon see Benue r. Nigeria 38
Bentinck I. Australia 44 17.04S139.30E
Benton Harbor U.S.A. 55 42.07N 86.27W
Benue d. Nigeria 38 7.20N 8.00E
Benue r. Nigeria 38 7.52N 6.45E
Ben Wyvis mtn. U.K. 6 57.40N 4.35W
Benxi China 25 41.21N123.45E
Beograd Yugo. 15 44.49N 20.28E
Beowawe U.S.A. 54 40.35N116.29W
Berat Albania 13 40.42N 19.59E
Berau, Teluk b. Indonesia 27 2.20S133.00E
Berbera Somali Rep. 35 10.28N 45.02E
Berbérati C.A.R. 36 4.19N 15.51E
Berceto Italy 9 44.31N 9.59E
Berchem Belgium 8 50.48N 3.32E
Berck France 11 50.25N 1.36E
Bercu France 8 50.32N 3.15E
Berdichev Ukraine 15 49.54N 28.39E
Berdsk Russian Fed. 20 54.51N 82.51E
Berdyansk Ukraine 19 46.45N 36.47E
Beregovo Ukraine 15 48.13N 22.39E
Bereko Tanzania 37 4.27S 35.43E
Beresford Australia 46 29.14S136.40E
Berettyóújfalu Hungary 15 47.14N 21.32E
Bereza Belorussia 15 52.32N 25.00E
Berezhany Ukraine 15 49.27N 24.56E
Berezina r. Belorussia 15 54.10N 28.10E
Berezna Ukraine 15 51.34N 31.46E
Berezniki Russian Fed. 18 59.26N 56.49E
Berezno Ukraine 15 51.00N 26.41E
Berezovka Ukraine 15 47.12N 30.56E
Berezovo Russian Fed. 20 63.58N 65.00E
Berga Spain 10 42.06N 1.48E
Berga Sweden 17 57.14N 16.03E
Bergama Turkey 13 39.08N 27.10E
Bergamo Italy 9 45.42N 9.40E
Bergen Germany 14 54.25N 13.26E
Bergen Neth. 8 52.40N 4.41E
Bergen Norway 17 60.23N 5.20E
Bergen op Zoom Neth. 8 51.30N 4.17E
Bergerac France 11 44.50N 0.29E
Bergheim Germany 8 50.58N 6.39E
Berghem Neth. 8 51.46N 5.32E
Bergisch Gladbach Germany 8 50.59N 7.10E
Bergkamen Germany 8 51.35N 7.39E
Bergkvara Sweden 17 56.23N 16.05E
Bergland U.S.A. 55 46.36N 89.33W
Bergues France 8 50.58N 2.21E
Bergum Neth. 8 53.14N 5.59E
Berhampore India 29 24.06N 88.18E
Berhampur India 29 19.21N 84.51E
Bering Sea N. America / Asia 50 65.00N170.00W
Bering Str. Russian Fed. / U.S.A 50 65.00N170.00W
Berislav Ukraine 19 46.51N 33.26E
Berja Spain 10 36.50N 2.56W
Berkåk Norway 16 62.48N 10.03E
Berkel r. Neth. 8 52.10N 6.12E
Berkeley U.S.A. 54 37.57N122.18W
Berkner I. Antarctica 64 79.30S 50.00W
Berkshire d. U.K. 5 51.25N 1.03W
Berkshire Downs hills U.K. 5 51.32N 1.36W
Berlin Germany 14 52.32N 13.25E
Berlin d. Germany 14 52.30N 13.20E
Berlin N.H. U.S.A. 55 44.29N 71.10W
Bermagui Australia 47 36.28S150.03E
Bermejo r. San Juan Argentina 62 31.40S 67.15W
Bermejo r. Tucumán Argentina 62 26.47S 58.30W
Bern Switz. 14 46.57N 7.26E
Bernard L. Canada 55 45.44N 79.24W
Bernay France 9 48.06N 0.36E
Bernburg Germany 14 51.48N 11.44E
Berne see Bern Switz. 11
Bernier I. Australia 42 24.51S113.09E
Bernina mtn. Italy / Switz. 9 46.22N 9.57E
Bernkastel Germany 8 49.55N 7.05E
Beroun Czech Republic 14 49.58N 14.04E
Berrechid Morocco 34 33.17N 7.35W
Berri Australia 46 34.17S140.36E
Berridale Australia 47 36.21S148.51E
Berrigan Australia 47 35.41S145.48E
Berry Head U.K. 5 50.24N 3.28W
Bersenbrück Germany 8 52.36N 7.58E
Bershad Ukraine 15 48.20N 29.30E
Berté, Lac l. Canada 55 50.47N 68.30W
Bertinoro Italy 9 44.09N 12.08E
Bertoua Cameroon 38 4.34N 13.42E
Bertraghboy B. Rep. of Ire. 7 53.23N 9.52W
Berwick-upon-Tweed U.K. 4 55.46N 2.00W
Besalampy Madagascar 37 16.45S 44.30E
Besançon France 11 47.14N 6.02E
Bessarabia f. Moldavia 15 46.30N 28.40E
Bessemer U.S.A. 53 33.22N 87.00W
Betanzos Spain 10 43.17N 8.13W
Bétaré Oya Cameroon 38 5.34N 14.09E
Bethal R.S.A. 39 26.26S 29.27E
Bethany Beach town U.S.A. 55 38.31N 75.04W
Bethel Alas. U.S.A. 50 60.48N161.46W
Bethlehem R.S.A. 39 28.13S 28.18E
Bethlehem U.S.A. 55 40.36N 75.22W
Béthune France 8 50.32N 2.38E
Béthune r. France 9 49.53N 1.09E
Betim Brazil 59 19.55S 44.07W
Betroka Madagascar 36 23.16S 46.06E
Bet She'an Israel 32 32.30N 35.30E
Bet Shemesh Israel 32 31.45N 35.00E
Betsiamites Canada 55 48.56N 68.38W
Bettles U.S.A. 50 66.53N151.51W
Betzdorf Germany 8 50.48N 7.54E
Beulah Australia 46 35.59S142.26E
Beuvron r. France 9 47.29N 3.31E
Beverley Australia 43 32.06S116.56E
Beverley U.K. 4 53.52N 0.26W
Beverley Hills town U.S.A. 54 34.04N118.26W
Beverly Mass. U.S.A. 55 42.33N 70.53W
Beverwijk Neth. 8 52.29N 4.40E
Bewcastle Fells hills U.K. 4 55.05N 2.50W
Bexhill U.K. 5 50.51N 0.29E
Bexley U.K. 5 51.26N 0.10E
Beyla Guinea 34 8.42N 8.39W
Beyneu Kazakhstan 19 45.16N 55.04E
Beypazari Turkey 30 40.10N 31.56E
Beyşehir Gölü l. Turkey 30 37.47N 31.30E
Bezhanovo Bulgaria 13 43.13N 24.26E
Bezhetsk Russian Fed. 18 57.49N 36.40E
Bezhitsa Russian Fed. 18 53.19N 34.17E
Béziers France 11 43.21N 3.13E
Bhadrakh India 29 21.04N 86.30E
Bhāgalpur India 29 25.14N 86.59E
Bhamo Burma 29 24.15N 97.15E
Bhatinda India 28 30.12N 74.57E
Bhatkal India 28 13.58N 74.34E
Bhātpāra India 29 22.51N 88.31E
Bhaunagar India 28 21.46N 72.14E
Bhīlwāra India 28 25.21N 74.38E
Bhima r. India 28 16.30N 77.10E
Bhopāl India 28 23.17N 77.28E
Bhor India 28 18.12N 73.53E
Bhubaneswar India 29 20.15N 85.50E
Bhuj India 28 23.12N 69.54E
Bhutan Asia 29 27.25N 89.50E
Biak Indonesia 27 1.10S136.05E
Biak i. Indonesia 27 0.55S136.00E
Biala Podlaska Poland 15 52.02N 23.06E
Bialogard Poland 14 54.00N 16.00E
Bialystok Poland 15 53.09N 23.10E
Biarritz France 11 43.29N 1.33W
Biasca Switz. 9 46.22N 8.58E
Bibā Egypt 32 28.56N 30.59E
Biberach Germany 14 48.20N 9.30E
Bic Canada 55 48.23N 68.43W
Bicas Brazil 59 21.44S 43.04W
Bicester U.K. 5 51.53N 1.09W
Bida Nigeria 38 9.06N 5.59E
Bīdar India 28 17.54N 77.33E
Biddeford U.S.A. 55 43.30N 70.26W
Bideford U.K. 5 51.01N 4.13W
Biel Switz. 11 47.09N 7.16E
Bielefeld Germany 14 52.02N 8.32E
Biella Italy 9 45.34N 8.03E
Bielsko-Biala Poland 15 49.49N 19.02E
Bielsk Podlaski Poland 15 52.47N 23.12E
Bienville, Lac l. Canada 51 55.05N 72.40W
Bié Plateau f. Angola 36 13.00S 16.00E
Big Bald Mtn. Canada 55 47.12N 66.25W
Big Bear Lake town U.S.A. 54 34.15N116.53W
Big Belt Mts. U.S.A. 54 46.40N111.25W
Bigbury B. U.K. 5 50.15N 3.56W
Biggar Canada 50 52.04N107.59W
Biggar U.K. 6 55.38N 3.31W
Bighorn r. U.S.A. 54 46.09N107.28W
Bighorn L. U.S.A. 54 45.06N108.08W
Bighorn Mts. U.S.A. 54 44.00N107.30W
Bight, Head of b. Australia 45 31.29S131.16E
Bignasco Switz. 9 46.20N 8.36E
Big Pine U.S.A. 54 37.10N118.17W
Big Piney U.S.A. 54 42.32N110.07W
Big Salmon Canada 50 61.53N134.55W
Big Sandy U.S.A. 54 48.11N110.07W
Big Smoky Valley f. U.S.A. 54 38.30N117.15W
Big Snowy Mtn. U.S.A. 54 46.50N109.30W
Big Spring town U.S.A. 52 32.15N101.30W
Big Sur U.S.A. 54 36.15N121.48W
Big Timber U.S.A. 54 45.50N109.57W
Big Trout L. Canada 51 53.45N 90.00W
Bihać Bosnia-Herzegovina 12 44.49N 15.53E
Bihar India 29 25.13N 85.31E
Bihar d. India 29 24.15N 86.00E
Biharamulo Tanzania 37 2.34S 31.20E
Bihor mtn. Romania 15 46.26N 22.43E
Bijagós, Arquipélago dos is. Guinea Bissau 34 11.30N 16.00W
Bijāpur India 28 16.52N 75.47E
Bijār Iran 31 35.52N 47.39E
Bijāwar India 29 24.36N 79.30E
Bijeljina Bosnia-Herzegovina 13 44.45N 19.13E
Bikaner India 28 28.01N 73.22E
Bikin Russian Fed. 25 46.52N134.15E
Bilāspur India 29 22.03N 82.12E
Bilauktaung Range mts. Burma 29 13.20N 99.30E
Bilbao Spain 10 43.15N 2.56W
Bilbays Egypt 32 30.25N 31.34E
Bilbo see Bilbao Spain 10
Bilecik Turkey 30 40.10N 29.59E
Bilibino Russian Fed. 21 68.02N166.15E
Billabong Creek r. Australia 46 35.04S144.06E
Billingham U.K. 4 54.36N 1.18W
Billings U.S.A. 54 45.47N108.27W
Bill of Portland c. U.K. 5 50.32N 2.28W
Bilma Niger 38 18.46N 12.50E
Biloela Australia 44 24.24S150.30E
Biloxi U.S.A. 53 30.30N 88.53W
Bilqās Qism Awwal Egypt 32 31.14N 31.22E
Bilto Norway 16 69.26N 21.35E
Bimberi, Mt. Australia 47 35.40S148.47E
Bina-Etāwa India 29 24.09N 78.10E
Binaiya mtn. Indonesia 27 3.10S129.30E
Bīnālūd, Kūh-e mts. Iran 31 36.15N 59.00E
Binbee Australia 44 20.20S147.55E
Binche Belgium 8 50.25N 4.10E
Bindura Zimbabwe 39 17.18S 31.20E
Binga Zimbabwe 39 17.38S 27.19E
Binga, Mt. Zimbabwe 39 19.47S 33.03E
Bingara Australia 47 29.51S150.38E
Bingen Germany 8 49.58N 7.55E
Bingerville Ivory Coast 38 5.20N 3.53W
Bingham U.K. 4 52.57N 0.57W
Bingham U.S.A. 55 45.03N 69.53W
Binghamton U.S.A. 55 42.08N 75.54W
Bingkor Malaysia 26 5.26N116.15E
Bingöl Turkey 19 38.54N 40.29E
Bingol Daglari mtn. Turkey 30 39.21N 41.22E
Binh Dinh Vietnam 26 13.55N109.07E
Binjai Indonesia 26 3.37N 98.25E
Binji Nigeria 38 13.12N 4.55E
Binnaway Australia 47 31.32S149.23E
Bintan i. Indonesia 26 1.10N104.30E
Bintulu Malaysia 26 3.12N113.01E
Binzert Tunisia 34 37.17N 9.51E
Biograd Croatia 12 43.56N 15.27E
Bioko I. Equat. Guinea 38 3.25N 8.45E
Bi'r Abū 'Uwayqilah well Egypt 32 30.50N 34.07E
Bi'r ad Dakhal well Egypt 32 28.40N 32.24E
Birāk Libya 34 27.32N 14.17E
Bi'r al Jidy well Egypt 32 30.13N 33.03E
Bi'r al Jufayr well Egypt 32 30.49N 32.40E
Bi'r al 'Udayd well Egypt 32 28.59N 34.05E
Birao C.A.R. 35 10.17N 22.47E
Bi'r aş Şafrā' well Egypt 32 28.46N 34.20E
Bi'r ath Thamadah well Egypt 32 30.10N 33.28E
Bi'r Buerāt well Egypt 32 28.59N 32.10E
Bi'r Bukhayt well Egypt 32 29.13N 32.17E
Birchip Australia 46 35.59S142.59E
Birch Mts. Canada 50 57.30N112.30W
Birdsville Australia 44 25.54S139.22E
Birecik Turkey 30 37.03N 37.59E
Birhan mtn. Ethiopia 35 11.00N 37.50E
Bi'r Ḥasanah well Egypt 32 30.29N 33.47E
Bi'r Ḥooker well Egypt 32 30.23N 30.20E
Bīrjand Iran 31 32.54N 59.10E
Bi'r Jifjāfah well Egypt 32 30.28N 33.11E
Birk, Wādī r. Saudi Arabia 31 24.08N 47.35E
Birkenfeld Rhein.-Pfalz Germany 8 49.39N 7.10E
Birkenhead U.K. 4 53.24N 3.01W
Birksgate Range mts. Australia 42 27.10S129.45E
Bi'r Kusaybah well Egypt 32 22.41N 29.55E
Bîrlad Romania 15 46.14N 27.40E
Bi'r Lahfān well Egypt 32 31.01N 33.52E
Birmingham U.K. 5 52.30N 1.55W
Birmingham Ala. U.S.A. 53 33.30N 86.55W
Bir Mogreïn Mauritania 34 25.14N 11.35W
Birni Benin 38 9.59N 1.34E
Birnin Gwari Nigeria 38 11.02N 6.47E
Birnin Kebbi Nigeria 38 12.30N 4.11E
Birni N'Konni Niger 38 13.49N 5.19E
Birobidzhan Russian Fed. 25 48.49N132.54E
Birr Rep. of Ire. 7 53.06N 7.56W
Birrie r. Australia 47 29.43S146.37E
Birsk Russian Fed. 18 55.28N 55.31E
Bi'r Tābah well Egypt 32 29.30N 34.53E
Bi'r Umm Sa'īd well Egypt 32 29.40N 33.34E
Bi'r Umm 'Umayyid well Egypt 32 27.53N 32.30E
Biržai Lithuania 18 56.10N 24.48E
Biscay, B. of France 11 45.30N 4.00W
Bisceglie Italy 13 41.14N 16.31E
Bishkek Kyrgyzstan 24 42.53N 74.46E
Bishop Calif. U.S.A. 54 37.22N118.24W
Bishop Auckland U.K. 4 54.40N 1.40W
Bishop's Stortford U.K. 5 51.53N 0.09E
Bisina, L. Uganda 37 1.35N 34.08E
Biskra Algeria 34 34.48N 5.40E
Bismarck U.S.A. 52 46.50N100.48W
Bismarck Range mts. P.N.G. 27 6.00S145.00E
Bismarck Sea Pacific Oc. 27 4.00S146.30E
Bīsotūn Iran 31 34.22N 47.29E
Bispgården Sweden 16 63.02N 16.40E
Bissau Guinea Bissau 34 11.52N 15.39W
Bistriţa Romania 15 47.08N 24.30E
Bistriţa r. Romania 15 46.30N 26.54E
Bitam Gabon 36 2.05N 11.30E
Bitburg Germany 8 49.58N 6.31E
Bitlis Turkey 30 38.23N 42.04E
Bitola Macedonia 13 41.02N 21.21E
Bitter Creek town U.S.A. 54 41.31N109.27W
Bitterfontein R.S.A. 39 31.02S 18.14E
Bitterroot Range mts. U.S.A. 54 47.06N115.10W
Biu Nigeria 38 10.36N 12.11E
Biumba Rwanda 37 1.38S 30.02E
Biwa ko l. Japan 23 35.10N136.00E
Biyalā Egypt 32 31.11N 31.13E
Biysk Russian Fed. 20 52.35N 85.16E
Bizerte see Binzert Tunisia 34
Bjelovar Croatia 13 45.54N 16.51E
Bjorli Norway 17 62.16N 8.13E
Björna Sweden 16 63.32N 18.36E
Björnafjorden est. Norway 17 60.06N 5.22E
Bjørnøya i. Arctic Oc. 64 74.30N 19.00E
Black r. Ark. U.S.A. 53 35.30N 91.20W
Blackall Australia 44 24.25S145.28E
Blackburn U.K. 4 53.44N 2.30W
Blackfoot U.S.A. 54 43.11N112.20W
Black Mtn. U.K. 5 51.52N 3.50W
Black Mts. U.K. 5 51.52N 3.09W
Blackpool U.K. 4 53.48N 3.03W
Black River town Jamaica 57 18.02N 77.52W
Black River town Mich. U.S.A. 55 44.51N 83.21W
Black Rock town U.S.A. 54 38.41N112.59W
Black Rock Desert U.S.A. 54 41.10N119.00W
Black Sand Desert see Karakumy, Peski Turkmenistan 31
Black Sea Europe 15 44.00N 30.00E
Blacksod B. Rep. of Ire. 7 54.04N 10.00W
Black Sugarloaf Mt. Australia 47 31.24S151.34E
Blackville Australia 47 31.34S150.10E
Black Volta r. Ghana 38 8.14N 2.11W
Blackwater Australia 44 23.34S148.53E
Blackwater r. Waterford Rep. of Ire. 7 51.58N 7.52W
Blackwood r. Australia 43 34.15S115.10E
Blaenau Ffestiniog U.K. 4 53.00N 3.57W
Blagoevgrad Bulgaria 13 42.02N 23.04E
Blagoveshchensk Russian Fed. 25 50.19N127.30E
Blain France 9 47.29N 1.46W
Blair Athol Australia 44 22.42S147.33E
Blair Atholl U.K. 6 56.46N 3.51W
Blairgowrie U.K. 6 56.36N 3.21W
Blanc, Cap c. Mauritania 34 20.44N 17.05W
Blanc, Mont mtn. Europe 11 45.50N 6.52E
Blanca, Bahía b. Argentina 63 39.20S 62.00W
Blanca, Sierra mtn. U.S.A. 52 33.23N105.48W
Blanchard U.S.A. 54 48.01N116.59W
Blanche, L. Australia 46 29.15S139.40E
Blanchetown Australia 46 34.21S139.38E
Blanco, C. Argentina 63 47.12S 65.20W
Blanco, C. Costa Rica 57 9.36N 85.06W
Blanco, C. U.S.A. 54 42.50N124.34W
Bland r. Australia 47 33.42S147.30E
Blandford Forum U.K. 5 50.52N 2.10W
Blankenberge Belgium 8 51.18N 3.08E
Blansko Czech Republic 14 49.22N 16.39E
Blantyre Malaŵi 37 15.46S 35.00E
Blarney Rep. of Ire. 7 51.56N 8.34W
Blatnica Bulgaria 15 43.42N 28.31E
Blavet r. France 11 47.43N 3.18W
Blaye France 11 45.08N 0.40W
Blayney Australia 47 33.32S149.19E
Blednaya, Gora mtn. Russian Fed. 20 76.23N 65.08E
Bleiburg Austria 14 46.35N 14.48E
Blekinge d. Sweden 17 56.20N 15.00E
Blenheim New Zealand 48 41.32S173.58E
Bléré France 9 47.20N 0.59E
Blerick Neth. 8 51.22N 6.08E
Bletchley U.K. 5 51.59N 0.45W
Blida Algeria 34 36.30N 2.50E
Bligh Entrance Australia 44 9.18S144.10E
Blind River town Canada 55 46.10N 82.58W
Blinman Australia 46 31.05S138.11E
Blitar Indonesia 26 8.06S112.12E
Blitta Togo 38 8.23N 1.06E
Bloemfontein R.S.A. 39 29.07S 26.14E
Bloemhof R.S.A. 39 27.37S 25.34E
Blois France 9 47.36N 1.20E
Blönduós Iceland 16 65.39N 20.18W
Bloody Foreland c. Rep. of Ire. 7 55.09N 8.17W
Bloomington Ill. U.S.A. 53 40.29N 89.00W
Bloomington Ind. U.S.A. 55 39.10N 86.31W
Bloomsburg U.S.A. 55 41.00N 76.27W
Bluefield U.S.A. 53 37.14N 81.17W
Bluefields Nicaragua 57 12.00N 83.49W
Blue Mts. Australia 47 33.16S150.19E
Blue Mts. U.S.A. 54 45.30N118.15W
Blue Mud B. Australia 44 13.26S135.56E
Blue Nile r. see Azraq, Al Baḩr al r. Sudan 35
Bluenose L. Canada 50 68.30N119.35W
Blue Stack Mts. Rep. of Ire. 7 54.44N 8.09W
Bluff New Zealand 48 46.38S168.21E
Bluff U.S.A. 54 37.17N109.33W
Bluff Knoll mtn. Australia 43 34.25S118.15E
Blumenau Brazil 59 26.55S 49.07W
Blyth Northum. U.K. 4 55.07N 1.29W
Blythe U.S.A. 54 33.37N114.36W
Bö Nordland Norway 16 68.38N 14.35E
Bö Telemark Norway 17 59.25N 9.04E
Bo Sierra Leone 34 7.58N 11.45W
Boa Esperança Brazil 59 21.03S 45.37W
Boa Esperança, Représa da resr. Brazil 61 6.45S 44.15W
Boane Mozambique 39 26.02S 32.19E
Boa Vista Brazil 60 2.51N 60.43W
Bobadah Australia 47 32.18S146.42E
Bobadilla Spain 10 37.02N 4.44W
Bobbili India 29 18.34N 83.22E
Bobbio Italy 9 44.46N 9.23E
Bobo-Dioulasso Burkina 38 11.11N 4.18W
Bobonong Botswana 39 21.59S 28.29E
Bobr Belorussia 15 54.19N 29.18E
Bóbr r. Poland 14 52.04N 15.04E
Bobruysk Belorussia 15 53.08N 29.10E
Bôca do Acre Brazil 60 8.45S 67.23W
Bocaranga C.A.R. 36 7.01N 15.35E
Bochnia Poland 15 49.58N 20.26E
Bocholt Germany 8 51.49N 6.37E
Bochum Germany 8 51.28N 7.11E
Bochum R.S.A. 39 23.12S 29.12E
Bockum-Hövel Germany 8 51.42N 7.41E
Boconó Venezuela 60 9.17N 70.17W
Bodalla Australia 47 36.05S150.03E
Bodallin Australia 43 31.22S118.52E
Bodélé f. Chad 34 16.50N 17.10E
Boden Sweden 16 65.50N 21.42E
Bodensee l. Europe 14 47.40N 9.30E
Bode Sadu Nigeria 38 8.57N 4.49E
Bodfish U.S.A. 54 35.36N118.30W
Bodmin U.K. 5 50.28N 4.44W
Bodmin Moor U.K. 5 50.53N 4.35W
Bodö Norway 16 67.18N 14.26E
Bodrum Turkey 30 37.03N 27.28E
Boende Zaïre 36 0.15S 20.49E
Bogalusa U.S.A. 53 30.56N 89.53W
Bogan r. Australia 47 30.00S146.20E
Bogan Gate town Australia 47 33.08S147.50E
Bogenfels Namibia 39 27.26S 15.22E
Boggabilla Australia 47 28.36S150.21E
Boggabri Australia 47 30.42S150.02E
Boggeragh Mts. Rep. of Ire. 7 52.03N 8.53W
Bogia P.N.G. 27 4.16S145.00E
Bognes Norway 16 68.15N 16.00E
Bognor Regis U.K. 5 50.47N 0.40W
Bog of Allen f. Rep. of Ire. 7 53.17N 7.00W
Bogong, Mt. Australia 47 36.45S147.21E
Bogor Indonesia 26 6.34S106.45E
Bogotá Colombia 60 4.38N 74.05W
Bogué Mauritania 34 16.40N 14.10W
Boguslav Ukraine 15 49.32N 30.52E
Bo Hai b. China 25 38.30N119.30E
Bohain France 8 49.59N 3.28E
Bohemian Forest see Böhmerwald mts. Germany 14
Böhmerwald mts. Germany 14 49.20N 13.10E
Bohol i. Phil. 27 9.45N124.10E
Boiaçu Brazil 60 0.27S 61.46W
Boigu i. Australia 44 9.16S142.12E
Bois, Lac des l. Canada 50 66.40N125.15W
Boise U.S.A. 54 43.37N116.13W
Bois-Guillaume France 9 49.28N 1.08E
Boizenburg Germany 14 53.22N 10.43E
Bojador, Cabo c. W. Sahara 34 26.08N 14.30W
Bojeador, C. Phil. 27 18.30N120.50E
Bojnūrd Iran 31 37.28N 57.20E
Bokani Nigeria 38 9.27N 5.13E
Boké Guinea 34 10.57N 14.13W
Bokhara r. Australia 47 29.55S146.42E
Boknafjorden est. Norway 17 59.10N 5.35E
Bol Chad 38 13.27N 14.40E
Bolama Guinea Bissau 34 11.35N 15.30W
Bolanda, Jabal mtn. Sudan 35 7.44N 25.28E
Bolbec France 9 49.34N 0.28E
Bole Ghana 38 9.03N 2.23W
Bolesławiec Poland 14 51.16N 15.34E
Bolgatanga Ghana 38 10.42N 0.52W
Bolgrad Ukraine 15 45.42N 28.40E
Bolívar Argentina 63 36.14S 61.07W
Bolivia S. America 62 17.00S 65.00W
Bollnäs Sweden 17 61.21N 16.25E
Bollon Australia 45 28.02S147.28E
Bollstabruk Sweden 16 62.59N 17.42E
Bolmen l. Sweden 17 56.55N 13.40E
Bologna Italy 9 44.30N 11.20E
Bologoye Russian Fed. 18 57.58N 34.00E
Bolomba Zaïre 36 0.30N 19.13E
Bolsena, Lago di l. Italy 12 42.36N 11.55E
Bolshaya Glushitsa Russian Fed. 18 52.28N 50.30E
Bolshaya Pyssa Russian Fed. 18 64.11N 48.44E
Bolsherechye Russian Fed. 20 56.07N 74.40E
Bol'shevik, Ostrov i. Russian Fed. 21 78.30N102.00E
Bolshezemelskaya Tundra f. Russian Fed. 18 67.00N 56.10E
Bolshoy Atlym Russian Fed. 20 62.17N 66.30E
Bol'shoy Balkhan, Khrebet mts. Turkmenistan 31 39.38N 54.30E
Bol'shoy Irgiz r. Russian Fed. 18 52.00N 47.20E
Bol'shoy Lyakhovskiy, Ostrov i. Russian Fed. 21 73.30N142.00E
Bol'shoy Onguren Russian Fed. 21 53.40N107.40E
Bolshoy Uzen r. Kazakhstan 19 49.00N 49.40E
Bolsover U.K. 4 53.14N 1.18W
Bolton U.K. 4 53.35N 2.26W
Bolu Turkey 30 40.45N 31.38E
Bolus Head Rep. of Ire. 7 51.47N 10.20W
Bolvadin Turkey 30 38.43N 31.02E
Bolzano Italy 9 46.30N 11.20E
Boma Zaïre 36 5.50S 13.03E
Bomaderry Australia 47 34.21S150.34E
Bomadi Nigeria 38 5.13N 6.01E
Bombala Australia 47 36.55S149.16E
Bombay India 28 18.56N 72.51E
Bombo Uganda 37 0.34N 32.32E
Bom Despacho Brazil 59 19.46S 45.15W
Bomi China 24 29.50N 95.45E
Bömlafjorden est. Norway 17 59.39N 5.20E
Bömlo i. Norway 17 59.46N 5.13E
Bomokandi r. Zaïre 37 3.37N 26.09E
Bonaire i. Neth. Antilles 60 12.15N 68.27W
Bonanza U.S.A. 54 40.01N109.11W
Bonaparte Archipelago is. Australia 42 14.17S125.18E
Bonar-Bridge town U.K. 6 57.53N 4.21W
Bonavista Canada 51 48.38N 53.08W
Bon Bon Australia 46 30.26S135.28E
Bondeno Italy 9 44.53N 11.25E
Bondo Zaïre 36 3.47N 23.45E
Bondoukou Ivory Coast 38 8.03N 2.15W
Bone, Teluk b. Indonesia 27 4.00S120.50E
Bo'ness U.K. 6 56.01N 3.36W
Bongouanou Ivory Coast 38 6.44N 4.10W
Bonifacio, Str. of Med. Sea 12 41.18N 9.10E
Bonn Germany 8 50.44N 7.06E
Bonners Ferry U.S.A. 54 48.41N116.18W
Bonnétable France 9 48.11N 0.26E
Bonneval France 9 48.11N 1.24E
Bonneville Salt Flats f. U.S.A. 54 40.45N113.52W
Bonney, L. Australia 46 37.47S140.23E
Bonnie Rock town Australia 43 30.32S118.21E
Bonny Nigeria 38 4.25N 7.10E
Bonny, Bight of Africa 38 2.58N 7.00E
Bonshaw Australia 47 29.08S150.53E
Bontang Indonesia 26 0.05N117.31E
Bonthe Sierra Leone 34 7.32N 12.30W
Bonython Range mts. Australia 42 23.51S129.00E
Bookaloo Australia 46 31.56S137.21E
Booleroo Centre Australia 46 32.53S138.21E
Booligal Australia 47 33.54S144.54E
Boom Belgium 8 51.07N 4.21E
Boomrivier R.S.A. 39 29.34S 20.26E
Boonville N.Y. U.S.A. 55 43.29N 75.20W
Boorabbin Australia 43 31.14S120.21E
Boorindal Australia 47 30.23S146.11E
Booroorban Australia 47 34.56S144.46E
Boorowa Australia 47 34.26S148.48E
Boort Australia 46 36.08S143.46E
Boothia, G. of Canada 51 70.00N 90.00W
Boothia Pen. Canada 51 70.30N 95.00W
Bootra Australia 46 30.00S143.00E
Bopeechee Australia 46 29.36S137.23E
Bophuthatswana Africa 39 27.00S 23.30E
Boppard Germany 8 50.13N 7.35E
Bor Czech Republic 14 49.43N 12.47E
Bor Yugo. 13 44.05N 22.07E
Borah Peak mtn. U.S.A. 54 44.08N113.38W
Borås Sweden 17 57.43N 12.55E
Borāzjān Iran 31 29.14N 51.12E
Borba Brazil 60 4.24S 59.41W
Bordeaux France 11 44.50N 0.34W
Borden Australia 43 34.05S118.16E
Borden I. Canada 50 78.30N111.00W
Borden Pen. Canada 51 73.00N 83.00W
Borders d. U.K. 6 55.30N 2.53W
Bordertown Australia 46 36.18S140.49E
Bordheyri Iceland 16 65.12N 21.06W
Bordighera Italy 9 43.46N 7.39E
Bordj Flye Sainte Marie Algeria 34 27.17N 2.59E
Bordö i. Faroe Is. 16 62.10N 7.13W

Borga Finland 17 60.24N 25.40E
Borga Sweden 16 64.49N 15.05E
Börgefjell mtn. Norway 16 65.20N 13.45E
Börgefjell Nat. Park Norway 16 65.00N 13.58E
Borger Neth. 8 52.57N 6.46E
Borger U.S.A. 52 35.39N101.24W
Borgholm Sweden 17 56.53N 16.39E
Borghorst Germany 8 52.08N 7.27E
Borgo Italy 9 46.03N 11.27E
Borgomanero Italy 9 45.42N 8.28E
Borgo San Dalmazzo Italy 9 44.20N 7.30E
Borgo San Lorenzo Italy 9 43.57N 11.23E
Borgosesia Italy 9 45.43N 8.16E
Borgo Val di Taro Italy 9 44.29N 9.46E
Borgund Norway 17 61.03N 7.49E
Borislav Ukraine 15 49.18N 23.28E
Borisoglebsk Russian Fed. 19 51.23N 42.02E
Borisov Belorussia 15 54.09N 28.30E
Borispol Ukraine 15 50.21N 30.59E
Borja Peru 60 4.20S 77.40W
Borken Germany 8 51.50N 6.52E
Borkum Germany 8 53.34N 6.41E
Borkum i. Germany 8 53.35N 6.45E
Borlänge Sweden 17 60.29N 15.25E
Borley, C. Antarctica 64 66.15S 55.00E
Bormio Italy 9 46.28N 10.22E
Borndiep g. Neth. 8 53.28N 5.35E
Borneo i. Asia 26 1.00N114.00E
Bornheim Germany 8 50.45N 7.00E
Bornholm i. Denmark 17 55.10N 15.00E
Borno d. Nigeria 38 11.20N 12.40E
Bornu, Plain of f. Nigeria 38 12.30N 13.00E
Boro r. Sudan 35 8.50N 28.00E
Borodyanka Ukraine 15 50.38N 29.59E
Boromo Burkina 38 11.43N 2.53W
Boroughbridge U.K. 4 54.06N 1.23W
Borovichi Russian Fed. 18 58.22N 34.00E
Borrika Australia 46 35.00S140.05E
Borroloola Australia 44 16.04S136.17E
Borşa Romania 15 46.56N 23.40E
Borşa Romania 15 47.39N 24.40E
Borth U.K. 5 52.29N 4.03W
Borüjerd Iran 31 33.54N 48.47E
Bory Tucholskie f. Poland 15 53.45N 17.30E
Borzhomi Georgia 19 41.49N 43.23E
Borzna Ukraine 19 51.15N 32.25E
Borzya Russian Fed. 21 50.24N116.35E
Bosa Italy 12 40.18N 8.29E
Bosanska Gradiška Croatia 13 45.09N 17.15E
Bosanski Novi Bosnia-Herzegovina 14 45.03N 16.23E
Boscastle U.K. 5 50.42N 4.42W
Boshof R.S.A. 39 28.32S 25.12E
Bosna r. Bosnia-Herzegovina 13 45.04N 18.27E
Bosnia-Herzegovina Europe 13 44.00N 18.10E
Bosnik Indonesia 27 1.09S136.14E
Bōsō-hantō pen. Japan 23 35.08N140.00E
Bosporus str. see Istanbul Bogazi str. Turkey 13
Bossangoa C.A.R. 36 6.27N 17.21E
Bosso Niger 38 13.43N 13.19E
Bosten Hu l. China 24 42.00N 87.00E
Boston U.K. 4 52.59N 0.02W
Boston U.S.A. 55 42.21N 71.04W
Botany B. Australia 47 34.04S151.08E
Botev mtn. Bulgaria 13 42.43N 24.55E
Botevgrad Bulgaria 13 42.55N 23.57E
Bothnia, G. of Europe 16 63.30N 20.30E
Botletle r. Botswana 39 21.06S 24.47E
Botoşani Romania 15 47.44N 26.41E
Botou Burkina 38 12.47N 2.02E
Botrange mtn. Belgium 8 50.30N 6.04E
Botro Ivory Coast 38 7.51N 5.19W
Botswana Africa 39 22.00S 24.15E
Bottrop Germany 8 51.31N 6.55E
Botucatu Brazil 59 22.52S 48.30W
Bouaflé Ivory Coast 38 7.01N 5.47W
Bouaké Ivory Coast 38 7.42N 5.00W
Bouar C.A.R. 38 5.58N 15.35E
Bou Arfa Morocco 34 32.30N 1.59W
Bouchoir France 9 49.45N 2.41E
Bougainville i. Pacific Oc. 40 6.00S155.00E
Bougouni Mali 34 11.25N 7.28W
Bouillon Belgium 8 49.48N 5.03E
Boulder Australia 43 30.55S121.32E
Boulder U.S.A. 52 40.01N105.17W
Boulder City U.S.A. 54 35.59N114.50W
Boulia Australia 44 22.54S139.54E
Boulogne France 11 50.43N 1.37E
Boulogne-Billancourt France 9 48.50N 2.15E
Boultoum Niger 38 14.45N 10.25E
Boumba r. Cameroon 38 2.00N 15.10E
Bouna Ivory Coast 38 9.19N 2.53W
Boundary Peak mtn. U.S.A. 54 37.51N118.21W
Bountiful U.S.A. 54 40.53N111.53W
Bouraga well Mali 38 19.00N 3.36W
Bourem Mali 38 16.59N 0.20W
Bourg France 11 46.12N 5.13E
Bourganeuf France 11 45.57N 1.44E
Bourges France 11 47.05N 2.23E
Bourg Madame France 11 42.26N 1.55E
Bourgogne d. France 11 47.10N 4.20E
Bourgogne, Canal de France 9 47.58N 3.30E
Bourgoin France 11 45.35N 5.17E
Bourgueil France 9 47.17N 0.10E
Bourke Australia 47 30.09S145.59E
Bournemouth U.K. 5 50.43N 1.53W
Boussac France 11 46.22N 2.13E
Bouvard, C. Australia 43 32.40S115.34E
Bovill U.S.A. 54 46.51N116.24W
Bovril Argentina 63 31.22S 59.25W
Bowelling Australia 43 33.25S116.27E
Bowen Australia 44 20.00S148.15E
Bowen, Mt. Australia 47 37.11S148.34E
Bowling Green U.S.A. 53 37.00N 86.29W
Bowling Green, C. Australia 44 19.19S146.25E
Bowman I. Antarctica 64 65.00S104.00E
Bowral Australia 47 34.30S150.24E
Bowser Australia 47 36.19S146.23E
Boxholm Sweden 17 58.12N 15.03E
Bo Xian China 25 33.40N115.50E
Box Tank Australia 46 32.13S142.17E
Boxtel Neth. 8 51.36N 5.20E
Boyabat Turkey 30 41.27N 34.45E
Boyanup Australia 43 33.29S115.40E
Boyarka Ukraine 15 50.20N 30.26E
Boyd r. Australia 47 29.51S152.25E
Boyle Rep. of Ire. 7 53.58N 8.19W
Boyne r. Rep. of Ire. 7 53.43N 6.17W
Boyoma Falls f. Zaïre 36 0.18N 25.30E
Boyup Brook Australia 43 33.50S116.22E
Bozca Ada i. Turkey 13 39.49N 26.03E
Bozeman U.S.A. 54 45.41N111.02W
Bozen see Bolzano Italy 9
Bra Italy 9 44.42N 7.51E
Brabant d. Belgium 8 50.47N 4.30E
Brač i. Croatia 13 43.20N 16.38E
Bracadale, Loch U.K. 6 57.22N 6.30W
Bracebridge Canada 55 45.02N 79.19W
Bracieux France 9 47.33N 1.33E
Bräcke Sweden 16 62.44N 15.30E
Brad Romania 13 46.06N 22.48E
Bradano r. Italy 13 40.23N 16.52E
Bradenton U.S.A. 53 27.29N 82.33W
Bradford Canada 55 44.07N 79.34W
Bradford U.K. 4 53.47N 1.45W
Bradford Penn. U.S.A. 55 41.58N 78.39W
Bradworthy U.K. 5 50.54N 4.22W
Braemar U.K. 6 57.01N 3.24W
Braga Portugal 10 41.32N 8.26W
Bragado Argentina 63 35.10S 60.30W
Bragança Brazil 61 1.03S 46.46W
Bragança Portugal 10 41.47N 6.46W
Bragança Paulista Brazil 59 22.59S 46.32W
Bragin Belorussia 15 51.49N 30.16E
Brahmaputra r. Asia 29 23.50N 89.45E
Braidwood Australia 47 35.27S149.50E
Brăila Romania 15 45.18N 27.58E
Brainerd U.S.A. 53 46.20N 94.10W
Braintree U.K. 5 51.53N 0.32E
Brålanda Sweden 17 58.34N 12.22E
Bramfield Australia 46 33.37S134.59E
Brampton Canada 55 43.41N 79.46W
Brampton U.K. 4 54.56N 2.43W
Bramsche Germany 8 52.26N 7.59E
Branco r. Brazil 60 1.00S 62.00W
Brandberg mtn. Namibia 39 21.08S 14.35E
Brandbu Norway 17 60.28N 10.30E
Brande Denmark 17 55.57N 9.07E
Brandenburg Germany 14 52.25N 12.34E
Brandenburg d. Germany 14 52.15N 13.10E
Brandfort R.S.A. 39 28.41S 26.27E
Brandon Canada 51 49.50N 99.57W
Brandon Mtn. Rep. of Ire. 7 52.14N 10.15W
Brandon Pt. Rep. of Ire. 7 52.17N 10.11W
Braniewo Poland 15 54.24N 19.50E
Bransby Australia 46 28.40S142.00E
Brasil, Planalto mts. Brazil 61 17.02S 50.00W
Brasiléia Brazil 60 11.00S 68.44W
Brasília Brazil 61 15.45S 47.57W
Braşov Romania 15 45.40N 25.35E
Brass Nigeria 38 4.20N 6.15E
Brasschaat Belgium 8 51.18N 4.28E
Bratislava Slovakia 15 48.10N 17.10E
Bratsk Russian Fed. 21 56.20N101.15E
Bratsk Vodokhranilishche resr. Russian Fed. 21 54.40N103.00E
Bratslav Ukraine 15 48.49N 28.51E
Braunau Austria 14 48.15N 13.02E
Braunschweig Germany 14 52.15N 10.30E
Braunton U.K. 5 51.06N 4.09W
Bravo del Norte, Rio r. Mexico see Rio Grande r. Mexico/U.S.A. 56
Brawley U.S.A. 54 32.59N115.31W
Bray France 9 48.25N 3.14E
Bray Rep. of Ire. 7 53.12N 6.07W
Bray Head Kerry Rep. of Ire. 7 51.53N 10.26W
Brazilian Highlands see Brasil, Planalto mts. Brazil 61
Brazos r. U.S.A. 53 28.55N 95.20W
Brazzaville Congo 36 4.14S 15.14E
Brčko Bosnia-Herzegovina 15 44.53N 18.48E
Brda r. Poland 15 53.07N 18.08E
Breadalbane f. U.K. 6 56.30N 4.20W
Bream B. New Zealand 48 36.00S174.30E
Brécey France 9 48.44N 1.10W
Brechin U.K. 6 56.44N 2.40W
Breckland f. U.K. 5 52.28N 0.40E
Břeclav Czech Republic 14 48.46N 16.53E
Brecon U.K. 5 51.57N 3.23W
Brecon Beacons mts. U.K. 5 51.53N 3.27W
Breda Neth. 8 51.35N 4.46E
Bredasdorp R.S.A. 39 34.31S 20.03E
Bredbo Australia 47 35.57S149.10E
Bregenz Austria 14 47.31N 9.46E
Bregovo Bulgaria 13 44.08N 22.39E
Bréhal France 9 48.53N 1.30W
Breidhafjördhur est. Iceland 16 65.15N 23.00W
Breim Norway 17 61.44N 6.25E
Brekstad Norway 16 63.42N 9.40E
Bremangerland i. Norway 17 61.51N 5.02E
Bremen Germany 14 53.05N 8.48E
Bremer Bay town Australia 43 34.21S119.20E
Bremerhaven Germany 14 53.33N 8.35E
Bremer Range mts. Australia 43 32.40S120.55E
Bremerton U.S.A. 54 47.34N122.38W
Brenner Pass Italy/Austria 14 47.00N 11.30E
Breno Italy 9 45.57N 10.18E
Brent Canada 55 46.02N 78.29W
Brenta r. Italy 9 45.25N 12.15E
Brentwood U.K. 5 51.38N 0.18E
Brescia Italy 9 45.33N 10.12E
Breskens Neth. 8 51.24N 3.34E
Bressay i. U.K. 6 60.08N 1.05W
Bressuire France 11 46.50N 0.28W
Brest Belorussia 15 52.08N 23.40E
Brest France 11 48.23N 4.30W
Bretagne d. France 11 48.15N 2.30W
Breteuil France 9 49.38N 2.18E
Breteuil-sur-Iton France 9 48.50N 0.55E
Brett, C. New Zealand 48 35.15S174.20E
Breuil-Cervinia Italy 9 45.56N 7.38E
Brevik Norway 17 59.04N 9.42E
Brewarrina Australia 47 29.57S147.54E
Brewer U.S.A. 55 44.48N 68.46W
Brezovo Bulgaria 13 42.20N 25.06E
Bria C.A.R. 35 6.32N 21.59E
Briançon France 11 44.53N 6.39E
Briare France 9 47.38N 2.44E
Bribbaree Australia 47 34.07S147.51E
Brichany Moldavia 15 48.20N 27.01E
Bricquebec France 9 49.28N 1.38W
Bride I.o.M Europe 4 54.23N 4.24W
Bridgend U.K. 5 51.30N 3.35W
Bridgeport Calif. U.S.A. 54 38.10N119.13W
Bridgeport Conn. U.S.A. 55 41.12N 73.12W
Bridger U.S.A. 54 45.18N108.55W
Bridgetown Australia 43 33.57S116.08E
Bridgetown Barbados 57 13.06N 59.37W
Bridgetown Rep. of Ire. 7 52.14N 6.33W
Bridgewater Canada 51 44.23N 64.31W
Bridgewater, C. Australia 46 38.25S141.28E
Bridgnorth U.K. 5 52.33N 2.25W
Bridgwater U.K. 5 51.08N 3.00W
Bridlington U.K. 4 54.06N 0.11W
Brie f. France 9 48.40N 3.20E
Brienne-le-Château France 9 48.24N 4.32E
Brig Switz. 9 46.19N 8.00E
Brigg U.K. 4 53.33N 0.30W
Brigham City U.S.A. 54 41.31N112.01W
Bright Australia 47 36.42S146.58E
Brighton U.K. 5 50.50N 0.09W
Brindisi Italy 13 40.38N 17.57E
Brinkworth Australia 46 33.42S138.24E
Brionne France 9 49.12N 0.43E
Briouze France 9 48.42N 0.22W
Brisbane Australia 47 27.30S153.00E
Brisighella Italy 9 44.13N 11.46E
Bristol U.K. 5 51.26N 2.35W
Bristol Tenn. U.S.A. 53 36.35N 82.12W
Bristol B. U.S.A. 50 58.00N158.50W
Bristol Channel U.K. 5 51.17N 3.20W
British Antarctic Territory Antarctica 64 70.00S 50.00W
British Columbia d. Canada 50 55.00N125.00W
British Mts. Canada 50 69.00N140.20W
British Virgin Is. C. America 57 18.30N 64.30W
Britstown R.S.A. 39 30.34S 23.30E
Britt Canada 55 45.46N 80.35W
Brive France 11 45.09N 1.32E
Briviesca Spain 10 42.33N 3.19W
Brixham U.K. 5 50.24N 3.31W
Brno Czech Republic 14 49.11N 16.39E
Broach India 28 21.42N 72.58E
Broad Arrow Australia 43 30.32S121.20E
Broad B. U.K. 6 58.15N 6.15W
Broadback r. Canada 55 51.20N 78.50W
Broadford Australia 47 37.16S145.03E
Broadmere Australia 44 25.30S149.30E
Broad Sd. Australia 44 22.20S149.50E
Broadsound Range mts. Australia 44 22.30S149.30E
Broadway U.K. 5 52.02N 1.51W
Brochet Canada 51 57.53N101.40W
Brockton U.S.A. 55 42.05N 71.01W
Brockville Canada 55 44.35N 75.41W
Brockway Mont. U.S.A. 54 47.15N105.45W
Brod Croatia 15 45.09N 18.02E
Brodeur Pen. Canada 51 73.00N 88.00W
Brodick U.K. 6 55.34N 5.09W
Brodnica Poland 15 53.16N 19.23E
Brody Ukraine 15 50.05N 25.08E
Broglie France 9 49.01N 0.32E
Broke Inlet Australia 43 34.55S116.25E
Broken B. Australia 47 33.34S151.18E
Broken Hill town Australia 46 31.57S141.30E
Bromley U.K. 5 51.24N 0.02E
Bromsgrove U.K. 5 52.20N 2.03W
Brönderslev Denmark 17 57.16N 9.58E
Brong-Ahafo d. Ghana 38 7.45N 1.30W
Brönnöysund Norway 16 65.30N 12.10E
Brooke's Point town Phil. 26 8.50N117.52E
Brookhaven U.S.A. 53 31.36N 90.28W
Brookings Oreg. U.S.A. 54 42.03N124.17W
Brookings S.Dak. U.S.A. 53 44.19N 96.47W
Brooks Canada 50 50.35N111.53W
Brooks Range mts. U.S.A. 50 68.50N152.00W
Brookton Australia 43 32.22S117.01E
Broom, Loch U.K. 6 57.52N 5.07W
Broome Australia 42 17.58S122.15E
Broome, Mt. Australia 42 17.21S125.23E
Broomehill town Australia 43 33.50S117.35E
Brora U.K. 6 58.01N 3.52W
Brora r. U.K. 6 58.00N 3.51W
Brosna r. Rep. of Ire. 7 53.13N 7.58W
Brothers U.S.A. 54 43.49N120.36W
Brou France 9 48.13N 1.11E
Brough England U.K. 4 54.32N 2.19W
Brough Scotland U.K. 6 60.29N 1.12W
Broughton r. Australia 46 33.21S137.46E
Broughton in Furness U.K. 4 54.17N 3.12W
Brouwershaven Neth. 8 51.44N 3.53E
Brovary Ukraine 15 50.30N 30.45E
Brovst Denmark 17 57.06N 9.32E
Brown, Mt. Australia 46 32.33S138.02E
Browning U.S.A. 54 48.34N113.01W
Brownwood U.S.A. 52 31.42N 98.59W
Bruay-en-Artois France 8 50.29N 2.36E
Bruce Pen. Canada 55 44.50N 81.20W
Bruce Rock town Australia 43 31.52S118.09E
Bruges see Brugge Belgium 8
Brugge Belgium 8 51.13N 3.14E
Brühl Germany 8 50.50N 6.55E
Brumadinho Brazil 59 20.09S 44.11W
Brumado Brazil 61 14.13S 41.40W
Brunei Asia 26 4.56N114.58E
Brünen Germany 8 51.45N 6.41E
Brunflo Sweden 16 63.04N 14.50E
Brunner New Zealand 48 42.28S171.12E
Brunsbüttel Germany 14 53.44N 9.05E
Brunssum Neth. 8 50.57N 5.59E
Brunswick Ga. U.S.A. 53 31.09N 81.21W
Brunswick Maine U.S.A. 55 43.55N 69.58W
Brunswick B. Australia 42 15.05S125.00E
Brunswick Junction Australia 43 33.15S115.45E
Bruny I. Australia 45 43.15S147.16E
Brusilovka Kazakhstan 19 50.39N 54.59E
Brussel see Bruxelles Belgium 8
Brussels see Bruxelles Belgium 8
Bruthen Australia 47 37.44S147.49E
Bruton U.K. 5 51.06N 2.28W
Bruxelles Belgium 8 50.50N 4.23E
Bryan Ohio U.S.A. 55 41.30N 84.34W
Bryan Tex. U.S.A. 53 30.41N 96.24W
Bryan, Mt. Australia 46 33.26S138.27E
Bryansk Russian Fed. 18 53.15N 34.09E
Bryne Norway 17 58.44N 5.39E
Bryson Canada 55 45.41N 76.37W
Bryson, Lac l. Canada 55 46.19N 77.27W
Brzeg Poland 15 50.52N 17.27E
Bsharri Lebanon 32 34.15N 36.00E
Bua r. Malaŵi 37 12.42S 34.15E
Bu'ayrāt al Ḥasūn Libya 34 31.24N 15.44E
Būbiyān, Jazīrat i. Kuwait 31 29.45N 48.15E
Bubye r. Zimbabwe 39 22.18S 31.00E
Bucak Turkey 30 37.28N 30.36E
Bucaramanga Colombia 60 7.08N 73.10W
Buchach Ukraine 15 49.09N 25.20E
Buchanan Liberia 34 5.57N 10.02W
Buchanan, L. Australia 44 21.28S145.52E
Buchan Ness c. U.K. 6 57.28N 1.47W
Buchans Canada 51 48.49N 56.52W
Bucharest see Bucureşti Romania 15
Buchloe Germany 14 48.02N 10.44E
Buchy France 9 49.35N 1.22E
Buckambool Mt. Australia 47 31.55S145.40E
Buckhaven and Methil U.K. 4 56.11N 3.03W
Buckie U.K. 6 57.40N 2.58W
Buckingham U.K. 5 52.00N 0.59W
Buckingham B. Australia 44 12.10S135.46E
Buckinghamshire d. U.K. 5 51.50N 0.48W
Buckland Tableland f. Australia 44 25.00S148.00E
Buckleboo Australia 46 32.55S136.12E
Bucquoy France 8 50.09N 2.43E
Bu Craa W. Sahara 34 26.21N 12.57W
Bucureşti Romania 15 44.25N 26.06E
Bucyrus U.S.A. 55 40.47N 82.57W
Bud Norway 16 62.54N 6.56E
Budapest Hungary 15 47.30N 19.03E
Budaun India 29 28.02N 79.07E
Budda Australia 46 31.12S144.16E
Budd Coast f. Antarctica 64 67.00S112.00E
Bude U.K. 5 50.49N 4.33W
Bude B. U.K. 5 50.50N 4.40W
Budennovsk Russian Fed. 19 44.50N 44.10E
Buea Cameroon 38 4.09N 9.13E
Buenaventura Colombia 60 3.54N 77.02W
Buenaventura Mexico 56 29.51N107.29W
Buenos Aires Argentina 63 34.40S 58.25W
Buenos Aires d. Argentina 63 36.30S 59.00W
Buenos Aires, L. Argentina/Chile 63 46.35S 72.00W
Buffalo N.Y. U.S.A. 55 42.52N 78.55W
Buffalo Wyo. U.S.A. 54 44.21N106.42W
Bug r. Poland 15 52.29N 21.11E
Buga Colombia 60 3.53N 76.17W
Bugaldie Australia 47 31.02S149.08E
Bugembe Uganda 37 0.26N 33.16E
Bugene Tanzania 37 1.34S 31.07E
Buggs Island l. U.S.A. 53 36.35N 78.20W
Bugrino Russian Fed. 18 68.45N 49.15E
Bugt China 25 48.45N121.58E
Bugulma Russian Fed. 18 54.32N 52.46E
Buguma Nigeria 38 4.43N 6.53E
Buguruslan Russian Fed. 18 53.36N 52.30E
Buhera Zimbabwe 39 19.21S 31.25E
Buhuşi Romania 15 46.43N 26.41E
Builth Wells U.K. 5 52.09N 3.24W
Buinsk Russian Fed. 18 54.58N 48.15E
Bu'in-Sofiā Iran 31 35.51N 46.02E
Buitenpost Neth. 8 53.15N 6.09E
Buji P.N.G. 44 9.07S142.26E
Bujumbura Burundi 37 3.22S 29.21E
Bukavu Zaïre 37 2.30S 28.49E
Bukene Tanzania 37 4.13S 32.52E
Bukhara Uzbekistan 31 39.47N 64.26E
Buki Ukraine 15 49.02N 30.29E
Bukima Tanzania 37 1.48S 33.25E
Bukittinggi Indonesia 26 0.18S100.20E
Bukoba Tanzania 37 1.20S 31.49E
Bukuru Nigeria 38 9.48N 8.52E
Būl, Kūh-e mtn. Iran 31 30.48N 52.45E
Bula Indonesia 27 3.07S130.27E
Bulahdelah Australia 47 32.25S152.13E
Bulan Phil. 27 12.40N123.53E
Bulawayo Zimbabwe 39 20.10S 28.43E
Buldern Germany 8 51.52N 7.21E
Bulgan Mongolia 24 48.34N103.12E
Bulgaria Europe 13 42.30N 25.00E
Bullabulling Australia 43 31.05S120.52E
Bullara Australia 42 22.40S114.03E
Buller r. New Zealand 48 41.45S171.35E
Buller, Mt. Australia 47 37.11S146.26E
Bullfinch Australia 43 30.59S119.06E
Bulli Australia 47 34.20S150.55E
Bull Mts. U.S.A. 54 46.05N109.00W
Bulloo r. Australia 46 28.43S142.27E
Bulloo Downs town Australia 46 28.30S142.45E
Bulolo P.N.G. 27 7.13S146.35E
Bultfontein R.S.A. 39 28.17S 26.09E
Bulu Indonesia 27 4.34N126.45E
Bulu, Gunung mtn. Indonesia 26 3.00N116.00E
Bulun Russian Fed. 21 70.50N127.20E
Bulunde Tanzania 37 4.19S 32.57E
Bumba Zaïre 35 2.15N 22.32E
Buna Kenya 37 2.49N 39.27E
Buna P.N.G. 44 8.40S148.25E
Bunbury Australia 43 33.20S115.34E
Buncrana Rep. of Ire. 7 55.08N 7.27W
Bundaberg Australia 44 24.50S152.21E
Bundaleer Australia 47 28.39S146.31E
Bundarra Australia 47 30.11S151.04E
Bunde Germany 8 53.12N 7.16E
Bundella Australia 47 31.35S149.59E
Bundoran Rep. of Ire. 7 54.28N 8.17W
Bungay U.K. 5 52.27N 1.26E
Bungu Tanzania 37 7.37S 39.07E
Buni Nigeria 38 11.20N 11.59E
Bunia Zaïre 37 1.30N 30.10E
Buninyong Australia 46 37.41S143.58E
Bunyala Kenya 37 0.07N 34.00E
Bunyan Australia 47 36.11S149.09E
Buol Indonesia 27 1.12N121.28E
Buqayq Saudi Arabia 31 25.55N 49.40E
Bura Coast Kenya 37 1.09S 39.55E
Bura Coast Kenya 37 3.30S 38.19E
Burakin Australia 43 30.30S117.08E
Buraydah Saudi Arabia 31 26.18N 43.58E
Burcher Australia 47 33.32S147.18E
Burdur Turkey 19 37.44N 30.17E
Burdwān India 29 23.15N 87.52E
Burg Germany 14 52.17N 11.51E
Burgas Bulgaria 13 42.30N 27.29E
Burgenland d. Austria 14 47.30N 16.20E
Burgess Hill U.K. 5 50.57N 0.07W
Burgos Spain 10 42.21N 3.41W
Burgsteinfurt Germany 8 52.09N 7.21E
Burgsvik Sweden 17 57.03N 18.16E
Burhānpur India 28 21.18N 76.08E
Buri Brazil 59 23.46S 48.39W
Burias i. Phil. 27 12.50N123.10E
Burica, Punta c. Panama 57 8.05N 82.50W
Burke r. Australia 44 23.12S139.33E
Burketown Australia 44 17.44S139.22E
Burkina Africa 38 12.30N 2.00W
Burley U.S.A. 54 42.32N113.48W
Burlington Canada 55 43.19N 79.48W
Burlington Iowa U.S.A. 53 40.50N 91.07W
Burlington Vt. U.S.A. 55 44.29N 73.13W
Burma Asia 29 21.00N 96.30E
Burngup Australia 43 33.00S118.39E
Burnham-on-Crouch U.K. 5 51.37N 0.50E
Burnham-on-Sea U.K. 5 51.15N 3.00W
Burnie Australia 45 41.03S145.55E
Burnley U.K. 4 53.47N 2.15W
Burns Oreg. U.S.A. 54 43.35N119.03W
Burnside r. Canada 50 66.51N108.04W
Buronga Australia 46 34.08S142.11E
Burra Australia 46 33.40S138.57E
Burracoppin Australia 43 31.22S118.30E
Burragorang, L. Australia 47 33.58S150.27E
Burren Junction Australia 47 30.08S148.59E
Burrewarra Pt. Australia 47 35.56S150.12E
Burriana Spain 10 39.54N 0.05W
Burrinjuck Australia 47 35.01S148.33E
Burrinjuck Resr. Australia 47 35.00S148.40E
Burry Port U.K. 5 51.41N 4.17W
Bursa Turkey 13 40.11N 29.04E
Būr Safājah Egypt 30 26.44N 33.56E
Būr Sa'īd Egypt 32 31.17N 32.18E
Būr Sūdān Sudan 35 19.39N 37.01E
Burta Australia 46 32.30S141.05E
Būr Tawfīq Egypt 32 29.57N 32.34E
Burton upon Trent U.K. 4 52.58N 1.39W
Burtundy Australia 46 33.45S142.22E
Buru i. Indonesia 27 3.30S126.30E
Burullus, Buḥayrat al l. Egypt 32 31.30N 30.45E
Burundi Africa 37 3.00S 30.00E
Bururi Burundi 37 3.58S 29.35E
Burutu Nigeria 38 5.20N 5.31E
Bury G.M. U.K. 4 53.36N 2.19W
Bury St. Edmunds U.K. 5 52.15N 0.42E
Busalla Italy 9 44.34N 8.57E
Busca Italy 9 44.31N 7.29E
Būsh Egypt 32 29.09N 31.07E
Būshehr Iran 31 28.57N 50.52E
Bushmanland f. R.S.A. 39 29.25S 19.40E
Busigny France 8 50.03N 3.29E
Buskerud Norway 17 60.20N 9.00E
Buşrá ash Shām Syria 32 32.30N 36.29E
Busselton Australia 43 33.43S115.15E
Bussum Neth. 8 52.17N 5.10E
Bustard Head c. Australia 44 24.02S151.48E
Busto Arsizio Italy 9 45.37N 8.51E
Buta Zaïre 35 2.49N 24.50E
Butari Rwanda 37 2.38S 29.43E
Bute Australia 46 33.24S138.01E
Bute i. U.K. 6 55.51N 5.07W
Bute, Sd. of U.K. 6 55.44N 5.10W
Butiaba Uganda 37 1.48N 31.15E
Buton i. Indonesia 27 5.00S122.50E
Butte Mont. U.S.A. 54 46.00N112.32W
Butterworth Malaysia 26 5.24N100.22E
Buttevant Rep. of Ire. 7 52.14N 8.41W
Butt of Lewis c. U.K. 6 58.31N 6.15W
Butty Head Australia 43 33.52S121.35E
Butuan Phil. 27 8.56N125.31E
Buur Gaabo Somali Rep. 37 1.10S 41.50E
Buur Hakaba Somali Rep. 37 2.43N 44.10E
Buxton U.K. 4 53.16N 1.54W
Buy Russian Fed. 18 58.23N 41.27E
Buyaga Russian Fed. 21 59.42N126.59E
Buynaksk Russian Fed. 19 42.48N 47.07E
Büyük Menderes r. Turkey 13 37.30N 27.05E
Buzachi, Poluostrov pen. Kazakhstan 19 45.00N 51.55E
Buzancy France 9 49.30N 4.59E
Buzău Romania 15 45.10N 26.49E
Buzău r. Romania 15 45.24N 27.48E
Buzaymah Libya 35 24.55N 22.02E
Buzi r. Mozambique 39 19.52S 34.00E
Buzuluk Russian Fed. 18 52.49N 52.19E
Bwasiaia P.N.G. 44 10.06S150.48E
Byala Bulgaria 13 42.53N 27.55E

Byam Martin I. Canada **50** 75.15N104.00W
Bydgoszcz Poland **15** 53.16N 17.33E
Bygland Norway **17** 58.48N 7.50E
Bykhov Belorussia **15** 53.30N 30.15E
Bykle Norway **17** 59.21N 7.20E
Bylot I. Canada **51** 73.00N 78.30W
Byrd Land *f.* Antarctica **64** 79.30S125.00W
Byrock Australia **47** 30.40S146.25E
Byron, C. Australia **47** 28.37S153.40E
Byron Bay *town* Australia **47** 28.43S153.34E
Byrranga, Gory *mts.* Russian Fed. **21** 74.50N101.00E
Byske Sweden **16** 64.57N 21.12E
Byske *r.* Sweden **16** 64.57N 21.13E
Byten Belorussia **15** 52.50N 25.28E
Bytom Poland **15** 50.22N 18.54E
Bzipi Georgia **19** 43.15N 40.24E

C

Cabanatuan Phil. **27** 15.30N120.58E
Cabimas Venezuela **60** 10.26N 71.27W
Cabinda Angola **36** 5.34S 12.12E
Cabinet Mts. U.S.A. **54** 48.08N115.46W
Cabo Delgado *d.* Mozambique **37** 12.30S 39.00E
Cabo Frio *town* Brazil **59** 22.51S 42.03W
Cabonga, Résr. Canada **55** 47.35N 76.35W
Caboolture Australia **45** 27.05S152.57E
Cabo Pantoja Peru **60** 1.00S 75.10W
Cabot Str. Canada **51** 47.00N 59.00W
Cabras Italy **12** 39.56N 8.32E
Cabrera *i.* Spain **10** 39.08N 2.56E
Cabrera, Sierra *mts.* Spain **10** 42.10N 6.30W
Cabriel *r.* Spain **10** 39.13N 1.07W
Cabruta Venezuela **60** 7.40N 66.16W
Čačak Yugo. **15** 43.53N 20.21E
Caçapava Brazil **59** 23.05S 45.40W
Cáceres Brazil **61** 16.05S 57.40W
Cáceres Spain **10** 39.29N 6.23W
Cacharí Argentina **63** 36.23S 59.29W
Cachoeira Brazil **61** 12.35S 38.59W
Cachoeira do Sul Brazil **59** 30.03S 52.52W
Cachoeiro de Itapemirim Brazil **59** 20.51S 41.07W
Cacín *r.* Spain **10** 37.10N 4.01W
Caconda Angola **36** 13.46S 15.06E
Čadca Slovakia **15** 49.26N 18.48E
Cader Idris *mtn.* U.K. **5** 52.40N 3.55W
Cadí, Serra del *mts.* Spain **10** 42.12N 1.35E
Cadibarrawirracanna, L. Australia **46** 28.52S135.27E
Cadillac U.S.A. **55** 44.15N 85.23W
Cadiz Phil. **27** 10.57N123.18E
Cádiz Spain **10** 36.32N 6.18W
Cádiz, Golfo de *g.* Spain **10** 37.00N 7.10W
Cadoux Australia **43** 30.47S117.05E
Caen France **9** 49.11N 0.22W
Caernarfon U.K. **4** 53.08N 4.17W
Caernarfon B. U.K. **4** 53.05N 4.25W
Caerphilly U.K. **5** 51.34N 3.13W
Caeté Brazil **59** 19.54S 43.37W
Cagayan de Oro Phil. **27** 8.29N124.40E
Cagliari Italy **12** 39.14N 9.07E
Cagliari, Golfo di *g.* Italy **12** 39.07N 9.15E
Cagnes France **9** 43.40N 7.09E
Caguán *r.* Colombia **60** 0.08S 74.18W
Caguas Puerto Rico **57** 18.08N 66.00W
Caha Mts. Rep. of Ire. **7** 51.44N 9.45W
Caherciveen Rep. of Ire. **7** 51.51N 10.14W
Cahir Rep. of Ire. **7** 52.23N 7.56W
Cahora Bassa Dam Mozambique **37** 15.36S 32.41E
Cahore Pt. Rep. of Ire. **7** 52.34N 6.12W
Cahors France **11** 44.28N 0.26E
Cahuapanas Peru **60** 5.15S 77.00W
Caianda Angola **36** 11.02S 23.29E
Caibarién Cuba **57** 22.31N 79.28W
Caicó Brazil **61** 6.25S 37.04W
Caicos Is. Turks & Caicos Is. **57** 21.30N 72.00W
Caird Coast *f.* Antarctica **64** 75.00S 20.00W
Cairngorms *mts.* U.K. **6** 57.04N 3.30W
Cairns Australia **44** 16.51S145.43E
Cairo *see* Al Qāhirah Egypt **32**
Cairo Ill. U.S.A. **53** 37.02N 89.02W
Cairo Montenotte Italy **9** 44.24N 8.16E
Caiwarro Australia **47** 28.38S144.45E
Cajamarca Peru **60** 7.09S 78.32W
Cajàzeiras Brazil **61** 6.52S 38.31W
Cajuru Brazil **59** 21.15S 47.18W
Čakovec Croatia **14** 46.23N 16.26E
Calabar Nigeria **38** 4.56N 8.22E
Calabozo Venezuela **60** 8.58N 67.28W
Calabria *d.* Italy **13** 39.00N 16.30E
Calafat Romania **15** 43.59N 22.57E
Calafate Argentina **63** 50.20S 72.16W
Calahorra Spain **10** 42.18N 1.58W
Calais France **3** 50.57N 1.52E
Calama Brazil **60** 8.03S 62.53W
Calama Chile **62** 22.30S 68.55W
Calamar Colombia **60** 10.15N 74.55W
Calamian Group *is.* Phil. **27** 12.00N120.05E
Cala Millor Spain **10** 39.35N 3.22E
Calamocha Spain **10** 40.54N 1.18W
Calapan Phil. **27** 13.23N121.10E
Călăraşi Romania **15** 44.11N 27.21E
Calatayud Spain **10** 41.21N 1.39W
Calau Germany **14** 51.45N 13.56E
Calbayog Phil. **27** 12.04N124.58E
Calcutta India **29** 22.35N 88.21E
Caldaro Italy **9** 46.25N 11.14E
Caldas Colombia **60** 6.05N 75.36W
Caldas da Rainha Portugal **10** 39.24N 9.08W
Caldera Chile **62** 27.04S 70.50W
Caldwell Idaho U.S.A. **54** 43.40N116.41W
Caldwell Ohio U.S.A. **55** 39.44N 81.32W
Caledon *r.* R.S.A. **39** 30.27S 26.12E
Caledon B. Australia **44** 12.58S136.52E
Calella Spain **10** 41.37N 2.40E
Calexico Mexico **54** 32.40N115.30W
Calf of Man *i.* I.o.M Europe **4** 54.03N 4.49W
Calgary Canada **50** 51.05N114.05W
Cali Colombia **60** 3.24N 76.30W
Caliente U.S.A. **54** 37.37N114.31W
California *d.* U.S.A. **54** 37.29N119.58W
California, G. of *see* California, Golfo de *g.* Mexico **56**
California, Golfo de *g.* Mexico **56** 28.00N112.00W
Calingasta Argentina **62** 31.15S 69.30W
Calingiri Australia **43** 31.07S116.27E
Callabonna, L. Australia **46** 29.47S140.07E
Callabonna Creek *r.* Australia **46** 29.37S140.08E
Callander U.K. **6** 56.15N 4.13W
Callao Peru **62** 12.05S 77.08W
Caloocan Phil. **27** 14.38N120.58E
Caloundra Australia **45** 26.47S153.08E
Caltagirone Italy **12** 37.14N 14.30E
Caltanissetta Italy **12** 37.30N 14.05E
Calulo Angola **36** 10.05S 14.56E
Calvados *d.* France **9** 49.10N 0.30W
Calvi France **11** 42.34N 8.44E
Calvinia R.S.A. **39** 31.29S 19.44E
Cam *r.* U.K. **5** 52.34N 0.21E
Camacupa Angola **36** 12.01S 17.22E
Camagüey Cuba **57** 21.25N 77.55W
Camagüey, Archipiélago de Cuba **57** 22.30N 78.00W
Camaiore Italy **9** 43.56N 10.18E
Camarès France **11** 43.49N 2.53E
Camaret-sur-Mer France **11** 48.16N 4.37W
Camarón, C. Honduras **57** 15.59N 85.00W
Camarones Argentina **63** 44.45S 65.40W
Camas U.S.A. **54** 45.35N122.24W
Cambay India **28** 22.18N 72.37E
Camberley U.K. **5** 51.21N 0.45W
Cambodia Asia **26** 12.00N105.00E
Camborne U.K. **5** 50.12N 5.19W
Cambrai Australia **46** 34.39S139.17E
Cambrai France **11** 50.10N 3.14E
Cambria U.S.A. **54** 35.34N121.05W
Cambrian Mts. U.K. **5** 52.33N 3.33W
Cambridge New Zealand **48** 37.53S175.29E
Cambridge U.K. **5** 52.13N 0.08E
Cambridge Idaho U.S.A. **54** 44.34N116.41W
Cambridge Mass. U.S.A. **55** 42.22N 71.06W
Cambridge Md. U.S.A. **55** 38.34N 76.04W
Cambridge Bay *town* Canada **50** 69.09N105.00W
Cambridge G. Australia **42** 15.00S128.05E
Cambridgeshire *d.* U.K. **5** 52.15N 0.05E
Cambundi-Catembo Angola **36** 10.09S 17.35E
Camden U.K. **5** 51.33N 0.10W
Camden N.J. U.S.A. **55** 39.57N 75.07W
Camelford U.K. **5** 50.37N 4.41W
Cameron Ariz. U.S.A. **54** 35.51N111.25W
Cameron Hills Canada **50** 59.48N118.00W
Cameron Mts. New Zealand **48** 45.50S167.00E
Cameroon Africa **34** 6.00N 12.30E
Cameroun, Mont *mtn.* Cameroon **38** 4.20N 9.05E
Cametá Brazil **61** 2.12S 49.30W
Camiri Bolivia **62** 20.03S 63.31W
Camocim Brazil **61** 2.55S 40.50W
Camooweal Australia **44** 19.55S138.07E
Camopi Guiana **61** 3.12N 52.15W
Campana Argentina **63** 34.10S 58.57W
Campana, Isla *i.* Chile **63** 48.25S 75.20W
Campania *d.* Italy **12** 41.00N 14.30E
Campbell, C. New Zealand **48** 41.45S174.15E
Campbellton Canada **55** 48.00N 66.41W
Campbell Town Australia **47** 41.55S147.30E
Campbelltown Australia **47** 34.04S150.49E
Campbeltown U.K. **6** 55.25N 5.36W
Campeche Mexico **56** 19.50N 90.30W
Campeche *d.* Mexico **56** 19.00N 90.00W
Campeche, Bahía de *b.* Mexico **56** 19.30N 94.00W
Campeche B. *see* Campeche, Bahía de *b.* Mexico **56**
Camperdown Australia **46** 38.15S143.14E
Campina Grande Brazil **61** 7.15S 35.50W
Campinas Brazil **59** 22.54S 47.06W
Campo Cameroon **38** 2.22N 9.50E
Campobasso Italy **12** 41.34N 14.39E
Campo Belo Brazil **59** 20.52S 45.16W
Campo Gallo Argentina **62** 26.35S 62.50W
Campo Grande Brazil **62** 20.24S 54.35W
Campo Maior Brazil **61** 4.50S 42.12W
Campo Maior Portugal **10** 39.01N 7.04W
Campos Brazil **59** 21.45S 41.18W
Campos Belos Brazil **61** 13.09S 47.03W
Campos do Jordão Brazil **59** 23.28S 46.10W
Cam Ranh Vietnam **26** 11.54N109.14E
Camrose Canada **50** 53.01N112.48W
Canada N. America **50** 60.00N105.00W
Cañada de Gómez Argentina **62** 32.49S 61.25W
Canadian *r.* U.S.A. **53** 35.20N 95.40W
Çanakkale Turkey **13** 40.09N 26.26E
Çanakkale Boğazi *str.* Turkey **13** 40.15N 26.30E
Canal du Midi France **11** 43.18N 2.00E
Cananea Mexico **56** 30.57N110.18W
Canarias, Islas *is.* Atlantic Oc. **34** 29.00N 15.00W
Canastra, Serra da *mts.* Brazil **59** 20.05S 46.30W
Canaveral, C. U.S.A. **53** 28.28N 80.28W
Canavieiras Brazil **61** 15.44S 38.58W
Canbelego Australia **47** 31.33S146.19E
Canberra Australia **47** 35.18S149.08E
Canby Calif. U.S.A. **54** 41.27N120.52W
Cancale France **9** 48.40N 1.50W
Cancon France **11** 44.32N 0.38E
Candé France **9** 47.34N 1.02W
Candeias Brazil **59** 20.44S 45.18W
Candeleda Spain **10** 40.10N 5.14W
Canelli Italy **9** 44.43N 8.17E
Canelones Uruguay **63** 34.32S 56.17W
Cañete Peru **60** 13.00S 76.30W
Cangas de Narcea Spain **10** 43.11N 6.33W
Canguçu Brazil **62** 31.24S 52.41W
Caniapiscau, Résr Canada **51** 54.10N 69.55W
Çankiri Turkey **30** 40.35N 33.37E
Canna *i.* U.K. **6** 57.03N 6.30W
Cannes France **11** 43.33N 7.00E
Cannich U.K. **6** 57.20N 4.45W
Cannock U.K. **5** 52.42N 2.02W
Cann River *town* Australia **47** 37.35S149.06E
Canõas Brazil **59** 29.55S 51.10W
Canonba Australia **47** 31.19S147.22E
Canon City U.S.A. **52** 38.27N105.14W
Canopus Australia **46** 33.30S140.57E
Canossa *site* Italy **9** 44.35N 10.27E
Canowindra Australia **47** 33.34S148.30E
Cantabria *d.* Spain **10** 43.10N 4.15W
Cantabria, Sierra de *mts.* Spain **10** 42.40N 2.30W
Cantábrica, Cordillera *mts.* Spain **10** 42.55N 5.10W
Cantagalo Brazil **59** 21.59S 42.22W
Cantaura Venezuela **60** 9.22N 64.24W
Canterbury *d.* New Zealand **48** 43.30S172.00E
Canterbury U.K. **5** 51.17N 1.05E
Canterbury Bight New Zealand **48** 44.15S172.00E
Can Tho Vietnam **26** 10.03N105.46E
Canton *see* Guangzhou China **25**
Canton Ohio U.S.A. **55** 40.48N 81.23W
Cantù Italy **9** 45.44N 9.08E
Cantua Creek *town* U.S.A. **54** 36.30N120.19W
Cañuelas Argentina **63** 35.03S 58.44W
Canumã *r.* Brazil **60** 3.55S 59.10W
Canutama Brazil **60** 6.32S 64.20W
Cany-Barville France **9** 49.47N 0.38E
Canyon Wyo. U.S.A. **54** 44.43N110.32W
Cao Bang Vietnam **26** 22.40N106.16E
Caorle Italy **9** 45.36N 12.53E
Capanema Brazil **61** 1.08S 47.07W
Cap-Chat Canada **55** 48.56N 66.53W
Cap-de-la-Madeleine *town* Canada **55** 46.22N 72.31W
Cape Barren I. Australia **45** 40.25S148.15E
Cape Borda Australia **46** 35.44S136.37E
Cape Breton I. Canada **51** 46.00N 61.00W
Cape Coast *town* Ghana **38** 5.10N 1.13W
Cape Cod B. U.S.A. **55** 41.50N 70.17W
Cape Crawford *town* Australia **44** 16.38S135.43E
Cape Dyer *town* Canada **51** 66.30N 61.20W
Cape Girardeau *town* U.S.A. **53** 37.19N 89.31W
Cape Johnson Depth Pacific Oc. **27** 10.20N127.20E
Capellen Lux. **8** 49.39N 5.59E
Cape Province *d.* R.S.A. **39** 31.30S 23.30E
Cape Town R.S.A. **39** 33.55S 18.27E
Cape York Pen. Australia **44** 12.40S142.20E
Cap-Haïtien *town* Haiti **57** 19.47N 72.17W
Capim *r.* Brazil **61** 1.40S 47.47W
Capoompeta, Mt. Australia **47** 29.22S151.59E
Cappoquin Rep. of Ire. **7** 52.09N 7.52W
Capraia *i.* Italy **12** 43.03N 9.50E
Caprera *i.* Italy **12** 41.48N 9.27E
Capri *i.* Italy **12** 40.33N 14.13E
Caprivi Strip *f.* Namibia **39** 17.50S 23.10E
Captains Flat Australia **47** 35.34S149.28E
Caqueta *r.* Colombia **60** 1.20S 70.50W
Caracal Romania **15** 44.08N 24.18E
Caracas Venezuela **60** 10.35N 66.56W
Caragabal Australia **47** 33.49S147.46E
Caraguatatuba Brazil **59** 23.39S 45.26W
Carandaí Brazil **59** 20.55S 43.46W
Carangola Brazil **59** 20.44S 42.03W
Caransebeş Romania **15** 45.25N 22.13E
Caratasca, Laguna de *b.* Honduras **57** 15.10N 84.00W
Caratinga Brazil **59** 19.50S 42.06W
Caravaca Spain **10** 38.06N 1.51W
Caravaggio Italy **9** 45.30N 9.38E
Caraveli Peru **60** 15.45S 73.25W
Carballo Spain **10** 43.13N 8.41W
Carbenyabba Creek *r.* Australia **46** 29.02S143.28E
Carbonara, Capo *c.* Italy **12** 39.06N 9.32E
Carbondale Penn. U.S.A. **55** 41.35N 75.30W
Carbonear Canada **51** 47.45N 53.13W
Carbonia Italy **12** 39.11N 8.32E
Carcassonne France **11** 43.13N 2.21E
Carcross Canada **50** 60.11N134.41W
Cárdenas Cuba **57** 23.02N 81.12W
Cárdenas Mexico **56** 22.00N 99.40W
Cardenete Spain **10** 39.46N 1.42W
Cardiff U.K. **5** 51.28N 3.11W
Cardigan U.K. **5** 52.06N 4.41W
Cardigan B. U.K. **5** 52.30N 4.30W
Cardona Spain **10** 41.56N 1.40E
Cardona Uruguay **63** 33.53S 57.23W
Cardwell Australia **44** 18.21S146.04E
Carei Romania **15** 47.42N 22.28E
Carentan France **9** 49.18N 1.14W
Carey U.S.A. **54** 43.18N113.56W
Carey, L. Australia **43** 29.05S122.15E
Carhaix France **11** 48.16N 3.35W
Carhué Argentina **63** 37.11S 62.45W
Caribbean Sea C. America **57** 15.00N 75.00W
Caribou U.S.A. **55** 46.52N 68.01W
Caribou Mts. Canada **50** 58.30N115.00W
Carignan France **9** 49.38N 5.10E
Carinda Australia **47** 30.29S147.45E
Carinhanha Brazil **61** 14.18S 43.47W
Carini Italy **12** 38.08N 13.11E
Caritianas Brazil **60** 9.25S 63.06W
Carleton Place Canada **55** 45.08N 76.09W
Carlingford Rep. of Ire. **7** 54.03N 6.12W
Carlingford Lough Rep. of Ire. **7** 54.03N 6.09W
Carlisle U.K. **4** 54.54N 2.55W
Carlos Reyles Uruguay **63** 33.03S 56.29W
Carlow Rep. of Ire. **7** 52.50N 6.46W
Carlow *d.* Rep. of Ire. **7** 52.43N 6.50W
Carlsbad Calif. U.S.A. **54** 33.10N117.21W
Carlsbad N.Mex. U.S.A. **52** 32.25N104.14W
Carmacks Canada **50** 62.04N136.21W
Carmagnola Italy **9** 44.51N 7.43E
Carmarthen U.K. **5** 51.52N 4.20W
Carmarthen B. U.K. **5** 52.30N 4.30W
Carmaux France **11** 44.03N 2.09E
Carmel Head U.K. **4** 53.24N 4.35W
Carmelo Uruguay **63** 34.00S 58.17W
Carmen Colombia **60** 9.46N 75.06W
Carmen Mexico **56** 18.38N 91.50W
Carmen Uruguay **63** 33.15S 56.01W
Carmen, Isla *i.* Mexico **56** 25.55N111.10W
Carmen, Isla del *i.* Mexico **56** 18.35N 91.40W
Carmen de Areco Argentina **63** 34.20S 59.50W
Carmen de Patagones Argentina **63** 40.48S 63.00W
Carmichael U.S.A. **54** 38.38N121.19W
Carmila Australia **44** 21.55S149.25E
Carmo Brazil **59** 21.56S 42.37W
Carmody, L. Australia **43** 32.27S119.20E
Carmona Spain **10** 37.28N 5.38W
Carnac France **11** 47.35N 3.05W
Carnarvon Australia **42** 24.53S113.40E
Carnarvon R.S.A. **39** 30.58S 22.07E
Carndonagh Rep. of Ire. **7** 55.15N 7.15W
Carnegie Australia **42** 25.43S122.59E
Carnegie, L. Australia **42** 26.15S123.00E
Carnew Rep. of Ire. **7** 52.43N 6.31W
Carniche, Alpi *mts.* Austria / Italy **12** 46.40N 12.48E
Car Nicobar *i.* India **29** 9.06N 92.57E
Carnot C.A.R. **36** 4.59N 15.56E
Carnot, C. Australia **46** 34.57S135.38E
Carnoustie U.K. **6** 56.30N 2.44W
Carnsore Pt. Rep. of Ire. **7** 52.10N 6.21W
Carolina Brazil **61** 7.20S 47.25W
Carolina Puerto Rico **57** 18.23N 65.57W
Carolina R.S.A. **39** 26.04S 30.07E
Caroline Is. Pacific Oc. **40** 7.50N145.00E
Caroní *r.* Venezuela **60** 8.20N 62.42W
Carora Venezuela **60** 10.12N 70.07W
Carpathians *mts.* Europe **15** 48.45N 23.45E
Carpaţii Meridionali *mts.* Romania **15** 45.35N 24.40E
Carpentaria, G. of Australia **44** 14.00S139.00E
Carpentras France **11** 44.03N 5.03E
Carpi Italy **9** 44.47N 10.53E
Carpio Spain **10** 41.13N 5.07W
Carquefou France **9** 47.18N 1.30W
Carra, Lough Rep. of Ire. **7** 53.41N 9.15W
Carrara Italy **9** 44.04N 10.06E
Carrathool Australia **47** 34.25S145.24E
Carrauntoohil *mtn.* Rep. of Ire. **7** 52.00N 9.45W
Carrickfergus U.K. **7** 54.43N 5.49W
Carrickmacross Rep. of Ire. **7** 53.58N 6.43W
Carrick-on-Shannon Rep. of Ire. **7** 53.57N 8.06W
Carrick-on-Suir Rep. of Ire. **7** 52.21N 7.26W
Carrieton Australia **46** 32.28S138.34E
Carrowmore Lough Rep. of Ire. **7** 54.11N 9.47W
Carrum Australia **47** 38.05S145.08E
Çarşamba Turkey **30** 41.13N 36.43E
Çarşamba *r.* Turkey **30** 37.52N 31.48E
Carson City U.S.A. **54** 39.10N119.46W
Carstairs U.K. **6** 55.42N 3.41W
Cartagena Colombia **60** 10.24N 75.33W
Cartagena Spain **10** 37.36N 0.59W
Cartago Colombia **60** 4.45N 75.55W
Cartago Costa Rica **57** 9.50N 83.52W
Carter U.S.A. **54** 41.27N110.25W
Carteret France **9** 49.22N 1.48W
Carterton New Zealand **48** 41.01S175.31E
Cartwright Canada **51** 53.42N 57.01W
Caruarú Brazil **61** 8.15S 35.55W
Carúpano Venezuela **60** 10.39N 63.14W
Carvin France **8** 50.30N 2.58E
Carvoeiro Brazil **60** 1.24S 61.59W
Caryapundy Swamp Australia **46** 29.00S142.36E
Casablanca Morocco **34** 33.39N 7.35W
Casa Branca Brazil **59** 21.45S 47.06W
Casa Grande U.S.A. **54** 32.53N111.45W
Casale Italy **9** 45.08N 8.27E
Casarano Italy **13** 40.00N 18.10E
Cascade Idaho U.S.A. **54** 44.31N116.02W
Cascade Mont. U.S.A. **54** 47.16N111.42W
Cascade Pt. New Zealand **48** 44.01S168.22E
Cascade Range *mts.* U.S.A. **52** 46.15N121.00W
Caserta Italy **12** 41.06N 14.21E
Cashel Tipperary Rep. of Ire. **7** 52.31N 7.54W
Casilda Argentina **63** 33.03S 61.10W
Casimiro de Abreu Brazil **59** 22.28S 42.12W
Casino Australia **47** 28.50S153.02E
Casma Peru **60** 9.30S 78.20W
Caspe Spain **10** 41.14N 0.03W
Casper U.S.A. **54** 42.51N106.19W
Caspian Depression *f.* Kazakhstan / Russian Fed. **19** 47.00N 48.00E
Caspian Sea Europe / Asia **19** 42.00N 51.00E
Cassano allo Ionio Italy **13** 39.47N 16.20E
Cass City U.S.A. **55** 43.37N 83.11W
Cassilis Australia **47** 32.01S149.59E
Castaños Mexico **56** 26.48N101.26W
Castelfranco Veneto Italy **9** 45.40N 11.55E
Casteljaloux France **11** 44.19N 0.06W
Castell' Arquato Italy **9** 44.51N 9.52E
Castelli Argentina **63** 36.07S 57.50W
Castellón Spain **10** 39.59N 0.03W
Castelmassa Italy **9** 45.01N 11.18E
Castelnovo ne'Monti Italy **9** 44.26N 10.24E
Castelnuovo di Garfagnana Italy **9** 44.06N 10.24E
Castelo Brazil **59** 20.33S 41.14W
Castelo Branco Portugal **10** 39.50N 7.30W
Castel San Giovanni Italy **9** 45.04N 9.26E
Castelvetrano Italy **12** 37.41N 12.47E
Casterton Australia **46** 37.35S141.25E
Castets France **11** 43.53N 1.09W
Castilla Peru **60** 5.16S 80.36W
Castilla la Mancha *d.* Spain **10** 40.00N 3.45W
Castilla y León *d.* Spain **10** 41.50N 4.15W
Castilletes Colombia **60** 11.55N 71.20W
Castlebar Rep. of Ire. **7** 53.52N 9.19W
Castleblayney Rep. of Ire. **7** 54.08N 6.46W
Castle Douglas U.K. **6** 54.56N 3.56W
Castleford U.K. **4** 53.43N 1.21W
Castlegate U.S.A. **54** 39.44N110.52W
Castleisland Rep. of Ire. **7** 52.13N 9.28W
Castlemaine Australia **46** 37.05S144.19E
Castlerea Rep. of Ire. **7** 53.45N 8.30W
Castlereagh *r.* Australia **47** 30.12S147.32E
Castle Rock *town* Wash. U.S.A. **54** 46.17N122.54W
Castletown I.o.M Europe **4** 54.04N 4.38W
Castletownshend Rep. of Ire. **7** 51.32N 9.12W
Castres France **11** 43.36N 2.14E
Castries St. Lucia **57** 14.01N 60.59W
Castro Chile **63** 42.30S 73.46W
Castro del Río Spain **10** 37.41N 4.29W
Casula Mozambique **37** 15.26S 33.32E
Cataguases Brazil **59** 21.23S 42.39W
Çatalca Turkey **13** 41.09N 28.29E
Cataluña *d.* Spain **10** 42.00N 2.00E
Catamarca Argentina **62** 28.30S 65.45W
Catamarca *d.* Argentina **62** 27.45S 67.00W
Catanduanes *i.* Phil. **27** 13.45N124.20E
Catanduva Brazil **59** 21.03S 49.00W
Catania Italy **12** 37.31N 15.05E
Catanzaro Italy **13** 38.55N 16.35E
Catarman Phil. **27** 12.28N124.50E
Catbalogan Phil. **27** 11.46N124.55E
Catete Angola **36** 9.09S 13.40E
Cathcart Australia **47** 36.49S149.25E
Cathcart R.S.A. **39** 32.17S 27.08E
Cat I. Bahamas **57** 24.30N 75.30W
Catoche, C. Mexico **57** 21.38N 87.08W
Catonsville U.S.A. **55** 39.16N 76.44W
Catriló Argentina **63** 36.23S 63.24W
Catterick U.K. **4** 54.23N 1.38W
Cattolica Italy **9** 43.58N 12.44E
Catuane Mozambique **39** 26.49S 32.17E
Cauca *r.* Colombia **60** 8.57N 74.30W
Caucasus *mts.* Europe **19** 43.00N 44.00E
Caudry France **11** 50.07N 3.22E
Cauquenes Chile **63** 35.58S 72.21W
Caura *r.* Venezuela **60** 7.38N 64.53W
Cavaillon France **11** 43.50N 5.02E
Cavalese Italy **9** 46.17N 11.26E
Cavan Rep. of Ire. **7** 54.00N 7.22W
Cavan *d.* Rep. of Ire. **7** 53.58N 7.10W
Cavarzere Italy **9** 45.08N 12.05E
Caviana, Ilha *i.* Brazil **61** 0.02N 50.00W
Cawndilla L. Australia **46** 32.30S142.18E
Caxambu Brazil **59** 21.59S 44.54W
Caxias Brazil **61** 4.53S 43.20W
Caxias do Sul Brazil **59** 29.14S 51.10W
Caxito Angola **36** 8.32S 13.38E
Cayambe Ecuador **60** 0.03N 78.08W
Cayenne Guiana **61** 4.55N 52.18W
Cayman Brac *i.* Cayman Is. **57** 19.44N 79.48W
Cayman Is. C. America **57** 19.00N 81.00W
Cazères France **11** 43.13N 1.05E
Ceara *d.* Brazil **61** 4.50S 39.00W
Cebollera, Sierra de *mts.* Spain **10** 41.58N 2.30W
Cebu Phil. **27** 10.17N123.56E
Cebu *i.* Phil. **27** 10.15N123.45E
Cecina Italy **12** 43.18N 10.30E
Cedar City U.S.A. **52** 37.40N113.04W
Cedar Falls *town* U.S.A. **53** 42.34N 92.26W
Cedar Rapids *town* U.S.A. **53** 41.59N 91.31W
Cedros, Isla *i.* Mexico **56** 28.10N115.15W
Ceduna Australia **46** 32.07S133.42E
Ceerigaabo Somali Rep. **35** 10.40N 47.20E
Cefalù Italy **12** 38.01N 14.03E
Cegléd Hungary **15** 47.10N 19.48E
Celaya Mexico **56** 20.32N100.48W
Celebes *i.* *see* Sulawesi *i.* Indonesia **27**
Celebes Sea Indonesia **27** 3.00N122.00E
Celina U.S.A. **55** 40.34N 84.35W
Celje Slovenia **12** 46.15N 15.16E
Celle Germany **14** 52.37N 10.05E
Celtic Sea Europe **3** 50.00N 8.00W
Cemaes Head U.K. **5** 52.08N 4.42W
Cenderawasih, Teluk *b.* Indonesia **27** 2.20S135.50E
Ceno *r.* Italy **9** 44.41N 10.05E
Cento Italy **9** 44.43N 11.17E
Central *d.* Botswana **39** 21.45S 26.15E
Central *d.* Ghana **38** 5.30N 1.10W
Central *d.* Kenya **37** 0.30S 37.00E
Central *d.* U.K. **6** 56.10N 4.20W
Central *d.* Zambia **37** 14.30S 29.30E
Central, Cordillera *mts.* Bolivia **62** 18.30S 65.00W
Central, Cordillera *mts.* Colombia **60** 5.00N 75.20W
Central African Republic Africa **34** 6.30N 20.00E
Central I. Kenya **37** 3.30N 36.02E
Centralia Ill. U.S.A. **53** 38.32N 89.08W
Centralia Wash. U.S.A. **54** 46.43N122.58W
Central Makran Range *mts.* Pakistan **28** 26.40N 64.30E
Central Siberian Plateau *see* Sredne Sibirskoye Ploskogor'ye Russian Fed. **21**
Centre *d.* Burkina **38** 11.50N 1.10W
Centre *d.* France **11** 47.40N 1.45E
Centre Est *d.* Burkina **38** 11.20N 0.10W
Centre Nord *d.* Burkina **38** 13.30N 1.00W
Centre Ouest *d.* Burkina **38** 12.00N 2.20W
Ceram *i.* *see* Seram *i.* Indonesia **27**
Ceram Sea *see* Seram, Laut *sea* Pacific Oc. **27**
Ceres U.S.A. **54** 37.35N120.57W
Ceresole Reale Italy **9** 45.26N 7.15E
Ceretè Colombia **60** 8.54N 75.51W
Cerignola Italy **12** 41.17N 15.53E
Cérilly France **11** 46.37N 2.50E
Cerisiers France **9** 48.08N 3.29E
Cerknica Slovenia **12** 45.48N 14.22E
Cernavodă Romania **15** 44.20N 28.02E

Cerritos Mexico **56** 22.26N100.17W
Cerro de Pasco Peru **60** 10.43S 76.15W
Cervera Lérida Spain **10** 41.40N 1.16E
Cervia Italy **9** 44.15N 12.22E
Cervignano del Friuli Italy **9** 45.49N 13.20E
Cesena Italy **9** 44.08N 12.15E
Cesenatico Italy **9** 44.12N 12.24E
Cēsis Latvia **18** 57.18N 25.18E
České Budějovice Czech Republic **14** 49.00N 14.30E
Český Krumlov Czech Republic **14** 48.49N 14.19E
Cessnock Australia **47** 32.51S151.21E
Cetinje Yugo. **13** 42.24N 18.55E
Ceuta Spain **10** 35.53N 5.19W
Ceva Italy **9** 44.23N 8.01E
Cévennes *mts.* France **11** 44.25N 4.05E
Ceyhan Turkey **30** 37.02N 35.48E
Ceyhan *r.* Turkey **30** 36.54N 34.58E
Chablis France **9** 47.47N 3.48E
Chacabuco Argentina **63** 34.38S 60.29W
Chachani *mtn.* Peru **60** 16.12S 71.32W
Chachapoyas Peru **60** 6.13S 77.54W
Chaco *d.* Argentina **62** 26.30S 60.00W
Chad Africa **34** 13.00N 19.00E
Chad, L. Africa **38** 13.30N 14.00E
Chadron U.S.A. **52** 42.50N103.02W
Chafe Nigeria **38** 11.56N 6.55E
Chagda Russian Fed. **21** 58.44N130.38E
Chahār Borjak Afghan. **28** 30.17N 62.03E
Chajarí Argentina **63** 30.45S 57.59W
Chake Chake Tanzania **37** 5.13S 39.46E
Chakhânsūr Afghan. **31** 31.10N 62.02E
Chala Peru **60** 15.48S 74.20W
Chaleur B. Canada **55** 48.00N 65.45W
Chalhuanca Peru **60** 14.20S 73.10W
Challans France **11** 46.51N 1.52W
Challenger Depth Pacific Oc. **27** 11.19N142.15E
Challis U.S.A. **54** 44.30N114.14W
Chalonnes-sur-Loire France **9** 47.21N 0.46W
Châlons-sur-Marne France **9** 48.58N 4.22E
Chalon-sur-Saône France **11** 46.47N 4.51E
Cham Germany **14** 49.13N 12.41E
Chama Zambia **37** 11.09S 33.10E
Chambal *r.* India **29** 26.30N 79.20E
Chambersburg U.S.A. **55** 39.56N 77.39W
Chambéry France **11** 45.34N 5.55E
Chambeshi Zambia **37** 10.57S 31.04E
Chambeshi *r.* Zambia **37** 11.15S 30.37E
Chambly France **9** 49.10N 2.15E
Chamical Argentina **62** 30.22S 66.19W
Chamonix France **11** 45.55N 6.52E
Champagne-Ardenne *d.* France **8** 49.42N 4.30E
Champaign U.S.A. **53** 40.07N 88.14W
Champéry Switz. **9** 46.10N 6.52E
Champlain, L. U.S.A. **55** 44.45N 73.15W
Champotón Mexico **56** 19.21N 90.43W
Chañaral Chile **62** 26.21S 70.37W
Chandeleur Is. U.S.A. **53** 29.50N 88.50W
Chandīgarh India **28** 30.44N 76.54E
Chāndpur Bangla. **29** 22.08N 91.55E
Chandrapur India **29** 19.58N 79.21E
Chānf Iran **31** 26.40N 60.31E
Changchun China **25** 43.50N125.20E
Changde China **25** 29.03N111.35E
Chang Jiang *r.* China **25** 31.40N121.15E
Changjin N. Korea **25** 40.21N127.20E
Changning China **25** 26.24N112.24E
Changping China **25** 40.12N116.12E
Changsha China **25** 28.10N113.00E
Changting China **25** 25.47N116.17E
Changzhi China **25** 36.09N113.12E
Changzhou China **25** 31.45N119.57E
Channel Is. Europe **5** 49.28N 2.13W
Channel Is. U.S.A. **54** 34.00N120.00W
Channel-Port-aux-Basques *town* Canada **51** 47.35N 59.10W
Channing Mich. U.S.A. **55** 46.08N 88.06W
Chantada Spain **10** 42.36N 7.46W
Chanthaburi Thailand **29** 12.38N102.12E
Chantilly France **9** 49.12N 2.28E
Chao'an China **25** 23.43N116.35E
Chaonde Mozambique **37** 13.43S 40.31E
Chao Phraya *r.* Thailand **29** 13.30N100.25E
Chaoyang Guangdong China **25** 23.17N116.33E
Chapada das Mangabeiras *mts.* Brazil **61** 10.00S 46.30W
Chapada Diamantina Brazil **59** 13.30S 42.30W
Chapala, Lago de *l.* Mexico **56** 20.00N103.00W
Chapayevo Kazakhstan **19** 50.12N 51.09E
Chapayevsk Russian Fed. **18** 52.58N 49.44E
Chapelle-d'Angillon France **9** 47.22N 2.26E
Chapicuy Uruguay **63** 31.39S 57.54W
Chapleau Canada **55** 47.50N 83.24W
Chāpra India **29** 25.46N 84.45E
Chaqui Bolivia **62** 19.36S 65.32W
Characot I. Antarctica **64** 70.00S 75.00W
Charcas Mexico **56** 23.08N101.07W
Chard U.K. **5** 50.52N 2.59W
Chardzhou India **29** 26.52N 92.46E
Chardzhou Turkmenistan **31** 39.09N 63.34E
Charente *r.* France **11** 45.57N 1.00W
Chari *r.* Chad **38** 13.00N 14.30E
Chārīkār Afghan. **28** 35.02N 69.13E
Charing U.K. **5** 51.12N 0.49E
Charleroi Belgium **8** 50.25N 4.27E
Charlesbourg Canada **55** 46.53N 71.16W
Charles Pt. Australia **42** 12.23S130.37E
Charleston S.C. U.S.A. **53** 32.48N 79.58W
Charleston W.Va. U.S.A. **55** 38.23N 81.40W
Charlestown Rep. of Ire. **7** 53.57N 8.48W
Charlestown Ind. U.S.A. **55** 38.28N 85.40W
Charleville Australia **44** 26.25S146.13E
Charleville-Mézières France **9** 49.46N 4.43E
Charlieu France **11** 46.10N 4.10E
Charlotte N.C. U.S.A. **53** 35.05N 80.50W
Charlottesville U.S.A. **53** 38.02N 78.29W
Charlottetown Canada **51** 46.14N 63.09W
Charlton Australia **46** 36.18S143.27E
Charly-sur-Marne France **9** 48.58N 3.17E
Charolles France **11** 46.26N 4.17E
Charters Towers Australia **44** 20.05S146.16E
Chartres France **9** 48.27N 1.30E
Chascomús Argentina **63** 35.35S 58.00W
Châteaubriant France **9** 47.43N 1.22W
Château-du-Loir France **9** 47.42N 0.25E
Châteaudun France **9** 48.04N 1.20E
Château Gontier France **9** 47.50N 0.42W
Château Landon France **9** 48.09N 2.42E
Château-la-Vallière France **9** 47.33N 0.19E
Châteauneuf-en-Thymerais France **9** 48.35N 1.15E
Châteauneuf-sur-Loire France **9** 47.52N 2.14E
Chateauneuf-sur-Sarthe France **9** 47.41N 0.30W
Château-Porcien France **9** 49.32N 4.15E
Château Renault France **9** 47.35N 0.55E
Châteauroux France **11** 46.49N 1.41E
Château-Thierry France **9** 49.03N 3.24E
Châtelet Belgium **8** 50.24N 4.32E
Châtellerault France **11** 46.49N 0.33E
Chatham N.B. Canada **55** 47.02N 65.30W
Chatham Ont. Canada **55** 42.24N 82.11W
Chatham U.K. **5** 51.23N 0.32E
Chatham Is. Pacific Oc. **40** 44.00S176.35W
Châtillon Italy **9** 45.45N 7.37E
Châtillon-Coligny France **9** 47.50N 2.51E
Châtillon-sur-Seine France **9** 47.52N 4.35E
Chattahoochee *r.* U.S.A. **53** 30.52N 84.57W
Chattanooga U.S.A. **53** 35.01N 85.18W
Chatteris U.K. **5** 52.27N 0.03E
Chaulnes France **9** 49.49N 2.48E
Chaumont France **11** 48.07N 5.08E
Chaumont-en-Vexin France **9** 49.16N 1.53E
Chauny France **9** 49.37N 3.13E
Chausy Belorussia **15** 53.49N 30.57E
Chavanges France **9** 48.31N 4.34E
Chaves Brazil **61** 0.10S 49.55W
Chaves Portugal **10** 41.44N 7.28W
Chawang Thailand **29** 8.25N 99.32E
Cheb Czech Republic **14** 50.04N 12.20E
Cheboksary Russian Fed. **18** 56.08N 47.12E
Cheboygan U.S.A. **55** 45.40N 84.28W
Chebsara Russian Fed. **18** 59.14N 38.59E
Chech, Erg *des.* Africa **34** 25.00N 2.15W
Chechersk Belorussia **15** 52.54N 30.54E
Checiny Poland **15** 50.48N 20.28E
Chegdomyn Russian Fed. **21** 51.09N133.01E
Chegga *well* Mauritania **34** 25.30N 5.46W
Chegutu Zimbabwe **39** 18.09S 30.07E
Chehalis U.S.A. **54** 46.40N122.58W
Cheiron, Cime du *mtn.* France **9** 43.49N 6.58E
Cheju S. Korea **25** 33.31N126.29E
Cheju do *i.* S. Korea **25** 33.20N126.30E
Cheleken Turkmenistan **31** 39.26N 53.11E
Chelforó Argentina **63** 39.04S 66.33W
Chelkar Kazakhstan **20** 47.48N 59.39E
Chelles France **9** 48.53N 2.36E
Chełm Poland **15** 51.10N 23.28E
Chelmsford U.K. **5** 51.44N 0.28E
Chełmża Poland **15** 53.12N 18.37E
Cheltenham U.K. **5** 51.53N 2.07W
Chelva Spain **10** 39.45N 1.00W
Chelyabinsk Russian Fed. **20** 55.10N 61.25E
Chelyuskin, Mys *c.* Russian Fed. **21** 77.20N106.00E
Chemainus Canada **54** 48.55N123.48W
Chemba Mozambique **37** 17.11S 34.53E
Chemnitz Germany **14** 50.50N 12.55E
Chemult U.S.A. **54** 43.13N121.47W
Chën, Gora *mtn.* Russian Fed. **21** 65.30N141.20E
Chenāb *r.* Asia **28** 29.26N 71.09E
Cheney U.S.A. **54** 47.29N117.34W
Chengde China **25** 40.48N118.06E
Chengdu China **29** 30.37N104.06E
Chen Xian China **25** 25.48N113.02E
Chepen Peru **60** 7.15S 79.20W
Chepstow U.K. **5** 51.38N 2.40W
Cher *r.* France **9** 47.12N 2.04E
Cherbourg France **9** 49.38N 1.37W
Cherdyn Russian Fed. **18** 60.25N 55.22E
Cheremkhovo Russian Fed. **21** 53.08N103.01E
Cherepovets Russian Fed. **18** 59.05N 37.55E
Cherikov Belorussia **15** 53.35N 31.23E
Cherkassy Ukraine **19** 49.27N 32.04E
Cherkessk Russian Fed. **19** 44.14N 42.05E
Cherkovitsa Bulgaria **13** 43.41N 24.49E
Cherlak Russian Fed. **20** 54.10N 74.52E
Chernigov Ukraine **15** 51.30N 31.18E
Chernikovsk Russian Fed. **18** 54.51N 56.06E
Chernobyl Ukraine **15** 51.17N 30.15E
Chernovtsy Ukraine **15** 48.19N 25.52E
Chernyakhov Ukraine **15** 50.30N 28.38E
Chernyakhovsk Russian Fed. **17** 54.38N 21.49E
Cherquenco Chile **63** 38.41S 72.00W
Cherry Creek *town* Nev. U.S.A. **54** 39.54N113.53W
Cherskogo, Khrebet *mts.* Russian Fed. **21** 65.50N143.00E
Chertkovo Russian Fed. **19** 49.22N 40.12E
Chertsey U.K. **5** 51.23N 0.27W
Chervonograd Ukraine **15** 50.25N 24.10E
Cherwell *r.* U.K. **5** 51.44N 1.15W
Chesapeake B. U.S.A. **53** 38.40N 76.25W
Chesham U.K. **5** 51.43N 0.38W
Cheshire *d.* U.K. **4** 53.14N 2.30W
Chëshskaya Guba *g.* Russian Fed. **18** 67.20N 46.30E
Chesil Beach *f.* U.K. **5** 50.37N 2.33W
Chester U.K. **4** 53.12N 2.53W
Chester Mont. U.S.A. **54** 48.31N110.58W
Chester Penn. U.S.A. **55** 39.51N 75.21W
Chesterfield U.K. **4** 53.14N 1.26W
Chesterfield Inlet *town* Canada **51** 63.00N 91.00W
Chesuncook L. U.S.A. **55** 46.00N 69.20W
Chetumal Mexico **57** 18.30N 88.17W
Chetumal B. Mexico **57** 18.30N 88.00W
Cheviot New Zealand **48** 42.49S173.16E
Cheviot U.S.A. **55** 39.10N 84.32W
Cheyenne *r.* U.S.A. **52** 44.40N101.15W
Cheyenne Wyo. U.S.A. **52** 41.08N104.49W
Cheyne B. Australia **43** 34.35S118.50E
Chhindwāra India **29** 22.04N 78.58E
Chiang Mai Thailand **29** 18.48N 98.59E
Chiapas *d.* Mexico **56** 16.30N 93.00W
Chiari Italy **9** 45.32N 9.56E
Chiavari Italy **9** 44.19N 9.19E
Chiavenna Italy **9** 46.19N 9.24E
Chiba Japan **23** 35.36N140.07E
Chiba *d.* Japan **23** 35.10N140.00E
Chibemba Angola **36** 15.43S 14.07E
Chibougamau Canada **55** 49.53N 74.24W
Chibougamau Lac *l.* Canada **55** 49.50N 74.19W
Chibougamau Prov. Park Canada **55** 49.24N 73.48W
Chibuk Nigeria **38** 10.52N 12.50E
Chibuto Mozambique **39** 24.41S 33.32E
Chicago U.S.A. **53** 41.50N 87.45W
Chichagof I. U.S.A. **50** 57.55N135.45W
Chichester U.K. **5** 50.50N 0.47W
Chichibu Japan **23** 35.59N139.05E
Chickasha U.S.A. **52** 35.03N 97.57W
Chiclana Spain **10** 36.26N 6.09W
Chiclayo Peru **60** 6.47S 79.47W
Chico *r.* Chubut Argentina **63** 43.45S 66.10W
Chico *r.* Santa Cruz Argentina **63** 50.03W 68.35W
Chico U.S.A. **54** 39.44N121.50W
Chicomo Mozambique **39** 24.33S 34.11E
Chicoutimi-Jonquière Canada **55** 48.26N 71.04W
Chicualacuala Mozambique **39** 22.06S 31.42E
Chidambaram India **29** 11.24N 79.42E
Chidenguele Mozambique **39** 24.54S 34.13E
Chidley, C. Canada **51** 60.30N 65.00W
Chiemsee *l.* Germany **14** 47.55N 12.30E
Chiengi Zambia **37** 8.42S 29.07E
Chieri Italy **9** 45.01N 7.49E
Chieti Italy **12** 42.22N 14.12E
Chifeng China **25** 41.17N118.56E
Chigasaki Japan **23** 35.19N139.24E
Chiguana Bolivia **62** 21.05S 67.58W
Chigubo Mozambique **39** 22.38S 33.18E
Chihuahua Mexico **56** 28.38N106.05W
Chihuahua *d.* Mexico **56** 28.40N106.00W
Chiili Kazakhstan **20** 44.10N 66.37E
Chikumbi Zambia **37** 15.14S 28.21E
Chikwawa Malaŵi **37** 16.00S 34.54E
Chīl *r.* Iran **31** 25.12N 61.30E
Chilapa Mexico **56** 17.38N 99.11W
Chilcoot U.S.A. **54** 39.49N120.08W
Childers Australia **44** 25.14S152.17E
Chile S. America **62** 32.30S 71.00W
Chile Chico Chile **63** 46.33S 71.44W
Chilko L. Canada **50** 51.20N124.05W
Chillagoe Australia **44** 17.09S144.32E
Chillán Chile **63** 36.36S 72.07W
Chillicothe Ohio U.S.A. **55** 39.20N 82.59W
Chilliwack Canada **54** 49.10N122.00W
Chiloé, Isla de *i.* Chile **63** 43.00S 73.00W
Chilonga Zambia **37** 12.02S 31.17E
Chilpancingo Mexico **56** 17.33N 99.30W
Chiltern Australia **47** 36.11S146.36E
Chiltern Hills U.K. **5** 51.40N 0.53W
Chilumba Malaŵi **37** 10.25S 34.18E
Chilwa, L. Malaŵi **37** 15.15S 35.45E
Chimanimani Zimbabwe **39** 19.48S 32.52E
Chimay Belgium **8** 50.03N 4.20E
Chimbas Argentina **62** 31.28S 68.30W
Chimbay Uzbekistan **20** 42.56N 59.46E
Chimborazo *mtn.* Ecuador **60** 1.29S 78.52W
Chimbote Peru **60** 9.04S 78.34W
Chimishliya Moldavia **15** 46.30N 28.50E
Chimkent Kazakhstan **24** 42.16N 69.05E
Chimoio Mozambique **39** 19.04S 33.29E
China Asia **24** 33.00N103.00E
China Lake *town* U.S.A. **54** 35.46N117.39W
Chinandega Nicaragua **57** 12.35N 87.10W
Chinati Peak U.S.A. **52** 29.57N104.29W
Chincha Alta Peru **60** 13.25S 76.07W
Chinchilla Australia **45** 26.44S150.39E
Chinchón Spain **10** 40.09N 3.26W
Chindio Mozambique **37** 17.46S 35.23E
Chindwin *r.* Burma **24** 21.30N 95.12E
Chinga Mozambique **37** 15.14S 38.40E
Chingleput India **29** 12.42N 79.59E
Chingola Zambia **37** 12.29S 27.53E
Chingombe Zambia **37** 14.25S 29.56E
Chin Hills Burma **29** 22.40N 93.30E
Chinhoyi Zimbabwe **39** 17.22S 30.10E
Chinkapook Australia **46** 35.11S142.57E
Chinle U.S.A. **54** 36.09N109.33W
Chinon France **11** 47.10N 0.15E
Chinook U.S.A. **54** 48.35N109.14W
Chino Valley *town* U.S.A. **54** 34.45N112.27W
Chinsali Zambia **37** 10.33S 32.05E
Chintheche Malaŵi **37** 11.50S 34.13E
Chiny Belgium **8** 49.45N 5.20E
Chiôco Mozambique **37** 16.27S 32.49E
Chioggia Italy **9** 45.13N 12.17E
Chipata Zambia **37** 13.37S 32.40E
Chipera Mozambique **37** 15.20S 32.35E
Chipie *r.* Canada **55** 51.30N 83.16W
Chipinge Zimbabwe **39** 20.12S 32.38E
Chippenham U.K. **5** 51.27N 2.07W
Chipping Norton U.K. **5** 51.56N 1.32W
Chiquian Peru **60** 10.10S 77.00W
Chiquinquirá Colombia **60** 5.37N 73.50W
Chir *r.* Russian Fed. **19** 48.34N 42.53E
Chirchik Uzbekistan **24** 41.28N 69.31E
Chiredzi Zimbabwe **39** 21.03S 31.39E
Chiredzi *r.* Zimbabwe **39** 21.10S 31.50E
Chiriquí *mtn.* Panama **57** 8.49N 82.38W
Chiriquí, Laguna de *b.* Panama **57** 9.00N 82.00W
Chiromo Malaŵi **37** 16.28S 35.10E
Chirripó *mtn.* Costa Rica **57** 9.31N 83.30W
Chirundu Zimbabwe **37** 16.04S 28.51E
Chisamba Zambia **37** 14.58S 28.23E
Chisasibi Canada **51** 53.50N 79.01W
Chişinau *see* Kishinev Moldavia **15**
Chisone *r.* Italy **9** 44.49N 7.25E
Chistopol Russian Fed. **18** 55.25N 50.38E
Chita Russian Fed. **25** 52.03N113.35E
Chitipa Malaŵi **37** 9.41S 33.19E
Chitorgarh India **28** 24.53N 74.38E
Chitrāl Pakistan **28** 35.52N 71.58E
Chittagong Bangla. **29** 22.20N 91.48E
Chittoor India **29** 13.13N 79.06E
Chiuta, L. Malaŵi / Mozambique **37** 14.45S 35.50E
Chivasso Italy **9** 45.11N 7.53E
Chivhu Zimbabwe **39** 19.01S 30.53E
Chivilcoy Argentina **63** 34.52S 60.02W
Chiwanda Tanzania **37** 11.21S 34.55E
Chobe *d.* Botswana **39** 18.30S 25.15E
Chobe *r.* Namibia / Botswana **39** 17.48S 25.12E
Chobe Swamp *f.* Namibia **39** 18.20S 23.40E
Chocolate Mts. U.S.A. **54** 33.20N115.15W
Chocope Peru **60** 7.47S 79.12W
Choele-Choel Argentina **63** 39.15S 65.30W
Chōfu Japan **23** 35.39N139.33E
Choix Mexico **56** 26.43N108.17W
Chojnice Poland **15** 53.42N 17.32E
Cholet France **11** 47.04N 0.53W
Cholon Vietnam **26** 10.45N106.39E
Choluteca Honduras **57** 13.16N 87.11W
Choma Zambia **36** 16.51S 27.04E
Chomutov Czech Republic **14** 50.28N 13.25E
Chon Buri Thailand **29** 13.21N101.01E
Chone Ecuador **60** 0.44S 80.04W
Ch'ŏngjin N. Korea **25** 41.55N129.50E
Ch'ŏngju S. Korea **25** 36.39N127.31E
Chongqing China **29** 29.31N106.35E
Chŏnju S. Korea **25** 35.50N127.05E
Chonos, Archipelago de los *is.* Chile **63** 45.00S 74.00W
Chorley U.K. **4** 53.39N 2.39W
Chorokh *r.* Georgia **19** 41.36N 41.35E
Chortkov Ukraine **15** 49.01N 25.42E
Chorzów Poland **15** 50.19N 18.56E
Chosica Peru **60** 11.55S 76.38W
Chos Malal Argentina **63** 37.20S 70.15W
Choszczno Poland **14** 53.10N 15.26E
Choteau U.S.A. **54** 47.49N112.11W
Chott Djerid *f.* Tunisia **34** 33.30N 8.30E
Chott ech Chergui *f.* Algeria **34** 34.00N 0.30E
Chott Melrhir *f.* Algeria **34** 34.15N 7.00E
Choum Mauritania **34** 21.10N 13.00W
Chowchilla U.S.A. **54** 37.07N120.16W
Christchurch New Zealand **48** 43.33S172.40E
Christchurch U.K. **5** 50.44N 1.47W
Christianshåb Greenland **51** 68.50N 51.00W
Christmas Creek *town* Australia **42** 18.55S125.56E
Christmas I. Indian Oc. **26** 10.30S105.40E
Chrudim Czech Republic **14** 49.57N 15.48E
Chu *r.* Kazakhstan **24** 42.30N 76.10E
Chubbuck U.S.A. **54** 42.55N112.20W
Chūbu *d.* Japan **23** 35.25N137.40E
Chubut *d.* Argentina **63** 44.00S 68.00W
Chubut *r.* Argentina **63** 43.18S 65.06W
Chudleigh U.K. **5** 50.35N 3.36W
Chudnov Ukraine **15** 50.05N 28.01E
Chudovo Russian Fed. **18** 59.10N 31.41E
Chuiquimula Guatemala **57** 15.52N 89.50W
Chukai Malaysia **26** 4.16N103.24E
Chukotskiy Poluostrov *pen.* Russian Fed. **21** 66.00N174.30W
Chukudukraal Botswana **39** 22.30S 23.22E
Chula Vista U.S.A. **54** 32.39N117.05W
Chulman Russian Fed. **21** 56.54N124.55E
Chulucanas Peru **60** 5.08S 80.00W
Chulym Russian Fed. **20** 55.09N 80.59E
Chum Russian Fed. **18** 67.05N 63.15E
Chumbicha Argentina **62** 28.50S 66.18W
Chumikan Russian Fed. **21** 54.40N135.15E
Chumphon Thailand **29** 10.35N 99.14E
Chuna *r.* Russian Fed. **21** 58.00N 94.00E
Ch'unch'ŏn S. Korea **25** 37.53N127.45E
Chungking *see* Chongqing China **29**
Chunya Tanzania **37** 8.31S 33.28E
Chuquicamata Chile **62** 22.20S 68.56W
Chuquisaca *d.* Bolivia **62** 21.00S 64.00W
Chur Switz. **11** 46.52N 9.32E
Churchill Canada **51** 58.45N 94.00W
Churchill *r.* Man. Canada **51** 58.20N 94.15W
Churchill *r.* Nfld. Canada **51** 53.20N 60.00W
Churchill, C. Canada **51** 58.50N 93.00W
Churchill L. Canada **50** 56.00N108.00W
Churchill Peak *mtn.* Canada **50** 58.10N125.00W
Church Stretton U.K. **5** 52.32N 2.49W
Chusovoy Russian Fed. **18** 58.18N 57.50E
Chuxiong China **29** 25.03N101.33E
Ciechanów Poland **15** 52.53N 20.38E
Ciego de Avila Cuba **57** 21.51N 78.47W
Ciénaga Colombia **60** 11.11N 74.15W
Cienfuegos Cuba **57** 22.10N 80.27W
Cieszyn Poland **15** 49.45N 18.38E
Cieza Spain **10** 38.14N 1.25W
Cifuentes Spain **10** 40.47N 2.37W
Cigüela *r.* Spain **10** 39.47N 3.00W
Cijara, Embalse de *resr.* Spain **10** 39.20N 4.50W
Cilacap Indonesia **26** 7.44S109.00E
Cimarron *r.* U.S.A. **53** 36.15N 96.55W
Cimone, Monte *mtn.* Italy **9** 44.12N 10.42E
Cimpina Romania **13** 45.08N 25.44E
Cimpulung Romania **13** 45.16N 25.03E
Cinca *r.* Spain **10** 41.22N 0.20E
Cincinnati U.S.A. **55** 39.10N 84.30W
Ciney Belgium **8** 50.17N 5.06E
Cinto, Monte *mtn.* France **11** 42.23N 8.57E
Cipolletti Argentina **63** 38.56S 67.59W
Circle U.S.A. **54** 47.25N105.35W
Circleville Ohio U.S.A. **55** 39.36N 82.57W
Circleville Utah U.S.A. **54** 38.10N112.16W
Cirebon Indonesia **26** 6.46S108.33E
Cirencester U.K. **5** 51.43N 1.59W
Ciriè Italy **9** 45.14N 7.36E
Cirò Marina Italy **13** 39.22N 17.08E
Ciskei Africa **39** 32.45S 27.00E
Cittadella Italy **9** 45.39N 11.47E
Cittanova Italy **12** 38.21N 16.05E
Ciudad Bolívar Venezuela **60** 8.06N 63.36W
Ciudad Camargo Mexico **56** 27.40N105.10W
Ciudad de México Mexico **56** 19.25N 99.10W
Ciudadela Spain **10** 40.00N 3.50E
Ciudad Guayana Venezuela **60** 8.22N 62.40W
Ciudad Guerrero Mexico **56** 28.33N107.28W
Ciudad Guzmán Mexico **56** 19.41N103.29W
Ciudad Ixtepec Mexico **56** 16.32N 95.10W
Ciudad Jiménez Mexico **54** 27.08N104.55W
Ciudad Juárez Mexico **56** 31.44N106.29W
Ciudad Madero Mexico **56** 22.19N 97.50W
Ciudad Mante Mexico **56** 22.44N 98.57W
Ciudad Obregón Mexico **56** 27.29N109.56W
Ciudad Ojeda Venezuela **60** 10.05N 71.17W
Ciudad Piar Venezuela **60** 7.27N 63.19W
Ciudad Real Spain **10** 38.59N 3.55W
Ciudad Rodrigo Spain **10** 40.36N 6.33W
Ciudad Victoria Mexico **56** 23.43N 99.10W
Civitanova Italy **12** 43.19N 13.40E
Civitavecchia Italy **12** 42.06N 11.48E
Civray France **11** 46.09N 0.18E
Çivril Turkey **30** 38.18N 29.43E
Cizre Turkey **30** 37.21N 42.11E
Clackline Australia **43** 31.43S116.31E
Clacton on Sea U.K. **5** 51.47N 1.10E
Claire, L. Canada **50** 58.30N112.00W
Clamecy France **9** 47.27N 3.31E
Clara Rep. of Ire. **7** 53.21N 7.37W
Clare N.S.W. Australia **46** 33.27S143.55E
Clare S.A. Australia **46** 33.50S138.38E
Clare *d.* Rep. of Ire. **7** 52.52N 8.55W
Clare *r.* Rep. of Ire. **7** 53.17N 9.04W
Clare U.S.A. **55** 43.49N 84.47W
Clare I. Rep. of Ire. **7** 53.48N 10.00W
Claremorris Rep. of Ire. **7** 53.44N 9.00W
Clarence *r.* Australia **47** 29.25S153.02E
Clarence *r.* New Zealand **48** 42.10S173.55E
Clarence I. Antarctica **64** 61.30S 53.50W
Clarence Str. Australia **42** 12.00S131.00E
Clarie Coast *f.* Antarctica **64** 67.00S133.00E
Clark, L. U.S.A. **50** 60.15N154.15W
Clarke I. Australia **45** 40.30S148.10E
Clark Fork *r.* U.S.A. **54** 48.09N116.15W
Clarksburg U.S.A. **55** 39.16N 80.22W
Clarksdale U.S.A. **53** 34.12N 90.33W
Clarkston U.S.A. **54** 46.26N117.02W
Clarksville Tenn. U.S.A. **53** 36.31N 87.21W
Clary France **8** 50.05N 3.21E
Clayton *r.* Australia **46** 29.06S137.59E
Clayton Idaho U.S.A. **54** 44.16N114.25W
Clayton N.Mex. U.S.A. **52** 36.27N103.12W
Clear, C. Rep. of Ire. **3** 51.25N 9.32W
Clearfield Utah U.S.A. **54** 41.07N112.01W
Clear I. Rep. of Ire. **7** 51.26N 9.30W
Clear L. U.S.A. **54** 39.02N122.50W
Clearwater U.S.A. **53** 27.57N 82.48W
Clearwater Mts. U.S.A. **54** 46.00N115.30W
Cle Elum U.S.A. **54** 47.12N120.56W
Cleethorpes U.K. **4** 53.33N 0.02W
Clermont Australia **44** 22.49S147.39E
Clermont France **9** 49.23N 2.24E
Clermont-en-Argonne France **9** 49.05N 5.05E
Clermont-Ferrand France **11** 45.47N 3.05E
Clervaux Lux. **8** 50.04N 6.01E
Cles Italy **9** 46.22N 11.02E
Cleve Australia **46** 33.37S136.32E
Clevedon U.K. **5** 51.26N 2.52W
Cleveland *d.* U.K. **4** 54.37N 1.08W
Cleveland Miss. U.S.A. **53** 33.43N 90.46W
Cleveland Ohio U.S.A. **55** 41.30N 81.41W
Cleveland Tenn. U.S.A. **53** 35.10N 84.51W
Cleveland, C. Australia **44** 19.11S147.01E
Cleveland Heights *town* U.S.A. **55** 41.30N 81.34W
Cleveland Hills U.K. **4** 54.25N 1.10W
Cleveleys U.K. **4** 53.52N 3.01W
Clew B. Rep. of Ire. **7** 53.50N 9.47W
Clifden Rep. of Ire. **7** 53.29N 10.02W
Cliffy Head Australia **43** 34.58S116.24E
Clifton Ariz. U.S.A. **54** 33.03N109.18W
Clinton B.C. Canada **50** 51.05N121.35W
Clinton New Zealand **48** 46.13S169.23E
Clinton Iowa U.S.A. **53** 41.51N 90.12W
Clinton Okla. U.S.A. **52** 35.32N 98.59W
Clisham *mtn.* U.K. **6** 57.58N 6.50W
Cliza Bolivia **62** 17.36S 65.56W
Cloghan Offaly Rep. of Ire. **7** 53.13N 7.54W
Clogher Head Kerry Rep. of Ire. **7** 52.09N 10.28W
Clonakilty Rep. of Ire. **7** 51.37N 8.54W
Cloncurry Australia **44** 20.42S140.30E
Clones Rep. of Ire. **7** 54.11N 7.16W
Clonmel Rep. of Ire. **7** 52.21N 7.44W
Clonroche Rep. of Ire. **7** 52.27N 6.45W
Cloppenburg Germany **8** 52.52N 8.02E
Clorinda Argentina **62** 25.20S 57.40W
Cloud Peak *mtn.* U.S.A. **54** 44.25N107.10W
Cloughton U.K. **4** 54.20N 0.27W
Cloverdale U.S.A. **54** 38.48N123.01W
Clovis Calif. U.S.A. **54** 36.49N119.42W
Clovis N.Mex. U.S.A. **52** 34.14N103.13W
Clowne U.K. **4** 53.18N 1.16W
Cluj-Napoca Romania **15** 46.47N 23.37E
Clunes Australia **46** 37.16S143.47E
Cluny France **11** 46.26N 4.39E
Clusone Italy **9** 45.53N 9.57E
Clutha *r.* New Zealand **48** 46.18S169.05E
Clwyd *d.* U.K. **4** 53.07N 3.20W
Clwyd *r.* U.K. **4** 53.19N 3.30W
Clyde Canada **51** 70.30N 68.30W
Clyde New Zealand **48** 45.11S169.19E
Clyde *r.* U.K. **6** 55.58N 4.53W
Clydebank U.K. **6** 55.53N 4.23W
Coachella U.S.A. **54** 33.41N116.10W

Coahuila *d.* Mexico **56** 27.00N103.00W
Coalinga U.S.A. **54** 36.09N120.21W
Coalville U.K. **5** 52.43N 1.21W
Coast *d.* Kenya **37** 3.00S 39.30E
Coast Mts. Canada **50** 55.30N128.00W
Coast Range *mts.* U.S.A. **54** 42.40N123.30W
Coatbridge U.K. **6** 55.52N 4.02W
Coats I. Canada **51** 62.30N 83.00W
Coats Land *f.* Antarctica **64** 77.00S 25.00W
Coatzacoalcos Mexico **56** 18.10N 94.25W
Cobalt Canada **55** 47.24N 79.41W
Cobán Guatemala **56** 15.28N 90.20W
Cobar Australia **47** 31.32S145.51E
Cobargo Australia **47** 36.24S149.52E
Cobden Australia **46** 38.21S143.07E
Cobden Canada **55** 45.38N 76.53W
Cobh Rep. of Ire. **7** 51.50N 8.18W
Cobham L. Australia **46** 30.09S142.05E
Cobija Bolivia **62** 11.02S 68.44W
Cobourg Canada **55** 43.58N 78.11W
Cobourg Pen. Australia **44** 11.20S132.15E
Cobram Australia **47** 35.56S145.40E
Cobre U.S.A. **54** 41.07N114.25W
Cobue Mozambique **37** 12.10S 34.50E
Coburg Germany **14** 50.15N 10.58E
Coburg I. Canada **51** 76.00N 79.25W
Cochabamba Bolivia **62** 17.24S 66.09W
Cochabamba *d.* Bolivia **62** 17.30S 65.40W
Cochem Germany **8** 50.08N 7.10E
Cochrane Ont. Canada **55** 49.04N 81.02W
Cochrane Chile **63** 47.20S 72.30W
Cockaleechie Australia **46** 34.07S135.53E
Cockburn Australia **46** 32.05S141.00E
Cockburnspath U.K. **6** 55.56N 2.22W
Cocklebiddy Australia **43** 32.02S126.05E
Coco *r.* Honduras **57** 14.58N 83.15W
Cocoparra Range *mts.* Australia **47** 34.00S146.00E
Cod, C. U.S.A. **55** 41.42N 70.15W
Codăeşti Romania **15** 46.52N 27.46E
Codajás Brazil **60** 3.55S 62.00W
Codigoro Italy **9** 44.49N 12.08E
Codó Brazil **61** 4.28S 43.51W
Codogno Italy **9** 45.09N 9.42E
Codroipo Italy **9** 45.58N 12.59E
Cody U.S.A. **54** 44.32N109.03W
Coen Australia **44** 13.56S143.12E
Coesfeld Germany **8** 51.55N 7.13E
Coeur d'Alene U.S.A. **52** 47.40N116.46W
Coevorden Neth. **8** 52.39N 6.45E
Coffin B. Australia **46** 34.27S135.19E
Coffin Bay Pen. Australia **46** 34.30S135.14E
Coff's Harbour Australia **47** 30.19S153.05E
Cofre de Perote *mtn.* Mexico **56** 19.30N 97.10W
Coghinas *r.* Italy **12** 40.57N 8.50E
Cognac France **11** 45.42N 0.19W
Cohoes U.S.A. **55** 42.46N 73.42W
Cohuna Australia **46** 35.47S144.15E
Coiba, Isla de *i.* Panama **57** 7.23N 81.45W
Coihaique Chile **63** 45.35S 72.08W
Coimbatore India **28** 11.00N 76.57E
Coimbra Brazil **59** 19.55S 57.47W
Coimbra Portugal **10** 40.12N 8.25W
Coín Spain **10** 36.40N 4.45W
Cojimies Ecuador **60** 0.20N 80.00W
Cokeville U.S.A. **54** 42.05N110.57W
Colac Australia **46** 38.22S143.38E
Colatina Brazil **59** 19.35S 40.37W
Colbeck, C. Antarctica **64** 77.20S159.00W
Colchester U.K. **5** 51.54N 0.55E
Coldstream U.K. **6** 55.39N 2.15W
Coldwater U.S.A. **55** 41.57N 85.01W
Coldwell Canada **55** 48.46N 86.31W
Coleambally Australia **47** 34.48S145.53E
Coleman *r.* Australia **44** 15.06S141.38E
Colenso R.S.A. **39** 28.43S 29.49E
Coleraine Australia **46** 37.36S141.42E
Coleraine U.K. **7** 55.08N 6.40W
Colesberg R.S.A. **39** 30.43S 25.05E
Colico Italy **9** 46.08N 9.22E
Colima Mexico **56** 19.14N103.41W
Colima *d.* Mexico **56** 19.05N104.00W
Colinas Brazil **61** 6.02S 44.14W
Coll *i.* U.K. **6** 56.38N 6.34W
Collarenebri Australia **47** 29.33S148.36E
College U.S.A. **50** 64.54N147.55W
College Park *town* Md. U.S.A. **55** 39.00N 76.55W
Collerina Australia **47** 29.22S146.32E
Collie N.S.W. Australia **47** 31.41S148.22E
Collie W.A. Australia **43** 33.21S116.09E
Collie Cardiff Australia **43** 33.27S116.09E
Collier B. Australia **42** 16.10S124.15E
Collingwood Canada **55** 44.29N 80.13W
Collingwood New Zealand **48** 40.41S172.41E
Collingwood B. P.N.G. **44** 9.20S149.30E
Collinsville Australia **44** 20.34S147.51E
Collin Top *mtn.* U.K. **7** 54.58N 6.08W
Collon Rep. of Ire. **7** 53.47N 6.30W
Collooney Rep. of Ire. **7** 54.11N 8.29W
Colmar France **11** 48.05N 7.21E
Colmenar Viejo Spain **10** 40.39N 3.46W
Colne *r.* Essex U.K. **5** 51.50N 0.59E
Colnett, C. Mexico **56** 31.00N116.20W
Colnett, Cabo *c.* Mexico **54** 31.00N116.20W
Colo *r.* Australia **47** 33.26S150.53E
Cologne *see* Köln Germany **8**
Colombia S. America **60** 4.00N 72.30W
Colombo Sri Lanka **29** 6.55N 79.52E
Colón Argentina **63** 32.15S 58.10W
Colón Panama **60** 9.21N 79.54W
Colona Australia **45** 31.38S132.05E
Colonia del Sacramento Uruguay **63** 34.28S 57.51W
Colonia Las Heras Argentina **63** 46.33S 68.57W
Colonia Lavelleja Uruguay **63** 31.06S 57.01W
Colonsay *i.* U.K. **6** 56.04N 6.13W
Colorado *r.* Argentina **63** 39.50S 62.02W
Colorado *d.* U.S.A. **52** 39.07N105.27W
Colorado *r.* Ariz. U.S.A. **54** 31.45N114.40W
Colorado *r.* Tex. U.S.A. **53** 28.30N 96.00W
Colorado Plateau *f.* U.S.A. **54** 36.30N108.00W
Colorado Springs *town* U.S.A. **52** 38.50N104.49W
Columbia Mo. U.S.A. **53** 38.58N 92.20W
Columbia *r.* U.S.A. **54** 46.15N124.05W
Columbia S.C. U.S.A. **53** 34.00N 81.00W
Columbia Tenn. U.S.A. **53** 35.37N 87.02W
Columbia Basin *f.* U.S.A. **54** 46.55N117.36W
Columbia Falls *town* U.S.A. **54** 48.23N114.11W
Columbia Plateau *f.* U.S.A. **54** 44.00N117.30W
Columbretes, Islas *is.* Spain **10** 39.50N 0.40E
Columbus Ga. U.S.A. **53** 32.28N 84.59W
Columbus Ind. U.S.A. **55** 39.12N 85.57W
Columbus Miss. U.S.A. **53** 33.30N 88.27W
Columbus Mont. U.S.A. **54** 45.38N109.15W
Columbus Ohio U.S.A. **55** 39.59N 83.03W
Colville *r.* U.S.A. **50** 70.06N151.30W
Colwyn Bay *town* U.K. **4** 53.18N 3.43W
Comacchio Italy **9** 44.42N 12.11E
Comacchio, Valli di *b.* Italy **9** 44.38N 12.06E
Comayagua Honduras **57** 14.30N 87.39W
Comblain-au-Pont Belgium **8** 50.29N 5.32E
Combles France **8** 50.01N 2.52E
Combourg France **9** 48.25N 1.45W
Comboyne Australia **47** 31.35S152.27E
Comeragh Mts. Rep. of Ire. **7** 52.17N 7.34W
Comilla Bangla. **29** 23.28N 91.10E
Comitán Mexico **56** 16.15N 92.08W
Commentry France **11** 46.17N 2.44E
Commonwealth Territory *d.* Australia **47** 35.00S151.00E
Como Italy **9** 45.48N 9.04E
Como, Lago di *l.* Italy **9** 46.05N 9.17E
Comodoro Rivadavia Argentina **63** 45.50S 67.30W
Comorin, C. India **28** 8.04N 77.35E
Comoros Africa **37** 12.15S 44.00E
Compiègne France **9** 49.24N 2.50E
Conakry Guinea **34** 9.30N 13.43W
Concarneau France **11** 47.53N 3.55W
Conceição do Araguaia Brazil **61** 8.15S 49.17W
Concepción Argentina **62** 27.20S 65.36W
Concepción Chile **63** 36.50S 73.03W
Concepción Paraguay **62** 23.22S 57.26W
Concepción del Oro Mexico **56** 24.38N101.25W
Concepción del Uruguay Argentina **63** 32.30S 58.14W
Conception, Pt. U.S.A. **54** 34.27N120.27W
Conception B. Namibia **39** 23.53S 14.28E
Conches France **9** 48.58N 0.58E
Conchillas Uruguay **63** 34.15S 58.04W
Conchos *r.* Mexico **56** 29.32N104.25W
Concord N.H. U.S.A. **55** 43.12N 71.32W
Concordia Argentina **63** 31.24S 58.02W
Concórdia Brazil **60** 4.35S 66.35W
Concordia U.S.A. **52** 39.35N 97.39W
Condé France **9** 48.51N 0.33W
Condé-sur-l'Escaut France **8** 50.28N 3.35E
Condobolin Australia **47** 33.03S147.11E
Condom France **11** 43.58N 0.22E
Conegliano Italy **9** 45.53N 12.18E
Confolens France **11** 46.01N 0.40E
Congleton U.K. **4** 53.10N 2.12W
Congo Africa **36** 1.00S 16.00E
Congonhas Brazil **59** 20.30S 43.53W
Coningsby U.K. **4** 53.07N 0.09W
Coniston U.K. **4** 54.22N 3.06W
Conn, Lough Rep. of Ire. **7** 54.01N 9.15W
Connah's Quay *town* U.K. **4** 53.13N 3.03W
Conneaut U.S.A. **55** 41.58N 80.34W
Connecticut *d.* U.S.A. **55** 41.45N 72.45W
Connecticut *r.* U.S.A. **55** 41.17N 72.21W
Connellsville U.S.A. **55** 40.01N 79.35W
Connemara *f.* Rep. of Ire. **7** 53.32N 9.56W
Conner, Mt. Australia **44** 25.35S131.49E
Conon *r.* U.K. **6** 57.33N 4.33W
Conrad U.S.A. **54** 48.10N111.57W
Conselheiro Lafaiete Brazil **59** 20.40S 43.48W
Consett U.K. **4** 54.52N 1.50W
Con Son *is.* Vietnam **26** 8.30N106.30E
Constance, L. *see* Bodensee Europe **14**
Constanţa Romania **13** 44.10N 28.31E
Constantina Spain **10** 37.54N 5.36W
Constantine Algeria **34** 36.22N 6.38E
Constitución Chile **63** 35.20S 72.25W
Constitución Uruguay **63** 31.05S 57.50W
Consuegra Spain **10** 39.28N 3.43W
Contact U.S.A. **54** 41.48N114.46W
Contamana Peru **60** 7.19S 75.00W
Contas *r.* Brazil **61** 14.15S 39.00W
Contreras, Embalse de *resr.* Spain **10** 39.32N 1.30W
Contres France **9** 47.25N 1.26E
Contwoyto L. Canada **50** 65.42N110.50W
Conty France **9** 49.44N 2.09E
Conway N.H. U.S.A. **55** 43.59N 71.07W
Conway, L. Australia **46** 28.17S135.35E
Coober Pedy Australia **46** 29.01S134.43E
Cook, C. Canada **50** 50.08N127.55W
Cook, Mt. New Zealand **48** 43.45S170.12E
Cooke, Mt. Australia **43** 32.26S116.18E
Cookhouse R.S.A. **39** 32.44S 25.47E
Cook Inlet U.S.A. **50** 60.30N152.00W
Cook Is. Pacific Oc. **40** 15.00S160.00W
Cookstown U.K. **7** 54.39N 6.46W
Cook Str. New Zealand **48** 41.15S174.30E
Cooktown Australia **44** 15.29S145.15E
Coolabah Australia **47** 31.02S146.45E
Coolah Australia **47** 31.48S149.45E
Coolamara Australia **46** 31.59S143.42E
Coolamon Australia **47** 34.48S147.12E
Coolangatta Australia **47** 28.10S153.26E
Coolgardie Australia **43** 31.01S121.12E
Coolidge U.S.A. **54** 32.59N111.31W
Cooma Australia **47** 36.15S149.07E
Coombah Australia **46** 32.58S141.39E
Coomberdale Australia **43** 30.29S116.03E
Coonabarabran Australia **47** 31.16S149.18E
Coonalpyn Australia **46** 35.41S139.52E
Coonamble Australia **47** 30.55S148.26E
Coonana Australia **43** 31.01S123.05E
Coonawarra Australia **46** 37.16S140.50E
Coondambo Australia **46** 31.07S135.20E
Cooper Creek *r.* Australia **46** 28.33S137.46E
Coorow Australia **43** 29.53S116.01E
Coos Bay *town* U.S.A. **54** 43.22N124.13W
Cootamundra Australia **47** 34.41S148.03E
Cootehill Rep. of Ire. **7** 54.05N 7.05W
Copainalá Mexico **56** 17.05N 93.12W
Copán *ruins* Honduras **57** 14.52N 89.10W
Copenhagen *see* København Denmark **17**
Copiapó Chile **62** 27.22S 70.20W
Copparo Italy **9** 44.54N 11.49E
Copperbelt *d.* Zambia **37** 13.00S 28.00E
Copper Belt *f.* Zambia **37** 12.40S 28.00E
Copper Center U.S.A. **50** 61.58N145.19W
Copper Cliff *town* Canada **55** 46.28N 81.04W
Copper Harbor U.S.A. **55** 47.28N 87.54W
Coppermine *r.* Canada **50** 67.54N115.10W
Coppermine *see* Qurlurtuuq *town* Canada **50**
Copper Queen Zimbabwe **39** 17.31S 29.20E
Copperton R.S.A. **39** 30.00S 22.15E
Coqên China **29** 31.20N 85.25E
Coquet *r.* U.K. **4** 55.21N 1.35W
Coquille U.S.A. **54** 43.11N124.11W
Coquimbo Chile **62** 29.58S 71.21W
Corabia Romania **13** 43.45N 24.29E
Coracora Peru **60** 15.02S 73.48W
Coraki Australia **47** 23.00S153.17E
Coral Bay *town* Australia **42** 23.02S113.48E
Coral Harbour *town* Canada **51** 64.10N 83.15W
Coral Sea Pacific Oc. **44** 14.30S149.30E
Corangamite, L. Australia **46** 38.10S143.25E
Corbeil France **9** 48.37N 2.29E
Corbeny France **9** 49.28N 3.49E
Corbigny France **9** 47.15N 3.40E
Corby U.K. **5** 52.29N 0.41W
Corcubión Spain **10** 42.56N 9.12W
Córdoba Argentina **62** 31.25S 64.10W
Córdoba *d.* Argentina **62** 30.30S 64.30W
Córdoba Mexico **56** 18.55N 96.55W
Córdoba Spain **10** 37.53N 4.46W
Córdoba, Sierras de *mts.* Argentina **62** 30.30S 64.40W
Cordova U.S.A. **50** 60.33N139.44W
Corentyne *r.* Guyana **61** 5.10N 57.20W
Corfield Australia **44** 21.43S143.22E
Corfu *i.* *see* Kérkira *i.* Greece **13**
Coricudgy, Mt. Australia **47** 32.51S150.25E
Corigliano Italy **13** 39.36N 16.31E
Corindi Australia **47** 30.00S153.21E
Corinth Miss. U.S.A. **53** 34.58N 88.30W
Corinto Nicaragua **57** 12.29N 87.14W
Cork Rep. of Ire. **7** 51.54N 8.28W
Cork *d.* Rep. of Ire. **7** 52.00N 8.40W
Cork Harbour *est.* Rep. of Ire. **7** 51.50N 8.17W
Cormeilles France **9** 49.15N 0.23E
Corner Brook *town* Canada **51** 48.58N 57.58W
Corner Inlet *b.* Australia **47** 38.43S146.20E
Corning N.Y. U.S.A. **55** 42.09N 77.04W
Corno, Monte *mtn.* Italy **12** 42.29N 13.33E
Cornwall Canada **55** 45.02N 74.45W
Cornwall *d.* U.K. **5** 50.26N 4.40W
Cornwallis I. Canada **51** 75.00N 95.00W
Coro Venezuela **60** 11.27N 69.41W
Coroatá Brazil **61** 4.08S 44.08W
Coroico Bolivia **62** 16.10S 67.44W
Coromandel New Zealand **48** 36.46S175.30E
Coromandel Pen. New Zealand **48** 36.45S175.30E
Coronation G. Canada **50** 68.00N112.00W
Coronda Argentina **63** 31.55S 60.55W
Coronel Chile **63** 37.01S 73.08W
Coronel Brandsen Argentina **63** 35.10S 58.15W
Coronel Pringles Argentina **63** 37.56S 61.25W
Coronel Suárez Argentina **63** 37.30S 61.52W
Coropuna *mtn.* Peru **60** 15.31S 72.45W
Corowa Australia **47** 36.00S146.20E
Corozal Belize **57** 18.23N 88.23W
Corpus Christi U.S.A. **53** 27.47N 97.26W
Correggio Italy **9** 44.46N 10.47E
Correntes, Cabo das *c.* Mozambique **39** 24.11S 35.35E
Corrib, Lough Rep. of Ire. **7** 53.26N 9.14W
Corrientes Argentina **62** 27.30S 58.48W
Corrientes *d.* Argentina **62** 28.00S 57.00W
Corrientes, Cabo *c.* Colombia **60** 5.30N 77.34W
Corrigin Australia **43** 32.21S117.52E
Corry U.S.A. **55** 41.56N 79.39W
Corryong Australia **47** 36.11S147.58E
Corse *d.* France **11** 42.00N 9.10E
Corse *i.* France **11** 42.00N 9.10E
Corse, Cap *c.* France **11** 43.00N 9.21E
Corsham U.K. **5** 51.25N 2.11W
Corsica *i.* *see* Corse *i.* France **11**
Corsicana U.S.A. **53** 32.05N 96.27W
Corte France **11** 42.18N 9.08E
Cortegana Spain **10** 37.55N 6.49W
Cortez Colo. U.S.A. **54** 37.21N108.35W
Cortez Nev. U.S.A. **54** 40.09N116.38W
Cortina Italy **12** 46.32N 12.08E
Cortland N.Y. U.S.A. **55** 42.36N 76.11W
Cortona Italy **12** 43.16N 11.59E
Coruche Portugal **10** 38.58N 8.31W
Çoruh Nehri *r.* Turkey *see* Chorokh *r.* Georgia **30**
Çorum Turkey **30** 40.31N 34.57E
Corumbá Brazil **62** 19.00S 57.27W
Corumbá *r.* Brazil **59** 18.15S 48.55W
Corvallis U.S.A. **54** 44.34N123.16W
Corwen U.K. **4** 52.59N 3.23W
Cosenza Italy **12** 39.17N 16.14E
Cosne France **9** 47.25N 2.55E
Coso Junction U.S.A. **54** 36.03N117.58W
Cosson *r.* France **9** 47.30N 1.15E
Costa Brava *f.* Spain **10** 41.30N 3.00E
Costa del Sol *f.* Spain **10** 36.30N 4.00W
Costa Mesa U.S.A. **54** 33.39N117.55W
Costa Rica C. America **57** 10.00N 84.00W
Costeşti Romania **13** 44.40N 24.53E
Cotabato Phil. **27** 7.14N124.15E
Cotagaita Bolivia **62** 20.50S 65.41W
Côte d'Azur *f.* France **11** 43.20N 6.45E
Côte d'Ivoire *see* Ivory Coast Africa **34**
Côte-d'Or *d.* France **9** 47.30N 4.50E
Côte d'Or *f.* France **9** 47.10N 4.50E
Cotonou Benin **38** 6.24N 2.31E
Cotopaxi *mtn.* Ecuador **60** 0.40S 78.28W
Cotswold Hills U.K. **5** 51.50N 2.00W
Cottage Grove U.S.A. **54** 43.48N123.03W
Cottbus Germany **14** 51.43N 14.21E
Cottonvale Australia **47** 28.32S151.57E
Cottonwood U.S.A. **54** 34.45N112.01W
Coucy France **9** 49.31N 3.19E
Couer d'Alene U.S.A. **54** 47.41N117.00W
Couesnon *r.* France **9** 48.37N 1.31W
Coulagh B. Rep. of Ire. **7** 51.42N 10.00W
Coulee City U.S.A. **54** 47.37N119.17W
Coulommiers France **9** 48.49N 3.05E
Coulonge *r.* Canada **55** 45.51N 76.45W
Council U.S.A. **50** 64.55N163.44W
Council Bluffs U.S.A. **53** 41.14N 95.54W
Coupar Angus U.K. **6** 56.33N 3.17W
Courland Lagoon Russian Fed./Lithuania **17** 55.00N 21.00E
Courson-les-Carrières France **9** 47.36N 3.30E
Courtalain France **9** 48.05N 1.09E
Courtenay Canada **50** 49.41N125.00W
Courtrai *see* Kortrijk Belgium **8**
Coutances France **9** 49.03N 1.29W
Coutras France **11** 45.02N 0.07W
Couvin Belgium **8** 50.03N 4.30E
Cové Benin **38** 7.16N 2.20E
Coventry U.K. **5** 52.25N 1.31W
Covilhã Portugal **10** 40.17N 7.30W
Covington Ky. U.S.A. **55** 39.04N 84.30W
Cowal, L. Australia **47** 33.36S147.22E
Cowan, L. Australia **43** 32.00S122.00E
Cowangie Australia **46** 35.14S141.28E
Cowansville Canada **55** 45.13N 72.44W
Cowcowing Lakes Australia **43** 31.01S117.18E
Cowdenbeath U.K. **6** 56.07N 3.21W
Cowell Australia **46** 33.41S136.55E
Cowes Australia **47** 38.27S145.15E
Cowes U.K. **5** 50.45N 1.18W
Cowra Australia **47** 33.50S148.45E
Cox *r.* Australia **44** 15.19S135.25E
Coxim Brazil **62** 18.28S 54.37W
Cox's Bāzār Bangla. **29** 21.25N 91.59E
Coyuca de Catalán Mexico **56** 18.20N100.39W
Cozes France **11** 45.35N 0.50W
Cozumel, Isla de *i.* Mexico **57** 20.30N 87.00W
Cradock Australia **46** 31.59S138.34E
Cradock R.S.A. **39** 32.10S 25.35E
Craig Colo. U.S.A. **54** 40.31N107.33W
Craigavon U.K. **7** 54.28N 6.25W
Craignure U.K. **6** 56.28N 5.42W
Craigsville U.S.A. **55** 38.04N 79.23W
Crail U.K. **6** 56.16N 2.38W
Crailsheim Germany **14** 49.09N 10.06E
Craiova Romania **13** 44.18N 23.46E
Cranbourne Australia **47** 38.07S145.19E
Cranbrook Australia **43** 34.15S117.32E
Cranbrook Canada **50** 49.29N115.48W
Crane U.S.A. **54** 43.25N118.34W
Cranston U.S.A. **55** 41.47N 71.26W
Craon France **9** 47.50N 0.58W
Craonne France **9** 49.27N 3.46E
Crater L. U.S.A. **54** 42.56N122.06W
Crateús Brazil **61** 5.10S 40.39W
Crati *r.* Italy **13** 39.43N 16.29E
Crato Amazonas Brazil **60** 7.25S 63.00W
Crato Ceará Brazil **61** 7.10S 39.25W
Craughwell Rep. of Ire. **7** 53.14N 8.44W
Crawfordsville U.S.A. **55** 40.03N 86.54W
Crawley U.K. **5** 51.07N 0.10W
Crazy Mts. U.S.A. **54** 46.08N110.20W
Crécy France **11** 50.15N 1.53E
Crécy-sur-Serre France **9** 49.42N 3.37E
Cree *r.* Canada **50** 59.00N105.47W
Creede U.S.A. **54** 37.51N106.56W
Cree L. Canada **50** 57.20N108.30W
Creil France **9** 49.16N 2.29E
Crema Italy **9** 45.22N 9.41E
Cremona Italy **9** 45.08N 10.03E
Crépy France **9** 49.36N 3.31E
Crépy-en-Valois France **9** 49.14N 2.54E
Cres *i.* Croatia **12** 44.50N 14.20E
Cres *town* Croatia **12** 44.58N 14.25E
Crescent U.S.A. **54** 43.29N121.41W
Crescent City U.S.A. **54** 41.45N124.12W
Crescent Head *town* Australia **47** 31.10S152.59E
Crespo Argentina **63** 32.02S 60.20W
Cressy Australia **46** 38.02S143.38E
Crest France **11** 44.44N 5.02E
Creston Iowa U.S.A. **53** 41.04N 94.20W
Creswick Australia **46** 37.25S143.54E
Crete *i.* *see* Kríti *i.* Greece **13**
Crete, Sea of *see* Kritikón Pélagos *sea* Greece **13**
Creus, Cabo de *c.* Spain **10** 42.20N 3.19E
Creuse *r.* France **11** 47.00N 0.35E
Crewe U.K. **4** 53.06N 2.28W
Crianlarich U.K. **6** 56.23N 4.37W
Criccieth U.K. **4** 52.55N 4.15W
Criciúma Brazil **59** 28.40S 49.23W
Crieff U.K. **6** 56.23N 3.52W
Crimea *pen.* *see* Krym *pen.* Ukraine **19**
Crinan U.K. **6** 56.06N 5.34W
Cristóbal Colón *mtn.* Colombia **60** 10.53N 73.48W
Crişu Alb *r.* Romania **15** 46.42N 21.17E
Crna *r.* Macedonia **13** 41.33N 21.58E
Crna Gora *d.* Yugo. **13** 43.00N 19.30E
Croaghnameal *mtn.* Rep. of Ire. **7** 54.40N 7.57W
Croatia Europe **13** 45.10N 15.30E
Crocodile *r.* R.S.A. **39** 24.11S 26.48E
Croker I. Australia **44** 11.12S132.32E
Cromarty U.K. **6** 57.40N 4.02W
Cromarty Firth *est.* U.K. **6** 57.41N 4.10W
Cromer U.K. **4** 52.56N 1.18E
Cromwell New Zealand **48** 45.03S169.14E
Crooked I. Bahamas **57** 22.45N 74.00W
Crookhaven Rep. of Ire. **7** 51.29N 9.45W
Crookwell Australia **47** 34.27S149.28E
Croom Rep. of Ire. **7** 52.31N 8.43W
Croppa Creek *town* Australia **47** 29.08S150.20E
Crosby I.o.M Europe **4** 54.11N 4.34W
Cross Fell *mtn.* U.K. **4** 54.43N 2.28W
Cross River *d.* Nigeria **38** 5.45N 8.25E
Cross Sd. U.S.A. **50** 58.10N136.30W
Crotone Italy **13** 39.05N 17.06E
Crow Agency U.S.A. **54** 45.36N107.27W
Crowl Creek *r.* Australia **47** 31.58S144.53E
Crowsnest Pass Canada **50** 49.40N114.41W
Croyde U.K. **5** 51.07N 4.13W
Croyden Australia **41** 18.12S142.14E
Croydon Australia **44** 18.12S142.14E
Croydon U.K. **5** 51.23N 0.06W
Crucero U.S.A. **54** 35.03N116.10W
Cruz, Cabo *c.* Cuba **57** 19.52N 77.44W
Cruz Alta Brazil **59** 28.38S 53.38W
Cruz del Eje Argentina **62** 30.44S 64.49W
Cruzeiro Brazil **59** 22.33S 44.59W
Cruzeiro do Sul Brazil **60** 7.40S 72.39W
Crystal Brook *town* Australia **46** 33.21S138.13E
Csorna Hungary **15** 47.37N 17.16E
Csurgó Hungary **15** 46.16N 17.06E
Cuamba Mozambique **37** 14.48S 36.32E
Cuando *r.* Angola **36** 18.30S 23.32E
Cuangar Angola **39** 17.34S 18.39E
Cuango *r.* *see* Kwango *r.* Angola **36**
Cuanza *r.* Angola **36** 9.22S 13.09E
Cuaró Uruguay **63** 30.37S 56.54W
Cuaró *r.* Uruguay **63** 30.15S 57.01W
Cuba C. America **57** 22.00N 79.00W
Cuballing Australia **43** 32.50S117.07E
Cubango *r.* *see* Okavango *r.* Angola **36**
Cubo Mozambique **39** 23.48S 33.55E
Cuckfield U.K. **5** 51.00N 0.08W
Cucuí Brazil **60** 1.12N 66.50W
Cúcuta Colombia **60** 7.55N 72.31W
Cuddalore India **29** 11.43N 79.46E
Cue Australia **42** 27.25S117.54E
Cuenca Ecuador **60** 2.54S 79.00W
Cuenca Spain **10** 40.04N 2.07W
Cuenca, Serranía de *mts.* Spain **10** 40.25N 2.00W
Cuernavaca Mexico **56** 18.57N 99.15W
Cuero U.S.A. **53** 29.06N 97.19W
Cuiabá Brazil **61** 15.32S 56.05W
Cuiabá *r.* Brazil **62** 18.00S 57.25W
Cuillin Hills U.K. **6** 57.12N 6.13W
Cuito *r.* Angola **39** 18.01S 20.50E
Culcairn Australia **47** 35.40S147.03E
Culemborg Neth. **8** 51.57N 5.14E
Culgoa *r.* Australia **47** 29.56S146.20E
Culiacán Mexico **56** 24.48N107.24W
Cullen U.K. **6** 57.41N 2.50W
Cullera Spain **10** 39.10N 0.15W
Cullin Sd. U.K. **6** 57.03N 6.13W
Culloden Moor U.K. **6** 57.29N 3.55W
Culpeper U.S.A. **55** 38.28N 77.53W
Culuene *r.* Brazil **61** 12.56S 52.51W
Culver, Pt. Australia **43** 32.52S124.41E
Cumaná Venezuela **60** 10.29N 64.12W
Cumberland Md. U.S.A. **55** 39.39N 78.46W
Cumberland *r.* U.S.A. **53** 37.16N 88.25W
Cumberland, L. U.S.A. **53** 37.00N 85.00W
Cumberland Pen. Canada **51** 66.50N 64.00W
Cumberland Sd. Canada **51** 65.00N 65.30W
Cumbernauld U.K. **6** 55.57N 4.00W
Cumbria *d.* U.K. **4** 54.30N 3.00W
Cumbrian Mts. U.K. **4** 54.32N 3.05W
Cuminá *r.* Brazil **61** 1.30S 56.00W
Cummins Australia **46** 34.16S135.44E
Cumnock Australia **47** 32.56S148.46E
Cumnock U.K. **6** 55.27N 4.15W
Cunderdin Australia **43** 31.39S117.15E
Cunene *d.* Angola **39** 16.00S 16.00E
Cunene *r.* Angola **39** 17.15S 11.50E
Cuneo Italy **9** 44.22N 7.32E
Cungena Australia **46** 32.33S134.40E
Cunnamulla Australia **47** 28.04S145.40E
Cuokkaraš'ša *mtn.* Norway **16** 69.57N 24.32E
Cuorgnè Italy **9** 45.23N 7.39E
Cupar U.K. **6** 56.19N 3.01W
Cupica, Golfo de *g.* Colombia **60** 6.35N 77.25W
Curaçao *i.* Neth. Antilles **60** 12.15N 69.00W
Curacautín Chile **63** 38.26S 71.53W
Curaco *r.* Argentina **63** 38.49S 65.01W
Curanilahue Chile **63** 37.28S 73.21W
Curaray *r.* Peru **60** 2.20S 74.05W
Curban Australia **47** 31.33S148.36E
Curdlawidny L. Australia **46** 30.16S136.20E
Cure *r.* France **9** 47.40N 3.41E
Curiapo Venezuela **60** 8.33N 61.05W
Curicó Chile **63** 34.59S 71.14W
Curitiba Brazil **59** 25.24S 49.16W
Curlewis Australia **47** 31.08S150.16E
Curnamona Australia **46** 31.40S139.35E
Currane, Lough Rep. of Ire. **7** 51.50N 10.07W
Currant U.S.A. **54** 38.44N115.30W
Curranyalpa Australia **47** 30.57S144.33E
Currie Australia **45** 39.56S143.52E
Currie U.S.A. **54** 40.17N114.44W
Curtin Australia **43** 30.50S122.05E
Curtis I. Australia **44** 23.38S151.09E
Curuá *r.* Brazil **61** 5.23S 54.22W
Cururupu Brazil **61** 1.50S 44.52W
Curuzú Cuatiá Argentina **63** 29.50S 58.05W
Curvelo Brazil **59** 18.45S 44.27W
Cushendall U.K. **7** 55.06N 6.05W
Cusna, Monte *mtn.* Italy **9** 44.17N 10.23E
Cut Bank U.S.A. **54** 48.38N112.20W
Cuttaburra Creek *r.* Australia **47** 29.18S145.00E
Cuttack India **29** 20.26N 85.56E

Cuxhaven Germany **14** 53.52N 8.42E
Cuyuni *r.* Guyana **60** 6.24N 58.38W
Cuzco Peru **60** 13.32S 71.57W
Cwmbran U.K. **5** 51.39N 3.01W
Cyclades *is. see* Kikládhes *is.* Greece **13**
Cynthiana U.S.A. **55** 38.22N 84.18W
Cyprus Asia **32** 35.00N 33.00E
Cyrenaica *f. see* Barqah *f.* Libya **35**
Czech Republic Europe **14** 49.30N 15.00E
Czeremcha Poland **15** 52.32N 23.15E
Czersk Poland **15** 53.48N 18.00E
Częstochowa Poland **15** 50.49N 19.07E

D

Da'an China **25** 45.30N124.18E
Ḍab'ah Jordan **32** 31.36N 36.04E
Dabakala Ivory Coast **38** 8.19N 4.24W
Dabbāgh, Jabal *mtn.* Saudi Arabia **32** 27.51N 35.43E
Dacca *see* Dhākā Bangla. **29**
Dachau Germany **14** 48.15N 11.26E
Dadanawa Guyana **60** 2.30N 59.30W
Dādu Pakistan **28** 26.44N 67.47E
Dadu He *r.* China **29** 28.47N104.40E
Daet Phil. **27** 14.07N122.58E
Dagali Norway **17** 60.25N 8.27E
Dagana Senegal **34** 16.28N 15.35W
Dagua P.N.G. **27** 3.25S143.20E
Daguan China **24** 27.44N103.53E
Dagupan Phil. **27** 16.02N120.21E
Daguragu Australia **42** 17.33S130.30E
Da Hinggan Ling *mts.* China **25** 50.00N122.10E
Dahlak Archipelago *is.* Eritrea **35** 15.45N 40.30E
Dahlem Germany **14** 50.23N 6.33E
Dahūk Iraq **30** 36.52N 43.00E
Daimiel Spain **10** 39.05N 3.35W
Daitō Japan **23** 34.42N135.38E
Dajarra Australia **44** 21.42S139.31E
Dajing China **25** 28.24N121.08E
Dakar Senegal **34** 14.38N 17.27W
Dakhal, Wādī ad *r.* Egypt **32** 28.49N 32.45E
Dākhilah, Al Wāḥāt ad *oasis* Egypt **30** 25.30N 28.10E
Dakhla W. Sahara **34** 23.43N 15.57W
Dakingari Nigeria **38** 11.40N 4.06E
Dakovica Yugo. **13** 42.23N 20.25E
Dakwa Zaïre **36** 4.00N 26.26E
Dal *r.* Sweden **17** 60.38N 17.27E
Dalandzadgad Mongolia **24** 43.34N104.20E
Da Lat Vietnam **26** 11.56N108.25E
Dalbeattie U.K. **6** 54.55N 3.49W
Dalby Australia **45** 27.11S151.12E
Dalby Sweden **17** 55.40N 13.20E
Dale Hordaland Norway **17** 60.35N 5.49E
Dale Sogn og Fj. Norway **17** 61.22N 5.24E
Dalen Norway **17** 59.27N 8.00E
Dalhousie Canada **55** 48.03N 66.22W
Dali China **24** 25.33N100.09E
Dali China **24** 25.42N100.11E
Dalian China **25** 38.53N121.37E
Dalkeith U.K. **6** 55.54N 3.04W
Dallas Oreg. U.S.A. **54** 44.55N123.19W
Dallas Tex. U.S.A. **53** 32.47N 96.48W
Dalmally U.K. **6** 56.25N 4.58W
Dalmellington U.K. **6** 55.19N 4.24W
Dalnerechensk Russian Fed. **25** 45.55N133.45E
Daloa Ivory Coast **34** 6.56N 6.28W
Dalou Shan *mts.* China **24** 28.00N106.40E
Dalrymple, Mt. Australia **44** 21.02S148.38E
Dalton Canada **55** 48.10N 84.04W
Daltonganj India **29** 24.02N 84.07E
Dalvik Iceland **16** 65.58N 18.28W
Dalwhinnie U.K. **6** 56.56N 4.15W
Daly *r.* Australia **42** 13.20S130.19E
Daly City U.S.A. **54** 37.42N122.29W
Daly Waters *town* Australia **44** 16.15S133.22E
Damā, Wādī *r.* Saudi Arabia **30** 27.04N 35.48E
Damān India **28** 20.25N 72.58E
Damanhūr Egypt **32** 31.03N 30.28E
Damar *i.* Indonesia **27** 7.10S128.30E
Damascus *see* Dimashq Syria **32**
Damaturu Nigeria **38** 11.49N 11.50E
Damāvand, Qolleh-ye *mtn.* Iran **31** 35.47N 52.04E
Damba Angola **36** 6.44S 15.17E
Dāmghān Iran **31** 36.09N 54.22E
Dammartin-en-Goële France **9** 49.03N 2.41E
Damongo Ghana **38** 9.06N 1.48W
Dampier Australia **42** 20.40S116.42E
Dampier, Selat *str.* Pacific Oc. **27** 0.30S130.50E
Dampier Land Australia **42** 17.20S123.00E
Damqawt Yemen **28** 16.34N 52.54E
Da Nang Vietnam **26** 16.04N108.14E
Danba China **24** 30.57N101.55E
Danbury Conn. U.S.A. **55** 41.24N 73.26W
Dandaragan Australia **43** 30.40S115.42E
Dandenong Australia **47** 37.59S145.14E
Dandong China **25** 40.06N124.25E
Dangriga Belize **57** 16.58N 88.13W
Daniel U.S.A. **54** 42.52N110.04W
Danilov Russian Fed. **18** 58.10N 40.12E
Daning China **25** 36.32N110.47E
Danisa Hills Kenya **37** 3.10N 39.37E
Danja Nigeria **38** 11.29N 7.30E
Danlí Honduras **57** 14.02N 86.30W
Dannenberg Germany **14** 53.06N 11.05E
Dannevirke New Zealand **48** 40.12S176.08E
Dannhauser R.S.A. **39** 28.00S 30.03E
Dansville U.S.A. **55** 42.34N 77.41W
Danube *r.* Europe **15** 45.26N 29.38E
Danube, Mouths of the *see* Dunării, Delta *f.* Romania **15**
Danville Va. U.S.A. **53** 36.34N 79.25W
Dan Xian China **25** 19.31N109.33E
Daoukro Ivory Coast **38** 7.10N 3.58W
Dapango Togo **38** 10.51N 0.15E
Da Qaidam China **24** 37.44N 95.08E
Daqq-e Patargān *f.* Iran **31** 33.30N 60.40E
Dar'ā Syria **32** 32.37N 36.06E
Dārāb Iran **31** 28.45N 54.34E
Darabani Romania **15** 48.11N 26.35E
Dārān Iran **31** 33.00N 50.27E
Darband, Kūh-e *mtn.* Iran **31** 31.33N 57.08E
Darbhanga India **29** 26.10N 85.54E
Darby Mont. U.S.A. **54** 46.01N114.11W
Dardanelles *see* Çanakkale Bogazi *str.* Turkey **13**
Dar es Salaam Tanzania **37** 6.51S 39.18E
Dar es Salaam *d.* Tanzania **37** 34.04S142.40E
Dareton Australia **46** 34.04S142.04E
Darfield New Zealand **48** 43.29S172.07E
Dargan Ata Turkmenistan **20** 40.30N 62.10E
Dargaville New Zealand **48** 35.57S173.53E
Dargo Australia **47** 37.30S147.16E
Darhan Mongolia **24** 49.34N106.23E
Darién, Golfo del *g.* Colombia **60** 9.20N 77.30W
Darjeeling India **29** 27.02N 88.20E
Darkan Australia **43** 33.19S116.42E
Darke Peak *mtn.* Australia **46** 33.28S136.12E
Darling *r.* Australia **46** 34.05S141.57E
Darling Downs *f.* Australia **45** 28.00S149.45E
Darling Range *mts.* Australia **43** 32.00S116.30E
Darlington U.K. **4** 54.33N 1.33W
Darlington Point *town* Australia **47** 34.36S146.01E
Darłowe Poland **14** 54.26N 16.23E
Darmstadt Germany **14** 49.52N 8.30E
Darnah Libya **35** 32.45N 22.39E
Darnétal France **9** 49.27N 1.09E
Darnick Australia **46** 32.55S143.39E
Darnley, C. Antarctica **64** 68.00S 69.00E
Daroca Spain **10** 41.09N 1.25W
Darreh Gaz Iran **31** 37.22N 59.08E
Dartmoor Australia **46** 37.58S141.19E
Dartmoor Forest *hills* U.K. **5** 50.33N 3.55W
Dartmouth Canada **51** 44.40N 63.34W
Dartmouth U.K. **5** 50.21N 3.35W
Dartmouth Resr. Australia **47** 36.36S147.38E
Dartry Mts. Rep. of Ire. **7** 54.23N 8.25W
Daru P.N.G. **44** 9.04S143.12E
Darvaza Turkmenistan **20** 40.12N 58.24E
Darvel, Teluk *b.* Malaysia **26** 4.40N118.30E
Darwen U.K. **4** 53.42N 2.29W
Darwin Australia **44** 12.23S130.44E
Daryācheh-ye Bakhtegān *l.* Iran **31** 29.20N 54.05E
Daryācheh-ye Namak *l.* Iran **31** 34.45N 51.36E
Daryācheh-ye Orūmīyeh *l.* Iran **31** 37.40N 45.28E
Daryācheh-ye Sīstān *f.* Iran **31** 31.00N 61.15E
Dasht *r.* Pakistan **28** 25.07N 61.45E
Dashte-e Mārgow *des.* Afghan. **31** 30.45N 63.00E
Dasht-e Kavīr *des.* Iran **31** 34.40N 55.00E
Dasht-e Lūt *des.* Iran **31** 31.30N 58.00E
Dassa-Zoumé Benin **38** 7.50N 2.13E
Dastgardān Iran **31** 34.19N 56.51E
Dastjerd Iran **31** 34.33N 50.15E
Datong China **25** 40.12N113.12E
Datteln Germany **8** 51.40N 7.20E
Datu, Tanjung *c.* Malaysia **26** 2.00N109.30E
Datu Piang Phil. **27** 7.02N124.30E
Daugavpils Latvia **18** 55.52N 26.31E
Daun Germany **8** 50.11N 6.50E
Dauphin Canada **51** 51.09N100.05W
Dauphiné, Alpes du *mts.* France **11** 44.35N 5.45E
Daura Nigeria **38** 13.05N 8.18E
Dāvangere India **28** 14.30N 75.52E
Davao Phil. **27** 7.05N125.38E
Davao G. Phil. **27** 6.30N126.00E
Davenport U.S.A. **53** 41.40N 90.36W
Daventry U.K. **5** 52.16N 1.10W
David Panama **57** 8.26N 82.26W
David-Gorodok Belorussia **15** 52.04N 27.10E
Davis U.S.A. **54** 38.33N121.44W
Davis Creek *town* U.S.A. **54** 41.44N120.24W
Davis Sea Antarctica **64** 66.00S 90.00E
Davis Str. N. America **51** 66.00N 58.00W
Davlekanovo Russian Fed. **18** 54.12N 55.00E
Davos Switz. **14** 46.47N 9.50E
Dawei *see* Tavoy Burma **29**
Dawlish U.K. **5** 50.34N 3.28W
Dawna Range *mts.* Burma **29** 16.10N 98.30E
Dawson Canada **50** 64.04N139.24W
Dawson Creek *town* Canada **50** 55.44N120.15W
Dawson Range *f.* Canada **50** 62.40N139.00W
Dawu China **24** 31.00N101.09E
Dax France **11** 43.43N 1.03W
Daxian China **29** 31.10N107.28E
Daylesford Australia **46** 37.22S144.12E
Dayman *r.* Uruguay **63** 31.25S 58.00W
Dayr az Zawr Syria **30** 35.20N 40.08E
Dayton Ohio U.S.A. **55** 39.45N 84.10W
Dayton Wash. U.S.A. **54** 46.19N117.59W
Daytona Beach *town* U.S.A. **53** 29.11N 81.01W
De Aar R.S.A. **39** 30.39S 24.01E
Dead Sea Jordan **32** 31.25N 35.30E
Deal U.K. **5** 51.13N 1.25E
Deán Funes Argentina **62** 30.25S 64.20W
Dearborn U.S.A. **55** 42.18N 83.14W
Dease Arm *b.* Canada **50** 66.52N119.37W
Death Valley *f.* U.S.A. **54** 36.30N117.00W
Death Valley *town* U.S.A. **54** 36.18N116.25W
Death Valley Nat. Monument U.S.A. **54** 36.30N117.00W
Deauville France **9** 49.21N 0.04E
Debar Macedonia **13** 41.31N 20.31E
Debica Poland **15** 50.04N 21.24E
Deblin Poland **15** 51.35N 21.50E
Deborah, L. Australia **43** 30.45S119.07E
Debrecen Hungary **15** 47.30N 21.37E
Debre Tabor Ethiopia **35** 11.50N 38.05E
Decatur Ill. U.S.A. **53** 39.44N 88.57W
Decatur Ind. U.S.A. **55** 40.50N 84.57W
Deccan *f.* India **28** 18.30N 77.30E
Decelles, Lac *l.* Canada **55** 47.40N 78.08W
Děčín Czech Republic **14** 50.48N 14.15E
Decize France **14** 46.50N 3.27E
De Cocksdorp Neth. **8** 53.12N 4.52E
Deda Romania **15** 46.57N 24.53E
Dédi Ivory Coast **38** 8.34N 3.33W
Dedza Malaŵi **37** 14.20S 34.24E
Dee *r.* D. and G. U.K. **6** 54.50N 4.05W
Dee *r.* Grampian U.K. **6** 57.07N 2.04W
Dee *r.* Wales U.K. **4** 53.13N 3.05W
Deep River *town* Canada **55** 46.06N 77.30W
Deepwater Australia **47** 29.26S151.51E
Deep Well Australia **44** 24.25S134.05E
Deer Lodge U.S.A. **54** 46.24N112.44W
Deesa India **28** 24.15N 72.10E
Deeth U.S.A. **54** 41.04N115.18W
Defiance U.S.A. **55** 41.17N 84.21W
Deggendorf Germany **14** 48.51N 12.59E
De Grey *r.* Australia **42** 20.12S119.11E
Deh Bīd Iran **31** 30.38N 53.12E
Dehra Dūn India **29** 30.19N 78.00E
Deinze Belgium **8** 50.59N 3.32E
Dej Romania **15** 47.08N 23.55E
Deje Sweden **17** 59.36N 13.28E
Dekina Nigeria **38** 7.43N 7.04E
Delano U.S.A. **54** 35.41N119.15W
Delaware *d.* U.S.A. **55** 39.10N 75.30W
Delaware *r.* U.S.A. **55** 39.20N 75.25W
Delaware *town* U.S.A. **55** 40.18N 83.06W
Delaware B. U.S.A. **55** 39.05N 75.15W
Delegate Australia **47** 37.03S148.58E
Delfinópolis Brazil **59** 20.21S 46.51W
Delft Neth. **8** 52.01N 4.23E
Delfzijl Neth. **8** 53.20N 6.56E
Delgado, C. Mozambique **37** 10.45S 40.38E
Delhi India **28** 28.40N 77.14E
Delicias Mexico **56** 28.13N105.28W
Delingha China **24** 37.16N 97.12E
Delmenhorst Germany **14** 53.03N 8.37E
De Long Mts. U.S.A. **50** 68.20N162.00W
Delphos U.S.A. **55** 40.50N 84.21W
Del Rio U.S.A. **52** 29.23N100.56W
Delta *d.* Nigeria **38** 5.30N 6.00E
Delta Colo. U.S.A. **54** 38.44N108.04W
Delta Utah U.S.A. **54** 39.21N112.35W
Delungra Australia **47** 29.38S150.50E
Demer *r.* Belgium **8** 50.59N 4.42E
Deming U.S.A. **52** 32.16N107.45W
Demmin Germany **14** 53.54N 13.02E
Demonte Italy **9** 44.19N 7.17E
Demotte U.S.A. **55** 41.07N 87.14W
Denain France **8** 50.20N 3.24E
Denakil *f.* Ethiopia **35** 13.00N 41.00E
Denbigh U.K. **4** 53.11N 3.25W
Den Burg Neth. **8** 53.03N 4.47E
Dendermonde Belgium **8** 51.01N 4.07E
Dendre *r.* Belgium **8** 51.01N 4.07E
Denham Australia **42** 25.54S113.35E
Denham Range *mts.* Australia **44** 21.55S147.46E
Den Helder Neth. **8** 52.58N 4.46E
Denia Spain **10** 38.51N 0.07E
Deniliquin Australia **47** 35.33S144.58E
Denizli Turkey **30** 37.46N 29.05E
Denman Australia **47** 32.23S150.42E
Denmark Australia **43** 34.54S117.25E
Denmark Europe **17** 55.50N 10.00E
Den Oever Neth. **8** 52.56N 5.01E
Denpasar Indonesia **26** 8.40S115.14E
Denton Mont. U.S.A. **54** 47.19N109.57W
D'Entrecasteaux, Pt. Australia **43** 34.50S116.00E
D'Entrecasteaux Is. P.N.G. **44** 9.30S150.40E
Denver U.S.A. **52** 39.43N105.01W
Deo *r.* Cameroon **38** 8.33N 12.45E
Deogarh Orissa India **29** 21.22N 84.45E
De Peel *f.* Belgium **8** 51.30N 5.50E
Depew U.S.A. **55** 42.54N 78.41W
Dêqên China **24** 28.45N 98.58E
Dera Ghāzi Khān Pakistan **28** 30.05N 70.44E
Dera Ismāīl Khān Pakistan **28** 31.51N 70.56E
Derazhnya Ukraine **15** 49.18N 27.28E
Derbent Russian Fed. **31** 42.03N 48.18E
Derby Tas. Australia **45** 41.08S147.47E
Derby W.A. Australia **42** 17.19S123.38E
Derby U.K. **4** 52.55N 1.28W
Derbyshire *d.* U.K. **4** 52.55N 1.28W
Derg, Lough Donegal Rep. of Ire. **7** 54.37N 7.55W
Derg, Lough Tipperary Rep. of Ire. **7** 52.57N 8.18W
Déroute, Passage de la *str.* France / U.K. **5** 49.10N 1.45W
Derrynasaggart Mts. Rep. of Ire. **7** 51.58N 9.15W
Derryveagh Mts. Rep. of Ire. **7** 55.00N 8.07W
Derval France **9** 47.40N 1.40W
Derwent *r.* Cumbria U.K. **4** 54.38N 3.34W
Derwent *r.* N. Yorks. U.K. **4** 53.44N 0.57W
Desaguadero *r.* Bolivia **62** 18.24S 67.05W
Deschutes *r.* U.S.A. **54** 45.38N120.54W
Desē Ethiopia **35** 11.05N 39.40E
Deseado Argentina **63** 47.39S 65.20W
Deseado *r.* Argentina **63** 47.45S 65.50W
Desenzano del Garda Italy **9** 45.28N 10.32E
Desert Center U.S.A. **54** 33.44N115.25W
Des Moines Iowa U.S.A. **53** 41.35N 93.35W
Desna *r.* Ukraine **15** 50.32N 30.37E
Dessau Germany **14** 51.51N 12.15E
Dete Zimbabwe **39** 18.39S 26.49E
Detroit U.S.A. **55** 42.23N 83.05W
Deurne Belgium **8** 51.13N 4.26E
Deurne Neth. **8** 51.29N 5.44E
Deutsche Bucht *b.* Germany **14** 54.00N 8.15E
Deva Romania **15** 45.54N 22.55E
Deventer Neth. **8** 52.15N 6.10E
Deveron *r.* U.K. **6** 57.40N 2.30W
Devil's Bridge U.K. **5** 52.23N 3.50W
Devils Lake *town* U.S.A. **52** 48.08N 98.50W
Devin Bulgaria **13** 41.44N 24.24E
Devizes U.K. **5** 51.21N 2.00W
Devon *d.* U.K. **5** 50.50N 3.40W
Devon I. Canada **51** 75.00N 86.00W
Devonport Australia **45** 41.09S146.16E
Devrez *r.* Turkey **30** 41.07N 34.25E
Dewsbury U.K. **4** 53.42N 1.38W
Dey-Dey L. Australia **45** 29.12S131.02E
Dez *r.* Iran **31** 31.38N 48.54E
Dezfūl Iran **31** 32.24N 48.27E
Dezhou China **25** 37.29N116.11E
Dezh Shāhpūr Iran **31** 35.31N 46.10E
Dhahab Egypt **32** 28.30N 34.31E
Dhahran *see* Aẓ Ẓahrān Saudi Arabia **31**
Dhākā Bangla. **29** 23.43N 90.25E
Dhānbād India **29** 23.47N 86.32E
Dhaulāgiri *mtn.* Nepal **29** 28.39N 83.28E
Dhodhekánisos *is.* Greece **13** 37.00N 27.00E
Dholpur India **28** 26.43N 77.54E
Dhule India **28** 20.52N 74.50E
Diamante Argentina **63** 32.05S 60.35W
Diamantina *r.* Australia **44** 26.45S139.10E
Diamantina Brazil **59** 18.17S 43.37W
Diamantina, Chapada *hills* Brazil **61** 13.00S 42.30W
Diamantino Brazil **59** 14.25S 56.29W
Diane Bank *is.* Australia **44** 15.50S149.48E
Diapaga Burkina **38** 12.04N 1.48E
Dibi Cameroon **38** 7.09N 13.43E
Dibrugarh India **29** 27.29N 94.56E
Dickinson U.S.A. **52** 46.53N102.47W
Dicle *r.* Turkey *see* Dijlah *r.* Asia **30**
Didcot U.K. **5** 51.36N 1.14W
Die France **11** 44.45N 5.23E
Diekirch Lux. **8** 49.52N 6.10E
Diélette France **9** 49.33N 1.52W
Diemen Neth. **8** 52.22N 4.58E
Diemuchuoke Jammu & Kashmir **29** 32.42N 79.29E
Dien Bien Phu Vietnam **26** 21.23N103.02E
Diepholz Germany **14** 52.35N 8.21E
Dieppe France **9** 49.55N 1.05E
Dierdorf Germany **8** 50.33N 7.38E
Dieren Neth. **8** 52.03N 6.06E
Diesdorf Germany **14** 52.45N 10.52E
Diest Belgium **8** 50.59N 5.03E
Dieuze France **11** 48.49N 6.43E
Dif Kenya **37** 1.04N 40.57E
Diffa Niger **38** 13.19N 12.35E
Diffa *d.* Niger **38** 16.00N 13.00E
Digne France **11** 44.05N 6.14E
Digoin France **11** 46.29N 3.59E
Digul *r.* Indonesia **27** 7.10S139.08E
Dijlah *r.* Asia **31** 31.00N 47.27E
Dijle *r.* Belgium **8** 51.02N 4.25E
Dijon France **11** 47.20N 5.02E
Dikhil Djibouti **35** 11.06N 42.22E
Dikili Turkey **13** 39.05N 26.52E
Dikirnis Egypt **32** 31.05N 31.35E
Dikodougou Ivory Coast **38** 9.00N 5.45W
Diksmuide Belgium **8** 51.01N 2.52E
Dikwa Nigeria **38** 12.01N 13.55E
Dili Indonesia **27** 8.35S125.35E
Dilling Sudan **35** 12.03N 29.39E
Dillingham U.S.A. **50** 59.02N158.29W
Dillon U.S.A. **54** 45.13N112.38W
Dimashq Syria **32** 33.30N 36.19E
Dimbokro Ivory Coast **38** 6.43N 4.46W
Dimboola Australia **46** 36.27S142.02E
Dîmbovița *r.* Romania **15** 44.13N 26.22E
Dimitrovgrad Bulgaria **13** 42.01N 25.34E
Dimona Israel **32** 31.04N 35.01E
Dinagat *i.* Phil. **27** 10.15N125.30E
Dinan France **11** 48.27N 2.02W
Dinant Belgium **8** 50.16N 4.55E
Dinar Turkey **30** 38.05N 30.09E
Dīnār, Kūh-e *mtn.* Iran **31** 30.45N 51.39E
Dinara Planina *mts.* Europe **14** 44.00N 16.30E
Dindigul India **28** 10.23N 78.00E
Dingle Rep. of Ire. **7** 52.09N 10.17W
Dingle B. Rep. of Ire. **7** 52.05N 10.12W
Dingolfing Germany **14** 48.38N 12.31E
Dingwall U.K. **6** 57.35N 4.26W
Dinokwe Botswana **39** 23.24S 26.40E
Dinuba U.S.A. **54** 36.32N119.23W
Diö Sweden **17** 56.38N 14.13E
Diourbel Senegal **34** 14.30N 16.10W
Dipolog Phil. **27** 8.34N123.28E
Dirdal Norway **17** 58.47N 6.14E
Diré Mali **38** 16.16N 3.24W
Direction, C. Australia **44** 12.51S143.32E
Dirē Dawa Ethiopia **35** 9.35N 41.50E
Dirico Angola **39** 17.58S 20.40E
Dirk Hartog I. Australia **42** 25.50S113.00E
Dirranbandi Australia **47** 28.35S148.10E
Disappointment, L. Australia **42** 23.30S122.55E
Disaster B. Australia **47** 37.20S149.58E
Discovery Canada **50** 63.10N113.58W
Discovery B. Australia **46** 38.12S141.07E
Disko *i.* Greenland **51** 69.45N 53.00W
Diss U.K. **5** 52.23N 1.06E
Distrito Federal *d.* Brazil **61** 15.45S 47.50W
Distrito Federal *d.* Mexico **56** 19.20N 99.10W
Disūq Egypt **32** 31.09N 30.39E
Diu India **28** 20.41N 70.59E
Diver Canada **55** 46.43N 79.30W
Dives *r.* France **9** 49.19N 0.05W
Divinópólis Brazil **59** 20.08S 44.55W
Divnoye Russian Fed. **19** 45.55N 43.21E
Divo Ivory Coast **38** 5.48N 5.15W
Divriği Turkey **30** 39.23N 38.06E
Dixcove Ghana **38** 4.49N 1.57W
Dixie U.S.A. **54** 45.34N115.28W
Dixon Entrance *str.* Canada / U.S.A. **50** 54.10N133.30W
Diyālā *r.* Iraq **31** 33.13N 44.33E
Diyarbakir Turkey **30** 37.55N 40.14E
Djado Niger **34** 21.00N 12.20E
Djado, Plateau du *f.* Niger **34** 22.00N 12.30E
Djambala Congo **36** 2.33S 14.38E
Djanet Algeria **34** 24.34N 9.29E
Djelfa Algeria **34** 34.43N 3.14E
Djénne Mali **38** 13.55N 4.31W
Djibo Burkina **38** 14.09N 1.38W
Djibouti Africa **35** 12.00N 42.50E
Djibouti *town* Djibouti **35** 11.35N 43.11E
Djougou Benin **38** 9.40N 1.47E
Djugu Zaïre **37** 1.55N 30.31E
Djúpivogur Iceland **16** 64.41N 14.16W
Dmitriya Lapteva, Proliv *str.* Russian Fed. **21** 73.00N142.00E
Dnepr *r.* Ukraine **15** 50.00N 31.00E
Dneprodzerzhinsk Ukraine **19** 48.30N 34.37E
Dnepropetrovsk Ukraine **19** 48.29N 35.00E
Dneprovskaya Nizmennost *f.* Belorussia **15** 52.30N 29.45E
Dneprovsko-Bugskiy Kanal Belorussia **15** 52.03N 25.35E
Dnestr *r.* Ukraine **15** 46.21N 30.20E
Dnieper *see* Dnepr *r.* Belorussia **15**
Dniester *see* Dnestr *r.* Ukraine **15**
Dno Russian Fed. **18** 57.50N 30.00E
Doba Chad **34** 8.40N 16.50E
Dobele Latvia **17** 56.37N 23.16E
Dobo Indonesia **27** 5.46S134.13E
Doboj Bosnia-Herzegovina **15** 44.44N 18.02E
Dobrich Bulgaria **13** 43.34N 27.52E
Dobrodzień Poland **15** 50.44N 18.27E
Dobruja *f.* Romania **15** 44.30N 28.15E
Dobrush Belorussia **15** 52.24N 31.19E
Dobryanka Russian Fed. **18** 58.30N 56.26E
Doce *r.* Brazil **59** 19.32S 39.57W
Docking U.K. **4** 52.55N 0.39E
Doda, Lac *l.* Canada **55** 49.24N 75.13W
Dodecanese *is. see* Dhodhekánisos *is.* Greece **13**
Dodge City U.S.A. **52** 37.45N100.02W
Dodman Pt. U.K. **5** 50.13N 4.48W
Dodoma Tanzania **37** 6.10S 35.40E
Dodoma *d.* Tanzania **37** 6.00S 36.00E
Dodson U.S.A. **54** 48.24N108.15W
Doetinchem Neth. **8** 51.57N 6.17E
Dogai Coring *l.* China **29** 34.30N 89.00E
Doğubayazit Turkey **31** 39.32N 44.08E
Doha *see* Ad Dawḥah Qatar **31**
Dokkum Neth. **8** 53.20N 6.00E
Dolbeau Canada **55** 48.52N 72.15W
Dol-de-Bretagne France **9** 48.33N 1.45W
Dole France **11** 47.05N 5.30E
Dolgellau U.K. **5** 52.44N 3.53W
Dolina Ukraine **15** 49.00N 23.59E
Dolinskaya Ukraine **19** 48.06N 32.46E
Dollard *b.* Germany **8** 53.20N 7.10E
Dolny Kubín Slovakia **15** 49.12N 19.17E
Dolomiti *mts.* Italy **9** 46.25N 11.50E
Dolores Argentina **63** 36.19S 57.40W
Dolores Uruguay **63** 33.33S 58.13W
Dolores U.S.A. **54** 37.28N108.30W
Dolphin and Union Str. Canada **50** 69.20N118.00W
Doma Nigeria **38** 8.23N 8.21E
Domadare Somali Rep. **37** 1.48N 41.13E
Domažlice Czech Republic **14** 49.27N 12.56E
Dombås Norway **17** 62.05N 9.08E
Dombey, C. Australia **46** 37.12S139.43E
Dombóvár Hungary **15** 46.23N 18.08E
Domburg Neth. **8** 51.35N 3.31E
Domfront France **9** 48.36N 0.39W
Dominica Windward Is. **57** 15.30N 61.30W
Dominican Republic C. America **57** 18.00N 70.00W
Dommel *r.* Neth. **8** 51.44N 5.17E
Domo Ethiopia **35** 7.54N 46.52E
Domodossola Italy **9** 46.07N 8.17E
Domuyo *mtn.* Argentina **63** 36.37S 70.28W
Don *r.* Russian Fed. **19** 47.06N 39.16E
Don *r.* England U.K. **4** 53.41N 0.50W
Don *r.* Scotland U.K. **6** 57.10N 2.05W
Donaghadee U.K. **7** 54.39N 5.33W
Donald Australia **46** 36.25S143.04E
Donau *r.* Germany *see* Danube *r.* Europe **14**
Donaueschingen Germany **14** 47.57N 8.29E
Donauwörth Germany **14** 48.44N 10.48E
Don Benito Spain **10** 38.57N 5.52W
Doncaster U.K. **4** 53.31N 1.09W
Dondo Mozambique **39** 19.39S 34.39E
Donegal Rep. of Ire. **7** 54.39N 8.06W
Donegal *d.* Rep. of Ire. **7** 54.52N 8.00W
Donegal B. Rep. of Ire. **7** 54.32N 8.18W
Donegal Pt. Rep. of Ire. **7** 52.43N 9.38W
Donetsk Ukraine **19** 48.00N 37.50E
Donga Nigeria **38** 7.45N 10.05E
Donga *r.* Nigeria **38** 8.20N 10.00E
Dongara Australia **43** 29.15S114.56E
Dongbei Pingyuan *f.* China **25** 42.30N123.00E
Dongchuan China **24** 26.10N103.02E
Dongfang China **25** 19.04N108.39E
Donggala Indonesia **26** 0.48S119.45E
Dong Hoi Vietnam **26** 17.32N106.35E
Dongkalang Indonesia **27** 0.12N120.07E
Dongou Congo **36** 2.05N 18.00E
Dongsheng China **25** 39.49N109.59E
Dongtai China **25** 32.51N120.18E
Dongting Hu *l.* China **25** 29.40N113.00E
Donington U.K. **4** 52.55N 0.12W
Donja Stubica Croatia **14** 45.59N 15.58E
Dönna *i.* Norway **16** 66.05N 12.30E
Donnacona Canada **55** 46.41N 71.45W
Donnybrook Australia **43** 33.34S115.47E
Donnybrook R.S.A. **39** 29.55S 29.51E
Donostia *see* San Sebastián Spain **10**
Doodlakine Australia **43** 31.41S117.23E
Doon, Loch U.K. **6** 55.15N 4.23W
Dora, L. Australia **42** 22.05S122.55E
Dora Baltea *r.* Italy **9** 45.11N 8.05E
Dora Riparia *r.* Italy **9** 45.05N 7.44E
Dorchester U.K. **5** 50.52N 2.28W
Dorchester, C. Canada **51** 65.29N 77.30W
Dordogne *r.* France **11** 45.03N 0.34W
Dordrecht Neth. **8** 51.48N 4.40E
Dordrecht R.S.A. **39** 31.22S 27.02E
Dore, Mont *mtn.* France **11** 45.32N 2.49E
Dori Burkina **38** 14.03N 0.02W

Dorking U.K. 5 51.14N 0.20W
Dormagen Germany 8 51.05N 6.50E
Dormans France 9 49.04N 3.38E
Dornie U.K. 6 57.16N 5.31W
Dornoch U.K. 6 57.52N 4.02W
Dornoch Firth *est.* U.K. 6 57.50N 4.04W
Dornum Germany 8 53.39N 7.26E
Doro Mali 38 16.09N 0.51W
Dorohoi Romania 15 47.57N 26.24E
Dörpen Germany 8 52.58N 7.20E
Dorre I. Australia 42 25.08S113.06E
Dorrigo Australia 47 30.20S152.41E
Dorris U.S.A. 54 41.58N121.55W
Dorset *d.* U.K. 5 50.48N 2.25W
Dorset, C. Canada 51 64.10N 76.40W
Dorsten Germany 8 51.38N 6.58E
Dortmund Germany 8 51.32N 7.27E
Dortmund-Ems Kanal Germany 8 52.20N 7.30E
Dos Bahías, C. Argentina 63 44.55S 65.32W
Dosquet Canada 55 46.28N 71.33W
Dosso Niger 38 13.03N 3.10E
Dosso *d.* Niger 38 13.00N 3.15E
Dossor Kazakhstan 19 47.31N 53.01E
Dothan U.S.A. 53 31.12N 85.25W
Douai France 8 50.22N 3.05E
Douala Cameroon 38 4.05N 9.43E
Douarnenez France 11 48.05N 4.20W
Doubs *r.* France 11 46.57N 5.03E
Doubtless B. New Zealand 48 35.10S173.30E
Doudeville France 9 49.43N 0.48E
Douentza Mali 38 14.58N 2.48W
Douglas I.o.M Europe 4 54.09N 4.29W
Douglas R.S.A. 39 29.03S 23.45E
Douglas Ariz. U.S.A. 52 31.21N109.33W
Douglas Mich. U.S.A. 55 42.38N 86.13W
Douglas Creek *r.* Australia 46 28.35S136.50E
Doulaincourt France 11 48.19N 5.12E
Doulevant-le-Château France 9 48.23N 4.55E
Doumé Cameroon 38 4.13N 13.30E
Douna Mali 38 12.40N 6.00W
Dounreay U.K. 6 58.35N 3.42W
Dourados Brazil 62 22.09S 54.52W
Dourdan France 9 48.32N 2.01E
Douro *r.* Portugal 10 41.10N 8.40W
Douvres France 9 49.17N 0.23W
Dove *r.* U.K. 4 52.50N 1.35W
Dover U.K. 5 51.07N 1.19E
Dover Del. U.S.A. 55 39.10N 75.32W
Dover N.H. U.S.A. 55 43.12N 70.56W
Dover Ohio U.S.A. 55 40.32N 81.30W
Dover, Pt. Australia 43 32.32S125.30E
Dover, Str. of U.K. 5 51.00N 1.30E
Dovey *r.* U.K. 5 52.33N 3.56W
Dovrefjell *mts.* Norway 17 62.06N 9.25E
Dovsk Belorussia 15 53.07N 30.29E
Dowa Malaŵi 37 13.40S 33.55E
Dowagiac U.S.A. 55 41.58N 86.06W
Dowerin Australia 43 31.15S117.00E
Dowlatābād Iran 31 28.19N 56.40E
Down *d.* U.K. 7 54.20N 6.00W
Downey U.S.A. 54 42.26N112.07W
Downham Market U.K. 5 52.36N 0.22E
Downpatrick U.K. 7 54.21N 5.43W
Downpatrick Head Rep. of Ire. 7 54.20N 9.22W
Dowra Rep. of Ire. 7 54.11N 8.02W
Dozois, Résr. Canada 55 47.30N 77.00W
Drâa, Oued *wadi* Morocco 34 28.40N 11.06W
Drachten Neth. 8 53.05N 6.06E
Drăgășani Romania 15 44.40N 24.16E
Dragoman, Pasul *pass* Bulgaria/Yugo. 13 42.56N 22.52E
Dragon's Mouth *str.* Trinidad 60 11.00N 61.35W
Dragovishtitsa Bulgaria 13 42.22N 22.39E
Draguignan France 11 43.32N 6.28E
Drake Australia 47 28.55S152.24E
Drakensberg *mts.* R.S.A./Lesotho 39 30.00S 29.05E
Dráma Greece 13 41.09N 24.11E
Drammen Norway 17 59.44N 10.15E
Drau *r.* Austria *see* Drava *r.* Slovenia/Croatia 14
Drava *r.* Slovenia/Croatia 15 45.34N 18.56E
Drenthe *d.* Neth. 8 52.52N 6.30E
Dresden Germany 14 51.03N 13.45E
Dreux France 9 48.44N 1.23E
Driftwood Canada 55 49.08N 81.23W
Drin *r.* Albania 13 41.45N 19.34E
Drina *r.* Bosnia-Herzegovina 15 44.53N 19.20E
Dröbak Norway 17 59.39N 10.39E
Drogheda Rep. of Ire. 7 53.42N 6.23W
Drogobych Ukraine 15 49.10N 23.30E
Droitwich U.K. 5 52.16N 2.10W
Drokiya Moldavia 15 48.07N 27.49E
Dromedary, C. Australia 47 36.18S150.15E
Dronero Italy 9 44.28N 7.22E
Dronfield U.K. 4 53.18N 1.29W
Dronne *r.* France 11 45.02N 0.09W
Dronning Maud Land *f.* Antarctica 64 74.00S 10.00E
Drumheller Canada 50 51.28N112.40W
Drum Hills Rep. of Ire. 7 52.03N 7.42W
Drummond Range *mts.* Australia 44 23.30S147.15E
Drummondville Canada 55 45.52N 72.30W
Drummore U.K. 6 54.41N 4.54W
Druskininkai Lithuania 15 53.48N 23.58E
Drut *r.* Belorussia 15 53.03N 30.42E
Drvar Bosnia-Herzegovina 14 44.22N 16.24E
Drymen U.K. 6 56.04N 4.27W
Drysdale *r.* Australia 42 13.59S126.51E
Dschang Cameroon 38 5.28N 10.02E
Duaringa Australia 44 23.42S149.40E
Ḑubā Saudi Arabia 30 27.21N 35.40E
Dubai *see* Dubayy U.A.E. 31
Dubawnt *r.* Canada 51 62.50N102.00W
Dubawnt L. Canada 51 62.50N102.00W
Dubayy U.A.E. 31 25.13N 55.17E
Dubbo Australia 47 32.16S148.41E
Dubica Croatia 14 45.11N 16.48E
Dublin Rep. of Ire. 7 53.21N 6.18W
Dublin *d.* Rep. of Ire. 7 53.20N 6.18W
Dublin U.S.A. 53 32.31N 82.54W
Dublin B. Rep. of Ire. 7 53.20N 6.09W
Dubno Ukraine 15 50.28N 25.40E
Dubois Idaho U.S.A. 54 44.10N112.14W
Du Bois Penn. U.S.A. 55 41.07N 78.46W
Dubovka Russian Fed. 19 49.04N 44.48E
Dubréka Guinea 34 9.50N 13.32W
Dubrovitsa Ukraine 15 51.38N 26.40E
Dubrovnik Croatia 13 42.40N 18.07E
Dubuque U.S.A. 53 42.31N 90.41W
Duchesne U.S.A. 54 40.10N110.24W
Duchess Australia 41 21.22S139.52E
Duchess Australia 44 21.22S139.52E
Du Couëdic, C. Australia 46 36.00S136.10E
Dudinka Russian Fed. 21 69.27N 86.13E
Dudley U.K. 5 52.30N 2.05W
Duero *r.* Spain *see* Douro *r.* Portugal 10
Duff Creek *town* Australia 46 28.28S135.51E
Dufftown U.K. 6 57.27N 3.09W
Duga Resa Croatia 14 45.27N 15.30E
Dugi *i.* Croatia 14 44.04N 15.00E
Duifken Pt. Australia 44 12.33S141.38E
Duisburg Germany 8 51.26N 6.45E
Duitama Colombia 60 5.50N 73.01W
Duiveland *i.* Neth. 8 51.39N 4.00E
Dujuuma Somali Rep. 37 1.14N 42.37E
Dukhān Qatar 31 25.24N 50.47E
Dukou China 24 26.33N101.44E
Dulce *r.* Argentina 62 30.40S 62.00W
Duleek Rep. of Ire. 7 53.39N 6.24W
Dülmen Germany 8 51.49N 7.17E
Dulovo Bulgaria 15 43.49N 27.09E
Duluth U.S.A. 53 46.50N 92.10W.
Dūmā Syria 32 33.33N 36.24E
Dumaguete Phil. 27 9.20N123.18E
Dumai Indonesia 26 1.41N101.27E
Dumaran *i.* Phil. 26 10.33N119.50E
Dumaresq *r.* Australia 47 28.40S150.28E
Dumaring Indonesia 26 1.36N118.12E
Dumbarton U.K. 6 55.57N 4.35W
Dumbleyung Australia 43 33.18S117.42E
Dumbrăveni Romania 15 46.14N 24.35E
Dumfries U.K. 6 55.04N 3.37W
Dumfries and Galloway *d.* U.K. 6 55.05N 3.40W
Dumyāṭ Egypt 32 31.26N 31.48E
Duna *r.* Hungary *see* Danube *r.* Europe 15
Dunaföldvár Hungary 15 46.48N 18.55E
Dunajec *r.* Poland 15 50.15N 20.44E
Dunajská Streda Slovakia 15 48.01N 17.35E
Dunany Pt. Rep. of Ire. 7 53.51N 6.15W
Dunărea *r.* Romania *see* Danube *r.* Europe 15
Dunării, Delta *f.* Romania 15 45.05N 29.45E
Dunav *r.* Bulgaria *see* Danube *r.* Europe 15
Dunav *r.* Yugo. *see* Danube *r.* Europe 15
Dunbar U.K. 6 56.00N 2.31W
Dunblane U.K. 6 56.12N 3.59W
Dunboyne Rep. of Ire. 7 53.26N 6.30W
Duncan Canada 54 48.45N123.40W
Duncan U.S.A. 52 34.30N 97.57W
Duncansby Head U.K. 6 58.39N 3.01W
Dundalk Rep. of Ire. 7 54.01N 6.25W
Dundalk U.S.A. 55 39.15N 76.31W
Dundalk B. Rep. of Ire. 7 53.55N 6.17W
Dundas, L. Australia 43 32.35S121.50E
Dundas Str. Australia 44 11.20S131.35E
Dundee R.S.A. 39 28.09S 30.14E
Dundee U.K. 6 56.28N 3.00W
Dundrum U.K. 7 54.16N 5.51W
Dundrum B. U.K. 7 54.12N 5.46W
Dunedin New Zealand 48 45.52S170.30E
Dunedoo Australia 47 31.60S149.25E
Dunfermline U.K. 6 56.04N 3.29W
Dungannon U.K. 7 54.31N 6.47W
Dungarvan Rep. of Ire. 7 52.06N 7.39W
Dungeness *c.* U.K. 5 50.55N 0.58E
Dungiven U.K. 7 54.56N 6.56W
Dungog Australia 47 32.24S151.46E
Dungu Zaïre 37 3.40N 28.40E
Dunhuang China 24 40.00N 94.40E
Dunkeld Qld. Australia 45 26.55S148.00E
Dunkeld Vic. Australia 46 37.40S142.23E
Dunkeld U.K. 6 56.34N 3.36W
Dunkerque France 8 51.02N 2.23E
Dunk I. Australia 44 17.56S146.10E
Dunkirk *see* Dunkerque France 8
Dunkirk U.S.A. 55 42.29N 79.21W
Dunkwa Central Ghana 38 5.59N 1.45W
Dun Laoghaire Rep. of Ire. 7 53.17N 6.09W
Dunleer Rep. of Ire. 7 53.49N 6.24W
Dunmahon Rep. of Ire. 7 52.09N 7.23W
Dunmarra Australia 44 16.37S133.22E
Dunmore U.S.A. 55 41.25N 75.38W
Dunnet Head U.K. 6 58.40N 3.23W
Dunolly Australia 46 36.50S143.45E
Dunoon U.K. 6 55.57N 4.57W
Dunqulah Sudan 35 19.10N 30.27E
Duns U.K. 6 55.47N 2.20W
Dunsborough Australia 43 33.37S115.06E
Dunshaughlin Rep. of Ire. 7 53.30N 6.34W
Dunstable U.K. 5 51.53N 0.32W
Dunstan Mts. New Zealand 48 44.45S169.45E
Dupont U.S.A. 55 38.53N 85.30W
Duque de Caxias Brazil 59 22.47S 43.18W
Durance *r.* France 11 43.55N 4.48E
Durango Mexico 56 24.01N104.00W
Durango *d.* Mexico 56 24.01N104.00W
Durango Spain 10 43.13N 2.40W
Durango U.S.A. 54 37.16N107.53W
Durant U.S.A. 53 33.59N 96.24W
Durazno Uruguay 63 33.22S 56.31W
Durban R.S.A. 39 29.50S 30.59E
Durbe Latvia 17 56.35N 21.21E
Düren Germany 8 50.48N 6.30E
Durg India 29 21.11N 81.17E
Durham U.K. 4 54.47N 1.34W
Durham *d.* U.K. 4 54.42N 1.45W
Durham N.C. U.S.A. 53 36.00N 78.54W
Durham N.H. U.S.A. 55 43.08N 70.56W
Durlston Head *c.* U.K. 5 50.35N 1.58W
Durmitor *mtn.* Yugo. 13 43.08N 19.03E
Durness U.K. 6 58.33N 4.45W
Durrës Albania 13 41.19N 19.27E
Durrow Rep. of Ire. 7 52.51N 7.25W
Dursey Head Rep. of Ire. 7 51.35N 10.15W
Durūz, Jabal ad *mtn.* Syria 32 32.42N 36.42E
D'Urville I. New Zealand 48 40.45S173.50E
Dushak Turkmenistan 20 37.13N 60.01E
Dushanbe Tajikistan 24 38.38N 68.51E
Duskotna Bulgaria 13 42.52N 27.10E
Düsseldorf Germany 8 51.13N 6.47E
Dutlhe Botswana 39 23.55S 23.47E
Dutton, L. Australia 46 31.49S137.08E
Duvno Bosnia-Herzegovina 15 43.43N 17.14E
Duyun China 24 26.16N107.29E
Dvina *r.* Europe 20 57.03N 24.02E
Dvinskaya Guba *b.* Russian Fed. 18 64.40N 39.30E
Dwarda Australia 43 32.45S116.23E
Dwārka India 28 22.14N 68.58E
Dwellingup Australia 43 32.42S116.04E
Dyatlovichi Belorussia 15 52.08N 30.49E
Dyatlovo Belorussia 15 53.28N 25.28E
Dyer, C. Canada 51 67.45N 61.45W
Dyérem *r.* Cameroon 38 6.36N 13.10E
Dyer Plateau Antarctica 64 70.00S 65.00W
Dyersburg U.S.A. 53 36.02N 89.21W
Dyfed *d.* U.K. 5 52.00N 4.17W
Dykh Tau *mtn.* Russian Fed. 19 43.04N 43.10E
Dymer Ukraine 15 50.50N 30.20E
Dyulevo Bulgaria 13 42.22N 27.10E
Dyultydag *mtn.* Russian Fed. 31 41.55N 46.52E
Dzamïn Üüd Mongolia 25 43.50N111.53E
Dzerzhinsk Belorussia 15 53.40N 27.01E
Dzerzhinsk Russian Fed. 18 56.15N 43.30E
Dzhambul Kazakhstan 24 42.50N 71.25E
Dzhankoy Ukraine 19 45.42N 34.23E
Dzhardzhan Russian Fed. 21 68.49N124.08E
Dzhelinde Russian Fed. 21 70.09N114.00E
Dzhetygara Kazakhstan 20 52.14N 61.10E
Dzhezkazgan Kazakhstan 20 47.48N 67.24E
Dzhizak Uzbekistan 20 40.06N 67.45E
Dzhugdzhur, Khrebet *mts.* Russian Fed. 21 57.30N138.00E
Dzhurin Ukraine 15 48.40N 28.16E
Działdowo Poland 15 53.15N 20.10E
Dzierzoniów Poland 14 50.44N 16.39E
Dzodze Ghana 38 6.14N 1.00E

E

Eabamet L. Canada 53 51.30N 87.55W
Eagle U.S.A. 54 39.39N106.50W
Eagle L. U.S.A. 55 46.17N 69.20W
Eagle Lake *town* U.S.A. 55 47.02N 68.36W
Eagle Pass *town* U.S.A. 52 28.44N100.31W
Ealing U.K. 5 51.31N 0.20W
Earlimart U.S.A. 54 35.53N119.16W
Earn *r.* U.K. 6 56.21N 3.18W
Earn, Loch U.K. 6 56.23N 4.12W
Easingwold U.K. 4 54.08N 1.11W
Easky Rep. of Ire. 7 54.17N 8.58W
East Alligator *r.* Australia 44 12.25S132.58E
East Anglian Heights *hills* U.K. 5 52.03N 0.15E
Eastbourne U.K. 5 50.46N 0.18E
East C. New Zealand 48 37.45S178.30E
East China Sea Asia 25 29.00N125.00E
Eastern *d.* Ghana 38 6.20N 0.45W
Eastern *d.* Kenya 37 0.00 38.00E
Eastern Desert *see* Sharqīyah, Aş Şaḩrā' ash *des.* Egypt 32
Eastern Ghāts *mts.* India 29 16.30N 80.30E
East Falkland *i.* Falkland Is. 63 51.45W 58.50W
East Grinstead U.K. 5 51.08N 0.01W
East Ilsley U.K. 5 51.33N 1.15W
East Kilbride U.K. 6 55.46N 4.09W
East Lansing U.S.A. 55 42.45N 84.30W
Eastleigh U.K. 5 50.58N 1.21W
East London R.S.A. 39 33.00S 27.54E
Eastmain Canada 51 52.15N 78.30W
Eastmain *r.* Canada 51 52.15N 78.30W
Easton Penn. U.S.A. 55 40.41N 75.13W
Easton Wash. U.S.A. 54 47.14N121.11W
East Retford U.K. 4 53.19N 0.55W
East Sussex *d.* U.K. 5 50.56N 0.12E
Eau-Claire, Lac à l' *l.* Canada 51 56.10N 74.30W
Eauripik *i.* Federated States of Micronesia 27 6.42N143.04E
Eban Nigeria 38 9.41N 4.54E
Ebbw Vale U.K. 5 51.47N 3.12W
Eberswalde Germany 14 52.50N 13.50E
Ebinur Hu *l.* China 24 45.00N 83.00E
Eboli Italy 12 40.37N 15.04E
Ebolowa Cameroon 38 2.56N 11.11E
Ebony Namibia 39 22.05S 15.15E
Ebro *r.* Spain 10 40.43N 0.54E
Ebro, Delta del *f.* Spain 10 40.43N 0.54E
Ecclefechan U.K. 4 55.03N 3.18W
Echternach Lux. 8 49.49N 6.25E
Echuca Australia 47 36.10S144.20E
Écija Spain 10 37.33N 5.04W
Écommoy France 9 47.50N 0.16E
Ecuador S. America 60 1.40S 79.00W
Ed Sweden 17 58.55N 11.55E
Edam Neth. 8 52.30N 5.02E
Eddrachillis B. U.K. 6 58.17N 5.15W
Eddystone Pt. Australia 45 40.58S148.12E
Ede Neth. 8 52.03N 5.40E
Ede Nigeria 38 7.45N 4.26E
Edea Cameroon 38 3.47N 10.13E
Eden Australia 47 37.04S149.54E
Eden *r.* Cumbria U.K. 4 54.57N 3.02W
Eden U.S.A. 54 42.03N109.26W
Edenburg R.S.A. 39 29.44S 25.55E
Edendale New Zealand 48 46.19S168.47E
Edenderry Rep. of Ire. 7 53.21N 7.05W
Edenhope Australia 46 37.04S141.20E
Edeowie Australia 46 31.28S138.29E
Eder *r.* Germany 14 51.13N 9.27E
Ederny U.K. 7 54.32N 7.40W
Edgeöya *i.* Arctic Oc. 64 77.45N 22.30E
Edgeworthstown Rep. of Ire. 7 53.42N 7.38W
Édhessa Greece 13 40.47N 22.03E
Ediacara Australia 46 30.18S137.50E
Edinburgh U.K. 6 55.57N 3.13W
Edirne Turkey 13 41.40N 26.35E
Edithburgh Australia 46 35.06S137.44E
Edjudina Australia 43 29.48S122.23E
Edmonton Canada 50 53.34N113.25W
Edmundston Canada 55 47.22N 68.20W
Edo *r.* Japan 23 35.37N139.53E
Edo *d.* Nigeria 38 6.20N 5.55E
Edolo Italy 9 46.11N 10.20E
Edremit Turkey 13 39.35N 27.02E
Edsbruk Sweden 17 58.02N 16.28E
Edson Canada 50 53.35N116.26W
Edward, L. Uganda/Zaïre 37 0.30S 29.30E
Edwards Plateau *f.* U.S.A. 52 30.30N100.30W
Eeklo Belgium 8 51.11N 3.34E
Eel *r.* U.S.A. 54 40.40N124.20W
Egaña Argentina 63 36.57S 59.06W
Egbe Nigeria 38 8.13N 5.31E
Eger Hungary 15 47.54N 20.23E
Egersund Norway 17 58.27N 6.00E
Egerton, Mt. Australia 42 24.44S117.40E
Egmont, Mt. New Zealand 48 39.20S174.05E
Eğridir Turkey 30 37.52N 30.51E
Eğridir Gölü *l.* Turkey 30 38.04N 30.55E
Egypt Africa 35 26.30N 29.30E
Éibar Spain 10 43.11N 2.28W
Eidsvåg Norway 16 62.47N 8.03E
Eidsvold Australia 44 25.23S151.08E
Eifel *f.* Germany 8 50.10N 6.45E
Eigg *i.* U.K. 6 56.53N 6.09W
Eighty Mile Beach *f.* Australia 42 19.00S121.00E
Eil, Loch U.K. 6 56.51N 5.12W
Eildon, L. Australia 47 37.10S146.00E
Einasleigh Australia 44 18.31S144.05E
Eindhoven Neth. 8 51.26N 5.30E
Eirunepé Brazil 60 6.40S 69.52W
Eiseb *r.* Namibia 39 20.26S 20.05E
Eisenach Germany 14 50.59N 10.19E
Eisenerz Austria 14 47.33N 14.53E
Eisenhut *mtn.* Austria 14 47.00N 13.45E
Eisenhüttenstadt Germany 14 52.09N 14.41E
Eišiškes Lithuania 15 54.09N 24.55E
Eisleben Germany 14 51.32N 11.33E
Eitorf Germany 8 50.46N 7.27E
Ejin Qi China 24 41.50N100.50E
Ejura Ghana 38 7.24N 1.20W
Eket Nigeria 38 4.39N 7.56E
Eketahuna New Zealand 48 40.39S175.44E
Ekibastuz Kazakhstan 20 51.45N 75.22E
Ekimchan Russian Fed. 21 53.09N133.00E
Eksjö Sweden 17 57.40N 14.47E
Ekträsk Sweden 16 64.29N 19.50E
El Aaiún W. Sahara 34 27.10N 13.11W
Elands *r.* R.S.A. 39 24.52S 29.20E
El Arenal Spain 10 39.30N 2.45E
El Asnam Algeria 34 36.20N 1.30E
Elat Israel 32 29.33N 34.56E
Elâzig Turkey 30 38.41N 39.14E
Elba *i.* Italy 12 42.47N 10.17E
El Barril Mexico 56 28.22N113.00W
Elbasan Albania 13 41.07N 20.04E
El Baúl Venezuela 60 8.59N 68.16W
Elbe *r.* Germany 14 53.33N 10.00E
El Beni *d.* Bolivia 62 14.00S 65.30W
Elbert, Mt. U.S.A. 52 39.07N106.27W
Elbeuf France 9 49.17N 1.01E
Elbistan Turkey 30 38.14N 37.11E
Elbląg Poland 15 54.10N 19.25E
Elbrus *mtn.* Russian Fed. 19 43.21N 42.29E
Elburg Neth. 8 52.27N 5.50E
Elburz Mts. *see* Alborz, Reshteh-ye Kūhhā-ye Iran 31
El Cajon U.S.A. 54 32.48N116.58W
El Callao Venezuela 60 7.18N 61.48W
El Centro U.S.A. 54 32.48N115.34W
Elche Spain 10 38.16N 0.41W
Elcho I. Australia 44 11.55S135.45E
El Cuy Argentina 63 39.57S 68.20W
Elda Spain 10 38.29N 0.47W
Elde *r.* Germany 14 53.17N 12.40E
Elder, L. Australia 46 30.39S140.13E
El Djouf *des.* Mauritania 34 20.30N 7.30W
El Dorado Ark. U.S.A. 53 33.12N 92.40W
El Dorado Venezuela 60 6.45N 61.37W
Eldoret Kenya 37 0.31N 35.17E
Eleja Latvia 17 56.26N 23.42E
Elektrostal Russian Fed. 18 55.46N 38.30E
Elephant Butte Resr. U.S.A. 52 33.19N107.10W
Elephant I. Antarctica 64 61.00S 55.00W
Eleuthera I. Bahamas 57 25.00N 76.00W
Elevtheroúpolis Greece 13 40.55N 24.16E
El Ferrol Spain 10 43.29N 8.14W
Elgå Norway 17 62.11N 11.07E
Elgin U.K. 6 57.39N 3.20W
Elgin Nev. U.S.A. 54 37.21N114.30W
Elgin Oreg. U.S.A. 54 45.34N117.55W
El Golea Algeria 34 30.35N 2.51E
Elgon, Mt. Kenya/Uganda 37 1.07N 34.35E
Elim Namibia 39 17.47S 15.30E
Elista Russian Fed. 19 46.18N 44.14E
Elizabeth Australia 46 34.45S138.39E
Elizabeth N.J. U.S.A. 55 40.40N 74.13W
Elizabeth W.Va. U.S.A. 55 39.04N 81.24W
Elizabeth City U.S.A. 53 36.18N 76.18W
El Jadida Morocco 34 33.16N 8.30W
Elk Poland 15 53.50N 22.22E
El Kairouan Tunisia 34 35.40N 10.04E
Elkhart Ind. U.S.A. 55 41.52N 85.56W
Elkhovo Bulgaria 13 42.10N 26.35E
Elkins W.Va. U.S.A. 55 38.55N 79.51W
Elko U.S.A. 54 40.50N115.46W
Elleker Australia 43 34.55S117.40E
Ellen, Mt. U.S.A. 52 38.06N110.50W
Ellendale Australia 42 17.56S124.48E
Ellensburg U.S.A. 54 47.00N120.32W
Ellesmere I. Canada 51 78.00N 82.00W
Ellesmere Port U.K. 4 53.17N 2.55W
Elliot R.S.A. 39 31.19S 27.49E
Elliot Lake *town* Canada 55 46.33N 82.39W
Elliott Australia 44 17.33S133.31E
Elliston Australia 46 33.39S134.55E
Ellon U.K. 6 57.22N 2.05W
El Mahdia Tunisia 34 35.30N 11.04E
Elmali Turkey 30 36.43N 29.56E
Elmina Ghana 38 5.07N 1.21W
Elmira U.S.A. 55 42.06N 76.49W
Elmore Australia 47 36.30S144.40E
Elmshorn Germany 14 53.46N 9.40E
Eloy U.S.A. 54 32.45N111.33W
El Paso U.S.A. 52 31.45N106.29W
El Portal U.S.A. 54 37.41N119.47W
El Real Panama 57 8.06N 77.42W
El Reno U.S.A. 52 35.32N 97.57W
El Roba Kenya 37 3.57N 40.01E
El Salvador C. America 57 13.30N 89.00W
Elsas Canada 55 48.32N 82.55W
Elsdorf Germany 8 50.56N 6.35E
Elsinore U.S.A. 54 38.41N112.09W
El Tabacal Argentina 62 23.15S 64.14W
El Tigre Venezuela 60 8.44N 64.18W
Elton, Ozero *l.* Russian Fed. 19 49.10N 46.34E
El Turbio Argentina 63 51.41S 72.05W
Elūru India 29 16.45N 81.10E
Elvas Portugal 10 38.53N 7.10W
Elvdal Norway 17 61.38N 11.56E
Elverum Norway 17 60.53N 11.34E
Elvira Argentina 63 35.15S 59.30W
El Wak Kenya 37 2.45N 40.52E
Ely Nev. U.S.A. 54 39.15N114.53W
Elyria U.S.A. 55 41.22N 82.06W
Emāmshahr Iran 31 36.25N 55.00E
Emån *r.* Sweden 17 57.08N 16.30E
Emba Kazakhstan 20 48.47N 58.05E
Emba *r.* Kazakhstan 19 46.38N 53.00E
Embarcación Argentina 62 23.15S 64.10W
Embleton U.K. 4 55.30N 1.37W
Embrun France 11 44.34N 6.30E
Embu Kenya 37 0.32S 37.28E
Emden Germany 8 53.23N 7.13E
Emerald Australia 44 23.32S148.10E
Emerson Canada 51 49.00N 97.12W
Emi Koussi *mtn.* Chad 34 19.58N 18.30E
Emilia-Romagna *d.* Italy 9 44.35N 11.00E
Emlichheim Germany 8 52.37N 6.50E
Emmaboda Sweden 17 56.38N 15.32E
Emmaste Estonia 17 58.42N 22.36E
Emmaville Australia 47 29.25S151.39E
Emmeloord Neth. 8 52.43N 5.46E
Emmen Neth. 8 52.48N 6.55E
Emmerich Germany 8 51.49N 6.16E
Emmett U.S.A. 54 43.52N116.30W
Emory Peak *mtn.* U.S.A. 52 29.15N103.19W
Empangeni R.S.A. 39 28.45S 31.54E
Empedrado Argentina 62 27.59S 58.47W
Emporia Kans. U.S.A. 53 38.24N 96.10W
Ems *r.* Germany 8 53.14N 7.25E
Emsdale Canada 55 45.32N 79.19W
Emsdetten Germany 8 52.14N 7.32E
Ems-Jade Kanal Germany 8 53.28N 7.40E
Emyvale Rep. of Ire. 7 54.20N 6.59W
Enard B. U.K. 6 58.05N 5.20W
Encarnación Paraguay 59 27.20S 55.50W
Enchi Ghana 38 5.53N 2.48W
Encontrados Venezuela 60 9.03N 72.14W
Encounter B. Australia 46 35.35S138.44E
Endeavour Str. Australia 44 10.50S142.15E
Endeh Indonesia 27 8.51S121.40E
Enderby Land *f.* Antarctica 64 67.00S 53.00E
Endicott U.S.A. 55 42.06N 76.03W
Endicott Mts. U.S.A. 50 68.00N152.00W
Endola Namibia 39 17.37S 15.50E
Eneabba Australia 43 29.48S115.16E
Enfield U.K. 5 51.40N 0.05W
Engaño, C. Phil. 27 18.30N122.20E
Engcobo R.S.A. 39 31.39S 28.01E
'En Gedi Israel 32 31.28N 35.23E
Engels Russian Fed. 19 51.30N 46.07E
Enggano *i.* Indonesia 26 5.20S102.15E
Enghien Belgium 8 50.42N 4.02E
England U.K. 4 53.00N 2.00W
English Bāzār India 29 25.00N 88.12E
English Channel U.K. 5 50.15N 1.00W
English River *town* Canada 55 49.14N 90.58W
Enid U.S.A. 52 36.24N 97.54W
Enkhuizen Neth. 8 52.42N 5.17E
Enköping Sweden 17 59.38N 17.04E
Enna Italy 12 37.34N 14.15E
Ennadai L. Canada 51 60.53N101.15W
Enngonia Australia 47 29.20S145.53E
Ennis Rep. of Ire. 7 52.51N 9.00W
Enniscorthy Rep. of Ire. 7 52.30N 6.35W
Enniskillen U.K. 7 54.21N 7.40W
Ennistymon Rep. of Ire. 7 52.56N 9.18W
Enns *r.* Austria 14 48.14N 14.22E
Enontekiö Finland 16 68.23N 23.38E
Ensay Australia 47 37.24S147.52E
Enschede Neth. 8 52.13N 6.54E
Ensenada Argentina 63 34.51S 57.55W
Ensenada Baja Calif. Norte Mexico 56 31.52N116.37W
Enshi China 25 30.18N109.29E
Enshū-nada *sea* Japan 23 34.30N137.30E
Entebbe Uganda 37 0.08N 32.29E
Entre Ríos *d.* Argentina 63 32.10S 59.00W
Entre Rios de Minas Brazil 59 20.39S 44.06W
Enugu Nigeria 38 6.20N 7.29E
Enugu *d.* Nigeria 38 6.30N 7.30E
Envermeu France 9 49.53N 1.15E
Envigado Colombia 60 6.09N 75.35W
Enza *r.* Italy 9 44.54N 10.31E
Enzan Japan 23 35.42N138.44E
Eolie, Isole *is.* Italy 12 38.35N 14.45E

Epe Neth. 8 52.21N 5.59E
Epernay France 9 49.02N 3.58E
Ephraim U.S.A. 54 39.22N111.35W
Ephrata Wash. U.S.A. 54 47.19N119.33W
Épila Spain 10 41.36N 1.17W
Épinal France 11 48.10N 6.28E
Epping U.K. 5 51.42N 0.07E
Epsom U.K. 5 51.20N 0.16W
Epte r. France 9 49.04N 1.37E
Equatorial Guinea Africa 34 1.30N 10.30E
Equerdreville France 9 49.40N 1.40W
Era, Ozero l. Russian Fed. 19 47.38N 45.18E
Eraclea Italy 9 45.35N 12.40E
Erciyaş Dagi mtn. Turkey 30 38.33N 35.25E
Erdre r. France 9 47.27N 1.34W
Erebus, Mt. Antarctica 64 77.40S167.20E
Erechim Brazil 59 27.35S 52.15W
Eregli Konya Turkey 30 37.30N 34.02E
Eregli Zonguldak Turkey 30 41.17N 31.26E
Erenhot China 25 43.50N112.00E
Erft r. Germany 8 51.12N 6.45E
Erfurt Germany 14 50.58N 11.02E
Ergani Turkey 30 38.17N 39.44E
Ergene r. Turkey 13 41.02N 26.22E
Erica Neth. 8 52.44N 6.56E
Erie U.S.A. 55 42.07N 80.05W
Erie, L. Canada/U.S.A. 55 42.15N 81.00W
Eriskay i. U.K. 6 57.04N 7.17W
Eritrea Africa 35 15.30N 38.00E
Erkelenz Germany 8 51.05N 6.18E
Erlangen Germany 14 49.36N 11.02E
Erldunda Australia 44 25.14S133.12E
Ermelo Neth. 8 52.19N 5.38E
Ermelo R.S.A. 39 26.30S 29.59E
Ernée France 9 48.18N 0.56W
Erode India 28 11.21N 77.43E
Er Rachidia Morocco 34 31.58N 4.25W
Errego Mozambique 37 16.02S 37.11E
Errigal Mtn. Rep. of Ire. 7 55.02N 8.08W
Erris Head Rep. of Ire. 7 54.19N 10.00W
Ertix He r. Kazakhstan 24 48.00N 84.20E
Erudina Australia 46 31.30S139.23E
Ervy-le-Châtel France 9 48.02N 3.55E
Erzgebirge mts. Germany 14 50.30N 12.50E
Erzin Russian Fed. 24 50.16N 95.14E
Erzincan Turkey 30 39.44N 39.30E
Erzurum Turkey 30 39.57N 41.17E
Esbjerg Denmark 17 55.28N 8.27E
Esbo see Espoo Finland 17
Escalante U.S.A. 54 37.47N111.36W
Escanaba U.S.A. 55 45.47N 87.04W
Esch Lux. 8 49.31N 5.59E
Eschweiler Germany 8 50.49N 6.16E
Escondido r. Nicaragua 57 11.58N 83.45W
Escondido U.S.A. 54 33.07N117.05W
Escuintla Guatemala 56 14.18N 90.47W
Esens Germany 8 53.40N 7.40E
Eşfahān Iran 31 32.42N 51.40E
Esher U.K. 5 51.23N 0.22W
Eshkanān Iran 31 27.10N 53.38E
Eshowe R.S.A. 39 28.53S 31.29E
Esk r. N. Yorks. U.K. 4 54.29N 0.37W
Eskifjördhur town Iceland 16 65.05N 14.00W
Eskilstuna Sweden 17 59.22N 16.30E
Eskimo Point town Canada 51 61.10N 94.15W
Eskişehir Turkey 30 39.46N 30.30E
Esla r. Spain 10 41.29N 6.03W
Eslāmābād-e-Gharb Iran 31 34.08N 46.35E
Eslöv Sweden 17 55.50N 13.20E
Esmeraldas Ecuador 60 0.56N 79.40W
Espanola Canada 55 46.15N 81.46W
Espe Kazakhstan 20 43.50N 74.10E
Esperance Australia 43 33.49S121.52E
Esperance B. Australia 43 33.51S121.53E
Esperanza Argentina 63 31.30S 61.00W
Espinal Colombia 60 4.08N 75.00W
Espinhaço, Serra do mts. Brazil 59 17.15S 43.10W
Espírito Santo d. Brazil 59 20.00S 40.30W
Espíritu Santo i. Vanuatu 40 15.50S166.50E
Espoo Finland 17 60.13N 24.40E
Espungabera Mozambique 39 20.28S 32.48E
Esquel Argentina 63 42.55S 71.20W
Esquimalt Canada 54 48.30N123.23W
Esquina Argentina 63 30.00S 59.30W
Essaouira Morocco 34 31.30N 9.47W
Essen Germany 8 51.27N 6.57E
Essequibo r. Guyana 60 6.30N 58.40W
Essex d. U.K. 5 51.46N 0.30E
Essex U.S.A. 54 34.45N115.15W
Essonne d. France 9 48.36N 2.20E
Essoyes France 9 48.04N 4.32E
Essoyla Russian Fed. 18 61.47N 33.11E
Est d. Burkina 38 12.45N 0.25E
Est, Pointe de l' c. Canada 51 49.08N 61.41W
Estados, Isla de los i. Argentina 63 54.45S 64.00W
Eşţahbānāt Iran 31 29.05N 54.03E
Estância Brazil 61 11.15S 37.28W
Estand, Kūh-e mtn. Iran 31 31.18N 60.03E
Este Italy 9 45.14N 11.39E
Estepona Spain 10 36.26N 5.09W
Esternay France 9 48.44N 3.34E
Estevan Canada 50 49.09N103.00W
Estissac France 9 48.16N 3.49E
Estivane Mozambique 39 24.07S 32.38E
Eston U.K. 4 54.34N 1.07W
Estonia Europe 18 59.00N 25.00E
Estoril Portugal 10 38.42N 9.23W
Estrela, Serra da mts. Portugal 10 40.20N 7.40W
Estremoz Portugal 10 38.50N 7.35W
Esztergom Hungary 15 47.48N 18.45E
Étables France 11 48.37N 2.50W
Etadunna Australia 46 28.43S138.38E
Étampes France 9 48.26N 2.10E
Étaples France 11 50.31N 1.39E
Ethel Creek town Australia 42 23.05S120.14E
Ethiopia Africa 35 10.00N 39.00E
Etive, Loch U.K. 6 56.27N 5.15W
Etna, Monte mtn. Italy 12 37.43N 14.59E
Etosha Game Res. Namibia 39 18.50S 15.40E
Etosha Pan f. Namibia 39 18.50S 16.20E
Étretat France 9 49.42N 0.12E
Ettelbrück Lux. 8 49.51N 6.06E
Euabalong Australia 47 33.07S146.28E
Euboea see Évvoia i. Greece 13
Eucla Australia 43 31.40S128.51E
Euclid U.S.A. 55 41.34N 81.33W
Eucumbene, L. Australia 47 36.05S148.45E
Eudunda Australia 46 34.09S139.04E
Eufaula Resr. U.S.A. 53 35.15N 95.35W
Eugene U.S.A. 54 44.02N123.05W
Eugenia, Punta c. Mexico 56 27.50N115.03W
Eugowra Australia 47 33.24S148.25E
Eupen Belgium 8 50.38N 6.04E
Euphrates r. see Nahr al Furāt r. Asia 31
Eure d. France 9 49.10N 1.00E
Eure r. France 9 48.18N 1.12E
Eure et Loire d. France 9 48.30N 1.30E
Eureka Calif. U.S.A. 54 40.47N124.09W
Eureka Nev. U.S.A. 54 39.31N115.58W
Eureka Utah U.S.A. 54 39.57N112.07W
Eurinilla r. Australia 46 30.50S140.01E
Euriowie Australia 46 31.22S141.42E
Euroa Australia 47 36.46S145.35E
Euro Disneyland France 9 48.50N 2.50E
Europa, Picos de mts. Spain 10 43.10N 4.40W
Euskirchen Germany 8 50.40N 6.47E
Euston Australia 46 34.34S142.49E
Evans, Lac l. Canada 55 50.50N 77.00W
Evans Head c. Australia 47 29.06S153.25E
Evanston Wyo. U.S.A. 54 41.16N110.58W
Evansville U.S.A. 55 38.00N 87.33W
Evelyn Creek r. Australia 46 28.20S134.50E
Everard, C. Australia 47 37.50S149.16E
Everard, L. Australia 46 31.25S135.05E
Everard Range mts. Australia 45 27.05S132.28E
Everest, Mt. Asia 29 27.59N 86.56E
Everett Wash. U.S.A. 54 47.59N122.13W
Evesham U.K. 5 52.06N 1.57W
Evijärvi Finland 16 63.22N 23.29E
Evje Norway 17 58.36N 7.51E
Évora Portugal 10 38.34N 7.54W
Évreux France 9 49.03N 1.11E
Évry France 9 48.38N 2.27E
Évvoia i. Greece 13 38.30N 23.50E
Ewe, Loch U.K. 6 57.48N 5.38W
Exe r. U.K. 5 50.40N 3.28W
Exeter U.K. 5 50.43N 3.31W
Exmoor Forest hills U.K. 5 51.08N 3.45W
Exmouth Australia 42 21.54S114.10E
Exmouth U.K. 5 50.37N 3.24W
Exmouth G. Australia 42 22.00S114.20E
Expedition Range mts. Australia 44 24.30S149.05E
Extremadura d. Spain 10 39.00N 6.00W
Exuma Is. Bahamas 57 24.00N 76.00W
Eyasi, L. Tanzania 37 3.40S 35.00E
Eye U.K. 5 52.19N 1.09E
Eyemouth U.K. 6 55.52N 2.05W
Eygurande France 11 45.40N 2.26E
Eyjafjördhur est. Iceland 16 65.54N 18.15W
Eyl Somali Rep. 35 8.00N 49.51E
Eyrarbakki Iceland 16 63.52N 21.09W
Eyre r. Australia 44 26.40S139.00E
Eyre, L. Australia 46 28.30S137.25E
Eyre Pen. Australia 46 34.00S135.45E
Ezequil Ramos Mexia, Embalse resr. Argentina 63 39.20S 69.00W

F

Fåberg Norway 17 61.10N 10.22E
Fåborg Denmark 17 55.06N 10.15E
Fabriano Italy 12 43.20N 12.54E
Facatativá Colombia 60 4.48N 74.32W
Facundo Argentina 63 45.19S 69.59W
Fada Chad 35 17.13N 21.30E
Fada-N'Gourma Burkina 38 12.03N 0.22E
Faenza Italy 9 44.17N 11.52E
Fafa Mali 38 15.20N 0.43E
Fafen r. Ethiopia 35 6.07N 44.20E
Făgăraş Romania 15 45.51N 24.58E
Fagernes Norway 17 60.59N 9.17E
Fagersta Sweden 17 60.00N 15.47E
Faguibine, Lac l. Mali 38 16.45N 3.54W
Fagus Egypt 32 30.44N 31.47E
Fā'id Egypt 32 30.19N 32.19E
Fairbanks U.S.A. 50 64.50N147.50W
Fairborn U.S.A. 55 39.48N 84.03W
Fairfield Calif. U.S.A. 54 38.15N122.03W
Fair Head U.K. 7 55.13N 6.09W
Fair Isle U.K. 6 59.32N 1.38W
Fairlie New Zealand 48 44.06S170.50E
Fairmont W.Va. U.S.A. 55 39.28N 80.08W
Fairview Utah U.S.A. 54 39.38N111.26W
Fairweather, Mt. U.S.A. 50 59.00N137.30W
Faisalābād Pakistan 28 31.25N 73.09E
Faizābād India 29 26.46N 82.08E
Fajr, Wādī r. Saudi Arabia 30 30.00N 38.25E
Fakenham U.K. 4 52.50N 0.51E
Fakfak Indonesia 27 2.55S132.17E
Falaise France 9 48.54N 0.11W
Falcarragh Rep. of Ire. 7 55.08N 8.06W
Falcone, Capo del c. Italy 12 40.57N 8.12E
Falesty Moldavia 15 47.30N 27.45E
Falkenberg Sweden 17 56.54N 12.28E
Falkirk U.K. 6 56.00N 3.48W
Falkland Is. Atlantic Oc. 63 51.45W 59.00W
Falkland Sd. str. Falkland Is. 63 51.45W 59.25W
Falköping Sweden 17 58.10N 13.31E
Fallbrook U.S.A. 54 33.23N117.15W
Fall River town U.S.A. 55 41.43N 71.08W
Falmouth U.K. 5 50.09N 5.05W
False B. R.S.A. 39 34.10S 18.40E
Falster i. Denmark 17 54.48N 11.58E
Fălticeni Romania 15 47.28N 26.18E
Falun Sweden 17 60.36N 15.38E
Famagusta see Ammókhostos Cyprus 32
Famoso U.S.A. 54 35.36N119.14W
Fannich, Loch U.K. 6 57.38N 5.00W
Fano Italy 9 43.50N 13.01E
Faradje Zaïre 37 3.45N 29.43E
Faradofay Madagascar 36 25.02S 47.00E
Farāfirah, Wāḩāt al oasis Egypt 30 27.15N 28.10E
Farāh Afghan. 31 32.23N 62.07E
Farāh r. Afghan. 31 31.25N 61.30E
Faraulep is. Federated States of Micronesia 27 8.36N144.33E
Fareham U.K. 5 50.52N 1.11W
Farewell, C. see Farvel, Kap c. Greenland 51
Farewell, C. New Zealand 48 40.30S172.35E
Fargo U.S.A. 53 46.52N 96.59W
Farina Australia 46 30.05S138.20E
Farkwa Tanzania 37 5.26S 35.15E
Farmington N.Mex. U.S.A. 54 36.44N108.12W
Farnborough U.K. 5 51.17N 0.46W
Farne Is. U.K. 4 55.38N 1.36W
Farnham U.K. 5 51.13N 0.49W
Faro Brazil 61 2.11S 56.44W
Faro Portugal 10 37.01N 7.56W
Faroe Is. Europe 16 62.00N 7.00W
Fårön i. Sweden 17 57.56N 19.08E
Fårösund Sweden 17 57.52N 19.03E
Farrell U.S.A. 55 41.13N 80.31W
Farrukhābād India 29 27.23N 79.35E
Fársala Greece 13 39.17N 22.22E
Fārsī Afghan. 31 33.47N 63.12E
Farsund Norway 17 58.05N 6.48E
Farvel, Kap c. Greenland 51 60.00N 44.20W
Fasā Iran 31 28.55N 53.38E
Fastov Ukraine 15 50.08N 29.59E
Făurei Romania 15 45.04N 27.15E
Fauske Norway 16 67.17N 15.25E
Favara Italy 12 37.19N 13.40E
Favignana i. Italy 12 37.57N 12.19E
Faxaflói b. Iceland 16 64.30N 22.50W
Faxe r. Sweden 16 63.15N 17.15E
Fayetteville Ark. U.S.A. 53 36.03N 94.10W
Fayetteville N.C. U.S.A. 53 35.03N 78.53W
Fdérik Mauritania 34 22.35N 12.30W
Feale r. Rep. of Ire. 7 52.28N 9.37W
Fear, C. U.S.A. 53 33.51N 77.59W
Fécamp France 9 49.45N 0.23E
Federación Argentina 63 31.00S 57.55W
Federal Argentina 63 30.55S 58.45W
Federal Capital Territory d. Nigeria 38 8.50N 7.00E
Federated States of Micronesia Pacific Oc. 40 10.00N155.00E
Fedovo Russian Fed. 18 62.22N 39.21E
Fedulki Russian Fed. 18 65.00N 66.10E
Feeagh, Lough Rep. of Ire. 7 53.56N 9.35W
Fehmarn i. Germany 14 54.30N 11.05E
Feia, Lagoa l. Brazil 59 22.00S 41.20W
Feijó Brazil 60 8.09S 70.21W
Feilding New Zealand 48 40.10S175.25E
Feira Zambia 37 15.30S 30.27E
Feira de Santana Brazil 61 12.17S 38.53W
Felanitx Spain 10 39.27N 3.08E
Feldkirch Austria 14 47.15N 9.38E
Felixstowe U.K. 5 51.58N 1.20E
Feltre Italy 9 46.01N 11.54E
Femunden l. Norway 17 62.12N 11.52E
Femundsenden Norway 17 61.55N 11.55E
Fengfeng China 25 36.34N114.19E
Fengjie China 25 31.00N109.30E
Fensfjorden est. Norway 17 60.51N 4.50E
Fenton U.S.A. 55 42.48N 83.42W
Fenyang China 25 37.14N111.43E
Feodosiya Ukraine 19 45.03N 35.23E
Ferdows Iran 31 34.00N 58.10E
Fère-Champenoise France 9 48.45N 3.59E
Fère-en-Tardenois France 9 48.12N 3.31E
Fergana Uzbekistan 24 40.23N 71.19E
Fergus Falls town U.S.A. 53 46.18N 96.00W
Fergusson I. P.N.G. 44 9.30S150.40E
Ferkéssédougou Ivory Coast 38 9.30N 5.10W
Fermanagh d. U.K. 7 54.21N 7.40W
Fermo Italy 12 43.09N 13.43E
Fermoselle Spain 10 41.19N 6.24W
Fermoy Rep. of Ire. 7 52.08N 8.17W
Fernlee Australia 47 28.12S147.05E
Ferrara Italy 9 44.49N 11.38E
Ferreñafe Peru 60 6.42S 79.45W
Ferret, Cap c. France 11 44.42N 1.16W
Ferrières France 9 48.05N 2.48E
Fès Morocco 34 34.05N 5.00W
Feshi Zaïre 36 6.08S 18.12E
Festubert Canada 55 47.12N 72.40W
Feteşti Romania 15 44.23N 27.50E
Fethiye Turkey 30 36.37N 29.06E
Fetlar i. U.K. 6 60.37N 0.52W
Feuilles, Rivière aux r. Canada 51 58.47N 70.06W
Fevzipaşa Turkey 30 37.07N 36.38E
Fianarantsoa Madagascar 36 21.26S 47.05E
Fidenza Italy 9 44.52N 10.03E
Fier Albania 13 40.43N 19.34E
Fife d. U.K. 6 56.10N 3.10W
Fife Ness c. U.K. 6 56.17N 2.36W
Figeac France 11 44.32N 2.01E
Figueira da Foz Portugal 10 40.09N 8.51W
Figueras Spain 10 42.16N 2.57E
Figueres see Figueras Spain 10
Fiji Pacific Oc. 40 18.00S178.00E
Filabusi Zimbabwe 39 20.34S 29.20E
Filey U.K. 4 54.13N 0.18W
Filiaşi Romania 15 44.33N 23.31E
Filiatrá Greece 13 37.09N 21.35E
Filingué Niger 38 14.21N 3.22E
Filipstad Sweden 17 59.43N 14.10E
Fillmore Calif. U.S.A. 54 34.24N118.55W
Finale Emilia Italy 9 44.50N 11.17E
Finale Ligure Italy 9 44.10N 8.20E
Findhorn r. U.K. 6 57.38N 3.37W
Findlay U.S.A. 55 41.02N 83.40W
Finisterre, Cabo de c. Spain 10 42.54N 9.16W
Finke Australia 44 25.35S134.34E
Finke r. Australia 45 27.00S136.10E
Finland Europe 18 64.30N 27.00E
Finland, G. of Finland/Estonia 17 59.30N 24.00E
Finlay r. Canada 50 56.30N124.40W
Finley Australia 47 35.40S145.34E
Finmark Canada 55 48.36N 89.44W
Finn r. Rep. of Ire. 7 54.50N 7.30W
Finnmark d. Norway 16 70.10N 26.00E
Finschhafen P.N.G. 27 6.35S147.51E
Finse Norway 17 60.36N 7.30E
Finspång Sweden 17 58.43N 15.47E
Fiorenzuola d'Arda Italy 9 44.56N 9.55E
Firat r. Turkey see Al Furāt r. Asia 30
Firenze Italy 12 43.46N 11.15E
Firenzuola Italy 9 44.07N 11.23E
Firozābād India 29 27.09N 78.24E
Firozpur India 28 30.55N 74.38E
Firth of Clyde est. U.K. 6 55.35N 4.53W
Firth of Forth est. U.K. 6 56.05N 3.00W
Firth of Lorn est. U.K. 6 56.20N 5.40W
Firth of Tay est. U.K. 6 56.24N 3.08W
Fīrūzābād Iran 31 28.50N 52.35E
Firyuza Turkmenistan 20 37.55N 58.03E
Fish r. Namibia 39 28.07S 17.45E
Fisher Str. Canada 51 63.00N 84.00W
Fishguard U.K. 5 51.59N 4.59W
Fiskenaesset Greenland 51 63.05N 50.40W
Fiskivötn f. Iceland 16 64.50N 20.45W
Fismes France 9 49.18N 3.41E
Fitz Roy Argentina 63 47.00S 67.15W
Fitzroy r. Australia 42 17.31S123.35E
Fitzroy Crossing Australia 42 18.13S125.33E
Fivizzano Italy 9 44.14N 10.08E
Fizi Zaïre 37 4.18S 28.56E
Fjällåsen Sweden 16 67.29N 20.10E
Fjällsjo r. Sweden 16 63.27N 17.06E
Flå Norway 17 60.25N 9.26E
Flagstaff U.S.A. 54 35.12N111.39W
Flåm Norway 17 60.50N 7.07E
Flamborough Head U.K. 4 54.06N 0.05W
Flaming Gorge Resr. U.S.A. 54 41.15N109.30W
Flandre f. Belgium 8 50.52N 3.00E
Flannan Is. U.K. 6 58.16N 7.40W
Flåsjön l. Sweden 16 64.06N 15.51E
Flathead L. U.S.A. 54 47.52N114.08W
Flattery, C. Australia 44 14.58S145.21E
Flattery, C. U.S.A. 52 48.23N124.43W
Fleetwood U.K. 4 53.55N 3.01W
Flekkefjord town Norway 17 58.17N 6.41E
Flen Sweden 17 59.04N 16.35E
Flensburg Germany 14 54.47N 9.27E
Flers France 9 48.45N 0.34W
Flevoland d. Neth. 8 52.25N 5.30E
Flinders r. Australia 44 17.30S140.45E
Flinders B. Australia 43 34.23S115.19E
Flinders I. S.A. Australia 46 33.44S134.30E
Flinders I. Tas. Australia 45 40.00S148.00E
Flinders Ranges mts. Australia 46 31.25S138.45E
Flinders Reefs Australia 44 17.37S148.31E
Flin Flon Canada 51 54.47N101.51W
Flint U.K. 4 53.15N 3.07W
Flint U.S.A. 55 43.03N 83.40W
Flint r. Ga. U.S.A. 53 30.52N 84.35W
Flinton Australia 45 27.54S149.34E
Flisa Norway 17 60.34N 12.06E
Florac France 11 44.19N 3.36E
Florence see Firenze Italy 12
Florence Ariz. U.S.A. 54 33.02N111.23W
Florence Oreg. U.S.A. 54 43.58N124.07W
Florence S.C. U.S.A. 53 34.12N 79.44W
Florence, L. Australia 46 28.52S138.08E
Florencia Colombia 60 1.37N 75.37W
Florennes Belgium 8 50.14N 4.35E
Florenville Belgium 8 49.42N 5.19E
Flores i. Indonesia 27 8.40S121.20E
Flores, Laut sea Indonesia 27 7.00S121.00E
Floreshty Moldavia 15 47.52N 28.12E
Flores Sea see Flores, Laut sea Indonesia 27
Floriano Brazil 61 6.45S 43.00W
Florianópolis Brazil 59 27.35S 48.34W
Florida Uruguay 63 34.06S 56.13W
Florida d. U.S.A. 53 29.00N 82.00W
Florina Australia 46 32.23S139.58E
Flórina Greece 13 40.48N 21.25E
Florö Norway 17 61.36N 5.00E
Fluessen l. Neth. 8 52.58N 5.23E
Flushing see Vlissingen Neth. 8
Fly r. P.N.G. 44 8.22S142.23E
Focşani Romania 15 45.40N 27.12E
Foggia Italy 12 41.28N 15.33E
Foggo Nigeria 38 11.21N 9.57E
Foix France 11 42.57N 1.35E
Folda est. N. Trönd. Norway 16 64.45N 11.20E
Folda est. Nordland Norway 16 67.36N 14.50E
Folégandros i. Greece 13 36.35N 24.55E
Foley Botswana 39 21.34S 27.21E
Foleyet Canada 55 48.05N 82.26W
Folgefonna glacier Norway 17 60.00N 6.20E
Foligno Italy 12 42.56N 12.43E
Folkestone U.K. 5 51.05N 1.11E
Folsom U.S.A. 54 38.41N121.15W
Fominskoye Russian Fed. 18 59.45N 42.03E
Fond du Lac Canada 50 59.20N107.09W
Fonsagrada Spain 10 43.08N 7.04W
Fonseca, Golfo de g. Honduras 57 13.10N 87.30W
Fontainebleau France 9 48.24N 2.42E
Fonte Boa Brazil 60 2.33S 65.59W
Fontenay France 11 46.28N 0.48W
Foochow see Fuzhou China 25
Forbach France 11 49.11N 6.54E
Forbes Australia 47 33.24S148.03E
Forchheim Germany 14 49.43N 11.04E
Förde Norway 17 61.27N 5.52E
Ford's Bridge Australia 47 29.46S145.25E
Forel, Mt. Greenland 51 67.00N 37.00W
Foreland Pt. U.K. 5 51.15N 3.47W
Forest of Bowland hills U.K. 4 53.57N 2.30W
Forest of Dean f. U.K. 5 51.48N 2.32W
Forfar U.K. 6 56.38N 2.54W
Forlì Italy 9 44.13N 12.02E
Formby Pt. U.K. 4 53.34N 3.07W
Formentera i. Spain 10 38.41N 1.30E
Formerie France 9 49.39N 1.44E
Formiga Brazil 59 20.30S 45.27W
Formosa Argentina 62 26.06S 58.14W
Formosa d. Argentina 62 25.00S 60.00W
Formosa see Taiwan Asia 25
Formosa Brazil 61 15.30S 47.22W
Formosa, Serra mts. Brazil 61 12.00S 55.20W
Fornovo di Taro Italy 9 44.42N 10.06E
Forres U.K. 6 57.37N 3.38W
Fors Sweden 17 60.13N 16.18E
Forsayth Australia 44 18.35S143.36E
Forssa Finland 17 60.49N 23.38E
Forst Germany 14 51.46N 14.39E
Forster Australia 47 32.12S152.30E
Forsyth U.S.A. 54 46.16N106.41W
Fort Albany Canada 51 52.15N 81.35W
Fortaleza Brazil 61 3.45S 38.35W
Fort Augustus U.K. 6 57.09N 4.41W
Fort Beaufort R.S.A. 39 32.46S 26.36E
Fort Benton U.S.A. 54 47.49N110.40W
Fort Chimo see Kuujjuak Canada 51
Fort Chipewyan Canada 50 58.46N111.09W
Fort Collins U.S.A. 52 40.35N105.05W
Fort Coulonge Canada 55 45.51N 76.44W
Fort-de-France Martinique 57 14.36N 61.05W
Fort Dodge U.S.A. 53 42.31N 94.10W
Forte dei Marmi Italy 9 43.57N 10.10E
Fortescue r. Australia 42 21.00S116.06E
Fort Frances Canada 51 48.37N 93.23W
Fort Franklin Canada 50 65.11N123.45W
Fort George see Chisasibi Canada 51
Fort Good Hope Canada 50 66.16N128.37W
Fort Grahame Canada 50 56.30N124.35W
Forth r. U.K. 6 56.06N 3.48W
Fort Harrison see Inukjuac Canada 51
Fort Klamath U.S.A. 54 42.42N122.00W
Fort Lallemand Algeria 34 31.13N 6.17E
Fort Lauderdale U.S.A. 53 26.08N 80.08W
Fort Liard Canada 50 60.14N123.28W
Fort MacKay Canada 50 57.12N111.41W
Fort MacMahon Algeria 34 29.51N 1.45E
Fort Maguire Malawi 37 13.38S 34.59E
Fort McMurray Canada 50 56.45N111.27W
Fort McPherson Canada 50 67.29N134.50W
Fort Miribel Algeria 34 29.31N 2.55E
Fort Morgan U.S.A. 52 40.15N103.48W
Fort Myers U.S.A. 53 26.39N 81.51W
Fort Nelson Canada 50 58.48N122.44W
Fort Norman Canada 50 64.55N125.29W
Fort Peck Dam U.S.A. 54 47.52N106.38W
Fort Peck Resr. U.S.A. 54 47.45N106.50W
Fort Pierce U.S.A. 53 27.28N 80.20W
Fort Portal Uganda 37 0.40N 30.17E
Fort Providence Canada 50 61.21N117.39W
Fort Randall U.S.A. 50 55.10N162.47W
Fort Reliance Canada 50 62.45N109.08W
Fort Resolution Canada 50 61.10N113.39W
Fortrose New Zealand 48 46.34S168.48E
Fortrose U.K. 6 57.34N 4.09W
Fort Rousset Congo 36 0.30S 15.48E
Fort Rupert see Waskaganish Canada 51
Fort Scott U.S.A. 53 37.52N 94.43W
Fort Severn Canada 51 56.00N 87.40W
Fort Shevchenko Kazakhstan 19 44.31N 50.15E
Fort Simpson Canada 50 61.46N121.15W
Fort Smith Canada 50 60.00N111.53W
Fort Smith d. Canada 50 63.30N118.00W
Fort Smith U.S.A. 53 35.22N 94.27W
Fort St. John Canada 50 56.14N120.55W
Fort Thomas U.S.A. 54 33.02N109.58W
Fortuna Calif. U.S.A. 54 40.36N124.09W
Fort Vermilion Canada 50 58.22N115.59W
Fort Wayne U.S.A. 55 41.05N 85.08W
Fort William U.K. 6 56.49N 5.07W
Fort Worth U.S.A. 53 32.45N 97.20W
Forty Mile town Canada 50 64.24N140.31W
Fort Yukon U.S.A. 50 66.35N145.20W
Foshan China 25 23.03N113.08E
Fossano Italy 9 44.33N 7.43E
Foster Australia 47 38.39S146.12E
Fostoria U.S.A. 55 41.10N 83.25W
Fougères France 9 48.21N 1.12W
Foula i. U.K. 6 60.08N 2.05W
Foulness I. U.K. 5 51.35N 0.55E
Foulwind, C. New Zealand 48 41.45S171.30E
Foumban Cameroon 38 5.43N 10.50E
Fourmies France 8 50.01N 4.02E
Foúrnoi i. Greece 13 37.34N 26.30E
Fouta Djalon f. Guinea 34 11.30N 12.30W
Foveaux Str. New Zealand 48 46.40S168.00E
Fowey U.K. 5 50.20N 4.39W
Fowlers B. Australia 45 31.59S132.27E
Foxe Basin b. Canada 51 67.30N 79.00W
Foxe Channel Canada 51 65.00N 80.00W
Foxe Pen. Canada 51 65.00N 76.00W
Fox Glacier town New Zealand 48 43.28S170.01E
Foxton New Zealand 48 40.27S175.18E
Foyle r. U.K. 7 55.00N 7.20W
Foyle, Lough U.K. 7 55.05N 7.10W
Foz do Iguaçu Brazil 59 25.33S 54.31W
Franca Brazil 59 20.33S 47.27W
Francavilla Fontana Italy 13 40.31N 17.35E
France Europe 11 47.00N 2.00E
Frances Australia 46 36.41S140.59E
Frances L. Canada 50 61.25N129.30W
Francesville U.S.A. 55 40.59N 86.54W
Franche-Comté d. France 11 47.10N 6.00E
Francia Uruguay 63 32.33S 56.37W
Francistown Botswana 39 21.12S 27.29E
Franeker Neth. 8 53.13N 5.31E

84

Godhra India 28 22.49N 73.40E
Godoy Cruz Argentina 63 32.55S 68.50W
Gods L. Canada 51 54.40N 94.20W
Godthåb Greenland 51 64.10N 51.40W
Goéland, Lac au l. Canada 55 49.47N 76.41W
Goes Neth. 8 51.30N 3.54E
Gogama Canada 55 47.35N 81.35W
Gogonou Benin 38 10.50N 2.50E
Gogra r. see Ghāghra India 29
Goiana Brazil 61 7.30S 35.00W
Goiânia Brazil 61 16.43S 49.18W
Goiás Brazil 61 15.57S 50.07W
Goiás d. Brazil 61 15.00S 48.00W
Goito Italy 9 45.15N 10.40E
Gojō Japan 23 34.21N135.42E
Gökçeada i. Turkey 13 40.10N 25.51E
Göksun Turkey 30 38.03N 36.30E
Gokteik Burma 29 22.26N 97.00E
Gokwe Zimbabwe 39 18.14S 28.54E
Gol Norway 17 60.42N 8.57E
Golan Heights mts. Syria 32 32.55N 35.42E
Golconda U.S.A. 54 40.57N117.30W
Gołdap Poland 15 54.19N 22.19E
Gold Beach town U.S.A. 54 42.25N124.25W
Golden Rep. of Ire. 7 52.30N 7.59W
Golden B. New Zealand 48 40.45S172.50E
Goldendale U.S.A. 54 45.49N120.50W
Golden Ridge town Australia 43 30.51S121.42E
Golden Vale f. Rep. of Ire. 7 52.30N 8.07W
Goldfield U.S.A. 54 37.42N117.14W
Goldsworthy Australia 42 20.20S119.30E
Goleniów Poland 14 53.36N 14.50E
Golets Skalisty mtn. Russian Fed. 21 56.00N130.40E
Golfito Costa Rica 57 8.42N 83.10W
Golfo degli Aranci town Italy 12 41.00N 9.38E
Golling Austria 14 47.36N 13.10E
Golmud China 24 36.22N 94.55E
Golovanevsk Ukraine 15 48.25N 30.30E
Golpāyegān Iran 31 33.23N 50.18E
Golspie U.K. 6 57.58N 3.58W
Goma Zaïre 37 1.37S 29.10E
Gombe Nigeria 38 10.17N 11.20E
Gombe r. Tanzania 37 4.43S 31.30E
Gomel Belorussia 15 52.25N 31.00E
Gómez Palacio Mexico 56 25.39N103.30W
Gomīshān Iran 31 37.04N 54.06E
Gonaïves Haiti 57 19.29N 72.42W
Gonâve, Golfe de la g. Haiti 57 19.20N 73.00W
Gonâve, Île de la i. Haiti 57 18.50N 73.00W
Gonbad-e Kāvūs Iran 31 37.15N 55.11E
Gonda India 29 27.08N 81.58E
Gonder Ethiopia 35 12.39N 37.29E
Gondia India 29 21.27N 80.12E
Gongbo'gyamda China 29 29.56N 93.23E
Gongga Shan mtn. China 24 29.30N101.30E
Gongola r. Nigeria 38 9.30N 12.06E
Gongolgon Australia 47 30.22S146.56E
Goñi Uruguay 63 33.31S 56.24W
Goniri Nigeria 38 11.30N 12.15E
Gonzaga Italy 9 44.57N 10.49E
Good Hope, C. of R.S.A. 39 34.21S 18.28E
Gooding U.S.A. 54 42.56N114.43W
Goodooga Australia 47 29.08S147.30E
Goodsprings U.S.A. 54 35.50N115.26W
Goole U.K. 4 53.42N 0.52W
Goolgowi Australia 47 33.59S145.42E
Goolma Australia 47 32.21S149.20E
Gooloogong Australia 47 33.36S148.27E
Goolwa Australia 46 35.31S138.45E
Goomalling Australia 43 31.19S116.49E
Goombalie Australia 47 29.59S145.24E
Goondiwindi Australia 47 28.30S150.17E
Goongarrie Australia 43 30.03S121.09E
Goor Neth. 8 52.16N 6.33E
Goose L. U.S.A. 54 41.57N120.25W
Göppingen Germany 14 48.43N 9.39E
Gorakhpur India 29 26.45N 83.23E
Gordon r. Australia 43 34.12S117.00E
Gordon Downs town Australia 42 18.43S128.33E
Gordonvale Australia 44 17.05S145.47E
Goré Chad 34 7.57N 16.31E
Gorē Ethiopia 35 8.08N 35.33E
Gore New Zealand 48 46.06S168.58E
Gorgān Iran 31 36.50N 54.29E
Gorgān r. Iran 31 37.00N 54.00E
Gori Georgia 31 41.59N 44.05E
Gorinchem Neth. 8 51.50N 4.59E
Gorizia Italy 12 45.58N 13.37E
Gorki see Nizhniy Novgorod Russian Fed 18
Gorkovskoye Vodokhranilishche resr. Russian Fed. 18 56.49N 43.00E
Görlitz Germany 14 51.09N 15.00E
Gorlovka Ukraine 19 48.17N 38.05E
Gorna Oryakhovitsa Bulgaria 13 43.07N 25.40E
Gorno Altaysk Russian Fed. 20 51.59N 85.56E
Gorno Filinskoye Russian Fed. 20 60.06N 69.58E
Gornyatskiy Russian Fed. 18 67.30N 64.03E
Gorodenka Ukraine 15 48.40N 25.30E
Gorodishche Belorussia 15 53.18N 26.00E
Gorodishche Belorussia 15 53.45N 29.45E
Gorodnitsa Ukraine 15 50.50N 27.19E
Gorodnya Ukraine 15 51.54N 31.37E
Gorodok Ukraine 15 49.48N 23.39E
Goroka P.N.G. 27 6.02S145.22E
Goroke Australia 46 36.43S141.30E
Gorokhov Ukraine 15 50.30N 24.46E
Gorongosa r. Mozambique 39 20.29S 34.36E
Gorontalo Indonesia 27 0.33N123.05E
Gort Rep. of Ire. 7 53.04N 8.49W
Goryn r. Ukraine 15 52.08N 27.17E
Gorzów Wielkopolski Poland 14 52.42N 15.12E
Gosford Australia 47 33.25S151.18E
Goslar Germany 14 51.54N 10.25E
Gospić Croatia 14 44.34N 15.23E
Gosport U.K. 5 50.48N 1.08W
Gossi Mali 38 15.49N 1.17W
Gostivar Macedonia 13 41.47N 20.24E
Gostynin Poland 15 52.26N 19.29E
Göta r. Sweden 17 57.42N 11.52E
Göta Kanal Sweden 17 58.50N 13.58E
Göteborg Sweden 17 57.43N 11.58E
Göteborg och Bohus d. Sweden 17 58.30N 11.30E
Gotemba Japan 23 35.18N138.56E
Götene Sweden 17 58.32N 13.29E
Gotha Germany 14 50.57N 10.43E
Gothenburg see Göteborg Sweden 17
Gothèye Niger 38 13.51N 1.31E
Gotland d. Sweden 17 57.30N 18.30E
Gotland i. Sweden 17 57.30N 18.33E
Göttingen Germany 14 51.32N 9.57E
Gouda Neth. 8 52.01N 4.43E
Gouin, Résr. Canada 55 48.38N 74.50W
Goulburn Australia 47 34.47S149.43E
Goulburn r. Australia 47 36.08S144.30E
Goulburn Is. Australia 44 11.33S133.26E
Goundam Mali 38 17.27N 3.39W
Gourdon France 11 44.45N 1.22E
Gouré Niger 38 13.59N 10.15E
Gourma-Rharous Mali 38 16.58N 1.50W
Gournay France 9 49.29N 1.44E
Governador Valadares Brazil 59 18.51S 42.00W
Gowanda U.S.A. 55 42.28N 78.57W
Gowd-e Zereh des. Afghan. 31 30.00N 62.00E
Gower pen. U.K. 5 51.37N 4.10W
Goya Argentina 62 29.10S 59.20W
Goyder r. Australia 44 12.38S135.11E
Gozo i. Malta 12 36.03N 14.16E
Graaff Reinet R.S.A. 39 32.15S 24.31E
Gračac Croatia 14 44.18N 15.51E
Grace, L. Australia 43 33.18S118.15E
Gracias á Dios, Cabo c. Honduras/Nicaragua 57 15.00N 83.10W
Grado Italy 9 45.40N 13.23E
Grado Spain 10 43.23N 6.04W
Grafton Australia 47 29.40S152.56E
Grafton N.Dak. U.S.A. 53 48.28N 97.25W
Grafton W.Va. U.S.A. 55 39.21N 80.03W
Graham, Mt. U.S.A. 54 32.42N109.52W
Graham Land f. Antarctica 64 67.00S 60.00W
Grahamstown R.S.A. 39 33.18S 26.30E
Graiguenamanagh Rep. of Ire. 7 52.33N 6.57W
Grajaú r. Brazil 61 3.41S 44.48W
Grampian d. U.K. 6 57.22N 2.35W
Grampian Mts. U.K. 6 56.55N 4.00W
Grampians mts. Australia 46 37.12S142.34E
Granada Nicaragua 57 11.58N 85.59W
Granada Spain 10 37.10N 3.35W
Granby Canada 55 45.23N 72.44W
Gran Canaria i. Canary Is. 34 28.00N 15.30W
Gran Chaco f. S. America 62 22.00S 60.00W
Grand r. S.Dak. U.S.A. 52 45.40N100.32W
Grand Bahama I. Bahamas 57 26.35N 78.00W
Grand Bassam Ivory Coast 38 5.14N 3.45W
Grand Canyon f. U.S.A. 54 36.10N112.45W
Grand Canyon town U.S.A. 54 36.03N112.09W
Grand Canyon Nat. Park U.S.A. 54 36.15N112.58W
Grand Cayman i. Cayman Is. 57 19.20N 81.30W
Grand Couronne France 9 49.21N 1.00E
Grande r. Bolivia 62 15.10S 64.55W
Grande r. Bahia Brazil 61 11.05S 43.09W
Grande r. Minas Gerais Brazil 62 20.00S 51.00W
Grande, Bahía b. Argentina 63 51.30S 67.30W
Grande, Ilha i. Brazil 59 23.07S 44.16W
Grande Cascapédia Canada 55 48.21N 65.52W
Grande Comore i. Comoros 37 11.35S 43.20E
Grande do Gurupá, Ilha i. Brazil 61 1.00S 51.30W
Grande Prairie town Canada 50 55.10N118.52W
Grand Erg de Bilma des. Niger 38 18.30N 14.00E
Grandes, Salinas f. Argentina 62 29.37S 64.56W
Grandes Bergeronnes Canada 55 48.16N 69.35W
Grand Falls town Nfld. Canada 51 48.57N 55.40W
Grand Falls town N.B. Canada 55 46.55N 67.45W
Grand Forks U.S.A. 53 47.57N 97.05W
Grand Fougeray France 9 47.44N 1.44W
Grand Island town U.S.A. 52 40.56N 98.21W
Grand Junction U.S.A. 54 39.05N108.33W
Grand L. N.B. Canada 55 45.38N 67.38W
Grand L. U.S.A. 55 45.15N 67.50W
Grand Lahou Ivory Coast 38 5.09N 5.01W
Grand Manan I. Canada 55 44.38N 66.50W
Grand Marais U.S.A. 53 47.55N 90.15W
Grand' Mère Canada 55 46.37N 72.41W
Grândola Portugal 10 38.10N 8.34W
Grand Rapids town Canada 51 53.08N 99.20W
Grand Rapids town Mich. U.S.A. 55 42.57N 85.40W
Grand St. Bernard, Col du pass Italy/Switz. 9 45.52N 7.11E
Grand Teton mtn. U.S.A. 54 43.44N110.48W
Grand Teton Nat. Park U.S.A. 54 43.30N110.37W
Grand Traverse B. U.S.A. 55 45.02N 85.30W
Grand Valley town U.S.A. 54 39.27N108.03W
Grandville U.S.A. 55 42.54N 85.48W
Grangemouth U.K. 6 56.01N 3.44W
Granger U.S.A. 54 41.35N109.58W
Grängesberg Sweden 17 60.05N 14.59E
Grangeville U.S.A. 54 45.56N116.07W
Granite Peak town Australia 42 25.38S121.21E
Granite Peak mtn. U.S.A. 52 45.10N109.50W
Granity New Zealand 48 41.38S171.51E
Granja Brazil 61 3.06S 40.50W
Gränna Sweden 17 58.01N 14.28E
Granollers Spain 10 41.37N 2.18E
Granön Sweden 16 64.15N 19.19E
Gran Paradiso mtn. Italy 9 45.31N 7.15E
Grant Mich. U.S.A. 55 43.20N 85.49W
Grantham U.K. 4 52.55N 0.39W
Grantown-on-Spey U.K. 6 57.20N 3.38W
Grant Range mts. U.S.A. 54 38.25N115.30W
Grants U.S.A. 54 35.09N107.52W
Grants Pass town U.S.A. 54 42.26N123.19W
Grantsville U.S.A. 55 38.55N 81.07W
Granville France 9 48.50N 1.35W
Gras, Lac de l. Canada 50 64.30N110.30W
Graskop R.S.A. 39 24.55S 30.50E
Grasse France 11 43.40N 6.56E
Grasset, L. Canada 55 49.53N 78.07W
Grass Valley town Calif. U.S.A. 54 39.13N121.04W
Grass Valley town Oreg. U.S.A. 54 45.22N120.47W
Grave Neth. 8 51.45N 5.45E
Grave, Pointe de c. France 11 45.35N 1.04W
Gravenhurst Canada 55 44.55N 79.22W
Gravesend Australia 47 29.35S150.20E
Gravesend U.K. 5 51.27N 0.24E
Gray France 11 47.27N 5.35E
Grayling U.S.A. 55 44.40N 84.43W
Grays U.K. 5 51.29N 0.20E
Graz Austria 14 47.05N 15.22E
Grdelica Yugo. 13 42.54N 22.04E
Great Abaco I. Bahamas 57 26.30N 77.00W
Great Artesian Basin f. Australia 44 26.30S143.02E
Great Australian Bight Australia 43 33.10S129.30E
Great Barrier I. New Zealand 48 36.15S175.30E
Great Barrier Reef f. Australia 44 16.30S146.30E
Great Basin f. U.S.A. 54 40.35N116.00W
Great Bear L. Canada 50 66.00N120.00W
Great Bend town U.S.A. 52 38.22N 98.46W
Great Bitter L. see Murrah al Kubrá, Al Buḩayrah al Egypt 32
Great Blasket I. Rep. of Ire. 7 52.05N 10.32W
Great Coco i. Burma 29 14.10N 93.25E
Great Divide Basin f. U.S.A. 54 42.00N108.10W
Great Dividing Range mts. Australia 47 29.00S152.00E
Great Driffield U.K. 4 54.01N 0.26W
Greater Antilles is. C. America 57 17.00N 70.00W
Greater London d. U.K. 5 51.31N 0.06W
Greater Manchester d. U.K. 4 53.30N 2.18W
Great Exuma i. Bahamas 57 23.00N 76.00W
Great Falls town U.S.A. 54 47.30N111.17W
Great Inagua I. Bahamas 57 21.00N 73.20W
Great Indian Desert see Thar Desert India/Pakistan 28
Great Karoo f. R.S.A. 39 32.40S 22.20E
Great Kei r. R.S.A. 39 32.39S 28.23E
Great L. Australia 45 41.50S146.43E
Great Malvern U.K. 5 52.07N 2.19W
Great Namaland f. Namibia 39 25.30S 17.20E
Great Nicobar i. India 29 7.00N 93.50E
Great Ouse r. U.K. 4 52.47N 0.23E
Great Ruaha r. Tanzania 37 7.55S 37.52E
Great Salt L. U.S.A. 54 41.10N112.30W
Great Salt Lake Desert U.S.A. 54 40.40N113.30W
Great Sandy Desert Australia 42 20.30S123.35E
Great Sandy Desert see An Nafūd des. Saudi Arabia 30
Great Slave L. Canada 50 61.30N114.20W
Great Victoria Desert Australia 43 29.00S127.30E
Great Whernside mtn. U.K. 4 54.09N 1.59W
Great Yarmouth U.K. 5 52.40N 1.45E
Great Zimbabwe ruins Zimbabwe 39 20.30S 30.30E
Gréboun, Mont mtn. Niger 38 20.01N 8.35E
Gredos, Sierra de mts. Spain 10 40.18N 5.20W
Greece Europe 13 39.00N 22.00E
Greeley U.S.A. 52 40.25N104.42W
Green r. U.S.A. 54 38.11N109.53W
Green Bay town U.S.A. 53 44.32N 88.00W
Greenbushes Australia 43 33.50S116.00E
Greencastle Ind. U.S.A. 55 39.39N 86.51W
Greene U.S.A. 55 42.20N 75.46W
Greenhills Australia 43 31.58S117.01E
Greening Canada 55 48.07N 74.55W
Greenland N. America 51 68.00N 45.00W
Greenlaw U.K. 6 55.43N 2.28W
Greenock U.K. 6 55.57N 4.45W
Greenore Pt. Rep. of Ire. 7 52.14N 6.19W
Greenough r. Australia 43 29.22S114.34E
Green River town Utah U.S.A. 54 38.59N110.10W
Green River town Wyo. U.S.A. 54 41.32N109.28W
Greensboro N.C. U.S.A. 53 36.03N 79.50W
Greensburg Ind. U.S.A. 55 39.20N 85.29W
Greenvale Australia 44 18.57S144.53E
Greenville Liberia 34 5.01N 9.03W
Greenville Ala. U.S.A. 53 31.50N 86.40W
Greenville Mich. U.S.A. 55 43.11N 85.13W
Greenville Miss. U.S.A. 53 33.23N 91.03W
Greenville S.C. U.S.A. 53 34.52N 82.25W
Greenville Tex. U.S.A. 53 33.09N 96.07W
Greenwood Miss. U.S.A. 53 33.31N 90.10W
Gregory r. Australia 44 17.53S139.17E
Gregory, L. S.A. Australia 46 28.55S139.00E
Gregory L. W.A. Australia 42 20.10S127.20E
Gregory Range mts. Australia 44 19.00S143.05E
Greifswald Germany 14 54.06N 13.24E
Gremikha Russian Fed. 18 68.03N 39.38E
Grenå Denmark 17 56.25N 10.53E
Grenada C. America 57 12.07N 61.40W
Grenade France 11 43.47N 1.10E
Grenfell Australia 47 33.53S148.11E
Grenoble France 11 45.11N 5.43E
Grenville, C. Australia 44 12.00S143.13E
Gretna U.K. 6 55.00N 3.04W
Greven Germany 8 52.07N 7.38E
Grevenbroich Germany 8 51.07N 6.33E
Grevesmühlen Germany 14 53.51N 11.10E
Grey r. New Zealand 48 42.28S171.13E
Grey, C. Australia 44 13.00S136.40E
Greybull U.S.A. 54 44.30N108.03W
Greymouth New Zealand 48 42.28S171.12E
Grey Range mts. Australia 45 27.30S143.59E
Greystones Rep. of Ire. 7 53.09N 6.04W
Greytown R.S.A. 39 29.04S 30.36E
Griffin U.S.A. 53 33.15N 84.17W
Griffith Australia 47 34.18S146.04E
Grignan France 11 44.25N 4.54E
Grigoriopol Moldavia 15 47.08N 29.18E
Grim, C. Australia 45 40.45S144.45E
Grimsby U.K. 4 53.35N 0.05W
Grimstad Norway 17 58.20N 8.36E
Grimsvötn mtn. Iceland 16 64.30N 17.10W
Grindavik Iceland 16 63.50N 22.27W
Grindsted Denmark 17 55.45N 8.56E
Griqualand East f. R.S.A. 39 30.40S 29.10E
Griqualand West f. R.S.A. 39 28.50S 23.30E
Griva Russian Fed. 18 60.35N 50.58E
Grobina Latvia 17 56.33N 21.10E
Groblershoop R.S.A. 39 28.55S 20.59E
Grodno Belorussia 15 53.40N 23.50E
Grodzisk Poland 14 52.14N 16.22E
Grodzyanka Belorussia 15 53.30N 28.41E
Groenlo Neth. 8 52.02N 6.36E
Groix, Île de i. France 11 47.38N 3.26W
Gronau Germany 8 52.14N 7.02E
Grong Norway 16 64.27N 12.19E
Groningen Neth. 8 53.13N 6.35E
Groningen d. Neth. 8 53.15N 6.45E
Groot r. C.P. R.S.A. 39 33.58S 25.03E
Groote Eylandt i. Australia 44 14.00S136.40E
Grootfontein Namibia 39 19.32S 18.07E
Groot Karasberge mts. Namibia 39 27.20S 18.50E
Grootlaagte r. Botswana 39 20.58S 21.42E
Groot Swartberge mts. R.S.A. 39 33.20S 22.00E
Grossenbrode Germany 14 54.23N 11.07E
Grossenhain Germany 14 51.17N 13.31E
Grosseto Italy 12 42.46N 11.08E
Gross Glockner mtn. Austria 14 47.05N 12.50E
Grote Nete r. Belgium 8 51.07N 4.20E
Groundhog r. Canada 55 49.43N 81.58W
Grouse Creek town U.S.A. 54 41.22N113.53W
Grover City U.S.A. 54 35.07N120.37W
Groznyy Russian Fed. 19 43.21N 45.42E
Grudziądz Poland 15 53.29N 18.45E
Grumeti r. Tanzania 37 2.05S 33.45E
Grünau Namibia 39 27.44S 18.18E
Grundarfjördhur town Iceland 16 64.55N 23.20W
Grungedal Norway 17 59.44N 7.43E
Gryazovets Russian Fed. 18 58.52N 40.12E
Gryfice Poland 14 53.56N 15.12E
Guachipas Argentina 62 25.31S 65.31W
Guacuí Brazil 59 20.44S 41.40W
Guadalajara Mexico 56 20.30N103.20W
Guadalajara Spain 10 40.37N 3.10W
Guadalcanal i. Solomon Is. 40 9.32S160.12E
Guadalete r. Spain 10 36.37N 6.15W
Guadalmena r. Spain 10 38.00N 3.50W
Guadalquivir r. Spain 10 36.50N 6.20W
Guadalupe Mexico 56 25.41N100.15W
Guadalupe, Isla de i. Mexico 52 29.00N118.16W
Guadalupe, Sierra de mts. Spain 10 39.30N 5.25W
Guadarrama r. Spain 10 39.55N 4.10W
Guadarrama, Sierra de mts. Spain 10 41.00N 3.50W
Guadeloupe i. Leeward Is. 57 16.20N 61.40W
Guadiana r. Portugal 10 37.10N 7.36W
Guadix Spain 10 37.19N 3.08W
Guafo, Golfo de g. Chile 63 43.35S 74.15W
Guainía r. Colombia 60 2.01N 67.07W
Guaíra Brazil 62 24.04S 54.15W
Guajará Mirim Brazil 60 10.48S 65.22W
Guajira, Península de la pen. Colombia 60 12.00N 72.00W
Gualeguay Argentina 63 33.10S 59.20W
Gualeguay r. Argentina 63 33.18S 59.38W
Gualeguaychu Argentina 63 33.00S 58.30W
Guam i. Mariana Is. 40 13.30N144.40E
Guamal Colombia 60 9.10N 74.15W
Guanajuato Mexico 56 21.00N101.16W
Guanajuato d. Mexico 56 21.00N101.00W
Guanare Venezuela 60 9.04N 69.45W
Guanarito Venezuela 60 8.43N 69.12W
Guane Cuba 57 22.13N 84.07W
Guangdong d. China 25 23.00N113.00E
Guanghua see Laohekou China 25
Guangxi Zhuangzu d. China 25 23.50N109.00E
Guangyuan China 29 32.26N105.52E
Guangzhou China 25 23.20N113.30E
Guanling China 29 25.57N105.38E
Guantánamo Cuba 57 20.09N 75.14W
Guan Xian Sichuan China 29 30.59N103.40E
Guaporé r. Bolivia/Brazil 62 12.00S 65.15W
Guaqui Bolivia 62 16.35S 68.51W
Guarabira Brazil 61 6.46S 35.25W
Guarapuava Brazil 59 25.22S 51.28W
Guaratinguetá Brazil 59 22.49S 45.09W
Guarda Portugal 10 40.32N 7.17W
Guardavalle Italy 13 38.30N 16.30E
Guardo Spain 10 42.47N 4.50W
Guareim r. Uruguay see Quarí r. Brazil 63
Guasipati Venezuela 60 7.28N 61.54W
Guastalla Italy 9 44.55N 10.39E
Guatemala C. America 57 15.40N 90.00W
Guatemala town Guatemala 56 14.38N 90.22W
Guatire Venezuela 60 10.28N 66.32W
Guaviare r. Colombia 60 4.00N 67.35W
Guaxupé Brazil 59 21.17S 46.44W
Guayaquil Ecuador 60 2.13S 79.54W
Guayaquil, Golfo de g. Ecuador 60 3.00S 80.35W
Guaymallén Argentina 63 32.54S 68.47W
Guaymas Mexico 56 27.56N110.54W
Guayquiraró r. Argentina 63 30.25S 59.36W
Gubakha Russian Fed. 18 58.55N 57.30E
Gubeikou China 25 40.41N117.09E
Gubin Poland 14 51.59N 14.42E
Gubio Nigeria 38 12.31N 12.44E
Guchab Namibia 39 19.40S 17.47E
Gúdar, Sierra de mts. Spain 10 40.27N 0.42W
Gudbrandsdalen f. Norway 17 61.30N 10.00E
Gudvangen Norway 17 60.52N 6.50E
Guecho Spain 10 43.21N 3.01W
Guelph Canada 55 43.33N 80.15W
Guéméné-sur-Scorff France 11 48.04N 3.13W
Guéret France 11 46.10N 1.52E
Guernica Spain 10 43.19N 2.40W
Guernsey i. U.K. 5 49.27N 2.35W
Guerra Mozambique 37 13.05S 35.12E
Guerrero d. Mexico 56 18.00N100.00W
Guiana S. America 61 3.40N 53.00W
Guiana Highlands S. America 60 4.00N 59.00W
Guichón Uruguay 63 32.21S 57.12W
Guildford Australia 43 31.55S115.55E
Guildford U.K. 5 51.14N 0.35W
Guilin China 25 25.21N110.11E
Guimarães Brazil 61 2.08S 44.36W
Guimarães Portugal 10 41.27N 8.18W
Guinan China 24 35.20N100.50E
Guinea Africa 34 10.30N 11.30W
Guinea, G. of Africa 38 3.00N 3.00E
Guinea Bissau Africa 34 11.30N 15.00W
Güines Cuba 57 22.50N 82.02W
Guingamp France 11 48.34N 3.09W
Guiping China 25 23.20N110.04E
Guiscard France 8 49.39N 3.01E
Guiscard France 9 49.39N 3.03E
Guise France 9 49.54N 3.38E
Guiuan Phil. 27 11.02N125.44E
Guiyang China 24 26.35N106.40E
Guizhou d. China 24 27.00N106.30E
Gujarat d. India 28 22.45N 71.30E
Gujrānwāla Pakistan 28 32.06N 74.11E
Gujrāt Pakistan 28 32.35N 74.06E
Gulargambone Australia 47 31.21S148.32E
Gulbarga India 28 17.22N 76.47E
Gulfport U.S.A. 53 30.21N 89.08W
Gulgong Australia 47 32.20S149.49E
Gulma Nigeria 38 12.41N 4.24E
Gulshad Kazakhstan 24 46.37N 74.22E
Gulu Uganda 37 2.46N 32.21E
Gulwe Tanzania 37 6.27S 36.27E
Gumel Nigeria 38 12.39N 9.23E
Gummersbach Germany 8 51.03N 7.32E
Gümüşhane Turkey 30 40.26N 39.26E
Guna India 28 24.39N 77.18E
Gunbar Australia 47 34.04S145.25E
Gundagai Australia 47 35.07S148.05E
Gundlupet India 28 11.48N 76.41E
Gungu Zaïre 36 5.43S 19.20E
Gunnedah Australia 47 30.59S150.15E
Gunning Australia 47 34.46S149.17E
Gunnison r. U.S.A. 54 39.03N108.35W
Gunnison Utah U.S.A. 54 39.09N111.49W
Guntersville L. U.S.A. 53 34.35N 86.00W
Guntūr India 29 16.20N 80.27E
Gunungsitoli Indonesia 26 1.17N 97.37E
Günzburg Germany 14 48.27N 10.16E
Gura Portiței f. Romania 15 44.40N 29.00E
Gurgueia r. Brazil 61 6.45S 43.35W
Gursköy i. Norway 16 62.16N 5.42E
Guruè Mozambique 37 15.30S 36.58E
Gürün Turkey 30 38.44N 37.15E
Gurupá Brazil 61 1.25S 51.39W
Gurupi r. Brazil 61 1.13S 46.06W
Guruve Zimbabwe 37 16.42S 30.40E
Guryev Kazakhstan 19 47.08N 51.59E
Gusau Nigeria 38 12.12N 6.40E
Gusev Russian Fed. 15 54.32N 22.12E
Guspini Italy 12 39.32N 8.38E
Gustav Holm, Kap c. Greenland 51 67.00N 34.00W
Güstrow Germany 14 53.48N 12.11E
Gütersloh Germany 14 51.54N 8.22E
Guyana S. America 60 4.40N 59.00W
Guyra Australia 47 30.14S151.40E
Guzhen Anhui China 25 33.19N117.19E
Gwa Burma 29 17.36N 94.35E
Gwabegar Australia 47 30.34S149.00E
Gwadabawa Nigeria 38 13.23N 5.15E
Gwādar Pakistan 28 25.09N 62.21E
Gwagwada Nigeria 38 10.15N 7.15E
Gwai Zimbabwe 39 19.15S 27.42E
Gwai r. Zimbabwe 39 17.59S 26.55E
Gwalior India 29 26.12N 78.09E
Gwanda Zimbabwe 39 20.59S 29.00E
Gwasero Nigeria 38 9.30N 8.30E
Gweebarra B. Rep. of Ire. 7 54.52N 8.28W
Gwent d. U.K. 5 51.44N 3.00W
Gweru Zimbabwe 39 19.25S 29.50E
Gwydir r. Australia 47 29.35S148.45E
Gwynedd d. U.K. 4 53.00N 4.00W
Gyandzha Azerbaijan 31 40.39N 46.20E
Gyangzê China 29 29.00N 89.40E
Gydanskiy Poluostrov pen. Russian Fed. 20 70.00N 78.30E
Gympie Australia 44 26.11S152.40E
Gyöngyös Hungary 15 47.47N 19.56E
Győr Hungary 15 47.41N 17.40E
Gypsumville Canada 51 51.45N 98.35W

H

Haan Germany 8 51.10N 7.02E
Haapajärvi Finland 16 63.45N 25.20E
Haapamäki Finland 16 62.15N 24.28E
Haapavesi Finland 16 64.08N 25.22E
Haapsalu Estonia 17 58.56N 23.33E
Hā Arava r. Israel/Jordan 32 30.30N 35.10E
Haarlem Neth. 8 52.22N 4.38E
Haarlem R.S.A. 39 33.46S 23.28E
Habahe China 24 47.53N 86.12E
Ḩabarūt Yemen 28 17.18N 52.44E
Habaswein Kenya 37 1.06N 39.26E
Habay-la-Neuve Belgium 8 49.45N 5.38E
Habikino Japan 23 34.33N135.37E
Habo Sweden 17 57.55N 14.04E

Hachinohe Japan **25** 40.30N141.30E
Hachiōji Japan **23** 35.39N139.20E
Hack, Mt. Australia **46** 30.44S138.45E
Hadano Japan **23** 35.22N139.14E
Ḩadd, Ra's al *c.* Oman **31** 22.32N 59.49E
Haddington U.K. **6** 55.57N 2.47W
Hadejia Nigeria **38** 12.30N 10.03E
Hadejia *r.* Nigeria **38** 12.47N 10.44E
Hadera Israel **32** 32.26N 34.55E
Haderslev Denmark **17** 55.15N 9.30E
Ḩaḑramawt *f.* Yemen **35** 16.30N 49.30E
Hadsten Denmark **17** 56.20N 10.03E
Hadsund Denmark **17** 56.43N 10.07E
Haedo, Cuchilla de *mts.* Uruguay **63** 31.50S 56.10W
Haegeland Norway **17** 58.15N 7.50E
Haeju N. Korea **25** 38.04N125.40E
Ḩafar al Bāţin Saudi Arabia **31** 28.28N 46.00E
Hafnarfjördhur *town* Iceland **16** 64.04N 21.58W
Haft Gel Iran **31** 31.28N 49.35E
Hagen Germany **8** 51.22N 7.27E
Hagerstown U.S.A. **55** 39.39N 77.43W
Hagfors Sweden **17** 60.02N 13.42E
Ha Giang Vietnam **26** 22.50N105.01E
Hags Head Rep. of Ire. **7** 52.56N 9.29W
Hague, Cap de la *c.* France **9** 49.44N 1.56W
Haguenau France **11** 48.49N 7.47E
Hai Duong Vietnam **26** 20.56N106.21E
Haifa *see* Hefa Israel **32**
Haikou China **25** 20.05N110.25E
Ḩā'il Saudi Arabia **30** 27.31N 41.45E
Hailar China **25** 49.15N119.41E
Hailsham U.K. **5** 50.52N 0.17E
Hailun China **25** 47.29N126.58E
Hailuoto *i.* Finland **16** 65.02N 24.42E
Hainan *d.* China **25** 18.30N109.40E
Hainaut *d.* Belgium **8** 50.30N 3.45E
Haines Alas. U.S.A. **50** 59.11N135.23W
Haines Oreg. U.S.A. **54** 44.55N117.56W
Haiphong Vietnam **26** 20.48N106.40E
Haiti C. America **57** 19.00N 73.00W
Hajdúböszörmény Hungary **15** 47.41N 21.30E
Hajdúszoboszló Hungary **15** 47.27N 21.24E
Hakkâri Turkey **31** 37.36N 43.45E
Hakodate Japan **25** 41.46N140.44E
Ḩalab Syria **30** 36.14N 37.10E
Ḩalabjah Iraq **31** 35.10N 45.59E
Ḩalbā Lebanon **32** 34.34N 36.05E
Halberstadt Germany **14** 51.54N 11.04E
Halden Norway **17** 59.09N 11.23E
Half Assini Ghana **38** 5.04N 2.53W
Halfmoon Bay *town* New Zealand **48** 46.45S168.08E
Haliburton Canada **55** 45.03N 78.03W
Haliburton Highlands Canada **55** 45.03N 78.03W
Halifax Canada **51** 44.38N 63.35W
Halifax U.K. **4** 53.43N 1.51W
Halīl *r.* Iran **28** 27.35N 58.44E
Halkett, C. U.S.A. **50** 71.00N152.00W
Halkirk U.K. **6** 58.30N 3.30W
Halladale *r.* U.K. **6** 58.34N 3.54W
Halland *d.* Sweden **17** 56.45N 13.00E
Halle Belgium **8** 50.45N 4.14E
Halle Germany **14** 51.28N 11.58E
Hällefors Sweden **17** 59.47N 14.30E
Hallingdal *f.* Norway **17** 60.30N 9.00E
Hall Lake *town* Canada **51** 68.40N 81.30W
Hällnäs Sweden **16** 64.19N 19.38E
Hall Pen. Canada **51** 63.30N 66.00W
Hallsberg Sweden **17** 59.04N 15.07E
Hall's Creek *town* Australia **42** 18.13S127.39E
Hallstavik Sweden **17** 60.03N 18.36E
Hallstead U.S.A. **55** 41.58N 75.45W
Halmahera *i.* Indonesia **27** 0.45N128.00E
Halmstad Sweden **17** 56.39N 12.50E
Halsa Norway **16** 63.03N 8.14E
Hälsingborg Sweden **17** 56.03N 12.42E
Haltern Germany **8** 51.45N 7.10E
Haltia Tunturi *mtn.* Finland **16** 69.17N 21.21E
Haltwhistle U.K. **4** 54.58N 2.27W
Ham France **9** 49.45N 3.04E
Ḩamaḑ, Wādī al *r.* Saudi Arabia **30** 25.49N 36.37E
Hamadān Iran **31** 34.47N 48.33E
Ḩamāh Syria **32** 35.09N 36.44E
Hamakita Japan **23** 34.48N137.47E
Hamamatsu Japan **23** 34.42N137.44E
Hamar Norway **17** 60.48N 11.06E
Hamaröy Norway **16** 68.05N 15.40E
Ḩamāţah, Jabal *mtn.* Egypt **30** 24.11N 35.01E
Hamborn Germany **8** 51.29N 6.46E
Hamburg Germany **14** 53.33N 10.00E
Hamburg R.S.A. **39** 33.17S 27.27E
Häme *d.* Finland **17** 61.20N 24.30E
Hämeenlinna Finland **17** 61.00N 24.27E
Hamelin B. Australia **43** 34.10S115.00E
Hameln Germany **14** 52.06N 9.21E
Hamersley Range *mts.* Australia **42** 22.00S118.00E
Hamhŭng N. Korea **25** 39.54N127.35E
Hami China **24** 42.40N 93.30E
Hamilton Australia **46** 37.45S142.04E
Hamilton *r.* Australia **45** 27.12S135.28E
Hamilton Canada **55** 43.15N 79.51W
Hamilton New Zealand **48** 37.46S175.18E
Hamilton U.K. **6** 55.46N 4.10W
Hamilton Mont. U.S.A. **54** 46.15N114.09W
Hamilton Ohio U.S.A. **55** 39.23N 84.33W
Hamley Bridge *town* Australia **46** 34.21S138.41E
Hamm Germany **8** 51.40N 7.49E
Ḩammār, Hawr al *l.* Iraq **31** 30.50N 47.00E
Hammerdal Sweden **16** 63.35N 15.20E
Hammerfest Norway **16** 70.40N 23.42E
Hammond Australia **46** 32.33S138.20E
Hammond N.Y. U.S.A. **55** 44.27N 75.42W
Hamoir Belgium **8** 50.25N 5.32E
Hampshire *d.* U.K. **5** 51.03N 1.20W
Ḩamrīn, Jabal *mts.* Iraq **31** 34.40N 44.10E
Hāmūn-e Jaz Mūrīān *l.* Iran **28** 27.20N 58.55E
Hanang *mtn.* Tanzania **37** 4.30S 35.21E
Hancheng China **25** 35.28N110.29E
Hancock Mich. U.S.A. **55** 47.08N 88.34W
Handa Japan **23** 34.53N136.56E
Handa Somali Rep. **35** 10.39N 51.08E
Handan China **25** 36.35N114.29E
Handeni Tanzania **37** 5.25S 38.04E
HaNegev *des.* Israel **32** 30.42N 34.55E
Hanford U.S.A. **54** 36.20N119.39W
Hanggin Houqi China **24** 40.52N107.04E
Hangö Finland **17** 59.50N 22.57E
Hangzhou China **25** 30.10N120.07E
Hankey R.S.A. **39** 33.50S 24.52E
Hanksville U.S.A. **54** 38.21N110.44W
Hānle Jammu & Kashmir **29** 32.48N 79.00E
Hanmer Springs *town* New Zealand **48** 42.31S172.50E
Hann, Mt. Australia **42** 15.55S125.57E
Hanna Canada **50** 51.38N111.54W
Hannah B. Canada **55** 51.05N 79.45W
Hannibal Mo. U.S.A. **53** 39.41N 91.25W
Hannover Germany **14** 52.23N 9.44E
Hannut Belgium **8** 50.40N 5.05E
Hanöbukten *b.* Sweden **17** 55.45N 14.30E
Ha Noi Vietnam **26** 21.01N105.53E
Hanover Canada **55** 44.09N 81.02W
Hanover R.S.A. **39** 31.04S 24.25E
Hanover Penn. U.S.A. **55** 39.48N 76.59W
Hanover, Isla *i.* Chile **63** 50.57S 74.40W
Han Pijesak Bosnia-Herzegovina **13** 44.04N 18.59E
Han Shui *r.* China **25** 30.45N114.24E
Hanson, L. Australia **46** 31.02S136.13E
Hantengri Feng *mtn.* China **24** 42.09N 80.12E
Hanzhong China **29** 33.10N107.02E
Haparanda Sweden **16** 65.50N 24.10E
Hapsu N. Korea **25** 41.12N128.48E
Ḩaql Saudi Arabia **32** 29.14N 34.56E
Ḩaraḑ Saudi Arabia **31** 24.12N 49.08E
Harare Zimbabwe **39** 17.49S 31.04E
Har-Ayrag Mongolia **25** 45.42N109.14E
Harbin China **25** 45.45N126.41E
Harbour Grace *town* Canada **51** 47.42N 53.13W
Harburg Germany **14** 53.27N 9.58E
Hardangerfjorden *est.* Norway **17** 60.10N 6.00E
Hardangerjökulen *mtn.* Norway **17** 60.33N 7.26E
Hardanger Vidda *f.* Norway **17** 60.20N 7.30E
Hardenberg Neth. **8** 52.36N 6.40E
Harderwijk Neth. **8** 52.21N 5.37E
Harding R.S.A. **39** 30.34S 29.52E
Hardman U.S.A. **54** 45.10N119.40W
Hardwār India **29** 29.58N 78.10E
Hardwicke B. Australia **46** 34.52S137.10E
Haren Germany **8** 52.48N 7.15E
Hārer Ethiopia **35** 9.20N 42.10E
Harfleur France **9** 49.30N 0.12E
Hargeysa Somali Rep. **35** 9.31N 44.02E
Har Hu *l.* China **24** 38.20N 97.40E
Hari *r.* Indonesia **26** 1.00S104.15E
Harīrūd *r.* Afghan. **28** 35.42N 61.12E
Harlech U.K. **4** 52.52N 4.08W
Harlem U.S.A. **54** 48.32N108.47W
Harlingen Neth. **8** 53.10N 5.25E
Harlow U.K. **5** 51.47N 0.08E
Harlowton U.S.A. **54** 46.26N109.50W
Harney Basin *f.* U.S.A. **54** 43.15N120.40W
Harney L. U.S.A. **54** 43.14N119.07W
Härnösand Sweden **16** 62.37N 17.55E
Har Nuur *l.* Mongolia **24** 48.00N 93.25E
Harricana *r.* Canada **55** 51.10N 79.45W
Harrington Australia **47** 31.50S152.43E
Harris *i.* U.K. **6** 57.50N 6.55W
Harris, L. Australia **46** 31.08S135.14E
Harris, Sd. of U.K. **6** 57.43N 7.05W
Harrisburg Oreg. U.S.A. **54** 44.16N123.10W
Harrisburg Penn. U.S.A. **55** 40.16N 76.52W
Harrismith Australia **43** 32.55S117.50E
Harrismith R.S.A. **39** 28.15S 29.07E
Harrison, C. Canada **51** 55.00N 58.00W
Harrogate U.K. **4** 53.59N 1.32W
Harrow U.K. **5** 51.35N 0.21W
Harstad Norway **16** 68.48N 16.30E
Hart, L. Australia **46** 31.08S136.24E
Hartford U.S.A. **55** 41.45N 72.42W
Hartland Canada **55** 46.18N 67.31W
Hartland U.K. **5** 50.59N 4.29W
Hartland Pt. U.K. **5** 51.01N 4.32W
Hartlepool U.K. **4** 54.42N 1.11W
Hartola Finland **17** 61.35N 26.01E
Harts Range *town* Australia **44** 23.06S134.55E
Har Us Nuur *l.* Mongolia **24** 48.10N 92.10E
Hārūt *r.* Afghan. **31** 31.36N 61.12E
Harvey Australia **43** 33.06S115.50E
Harwich U.K. **5** 51.56N 1.18E
Haryana *d.* India **28** 29.15N 76.00E
Ḩasā, Wādī al *r.* Jordan **32** 31.01N 35.29E
Hasa Oasis *see* Aḩsā', Wāḩat al *oasis* Saudi Arabia **31**
Hase *r.* Germany **8** 52.42N 7.17E
Haselünne Germany **8** 52.40N 7.30E
Hasenkamp Argentina **63** 31.30S 59.50W
Ḩasharūd Iran **31** 37.29N 47.05E
Hashimoto Japan **23** 34.19N135.37E
Haslemere U.K. **5** 51.05N 0.41W
Hasselt Belgium **8** 50.56N 5.20E
Hassi Messaoud Algeria **34** 31.43N 6.03E
Hässleholm Sweden **17** 56.09N 13.46E
Hastings Australia **47** 38.18S145.12E
Hastings New Zealand **48** 39.39S176.52E
Hastings U.K. **5** 50.51N 0.36E
Hastings Nebr. U.S.A. **52** 40.37N 98.22W
Hatches Creek *town* Australia **44** 20.56S135.12E
Hatfield Australia **46** 33.53S143.47E
Hatfield U.K. **5** 51.46N 0.13W
Ha Tinh Vietnam **26** 18.21N105.55E
Hattah Australia **46** 34.52S142.23E
Hattem Neth. **8** 52.29N 6.06E
Hatteras, C. U.S.A. **53** 35.14N 75.31W
Hattiesburg U.S.A. **53** 31.25N 89.19W
Hattingen Germany **8** 51.24N 7.09E
Hatton U.S.A. **54** 46.46N118.49W
Hatvan Hungary **15** 47.40N 19.41E
Hauge Norway **17** 58.18N 6.15E
Haugesund Norway **17** 59.25N 5.18E
Haugsdorf Austria **14** 48.42N 16.05E
Hauraki G. New Zealand **48** 36.30S175.00E
Haut Atlas *mts.* Morocco **34** 32.00N 5.50W
Haute Maurice Prov. Park Canada **55** 48.35N 74.21W
Haute-Normandie *d.* France **9** 49.30N 1.00E
Hauterive Canada **55** 49.11N 68.16W
Hautmont France **8** 50.16N 3.52E
Hauts Bassins *d.* Burkina **38** 10.45N 3.45W
Haut Zaïre *d.* Zaïre **37** 2.00N 27.00E
Havana *see* La Habana Cuba **57**
Havant U.K. **5** 50.51N 0.59W
Havel *r.* Germany **14** 52.51N 11.57E
Havelange Belgium **8** 50.23N 5.14E
Havelberg Germany **14** 52.50N 12.04E
Havelock New Zealand **48** 41.17S173.46E
Haverfordwest U.K. **5** 51.48N 4.59W
Haverhill U.K. **5** 52.06N 0.27E
Havlíčkuv Brod Czech Republic **14** 49.38N 15.35E
Havre U.S.A. **54** 48.33N109.41W
Hawaii *d.* U.S.A. **52** 21.00N156.00W
Hawaii *i.* Hawaii U.S.A. **52** 19.30N155.30W
Hawaiian Is. U.S.A. **52** 21.00N157.00W
Hawdon North, L. Australia **46** 37.09S139.54E
Hawea, L. New Zealand **48** 44.30S169.15E
Hawera New Zealand **48** 39.35S174.19E
Hawick U.K. **6** 55.25N 2.47W
Hawke B. New Zealand **48** 39.18S177.15E
Hawker Australia **46** 31.53S138.25E
Hawker Gate Australia **46** 29.46S141.00E
Hawke's Bay *d.* New Zealand **48** 39.00S176.35E
Ḩawrān, Wādī *r.* Iraq **30** 33.57N 42.35E
Ḩawsh 'Īsá Egypt **32** 30.55N 30.17E
Hawthorne U.S.A. **54** 38.32N118.38W
Hay Australia **47** 34.31S144.31E
Hay *r.* Australia **44** 25.00S138.00E
Haya *r.* Japan **23** 35.30N138.26E
Hayange France **11** 49.20N 6.02E
Hayden U.S.A. **54** 33.00N110.47W
Hayes *r.* Canada **51** 57.00N 92.30W
Hayes Creek *town* Australia **42** 13.27S131.25E
Hay-on-Wye U.K. **5** 52.04N 3.09W
Hay River *town* Canada **50** 60.51N115.42W
Haywards Heath *f.* U.K. **5** 51.00N 0.05E
Hazārān, Kūh-e *mtn.* Iran **31** 29.30N 57.18E
Hazelton Canada **50** 55.16N127.18W
Hazen U.S.A. **54** 39.34N119.03W
Hazleton U.S.A. **55** 40.58N 75.59W
Healdsburg U.S.A. **54** 38.37N122.52W
Healesville Australia **47** 37.40S145.31E
Healy U.S.A. **50** 63.52N148.58W
Heanor U.K. **4** 53.01N 1.20W
Hearst Canada **55** 49.42N 83.40W
Heathcote Australia **47** 36.54S144.42E
Hebei *d.* China **25** 39.20N117.15E
Hebel Australia **47** 28.55S147.49E
Hebi China **25** 35.57N114.08E
Hebron Canada **51** 58.05N 62.30W
Hebron *see* Al Khalīl Jordan **32**
Heby Sweden **17** 59.56N 16.53E
Hecate Str. Canada **50** 53.00N131.00W
Hechtel Belgium **8** 51.07N 5.22E
Hechuan China **29** 30.00N106.15E
Hede Sweden **17** 62.25N 13.30E
Hedemora Sweden **17** 60.17N 15.59E
Hedmark *d.* Norway **17** 61.20N 11.30E
Heemstede Neth. **8** 52.21N 4.38E
Heerde Neth. **8** 52.23N 6.02E
Heerenveen Neth. **8** 52.57N 5.55E
Heerlen Neth. **8** 50.53N 5.59E
Hefa Israel **32** 32.49N 34.59E
Hefei China **25** 31.55N117.18E
Hegang China **25** 47.36N130.30E
Heide Germany **14** 54.12N 9.06E
Heidelberg Germany **14** 49.25N 8.42E
Heidelberg C.P. R.S.A. **39** 34.05S 20.58E
Heilbron R.S.A. **39** 27.16S 27.57E
Heilbronn Germany **14** 49.08N 9.14E
Heilongjiang *d.* China **25** 47.15N128.50E
Heiloo Neth. **8** 52.37N 4.43E
Heinola Finland **17** 61.13N 26.02E
Heinsberg Germany **8** 51.04N 6.06E
Heishui China **25** 42.06N119.22E
Hejaz *f. see* Al Ḩijāz *f.* Saudi Arabia **30**
Hekinan Japan **23** 34.51N136.58E
Hekla, Mt. Iceland **16** 64.00N 19.45W
Hekou China **29** 22.39N103.57E
Helagsfjället *mtn.* Sweden **16** 62.58N 12.25E
Helena U.S.A. **54** 46.36N112.01W
Helen Reef *i.* Pacific Ocean **27** 2.43N131.46E
Helensburgh U.K. **6** 56.01N 4.44W
Helensville New Zealand **48** 36.40S174.27E
Hellendoorn Neth. **8** 52.24N 6.29E
Hellenthal Germany **8** 50.28N 6.25E
Hellesylt Norway **17** 62.05N 6.54E
Hellevoetsluis Neth. **8** 51.49N 4.08E
Hellín Spain **10** 38.31N 1.43W
Helmand *r.* Asia **28** 31.10N 61.20E
Helmond Neth. **8** 51.28N 5.40E
Helmsdale U.K. **6** 58.07N 3.40W
Helmsdale *r.* U.K. **6** 58.05N 3.39W
Helsingfors *see* Helsinki Finland **17**
Helsingör Denmark **17** 56.02N 12.37E
Helsinki Finland **17** 60.08N 25.00E
Helston U.K. **5** 50.07N 5.17W
Helvecia Argentina **63** 31.06S 60.05W
Hemel Hempstead U.K. **5** 51.46N 0.28W
Hemse Sweden **17** 57.14N 18.22E
Hemsedal Norway **17** 60.52N 8.34E
Henan *d.* China **25** 33.45N113.00E
Henares *r.* Spain **10** 40.26N 3.35W
Henbury Australia **44** 24.35S133.15E
Hendaye France **11** 43.22N 1.46W
Henderson Ky. U.S.A. **55** 37.50N 87.35W
Henderson Nev. U.S.A. **54** 36.02N114.59W
Hendrik Verwoerd Dam R.S.A. **39** 30.37S 25.29E
Hendrina R.S.A. **39** 26.09S 29.42E
Hengelo Neth. **8** 52.16N 6.46E
Hengyang China **25** 26.58N112.31E
Hénin-Beaumont France **8** 50.25N 2.55E
Hennebont France **11** 47.48N 3.16W
Henrietta Maria, C. Canada **51** 55.00N 82.15W
Hentiesbaai Namibia **39** 22.10S 14.19E
Henty Australia **47** 35.30S147.03E
Henzada Burma **29** 17.38N 95.35E
Heppner U.S.A. **54** 45.21N119.33W
Heqing China **29** 26.34N100.12E
Herāt Afghan. **31** 34.21N 62.10E
Herceg-Novi Yugo. **13** 42.27N 18.32E
Hereford U.K. **5** 52.04N 2.43W
Hereford and Worcester *d.* U.K. **5** 52.08N 2.30W
Herentals Belgium **8** 51.12N 4.42E
Herford Germany **14** 52.07N 8.40E
Hermannsburg Australia **44** 23.56S132.46E
Hermanus R.S.A. **39** 34.24S 19.16E
Hermidale Australia **47** 31.33S146.44E
Hermiston U.S.A. **54** 45.51N119.17W
Hermosillo Mexico **56** 29.04N110.58W
Herne Germany **8** 51.32N 7.12E
Herne Bay *town* U.K. **5** 51.23N 1.10E
Herning Denmark **17** 56.08N 8.59E
Heron Bay *town* Canada **55** 48.41N 86.28W
Herrera del Duque Spain **10** 39.10N 5.03W
Herstal Belgium **8** 50.14N 5.38E
Herten Germany **8** 51.36N 7.08E
Hertford U.K. **5** 51.48N 0.05W
Hertfordshire *d.* U.K. **5** 51.51N 0.05W
Hervey B. Australia **44** 25.00S153.00E
Herzliyya Israel **32** 32.10N 34.50E
Hesbaye *f.* Belgium **8** 50.32N 5.07E
Hesel Germany **8** 53.19N 7.35E
Hessen *d.* Germany **14** 50.30N 9.15E
Hesso Australia **46** 32.08S137.58E
Hetzerath Germany **8** 49.54N 6.50E
Hewett, C. Canada **51** 70.20N 68.00W
Hexham U.K. **4** 54.58N 2.06W
Hexigten Qi China **25** 43.17N117.24E
Heysham U.K. **4** 54.03N 2.53W
Heyuan China **25** 23.44N114.41E
Heywood Australia **46** 38.08S141.38E
Heywood U.K. **4** 53.36N 2.13W
Hiawatha Utah U.S.A. **54** 39.29N111.01W
Hibbing U.S.A. **53** 47.25N 92.55W
Hicks Bay *town* New Zealand **48** 37.35S178.18E
Hidalgo *d.* Mexico **56** 20.50N 98.30W
Hidalgo Tamaulipas Mexico **56** 24.15N 99.26W
Hidalgo del Parral Mexico **56** 26.56N105.40W
Hieradhsvotn *r.* Iceland **16** 65.45N 18.50W
Higashimatsuyama Japan **23** 36.02N139.24E
Higashimurayama Japan **23** 35.46N139.29E
Higashiōsaka Japan **23** 34.39N135.35E
Higginsville Australia **43** 31.46S121.43E
Highland *d.* U.K. **6** 57.42N 5.00W
High Peak *mtn.* U.K. **4** 53.22N 1.48W
High Willhays *mtn.* U.K. **5** 50.41N 4.00W
High Wycombe U.K. **5** 51.38N 0.46W
Hiiumaa *i.* Estonia **17** 58.52N 22.40E
Híjar Spain **10** 41.10N 0.27W
Hikone Japan **23** 35.15N136.15E
Hikurangi New Zealand **48** 35.36S174.17E
Hikurangi *mtn.* New Zealand **48** 37.50S178.10E
Hilden Germany **8** 51.10N 6.56E
Hildesheim Germany **14** 52.09N 9.58E
Hillegom Neth. **8** 52.19N 4.35E
Hill End Australia **47** 33.01S149.26E
Hillsboro Oreg. U.S.A. **54** 45.31N122.59W
Hillsdale U.S.A. **55** 41.56N 84.37W
Hillsport Canada **55** 49.27N 85.34W
Hillston Australia **47** 33.30S145.33E
Hilo Hawaii U.S.A. **52** 19.42N155.04W
Hiltrup Germany **8** 51.55N 7.36E
Hilversum Neth. **8** 52.14N 5.12E
Himachal Pradesh *d.* India **28** 31.45N 77.30E
Himalaya *mts.* Asia **29** 29.00N 84.00E
Himanka Finland **16** 64.04N 23.39E
Himarë Albania **13** 40.07N 19.44E
Ḩimş Syria **32** 34.44N 36.43E
Hinchinbrook I. Australia **44** 18.23S146.17E
Hinckley U.K. **5** 52.33N 1.21W
Hindmarsh, L. Australia **46** 36.03S141.53E
Hindu Kush *mts.* Asia **28** 36.40N 70.00E
Hindupur India **28** 13.49N 77.29E
Hines Creek *town* Canada **50** 56.15N118.36W
Hingol *r.* Pakistan **28** 25.25N 65.32E
Hinnöy *i.* Norway **16** 68.35N 15.50E
Hinojosa Spain **10** 38.30N 5.17W
Hinsdale Mont. U.S.A. **54** 48.24N107.05W
Hippolytushoef Neth. **8** 52.57N 4.58E
Hirakata Japan **23** 34.48N135.38E
Hīrākud *resr.* India **29** 21.32N 83.55E
Hiratsuka Japan **23** 35.19N139.21E
Hiroshima Japan **25** 34.23N132.27E
Hirson France **8** 49.56N 4.05E
Hîrşova Romania **15** 44.41N 27.57E
Hirtshals Denmark **17** 57.35N 9.58E
Hisai Japan **23** 34.40N136.28E
Hisār India **28** 29.10N 75.43E
Ḩismá *f.* Saudi Arabia **32** 28.45N 35.56E
Hispaniola *i.* C. America **57** 19.00N 71.00W
Ḩisyah Syria **32** 34.24N 36.45E
Hīt Iraq **30** 33.38N 42.50E
Hitchin U.K. **5** 51.57N 0.16W
Hitra *i.* Norway **16** 63.37N 8.46E
Hjälmaren *l.* Sweden **17** 59.15N 15.45E
Hjörring Denmark **17** 57.28N 9.59E
Hlotse Lesotho **39** 28.52S 28.02E
Ho Ghana **38** 6.38N 0.38E
Hoare B. Canada **51** 65.20N 62.30W
Hobart Australia **45** 42.54S147.18E
Hobart Ind. U.S.A. **55** 41.32N 87.14W
Hoboken Belgium **8** 51.11N 4.21E
Hobro Denmark **17** 56.38N 9.48E
Hobyo Somali Rep. **35** 5.20N 48.30E
Ho Chi Minh Vietnam **26** 10.46N106.43E
Hodgson Canada **51** 51.13N 97.34W
Hod HaSharon Israel **32** 32.15N 34.55E
Hódmezövásárhely Hungary **13** 46.26N 20.21E
Hoek van Holland Neth. **8** 51.59N 4.08E
Hoeryŏng N.Korea **23** 42.27N129.44E
Hof Germany **14** 50.19N 11.56E
Höfn Iceland **16** 64.16N 15.10W
Hofors Sweden **17** 60.33N 16.17E
Hofsjökull *mtn.* Iceland **16** 64.50N 19.00W
Hofsos Iceland **16** 65.53N 19.26W
Höganäs Sweden **17** 56.12N 12.33E
Hohhot China **25** 40.49N111.37E
Hoi An Vietnam **26** 15.54N108.19E
Hoima Uganda **37** 1.25N 31.22E
Hokitika New Zealand **48** 42.42S170.59E
Hokkaidō *i.* Japan **25** 43.30N143.20E
Hokksund Norway **17** 59.47N 9.59E
Hola Kenya **37** 1.29S 40.02E
Holbaek Denmark **17** 55.43N 11.43E
Holbrook Australia **47** 35.46S147.20E
Holbrook U.S.A. **54** 34.54N110.10W
Holguín Cuba **57** 20.54N 76.15W
Höljes Sweden **17** 60.54N 12.36E
Hollabrunn Austria **14** 48.34N 16.05E
Holland Mich. U.S.A. **55** 42.46N 86.06W
Holman Island *town* Canada **50** 70.43N117.43W
Holmavik Iceland **16** 65.43N 21.39W
Holmestrand Norway **17** 59.29N 10.18E
Holmön *i.* Sweden **16** 63.47N 20.53E
Holmsund Sweden **16** 63.41N 20.20E
Holon Israel **32** 32.01N 34.46E
Holroyd *r.* Australia **44** 14.10S141.36E
Holstebro Denmark **17** 56.21N 8.38E
Holstein Canada **55** 44.03N 80.45W
Holsteinsborg Greenland **51** 66.55N 53.30W
Holsworthy U.K. **5** 50.48N 4.21W
Holt U.K. **4** 52.55N 1.04E
Holten Neth. **8** 52.18N 6.26E
Holwerd Neth. **8** 53.22N 5.54E
Holy Cross U.S.A. **50** 62.12N159.47W
Holyhead U.K. **4** 53.18N 4.38W
Holyhead B. U.K. **4** 53.22N 4.40W
Holy I. England U.K. **4** 55.41N 1.47W
Holy I. Wales U.K. **4** 53.15N 4.38W
Holywood U.K. **7** 54.38N 5.50W
Hombori Mali **38** 15.20N 1.38W
Home B. Canada **51** 69.00N 66.00W
Home Hill *town* Australia **44** 19.40S147.25E
Homer Alas. U.S.A. **50** 59.40N151.37W
Homer Tunnel New Zealand **48** 44.40S168.15E
Homoine Mozambique **39** 23.45S 35.09E
Homoljske Planina *f.* Yugo. **15** 44.20N 21.45E
Honda Colombia **60** 5.15N 74.50W
Hondeklipbaai R.S.A. **39** 30.19S 17.12E
Hondo *r.* Mexico **57** 18.33N 88.22W
Honduras C. America **57** 14.30N 87.00W
Honduras, G. of Carib. Sea **57** 16.20N 87.30W
Honfleur France **9** 49.25N 0.14E
Hong Hà *r.* Vietnam **26** 20.15N106.36E
Hong Kong Asia **25** 22.30N114.10E
Hongshui He *r.* China **25** 23.20N110.04E
Honiton U.K. **5** 50.48N 3.13W
Honkajoki Finland **17** 62.00N 22.15E
Honolulu Hawaii U.S.A. **52** 21.19N157.50W
Honshū *i.* Japan **25** 36.00N138.00E
Hood Pt. Australia **43** 34.23S119.34E
Hood Range *mts.* Australia **47** 28.35S144.30E
Hoogeveen Neth. **8** 52.44N 6.29E
Hoogezand Neth. **8** 53.10N 6.47E
Hoogstade Belgium **8** 50.59N 2.42E
Hook Head Rep. of Ire. **7** 52.07N 6.55W
Hoopa U.S.A. **54** 41.03N123.40W
Hoopstad R.S.A. **39** 27.48S 25.52E
Hoorn Neth. **8** 52.38N 5.03E
Hoover Dam U.S.A. **54** 36.00N114.27W
Hope W.A. U.S.A. **53** 33.40N 93.36W
Hope, L. S.A. Australia **43** 32.31S120.25E
Hope, L. S.A. Australia **46** 28.23S139.19E
Hopedale Canada **51** 55.30N 60.10W
Hopefield R.S.A. **39** 33.04S 18.19E
Hopetoun Vic. Australia **46** 35.43S142.20E
Hopetoun W.A. Australia **43** 33.57S120.05E
Hopetown R.S.A. **39** 29.37S 24.04E
Hopkins *r.* Australia **46** 38.25S142.00E
Hopkins, L. Australia **42** 24.15S128.50E
Hopland U.S.A. **54** 38.58N123.07W
Hoquiam U.S.A. **54** 46.59N123.53W
Hordaland *d.* Norway **17** 60.30N 6.30E
Horde Germany **8** 51.29N 7.30E
Horlick Mts. Antarctica **64** 86.00S102.00W
Hormuz, Str. of Asia **31** 26.35N 56.20E
Horn Austria **14** 48.40N 15.40E
Horn, C. *see* Hornos, Cabo de *c.* S. America **63**
Hornavan *l.* Sweden **16** 66.10N 17.30E
Horncastle U.K. **4** 53.13N 0.08W
Horndal Sweden **17** 60.18N 16.25E
Hornell U.S.A. **55** 42.19N 77.39W
Hornepayne Canada **55** 49.14N 84.48W
Hornindal Norway **17** 61.58N 6.31E
Horn Mts. Canada **50** 62.15N119.15W
Hornos, Cabo de *c.* S. America **63** 55.47S 67.00W
Hornsby Australia **47** 33.11S151.06E
Hornsea U.K. **4** 53.55N 0.10W
Hořovice Czech Republic **14** 49.50N 13.54E
Horsens Denmark **17** 55.52N 9.52E
Horsham Australia **46** 36.45S142.15E
Horsham U.K. **5** 51.04N 0.20W
Horten Norway **17** 59.25N 10.30E
Horton *r.* Canada **50** 70.00N127.00W
Horton L. Canada **50** 67.30N122.28W
Hose, Pegunungan *mts.* Malaysia **26** 1.30N114.10E
Hoshiārpur India **28** 31.30N 75.59E
Hôsh 'Isa Egypt **32** 30.55N 30.17E

Hoskins P.N.G. **41** 5.30S150.27E
Hospitalet de Llobregat Spain **10** 41.20N 2.06E
Hoste, Isla *i.* Chile **63** 55.10S 69.00W
Hotan China **24** 37.07N 79.57E
Hotazel R.S.A. **39** 27.16S 22.57E
Hotham *r.* Australia **43** 32.58S116.22E
Hotham, Mt. Australia **47** 36.58S147.11E
Hoting Sweden **16** 64.07N 16.10E
Hot Springs *town* Ark. U.S.A. **53** 34.30N 93.02W
Hot Springs *town* S.Dak. U.S.A. **52** 43.26N103.29W
Hottah L. Canada **50** 65.04N118.29W
Houdan France **9** 48.47N 1.36E
Houffalize Belgium **8** 50.08N 5.50E
Houghton L. U.S.A. **55** 44.16N 84.48W
Houghton-le-Spring U.K. **4** 54.51N 1.28W
Houlton U.S.A. **55** 46.08N 67.51W
Houma U.S.A. **53** 29.35N 90.44W
Houndé Burkina **38** 11.34N 3.31W
Hourn, Loch U.K. **6** 57.06N 5.33W
Houston Tex. U.S.A. **53** 29.45N 95.25W
Hovd Mongolia **24** 46.40N 90.45E
Hove U.K. **5** 50.50N 0.10W
Hövsgöl Nuur *l.* Mongolia **24** 51.00N100.30E
Howe, C. Australia **47** 37.30S149.59E
Howitt, Mt. Australia **47** 37.15S146.40E
Howrah India **29** 22.35N 88.20E
Howth Head Rep. of Ire. **7** 53.22N 6.03W
Hoy *i.* U.K. **6** 58.51N 3.17W
Höyanger Norway **17** 61.13N 6.05E
Hoyos Spain **10** 40.09N 6.45W
Hradec Králové Czech Republic **14** 50.13N 15.50E
Hron *r.* Slovakia **15** 47.49N 18.45E
Hrubieszów Poland **15** 50.49N 23.55E
Huab *r.* Namibia **39** 20.55S 13.28E
Huabei Pingyuan *f.* China **25** 34.30N117.00E
Huacho Peru **60** 11.05S 77.36W
Huade China **25** 41.57N114.04E
Huai He *r.* China **25** 32.58N118.18E
Huainan China **25** 32.41N117.06E
Huajuápan Mexico **56** 17.50N 97.48W
Hualian Taiwan **25** 24.00N121.39E
Huallaga *r.* Peru **60** 5.02S 75.30W
Huamanrazo *mtn.* Peru **60** 12.54S 75.04W
Huambo Angola **36** 12.47S 15.44E
Huanan China **25** 46.13N130.31E
Huancané Peru **60** 15.10S 69.44W
Huancapi Peru **60** 13.35S 74.05W
Huancavelica Peru **60** 12.45S 75.03W
Huancayo Peru **60** 12.05S 75.12W
Huanggang China **25** 30.40N114.50E
Huang Hai *b.* N. Korea **25** 39.00N124.00E
Huang He *r.* China **25** 37.55N118.46E
Huanghua China **25** 38.22N117.20E
Huangshi China **25** 30.13N115.05E
Huanta Peru **60** 12.54S 74.13W
Huánuco Peru **60** 9.55S 76.11W
Huaráz Peru **60** 9.33S 77.31W
Huarmey Peru **60** 10.05S 78.05W
Huascaran *mtn.* Peru **60** 9.08S 77.36W
Huasco Chile **62** 28.28S 71.14W
Hubei *d.* China **25** 31.15N112.15E
Hubli India **28** 15.20N 75.14E
Hückelhoven Germany **8** 51.04N 6.10E
Hucknall U.K. **4** 53.03N 1.12W
Huddersfield U.K. **4** 53.38N 1.49W
Huddinge Sweden **17** 59.14N 17.59E
Hudiksvall Sweden **17** 61.44N 17.07E
Hudson N.Y. U.S.A. **55** 42.15N 73.47W
Hudson *r.* U.S.A. **55** 40.42N 74.02W
Hudson Wyo. U.S.A. **54** 42.54N108.35W
Hudson B. Canada **51** 58.00N 86.00W
Hudson Hope Canada **50** 56.02N121.55W
Hudson Mts. Antarctica **64** 76.00S 99.00W
Hudson Str. Canada **51** 62.00N 70.00W
Hue Vietnam **26** 16.28N107.35E
Huedin Romania **15** 46.52N 23.02E
Huehuetenango Guatemala **56** 15.19N 91.26W
Huelva Spain **10** 37.15N 6.56W
Huelva *r.* Spain **10** 37.25N 6.00W
Huércal-Overa Spain **10** 37.23N 1.56W
Huesca Spain **10** 42.02N 0.25W
Hugh *r.* Australia **44** 25.01S134.01E
Hughenden Australia **44** 20.51S144.12E
Hughes Australia **45** 30.40S129.32E
Hughes U.S.A. **50** 66.03N154.16W
Huiarau Range *mts.* New Zealand **48** 38.20S177.15E
Huimin China **25** 37.29N117.29E
Huisne *r.* France **9** 47.59N 0.11E
Huixtla Mexico **56** 15.09N 92.30W
Huizen Neth. **8** 52.18N 5.12E
Hukuntsi Botswana **39** 24.02S 21.48E
Ḩulayfā' Saudi Arabia **30** 26.00N 40.47E
Hulín Czech Republic **15** 49.19N 17.28E
Hull Canada **55** 45.26N 75.45W
Hüls Germany **8** 51.23N 6.30E
Hulst Neth. **8** 51.18N 4.01E
Hultsfred Sweden **17** 57.29N 15.50E
Hulun Nur *l.* China **25** 49.00N117.27E
Ḩulwān Egypt **32** 29.51N 31.20E
Humaitá Brazil **60** 7.31S 63.02W
Humansdorp R.S.A. **39** 34.02S 24.45E
Humber *r.* U.K. **4** 53.40N 0.12W
Humberside *d.* U.K. **4** 53.48N 0.35W
Humboldt *r.* U.S.A. **54** 40.02N118.31W
Hume, L. Australia **47** 36.06S147.05E
Hūmedān Iran **31** 25.24N 59.39E
Humenné Slovakia **15** 48.56N 21.55E
Humphreys Peak *mtn.* U.S.A. **54** 35.20N111.40W
Hūn Libya **34** 29.06N 15.57E
Húnaflói *b.* Iceland **16** 65.45N 20.50W
Hunan *d.* China **25** 27.30N111.30E
Hunedoara Romania **15** 45.45N 22.54E
Hungary Europe **15** 47.30N 19.00E
Hungerford Australia **46** 29.00S144.26E
Hungerford U.K. **5** 51.25N 1.30W
Hŭngnam N. Korea **25** 39.49N127.40E
Hunsberge *mts.* Namibia **39** 27.40S 17.12E
Hunse *r.* Neth. **8** 53.20N 6.18E
Hunsrück *mts.* Germany **8** 49.44N 7.05E
Hunstanton U.K. **4** 52.57N 0.30E
Hunte *r.* Germany **14** 52.30N 8.19E
Hunter *r.* Australia **47** 32.50S151.42E
Hunter I. Australia **45** 40.30S144.46E
Huntingdon U.K. **5** 52.20N 0.11W
Huntingdon Penn. U.S.A. **55** 40.29N 78.01W
Huntington Ind. U.S.A. **55** 40.54N 85.30W
Huntington Oreg. U.S.A. **54** 44.21N117.16W
Huntington Utah U.S.A. **54** 39.20N110.58W
Huntington W.Va. U.S.A. **55** 38.24N 82.26W
Huntington Beach *town* U.S.A. **54** 33.39N118.01W
Huntly New Zealand **48** 37.35S175.10E
Huntly U.K. **6** 57.27N 2.47W
Huntsville Canada **55** 45.20N 79.13W
Huntsville Ala. U.S.A. **53** 34.44N 86.35W
Huntsville Tex. U.S.A. **53** 34.44N 86.35W
Hunyani *r.* Mozambique **39** 15.41S 30.38E
Huon Pen. P.N.G. **27** 6.00S147.00E
Huonville Australia **45** 43.01S147.01E
Huron S.Dak. U.S.A. **52** 44.22N 98.12W
Huron, L. Canada / U.S.A. **55** 44.30N 82.15W
Húsavík Iceland **16** 66.03N 17.21W
Huşi Romania **15** 46.40N 28.04E
Huskvarna Sweden **17** 57.48N 14.16E
Husum Germany **14** 54.29N 9.04E
Hutchinson R.S.A. **39** 31.30S 23.10E
Hutchinson U.S.A. **52** 38.03N 97.56W
Huy Belgium **8** 50.31N 5.14E
Hvar *i.* Croatia **13** 43.10N 16.45E
Hvita *r.* Iceland **16** 64.33N 21.45W
Hwange Zimbabwe **39** 18.20S 26.29E
Hwange Nat. Park Zimbabwe **39** 19.00S 26.30E
Hyargas Nuur *l.* Mongolia **24** 49.30N 93.35E
Hyde U.K. **4** 53.26N 2.06W
Hyden Australia **43** 32.27S118.53E
Hyderābād India **29** 17.22N 78.26E
Hyderābād Pakistan **28** 25.23N 68.24E
Hydesville U.S.A. **54** 40.31N124.00W
Hyères France **11** 43.07N 6.08E
Hyères, Îles d' *is.* France **11** 43.01N 6.25E
Hyland, Mt. Australia **47** 30.09S152.25E
Hyllestad Norway **17** 61.10N 5.18E
Hyndman Peak U.S.A. **54** 43.50N114.10W
Hysham U.S.A. **54** 46.18N107.14W
Hythe Kent U.K. **5** 51.04N 1.05E
Hyvinkää Finland **17** 60.38N 24.52E

I

Ialomiţa *r.* Romania **15** 44.41N 27.52E
Iar Connacht *f.* Rep. of Ire. **7** 53.21N 9.22W
Iaşi Romania **15** 47.09N 27.38E
Iauaretê Brazil **60** 0.36N 69.12W
Iaupolo P.N.G. **44** 9.34S150.30E
Ibadan Nigeria **38** 7.23N 3.56E
Ibagué Colombia **60** 4.25N 75.20W
Ibar *r.* Yugo. **13** 43.44N 20.44E
Ibaraki Japan **23** 34.49N135.34E
Ibarra Ecuador **60** 0.23N 78.05W
Ibbenbüren Germany **8** 52.17N 7.44E
Ibi *r.* Japan **23** 35.03N136.42E
Ibi Nigeria **38** 8.11N 9.44E
Ibiapaba, Serra da *mts.* Brazil **61** 5.30S 41.00W
Ibicaraí Brazil **61** 14.52S 39.37W
Ibicuy Argentina **63** 33.45S 59.13W
Ibina *r.* Zaïre **37** 1.00N 28.40E
Ibitinga Brazil **59** 21.43S 48.47W
Ibiza *i.* Spain **10** 39.00N 1.23E
Ibiza *town* Spain **10** 38.55N 1.30E
Ibotirama Brazil **61** 12.13S 43.12W
Ibshawāy Egypt **32** 29.21N 30.40E
Içá *r.* Brazil **60** 3.07S 67.58W
Ica Peru **60** 14.02S 75.48W
Içana Brazil **60** 0.21N 67.19W
Içana *r.* Brazil **60** 0.00 67.10W
Iceland Europe **16** 64.45N 18.00W
Ichihara Japan **23** 35.31N140.05E
Ichikawa Japan **23** 35.44N139.55E
Ichinomiya Japan **23** 35.18N136.48E
Icoraci Brazil **61** 1.16S 48.28W
Idah Nigeria **38** 7.05N 6.45E
Idaho *d.* U.S.A. **54** 44.58N115.56W
Idaho Falls *town* U.S.A. **54** 43.30N112.02W
Idar-Oberstein Germany **8** 49.43N 7.19E
Ideles Algeria **34** 23.58N 5.53E
Idfū Egypt **30** 24.58N 32.50E
Ídhi Óros *mtn.* Greece **13** 35.13N 24.45E
Ídhra *i.* Greece **13** 37.20N 23.32E
Idmū Egypt **32** 28.09N 30.41E
Idre Sweden **17** 61.52N 12.43E
Ieper Belgium **8** 50.51N 2.53E
Ierápetra Greece **13** 35.00N 25.45E
Iesi Italy **12** 43.32N 13.15E
Iesolo Italy **9** 45.32N 12.38E
Ifakara Tanzania **37** 8.09S 36.41E
Ifalik *is.* Federated States of Micronesia **27** 7.15N144.27E
Ife Oyo Nigeria **38** 7.33N 4.34E
Iferouâne Niger **38** 19.04N 8.24E
Iga *r.* Japan **23** 34.45N136.01E
Iggesund Sweden **17** 61.38N 17.04E
Iglesias Italy **12** 39.18N 8.32E
Igli Algeria **34** 30.25N 2.12W
Igloolik Island *town* Canada **51** 69.05N 81.25W
Ignace Canada **51** 49.26N 91.40W
Iğneada Burnu *c.* Turkey **13** 41.50N 28.05E
Igoumenítsa Greece **13** 39.32N 20.14E
Igra Russian Fed. **18** 57.31N 53.09E
Iguaçu *r.* Brazil **59** 25.33S 54.35W
Iguaçu, Saltos do *f.* Brazil / Argentina **59** 25.35S 54.22W
Iguala Mexico **56** 18.21N 99.31W
Igualada Spain **10** 41.35N 1.37E
Iguassu Falls *see* Iguaçu, Saltos do *f.* Brazil / Argentina **59**
Iguatu Brazil **61** 6.22S 39.20W
Ihiala Nigeria **38** 5.51N 6.52E
Ihosy Madagascar **36** 22.24S 46.08E
Ii *r.* Finland **16** 65.19N 25.20E
Iida Japan **23** 35.31N137.50E
Iisalmi Finland **16** 63.34N 27.11E
Ijebu Ode Nigeria **38** 6.47N 3.54E
IJmuiden Neth. **8** 52.28N 4.37E
IJssel *r.* Zuid Holland Neth. **8** 51.54N 4.32E
IJssel *r.* Overijssel Neth. **8** 52.34N 5.50E
IJsselmeer *l.* Neth. **8** 52.45N 5.20E
Ijuí Brazil **59** 28.23S 53.55W
Ijzendijke Neth. **8** 51.19N 3.37E
Ijzer *r.* Belgium **8** 51.09N 2.44E
Ikaría *i.* Greece **13** 37.35N 26.10E
Ikdū Egypt **32** 31.18N 30.18E
Ikela Zaïre **36** 1.06S 23.04E
Ikerre Nigeria **38** 7.30N 5.14E
Ila Nigeria **38** 8.01N 4.55E
Ilagan Phil. **27** 17.07N121.53E
Īlām Iran **31** 33.27N 46.27E
Ilangali Tanzania **37** 6.50S 35.06E
Ilaro Nigeria **38** 6.53N 3.03E
Iława Poland **15** 53.37N 19.33E
Ilebo Zaïre **36** 4.20S 20.35E
Ilek *r.* Russian Fed. **19** 51.30N 54.00E
Ileret Kenya **37** 4.22N 36.13E
Ilesha Oyo Nigeria **38** 7.39N 4.45E
Ilfracombe Australia **44** 23.30S144.30E
Ilfracombe U.K. **5** 51.13N 4.08W
Ilhabela Brazil **59** 23.47S 45.20W
Ilha Grande, Baía da *b.* Brazil **59** 23.09S 44.30W
Ilha Grande, Reprêsa *resr.* Brazil **59** 23.10S 53.40W
Ilhéus Brazil **61** 14.50S 39.06W
Ili *r.* Kazakhstan **24** 45.00N 74.20E
Ilia Romania **15** 45.56N 22.39E
Iliamna L. U.S.A. **50** 59.30N155.00W
Ilich Russian Fed. **24** 40.50N 68.29E
Iligan Phil. **27** 8.12N124.13E
Ilintsy Ukraine **15** 49.08N 29.11E
Ilion U.S.A. **55** 43.01N 75.02W
Ilkley U.K. **4** 53.56N 1.49W
Illapel Chile **62** 31.38S 71.10W
Ille-et-Vilaine *d.* France **9** 48.10N 1.30W
Illéla Niger **38** 14.30N 5.09E
Iller *r.* Germany **14** 48.23N 9.58E
Illiers France **9** 48.18N 1.15E
Illinois *d.* U.S.A. **53** 40.00N 89.00W
Illizi Algeria **34** 26.20N 8.20E
Ilmajoki Finland **16** 62.44N 22.34E
Ilminster U.K. **5** 50.55N 2.56W
Ilo Peru **62** 17.38S 71.20W
Iloilo Phil. **27** 10.45N122.33E
Ilorin Nigeria **38** 8.32N 4.34E
Ilovlya Russian Fed. **19** 49.19N 44.01E
Imala Mozambique **37** 14.39S 39.34E
Imandra Russian Fed. **18** 67.53N 33.30E
Imandra, Ozero *l.* Russian Fed. **18** 67.30N 32.45E
Imbābah Egypt **32** 30.05N 31.12E
Īmī Ethiopia **35** 6.28N 42.18E
Immingham U.K. **4** 53.37N 0.12W
Imo *d.* Nigeria **38** 5.30N 7.20E
Imola Italy **9** 44.21N 11.42E
Imperatriz Brazil **61** 5.32S 47.28W
Imperia Italy **9** 43.53N 8.01E
Imperial Calif. U.S.A. **54** 32.51N115.34W
Imperial Dam U.S.A. **54** 32.55N114.30W
Imperial Valley *f.* U.S.A. **54** 32.50N115.30W
Impfondo Congo **36** 1.36N 17.58E
Imphāl India **29** 24.47N 93.55E
Imroz *i. see* Gökçeada *i.* Turkey **13**
Ina Japan **23** 35.50N137.57E
Ina *r.* Japan **23** 34.43N135.28E
In Abbangarit *well* Niger **38** 17.49N 6.15E
Inangahua Junction New Zealand **48** 41.53S171.58E
Inanwatan Indonesia **27** 2.08S132.10E
Inari *l.* Finland **16** 69.00N 28.00E
Inari *town* Finland **16** 68.54N 27.01E
Inazawa Japan **23** 35.15N136.47E
Inca Spain **10** 39.43N 2.54E
Incesu Turkey **30** 38.39N 35.12E
Inch'on S. Korea **25** 37.30N126.38E
Indals *r.* Sweden **16** 62.30N 17.20E
Indaw Burma **24** 24.14N 96.07E
Independence Calif. U.S.A. **54** 36.48N118.12W
Inderborskiy Kazakhstan **19** 48.32N 51.44E
India Asia **29** 23.00N 78.30E
Indiana *d.* U.S.A. **55** 40.00N 86.15W
Indiana *town* U.S.A. **55** 40.37N 79.09W
Indianapolis U.S.A. **55** 39.45N 86.10W
Indian Harbour Canada **51** 54.25N 57.20W
Indiga Russian Fed. **18** 67.40N 49.00E
Indigirka *r.* Russian Fed. **21** 71.00N148.45E
Indija Yugo. **15** 45.03N 20.05E
Indio U.S.A. **54** 33.43N116.13W
Indonesia Asia **26** 6.00S118.00E
Indore India **28** 22.42N 75.54E
Indragiri *r.* Indonesia **26** 0.30S103.08E
Indrāvati *r.* India **29** 18.45N 80.16E
Indre *r.* France **11** 47.16N 0.19W
Indus *r.* Pakistan **28** 24.00N 67.33E
Inebolu Turkey **30** 41.57N 33.45E
Inegöl Turkey **30** 40.06N 29.31E
Infiesto Spain **10** 43.21N 5.21W
I-n-Gall Niger **38** 16.47N 6.56E
Ingatestone U.K. **5** 51.41N 0.22E
Ingersoll Canada **55** 43.02N 80.53W
Ingham Australia **44** 18.35S146.12E
Ingleborough Qld. U.K. **4** 54.10N 2.23W
Inglewood Qld. Australia **47** 28.25S151.02E
Inglewood Vic. Australia **46** 36.33S143.53E
Inglewood New Zealand **48** 39.09S174.12E
Inglewood U.S.A. **54** 33.58N118.21W
Ingolstadt Germany **14** 48.46N 11.27E
Ingomar Australia **46** 29.38S134.48E
Ingulets Ukraine **19** 47.43N 33.16E
Ingwiller France **11** 48.52N 7.29E
Inhambane Mozambique **39** 23.51S 35.29E
Inhambane *d.* Mozambique **39** 22.20S 34.00E
Inhaminga Mozambique **39** 18.24S 35.00E
Inharrime Mozambique **39** 24.29S 35.01E
Inhassoro Mozambique **39** 21.32S 35.10E
Inirida *r.* Colombia **60** 3.59N 67.45W
Inishbofin *i.* Galway Rep. of Ire. **7** 53.38N 10.14W
Inisheer *i.* Rep. of Ire. **7** 53.04N 9.32W
Inishmaan *i.* Rep. of Ire. **7** 53.06N 9.36W
Inishmore *i.* Rep. of Ire. **7** 53.08N 9.43W
Inishowen Pen. Rep. of Ire. **7** 55.08N 7.20W
Inishturk *i.* Rep. of Ire. **7** 53.43N 10.08W
Injune Australia **44** 25.51S148.34E
Inn *r.* Europe **14** 48.33N 13.26E
Innaminka Australia **45** 27.43S140.46E
Inner Hebrides *is.* U.K. **6** 56.50N 6.45W
Inner Mongolia *d. see* Nei Monggol Zizhiqu *d.* China **25**
Inner Sd. U.K. **6** 57.30N 5.55W
Innisfail Australia **44** 17.32S146.02E
Innsbruck Austria **14** 47.17N 11.25E
Innset Norway **16** 68.41N 18.50E
Inongo Zaïre **36** 1.55S 18.20E
Inowrocław Poland **15** 52.49N 18.12E
I-n-Salah Algeria **34** 27.12N 2.29E
Insein Burma **26** 16.54N 96.08E
In Tasik *well* Mali **38** 18.03N 2.00E
Interlaken Switz. **14** 46.42N 7.52E
Intute Mozambique **37** 14.08S 39.55E
Inukjuak Canada **51** 58.25N 78.18W
Inuvik Canada **50** 68.16N133.40W
Inuvik *d.* Canada **50** 68.00N130.00W
Inuyama Japan **23** 35.23N136.56E
Inveraray U.K. **6** 56.24N 5.05W
Inverbervie U.K. **6** 56.51N 2.17W
Invercargill New Zealand **48** 46.26S168.21E
Inverell Australia **47** 29.46S151.10E
Invergordon U.K. **6** 57.42N 4.10W
Inverness U.K. **6** 57.27N 4.15W
Inverurie U.K. **6** 57.17N 2.23W
Inverway Australia **42** 17.49S129.40E
Investigator Group *is.* Australia **46** 33.45S134.30E
Investigator Str. Australia **46** 35.25S137.10E
Invinheima *r.* Brazil **62** 22.52S 53.20W
Inya Russian Fed. **20** 50.24N 86.47E
Inyangani *mtn.* Zimbabwe **39** 18.18S 32.50E
Inyonga Tanzania **37** 6.43S 32.02E
Ioánnina Greece **13** 39.39N 20.49E
Iona *i.* U.K. **6** 56.20N 6.25W
Ionia U.S.A. **55** 42.58N 85.06W
Ionian Is. *see* Iónioi Nísoi *is.* Greece **13**
Ionian Sea Med. Sea **13** 38.30N 18.45E
Iónioi Nísoi *is.* Greece **13** 38.45N 20.00E
Íos *i.* Greece **13** 36.42N 25.20E
Iowa *d.* U.S.A. **53** 42.00N 93.00W
Iowa City U.S.A. **53** 41.39N 91.30W
Ipatovo Russian Fed. **19** 45.44N 42.56E
Ipiales Colombia **60** 0.52N 77.38W
Ipiaú Brazil **61** 14.07S 39.43W
Ipixuna Brazil **60** 7.00S 71.30W
Ipoh Malaysia **26** 4.36N101.02E
Ippa *r.* Belorussia **15** 52.13N 29.08E
Ipswich Australia **47** 27.38S152.40E
Ipswich U.K. **5** 52.04N 1.09E
Ipu Brazil **61** 4.23S 40.44W
Ipuh Indonesia **26** 2.58S101.28E
Iquique Chile **62** 20.13S 70.10W
Iquitos Peru **60** 3.51S 73.13W
Irago-suidō *str.* Japan **23** 34.35N137.00E
Iráklion Greece **13** 35.20N 25.08E
Iran Asia **31** 32.00N 54.30E
Iran, Pegunungan *mts.* Indonesia / Malaysia **26** 3.20N115.00E
Īrānshahr Iran **31** 27.14N 60.42E
Irapuato Mexico **56** 20.40N101.40W
Iraq Asia **30** 33.00N 44.00E
Irayel Russian Fed. **18** 64.23N 55.25E
Irazú *mtn.* Costa Rica **57** 9.59N 83.52W
Irbid Jordan **32** 32.33N 35.51E
Irbīl Iraq **31** 36.12N 44.01E
Irian Jaya *d.* Indonesia **27** 4.00S138.00E
Iringa Tanzania **37** 7.49S 35.39E
Iringa *d.* Tanzania **37** 8.30S 35.00E
Iriomote jima *i.* Japan **25** 24.30N124.00E
Iriri *r.* Brazil **61** 3.50S 52.40W
Irish Sea U.K. / Rep. of Ire. **7** 53.30N 5.40W
Irkutsk Russian Fed. **24** 52.18N104.15E
Iron Baron Australia **46** 32.59S137.09E
Iron Gate *f.* Romania / Yugo. **15** 44.40N 22.30E
Iron Knob Australia **46** 32.44S137.08E
Iron Mountain *town* U.S.A. **55** 45.51N 88.03W
Iron Mts. Rep. of Ire. **7** 54.10N 7.56W
Iron River *town* U.S.A. **53** 46.05N 88.38W
Irons U.S.A. **55** 44.08N 85.55W
Ironton U.S.A. **55** 38.32N 82.40W
Ironwood U.S.A. **55** 46.25N 90.08W
Iroquois Falls *town* Canada **55** 48.47N 80.41W
Irosin Phil. **27** 12.45N124.02E
Irō-zaki *c.* Japan **23** 34.36N138.51E
Irpen Ukraine **15** 50.31N 30.29E
Irrapatana Australia **46** 29.03S136.28E
Irrawaddy *r.* Burma **29** 17.45N 95.25E
Irrawaddy Delta Burma **29** 16.30N 95.20E
Irsha *r.* Ukraine **15** 50.45N 29.30E
Irtysh *r.* Russian Fed. **20** 61.00N 68.40E
Iruma *r.* Japan **23** 35.57N139.30E
Irumu Zaïre **37** 1.29N 29.48E
Irún Spain **10** 43.20N 1.48W
Irvine U.K. **6** 55.37N 4.40W
Irvinestown U.K. **7** 54.29N 7.40W
Irwin, Pt. Australia **43** 35.03S116.20E
Isa Nigeria **38** 13.14N 6.24E
Isaac *r.* Australia **44** 22.52S149.20E
Isabelia, Cordillera *mts.* Nicaragua **57** 13.30N 85.00W
Ísafjördhur *town* Iceland **16** 66.05N 23.06W
Isaka Tanzania **37** 3.52S 32.54E
Isakogorka Russian Fed. **18** 64.23N 40.31E
Isar *r.* Germany **14** 48.48N 12.57E
Isbergues France **8** 50.38N 2.24E
Ischia *i.* Italy **12** 40.43N 13.54E
Ise Japan **23** 34.29N136.42E
Iseo, Lago d' *l.* Italy **9** 45.43N 10.04E
Isère *r.* France **11** 45.02N 4.54E
Iserlohn Germany **8** 51.23N 7.42E
Isernia Italy **12** 41.36N 14.14E
Ise-wan *b.* Japan **23** 34.45N136.40E
Iseyin Nigeria **38** 7.59N 3.36E
Isfahan *see* Eşfahān Iran **28**
Ishim Russian Fed. **20** 56.10N 69.30E
Ishim *r.* Russian Fed. **20** 57.50N 71.00E
Ishinomaki Japan **25** 38.25N141.18E
Ishpeming U.S.A. **55** 46.29N 87.40W
Isigny France **9** 49.18N 1.06W
Isiolo Kenya **37** 0.20N 37.36E
Isipingo Beach *town* R.S.A. **39** 30.00S 30.57E
Isiro Zaïre **37** 2.50N 27.40E
Iskenderun Turkey **30** 36.37N 36.08E
Iskenderun Körfezi *g.* Turkey **30** 36.40N 35.50E
Iskilip Turkey **30** 40.45N 34.28E
Iskŭr *r.* Bulgaria **13** 43.42N 24.27E
Isla *r.* U.K. **6** 56.32N 3.22W
Islāmābād Pakistan **28** 33.40N 73.08E
Island L. Australia **46** 31.30S136.40E
Island L. Canada **51** 53.58N 94.47W
Island Magee *pen.* U.K. **7** 54.48N 5.44W
Islands, B. of New Zealand **48** 35.15S174.15E
Islay *i.* U.K. **6** 55.45N 6.20W
Isle *r.* France **11** 45.02N 0.08W
Isle of Portland *f.* U.K. **5** 50.32N 2.25W
Isle of Wight *d.* U.K. **5** 50.40N 1.17W
Ismael Cortinas Uruguay **63** 33.58S 57.06W
Isnā Egypt **30** 25.16N 32.30E
Isoka Zambia **37** 10.06S 32.39E
Isola della Scala Italy **9** 45.16N 11.00E
Isparta Turkey **30** 37.46N 30.32E
Ispica Italy **12** 36.46N 14.55E
Israel Asia **32** 32.00N 34.50E
Israelite B. Australia **43** 33.40S123.55E
Israelite Bay *town* Australia **43** 33.37S123.48E
Issoire France **11** 45.33N 3.15E
Is-sur-Tille France **11** 47.30N 5.10E
Issyk Kul *l.* Kyrgyzstan **24** 43.30N 77.20E
Istanbul Turkey **13** 41.02N 28.58E
Istanbul Boğazi *str.* Turkey **13** 41.07N 29.04E
Isthmus of Kra Thailand **29** 10.10N 99.00E
Istiaía Greece **13** 38.57N 23.09E
Istok Yugo. **13** 42.47N 20.29E
Istra *pen.* Croatia **14** 45.12N 13.55E
Itabaiana Brazil **61** 7.20S 35.20W
Itabira Brazil **59** 19.39S 43.14W
Itabirito Brazil **59** 20.21S 43.45W
Itabuna Brazil **61** 14.48S 39.18W
Itacajuna *r.* Brazil **61** 5.20S 49.08W
Itacoatiara Brazil **60** 3.06S 58.22W
Itagüí Colombia **60** 6.10N 75.36W
Itaí Brazil **59** 23.23S 49.05W
Itaim *r.* Brazil **61** 6.43S 42.48W
Itaipu, Reprêsa *resr.* Brazil / Paraguay **59** 24.30S 54.20W
Itaituba Brazil **61** 4.17S 55.59W
Itajaí Brazil **59** 26.50S 48.39W
Itajubá Brazil **59** 22.24S 45.25W
Itaka Tanzania **37** 8.51S 32.48E
Italy Europe **12** 43.00N 12.00E
Itami Japan **23** 34.46N135.25E
Itapecerica Brazil **59** 20.28S 45.09W
Itapecuru Mirim Brazil **61** 3.24S 44.20W
Itaperuna Brazil **59** 21.14S 41.51W
Itapetinga Brazil **61** 15.17S 40.16W
Itapetininga Brazil **59** 23.36S 48.07W
Itapeva Brazil **59** 23.59S 48.59W
Itapicuru *r.* Brazil **61** 11.50S 37.30W
Itapira Brazil **59** 22.24S 46.56W
Itaqui Brazil **59** 29.07S 56.33W
Itatiba Brazil **59** 22.59S 46.51W
Itatinga Brazil **59** 23.06S 48.36W
Itatuba Brazil **60** 5.40S 63.20W
Itaúna Brazil **59** 20.04S 44.14W
Ithaca U.S.A. **55** 42.26N 76.30W
Itháki Greece **13** 38.23N 20.42E
Itmurinkol, Ozero *l.* Kazakhstan **19** 49.30N 52.17E
Itō Japan **23** 34.58N139.05E
Iton *r.* France **9** 49.09N 1.12E
Iţsa Egypt **32** 29.14N 30.47E
Itu Brazil **59** 23.17S 47.18W
Ituí *r.* Brazil **60** 4.38S 70.19W
Ituiutaba Brazil **59** 19.00S 49.25W
Ituri *r.* Zaïre **37** 1.45N 27.06E
Iturup *i.* Russian Fed. **25** 44.00N147.30E
Ituverava Brazil **59** 20.22S 47.48W
Ituxi *r.* Brazil **60** 7.20S 64.50W
Ityāy al Bārūd Egypt **32** 30.53N 30.40E
Itzehoe Germany **14** 53.56N 9.32E
Ivaí *r.* Brazil **59** 23.20S 53.23W
Ivalo Finland **16** 68.42N 27.30E
Ivalo *r.* Finland **16** 68.43N 27.36E
Ivanhoe Australia **46** 32.56S144.22E
Ivano-Frankovsk Ukraine **15** 48.55N 24.42E
Ivanovo Belorussia **15** 52.10N 25.13E
Ivanovo Russian Fed. **18** 57.00N 41.00E
Ivdel Russian Fed. **18** 60.45N 60.30E
Ivenets Belorussia **15** 53.50N 26.40E
Ivigtût Greenland **51** 61.10N 48.00W
Ivittuut *see* Ivigtût Greenland **51**
Iviza *i. see* Ibiza *i.* Spain **10**
Ivory Coast Africa **34** 8.00N 5.30W
Ivrea Italy **9** 45.28N 7.52E
Ivujivik Canada **51** 62.24N 77.55W
Ivybridge U.K. **5** 50.24N 3.56W
Iwata Japan **23** 34.42N137.48E
Iwo Nigeria **38** 7.38N 4.11E
Ixiamas Bolivia **62** 13.45S 68.09W
Izabal, Lago de *l.* Guatemala **57** 15.30N 89.00W

Izberbash Russian Fed. 19 42.31N 47.52E
Izhevsk Russian Fed. 18 56.49N 53.11E
Izhma Russian Fed. 18 65.03N 53.48E
Izhma r. Russian Fed. 18 65.16N 53.18E
Izmail Ukraine 15 45.20N 28.50E
Izmir Turkey 13 38.24N 27.09E
Izmir Körfezi g. Turkey 13 38.30N 26.45E
Izmit Turkey 30 40.48N 29.55E
Izozog, Bañados de f. Bolivia 62 18.30S 62.05W
Izozog Marshes f. see Izozog, Bañados de f. Bolivia 62
Izu-hantō pen. Japan 23 34.53N138.55E
Izumi Japan 23 34.29N135.26E
Izumi-ōtsu Japan 23 34.30N135.24E
Izumi-sano Japan 23 34.25N135.19E
Izumo r. Japan 23 34.38N136.33E
Izyaslav Ukraine 15 50.10N 26.46E
Izyum Ukraine 19 49.12N 37.19E

J

Jabal, Baḩr al r. Sudan 35 9.30N 30.20E
Jabalón r. Spain 10 38.55N 4.07W
Jabalpur India 29 23.10N 79.59E
Jabālyah Egypt 32 31.32N 34.29E
Jabbān, Arḑ al f. Jordan 32 32.08N 36.35E
Jabiru Australia 44 12.39S132.55E
Jablah Syria 32 35.22N 35.56E
Jablonec nad Nisou Czech Republic 14 50.44N 15.10E
Jaboticabal Brazil 59 21.15S 48.17W
Jaca Spain 10 42.34N 0.33W
Jacareí Brazil 59 23.17S 45.57W
Jackman U.S.A. 55 45.38N 70.16W
Jackson Mich. U.S.A. 55 42.15N 84.24W
Jackson Miss. U.S.A. 53 32.20N 90.11W
Jackson Ohio U.S.A. 55 39.03N 82.40W
Jackson Tenn. U.S.A. 53 35.37N 88.50W
Jackson Wyo. U.S.A. 54 43.29N110.38W
Jacksonville Fla. U.S.A. 53 30.20N 81.40W
Jacobābād Pakistan 28 28.16N 68.30E
Jacobina Brazil 61 11.13S 40.30W
Jacob Lake town U.S.A. 54 36.41N112.14W
Jacques Cartier, Mt. Canada 55 49.00N 65.55W
Jacuí r. Brazil 59 29.56S 51.13W
Jacundá r. Brazil 61 1.57S 50.26W
Jade Germany 8 53.21N 8.11E
Jadebusen b. Germany 8 53.30N 8.12E
Jaén Peru 60 5.21S 78.28W
Jaén Spain 10 37.46N 3.48W
Jaffa see Tel Aviv-Yafo Israel 32
Jaffa, C. Australia 46 36.58S139.39E
Jaffna Sri Lanka 29 9.38N 80.02E
Jagdalpur India 29 19.04N 82.05E
Jaguarão Brazil 59 32.30S 53.25W
Jahrom Iran 31 28.30N 53.30E
Jailolo Indonesia 27 1.05N127.29E
Jaipur India 28 26.53N 75.50E
Jajawijaya Mts. Asia 27 4.20S139.10E
Jājpur India 29 20.50N 86.20E
Jakarta Indonesia 26 6.08S106.45E
Jäkkvik Sweden 16 66.23N 17.00E
Jakobstad see Pietarsaari Finland 16
Jalālah al Baḩrīyah, Jabal mts. Egypt 32 29.20N 32.12E
Jalālat al Qiblīyah, Jabal al mts. Egypt 32 28.42N 32.23E
Jalapa Mexico 56 19.45N 96.48W
Jālgaon India 28 21.01N 75.39E
Jalingo Nigeria 38 8.54N 11.21E
Jalisco d. Mexico 56 21.00N103.00W
Jālna India 28 19.50N 75.58E
Jalón r. Spain 10 41.47N 1.02W
Jālor India 28 25.21N 72.37E
Jalpaiguri India 29 26.30N 88.50E
Jālū Libya 35 29.00N 21.30E
Jalūlā Iraq 31 34.16N 45.10E
Jamaame Somali Rep. 37 0.04N 42.46E
Jamaari Nigeria 38 11.44N 9.53E
Jamaica C. America 57 18.00N 77.00W
Jamālpur Bangla. 29 24.54N 89.57E
Jamanxim r. Brazil 61 4.43S 56.18W
Jambes Belgium 8 50.28N 4.52E
Jambi Indonesia 26 1.36S103.39E
Jambi d. Indonesia 26 2.00S102.30E
James r. S.Dak. U.S.A. 53 42.50N 97.15W
James B. Canada 51 53.00N 80.00W
James Bay Prov. Park Canada 55 51.24N 79.00W
Jamestown Australia 46 33.12S138.38E
Jamestown N.Dak. U.S.A. 52 46.54N 98.42W
Jamestown N.Y. U.S.A. 55 42.06N 79.14W
Jammerbugt b. Denmark 17 57.20N 9.30E
Jammu Jammu & Kashmir 28 32.44N 74.52E
Jammu & Kashmir Asia 28 33.30N 76.00E
Jāmnagar India 28 22.28N 70.06E
Jamsah Egypt 32 27.39N 33.35E
Jämsänkoski Finland 17 61.55N 25.11E
Jamshedpur India 29 22.47N 86.12E
Jämtland d. Sweden 16 63.00N 14.30E
Janda, Laguna de la l. Spain 10 36.15N 5.50W
Jándula r. Spain 10 38.08N 4.08W
Janesville U.S.A. 53 42.42N 89.02W
Jangamo Mozambique 39 24.06S 35.21E
Janīn Jordan 32 32.28N 35.18E
Jan Kempdorp R.S.A. 39 27.55S 24.48E
Jan Mayen i. Arctic Oc. 64 71.00N 9.00W
Januária Brazil 59 15.28S 44.23W
Janzé France 9 47.58N 1.30W
Japan Asia 25 36.00N136.00E
Japan, Sea of Asia 25 40.00N135.00E
Japurá r. Brazil 60 3.00S 64.50W
Jarama r. Spain 10 40.27N 3.32W
Jarash Jordan 32 32.17N 35.54E
Jardee Australia 43 34.18S116.04E
Jardine r. Australia 44 11.07S142.30E
Jardines de la Reina is. Cuba 57 20.30N 79.00W
Jardinópolis Brazil 59 20.59S 47.48W
Jargeau France 9 47.52N 2.07E
Jarocin Poland 15 51.59N 17.31E
Jarosław Poland 15 50.02N 22.42E
Jarrāḩī r. Iran 31 30.40N 48.23E
Järvenpää Finland 17 60.28N 25.06E
Jäsk Iran 31 25.40N 57.45E
Jasło Poland 15 49.45N 21.29E
Jasper Canada 50 52.55N118.05W
Jastrebarsko Croatia 14 45.40N 15.39E
Jastrowie Poland 14 53.26N 16.49E
Jászberény Hungary 15 47.30N 19.55E
Jataí Brazil 59 17.58S 51.45W
Játiva Spain 10 39.00N 0.32W
Jaú Brazil 59 22.11S 48.35W
Jauja Peru 60 11.50S 75.15W
Jaunjelgava Latvia 18 56.34N 25.02E
Jaunpur India 29 25.44N 82.41E
Java i. see Jawa i. Indonesia 26
Javari r. Peru 60 4.30S 71.20W
Java Sea see Jawa, Laut sea Indonesia 26
Java Trench f. Indonesia 26 10.00S110.00E
Jawa i. Indonesia 26 7.30S110.00E
Jawa, Laut sea Indonesia 26 5.00S111.00E
Jawa Barat d. Indonesia 26 7.15S107.00E
Jawa Tengah d. Indonesia 26 7.40S109.40E
Jawa Timur d. Indonesia 26 7.00S112.00E
Jayah, Wādī al see Hā 'Arava Jordan / Israel 32
Jayapura Indonesia 27 2.28S140.38E
Jazirah Doberai f. Indonesia 27 1.10S132.30E
Jazzīn Lebanon 32 33.32N 35.34E
Jean U.S.A. 54 35.46N115.20W
Jean Marie River town Canada 50 61.32N120.40W
Jebāl Bārez, Kūh-e mts. Iran 31 28.40N 58.10E
Jebba Nigeria 38 9.11N 4.49E
Jedburgh U.K. 6 55.29N 2.33W
Jedda see Jiddah Saudi Arabia 35
Jedrzejów Poland 15 50.39N 20.18E
Jefferson, Mt. Nev. U.S.A. 54 38.46N116.55W
Jefferson, Mt. Oreg. U.S.A. 54 44.40N121.47W
Jefferson City U.S.A. 53 38.33N 92.10W
Jeffersonville U.S.A. 55 38.16N 85.45W
Jega Nigeria 38 12.12N 4.23E
Jēkabpils Latvia 18 56.28N 25.58E
Jelenia Góra Poland 14 50.55N 15.45E
Jelgava Latvia 17 56.39N 23.42E
Jember Indonesia 26 8.07S113.45E
Jena Germany 14 50.56N 11.35E
Jenbach Austria 14 47.24N 11.47E
Jenolan Caves town Australia 47 33.53S150.03E
Jeparit Australia 46 36.09S141.59E
Jeppo Finland 16 63.24N 22.37E
Jequié Brazil 61 13.52S 40.06W
Jequitinhonha r. Brazil 59 16.46S 39.45W
Jerantut Malaysia 26 3.56N102.22E
Jérémie Haiti 57 18.40N 74.09W
Jerez Spain 10 38.20N 6.45W
Jerez de la Frontera Spain 10 36.41N 6.08W
Jericho see Arīḩā Jordan 32
Jerilderie Australia 47 35.23S145.41E
Jerome U.S.A. 54 42.43N114.31W
Jerramungup Australia 43 33.57S118.53E
Jersey i. U.K. 5 49.13N 2.08W
Jersey City U.S.A. 55 40.44N 74.04W
Jerusalem see Yerushalayim Israel / Jordan 32
Jervis B. Australia 47 35.05S150.44E
Jesenice Slovenia 12 46.27N 14.04E
Jessore Bangla. 29 23.10N 89.12E
Jesús Carranza Mexico 56 17.26N 95.02W
Jever Germany 8 53.34N 7.54E
Jevnaker Norway 17 60.15N 10.28E
Jeypore India 29 18.51N 82.41E
Jeziorak, Jezioro l. Poland 15 53.40N 19.04E
Jhang Sadar Pakistan 28 31.16N 72.19E
Jhānsi India 29 25.27N 78.34E
Jhelum r. Pakistan 28 31.04N 72.10E
Jialing Jiang r. China 29 29.33N106.30E
Jiamusi China 25 46.50N130.21E
Ji'an China 25 27.08N115.00E
Jiange China 29 32.04N105.26E
Jiangling China 25 30.20N112.20E
Jiangsu d. China 25 34.00N119.00E
Jiangxi d. China 25 27.25N115.20E
Jianyang Fujian China 25 27.20N117.50E
Jiaohe China 25 43.42N127.19E
Jiashan China 25 32.47N117.59E
Jiaxian China 25 38.02N110.29E
Jiaxing China 25 30.40N120.50E
Jiayi Taiwan 25 23.38N120.27E
Jiddah Saudi Arabia 35 21.30N 39.10E
Jigawa d. Nigeria 38 12.30N 9.30E
Jihlava Czech Republic 14 49.24N 15.35E
Jilib Somali Rep. 37 0.28N 42.50E
Jilin China 25 43.53N126.35E
Jilin d. China 25 44.50N125.00E
Jilong Taiwan 25 25.10N121.43E
Jīma Ethiopia 35 7.39N 36.47E
Jiménez Mexico 56 27.08N104.55W
Jimeta Nigeria 38 9.19N 12.25E
Jinan China 25 36.50N117.00E
Jindabyne Australia 47 36.24S148.37E
Jingdezhen China 25 29.16N117.11E
Jingellic Australia 47 35.54S147.44E
Jinggu Yunnan China 29 23.29N100.19E
Jinghong China 24 21.59N100.49E
Jing Xian China 25 26.35N109.41E
Jinhua China 25 29.06N119.40E
Jining Nei Monggol China 25 40.56N113.00E
Jining Shantung China 25 35.25N116.40E
Jinja Uganda 37 0.27N 33.10E
Jinotepe Nicaragua 57 11.50N 86.10W
Jinsha Jiang r. China 29 26.30N101.40E
Jinxi Liaoning China 25 40.54N120.36E
Jin Xian Liaoning China 25 39.04N121.45E
Jinzhou China 25 41.07N121.06E
Jipijapa Ecuador 60 1.23S 80.35W
Jirjā Egypt 30 26.20N 31.53E
Jitarning Australia 43 32.48S117.57E
Jiu r. Romania 13 43.44N 23.52E
Jiujiang China 25 29.41N116.03E
Jixi China 25 45.17N131.00E
Jīzān Saudi Arabia 35 16.56N 42.33E
Jizl, Wādī al r. Saudi Arabia 30 25.37N 38.20E
João Pessoa Brazil 61 7.06S 34.53W
Jódar Spain 10 37.50N 3.21W
Jodhpur India 28 26.18N 73.08E
Jodoigne Belgium 8 50.45N 4.52E
Joensuu Finland 18 62.35N 29.46E
Joetsu Japan 23 37.07N138.15E
Johannesburg R.S.A. 39 26.11S 28.04E
John Day U.S.A. 54 44.25N118.57W
John Day r. U.S.A. 54 45.44N120.39W
John O'Groats U.K. 6 58.39N 3.02W
Johnson City Tenn. U.S.A. 53 36.20N 82.23W
Johnston, L. Australia 43 32.25S120.30E
Johnstown Penn. U.S.A. 55 40.20N 78.55W
Johor Baharu Malaysia 26 1.29N103.40E
Joigny France 9 48.00N 3.20E
Joinville Brazil 59 26.20S 48.49W
Joinville France 11 48.27N 5.08E
Jokkmokk Sweden 16 66.37N 19.50E
Jökulsá á Brú r. Iceland 16 65.33N 14.23W
Jökulsá á Fjöllum r. Iceland 16 66.05N 16.32W
Jolfa Iran 31 32.40N 51.39E
Joliette Canada 55 46.02N 73.27W
Jolo i. Phil. 27 5.55N121.20E
Jolo town Phil. 27 6.03N121.00E
Jombang Indonesia 26 7.30S112.21E
Jomda China 29 31.30N 98.16E
Jonava Lithuania 17 55.05N 24.17E
Jonesboro Ark. U.S.A. 53 35.50N 90.41W
Jones Sd. Canada 51 76.00N 85.00W
Jönköping Sweden 17 57.47N 14.11E
Jönköping d. Sweden 17 57.30N 14.30E
Joplin U.S.A. 53 37.04N 94.31W
Jordan Asia 30 31.00N 36.00E
Jordan r. see Al Urdunn r. Asia 32
Jordan Mont. U.S.A. 54 47.19N106.55W
Jordan Valley town U.S.A. 54 42.58N117.03W
Jorhāt India 29 26.45N 94.13E
Jörn Sweden 16 65.04N 20.02E
Jos Nigeria 38 9.54N 8.53E
José de San Martín Argentina 63 44.04S 70.26W
José Enrique Rodó Uruguay 63 33.41S 57.34W
Joseph Bonaparte G. Australia 42 14.00S128.30E
Joseph City U.S.A. 54 34.57N110.20W
Jos Plateau f. Nigeria 38 10.00N 9.00E
Jotunheimen mts. Norway 17 61.38N 8.18E
Joué-lès-Tours France 9 47.21N 0.40E
Joure Neth. 8 52.59N 5.49E
Joverega Botswana 39 19.08S 24.15E
Juan Aldama Mexico 56 24.19N103.21W
Juan B. Arruabarrena Argentina 63 30.25S 58.15W
Juan de Fuca, Str. of Canada / U.S.A. 54 48.15N124.00W
Juan de Nova i. Madagascar 37 17.03S 42.45E
Juárez Argentina 63 37.40S 59.48W
Juàzeiro Brazil 61 9.25S 40.30W
Juàzeiro do Norte Brazil 61 7.10S 39.18W
Jūbā Sudan 35 4.50N 31.35E
Jūbāl, Maḑīq str. Egypt 32 27.40N 33.55E
Jubal, Str. of see Jūbāl, Maḑīq str. Egypt 32
Jubba r. Somali Rep. 37 0.20S 42.40E
Jubilee Downs town Australia 42 18.22S125.17E
Júcar r. Spain 10 39.10N 0.15W
Juchitán Mexico 56 16.27N 95.05W
Judenburg Austria 14 47.10N 14.40E
Judith Basin f. U.S.A. 54 47.10N109.58W
Juist Germany 8 53.41N 7.01E
Juist i. Germany 8 53.43N 7.00E
Juiz de Fora Brazil 59 21.47S 43.23W
Jujuy d. Argentina 62 23.00S 66.00W
Juklegga mtn. Norway 17 61.03N 8.13E
Juliaca Peru 60 15.29S 70.09W
Julia Creek town Australia 44 20.39S141.45E
Juliana Kanaal canal Neth. 8 51.00N 5.48E
Julianehåb Greenland 51 60.45N 46.00W
Jülich Germany 8 50.55N 6.21E
Jullundur India 28 31.18N 75.40E
Jumboo Somali Rep. 37 0.12S 42.38E
Jumet Belgium 8 50.27N 4.27E
Jumilla Spain 10 38.28N 1.19W
Jumla Nepal 29 29.17N 82.10E
Jumna r. see Yamuna India 28
Junāgadh India 28 21.32N 70.32E
Junan China 25 35.11N118.50E
Junction B. Australia 44 11.50S134.15E
Junction City Kans. U.S.A. 53 39.02N 96.51W
Junction City Oreg. U.S.A. 54 44.13N123.12W
Jundah Australia 44 24.50S143.02E
Jundiaí Brazil 59 23.10S 46.54W
Juneau U.S.A. 50 58.20N134.20W
Junee Australia 47 34.51S147.40E
Jungfrau mtn. Switz. 11 46.30N 8.00E
Junggar Pendi f. Asia 24 44.20N 86.30E
Junglinster Lux. 8 49.41N 6.13E
Junín Argentina 63 34.35S 60.58W
Junín de los Andes Argentina 63 39.57S 71.05W
Juniville France 9 49.24N 4.23E
Jūniyah Lebanon 32 33.59N 35.38E
Junnah, Jabal mts. Egypt 32 28.52N 34.15E
Junsele Sweden 16 63.40N 16.55E
Juntura U.S.A. 54 43.46N118.05W
Jura mts. Europe 11 46.55N 6.45E
Jura i. U.K. 6 55.58N 5.55W
Jura, Sd. of U.K. 6 56.00N 5.45W
Jurado Colombia 60 7.07N 77.46W
Jura Krakowska mts. Poland 15 50.30N 19.30E
Jurhen Ul Shan mts. China 29 34.00N 91.00E
Jūrmala Latvia 17 56.58N 23.42E
Juruá r. Brazil 60 2.33S 65.50W
Juruena Brazil 62 12.50S 58.58W
Juruena r. Brazil 61 7.20S 57.30W
Juruti Brazil 61 2.09S 56.04W
Jussey France 11 47.49N 5.54E
Jutaí r. Brazil 60 2.35S 67.00W
Juticalpa Honduras 57 14.45N 86.12W
Jutland pen. see Jylland pen. Denmark 17
Jūyom Iran 31 28.10N 53.52E
Juzur al Halaniyat is. Oman 28 17.30N 56.00E
Jwayyā Lebanon 32 33.14N 35.20E
Jylland pen. Denmark 17 56.00N 9.15E
Jyväskylä Finland 16 62.14N 25.44E

K

Ka r. Nigeria 38 11.35N 4.10E
Kaabong Uganda 37 3.28N 34.08E
Kaapstad see Cape Town R.S.A. 39
Kabaena i. Indonesia 27 5.25S122.00E
Kabala Sierra Leone 34 9.40N 11.36W
Kabale Uganda 37 1.13S 30.00E
Kabalega Falls f. Uganda 37 2.17N 31.46E
Kabalega Falls Nat. Park Uganda 37 2.15N 31.45E
Kabalo Zaïre 36 6.02S 27.00E
Kabambare Zaïre 37 4.40S 27.41E
Kabanga Zambia 37 17.36S 26.45E
Kabba Nigeria 38 7.50N 6.07E
Kabinakagami r. Canada 55 50.20N 84.20W
Kabīr Kūh mts. Iran 31 33.00N 47.00E
Kābol Afghan. 28 34.30N 69.10E
Kabongo Zaïre 36 7.22S 25.34E
Kabonzo Zaïre 37 6.41S 27.49E
Kabūd Gonbad Iran 31 37.02N 59.46E
Kabul see Kābol Afghan. 28
Kabunda Zaïre 37 12.27S 29.15E
Kabwe Zambia 37 14.27S 28.25E
Kāchā Kūh mts. Iran 31 29.30N 61.20E
Kachchh, G. of India 28 22.30N 69.30E
Kachiry Kazakhstan 20 53.07N 76.08E
Kade Ghana 38 6.08N 0.51W
Kadina Australia 46 33.58S137.14E
Kadioli Mali 38 10.38N 5.45W
Kadoma Zimbabwe 39 18.23S 29.52E
Kaduna Nigeria 38 10.28N 7.25E
Kaduna d. Nigeria 38 11.00N 7.35E
Kaduna r. Nigeria 38 8.45N 5.45E
Kāduqlī Sudan 35 11.01N 29.43E
Kadusam mtn. China 29 28.30N 96.45E
Kadzherom Russian Fed. 18 64.42N 55.59E
Kaédi Mauritania 34 16.12N 13.32W
Kaélé Cameroon 38 10.05N 14.28E
Kaesŏng N. Korea 25 37.59N126.30E
Kafanchan Nigeria 38 9.38N 8.20E
Kafirévs, Ákra c. Greece 13 38.11N 24.30E
Kafr ad Dawwār Egypt 32 31.08N 30.08E
Kafr al Baţţīkh Egypt 32 31.24N 31.44E
Kafr ash Shaykh Egypt 32 31.07N 30.56E
Kafr az Zayyāt Egypt 32 30.50N 30.49E
Kafr Salīm Egypt 32 31.09N 30.07E
Kafu r. Uganda 37 1.40N 32.07E
Kafue Zambia 37 15.40S 28.13E
Kafue r. Zambia 36 15.53S 28.55E
Kafue Dam Zambia 37 15.40S 27.10E
Kafunzo Uganda 37 1.05S 30.26E
Kaga Bandoro C.A.R. 36 7.00N 19.10E
Kagan Uzbekistan 20 39.45N 64.32E
Kagarlyk Ukraine 15 49.50N 30.50E
Kagera d. Tanzania 37 2.00S 31.20E
Kagizman Turkey 30 40.08N 43.07E
Kagoshima Japan 25 31.37N130.32E
Kagul Moldavia 15 45.54N 28.11E
Kahama Tanzania 37 3.48S 32.38E
Kahayan r. Indonesia 26 3.20S114.04E
Kahnūj Iran 31 27.55N 57.45E
Kahraman Maraş Turkey 30 37.34N 36.54E
Kai, Kepulauan is. Indonesia 27 5.45S132.55E
Kaiama Nigeria 38 9.37N 4.03E
Kaiapoi New Zealand 48 43.23S172.39E
Kaifeng China 25 34.47N114.20E
Kaikohe New Zealand 48 35.25S173.49E
Kaikoura New Zealand 48 42.24S173.41E
Kaikoura Range mts. New Zealand 48 42.00S173.40E
Kaimana Indonesia 27 3.39S133.44E
Kaimanawa Mts. New Zealand 48 39.10S176.15E
Kainantu P.N.G. 27 6.16S145.50E
Kainji Resr. Nigeria 38 10.00N 4.35E
Kaipara Harbour New Zealand 48 36.30S174.00E
Kaiserslautern Germany 8 49.27N 7.47E
Kaitaia New Zealand 48 35.08S173.18E
Kaitum r. Sweden 16 67.30N 21.05E
Kaizuka Japan 23 34.27N135.21E
Kajaani Finland 16 64.14N 27.41E
Kajabbi Australia 44 20.02S140.02E
Kajiado Kenya 37 1.50S 36.48E
Kajuru Nigeria 38 10.19N 7.40E
Kakamas R.S.A. 39 28.44S 20.35E
Kakamega Kenya 37 0.21N 34.47E
Kakamigahara Japan 23 35.28N136.48E
Kakegawa Japan 23 34.46N138.01E
Kakhovskoye Vodokhranilishche resr. Ukraine 19 47.33N 34.40E
Kākī Iran 31 28.19N 51.34E
Kākināda India 29 16.59N 82.20E
Kakonko Tanzania 37 3.19S 30.54E
Kakuma Kenya 37 3.38N 34.48E
Kakuto Uganda 37 0.54S 31.26E
Kala r. Finland 16 64.17N 23.55E
Kalaallit Nunaat see Greenland N.America 51
Kalabahi Indonesia 27 8.13S124.31E
Kalabáka Greece 13 39.42N 21.43E
Kalabity Australia 46 31.53S140.18E
Kalach-na-Donu Russian Fed. 19 48.43N 43.31E
Kalahari Desert Botswana 39 23.30S 22.00E
Kalahari Gemsbok Nat. Park R.S.A. 39 25.45S 20.25E
Kalajoki Finland 16 64.15N 23.57E
Kalakan Russian Fed. 21 55.10N116.45E
Kalámai Greece 13 37.02N 22.05E
Kalamazoo U.S.A. 55 42.17N 85.36W
Kalamera Tanzania 37 2.07S 33.43E
Kalamurra, L. Australia 46 28.00S138.00E
Kalannie Australia 43 30.21S117.04E
Kalarash Moldavia 15 47.18N 28.16E
Kalāt Pakistan 28 29.01N 66.38E
Kalbarri Australia 43 27.40S114.12E
Kalecik Turkey 30 40.06N 33.22E
Kalehe Zaïre 37 2.05S 28.53E
Kalemie Zaïre 37 5.57S 29.10E
Kalgan r. Australia 43 34.55S117.58E
Kalgoorlie Australia 43 30.49S121.29E
Kaliakra, Nos c. Bulgaria 13 43.23N 28.29E
Kalianda Indonesia 26 5.50S105.45E
Kalimantan d. Indonesia 26 1.00S113.00E
Kalimantan f. Indonesia 26 0.05N112.30E
Kalimantan Barat d. Indonesia 26 0.30N110.00E
Kalimantan Selatan d. Indonesia 26 2.30S115.30E
Kalimantan Tengah d. Indonesia 26 2.00S113.30E
Kalimantan Timur d. Indonesia 26 2.20N116.30E
Kálimnos i. Greece 13 37.00N 27.00E
Kaliningrad Russian Fed. 17 54.43N 20.30E
Kalinkovichi Belorussia 15 52.10N 29.13E
Kalinovka Ukraine 15 49.29N 28.30E
Kalispell U.S.A. 54 48.12N114.19W
Kalisz Poland 15 51.46N 18.02E
Kaliua Tanzania 37 5.08S 31.50E
Kalix r. Sweden 16 65.50N 23.11E
Kalkar Germany 8 51.45N 6.17E
Kalkfontein Botswana 39 22.08S 20.54E
Kalkrand Namibia 39 24.05S 17.34E
Kallsjön l. Sweden 16 63.35N 13.00E
Kalmar Sweden 17 56.40N 16.22E
Kalmar d. Sweden 17 57.20N 16.00E
Kalmarsund str. Sweden 17 56.40N 16.25E
Kalmthout Belgium 8 51.23N 4.28E
Kalmykovo Kazakhstan 19 49.02N 51.55E
Kalo P.N.G. 44 10.05S147.45E
Kalocsa Hungary 15 46.32N 18.59E
Kalole Zaïre 37 3.40S 27.22E
Kalomo Zambia 36 17.03S 26.29E
Kalonje Zambia 37 12.21S 31.06E
Kaltag U.S.A. 50 64.20N158.44W
Kaluga Russian Fed. 18 54.31N 36.16E
Kalumburu Australia 42 14.14S126.38E
Kalundborg Denmark 17 55.41N 11.06E
Kalush Ukraine 15 49.02N 24.20E
Kalutara Sri Lanka 29 6.35N 79.58E
Kama r. Russian Fed. 18 55.30N 52.00E
Kamakura Japan 23 35.19N139.33E
Kamanashi r. Japan 23 35.33N138.28E
Kamanjab Namibia 39 19.39S 14.50E
Kamba Nigeria 38 11.52N 3.42E
Kambalda Australia 43 31.12S121.40E
Kambarka Russian Fed. 18 56.18N 54.13E
Kamchatka, Poluostrov pen. Russian Fed. 21 56.00N160.00E
Kamen mtn. Russian Fed. 21 68.40N 94.20E
Kamenets Podolskiy Ukraine 15 48.40N 26.36E
Kamenka Russian Fed. 18 65.55N 44.02E
Kamenka Russian Fed. 18 53.10N 44.05E
Kamenka Bugskaya Ukraine 15 50.07N 24.30E
Kamen Kashirskiy Ukraine 15 51.32N 24.59E
Kamen-na-Obi Russian Fed. 20 53.46N 81.18E
Kamenskoye Russian Fed. 21 62.31N165.15E
Kamensk-Shakhtinskiy Russian Fed. 19 48.20N 40.16E
Kamensk-Ural'skiy Russian Fed. 20 56.29N 61.49E
Kāmet mtn. China 29 31.03N 79.25E
Kameyama Japan 23 34.51N136.27E
Kamiah U.S.A. 54 46.14N116.02W
Kamieskroon R.S.A. 39 30.12S 17.53E
Kamina Zaïre 36 8.46S 25.00E
Kamloops Canada 50 50.39N120.24W
Kamo r. Japan 23 35.00N139.52E
Kamp Germany 8 50.14N 7.37E
Kampa Indonesia 26 1.46S105.26E
Kampala Uganda 37 0.19N 32.35E
Kampar r. Indonesia 26 0.20N102.55E
Kampen Neth. 8 52.33N 5.55E
Kamp-Lintfort Germany 8 51.34N 6.38E
Kâmpóng Cham Cambodia 26 11.59N105.26E
Kâmpóng Chhnăng Cambodia 26 12.16N104.39E
Kâmpóng Saôm Cambodia 26 10.38N103.30E
Kâmpôt Cambodia 26 10.37N104.11E
Kampti Burkina 38 10.07N 3.22W
Kamsack Canada 51 51.34N101.54W
Kamskoye Vodokhranilishche resr. Russian Fed. 18 58.55N 56.20E
Kamyshin Russian Fed. 19 50.05N 45.24E
Kana r. Zimbabwe 39 18.30S 26.50E
Kanagawa d. Japan 23 35.25N139.10E
Kananga Zaïre 36 5.53S 22.26E
Kanash Russian Fed. 18 55.30N 47.27E
Kanawha r. U.S.A. 55 38.50N 82.08W
Kanazawa Japan 25 36.35N136.38E
Kanchanaburi Thailand 29 14.08N 99.31E
Kānchenjunga mtn. Asia 29 27.44N 88.11E
Kānchipuram India 29 12.50N 79.44E
Kandalaksha Russian Fed. 18 67.09N 32.31E
Kandalakshskaya Guba g. Russian Fed. 18 66.30N 34.00E
Kandangan Indonesia 26 2.50S115.15E
Kandi Benin 38 11.05N 2.59E
Kandira Turkey 30 41.05N 30.08E
Kandos Australia 47 32.53S149.59E
Kandrāch Pakistan 28 25.29N 65.29E
Kandreho Madagascar 37 17.29S 46.06E
Kandy Sri Lanka 29 7.18N 80.43E
Kane U.S.A. 55 41.40N 78.49W
Kanem d. Chad 38 15.10N 15.30E
Kanevka Russian Fed. 18 67.08N 39.50E
Kang Botswana 39 23.43S 22.51E
Kangaarsussuaq see Parry, Kap Greenland 51
Kangān Iran 31 27.50N 52.07E
Kangar Malaysia 26 6.28N100.10E
Kangaroo I. Australia 46 35.50S137.06E
Kangding China 24 30.05N102.04E

Kangean, Kepulauan *is.* Indonesia **26** 7.00S115.45E
Kangerlussuaq *see* Söndreströmfjord Greenland **51**
Kangiqsualujjuaq Canada **51** 58.35N 65.59W
Kangiqsujuaq Canada **51** 61.30N 72.00W
Kangirsuk Canada **51** 60.01N 70.01W
Kanin, Poluostrov *pen.* Russian Fed. **18** 68.00N 45.00E
Kaningo Kenya **37** 0.52S 38.31E
Kanin Nos, Mys *c.* Russian Fed. **18** 68.38N 43.20E
Kaniva Australia **46** 36.33S141.17E
Kanjiža Yugo. **15** 46.04N 20.04E
Kankakee U.S.A. **53** 41.08N 87.52W
Kankan Guinea **34** 10.22N 9.11W
Kānker India **29** 20.17N 81.30E
Kano *r.* Japan **23** 35.05N138.52E
Kano Nigeria **38** 12.00N 8.31E
Kano *d.* Nigeria **38** 11.45N 8.30E
Kanona Zambia **37** 13.03S 30.37E
Kanowna Australia **43** 30.36S121.36E
Kānpur India **29** 26.27N 80.14E
Kansas *d.* U.S.A. **52** 38.00N 99.00W
Kansas *r.* U.S.A. **53** 39.07N 94.36W
Kansas City Mo. U.S.A. **53** 39.02N 94.33W
Kansk Russian Fed. **21** 56.11N 95.20E
Kansŏng S. Korea **25** 38.20N128.28E
Kantché Niger **38** 13.31N 8.30E
Kantemirovka Russian Fed. **19** 49.40N 39.52E
Kantō *d.* Japan **23** 35.35N139.30E
Kantōheiya *f.* Japan **23** 36.02N140.10E
Kantō-sanchi *mts.* Japan **23** 36.00N138.35E
Kanye Botswana **39** 24.58S 25.17E
Kanyu Botswana **39** 20.05S 24.39E
Kaolack Senegal **34** 14.09N 16.08W
Kapchagay Kazakhstan **24** 43.51N 77.14E
Kapenguria Kenya **37** 1.13N 35.07E
Kapfenberg Austria **14** 47.27N 15.18E
Kapiri Mposhi Zambia **37** 13.59S 28.40E
Kapit Malaysia **26** 2.01N112.56E
Kapiti I. New Zealand **48** 40.50S174.50E
Kapongolo Zaïre **37** 7.51S 28.12E
Kaposvár Hungary **13** 46.22N 17.47E
Kapps Namibia **39** 22.22S 17.52E
Kapsabet Kenya **37** 0.12N 35.05E
Kapuas *r.* Indonesia **26** 0.13S109.12E
Kapunda Australia **46** 34.21S138.54E
Kapuskasing Canada **55** 49.25N 82.26W
Kaputar, Mt. Australia **47** 30.20S150.10E
Kapuvár Hungary **15** 47.36N 17.02E
Kara Russian Fed. **20** 69.12N 65.00E
Kara-Bogaz Gol, Zaliv *b.* Turkmenistan **31** 41.20N 53.40E
Karabük Turkey **30** 41.12N 32.36E
Karabutak Kazakhstan **20** 49.55N 60.05E
Karāchi Pakistan **28** 24.51N 67.02E
Karād India **28** 17.17N 74.12E
Karaganda Kazakhstan **20** 49.53N 73.07E
Karaginskiy, Ostrov *i.* Russian Fed. **21** 59.00N165.00E
Karakas Kazakhstan **24** 48.20N 83.30E
Karakelong *i.* Indonesia **27** 4.20N126.50E
Karakoram Pass Asia **29** 35.33N 77.51E
Karakoram Range *mts.* Jammu & Kashmir **28** 35.30N 76.30E
Karaköse *see* Ağri Turkey **19**
Karakumskiy Kanal *canal* Turkmenistan **31** 37.30N 65.48E
Karakumy, Peski *f.* Turkmenistan **31** 37.45N 60.00E
Karakuwisa Namibia **39** 18.56S 19.43E
Karaman Turkey **30** 37.11N 33.13E
Karamay China **24** 45.48N 84.30E
Karamea New Zealand **48** 41.15S172.07E
Karamea Bight *b.* New Zealand **48** 41.15S171.30E
Karamürsel Turkey **30** 40.42N 29.37E
Karand Iran **31** 34.16N 46.15E
Karasburg Namibia **39** 28.00S 18.46E
Karasjok Norway **16** 69.27N 25.30E
Karasuk Russian Fed. **20** 53.45N 78.01E
Karatau, Khrebet *mts.* Kazakhstan **19** 44.15N 52.10E
Karatobe Kazakhstan **19** 49.44N 53.30E
Karaton Kazakhstan **19** 46.26N 53.32E
Karazhal Kazakhstan **20** 48.00N 70.55E
Karbalā' Iraq **31** 32.37N 44.03E
Karcag Hungary **15** 47.19N 20.56E
Kardhítsa Greece **13** 39.22N 21.59E
Kärdla Estonia **17** 59.00N 22.42E
Karema Tanzania **37** 6.50S 30.25E
Karen India **29** 12.50N 92.55E
Karepino Russian Fed. **18** 61.05N 58.02E
Karesuando Finland **16** 68.25N 22.30E
Kargasok Russian Fed. **20** 59.07N 80.58E
Kargi Kenya **37** 2.31N 37.34E
Kargil Jammu & Kashmir **28** 34.32N 76.12E
Kargopol Russian Fed. **18** 61.32N 38.59E
Kari Nigeria **38** 11.17N 10.35E
Kariba Zimbabwe **37** 16.32S 28.50E
Kariba, L. Zimbabwe/Zambia **37** 16.50S 28.00E
Kariba Dam Zimbabwe/Zambia **37** 16.15S 28.55E
Karibib Namibia **39** 21.56S 15.52E
Kārikāl India **29** 10.58N 79.50E
Karimama Benin **38** 12.02N 3.15E
Karis Finland **17** 60.05N 23.40E
Karisimbi, Mt. Zaïre/Rwanda **37** 1.31S 29.25E
Kariya Japan **23** 34.59N136.59E
Kariyangwe Zimbabwe **39** 17.57S 27.30E
Karkaralinsk Kazakhstan **20** 49.21N 75.27E
Karkar I. P.N.G. **27** 4.40S146.00E
Karkas, Kūh-e *mtn.* Iran **31** 33.25N 51.40E
Karkheh *r.* Iran **31** 31.45N 47.52E
Karkinitskiy Zaliv *g.* Ukraine **19** 45.50N 32.45E
Karkoo Australia **46** 34.02S135.44E
Karlino Poland **14** 54.03N 15.51E
Karl-Marx-Stadt *see* Chemnitz Germany **14**
Karlovac Croatia **12** 45.30N 15.34E
Karlovy Vary Czech Republic **14** 50.14N 12.53E
Karlsborg Sweden **17** 58.32N 14.31E
Karlshamn Sweden **17** 56.10N 14.51E
Karlskoga Sweden **17** 59.20N 14.31E
Karlskrona Sweden **17** 56.10N 15.35E
Karlsruhe Germany **14** 49.00N 8.24E
Karlstad Sweden **17** 59.22N 13.30E
Karmöy *i.* Norway **17** 59.15N 5.15E
Karnafuli Resr. Bangla. **29** 22.40N 92.05E
Karnataka *d.* India **28** 14.45N 76.00E
Karnobat Bulgaria **13** 42.40N 27.00E
Kärnten *d.* Austria **14** 46.50N 13.50E
Karonga Malaŵi **37** 9.54S 33.55E
Karonie Australia **43** 30.58S122.32E
Karoonda Australia **46** 35.09S139.54E
Karos Dam R.S.A. **39** 28.27S 21.39E
Karpach Moldavia **15** 48.00N 27.10E
Kárpathos Greece **13** 35.30N 27.14E
Kárpathos *i.* Greece **13** 35.35N 27.08E
Karpineny Moldavia **15** 46.46N 28.18E
Karpinsk Russian Fed. **18** 59.48N 59.59E
Karpogory Russian Fed. **18** 64.01N 44.30E
Karragullen Australia **43** 32.05S116.03E
Karratha Australia **42** 20.44S116.50E
Karridale Australia **43** 34.12S115.04E
Kars Turkey **30** 40.35N 43.05E
Karsakpay Kazakhstan **20** 47.47N 66.43E
Kärsämäki Finland **16** 63.58N 25.46E
Kārsava Russian Fed. **18** 56.45N 27.40E
Karskoye More *sea* Russian Fed. **20** 73.00N 65.00E
Kartaly Russian Fed. **20** 53.06N 60.37E
Karufa Indonesia **27** 3.50S133.27E
Karumba Australia **44** 17.28S140.50E
Kārūn *r.* Iran **31** 30.25N 48.12E
Karungi Sweden **16** 66.03N 23.55E
Karungu Kenya **37** 0.50S 34.09E
Karviná Czech Republic **15** 49.50N 18.30E
Kasai *r.* Zaïre **36** 3.10S 16.13E
Kasama Zambia **37** 10.10S 31.11E
Kasane Botswana **39** 17.48S 25.09E
Kasanga Tanzania **37** 8.27S 31.10E
Kāsaragod India **28** 12.30N 75.00E
Kasba L. Canada **51** 60.18N102.07W
Kasese Uganda **37** 0.07N 30.06E
Kāshān Iran **31** 33.59N 51.31E
Kashi China **24** 39.29N 76.02E
Kashin Russian Fed. **18** 57.22N 37.39E
Kashiwa Japan **23** 35.52N139.59E
Kāshmar Iran **31** 35.12N 58.26E
Kasimov Russian Fed. **18** 54.55N 41.25E
Kaskinen Finland **16** 62.23N 21.13E
Kaskö *see* Kaskinen Finland **16**
Kásos *i.* Greece **13** 35.22N 26.56E
Kassalā Sudan **35** 15.24N 36.30E
Kassel Germany **14** 51.18N 9.30E
Kastamonu Turkey **30** 41.22N 33.47E
Kastoría Greece **13** 40.32N 21.15E
Kasugai Japan **23** 35.14N136.58E
Kasukabe Japan **23** 35.58N139.45E
Kasulu Tanzania **37** 4.34S 30.06E
Kasungu Malaŵi **37** 13.04S 33.29E
Kasūr Pakistan **28** 31.07N 74.30E
Katanning Australia **43** 33.42S117.33E
Katarniān Ghāt India **29** 28.20N 81.09E
Katchall *i.* India **29** 7.57N 93.22E
Katete Zambia **37** 14.08S 31.50E
Katha Burma **29** 24.11N 96.20E
Katherine Australia **44** 14.29S132.20E
Kathmandu Nepal **29** 27.42N 85.19E
Kati Mali **34** 12.41N 8.04W
Katima Rapids *f.* Zambia **39** 17.27S 24.13E
Katiola Ivory Coast **38** 8.10N 5.10W
Katonga *r.* Uganda **37** 0.03N 30.15E
Katoomba Australia **47** 33.42S150.23E
Katowice Poland **15** 50.15N 18.59E
Kātrīnā, Jabal *mtn.* Egypt **32** 28.30N 33.57E
Katrine, Loch U.K. **6** 56.15N 4.30W
Katrineholm Sweden **17** 59.00N 16.12E
Katsina Nigeria **38** 13.00N 7.32E
Katsina *d.* Nigeria **38** 12.25N 7.55E
Katsina Ala Nigeria **38** 7.10N 9.30E
Katsina Ala *r.* Nigeria **38** 7.50N 8.58E
Katsura *r.* Japan **23** 34.53N135.42E
Katsuura Japan **23** 35.08N140.18E
Kattegat *str.* Denmark/Sweden **17** 57.00N 11.20E
Katwijk aan Zee Neth. **8** 52.13N 4.27E
Kauai *i.* Hawaii U.S.A. **52** 22.05N159.30W
Kaub Germany **8** 50.07N 7.50E
Kaufbeuren Germany **14** 47.53N 10.37E
Kauhajoki Finland **16** 62.26N 22.11E
Kauhava Finland **16** 63.06N 23.05E
Kaukauveld *mts.* Namibia **39** 20.00S 20.15E
Kauliranta Finland **16** 66.26N 23.40E
Kaunas Lithuania **17** 54.54N 23.54E
Kaura Namoda Nigeria **38** 12.39N 6.38E
Kautokeino Norway **16** 69.00N 23.02E
Kavála Greece **13** 40.56N 24.24E
Kāvali India **29** 14.55N 80.01E
Kavarna Bulgaria **13** 43.26N 28.22E
Kavimba Botswana **39** 18.05S 24.34E
Kavkaz Russian Fed. **19** 45.20N 36.39E
Kaw Guiana **61** 4.29N 52.02W
Kawachi-nagano Japan **23** 34.25N135.32E
Kawagoe Japan **23** 35.55N139.29E
Kawaguchi Japan **23** 35.48N139.43E
Kawambwa Zambia **37** 9.47S 29.10E
Kawasaki Japan **23** 35.32N139.43E
Kawerau New Zealand **48** 38.05S176.42E
Kawhia New Zealand **48** 38.04S174.49E
Kaya Burkina **38** 13.04N 1.04W
Kayambi Zambia **37** 9.26S 32.01E
Kayan *r.* Indonesia **26** 2.47N117.46E
Kaycee U.S.A. **54** 43.43N106.38W
Kayenta U.S.A. **54** 36.44N110.17W
Kayes Mali **34** 14.26N 11.28W
Kayseri Turkey **30** 38.42N 35.28E
Kaysville U.S.A. **54** 41.02N111.56W
Kazachye Russian Fed. **21** 70.46N136.15E
Kazakhskiy Zaliv *b.* Kazakhstan **19** 42.43N 52.30E
Kazakhstan Asia **19** 48.00N 52.30E
Kazan Russian Fed. **18** 55.45N 49.10E
Kazanlŭk Bulgaria **13** 42.38N 25.26E
Kazatin Ukraine **15** 49.41N 28.49E
Kazaure Nigeria **38** 12.40N 8.25E
Kazbek *mtn.* Russian Fed. **19** 42.42N 44.30E
Kāzerūn Iran **31** 29.35N 51.39E
Kazhim Russian Fed. **18** 60.18N 51.34E
Kazincbarcika Hungary **15** 48.16N 20.37E
Kazo Japan **23** 36.07N139.36E
Kéa *i.* Greece **13** 37.36N 24.20E
Kearney U.S.A. **52** 40.42N 99.04W
Keban Turkey **30** 38.48N 38.45E
Kebbi *d.* Nigeria **38** 11.30N 3.45E
Kebnekaise *mtn.* Sweden **16** 67.53N 18.33E
K'ebri Dehar Ethiopia **35** 6.47N 44.17E
Kecskemét Hungary **15** 46.54N 19.42E
Kedainiai Lithuania **17** 55.17N 24.00E
Kedgwick Canada **55** 47.38N 67.21W
Kediri Indonesia **26** 7.55S112.01E
Kédougou Senegal **34** 12.35N 12.09W
Keele Peak *mtn.* Canada **50** 63.15N129.50W
Keene U.S.A. **55** 42.56N 72.17W
Keepit, L. Australia **47** 30.52S150.30E
Keer-Weer, C. Australia **44** 13.58S141.30E
Keetmanshoop Namibia **39** 26.34S 18.07E
Keewatin *d.* Canada **51** 65.00N 90.00W
Kefallinía *i.* Greece **13** 38.15N 20.33E
Kefar Sava Israel **32** 32.11N 34.54E
Keffi Nigeria **38** 8.52N 7.53E
Keflavík Iceland **16** 64.01N 22.35W
Keighley U.K. **4** 53.52N 1.54W
Keila Estonia **17** 59.18N 24.29E
Keimoes R.S.A. **39** 28.41S 20.58E
Keitele *l.* Finland **16** 62.55N 26.00E
Keith Australia **46** 36.06S140.22E
Keith U.K. **6** 57.32N 2.57W
Keith Arm *b.* Canada **50** 65.20N122.15W
Kelang Malaysia **26** 2.57N101.24E
Kelberg Germany **8** 50.17N 6.56E
Kelkit *r.* Turkey **30** 40.46N 36.32E
Keller U.S.A. **54** 48.03N118.40W
Kellerberrin Australia **43** 31.38S117.43E
Kellet, C. Canada **50** 71.59N125.34W
Kelloselkä Finland **16** 66.55N 28.50E
Kells Meath Rep. of Ire. **7** 53.44N 6.53W
Kelme Lithuania **17** 55.38N 22.56E
Kelowna Canada **50** 49.50N119.29W
Kelso U.K. **6** 55.36N 2.26W
Kelso Calif. U.S.A. **54** 35.01N115.39W
Kelso Wash. U.S.A. **54** 46.09N122.54W
Keluang Malaysia **26** 2.01N103.18E
Kelvedon U.K. **5** 51.50N 0.43E
Kem Russian Fed. **18** 64.58N 34.39E
Kema Indonesia **27** 1.22N125.08E
Ke Macina Mali **38** 14.05N 5.20W
Kemah Turkey **30** 39.35N 39.02E
Kemaliye Turkey **30** 39.16N 38.29E
Kemerovo Russian Fed. **20** 55.25N 86.10E
Kemi Finland **16** 65.49N 24.32E
Kemi *r.* Finland **16** 65.47N 24.30E
Kemijärvi Finland **16** 66.36N 27.24E
Kemmerer U.S.A. **54** 41.48N110.32W
Kempen *f.* Belgium **8** 51.05N 5.00E
Kemp Land *f.* Antarctica **64** 69.00S 57.00E
Kempsey Australia **47** 31.05S152.50E
Kempt, Lac *l.* Canada **55** 47.26N 74.30W
Kempten Germany **14** 47.44N 10.19E
Kenai U.S.A. **50** 60.33N151.15W
Kendal U.K. **4** 54.19N 2.44W
Kendall Australia **47** 31.28S152.40E
Kendari Indonesia **27** 3.57S122.36E
Kendenup Australia **43** 34.28S117.35E
Kendrick U.S.A. **54** 46.37N116.39W
Kenebri Australia **47** 30.45S149.02E
Kenema Sierra Leone **34** 7.57N 11.11W
Kengeja Tanzania **37** 5.24S 39.45E
Keng Tung Burma **29** 21.16N 99.39E
Kenhardt R.S.A. **39** 29.21S 21.08E
Kenilworth U.K. **5** 52.22N 1.35W
Kenitra Morocco **34** 34.20N 6.34W
Kenmare Rep. of Ire. **7** 51.53N 9.36W
Kennebec *r.* U.S.A. **55** 44.00N 69.50W
Kennet *r.* U.K. **5** 51.28N 0.57W
Kennewick U.S.A. **54** 46.12N119.07W
Kenogami *r.* Canada **55** 50.24N 84.20W
Keno Hill *town* Canada **50** 63.58N135.22W
Kenora Canada **51** 49.47N 94.26W
Kenosha U.S.A. **53** 42.34N 87.50W
Kenozero, Ozero *l.* Russian Fed. **18** 62.20N 37.00E
Kent *d.* U.K. **5** 51.12N 0.40E
Kent Ohio U.S.A. **55** 41.10N 81.20W
Kent Wash. U.S.A. **54** 47.23N122.14W
Kentau Kazakhstan **24** 43.28N 68.36E
Kentland U.S.A. **55** 40.46N 87.26W
Kenton U.S.A. **55** 40.38N 83.38W
Kent Pen. Canada **50** 68.30N107.00W
Kentucky *d.* U.S.A. **53** 38.00N 85.00W
Kentucky L. U.S.A. **53** 36.15N 88.00W
Kenya Africa **37** 1.00N 38.00E
Kenya, Mt. *see* Kirinyaga Kenya **37**
Keokuk U.S.A. **53** 40.23N 91.25W
Kepi Indonesia **27** 6.32S139.19E
Kepno Poland **15** 51.17N 17.59E
Keppel B. Australia **44** 23.21S150.55E
Kerala *d.* India **28** 10.30N 76.30E
Kerang Australia **46** 35.42S143.59E
Kerch Ukraine **19** 45.22N 36.27E
Kerchenskiy Proliv *str.* Ukraine/Russian Fed. **19** 45.15N 36.35E
Kerema P.N.G. **27** 7.59S145.46E
Kericho Kenya **37** 0.22S 35.19E
Kerinci, Gunung *mtn.* Indonesia **26** 1.45S101.20E
Kerio *r.* Kenya **37** 3.00N 36.14E
Kerkebet Eritrea **35** 16.13N 37.30E
Kerki Russian Fed. **18** 63.40N 54.00E
Kerki Turkmenistan **20** 37.53N 65.10E
Kérkira Greece **13** 39.37N 19.50E
Kérkira *i.* Greece **13** 39.35N 19.50E
Kerkrade Neth. **8** 50.52N 6.02E
Kermān Iran **31** 30.18N 57.05E
Kermānshāh Iran **31** 34.19N 47.04E
Kerme Körfezi *g.* Turkey **13** 36.52N 27.53E
Kerpen Germany **8** 50.52N 6.42E
Kerry *d.* Rep. of Ire. **7** 52.07N 9.35W
Kerry Head Rep. of Ire. **7** 52.24N 9.56W
Kerulen *r.* Mongolia **25** 48.45N117.00E
Kesagami L. Canada **55** 50.23N 80.15W
Keşan Turkey **13** 40.50N 26.39E
Keshod India **28** 21.18N 70.15E
Keskal India **29** 20.05N 81.35E
Keski-Suomi *d.* Finland **16** 62.30N 25.30E
Keswick U.K. **4** 54.35N 3.09W
Keszthely Hungary **15** 46.46N 17.15E
Ketapang Kalimantan Indonesia **26** 1.50S110.02E
Ketchikan U.S.A. **50** 55.25N131.40W
Ketchum U.S.A. **54** 43.41N114.22W
Kete Krachi Ghana **38** 7.50N 0.03W
Ketrzyn Poland **15** 54.06N 21.23E
Kettering U.K. **5** 52.24N 0.44W
Kettering U.S.A. **55** 39.41N 84.10W
Kettle Falls *town* U.S.A. **54** 48.36N118.03W
Keweenaw B. U.S.A. **55** 46.46N 88.26W
Keweenaw Pen. U.S.A. **55** 47.10N 88.30W
Key, Lough Rep. of Ire. **7** 54.00N 8.15W
Key Harbour Canada **55** 45.52N 80.48W
Keynsham U.K. **5** 51.25N 2.30W
Kezhma Russian Fed. **21** 58.58N101.08E
Kežmarok Slovakia **15** 49.08N 20.25E
Kgalagadi *d.* Botswana **39** 25.00S 21.30E
Kgatleng *d.* Botswana **39** 24.20S 26.20E
Khabarovsk Russian Fed. **25** 48.32N135.08E
Khairpur Sind Pakistan **28** 27.30N 68.50E
Khalkhāl Iran **31** 37.36N 48.36E
Khalkís Greece **13** 38.27N 23.36E
Khalmer Yu Russian Fed. **18** 67.58N 64.48E
Khalturin Russian Fed. **18** 58.38N 48.50E
Khalūf Oman **28** 20.31N 58.04E
Khambhāt, G. of India **28** 20.30N 72.00E
Khamkeut Laos **29** 18.14N104.44E
Khānaqīn Iraq **31** 34.22N 45.22E
Khandwa India **28** 21.49N 76.23E
Khāneh Khvodī Iran **31** 36.05N 56.04E
Khaniá Greece **13** 35.30N 24.02E
Khanka, Ozero *l.* Russian Fed. **25** 45.00N132.30E
Khankendy *see* Stepanakert Armenia **31**
Khanty-Mansiysk Russian Fed. **20** 61.00N 69.00E
Khān Yūnus Egypt **32** 31.21N 34.18E
Khapcheranga Russian Fed. **25** 49.46N112.20E
Kharagpur India **29** 22.23N 87.22E
Khārān *r.* Iran **31** 27.37N 58.48E
Khārijah, Al Wāḥāt al *oasis* Egypt **30** 24.55N 30.35E
Kharkov Ukraine **19** 50.00N 36.15E
Khār Kūh *mtn.* Iran **31** 31.37N 53.47E
Kharovsk Russian Fed. **18** 59.67N 40.07E
Khartoum *see* Al Kharṭūm Sudan **35**
Kharutayuvam Russian Fed. **18** 66.51N 59.31E
Khasavyurt Russian Fed. **19** 43.16N 46.36E
Khāsh *r.* Afghan. **31** 31.12N 62.00E
Khāsh Iran **31** 28.14N 61.15E
Khashgort Russian Fed. **18** 65.25N 65.40E
Khaskovo Bulgaria **13** 41.57N 25.33E
Khatanga Russian Fed. **21** 71.50N102.31E
Khatangskiy Zaliv *g.* Russian Fed. **21** 75.00N112.10E
Khemmarat Thailand **29** 16.04N105.10E
Khenifra Morocco **34** 33.00N 5.40W
Khersān *r.* Iran **31** 31.29N 48.53E
Kherson Ukraine **19** 46.39N 32.38E
Khíos Greece **13** 38.23N 26.07E
Khíos *i.* Greece **13** 38.23N 26.04E
Khiva Uzbekistan **31** 41.25N 60.49E
Khmelnik Ukraine **15** 49.36N 27.59E
Khmelnitskiy Ukraine **15** 49.25N 26.49E
Khodorov Ukraine **15** 49.20N 24.19E
Kholm Russian Fed. **18** 57.10N 31.11E
Kholmogory Russian Fed. **18** 63.51N 41.46E
Khomas-Hochland *mts.* Namibia **39** 22.50S 16.25E
Khonu Russian Fed. **21** 66.29N143.12E
Khoper *r.* Russian Fed. **19** 49.35N 42.17E
Khorixas Namibia **39** 20.24S 14.58E
Khorog Tajikistan **24** 37.32N 71.32E
Khorramābād Iran **31** 33.29N 48.21E
Khorramshahr Iran **31** 30.26N 48.09E
Khotimsk Belorussia **15** 53.24N 32.36E
Khotin Ukraine **15** 48.30N 26.31E
Khowrnag, Kūh-e *mtn.* Iran **31** 32.10N 54.38E
Khoyniki Belorussia **15** 51.54N 30.00E
Khudzhand Tajikistan **24** 40.14N 69.40E
Khuis Botswana **39** 26.37S 21.45E
Khulga *r.* Russian Fed. **18** 63.33N 61.53E
Khulna Bangla. **29** 22.49N 89.34E
Khurra Bārīk *r.* Iraq **30** 32.00N 44.15E
Khust Ukraine **15** 48.11N 23.19E
Khvor Iran **31** 33.47N 55.06E
Khvormuj Iran **31** 28.40N 51.20E
Khvoy Iran **31** 38.32N 45.02E
Khyber Pass Asia **28** 34.06N 71.05E
Kiama Australia **47** 34.41S150.49E
Kibali *r.* Zaïre **37** 3.37N 28.38E
Kibombo Zaïre **36** 3.58S 25.57E
Kibondo Tanzania **37** 3.35S 30.41E
Kibre Mengist Ethiopia **35** 5.52N 39.00E
Kibungu Rwanda **37** 2.10S 30.31E
Kibwesa Tanzania **37** 6.30S 29.57E
Kibwezi Kenya **37** 2.28S 37.57E
Kichiga Russian Fed. **21** 59.50N163.27E
Kicking Horse Pass Canada **50** 51.28N116.23W
Kidal Mali **38** 18.27N 1.25E
Kidderminster U.K. **5** 52.24N 2.13W
Kidete Morogoro Tanzania **37** 6.39S 36.42E
Kidsgrove U.K. **4** 53.06N 2.15W
Kiel Germany **14** 54.20N 10.08E
Kielce Poland **15** 50.52N 20.37E
Kielder *resr.* U.K. **4** 55.12N 2.30W
Kieler Bucht *b.* Germany **14** 54.30N 10.30E
Kiev *see* Kiyev Ukraine **15**
Kiffa Mauritania **34** 16.38N 11.28W
Kigali Rwanda **37** 1.59S 30.05E
Kigoma Tanzania **37** 4.52S 29.36E
Kigoma *d.* Tanzania **37** 4.45S 30.00E
Kigosi *r.* Tanzania **37** 4.37S 31.29E
Kiiminkin *r.* Finland **16** 65.12N 25.18E
Kikinda Yugo. **15** 45.51N 20.30E
Kikládhes *is.* Greece **13** 37.00N 25.00E
Kikori P.N.G. **27** 7.25S144.13E
Kikori *r.* P.N.G. **27** 7.10S144.05E
Kikwit Zaïre **36** 5.02S 18.51E
Kil Sweden **17** 59.30N 13.19E
Kilafors Sweden **17** 61.14N 16.34E
Kila Kila P.N.G. **27** 9.31S147.10E
Kilchu N. Korea **25** 40.55N129.21E
Kilcoy Australia **45** 26.57S152.33E
Kilcullen Rep. of Ire. **7** 53.08N 6.46W
Kildare Rep. of Ire. **7** 53.10N 6.55W
Kildare *d.* Rep. of Ire. **7** 53.10N 6.50W
Kildonan Zimbabwe **39** 17.22S 30.33E
Kilfinan U.K. **6** 55.58N 5.18W
Kilifi Kenya **37** 3.30S 39.50E
Kilimanjaro *d.* Tanzania **37** 3.45S 37.40E
Kilimanjaro *mtn.* Tanzania **37** 3.02S 37.20E
Kilindoni Tanzania **37** 7.55S 39.39E
Kilingi-Nõmme Estonia **17** 58.09N 24.58E
Kilis Turkey **30** 36.43N 37.07E
Kiliya Ukraine **15** 45.30N 29.16E
Kilkee Rep. of Ire. **7** 52.41N 9.40W
Kilkenny Rep. of Ire. **7** 52.39N 7.16W
Kilkenny *d.* Rep. of Ire. **7** 52.35N 7.15W
Kilkieran B. Rep. of Ire. **7** 53.20N 9.42W
Kilkís Greece **13** 40.59N 22.51E
Killala B. Rep. of Ire. **7** 54.15N 9.10W
Killard Pt. U.K. **7** 54.19N 5.31W
Killarney Australia **47** 28.18S152.15E
Killarney Rep. of Ire. **7** 52.04N 9.32W
Killary Harbour *est.* Rep. of Ire. **7** 53.38N 9.56W
Killin U.K. **6** 56.29N 4.19W
Killíni *mtn.* Greece **13** 37.56N 22.22E
Killorglin Rep. of Ire. **7** 52.07N 9.45W
Killybegs Rep. of Ire. **7** 54.38N 8.27W
Killyleagh U.K. **7** 54.24N 5.39W
Kilmarnock U.K. **6** 55.37N 4.30W
Kilmichael Pt. Rep. of Ire. **7** 52.44N 6.09W
Kilmore Australia **47** 37.18S144.58E
Kilninver U.K. **6** 56.21N 5.30W
Kilombero *r.* Tanzania **37** 8.30S 37.28E
Kilosa Tanzania **37** 6.49S 37.00E
Kilronan Rep. of Ire. **7** 53.08N 9.41W
Kilrush Rep. of Ire. **7** 52.39N 9.30W
Kilsyth U.K. **6** 55.59N 4.04W
Kilvo Sweden **16** 66.50N 21.04E
Kilwa Kivinje Tanzania **37** 8.45S 39.21E
Kilwa Masoko Tanzania **37** 8.55S 39.31E
Kimaan Indonesia **27** 7.54S138.51E
Kimba Australia **46** 33.09S136.25E
Kimberley R.S.A. **39** 28.44S 24.44E
Kimberley Plateau Australia **42** 17.20S127.20E
Kimito *i.* Finland **17** 60.10N 22.30E
Kimparana Mali **38** 12.52N 4.59W
Kimry Russian Fed. **18** 56.51N 37.20E
Kinabalu *mtn.* Malaysia **26** 6.10N116.40E
Kincardine Canada **55** 44.11N 81.38W
Kindia Guinea **34** 10.03N 12.49W
Kindu Zaïre **36** 3.00S 25.56E
Kinel Russian Fed. **18** 53.17N 50.42E
Kineshma Russian Fed. **18** 57.28N 42.08E
Kingaroy Australia **44** 26.33S151.50E
King City U.S.A. **54** 36.13N121.08W
King Edward *r.* Australia **42** 14.12S126.34E
King George Is. Canada **51** 57.20N 78.25W
King George Sd. Australia **43** 35.03S117.57E
King I. Australia **45** 39.50S144.00E
King Leopold Range *mts.* Australia **42** 17.00S125.30E
Kingman Ariz. U.S.A. **54** 35.12N114.04W
Kingoonya Australia **46** 30.54S135.18E
Kings *r.* U.S.A. **54** 36.03N119.49W
Kingsbridge U.K. **5** 50.17N 3.46W
Kings Canyon Australia **44** 24.15S131.33E
Kings Canyon Nat. Park U.S.A. **54** 36.48N118.30W
Kingsclere U.K. **5** 51.20N 1.14W
Kingscote Australia **46** 35.40S137.38E
King Sd. Australia **42** 17.00S123.30E
Kingsdown Kent U.K. **5** 51.21N 0.17E
Kingsley Dam U.S.A. **52** 41.15N101.30W
King's Lynn U.K. **4** 52.45N 0.25E
Kings Peaks *mts.* U.S.A. **54** 40.46N110.23W
Kingston Canada **55** 44.14N 76.30W
Kingston Jamaica **57** 17.58N 76.48W
Kingston New Zealand **48** 45.20S168.43E
Kingston N.Y. U.S.A. **55** 41.55N 74.00W
Kingston S.E. Australia **46** 36.50S139.50E
Kingston upon Hull U.K. **4** 53.45N 0.20W
Kingstown St. Vincent **57** 13.12N 61.14W
Kingsville U.S.A. **52** 27.32N 97.53W
Kingswood Avon U.K. **5** 51.27N 2.29W
Kings Worthy U.K. **5** 51.06N 1.18W
Kington U.K. **5** 52.12N 3.02W
Kingussie U.K. **6** 57.05N 4.04W
King William I. Canada **51** 69.00N 97.30W
King William's Town R.S.A. **39** 32.52S 27.23E
Kinloch Rannoch U.K. **6** 56.42N 4.11W
Kinna Sweden **17** 57.30N 12.41E
Kinnairds Head U.K. **6** 57.42N 2.00W
Kinnegad Rep. of Ire. **7** 53.28N 7.08W
Kino *r.* Japan **23** 34.13N135.09E
Kinross U.K. **6** 56.13N 3.27W
Kinsale Rep. of Ire. **7** 51.42N 8.32W

Kinshasa Zaïre 36 4.18S 15.18E
Kintyre pen. U.K. 6 55.35N 5.35W
Kinvara Rep. of Ire. 7 53.08N 8.56W
Kiparissía Greece 13 37.15N 21.40E
Kipawa, Lac l. Canada 55 46.55N 79.00W
Kipengere Range mts. Tanzania 37 9.15S 34.15E
Kipili Tanzania 37 7.30S 30.39E
Kipini Kenya 37 2.31S 40.32E
Kippure mtn. Rep. of Ire. 7 53.11N 6.20W
Kirby U.S.A. 54 43.49N108.10W
Kircheimbolanden Germany 8 49.39N 8.00E
Kirensk Russian Fed. 21 57.45N108.00E
Kirgiziya Step f. Kazakhstan 19 50.00N 57.10E
Kirgiz Steppe see Kirgiziya Step f. Kazakhstan 19
Kiribati Pacific Oc. 40 6.00S170.00W
Kirikkale Turkey 30 39.51N 33.32E
Kirillov Russian Fed. 18 59.53N 38.21E
Kirínia Cyprus 32 35.20N 33.20E
Kirinyaga mtn. Kenya 37 0.10S 37.19E
Kirkby Lonsdale U.K. 4 54.13N 2.36W
Kirkby Stephen U.K. 4 54.27N 2.23W
Kirkcaldy U.K. 6 56.07N 3.10W
Kirkcudbright U.K. 6 54.50N 4.03W
Kirkenes Norway 16 69.40N 30.03E
Kirkland Ariz. U.S.A. 54 34.26N112.43W
Kirkland Wash. U.S.A. 54 47.41N122.12W
Kirkland Lake town Canada 55 48.10N 80.00W
Kirklareli Turkey 13 41.44N 27.12E
Kirkpatrick, Mt. Antarctica 64 85.00S170.00E
Kirksville U.S.A. 53 40.12N 92.35W
Kirkūk Iraq 31 35.28N 44.26E
Kirkwall U.K. 6 58.59N 2.58W
Kirkwood R.S.A. 39 33.25S 25.24E
Kirn Germany 8 49.47N 7.28E
Kirov Russian Fed 18 53.59N 34.20E
Kirov Russian Fed 18 58.38N 49.38E
Kirovakan Armenia 31 40.49N 44.30E
Kirovo-Chepetsk Russian Fed. 18 58.40N 50.02E
Kirovograd Ukraine 19 48.31N 32.15E
Kirovsk Russian Fed. 18 67.37N 33.39E
Kirovskiy Russian Fed. 21 54.25N155.37E
Kirriemuir U.K. 6 56.41N 3.01W
Kirs Russian Fed. 18 59.21N 52.10E
Kirsanoy Kazakhstan 19 51.29N 52.30E
Kirşehir Turkey 30 39.09N 34.08E
Kiruna Sweden 16 67.51N 20.16E
Kisa Sweden 17 57.59N 15.37E
Kisaga Tanzania 37 4.26S 34.26E
Kisangani Zaïre 35 0.33N 25.14E
Kisaran Indonesia 26 2.47N 99.29E
Kisarazu Japan 23 35.23N139.55E
Kiselevsk Russian Fed. 20 54.01N 86.41E
Kishinev Moldavia 15 47.00N 28.50E
Kishiwada Japan 23 34.28N135.22E
Kishtwār Jammu & Kashmir 28 33.20N 75.48E
Kisii Kenya 37 0.40S 34.44E
Kisiju Tanzania 37 7.23S 39.20E
Kiskörös Hungary 15 46.38N 19.17E
Kiskunfélegyháza Hungary 15 46.43N 19.52E
Kiskunhalas Hungary 15 46.26N 19.30E
Kislovodsk Russian Fed. 19 43.56N 42.44E
Kismaayo Somali Rep. 37 0.25S 42.31E
Kiso Japan 23 35.02N136.45E
Kiso sammyaku mts. Japan 23 35.42N137.50E
Kissamos Greece 13 35.30N 23.38E
Kissidougou Guinea 34 9.48N 10.08W
Kissū, Jabal mtn. Sudan 35 21.35N 25.09E
Kistna r. see Krishna r. India 28
Kisumu Kenya 37 0.07S 34.47E
Kisvárda Hungary 15 48.13N 22.05E
Kita Mali 34 13.04N 9.29W
Kitab Uzbekistan 20 39.08N 66.51E
Kitakyūshū Japan 25 33.52N130.49E
Kitale Kenya 37 1.01N 35.01E
Kitchener Australia 43 31.01S124.20E
Kitchener Canada 55 43.27N 80.29W
Kitchigama r. Canada 55 51.12N 78.55W
Kitgum Uganda 37 3.17N 32.54E
Kíthira Greece 13 36.09N 23.00E
Kíthira i. Greece 13 36.15N 23.00E
Kíthnos i. Greece 13 37.25N 24.25E
Kitikmeot d. Canada 50 80.00N105.00W
Kitimat Canada 50 54.05N128.38W
Kitinen r. Finland 16 67.20N 27.27E
Kitsman Ukraine 15 48.30N 25.50E
Kittakittaooloo, L. Australia 46 28.09S138.09E
Kittanning U.S.A. 55 40.49N 79.32W
Kittery U.S.A. 55 43.05N 70.45W
Kittilä Finland 16 67.40N 24.54E
Kitui Kenya 37 1.22S 38.01E
Kitunda Tanzania 37 6.48S 33.17E
Kitwe Zambia 37 12.50S 28.04E
Kiunga Kenya 37 1.46S 41.30E
Kivijärvi l. Finland 16 63.10N 25.09E
Kivik Sweden 17 55.41N 14.15E
Kivu d. Zaïre 37 3.00S 27.00E
Kivu, L. Rwanda / Zaïre 37 2.00S 29.10E
Kiyev Ukraine 15 50.28N 30.29E
Kiyevskoye Vodokhranilishche resr. Ukraine 15 51.00N 30.25E
Kizel Russian Fed. 18 59.01N 57.42E
Kizema Russian Fed. 18 61.12N 44.52E
Kizil r. Turkey 30 41.45N 35.57E
Kizlyar Russian Fed. 19 43.51N 46.43E
Kizlyarskiy Zaliv b. Russian Fed. 19 44.33N 47.00E
Kizu r. Japan 23 34.53N135.42E
Kizyl-Arvat Turkmenistan 31 39.00N 56.23E
Kizyl Atrek Turkey 31 37.37N 54.49E
Kladno Czech Republic 14 50.10N 14.05E
Klagenfurt Austria 14 46.38N 14.20E
Klaipeda Lithuania 17 55.43N 21.07E
Klamath r. U.S.A. 54 41.33N124.04W
Klamath Falls town U.S.A. 54 42.14N121.47W
Klamath Mts. U.S.A. 54 41.40N123.20W
Klamono Indonesia 27 1.08S131.28E
Klar r. Sweden 17 59.23N 13.32E
Klatovy Czech Republic 14 49.24N 13.18E
Klawer R.S.A. 39 31.48S 18.34E
Kleinsee R.S.A. 39 29.41S 17.04E
Klerksdorp R.S.A. 39 26.51S 26.38E
Klevan Ukraine 15 50.44N 25.50E
Kleve Germany 8 51.47N 6.11E
Klickitat U.S.A. 54 45.49N121.09W
Klimovichi Belorussia 15 53.36N 31.58E
Klimpfjäll Sweden 16 65.04N 14.52E
Klin Russian Fed. 18 56.20N 36.45E
Klintehamn Sweden 17 57.24N 18.12E
Klintsy Russian Fed. 15 52.45N 32.15E
Klipdale R.S.A. 39 34.18S 19.58E
Klippan Sweden 17 56.08N 13.06E
Klipplaat R.S.A. 39 33.01S 24.19E
Kłobuck Poland 15 50.55N 18.57E
Kłodzko Poland 14 50.27N 16.39E
Klöfta Norway 17 60.04N 11.09E
Klondike Canada 50 64.02N139.24W
Kluczbork Poland 15 50.59N 18.13E
Knaresborough U.K. 4 54.01N 1.29W
Knighton U.K. 5 52.21N 3.02W
Knin Croatia 14 44.02N 16.10E
Knockadoon Head Rep. of Ire. 7 51.52N 7.52W
Knockalongy mtn. Rep. of Ire. 7 54.12N 8.45W
Knockmealdown Mts. Rep. of Ire. 7 52.15N 7.55W
Knokke Belgium 8 51.21N 3.17E
Knolls U.S.A. 54 40.44N113.18W
Knossos site Greece 13 35.20N 25.10E
Knoxville U.S.A. 53 36.00N 83.57W
Knutsford U.K. 4 53.18N 2.22W
Knyazhevo Russian Fed. 18 59.40N 43.51E
Knysna R.S.A. 39 34.02S 23.03E
Kōbe Japan 23 34.41N135.10E
København Denmark 17 55.43N 12.34E
Koblenz Germany 8 50.21N 7.36E
Kobrin Belorussia 15 52.16N 24.22E
Kobroor i. Indonesia 27 6.10S134.30E
Kočani Macedonia 13 41.55N 22.24E
Kočevje Slovenia 12 45.38N 14.52E
Kochi India 28 9.56N 76.15E
Kochkoma Russian Fed. 18 64.03N 34.14E
Kochmes Russian Fed. 18 66.12N 60.48E
Kodaira Japan 23 35.44N139.29E
Kodiak U.S.A. 50 57.49N152.30W
Kodiak I. U.S.A. 50 57.00N153.50W
Kodima Russian Fed. 18 62.24N 43.57E
Kodyma Ukraine 15 48.06N 29.04E
Koekelare Belgium 8 51.08N 2.59E
Koekenaap R.S.A. 39 31.30S 18.18E
Koersel Belgium 8 51.04N 5.19E
Koës Namibia 39 25.58S 19.07E
Koffiefontein R.S.A. 39 29.24S 25.00E
Köflach Austria 14 47.04N 15.05E
Koforidua Ghana 38 6.01N 0.12W
Kōfu Japan 23 35.39N138.35E
Koga Tanzania 37 6.10S 32.21E
Køge Denmark 17 55.27N 12.11E
Køge Bugt b. Greenland 51 65.00N 40.30W
Kogi d. Nigeria 38 7.15N 7.00E
Kohāt Pakistan 28 33.37N 71.30E
Kohīma India 29 25.40N 94.08E
Kohler Range mts. Antarctica 64 77.00S110.00W
Kohtla-Järve Estonia 18 59.28N 27.20E
Koito r. Japan 23 35.21N139.52E
Kojonup Australia 43 33.50S117.05E
Kokand Uzbekistan 24 40.33N 70.55E
Kokas Indonesia 27 2.45S132.26E
Kokchetav Kazakhstan 20 53.18N 69.25E
Kokemäki Finland 17 61.15N 22.21E
Kokenau Indonesia 27 4.42S136.25E
Kokka Sudan 35 20.00N 30.35E
Kokkola Finland 16 63.50N 23.07E
Koko Sokoto Nigeria 38 11.27N 4.35E
Kokoda P.N.G. 44 8.50S147.45E
Kokomo U.S.A. 55 40.30N 86.09W
Kokpekty Kazakhstan 24 48.45N 82.25E
Koksoak r. Canada 51 58.30N 68.15W
Kokstad R.S.A. 39 30.32S 29.25E
Kokuora Russian Fed. 21 71.33N144.50E
Kolaka Indonesia 27 4.04S121.38E
Kola Pen. see Kolskiy Poluostrov pen. Russian Fed. 18
Kolār India 29 13.10N 78.10E
Kolari Finland 16 67.20N 23.48E
Kolāyat India 28 27.50N 72.57E
Kolbio Kenya 37 1.11S 41.10E
Kolda Senegal 34 12.56N 14.55W
Kolding Denmark 17 55.31N 9.29E
Kolepom i. see Yos Sudarsa, Pulau i. Indonesia 27
Kolguyev, Ostrov i. Russian Fed. 18 69.00N 49.00E
Kolhāpur India 28 16.43N 74.15E
Kolia Ivory Coast 38 9.46N 6.28W
Kolín Czech Republic 14 50.02N 15.10E
Kolka Latvia 17 57.45N 22.35E
Kolki Ukraine 15 51.09N 25.40E
Kollam India 28 8.53N 76.38E
Köln Germany 8 50.56N 6.57E
Koło Poland 15 53.25N 21.56E
Koło Poland 15 52.12N 18.37E
Kołobrzeg Poland 14 54.10N 15.35E
Kologriv Russian Fed. 18 58.49N 44.19E
Kolomna Russian Fed. 18 55.05N 38.45E
Kolomyya Ukraine 15 48.31N 25.00E
Kolpashevo Russian Fed. 20 58.21N 82.59E
Kolpino Russian Fed. 18 59.44N 30.39E
Kolskiy Poluostrov pen. Russian Fed. 18 67.00N 38.00E
Kolsva Sweden 17 59.36N 15.50E
Koluszki Poland 15 51.44N 19.49E
Kolvereid Norway 16 64.53N 11.35E
Kolwezi Zaïre 36 10.44S 25.28E
Kolyma r. Russian Fed. 21 68.50N161.00E
Kolymskiy, Khrebet mts Russian Fed. 21 63.00N160.00E
Kom Kenya 37 1.06N 38.00E
Komadugu Gana r. Nigeria 38 13.06N 12.23E
Komadugu Yobe r. Niger / Nigeria 38 13.43N 13.19E
Komagane Japan 23 35.43N137.55E
Komaga-take mtn. Japan 23 35.47N137.48E
Komaki Japan 23 35.17N136.55E
Komárno Slovakia 15 47.45N 18.09E
Komarom Hungary 15 47.44N 18.08E
Komatipoort R.S.A. 39 25.25S 31.55E
Komló Hungary 15 46.12N 18.16E
Kommunarsk Ukraine 19 48.30N 38.47E
Kommunizma, Pik mtn. Tajikistan 24 38.39N 72.01E
Komotiní Greece 13 41.07N 25.26E
Komrat Moldavia 15 46.18N 28.40E
Komsberg mtn. R.S.A. 39 32.40S 20.48E
Komsomolets, Ostrov i. Russian Fed. 21 80.20N 96.00E
Komsomolets, Zaliv g. Kazakhstan 19 45.17N 53.30E
Komsomolsk-na-Amure Russian Fed. 21 50.32N136.59E
Kōnan Japan 23 35.20N136.53E
Kondakovo Russian Fed. 21 69.38N152.00E
Kondinin Australia 43 32.33S118.13E
Kondoa Tanzania 37 4.54S 35.49E
Kondopoga Russian Fed. 18 62.12N 34.17E
Kondratyevo Russian Fed. 21 57.22N 98.15E
Kondut Australia 43 30.44S117.06E
Kong Ivory Coast 38 8.54N 4.36W
Kong Christian den IX Land f. Greenland 51 68.20N 37.00W
Kong Frederik den VI Kyst f. Greenland 51 63.00N 44.00W
Kong Haakon VII Hav sea Antarctica 64 65.00S 25.00E
Kongolo Zaïre 36 5.20S 27.00E
Kongsberg Norway 17 59.39N 9.39E
Kongsvinger Norway 17 60.12N 12.00E
Kongur Shan mtn. China 24 38.40N 75.30E
Kongwa Tanzania 37 6.13S 36.28E
Konin Poland 15 52.13N 18.16E
Konjic Bosnia-Herzegovina 15 43.39N 17.57E
Könkämä r. Sweden / Finland 16 68.29N 22.30E
Konongo Ghana 38 6.38N 1.12W
Konosha Russian Fed. 18 60.58N 40.08E
Kōnosu Japan 23 36.03N139.31E
Konotop Ukraine 19 51.15N 33.14E
Końskie Poland 15 51.12N 20.26E
Konstanz Germany 14 47.40N 9.10E
Kontagora Nigeria 38 10.24N 5.22E
Kontcha Cameroon 38 7.59N 12.15E
Kontiomäki Finland 18 64.21N 28.10E
Kontum Vietnam 26 14.23N108.00E
Konya Turkey 30 37.51N 32.30E
Konz Germany 8 49.42N 6.34E
Konza Kenya 37 1.45S 37.07E
Koolkootinnie L. Australia 46 27.58S137.47E
Koolyanobbing Australia 43 30.48S119.29E
Koondrook Australia 46 35.39S144.11E
Koongawa Australia 46 33.11S135.52E
Koorawatha Australia 47 34.02S148.33E
Koorda Australia 43 30.50S117.51E
Kootjieskolk R.S.A. 39 31.14S 20.18E
Kópavogur Iceland 16 64.06N 21.53W
Koper Slovenia 14 45.33N 13.44E
Kopervik Norway 17 59.17N 5.18E
Kopet Dag, Khrebet mts. Turkmenistan 31 38.00N 58.00E
Köping Sweden 17 59.31N 16.00E
Kopparberg d. Sweden 17 60.50N 15.00E
Koppom Sweden 17 59.43N 12.09E
Koprivnica Croatia 14 46.10N 16.50E
Kopychintsy Ukraine 15 49.10N 25.58E
Kor r. Iran 31 29.40N 53.17E
Korba India 29 22.21N 82.41E
Korbach Germany 14 51.16N 8.53E
Korçë Albania 13 40.37N 20.45E
Korčula i. Croatia 13 42.56N 16.53E
Kord Kūy Iran 31 36.48N 54.07E
Korea Str. S. Korea / Japan 25 35.00N129.20E
Korets Ukraine 15 50.39N 27.10E
Korhogo Ivory Coast 38 9.22N 5.31W
Korim Indonesia 27 0.58S136.10E
Korinthiakós Kólpos g. Greece 13 38.15N 22.30E
Kórinthos Greece 13 37.56N 22.55E
Kōriyama Japan 25 37.23N140.22E
Korma Belorussia 15 53.08N 30.47E
Körmend Hungary 14 47.01N 16.37E
Kornat i. Croatia 12 43.48N 15.20E
Korneshty Moldavia 15 47.21N 28.00E
Kornsjö Norway 17 58.57N 11.39E
Koro Mali 38 14.01N 2.58W
Korocha Russian Fed. 19 50.50N 37.13E
Korogwe Tanzania 37 5.10S 38.35E
Koroit Australia 46 38.17S142.26E
Korong Vale town Australia 46 36.22S143.45E
Koror i. Belau 27 7.30N134.30E
Korosten Ukraine 15 51.00N 28.30E
Korostyshev Ukraine 15 50.19N 29.03E
Korsör Denmark 17 55.20N 11.09E
Korsze Poland 15 54.10N 21.09E
Kortrijk Belgium 8 50.49N 3.17E
Koryakskiy Khrebet mts. Russian Fed. 21 62.20N171.00E
Koryazhma Russian Fed. 18 61.19N 47.12E
Kos i. Greece 13 36.48N 27.10E
Kościan Poland 14 52.06N 16.38E
Kościerzyna Poland 15 54.08N 18.00E
Kosciusko, Mt. Australia 47 36.28S148.17E
Koshk-e Kohneh Afghan 31 34.52N 62.29E
Košice Slovakia 15 48.44N 21.15E
Koski Finland 17 60.39N 23.09E
Koslan Russian Fed. 18 63.29N 48.59E
Kossovo Belorussia 15 52.40N 25.18E
Kosta Sweden 17 56.51N 15.23E
Koster R.S.A. 39 25.51S 26.52E
Kostopol Ukraine 15 50.51N 26.22E
Kostroma Russian Fed. 18 57.46N 40.59E
Kostrzyn Poland 14 52.24N 17.11E
Kostyukovichi Belorussia 15 53.20N 32.01E
Kosyu Russian Fed. 18 65.36N 59.00E
Koszalin Poland 14 54.12N 16.09E
Kota Rāj. India 28 25.11N 75.58E
Kota Baharu Malaysia 26 6.07N102.15E
Kota Belud Malaysia 26 6.00N116.00E
Kotabumi Indonesia 26 4.52S104.59E
Kota Kinabalu Malaysia 26 5.59N116.04E
Kotelnich Russian Fed. 18 58.20N 48.10E
Kotelnikovo Russian Fed. 19 47.39N 43.08E
Kotel'nyy, Ostrov i. Russian Fed. 21 75.30N141.00E
Kotka Finland 18 60.26N 26.55E
Kotlas Russian Fed. 18 61.15N 46.28E
Kotlik U.S.A. 50 63.02N163.33W
Kotor Yugo. 13 42.28N 18.47E
Kotovsk Moldavia 15 46.50N 28.31E
Kotovsk Ukraine 15 47.42N 29.30E
Kottagūdem India 29 17.32N 80.39E
Kotuy r. Russian Fed. 21 71.40N103.00E
Kotzebue U.S.A. 50 66.51N162.40W
Kotzebue Sd. U.S.A. 50 66.20N163.00W
Koudougou Burkina 38 12.15N 2.21W
Koúklia Cyprus 32 34.42N 32.34E
Koumankou Mali 38 11.58N 6.06W
Koumbia Burkina 38 11.18N 3.38W
Koumbia Guinea 34 11.54N 13.40W
Koumongou Togo 38 10.10N 0.29E
Koupéla Burkina 38 12.09N 0.22W
Kouroussa Guinea 34 10.40N 9.50W
Kousseri Cameroon 34 12.07N 15.01E
Koutiala Mali 38 12.20N 5.23W
Kouto Ivory Coast 38 9.53N 6.25W
Kouvola Finland 18 60.54N 26.45E
Kovdor Russian Fed. 18 67.33N 30.30E
Kovel Ukraine 15 51.12N 24.48E
Kovpyta Ukraine 15 51.22N 30.51E
Kovrov Russian Fed. 18 56.23N 41.21E
Kovzha r. Russian Fed. 18 61.05N 36.27E
Kowanyama Australia 44 15.29S141.44E
Kowloon Hong Kong 25 22.20N114.15E
Koyukuk r. U.S.A. 50 64.50N157.30W
Kozan Turkey 30 37.27N 35.47E
Kozáni Greece 13 40.18N 21.48E
Kozelets Ukraine 15 50.54N 31.09E
Kozhikode India 28 11.15N 75.45E
Kozhim Russian Fed. 18 65.45N 59.30E
Kozhposelok Russian Fed. 18 63.10N 38.10E
Kpandu Ghana 38 7.02N 0.17E
Kpessi Togo 38 8.07N 1.17E
Krabi Thailand 26 8.04N 98.52E
Krâchéh Cambodia 26 12.30N106.03E
Kragerö Norway 17 58.52N 9.25E
Kragujevac Yugo. 13 44.01N 20.55E
Kraków Poland 15 50.03N 19.55E
Kraljevo Yugo. 13 43.44N 20.41E
Kramatorsk Ukraine 19 48.43N 37.33E
Kramfors Sweden 16 62.55N 17.50E
Kranj Slovenia 14 46.15N 14.21E
Kranskop R.S.A. 39 28.58S 30.52E
Krapkowice Poland 15 50.29N 17.56E
Krasavino Russian Fed. 18 60.58N 46.25E
Krasilov Ukraine 15 49.39N 26.59E
Kraskino Russian Fed. 25 42.42N130.48E
Krasnaya Gora Russian Fed. 15 53.00N 31.36E
Kraśnik Poland 15 50.56N 22.13E
Krasnodar Russian Fed. 19 45.02N 39.00E
Krasnograd Ukraine 19 49.22N 35.28E
Krasnokamsk Russian Fed. 18 58.05N 55.49E
Krasnoperekopsk Ukraine 19 45.56N 33.47E
Krasnoselkup Russian Fed. 20 65.45N 82.31E
Krasnoturinsk Russian Fed. 18 59.46N 60.10E
Krasnoufimsk Russian Fed. 18 56.40N 57.49E
Krasnouralsk Russian Fed. 20 58.25N 60.00E
Krasnovishersk Russian Fed. 18 60.25N 57.02E
Krasnovodsk Turkmenistan 31 40.01N 53.00E
Krasnovodskiy Poluostrov pen. Turkmenistan 31 40.30N 53.10E
Krasnovodskiy Zaliv g. Turkmenistan 31 39.50N 53.15E
Krasnoyarsk Russian Fed. 21 56.05N 92.46E
Krasnyy Yar Russian Fed. 19 46.32N 48.21E
Kratovo Macedonia 13 42.05N 22.11E
Krefeld Germany 8 51.20N 6.32E
Kremenchug Ukraine 19 49.03N 33.25E
Kremenchugskoye Vodokhranilishche resr. Ukraine 19 49.20N 32.30E
Kremenets Ukraine 15 50.05N 25.48E
Krems Austria 14 48.25N 15.36E
Krestovka Russian Fed. 18 66.24N 52.31E
Kretinga Lithuania 17 55.53N 21.13E
Kribi Cameroon 38 2.56N 9.56E
Krichev Belorussia 15 53.40N 31.44E
Krishna r. India 29 16.00N 81.00E
Kristiansand Norway 17 58.10N 8.00E
Kristianstad Sweden 17 56.02N 14.08E
Kristianstad d. Sweden 17 56.15N 13.35E
Kristiansund Norway 16 63.07N 7.45E
Kristiinankaupunki Finland 17 62.17N 21.23E
Kristinehamn Sweden 17 59.20N 14.07E
Kristinestad see Kristiinankaupunki Finland 17
Kristinovka Ukraine 15 48.50N 29.58E
Kríti i. Greece 13 35.15N 25.00E
Kritikón Pélagos sea Greece 13 36.00N 25.00E
Krivaja r. Bosnia-Herzegovina 15 44.27N 18.09E
Krivoy Rog Ukraine 19 47.55N 33.24E
Krk i. Croatia 14 45.04N 14.36E
Krnov Czech Republic 15 50.05N 17.41E
Kroken Norway 16 65.23N 14.15E
Krokom Sweden 16 63.20N 14.30E
Kronoberg d. Sweden 17 56.45N 14.15E
Kronprins Olav Kyst f. Antarctica 64 69.00S 42.00E
Kronshtadt Russian Fed. 18 60.00N 29.40E
Kroonstad R.S.A. 39 27.38S 27.12E
Kropotkin Russian Fed. 19 45.25N 40.35E
Krosno Poland 15 49.42N 21.46E
Krotoszyn Poland 15 51.42N 17.26E
Kruger Nat. Park R.S.A. 39 24.10S 31.36E
Krugersdorp R.S.A. 39 26.06S 27.46E
Krujë Albania 13 41.30N 19.48E
Krumbach Germany 14 48.14N 10.22E
Krung Thep see Bangkok Thailand 29
Krupki Belorussia 15 54.19N 29.05E
Kruševac Yugo. 15 43.34N 21.20E
Krym pen. Ukraine 19 45.30N 34.00E
Krymsk Russian Fed. 19 44.56N 38.00E
Krzyz Poland 14 52.54N 16.01E
Ksar el Boukhari Algeria 34 35.55N 2.47E
Kuala Dungun Malaysia 26 4.47N103.26E
Kualakapuas Indonesia 26 3.01S114.21E
Kuala Lipis Malaysia 26 4.11N102.00E
Kuala Lumpur Malaysia 26 3.08N101.42E
Kuala Trengganu Malaysia 26 5.10N103.10E
Kuandang Indonesia 27 0.53N122.58E
Kuantan Malaysia 26 3.50N103.19E
Kuba Azerbaijan 31 41.23N 48.33E
Kuban r. Russian Fed. 19 45.20N 37.17E
Kuching Malaysia 26 1.32N110.20E
Kudat Malaysia 26 6.45N116.47E
Kudus Indonesia 26 6.46S110.48E
Kufstein Austria 14 47.36N 12.11E
Kūhpāyeh Iran 31 32.42N 52.25E
Kūhrān, Kūh-e mtn. Iran 31 26.46N 58.15E
Kuivaniemi Finland 16 65.35N 25.11E
Kuke Botswana 39 23.19S 24.29E
Kukerin Australia 43 33.11S118.03E
Kukës Albania 13 42.05N 20.24E
Kūl r. Iran 31 28.00N 55.45E
Kula Turkey 30 38.33N 28.38E
Kulakshi Kazakhstan 19 47.09N 55.22E
Kulal, Mt. Kenya 37 2.44N 36.56E
Kuldīga Latvia 17 56.58N 21.59E
Kulgera Australia 44 25.50S133.18E
Kulin Australia 43 32.40S118.10E
Kulja Australia 43 30.28S117.17E
Kulkyne r. Australia 47 30.16S144.12E
Kulpara Australia 46 34.07S137.59E
Kulsary Kazakhstan 19 46.59N 54.02E
Kulu Turkey 19 39.06N 33.02E
Kulunda Russian Fed. 20 52.34N 78.58E
Kulwin Australia 46 35.02S142.40E
Kulyab Tajikistan 24 37.55N 69.47E
Kuma r. Russian Fed. 19 44.40N 46.55E
Kumagaya Japan 23 36.08N139.23E
Kumai Indonesia 26 2.45S111.44E
Kumamoto Japan 25 32.50N130.42E
Kumanovo Macedonia 13 42.08N 21.40E
Kumara New Zealand 48 42.38S171.11E
Kumarl Australia 43 32.47S121.33E
Kumasi Ghana 38 6.45N 1.35W
Kumayri Armenia 31 40.47N 43.49E
Kumba Cameroon 38 4.39N 9.26E
Kumbakonam India 29 10.59N 79.24E
Kum Dag Turkmenistan 31 39.14N 54.33E
Kumertau Russian Fed. 18 52.48N 55.46E
Kumi Uganda 37 1.26N 33.54E
Kumla Sweden 17 59.08N 15.08E
Kunashir i. Russian Fed. 25 44.25N146.00E
Kundelungu Mts. Zaïre 37 9.30S 27.50E
Kundip Australia 43 33.44S120.11E
Kungälv Sweden 17 57.52N 11.58E
Kungsbacka Sweden 17 57.29N 12.04E
Kungur Russian Fed. 18 57.27N 56.50E
Kunlun Shan mts. China 24 36.40N 88.00E
Kunming China 24 25.04N102.41E
Kunsan S. Korea 25 35.57N126.42E
Kununoppin Australia 43 31.09S117.53E
Kununurra Australia 41 15.42S128.50E
Kuolayarvi Russian Fed. 16 66.58N 29.12E
Kuopio Finland 18 62.51N 27.30E
Kupa r. Croatia 14 45.30N 16.20E
Kupang Indonesia 27 10.13S123.38E
Kupyansk Ukraine 19 49.41N 37.37E
Kuqa China 24 41.43N 82.58E
Kura r. Azerbaijan 31 39.18N 49.22E
Kuraymah Sudan 35 18.32N 31.48E
Kurchum Kazakhstan 24 48.35N 83.39E
Kurdistan f. Asia 31 37.00N 43.30E
Kŭrdzhali Bulgaria 13 41.38N 25.21E
Kuressaare Estonia 17 58.12N 22.30E
Kurgaldzhino Kazakhstan 20 50.35N 70.03E
Kurgan Russian Fed. 20 55.20N 65.20E
Kurikka Finland 16 62.37N 22.25E
Kurilskiye Ostrova is. Russian Fed. 25 46.00N150.30E
Kuring Kuru Namibia 39 17.36S 18.36E
Kurlovski Russian Fed. 18 55.26N 40.40E
Kurnool India 29 15.51N 78.01E
Kurow New Zealand 48 44.44S170.28E
Kurri Kurri Australia 47 32.49S151.29E
Kursk Russian Fed. 19 51.45N 36.14E
Kuršumlija Yugo. 13 43.09N 21.16E
Kuru Finland 17 61.52N 23.44E
Kuruman R.S.A. 39 27.28S 23.25E
Kuruman r. R.S.A. 39 26.53S 20.38E
Kusatsu Japan 23 35.02N135.57E
Kusel Germany 8 49.32N 7.21E
Kushchevskaya Russian Fed. 19 46.34N 39.39E
Kushida r. Japan 23 34.36N136.34E
Kushiro Japan 25 42.58N144.24E
Kushka Turkmenistan 31 35.14N 62.15E
Kuskokwim B. U.S.A. 50 59.45N162.25W
Kuskokwim Mts. U.S.A. 50 62.50N156.00W
Kustanay Kazakhstan 20 53.15N 63.40E
Küstenkanal Germany 8 53.05N 7.46E
Kūstī Sudan 35 13.11N 32.38E
Kütahya Turkey 30 39.25N 29.56E
Kutaisi Georgia 19 42.15N 42.44E
Kutná Hora Czech Republic 14 49.57N 15.16E
Kutno Poland 15 52.15N 19.23E
Kutu Zaïre 36 2.42S 18.09E
Kuujjuaq Canada 51 58.10N 68.15W
Kuujjuarapik Canada 51 55.25N 77.45W
Kuusamo Finland 18 65.57N 29.15E
Kuvango Angola 36 14.28S 16.25E
Kuwait Asia 31 29.20N 47.40E

Kuwait town see Al Kuwayt Kuwait 31
Kuwana Japan 23 35.04N136.42E
Kuybyshev see Samara Russian Fed. 18
Kuybyshevskoye Vodokhranilishche resr. Russian Fed. 18 55.00N 49.00E
Kuyeda Russian Fed. 18 56.25N 55.33E
Kuzey Anadolu Daglari mts. Turkey 30 40.32N 38.00E
Kuznetsk Russian Fed. 18 53.08N 46.36E
Kuzomen Russian Fed. 18 66.15N 36.51E
Kuzreka Russian Fed. 18 66.35N 34.48E
Kvaenangen est. Norway 16 69.50N 21.30E
Kwale Kenya 37 4.20S 39.25E
Kwangju S. Korea 25 35.07N126.52E
Kwango r. Zaïre 36 3.20S 17.23E
Kwara d. Nigeria 38 8.20N 5.35E
Kwatisore Indonesia 27 3.18S134.50E
Kwa Zulu f. R.S.A. 39 27.30S 32.00E
Kwekwe Zimbabwe 39 18.59S 29.46E
Kweneng d. Botswana 39 24.30S 25.40E
Kwethluk U.S.A. 50 60.49N161.27W
Kwidzyn Poland 15 53.45N 18.56E
Kwigillingok U.S.A. 50 59.51N163.08W
Kwiguk U.S.A. 50 62.45N164.28W
Kwinana Australia 43 32.15S115.48E
Kwoka mtn. Indonesia 27 1.30S132.30E
Kyabé Chad 34 9.28N 18.54E
Kyabram Australia 47 36.18S145.05E
Kyaka Tanzania 37 1.16S 31.27E
Kyakhta Russian Fed. 24 50.22N106.30E
Kyalite Australia 46 34.57S143.31E
Kyancutta Australia 46 33.08S135.34E
Kyaukpyu Burma 29 19.28N 93.30E
Kybybolite Australia 46 36.54S140.58E
Kychema Russian Fed. 18 65.32N 42.42E
Kyle of Lochalsh town U.K. 6 57.17N 5.43W
Kyll r. Germany 8 49.48N 6.42E
Kyllburg Germany 8 50.03N 6.36E
Kyluchevskaya mtn. Russian Fed. 21 56.00N160.30E
Kyneton Australia 46 37.14S144.28E
Kynuna Australia 44 21.35S141.55E
Kyoga, L. Uganda 37 1.30N 33.00E
Kyogle Australia 47 28.36S152.59E
Kyotera Uganda 37 0.40S 31.31E
Kyōto Japan 23 35.00N135.45E
Kyōto d. Japan 23 34.55N135.35E
Kyrgyzstan Asia 24 41.30N 75.00E
Kyrön r. Finland 16 63.14N 21.45E
Kyrta Russian Fed. 18 64.02N 57.40E
Kyūshū i. Japan 25 32.50N130.50E
Kyustendil Bulgaria 13 42.18N 22.39E
Kywong Australia 47 35.01S146.45E
Kyyjärvi Finland 16 63.02N 24.34E
Kyzyl Russian Fed. 24 51.42N 94.28E
Kyzyl Kum, Peski f. Uzbekistan 20 42.00N 64.30E
Kzyl Orda Kazakhstan 20 44.52N 65.28E
K2 mtn. Asia 24 35.53N 76.32E

L

Laas Caanood Somali Rep. 35 8.26N 47.24E
La Asunción Venezuela 60 11.06N 63.53W
Laâyoune see El Aaiún W. Sahara 34
La Baleine r. Canada 51 58.00N 57.50W
La Banda Argentina 62 27.44S 64.15W
La Bañeza Spain 10 42.17N 5.55W
Labao Indonesia 27 8.12S122.49E
La Barca Mexico 56 20.20N102.33W
La Barge U.S.A. 54 42.16N110.12W
La Bassée France 8 50.32N 2.49E
La Baule France 11 47.18N 2.23W
Labbezanga Mali 38 14.57N 0.42E
Labe r. Czech. see Elbe r. Germany 14
Labé Guinea 34 11.17N 12.11W
Labinsk Russian Fed. 19 44.39N 40.44E
La Blanquilla i. Venezuela 57 11.53N 64.38W
Labouheyre France 11 44.13N 0.55W
Laboulaye Argentina 63 34.05S 63.25W
Labrador f. Canada 51 54.00N 61.30W
Labrador City Canada 51 52.54N 66.50W
Labrador Sea Canada / Greenland 51 57.00N 53.00W
Lábrea Brazil 60 7.16S 64.47W
Labrit France 11 44.07N 0.33W
Labuan i. Malaysia 26 5.20N115.15E
Labuha Indonesia 27 0.37S127.29E
Labyrinth, L. Australia 46 30.43S135.07E
Lac d. Chad 38 13.30N 14.35E
La Calera Chile 63 32.47S 71.12W
La Capelle France 8 49.59N 3.57E
La Carlota Argentina 63 33.25S 63.18W
La Carolina Spain 10 38.16N 3.36W
Lacaune France 11 43.42N 2.41E
La Ceiba Honduras 57 15.45N 86.45W
Lacepede B. Australia 46 36.47S139.45E
Lac Giao Vietnam 26 12.41N108.02E
Lacha, Ozero l. Russian Fed. 18 61.25N 39.00E
La Charité France 11 47.11N 3.01E
La Chartre France 9 47.44N 0.35E
La Chaux-de-Fonds Switz. 14 47.07N 6.51E
Lach Dera r. Somali Rep. 37 0.01S 42.45E
Lachlan r. Australia 46 34.21S143.58E
Lackan Resr. Rep. of Ire. 7 53.09N 6.31W
Lackawanna U.S.A. 55 42.49N 78.49W
Lac la Biche town Canada 50 54.46N111.58W
La Cocha Argentina 62 27.45S 65.35W
Lacombe Canada 50 52.28N113.44W
La Concepción Venezuela 60 10.25N 71.41W
La Concordia Mexico 56 16.05N 92.38W
La Coruña Spain 10 43.22N 8.24W
La Crosse Wisc. U.S.A. 53 43.48N 91.15W
La Cruz Uruguay 63 33.56S 56.15W
La Demanda, Sierra de mts. Spain 10 42.10N 3.20W
Ladismith R.S.A. 39 33.29S 21.15E
Ladispoli Italy 12 41.56N 12.05E
Lādīz Iran 31 28.57N 61.18E
Ladoga l. see Ladozhskoye Ozero l. Russian Fed. 18
La Dorada Colombia 60 5.27N 74.40W
Ladozhskoye Ozero l. Russian Fed. 18 61.00N 32.00E
Ladushkin Russian Fed. 15 54.30N 20.05E
Ladva Vetka Russian Fed. 18 61.16N 34.23E
Ladybrand R.S.A. 39 29.11S 27.26E
Ladysmith Canada 50 48.58N123.49W
Ladysmith R.S.A. 39 28.32S 29.47E
Lae P.N.G. 27 6.45S146.30E
Laesö i. Denmark 17 57.16N 11.01E
La Estrada Spain 10 42.40N 8.30W
Lafayette Ind. U.S.A. 55 40.25N 86.54W
Lafayette La. U.S.A. 53 30.12N 92.18W
La Fère France 9 49.40N 3.22E
La Ferté-Bernard France 9 48.11N 0.40E
La Ferté-Gaucher France 9 48.47N 3.18E
La Ferté-Macé France 9 48.36N 0.22W
La Ferté-St. Aubin France 9 47.43N 1.56E
Lafia Nigeria 38 8.35N 8.34E
Lafiagi Nigeria 38 8.50N 5.23E
La Flèche France 9 47.42N 0.05W
Laforest Canada 55 47.02N 81.13W
La Fregeneda Spain 10 40.58N 6.54W
La Fuente de San Esteban Spain 10 40.48N 6.15W
Lagan r. U.K. 7 54.37N 5.44W
Lågen r. Akershus Norway 17 60.10N 11.28E
Lågen r. Vestfold Norway 17 59.03N 10.05E
Laghouat Algeria 34 33.50N 2.59E
Lagos Mexico 56 21.21N101.55W
Lagos Nigeria 38 6.27N 3.28E
Lagos d. Nigeria 38 6.32N 3.30E
Lagos Portugal 10 37.05N 8.40W
La Grande U.S.A. 54 45.20N118.05W
La Grande Résr. 2 Canada 51 53.35N 77.10W
La Grande Résr. 3 Canada 51 53.35N 74.55W
Lagrange Australia 42 18.46S121.49E
La Grange U.S.A. 53 33.02N 85.02W
La Guaira Venezuela 60 10.38N 66.55W
La Guerche-de-Bretagne France 9 47.56N 1.14W
Laguna Brazil 62 28.29S 48.47W
Laguna Dam U.S.A. 54 32.55N114.25W
Lagunas Chile 62 20.59S 69.37W
Lagunas Peru 60 5.10S 73.35W
La Habana Cuba 57 23.07N 82.25W
Lahad Datu Malaysia 26 5.05N118.20E
Lahat Indonesia 26 3.46S103.32E
La Haye-du-Puits France 9 49.18N 1.33W
Lāhījān Iran 31 37.12N 50.00E
Lahn r. Germany 8 50.18N 7.36E
Lahnstein Germany 8 50.17N 7.38E
Laholm Sweden 17 56.31N 13.02E
Lahore Pakistan 28 31.34N 74.22E
Lahti Finland 17 60.58N 25.40E
Laï Chad 34 9.22N 16.14E
Laiagam P.N.G. 27 5.31S143.39E
L'Aigle France 9 48.45N 0.38E
Laignes France 9 47.50N 4.22E
Laihia Finland 16 62.58N 22.01E
Laingsburg R.S.A. 39 33.11S 20.49E
Lainio r. Sweden 16 67.28N 22.50E
Lairg U.K. 6 58.01N 4.25W
Laisamis Kenya 37 1.38N 37.47E
Laissac France 11 44.23N 2.49E
Laitila Finland 17 60.53N 21.41E
Laizhou Wan b. China 25 37.30N119.30E
Lajes Brazil 59 27.48S 50.20W
La Junta U.S.A. 52 37.59N103.33W
Lak Bor r. Somali Rep. 37 0.32N 42.05E
Lake Biddy town Australia 43 33.01S118.51E
Lake Boga town Australia 46 35.27S143.39E
Lake Bolac town Australia 46 37.42S142.50E
Lake Brown town Australia 43 30.57S118.19E
Lake Cargelligo town Australia 47 33.19S146.23E
Lake Charles town U.S.A. 53 30.13N 93.13W
Lake City U.S.A. 53 30.05N 82.40W
Lake District f. U.K. 4 54.30N 3.10W
Lake Grace town Australia 43 33.06S118.28E
Lake Harbour town Canada 51 62.50N 69.50W
Lake King town Australia 43 33.05S119.40E
Lakeland town U.S.A. 53 28.02N 81.59W
Lake Mead Nat. Recreation Area U.S.A. 54 36.00N114.30W
Lake Nash town Australia 44 21.00S137.55E
Lake Placid town U.S.A. 55 44.17N 73.59W
Lakes Entrance town Australia 47 37.53S147.59E
Lakeshore U.S.A. 54 37.15N119.12W
Lakeside Utah U.S.A. 54 41.13N112.54W
Lake Superior Prov. Park Canada 55 47.43N 84.53W
Lakeview U.S.A. 54 42.11N120.21W
Lakewood N.J. U.S.A. 55 40.06N 74.12W
Lakewood Ohio U.S.A. 55 41.29N 81.50W
Lakhpat India 28 23.49N 68.47E
Lakonikós Kólpos g. Greece 13 36.35N 22.42E
Lakota Ivory Coast 38 5.50N 5.30W
Laksefjorden est. Norway 16 70.58N 27.00E
Lakselv Norway 16 70.03N 24.55E
Lakshadweep Is. Indian Oc. 28 11.00N 72.00E
Lalaua Mozambique 37 14.20S 38.30E
Lālehzār, Kūh-e mtn. Iran 31 29.26N 56.48E
La Libertad El Salvador 57 13.28N 89.20W
Lalín Spain 10 42.40N 8.05W
La Línea Spain 10 36.10N 5.21W
Lalitpur India 29 24.42N 78.24E
La Loupe France 9 48.28N 1.01E
La Louvière Belgium 8 50.29N 4.11E
Lamar U.S.A. 52 38.04N102.37W
Lambaréné Gabon 36 0.41S 10.13E
Lambayeque Peru 60 6.36S 79.50W
Lambay I. Rep. of Ire. 7 53.29N 6.01W
Lambert's Bay town R.S.A. 39 32.06S 18.16E
Lamé Chad 38 9.14N 14.33E
Lame Nigeria 38 10.27N 9.12E
Lamego Portugal 10 41.05N 7.49W
Lameroo Australia 46 35.20S140.33E
La Mesa Calif. U.S.A. 54 32.46N117.01W
Lamía Greece 13 38.53N 22.25E
Lammermuir Hills U.K. 6 55.51N 2.40W
Lammhult Sweden 17 57.09N 14.35E
Lamont U.S.A. 54 42.12N107.28W
Lamotrek i. Federated States of Micronesia 27 7.28N146.23E
Lamotte-Beuvron France 9 47.37N 2.01E
Lampa Peru 60 15.10S 70.30W
Lampazos Mexico 56 27.01N100.31W
Lampedusa i. Italy 12 35.30N 12.35E
Lampeter U.K. 5 52.06N 4.06W
Lampione i. Italy 12 35.33N 12.18E
Lamu Kenya 37 2.20S 40.54E
La Mure France 11 44.54N 5.47E
La Nao, Cabo de Spain 10 38.42N 0.15E
Lanark U.K. 6 55.41N 3.47W
Lancang Jiang r. China see Mekong r. Asia 24
Lancashire d. U.K. 4 53.53N 2.30W
Lancaster U.K. 4 54.03N 2.48W
Lancaster Calif. U.S.A. 54 34.42N118.08W
Lancaster Ohio U.S.A. 55 39.43N 82.37W
Lancaster Penn. U.S.A. 55 40.02N 76.19W
Lancaster Sd. Canada 51 74.00N 85.00W
Lancelin Australia 43 31.01S115.19E
Lanchow see Lanzhou China 24
Landau Bayern Germany 14 48.40N 12.43E
Landeck Austria 14 47.09N 10.35E
Landen Belgium 8 50.46N 5.04E
Lander r. Australia 44 20.25S132.00E
Lander U.S.A. 54 42.50N108.44W
Landerneau France 11 48.27N 4.16W
Landor Australia 42 25.06S116.50E
Landrecies France 8 50.08N 3.40E
Land's End c. U.K. 5 50.03N 5.45W
Landshut Germany 14 48.31N 12.10E
Landskrona Sweden 17 55.52N 12.50E
Langå Denmark 17 56.23N 9.55E
Langadhás Greece 13 40.45N 23.04E
Langanes c. Iceland 16 66.30N 14.30W
Langao China 25 33.22N109.04E
Langeais France 9 47.20N 0.24E
Langeland i. Denmark 17 55.00N 10.50E
Längelmävesi l. Finland 17 61.32N 24.22E
Langeoog i. Germany 8 53.46N 7.30E
Langesund Norway 17 59.00N 9.45E
Langholm U.K. 6 55.09N 3.00W
Langjökull ice cap Iceland 16 63.43N 20.03W
Langkawi i. Malaysia 26 6.20N 99.30E
Langlade Canada 55 48.14N 75.59W
Langon France 11 44.33N 0.14W
Langöy i. Norway 16 68.45N 15.00E
Langres France 11 47.53N 5.20E
Langsa Indonesia 26 4.28N 97.59E
Lang Son Vietnam 26 21.50N106.55E
Languedoc-Roussillon d. France 11 43.50N 3.30E
Lannion France 11 48.44N 3.27W
Lansing U.S.A. 55 42.44N 84.34W
Lanslebourg France 9 45.17N 6.52E
Lantewa Nigeria 38 12.15N 11.45E
Lanzarote i. Canary Is. 34 29.00N 13.55W
Lanzhou China 24 36.01N103.45E
Lanzo Torinese Italy 9 45.16N 7.28E
Laoag Phil. 27 18.14N120.36E
Lào Cai Vietnam 26 22.30N104.00E
Laohekou China 25 32.26N111.41E
Laois d. Rep. of Ire. 7 53.00N 7.20W
Laon France 9 49.34N 3.37E
La Oroya Peru 60 11.36S 75.54W
Laos Asia 26 19.00N104.00E
La Palma i. Canary Is. 34 28.50N 18.00W
La Palma Spain 10 37.23N 6.33W
La Pampa d. Argentina 63 37.00S 66.00W
La Paragua Venezuela 60 6.53N 63.22W
La Paz Entre Ríos Argentina 63 30.45S 59.38W
La Paz Mendoza Argentina 63 33.28S 67.34W
La Paz Bolivia 62 16.30S 68.09W
La Paz d. Bolivia 62 16.00S 68.10W
La Paz Mexico 56 24.10N110.18W
La Pedrera Colombia 60 1.18S 69.43W
Lapeer U.S.A. 55 43.03N 83.09W
La Peña, Sierra de mts. Spain 10 42.30N 0.50W
La Perouse Str. Russian Fed. 21 45.50N142.30E
La Pine U.S.A. 54 43.40N121.30W
Lapinjärvi Finland 17 60.38N 26.13E
Lapland f. Sweden / Finland 16 68.10N 24.10E
La Plata Argentina 63 34.55S 57.57W
La Plata, Río de est. Argentina / Uruguay 63 35.15S 56.45W
Lappajärvi l. Finland 16 63.08N 23.40E
Lappeenranta Finland 18 61.04N 28.05E
Lappi d. Finland 16 67.20N 26.00E
Laptevykh, More sea Russian Fed. 21 74.30N125.00E
Lapua Finland 16 62.57N 23.00E
La Push U.S.A. 54 47.55N124.38W
La Quiaca Argentina 62 22.05S 65.36W
L'Aquila Italy 12 42.22N 13.25E
Lār Iran 31 27.37N 54.16E
Lara Australia 46 38.01S144.26E
Larache Morocco 34 35.12N 6.10W
Laramie U.S.A. 52 41.19N105.35W
Lärbro Sweden 17 57.47N 18.47E
Larche, Col de France / Italy 9 44.25N 6.53E
Laredo U.S.A. 52 27.32N 99.22W
Largeau Chad 34 17.55N 19.07E
Largs U.K. 6 55.48N 4.52W
Lariang Indonesia 26 1.35S119.25E
La Rioja Argentina 62 29.25S 66.50W
La Rioja d. Argentina 62 29.00S 66.00W
La Rioja d. Spain 10 42.15N 2.25W
Lárisa Greece 13 39.36N 22.24E
Lark r. U.K. 5 52.26N 0.20E
Lārkāna Pakistan 28 27.32N 68.18E
Larnaca see Lárnax Cyprus 32
Lárnax Cyprus 32 34.54N 33.39E
Larne U.K. 7 54.51N 5.49W
La Robla Spain 10 42.50N 5.41W
La Roche Belgium 8 50.11N 5.35E
La Rochelle France 11 46.10N 1.10W
La Roche-sur-Yon France 11 46.40N 1.25W
La Roda Spain 10 39.13N 2.10W
La Romana Dom. Rep. 57 18.27N 68.57W
La Ronge Canada 50 55.07N105.18W
La Ronge, Lac l. Canada 50 55.07N105.15W
Laroquebrou France 11 44.58N 2.11E
Larrimah Australia 44 15.35S133.12E
Larvik Norway 17 59.04N 10.00E
La Sagra mtn. Spain 10 37.58N 2.35W
La Sarre Canada 55 48.49N 79.12W
Las Cruces U.S.A. 52 32.23N106.29W
La Seine, Baie de France 11 49.40N 0.30W
La Serena Chile 62 29.54S 71.16W
La Seyne France 11 43.06N 5.53E
Las Flores Argentina 63 36.02S 59.07W
Lāsh-e Joveyn Afghan. 31 31.43N 61.39E
Las Heras Argentina 63 32.50S 68.50W
Lashio Burma 29 22.58N 97.48E
Las Lomitas Argentina 62 24.43S 60.35W
Las Marismas f. Spain 10 37.00N 6.15W
Las Palmas Canary Is. 34 28.08N 15.27W
Las Perlas, Archipelago de Panama 57 8.45N 79.30W
La Spezia Italy 9 44.07N 9.49E
Las Piedras Uruguay 63 34.44S 56.13W
Las Plumas Argentina 63 43.40S 67.15W
Lassay France 9 48.26N 0.30W
Lassen Peak mtn. U.S.A. 54 40.29N121.31W
Lastoursville Gabon 36 0.50S 12.47E
Lastovo i. Croatia 13 42.45N 16.52E
Lastrup Germany 8 52.48N 7.55E
La Suze France 9 47.54N 0.02E
Las Vegas Nev. U.S.A. 54 36.11N115.08W
Las Vegas N.Mex. U.S.A. 52 35.36N105.13W
Latacunga Ecuador 60 0.58S 78.36W
La Tagua Colombia 60 0.03S 74.40W
Latakia see Al Lādhiqīyah Syria 32
La Teste-de-Buch France 11 44.38N 1.09W
Lathen Germany 8 52.54N 7.20E
Latina Italy 12 41.28N 12.52E
Latisana Italy 9 45.47N 13.00E
La Tortuga i. Venezuela 60 11.00N 65.20W
La Trobe, Mt. Australia 47 39.03S146.25E
La Tuque Canada 55 47.26N 72.47W
Latvia Europe 18 56.45N 25.00E
Lau Nigeria 38 9.14N 11.15E
Lauchhammer Germany 14 51.30N 13.48E
Lauenburg Germany 14 53.22N 10.33E
Laughlen, Mt. Australia 44 23.23S134.23E
Launceston Australia 45 41.25S147.07E
Launceston U.K. 5 50.38N 4.21W
La Unión Chile 63 40.15S 73.02W
La Unión Spain 10 37.38N 0.53W
Laura Australia 46 33.08S138.19E
La Urbana Venezuela 60 7.08N 66.56W
Laurel Miss. U.S.A. 53 31.41N 89.09W
Laurel Mont. U.S.A. 54 45.40N108.46W
Laurencekirk U.K. 6 56.50N 2.29W
Laurentides Prov. Park Canada 55 47.46N 71.40W
Laurieton Australia 47 31.38S152.46E
Lausanne Switz. 14 46.32N 6.39E
Laut i. Indonesia 26 3.45S116.20E
Lautaro Chile 63 38.31S 72.27W
Lauterecken Germany 8 49.39N 7.36E
Lavagh More mtn. Rep. of Ire. 7 54.45N 8.07W
Lava Hot Springs town U.S.A. 54 42.37N112.01W
Laval France 9 48.04N 0.45W
La Vega Dom. Rep. 57 19.15N 70.33W
La Vela Venezuela 60 11.27N 69.34W
La Vérendrye Prov. Park Canada 55 47.29N 77.06W
Laverton Australia 43 28.49S122.25E
Lavia Finland 17 61.36N 22.36E
Lavik Norway 17 61.06N 5.30E
Lavras Brazil 59 21.15S 44.59W
Lávrion Greece 13 37.44N 24.04E
Lawra Ghana 38 10.40N 2.49W
Lawrence New Zealand 48 45.55S169.42E
Lawrence Kans. U.S.A. 53 38.58N 95.15W
Lawrence Mass. U.S.A. 55 42.42N 71.09W
Lawton Okla. U.S.A. 52 34.36N 98.25W
Lawz, Jabal al mtn. Saudi Arabia 32 28.40N 35.20E
Laxå Sweden 17 58.59N 14.37E
Laytonville U.S.A. 54 39.41N123.29W
Lazio d. Italy 12 42.20N 12.00E
Leadhills U.K. 6 55.25N 3.46W
Leamington U.S.A. 54 39.31N112.17W
Learmonth Australia 42 22.13S114.04E
Leavenworth U.S.A. 53 39.19N 94.55W
Lebak Phil. 27 6.32N124.03E
Lebanon Asia 32 34.00N 36.00E
Lebanon Ind. U.S.A. 55 40.02N 87.28W
Lebanon Oreg. U.S.A. 54 44.32N122.54W
Lebanon Penn. U.S.A. 55 40.20N 76.25W
Lebanon Tenn. U.S.A. 53 36.11N 86.19W
Lebec U.S.A. 54 34.50N118.52W
Lebesby Norway 16 70.34N 27.00E
Le Blanc France 11 46.37N 1.03E
Łebork Poland 15 54.33N 17.44E
Lebrija Spain 10 36.55N 6.10W
Lebu Chile 63 37.37S 73.39W
Le Bugue France 11 44.55N 0.56E
Le Cateau France 8 50.07N 3.33E
Le Catelet France 8 50.00N 3.12E
Lecce Italy 13 40.21N 18.11E
Lecco Italy 9 45.51N 9.23E
Lech r. Germany 14 48.45N 10.51E
Le Chesne France 8 49.31N 4.46E
Lechiguanas, Islas de las is. Argentina 63 33.26S 59.42W
Le Creusot France 11 46.48N 4.27E
Lectoure France 11 43.56N 0.38E
Ledbury U.K. 5 52.03N 2.25W
Ledesma Spain 10 41.05N 6.00W
Le Dorat France 11 46.14N 1.05E
Leduc Canada 50 53.16N113.33W
Lee r. Rep. of Ire. 7 51.53N 8.25W
Leech L. U.S.A. 53 47.10N 94.30W
Leeds U.K. 4 53.48N 1.34W
Leek U.K. 4 53.07N 2.02W
Leer Germany 8 53.14N 7.27E
Leeston New Zealand 48 43.46S172.18E
Leeton Australia 47 34.33S146.24E
Leeuwarden Neth. 8 53.12N 5.48E
Leeuwin, C. Australia 43 34.22S115.08E
Leeward Is. C. America 57 18.00N 61.00W
Lefroy, L. Australia 43 31.15S121.40E
Legazpi Phil. 27 13.10N123.45E
Legges Tor mtn. Australia 45 41.32S147.40E
Legget U.S.A. 54 39.52N123.34W
Leghorn see Livorno Italy 12
Legion Mine Zimbabwe 39 21.23S 28.33E
Legionowo Poland 15 52.25N 20.56E
Legnago Italy 9 45.11N 11.18E
Legnano Italy 9 45.36N 8.54E
Legnica Poland 14 51.12N 16.10E
Le Grand-Lucé France 9 47.52N 0.28E
Le Grand-Quevilly France 9 49.25N 1.02E
Leh Jammu & Kashmir 28 34.09N 77.35E
Le Havre France 9 49.30N 0.06E
Lehrte Germany 14 52.22N 9.59E
Lehututu Botswana 39 23.54S 21.52E
Leibnitz Austria 14 46.48N 15.32E
Leicester U.K. 5 52.39N 1.09W
Leicestershire d. U.K. 5 52.29N 1.10W
Leichardt r. Australia 44 17.35S139.48E
Leiden Neth. 8 52.10N 4.30E
Leie r. Belgium 8 51.03N 3.44E
Leigh Creek r. Australia 46 29.49S138.10E
Leigh Creek town Australia 46 30.31S138.25E
Leighton Buzzard U.K. 5 51.55N 0.39W
Leikanger Norway 17 61.10N 6.52E
Leinster Australia 43 27.59S120.30E
Leipzig Germany 14 51.20N 12.20E
Leiria Portugal 10 39.45N 8.48W
Leitrim d. Rep. of Ire. 7 54.08N 8.00W
Leizhou Bandao pen. China 25 20.40N109.30E
Lek r. Neth. 8 51.55N 4.29E
Leksvik Norway 16 63.40N 10.40E
Lelchitsy Belorussia 15 51.48N 28.20E
Leleque Argentina 63 42.24S 71.04W
Le Lion-d'Angers France 9 47.38N 0.43W
Le Lude France 9 47.39N 0.09E
Lelystad Neth. 8 52.32N 5.29E
Léman, Lac l. Switz. 14 46.30N 6.30E
Le Mans France 9 48.01N 0.10E
Leme Brazil 59 22.10S 47.23W
Le Merlerault France 9 48.42N 0.18E
Lemesós Cyprus 32 34.40N 33.03E
Lemgo Germany 14 52.02N 8.54E
Lemhi Range mts. U.S.A. 54 44.30N113.25W
Lemmer Neth. 8 52.50N 5.43E
Lemmon U.S.A. 52 45.56N102.10W
Lemvig Denmark 17 56.32N 8.18E
Lena r. Russian Fed. 21 72.00N127.10E
Lendery Russian Fed. 18 63.24N 31.04E
Lendinara Italy 9 45.05N 11.36E
Lengerich Germany 8 52.12N 7.52E
Lenina, Kanal canal Russian Fed. 19 43.46N 45.00E
Lenina, Pik mtn. Tajikistan 24 40.14N 69.40E
Leningrad see Sankt-Peterburg Russian Fed. 18
Leninogorsk Kazakhstan 20 50.23N 83.32E
Leninsk Russian Fed. 19 48.42N 45.14E
Leninsk Kuznetskiy Russian Fed. 20 54.44N 86.13E
Lenkoran Azerbaijan 31 38.45N 48.50E
Lenmalu Indonesia 27 1.58S130.00E
Lenne r. Germany 8 51.24N 7.30E
Lens France 8 50.26N 2.50E
Lentini Italy 12 37.17N 15.00E
Lenvik Norway 16 69.22N 18.10E
Léo Burkina 38 11.05N 2.06W
Leoben Austria 14 47.23N 15.06E
Leominster U.K. 5 52.15N 2.43W
Leominster U.S.A. 55 42.32N 71.45W
León Mexico 56 21.10N101.42W
León Nicaragua 57 12.24N 86.52W
León Spain 10 42.35N 5.34W
Leonardville Namibia 39 23.21S 18.47E
Leonárison Cyprus 32 35.28N 34.08E
Leongatha Australia 47 38.29S145.57E
Leonora Australia 43 28.54S121.20E
Leopoldina Brazil 59 21.30S 42.38W
Leopoldsburg Belgium 8 51.08N 5.13E
Leovo Moldavia 15 46.29N 28.12E
Lepel Russian Fed. 18 54.48N 28.40E
Le Puy France 11 45.03N 3.54E
Le Quesnoy France 8 50.15N 3.39E
Lerbäck Sweden 17 58.56N 15.02E
Léré Chad 38 9.41N 14.17E
Lerici Italy 9 44.04N 9.55E
Lérida Spain 10 41.37N 0.38E
Lerma Spain 10 42.02N 3.46W
Le Roy Mich. U.S.A. 55 44.03N 85.29W
Lerwick U.K. 6 60.09N 1.09W
Les Andelys France 9 49.15N 1.25E
Les Cayes Haiti 57 18.15N 73.46W
Leschenault, C. Australia 43 31.50S115.23E
Les Ecrins mtn. France 11 44.50N 6.20E
Leshan China 29 29.34N103.42E
Leshukonskoye Russian Fed. 18 64.55N 45.50E
Lesjaskog Norway 17 62.15N 8.22E
Leskovac Yugo. 13 43.00N 21.56E
Lesotho Africa 39 29.00S 28.00E
Lesozavodsk Russian Fed. 25 45.30N133.29E
Les Pieux France 9 49.35N 1.50W
Les Riceys France 9 47.59N 4.22E
Les Sables d'Olonne France 11 46.30N 1.47W
Lessay France 9 49.14N 1.30W
Lesser Antilles is. C. America 57 13.00N 65.00W

Lesser Slave L. Canada 50 55.30N115.00W
Lesser Sunda Is. see Nusa Tenggara is. Indonesia 26
Lessines Belgium 8 50.43N 3.50E
Lesti r. Finland 16 64.04N 23.38E
Lésvos i. Greece 13 39.10N 26.16E
Leszno Poland 14 51.51N 16.35E
Letchworth U.K. 5 51.58N 0.13W
Lethbridge Canada 50 49.43N112.48W
Lethem Guyana 60 3.18N 59.46W
Leti, Kepulauan is. Indonesia 27 8.20S128.00E
Letiahau r. Botswana 39 21.16S 24.00E
Leticia Colombia 60 4.09S 69.57W
Le Tréport France 11 50.04N 1.22E
Letterkenny Rep. of Ire. 7 54.56N 7.45W
Leuk Switz. 9 46.19N 7.38E
Leuser mtn. Indonesia 26 3.50N 97.10E
Leuven Belgium 8 50.53N 4.45E
Leuze Hainaut Belgium 8 50.36N 3.37E
Leuze Namur Belgium 8 50.34N 4.53E
Levanger Norway 16 63.45N 11.19E
Levanto Italy 9 44.10N 9.38E
Levelland U.S.A. 52 33.35N102.23W
Lévêque, C. Australia 42 16.25S123.00E
Le Verdon France 11 45.33N 1.04W
Leverkusen Germany 8 51.02N 6.59E
Levice Slovakia 15 48.13N 18.37E
Levin New Zealand 48 40.37S175.18E
Lévis Canada 55 46.49N 71.12W
Lévka Cyprus 32 35.06N 32.51E
Levkás Greece 13 38.50N 20.41E
Levkás i. Greece 13 38.44N 20.37E
Levkosía Cyprus 32 35.11N 33.23E
Lewes U.K. 5 50.53N 0.02E
Lewis i. U.K. 6 58.10N 6.40W
Lewis Pass f. New Zealand 48 42.30S172.15E
Lewis Range mts. U.S.A. 54 48.30N113.15W
Lewiston Idaho U.S.A. 54 46.25N117.01W
Lewiston Maine U.S.A. 55 44.06N 70.13W
Lewistown Mont. U.S.A. 54 47.04N109.26W
Lewistown Penn. U.S.A. 55 40.36N 77.31W
Lexington Ky. U.S.A. 55 38.02N 84.30W
Lexington Oreg. U.S.A. 54 45.27N119.41W
Leyburn U.K. 4 54.19N 1.50W
Leydsdorp R.S.A. 39 23.59S 30.32E
Leyte i. Phil. 27 10.40N124.50E
Lezignan France 11 43.12N 2.46E
Lhasa China 29 29.41N 91.10E
Lhazê China 29 29.10N 87.45E
Lhokseumawe Indonesia 26 5.09N 97.09E
Liangdang China 24 33.56N106.12E
Lianyungang China 25 34.37N119.10E
Liaocheng China 25 36.29N115.55E
Liaodong Bandao pen. China 25 40.00N122.50E
Liaodong Wan b. China 25 40.20N121.00E
Liaoning d. China 25 41.30N123.00E
Liaoyang China 25 41.16N123.12E
Liaoyuan China 25 42.53N125.10E
Liard r. Canada 50 61.56N120.35W
Liart France 9 49.46N 4.20E
Libby U.S.A. 54 48.23N115.33W
Libenge Zaïre 34 3.39N 18.39E
Liberal U.S.A. 52 37.03N100.56W
Liberdade Brazil 59 22.01S 44.22W
Liberec Czech Republic 14 50.48N 15.05E
Liberia Africa 34 6.30N 9.30W
Liberia Costa Rica 57 10.39N 85.28W
Lībīyah, Aş Şahrā' al des. Africa 30 24.00N 25.30E
Libourne France 11 44.55N 0.14W
Libramont Belgium 8 49.56N 5.22E
Libreville Gabon 36 0.30N 9.25E
Libyan Desert see Lībīyah, Aş Şahrā' al Africa 30
Libyan Plateau see Aḑ Ḑiffah f. Africa 30
Licantén Chile 63 34.59S 72.00W
Licata Italy 12 37.07N 13.58E
Lichfield U.K. 5 52.40N 1.50W
Lichinga Mozambique 37 13.09S 35.17E
Lichtenburg R.S.A. 39 26.08S 26.09E
Lichtenvoorde Neth. 8 51.59N 6.32E
Lida Belorussia 15 53.50N 25.19E
Lida U.S.A. 54 37.29N117.29W
Lidköping Sweden 17 58.30N 13.10E
Liechtenstein Europe 14 47.08N 9.35E
Liège Belgium 8 50.38N 5.35E
Liège d. Belgium 8 50.32N 5.35E
Lienz Austria 14 46.50N 12.47E
Liepāja Latvia 17 56.31N 21.01E
Lier Belgium 8 51.08N 4.35E
Lierneux Belgium 8 50.18N 5.50E
Lieşti Romania 15 45.38N 27.32E
Liévin France 8 50.27N 2.49E
Lièvre, Rivière du r. Canada 55 45.31N 75.26W
Liffey r. Rep. of Ire. 7 53.21N 6.14W
Liffré France 9 48.13N 1.30W
Lightning Ridge town Australia 47 29.27S148.00E
Liguria d. Italy 9 42.25N 8.40E
Ligurian Sea Med. Sea 12 43.30N 9.00E
Lihou Reef and Cays Australia 44 17.25S151.40E
Lihue Hawaii U.S.A. 52 21.59N159.23W
Lihula Estonia 17 58.41N 23.50E
Lijiang China 29 26.50N100.15E
Likasi Zaïre 36 10.58S 26.47E
Lille France 8 50.39N 3.05E
Lille Baelt str. Denmark 17 55.20N 9.45E
Lillebonne France 9 49.31N 0.33E
Lillehammer Norway 17 61.08N 10.30E
Lillers France 8 50.34N 2.29E
Lillesand Norway 17 58.15N 8.24E
Lilleström Norway 17 59.57N 11.05E
Lillhärdal Sweden 17 61.51N 14.04E
Lillooet Canada 50 50.42N121.56W
Lilongwe Malaŵi 37 13.58S 33.49E
Liloy Phil. 27 8.08N122.40E
Lilydale Australia 46 32.58S139.59E
Lim r. Bosnia-Herzegovina 13 43.45N 19.13E
Lima Peru 60 12.06S 77.03W
Lima r. Portugal 10 41.40N 8.50W
Lima Sweden 17 60.56N 13.26E
Lima Mont. U.S.A. 54 44.38N112.36W
Lima Ohio U.S.A. 55 40.43N 84.06W
Limassol see Lemesós Cyprus 32
Limavady U.K. 7 55.03N 6.57W
Limay r. Argentina 63 39.02S 68.07W
Limbang Malaysia 26 4.50N115.00E
Limbe Cameroon 38 4.01N 9.12E
Limbourg Belgium 8 50.36N 5.57E
Limburg d. Belgium 8 50.36N 5.57E
Limburg d. Neth. 8 51.15N 5.45E
Limeira Brazil 59 22.34S 47.25W
Limerick Rep. of Ire. 7 52.40N 8.37W
Limerick d. Rep. of Ire. 7 52.40N 8.37W
Limfjorden str. Denmark 17 56.55N 9.10E
Liminka Finland 16 64.49N 25.24E
Limmen Bight Australia 44 14.45S135.40E
Límnos i. Greece 13 39.55N 25.14E
Limoges France 11 45.50N 1.15E
Limogne France 11 44.24N 1.46E
Limón Costa Rica 57 10.00N 83.01W
Limone Piemonte Italy 9 44.12N 7.34E
Limousin d. France 11 45.45N 1.30E
Limpopo r. Mozambique 39 25.14S 33.33E
Līnah Saudi Arabia 31 28.48N 43.45E
Linakhamari Russian Fed. 18 69.39N 31.21E
Linares Chile 63 35.51S 71.36W
Linares Mexico 56 24.54N 99.38W
Linares Spain 10 38.05N 3.38W
Lincang China 24 24.00N100.10E
Lincoln Argentina 63 34.55S 61.30W
Lincoln New Zealand 48 43.38S172.29E
Lincoln U.K. 4 53.14N 0.32W
Lincoln Nebr. U.S.A. 53 40.49N 96.41W
Lincoln N.H. U.S.A. 55 44.03N 71.40W
Lincoln City U.S.A. 54 44.59N124.00W
Lincoln Sea Greenland 64 82.00N 55.00W
Lincolnshire d. U.K. 4 53.14N 0.32W
Lincoln Wolds hills U.K. 4 53.22N 0.08W
Lindeman Group is. Australia 44 20.28S149.05E
Lindesnes c. Norway 17 58.00N 7.02E
Líndhos Greece 13 36.05N 28.02E
Lindi Tanzania 37 10.00S 39.41E
Lindsay Canada 55 44.21N 78.44W
Lindsay U.S.A. 54 36.12N119.05W
Linfen China 25 36.05N111.32E
Lingayen Phil. 27 16.02N120.14E
Lingbo Sweden 17 61.03N 16.41E
Lingen Germany 8 52.32N 7.19E
Lingga i. Indonesia 26 0.20S104.30E
Linguère Senegal 34 15.22N 15.11W
Linköping Sweden 17 58.25N 15.37E
Linnhe, Loch U.K. 6 56.35N 5.25W
Linosa i. Italy 12 35.52N 12.50E
Lins Brazil 59 21.40S 49.44W
Lintan China 24 34.39N103.40E
Linton Ind. U.S.A. 55 39.01N 87.10W
Lintorf Germany 8 51.19N 6.50E
Linxe France 11 43.56N 1.10W
Linxia China 24 35.31N103.08E
Linz Austria 14 48.19N 14.18E
Linz Germany 8 50.34N 7.19E
Lion, Golfe du g. France 11 43.12N 4.15E
Lions, G. of see Lion, Golfe du g. France 11
Lipetsk Russian Fed. 18 52.37N 39.36E
Liphook U.K. 5 51.05N 0.49W
Lipkany Moldavia 15 48.18N 26.48E
Lipova Romania 15 46.05N 21.40E
Lipovets Ukraine 15 49.11N 29.01E
Lippe r. Germany 8 51.38N 6.37E
Lippstadt Germany 14 51.41N 8.20E
Liptovský Mikuláš Slovakia 15 49.06N 19.37E
Liptrap, C. Australia 47 38.53S145.55E
Lira Uganda 37 2.15N 32.55E
Liri r. Italy 12 41.12N 13.45E
Liria Spain 10 39.37N 0.35W
Lisala Zaïre 35 2.08N 21.37E
Lisboa Portugal 10 38.44N 9.08W
Lisbon see Lisboa Portugal 10
Lisburn U.K. 7 54.30N 6.03W
Lisburne, C. U.S.A. 50 69.00N165.50W
Liscannor B. Rep. of Ire. 7 52.55N 9.24W
Lishui China 25 28.30N119.59E
Lisichansk Ukraine 19 48.53N 38.25E
Lisieux France 9 49.09N 0.14E
Liskeard U.K. 5 50.27N 4.29W
Liski Russian Fed. 19 51.00N 39.30E
Lismore N.S.W. Australia 47 28.48S153.17E
Lismore Vic. Australia 46 37.58S143.22E
Lismore Rep. of Ire. 7 52.08N 7.57W
Liss U.K. 5 51.03N 0.53W
Lisse Neth. 8 52.18N 4.33E
Listowel Rep. of Ire. 7 52.27N 9.30W
Litang Qu r. China 29 28.09N101.30E
Lithgow Australia 47 33.30S150.09E
Lithuania Europe 18 55.30N 24.00E
Little Andaman i. India 29 10.50N 92.38E
Little Belt Mts. U.S.A. 54 46.45N110.35W
Little Cayman i. Cayman Is. 57 19.40N 80.00W
Little Coco i. Burma 26 13.50N 93.10E
Little Colorado r. U.S.A. 54 36.11N111.48W
Little Current r. Canada 55 50.57N 84.36W
Little Current town Canada 55 45.58N 81.56W
Little Falls town N.Y. U.S.A. 55 43.03N 74.52W
Littlehampton U.K. 5 50.48N 0.32W
Little Inagua i. Bahamas 57 21.30N 73.00W
Little Karoo f. R.S.A. 39 33.40S 21.40E
Little Lake town U.S.A. 54 35.58N117.53W
Little Missouri r. U.S.A. 52 47.30N102.25W
Little Nicobar i. India 29 7.20N 93.40E
Little Ouse r. U.K. 5 52.34N 0.20E
Little Rock town U.S.A. 53 34.42N 92.17W
Little Topar Australia 46 31.44S142.14E
Liuli Tanzania 37 11.07S 34.34E
Liuzhou China 25 24.17N109.15E
Livarot France 9 49.01N 0.09E
Livermore, Mt. U.S.A. 52 30.39N104.11W
Liverpool Australia 47 33.57S150.52E
Liverpool Canada 51 44.03N 64.43W
Liverpool U.K. 4 53.25N 3.00W
Liverpool, C. Canada 51 73.38N 78.06W
Liverpool B. U.K. 4 53.30N 3.10W
Liverpool Range mts. Australia 47 31.45S150.45E
Livingston U.K. 6 55.54N 3.31W
Livingston Mont. U.S.A. 54 45.40N110.34W
Livingstone see Maramba Zambia 39
Livingstonia Malaŵi 37 10.35S 34.10E
Livo r. Finland 16 65.24N 26.48E
Livorno Italy 12 43.33N 10.18E
Liwale Tanzania 37 9.47S 38.00E
Lizard U.K. 5 49.58N 5.12W
Lizard I. Australia 44 14.39S145.28E
Lizard Pt. U.K. 5 49.57N 5.15W
Ljubljana Slovenia 12 46.04N 14.28E
Ljugarn Sweden 17 57.19N 18.42E
Ljungan r. Sweden 17 62.19N 17.23E
Ljungby Sweden 17 56.50N 13.56E
Ljungdalen Sweden 16 62.54N 12.45E
Ljusdal Sweden 17 61.50N 16.05E
Ljusnan r. Sweden 17 61.12N 17.08E
Ljusne Sweden 17 61.13N 17.08E
Llandeilo U.K. 5 51.54N 4.00W
Llandovery U.K. 5 51.59N 3.49W
Llandrindod Wells U.K. 5 52.15N 3.23W
Llandudno U.K. 4 53.19N 3.49W
Llanelli U.K. 5 51.41N 4.11W
Llanes Spain 10 43.25N 4.45W
Llangadfan U.K. 5 52.41N 3.28W
Llangollen U.K. 4 52.58N 3.10W
Llanidloes U.K. 5 52.28N 3.31W
Llanos f. S. America 60 7.30N 70.00W
Llanwrtyd Wells U.K. 5 52.06N 3.39W
Lleida see Lérida Spain 10
Llerena Spain 10 38.14N 6.00W
Lloret de Mar Spain 10 41.41N 2.53E
Lloydminster Canada 50 53.18N110.00W
Lobatse Botswana 39 25.12S 25.39E
Löbau Germany 14 51.05N 14.40E
Lobería Argentina 63 38.08S 58.48W
Lobito Angola 36 12.20S 13.34E
Lobonäs Sweden 17 61.33N 15.20E
Lobos Argentina 63 35.10S 59.05W
Locarno Switz. 14 46.10N 8.48E
Lochboisdale town U.K. 6 57.09N 7.19W
Lochem Neth. 8 52.10N 6.25E
Loches France 11 47.08N 1.00E
Lochgilphead U.K. 6 56.02N 5.26W
Lochinver U.K. 6 58.09N 5.15W
Lochmaddy town U.K. 6 57.36N 7.10W
Lochnagar mtn. U.K. 6 56.57N 3.15W
Lochranza U.K. 6 55.42N 5.18W
Lochy, Loch U.K. 6 56.58N 4.55W
Lock Australia 46 33.34S135.46E
Lockerbie U.K. 6 55.07N 3.21W
Lockhart Australia 47 35.16S146.42E
Lockhart, L. Australia 43 33.27S119.00E
Lockhart River town Australia 44 12.58S143.29E
Lock Haven U.S.A. 55 41.08N 77.27W
Lockport U.S.A. 55 43.11N 78.39W
Loc Ninh Vietnam 26 11.55N106.35E
Lodalskåpa mtn. Norway 17 61.47N 7.13E
Loddon r. Australia 46 35.40S143.59E
Lodeynoye Pole Russian Fed. 18 60.43N 33.30E
Lodge Grass U.S.A. 54 45.19N107.22W
Lodhrān Pakistan 28 29.32N 71.38E
Lodi Italy 9 45.19N 9.30E
Lodi Calif. U.S.A. 54 38.08N121.16W
Lodja Zaïre 36 3.29S 23.33E
Lodwar Kenya 37 3.06N 35.38E
Łódź Poland 15 51.49N 19.28E
Lofoten Vesterålen is. Norway 16 68.15N 13.50E
Log Russian Fed. 19 49.28N 43.51E
Loga Niger 38 13.40N 3.15E
Logan Utah U.S.A. 54 41.44N111.50W
Logan, Mt. Canada 50 60.45N140.00W
Logansport U.S.A. 55 40.45N 86.25W
Logone r. Cameroon / Chad 34 12.10N 15.00E
Logoysk Belorussia 15 54.08N 27.42E
Logroño Spain 10 42.28N 2.26W
Lögstör Denmark 17 56.58N 9.15E
Lohja Finland 17 60.15N 24.05E
Lohjanjärvi l. Finland 17 60.15N 23.55E
Loimaa Finland 17 60.51N 23.03E
Loir r. France 9 47.29N 0.32W
Loire r. France 9 47.18N 2.00W
Loiret d. France 9 47.55N 2.20E
Loir-et-Cher d. France 9 47.30N 1.30E
Loja Ecuador 60 3.59S 79.16W
Loja Spain 10 37.10N 4.09W
Löken Norway 17 59.48N 11.29E
Loken tekojärvi resr. Finland 16 67.55N 27.40E
Lokeren Belgium 8 51.06N 3.59E
Lokichar Kenya 37 2.23N 35.39E
Lokitaung Kenya 37 4.15N 35.45E
Lokka Finland 16 67.49N 27.44E
Løkken Denmark 17 57.22N 9.43E
Lökken Norway 16 63.06N 9.43E
Loknya Russian Fed. 18 56.49N 30.00E
Lokoja Nigeria 38 7.49N 6.44E
Lolland i. Denmark 17 54.46N 11.30E
Lom Bulgaria 15 43.49N 23.13E
Lom Norway 17 61.50N 8.33E
Loma U.S.A. 54 47.57N110.30W
Lomas de Zamora Argentina 63 34.46S 58.24W
Lombardia d. Italy 9 45.25N 10.00E
Lombok i. Indonesia 26 8.30S116.20E
Lomé Togo 38 6.10N 1.21E
Lomela Zaïre 36 2.15S 23.15E
Lomié Cameroon 38 3.09N 13.35E
Lomme France 8 50.38N 2.59E
Lommel Belgium 8 51.15N 5.18E
Lomond, Loch U.K. 6 56.07N 4.36W
Lompoc U.S.A. 54 34.38N120.27W
Łomża Poland 15 53.11N 22.04E
Londinières France 9 49.50N 1.24E
London Canada 55 42.59N 81.14W
London U.K. 5 51.32N 0.06W
Londonderry U.K. 7 55.00N 7.21W
Londonderry d. U.K. 7 55.00N 7.00W
Londonderry, C. Australia 42 13.58S126.55E
Londonderry, Isla i. Chile 63 55.03S 70.40W
Londrina Brazil 62 23.30S 51.13W
Lone Pine U.S.A. 54 36.36N118.04W
Longa, Proliv str. Russian Fed. 21 70.00N178.00E
Longarone Italy 9 46.16N 12.18E
Long Beach town Calif. U.S.A. 54 33.46N118.11W
Longchamps Belgium 8 50.05N 5.42E
Long Creek town U.S.A. 54 44.43N119.06W
Long Eaton U.K. 4 52.54N 1.16W
Longford Rep. of Ire. 7 53.44N 7.48W
Longford d. Rep. of Ire. 7 53.42N 7.45W
Long I. Bahamas 57 23.00N 75.00W
Long I. U.S.A. 55 40.46N 73.00W
Longido Tanzania 37 2.43S 36.41E
Longiram Indonesia 26 0.05S115.45E
Long L. Canada 55 49.29N 86.44W
Longlac town Canada 55 49.47N 86.24W
Longnawan Indonesia 26 1.54N114.53E
Longniddry U.K. 6 55.58N 2.53W
Longquan China 25 28.05N119.07E
Longreach Australia 44 23.26S144.15E
Longs Peak U.S.A. 52 40.15N105.37W
Longtown U.K. 4 55.01N 2.58W
Longué France 9 47.23N 0.06W
Longuyon France 8 49.27N 5.35E
Longview Tex. U.S.A. 53 32.30N 94.45W
Longview Wash. U.S.A. 54 46.08N122.57W
Longwy France 8 49.32N 5.46E
Longxi China 24 35.00N105.00E
Long Xuyen Vietnam 26 10.23N105.25E
Lonigo Italy 9 45.23N 11.23E
Löningen Germany 8 52.44N 7.46E
Lönsdal Norway 16 66.46N 15.26E
Lonsdale, L. Australia 46 37.05S142.15E
Lons-le-Saunier France 11 46.40N 5.33E
Looc Phil. 27 12.20N122.05E
Looe U.K. 5 50.51N 4.26W
Lookout, C. U.S.A. 53 34.34N 76.34W
Loolmalassin mtn. Tanzania 37 3.00S 35.45E
Loop Head Rep. of Ire. 7 52.33N 9.56W
Lop Buri Thailand 26 14.49N100.37E
Lopez, C. Gabon 36 0.36S 8.45E
Lop Nur l. China 24 40.30N 90.30E
Lopphavet est. Norway 16 70.30N 20.00E
Lopydino Russian Fed. 18 61.10N 52.02E
Lora Creek r. Australia 46 28.10S135.22E
Lorain U.S.A. 55 41.28N 82.11W
Loralai Pakistan 28 30.20N 68.41E
Lorca Spain 10 37.40N 1.41W
Lordsburg U.S.A. 52 32.21N108.43W
Lorena Brazil 59 22.44S 45.07W
Lorengau P.N.G. 27 2.01S147.15E
Lorenzo Geyres Uruguay 63 32.05S 57.55W
Loreto Brazil 61 7.05S 45.09W
Loreto Italy 12 43.26N 13.36E
Lorian Swamp Kenya 37 0.35N 39.40E
Lorient France 11 47.45N 3.21W
Lormes France 9 47.17N 3.49E
Lorne Australia 46 38.34S144.01E
Lorraine d. France 11 49.00N 6.20E
Lorris France 9 47.53N 2.31E
Lorup Germany 8 52.58N 7.39E
Los Andes Chile 63 32.50S 70.37W
Los Angeles Chile 63 37.28S 72.21W
Los Angeles U.S.A. 52 34.00N118.17W
Los Banos U.S.A. 54 37.04N120.51W
Los Blancos Argentina 62 23.40S 62.35W
Los Blancos Spain 10 37.37N 0.48W
Los Canarreos, Archipiélago de Cuba 57 21.40N 82.30W
Lošinj i. Croatia 12 44.36N 14.20E
Losinovka Ukraine 15 50.50N 31.57E
Los Mochis Mexico 56 25.45N108.57W
Los Olivos U.S.A. 54 34.40N120.06W
Los Roques is. Venezuela 60 12.00N 67.00W
Lossiemouth U.K. 6 57.43N 3.18W
Lost Cabin U.S.A. 54 43.19N107.36W
Los Teques Venezuela 60 10.25N 67.01W
Los Vilos Chile 62 31.55S 71.31W
Lot r. France 11 44.17N 0.22E
Lota Chile 63 37.05S 73.10W
Lotagipi Swamp Sudan 36 4.36N 34.55E
Lothian d. U.K. 6 55.50N 3.00W
Lotsani r. Botswana 39 22.42S 28.11E
Lötschberg Tunnel Switz. 11 46.25N 7.53E
Louang Namtha Laos 29 20.57N101.25E
Louangphrabang Laos 29 19.53N102.10E
Loubomo Congo 36 4.09S 12.40E
Loudéac France 11 48.11N 2.45W
Loué France 9 48.00N 0.09W
Loughborough U.K. 4 52.47N 1.11W
Loughrea Rep. of Ire. 7 53.12N 8.35W
Loughros More B. Rep. of Ire. 7 54.48N 8.32W
Louisburgh Rep. of Ire. 7 53.46N 9.49W
Louisiade Archipelago is. P.N.G. 44 11.00S153.00E
Louisiana d. U.S.A. 53 31.00N 92.30W
Louis Trichardt R.S.A. 39 23.03S 29.54E
Louisville Ky. U.S.A. 55 38.13N 85.48W
Loukhi Russian Fed. 18 66.05N 33.04E
Loulé Portugal 10 37.08N 8.02W
Loum Cameroon 38 4.46N 9.45E
Lourches France 8 50.19N 3.20E
Lourdes France 11 43.06N 0.02W
Louth Australia 47 30.34S145.09E
Louth d. Rep. of Ire. 7 53.55N 6.30W
Louth U.K. 4 53.23N 0.00
Louviers France 9 49.13N 1.10E
Louvigné-du-Désert France 9 48.29N 1.08W
Lövånger Sweden 16 64.22N 21.18E
Lovat r. Russian Fed. 18 58.06N 31.37E
Lovech Bulgaria 13 43.08N 24.44E
Lovell U.S.A. 54 44.50N108.24W
Lovelock U.S.A. 54 40.11N118.28W
Lovere Italy 9 45.49N 10.04E
Lovoi r. Zaïre 37 8.14S 26.40E
Lovozero Russian Fed. 18 68.01N 35.08E
Lovrin Romania 15 45.58N 20.48E
Lowell U.S.A. 55 42.39N 71.18W
Lower California pen. see Baja California pen. Mexico 56
Lower Egypt see Mişr Baḩrī f. Egypt 32
Lower Hutt New Zealand 48 41.13S174.55E
Lower Lough Erne U.K. 7 54.28N 7.48W
Lowestoft U.K. 5 52.29N 1.44E
Łowicz Poland 15 52.06N 19.55E
Loxton Australia 46 34.38S140.38E
Loyauté, Îles is. N. Cal. 40 21.00S167.00E
Loyoro Uganda 37 3.22N 34.16E
Loznica Yugo. 13 44.32N 19.13E
Luachimo Angola 36 7.25S 20.43E
Lualaba r. Zaïre 36 0.18N 25.30E
Luama r. Zaïre 37 4.45S 26.55E
Luanda Angola 36 8.50S 13.20E
Luangwa r. Zambia 37 15.32S 30.28E
Luanshya Zambia 37 13.09S 28.24E
Luan Xian China 25 39.45N118.44E
Luapula r. Zambia 37 9.25S 28.36E
Luarca Spain 10 43.33N 6.31W
Luau Angola 36 10.41S 22.09E
Lubango Angola 36 14.55S 13.30E
Lubbock U.S.A. 52 33.35N101.53W
Lubeck Australia 46 36.47S142.38E
Lübeck Germany 14 53.52N 10.40E
Lubenka Kazakhstan 19 50.22N 54.13E
Lubersac France 11 45.27N 1.24E
Lubika Zaïre 37 7.50S 29.12E
Lubin Poland 14 51.24N 16.13E
Lublin Poland 15 51.18N 22.31E
Lubliniec Poland 15 50.40N 18.41E
Lubny Ukraine 19 50.01N 33.00E
Lubumbashi Zaïre 37 11.44S 27.29E
Lucas González Argentina 63 32.25S 59.33W
Lucca Italy 9 43.50N 10.29E
Luce B. U.K. 6 54.45N 4.47W
Lucena Phil. 27 13.56N121.37E
Lucena Spain 10 37.25N 4.29W
Lucena del Cid Spain 10 40.09N 0.17W
Lučenec Slovakia 15 48.20N 19.40E
Lucera Italy 12 41.30N 15.20E
Lucerne U.S.A. 54 48.12N120.36W
Lucero Mexico 56 30.49N106.30W
Lucin U.S.A. 54 41.22N113.55W
Lucindale Australia 46 36.59S140.25E
Luckenwalde Germany 14 52.05N 13.11E
Lucknow India 29 26.50N 80.54E
Lucy Creek town Australia 44 22.25S136.20E
Lüda see Dalian China 25
Lüdenscheid Germany 8 51.13N 7.36E
Lüderitz Namibia 39 26.37S 15.09E
Ludhiāna India 28 30.56N 75.52E
Lüdinghausen Germany 8 51.46N 7.27E
Ludington U.S.A. 55 43.58N 86.27W
Ludlow U.K. 5 52.23N 2.42W
Ludogorie mts. Bulgaria 15 43.45N 27.00E
Luduş Romania 15 46.29N 24.05E
Ludvika Sweden 17 60.09N 15.11E
Ludwigsburg Germany 14 48.53N 9.11E
Ludwigshafen Germany 14 49.29N 8.27E
Luena Angola 36 11.46S 19.55E
Luena Zambia 37 10.40S 30.21E
Lufeng China 25 22.57N115.38E
Lufkin U.S.A. 53 31.21N 94.47W
Luga Russian Fed. 18 58.42N 29.49E
Lugano Switz. 9 46.01N 8.58E
Lugano, Lago di l. Switz./Italy 9 46.00N 9.00E
Lugansk Ukraine 19 48.35N 39.20E
Lugela Mozambique 37 16.25S 36.42E
Lugenda r. Mozambique 37 11.23S 38.30E
Luginy Ukraine 15 51.05N 28.21E
Lugnaquilla Mtn. Rep. of Ire. 7 52.58N 6.28W
Lugo Italy 9 44.25N 11.54E
Lugo Spain 10 43.00N 7.33W
Lugoj Romania 15 45.42N 21.56E
Luiana Angola 39 17.08S 22.59E
Luiana r. Angola 39 17.28S 23.02E
Luino Italy 9 46.00N 8.44E
Luiro r. Finland 16 67.18N 27.28E
Luków Poland 15 51.56N 22.23E
Lukoyanov Russian Fed. 18 55.03N 44.29E
Lukuga r. Zaïre 37 5.37S 26.58E
Lukumbule Tanzania 37 11.34S 37.24E
Lule r. Sweden 16 65.35N 22.03E
Luleå Sweden 16 65.34N 22.10E
Lüleburgaz Turkey 13 41.25N 27.23E
Lulua r. Zaïre 36 5.03S 21.07E
Lumberton N.Mex. U.S.A. 54 36.55N106.56W
Lumsden New Zealand 48 45.44S168.26E
Lund Sweden 17 55.42N 13.11E
Lund Nev. U.S.A. 54 38.52N115.00W
Lund Utah U.S.A. 54 38.01N113.28W
Lundazi Zambia 37 12.19S 33.11E
Lundy i. U.K. 5 51.10N 4.41W
Lune r. U.K. 4 54.03N 2.49W
Lüneburg Germany 14 53.15N 10.24E
Lünen Germany 8 51.37N 7.31E
Lunéville France 11 48.36N 6.30E
Luninets Belorussia 15 52.18N 26.50E
Luning U.S.A. 54 38.30N118.10W
Luofo Zaïre 37 0.12S 29.15E
Luogosanto Italy 12 41.02N 9.12E
Luoyang China 25 34.48N112.25E
Lupilichi Mozambique 37 11.45S 35.15E
Luquan China 29 25.35N102.30E
Lure France 11 47.42N 6.30E
Lurgan U.K. 7 54.28N 6.21W
Lurio Mozambique 37 13.30S 40.30E
Lurio r. Mozambique 37 13.32S 40.31E
Lusaka Zambia 37 15.20S 28.14E
Lusambo Zaïre 36 4.59S 23.26E

Lushnje Albania 13 40.56N 19.42E
Lushoto Tanzania 37 4.48S 38.20E
Lusk U.S.A. 52 42.46N104.27W
Luton U.K. 5 51.53N 0.25W
Lutsk Ukraine 15 50.42N 25.15E
Lutterworth U.K. 5 52.28N 1.12W
Luud *r.* Somali Rep. 35 10.25N 51.05E
Luuq Somali Rep. 37 3.56N 42.32E
Luvua *r.* Zaïre 37 6.45S 27.00E
Luwegu *r.* Tanzania 37 8.30S 37.28E
Luwingu Zambia 37 10.13S 30.05E
Luxembourg *d.* Belgium 8 49.58N 5.30E
Luxembourg Europe 8 49.50N 6.15E
Luxembourg *town* Lux. 8 49.37N 6.08E
Luxor *see* Al Uqşur Egypt 30
Luza Russian Fed. 18 60.41N 47.12E
Luza *r.* Russian Fed. 18 60.45N 46.25E
Luzarches France 9 49.07N 2.25E
Luzern Switz. 14 47.03N 8.17E
Luzhou China 29 28.25N105.20E
Luziânia Brazil 61 16.18S 47.57W
Luzon *i.* Phil. 27 17.50N121.00E
Luzon Str. Pacific Oc. 27 20.20N122.00E
Lvov Ukraine 15 49.50N 24.00E
Lyantonde Uganda 37 0.26S 31.08E
Lybster U.K. 6 58.18N 3.18W
Lycksele Sweden 16 64.36N 18.40E
Lydenburg R.S.A. 39 25.06S 30.27E
Lyme B. U.K. 5 50.40N 2.55W
Lyme Regis U.K. 5 50.44N 2.57W
Lymington U.K. 5 50.46N 1.32W
Lyna *r.* Poland 15 54.37N 21.14E
Lynchburg U.S.A. 53 37.24N 79.09W
Lyndhurst Australia 46 30.19S138.24E
Lyngdal Norway 17 58.08N 7.05E
Lyngen Norway 16 69.36N 20.10E
Lyngen *est.* Norway 16 69.35N 20.20E
Lynn U.S.A. 55 42.28N 70.57W
Lynn Lake *town* Canada 51 56.51N101.01W
Lynton U.K. 5 51.14N 3.50W
Lynx Canada 55 50.07N 86.00W
Lyon France 11 45.46N 4.50E
Lyons Australia 46 30.34S133.50E
Lyons *r.* Australia 42 25.02S115.09E
Lysefjorden *est.* Norway 17 59.00N 6.14E
Lysekil Sweden 17 58.16N 11.26E
Lysva Russian Fed. 18 58.07N 57.49E
Lysyanka Ukraine 15 49.16N 30.49E
Lysyye Gory Russian Fed. 19 51.32N 44.48E
Lytham St. Anne's U.K. 4 53.45N 3.01W
Lyubar Ukraine 15 49.58N 27.41E
Lyubech Ukraine 15 51.42N 30.41E
Lyubertsy Russian Fed. 18 55.38N 37.58E
Lyubeshov Ukraine 15 51.42N 25.32E
Lyushcha Belorussia 15 52.28N 26.41E

M

Ma *r.* Vietnam 26 19.47N105.56E
Maamakeogh *mtn.* Rep. of Ire. 7 54.17N 9.29W
Maamturk Mts. Rep. of Ire. 7 53.32N 9.42W
Ma'ān Jordan 32 30.11N 35.43E
Maarianhamina Finland 17 60.06N 19.57E
Maas *r.* Neth. 8 51.44N 4.42E
Maaseik Belgium 8 51.08N 5.48E
Maassluis Neth. 8 51.58N 4.12E
Maastricht Neth. 8 50.51N 5.42E
Maave Mozambique 39 21.06S 34.48E
Maaza Plateau Egypt 32 27.39N 31.45E
Mabalane Mozambique 39 23.49S 32.36E
Mablethorpe U.K. 4 53.21N 0.14E
Mabrouk Mali 38 19.29N 1.15W
Macá *mtn.* Chile 63 45.06S 73.12W
Macaé Brazil 59 22.21S 41.48W
Macalister *r.* Australia 47 37.55S146.50E
Macapá Brazil 61 0.04N 51.04W
Macarthur Australia 46 38.01S142.01E
Macau Asia 25 22.11N113.33E
Macau Brazil 61 5.05S 36.37W
Macclesfield U.K. 4 53.16N 2.09W
Macdiarmid Canada 55 49.27N 88.08W
Macdoel U.S.A. 54 41.50N122.00W
Macdonald, L. Australia 42 23.30S129.00E
Macdonnell Ranges *mts.* Australia 44 23.45S133.20E
Macduff U.K. 6 57.40N 2.29W
Macedon, Mt. Australia 47 37.27S144.34E
Macedonia Europe 13 41.35N 21.30E
Maceió Brazil 61 9.40S 35.44W
Macerata Italy 12 43.18N 13.30E
Macfarlane, L. Australia 46 31.55S136.42E
Macgillycuddy's Reeks *mts.* Rep. of Ire. 7 52.00N 9.43W
Machado Brazil 59 21.39S 45.33W
Machala Ecuador 60 3.20S 79.57W
Machattie, L. Australia 44 24.50S139.48E
Machece Mozambique 39 19.17S 35.33E
Macheke Zimbabwe 39 18.08S 31.49E
Macheng China 25 31.11N115.02E
Machevna Russian Fed. 21 60.46N171.40E
Machias Maine U.S.A. 55 44.43N 67.28W
Machida Japan 23 35.32N139.27E
Machilīpatnam India 29 16.13N 81.12E
Machiques Venezuela 60 10.04N 72.37W
Machiya *r.* Japan 23 35.01N136.42E
Machrihanish U.K. 6 55.25N 5.44W
Machynlleth U.K. 5 52.35N 3.51W
Maciá Argentina 63 32.11S 59.25W
Macia Mozambique 39 25.03S 33.10E
Macintyre *r.* Australia 47 28.50S150.50E
Mackay Australia 44 21.09S149.11E
MacKay U.S.A. 54 43.55N113.37W
Mackay, L. Australia 42 22.30S129.10E
Mackenzie *r.* Australia 44 22.48S149.15E
Mackenzie *r.* Canada 50 69.20N134.00W
Mackenzie King I. Canada 50 77.30N112.00W
Mackenzie Mts. Canada 50 64.00N130.00W
Mackinaw City U.S.A. 55 45.47N 84.43W
Mackinnon Road *town* Kenya 37 3.50S 39.03E
Macksville Australia 47 30.43S152.55E
Maclean Australia 45 29.27S153.14E
Maclear R.S.A. 39 31.04S 28.21E
Macleay *r.* Australia 47 30.52S153.01E
MacLeod, L. Australia 42 24.10S113.35E
Maçobere Mozambique 39 21.14S 32.50E
Macomer Italy 12 40.16N 8.45E
Mâcon France 11 46.18N 4.50E
Macon Ga. U.S.A. 53 32.47N 83.37W
Macquarie *r.* Australia 47 30.07S147.24E
Macquarie, L. Australia 47 33.05S151.35E
Macquarie Marshes Australia 47 30.50S147.32E
MacRobertson Land *f.* Antarctica 64 69.30S 64.00E
Macroom Rep. of Ire. 7 51.54N 8.58W
Macumba *r.* Australia 45 27.55S137.15E
Ma'dabā Jordan 32 31.44N 35.48E
Madagascar Africa 36 17.00S 46.00E
Madang P.N.G. 27 5.14S145.45E
Madaoua Niger 38 14.05N 6.27E
Madawaska U.S.A. 55 47.21N 68.20W
Madeira *i.* Atlantic Oc. 34 32.45N 17.00W
Madeira *r.* Brazil 60 3.20S 59.00W
Madeira, Arquipélago da *is.* Atlantic Oc. 34 32.40N 16.45W
Madeleine, Îles de la *is.* Canada 51 47.30N 61.45W
Madera U.S.A. 54 36.57N120.03W
Madgaon India 28 15.26N 73.50E
Madhya Pradesh *d.* India 29 23.00N 79.30E
Madibira Tanzania 37 8.13S 34.47E
Madigan G. Australia 46 28.55S137.48E
Madison Fla. U.S.A. 53 30.29N 83.39W
Madison Ind. U.S.A. 55 38.46N 85.22W
Madison Wisc. U.S.A. 53 43.04N 89.22W
Madison W.Va. U.S.A. 55 38.03N 81.50W
Madison Junction U.S.A. 54 44.39N110.51W
Madiun Indonesia 26 7.37S111.33E
Madoc Canada 55 44.30N 77.28W
Mado Gashi Kenya 37 0.40N 39.11E
Madoi China 24 34.28N 98.56E
Madonna di Campiglio Italy 9 46.14N 10.49E
Madrakah, Ra's al *c.* Oman 28 19.00N 57.50E
Madras India 29 13.05N 80.18E
Madras U.S.A. 54 44.38N121.08W
Madre, Laguna *b.* Mexico 56 25.00N 97.30W
Madre, Sierra *mts.* Mexico / Guatemala 56 15.20N 92.20W
Madre de Dios *r.* Bolivia 60 10.24S 65.30W
Madre del Sur, Sierra *mts.* Mexico 56 17.00N100.00W
Madre Occidental, Sierra *mts.* Mexico 56 25.00N105.00W
Madre Oriental, Sierra *mts.* Mexico 56 24.00N 99.00W
Madrid Spain 10 40.25N 3.43W
Madrid *d.* Spain 10 40.45N 3.40W
Madukani Tanzania 37 3.57S 35.49E
Madura *i.* Indonesia 26 7.00S113.30E
Madurai India 29 9.55N 78.07E
Maestra, Sierra *mts.* Cuba 57 20.10N 76.30W
Maevatanana Madagascar 36 16.56S 46.49E
Mafeteng Lesotho 39 29.51S 27.13E
Maffra Australia 47 37.58S146.59E
Mafia I. Tanzania 37 7.50S 39.50E
Mafikeng R.S.A. 39 25.52S 25.36E
Mafra Portugal 10 38.56N 9.20W
Magadan Russian Fed. 21 59.38N150.50E
Magadi Kenya 37 1.53S 36.18E
Magallanes, Estrecho de *str.* Chile 63 53.00S 71.00W
Magalluf Spain 10 39.30N 2.31E
Magangué Colombia 60 9.14N 74.46W
Magdalena Argentina 63 35.04S 57.32W
Magdalena Bolivia 62 13.50S 64.08W
Magdalena *r.* Colombia 60 10.56N 74.58W
Magdalena Mexico 56 30.38N110.59W
Magdalena, Isla *i.* Chile 63 44.42S 73.10W
Magdalene *mtn.* Malaysia 26 4.25N117.55E
Magdeburg Germany 14 52.08N 11.36E
Magé Brazil 59 22.37S 43.03W
Magelang Indonesia 26 7.28S110.11E
Magellan's Str. *see* Magallanes, Estrecho de *str.* Chile 63
Magenta Italy 9 45.28N 8.53E
Magenta, L. Australia 43 33.26S119.10E
Mageröya *i.* Norway 16 71.03N 25.45E
Maggiorasca, Monte *mtn.* Italy 9 44.33N 9.29E
Maggiore, Lago *l.* Italy 9 46.00N 8.40E
Maghâghah Egypt 32 28.39N 30.50E
Magherafelt U.K. 7 54.45N 6.38W
Magna U.S.A. 54 40.42N112.06W
Magnetic I. Australia 44 19.08S146.50E
Magnitogorsk Russian Fed. 18 53.28N 59.06E
Magny-en-Vexin France 9 49.09N 1.47E
Magog Canada 55 45.16N 72.09W
Magude Mozambique 39 25.01S 32.39E
Magué Mozambique 37 15.46S 31.42E
Magwe Burma 29 20.10N 95.00E
Mahābād Iran 31 36.44N 45.44E
Mahadday Weyne Somali Rep. 37 2.58N 45.32E
Mahagi Zaïre 37 2.16N 30.59E
Mahajanga Madagascar 36 15.43S 46.19E
Mahalapye Botswana 39 23.04S 26.47E
Maḩallāt Iran 31 33.54N 50.28E
Mahānadi *r.* India 29 20.17N 86.43E
Mahārāshtra *d.* India 28 20.00N 77.00E
Mahd adh Dhahab Saudi Arabia 30 23.30N 40.52E
Mahdia Guyana 60 5.10N 59.12W
Mahenge Tanzania 37 8.46S 36.38E
Mahia Pen. New Zealand 48 39.10S177.50E
Maho Sri Lanka 29 7.49N 80.17E
Mahón Spain 10 39.55N 4.18E
Maidenhead U.K. 5 51.32N 0.44W
Maidstone U.K. 5 51.17N 0.32E
Maiduguri Nigeria 38 11.53N 13.16E
Maignelay France 9 49.33N 2.31E
Maihar India 29 24.14N 80.50E
Main *r.* Germany 14 50.00N 8.19E
Main Channel *str.* Canada 55 45.22N 81.50W
Mai Ndombe *l.* Zaïre 36 2.00S 18.20E
Maine *d.* U.S.A. 55 45.15N 69.15W
Mainland *i.* Orkney Is. U.K. 6 59.00N 3.10W
Mainoru Australia 44 14.02S134.05E
Maintenon France 9 48.35N 1.35E
Mainz Germany 14 50.00N 8.16E
Maipo *mtn.* Argentina 63 34.10S 69.50W
Maipú Argentina 63 36.52S 57.54W
Maiquetía Venezuela 60 10.03N 66.57W
Maitland N.S.W. Australia 47 32.33S151.33E
Maitland S.A. Australia 46 34.21S137.42E
Majene Indonesia 26 3.33S118.59E
Majorca *i.* *see* Mallorca *i.* Spain 10
Majrūr Sudan 35 15.03N 30.31E
Majuba Hill R.S.A. 39 27.26S 29.48E
Makale Indonesia 26 3.06S119.53E
Makarikha Russian Fed. 18 66.17N 58.28E
Makaryev Russian Fed. 18 57.52N 43.40E
Makasar, Selat *str.* Indonesia 26 3.00S118.00E
Makassar Str. *see* Makasar, Selat *str.* Indonesia 26
Makat Kazakhstan 19 47.38N 53.16E
Makedonija *see* Macedonia Europe 13
Makere Tanzania 37 4.15S 30.26E
Makeyevka Ukraine 19 48.01N 38.00E
Makgadikgadi Salt Pan *f.* Botswana 39 20.50S 25.45E
Makhachkala Russian Fed. 19 42.59N 47.30E
Makhfar al Quwayrah Jordan 32 29.49N 35.18E
Makhrūq, Wādī al *r.* Jordan 32 31.30N 37.10E
Makinsk Kazakhstan 20 52.40N 70.28E
Makkah Saudi Arabia 35 21.26N 39.49E
Makó Hungary 15 46.13N 20.30E
Makokou Gabon 36 0.38N 12.47E
Makran *f.* Asia 31 26.30N 61.20E
Makrān Coast Range *mts.* Pakistan 28 25.40N 64.00E
Maksamaa Finland 16 63.14N 22.05E
Makuliro Tanzania 37 9.34S 37.26E
Makurdi Nigeria 38 7.44N 8.35E
Malabo Equat. Guinea 38 3.45N 8.48E
Malacca *see* Melaka Malaysia 26
Malacca, Str. of Indian Oc. 26 3.00N100.30E
Malad City U.S.A. 54 42.12N112.15W
Málaga Spain 10 36.43N 4.25W
Malakāl Sudan 35 9.31N 31.40E
Malakand Pakistan 28 34.34N 71.57E
Malang Indonesia 26 7.59S112.45E
Malanje Angola 36 9.36S 16.21E
Mälaren *l.* Sweden 17 59.30N 17.12E
Malartic Canada 55 48.09N 78.09W
Malatya Turkey 30 38.22N 38.18E
Malaŵi Africa 37 12.00S 34.00E
Malaŵi, L. Africa 37 12.00S 34.30E
Malaya Vishera Russian Fed. 18 58.53N 32.08E
Malāyer Iran 31 34.19N 48.51E
Malaysia Asia 26 5.00N110.00E
Malazgirt Turkey 30 39.09N 42.31E
Malbaie *r.* Canada 55 47.39N 70.09W
Malbooma Australia 46 30.41S134.11E
Malbork Poland 15 54.02N 19.01E
Malcolm Australia 43 28.56S121.30E
Malcolm, Pt. Australia 43 33.47S123.44E
Maldives Indian Oc. 28 6.20N 73.00E
Maldon U.K. 5 51.43N 0.41E
Maldonado Uruguay 59 34.57S 54.59W
Male Italy 9 46.21N 10.55E
Maléa, Ákra *c.* Greece 13 36.27N 23.11E
Mālegaon India 28 20.32N 74.38E
Malekula *i.* Vanuatu 40 16.15S167.30E
Malema Mozambique 37 14.55S 37.09E
Malenga Russian Fed. 18 63.50N 36.50E
Malesherbes France 9 48.18N 2.25E
Malgomaj *l.* Sweden 16 64.47N 16.12E
Malheur L. U.S.A. 54 43.20N118.45W
Mali Africa 34 17.30N 2.30E
Malili Indonesia 27 2.38S121.06E
Malin Ukraine 15 50.48N 29.08E
Malinau Indonesia 26 3.35N116.38E
Malindi Kenya 37 3.14S 40.08E
Malin Head Rep. of Ire. 7 55.23N 7.24W
Malin More Rep. of Ire. 7 54.42N 8.48W
Malita Phil. 27 6.19N125.39E
Mallacoota Australia 47 37.34S149.43E
Mallacoota Inlet *b.* Australia 47 37.34S149.43E
Mallaig U.K. 6 57.00N 5.50W
Mallawi Egypt 32 27.44N 30.50E
Mallorca *i.* Spain 10 39.35N 3.00E
Mallow Rep. of Ire. 7 52.08N 8.39W
Malm Norway 16 64.04N 11.12E
Malmberget Sweden 16 67.10N 20.40E
Malmédy Belgium 8 50.25N 6.02E
Malmesbury R.S.A. 39 33.28S 18.43E
Malmö Sweden 17 55.36N 13.00E
Malmöhus *d.* Sweden 17 55.45N 13.30E
Malmyzh Russian Fed. 18 56.34N 50.41E
Maloja Switz. 9 46.24N 9.41E
Malone U.S.A. 55 44.51N 74.17W
Malonga Zaïre 36 10.26S 23.10E
Malorita Belorussia 15 51.50N 24.08E
Målöy Norway 17 61.56N 5.07E
Malozemelskaya Tundra *f.* Russian Fed. 18 67.40N 50.10E
Malpas Australia 46 34.44S140.43E
Malta Europe 12 35.55N 14.25E
Malta Mont. U.S.A. 54 48.21N107.52W
Malta Channel Med. Sea 12 36.20N 14.45E
Maltby U.K. 4 53.25N 1.12W
Malton U.K. 4 54.09N 0.48W
Maluku *d.* Indonesia 27 4.00S129.00E
Maluku, Laut *sea* Pacific Oc. 27
Malumfashi Nigeria 38 11.48N 7.36E
Malung Sweden 17 60.40N 13.44E
Malvérnia Mozambique 36 22.06S 31.42E
Malvinas, Islas *see* Falkland Is. Atlantic Ocean 63
Mama Russian Fed. 21 58.20N112.55E
Mamadysh Russian Fed. 18 55.43N 51.20E
Mamaia Romania 15 44.15N 28.37E
Mambasa Zaïre 37 1.20N 29.05E
Mamberamo *r.* Indonesia 27 1.45S137.25E
Mambilima Falls *town* Zambia 37 10.32S 28.45E
Mamers France 9 48.21N 0.23E
Mamfe Cameroon 38 5.46N 9.18E
Mamonovo Russian Fed. 15 54.30N 19.59E
Mamore *r.* Bolivia 62 12.00S 65.15W
Mampong Ghana 38 7.06N 1.24W
Mamry, Jezioro *l.* Poland 15 54.08N 21.42E
Mamuju Indonesia 26 2.41S118.55E
Man Ivory Coast 34 7.31N 7.37W
Man, Isle of Europe 4 54.15N 4.30W
Mana *r.* Guiana 61 5.35N 53.55W
Manacapuru Brazil 60 3.16S 60.37W
Manacor Spain 10 39.32N 3.12E
Manado Indonesia 27 1.30N124.58E
Managua Nicaragua 57 12.06N 86.18W
Managua, Lago de *l.* Nicaragua 57 12.10N 86.30W
Manakara Madagascar 36 22.08S 48.01E
Manangatang Australia 46 35.02S142.54E
Manapouri, L. New Zealand 48 45.30S167.00E
Manau P.N.G. 27 8.02S148.00E
Manaus Brazil 60 3.06S 60.00W
Manawatu-Wanganui *d.* New Zealand 48 39.00S175.25E
Mancelona U.S.A. 55 44.54N 85.03W
Manche *d.* France 9 49.00N 1.10W
Manchester U.K. 4 53.30N 2.15W
Manchester Conn. U.S.A. 55 41.47N 72.31W
Manchester N.H. U.S.A. 55 42.59N 71.28W
Manchurian Plain *f.* *see* Dongbei Pingyuan *f.* China 25
Mancia Mozambique 36 19.04S 33.29E
Mand *r.* Iran 31 28.09N 51.16E
Manda Iringa Tanzania 37 10.30S 34.37E
Manda Mbeya Tanzania 37 7.59S 32.27E
Manda, Jabal *mtn.* Sudan 35 8.39N 24.27E
Mandal Norway 17 58.02N 7.27E
Mandala Peak Indonesia 27 4.45S140.15E
Mandalay Burma 29 21.57N 96.04E
Mandalgovi Mongolia 24 45.40N106.10E
Mandals *r.* Norway 17 58.02N 7.28E
Mandan U.S.A. 52 46.50N100.54W
Mandara Mts. Nigeria / Cameroon 38 10.30N 13.30E
Mandera Kenya 37 3.55N 41.50E
Mandora Australia 42 19.45S120.50E
Mandurah Australia 43 32.31S115.41E
Manduria Italy 13 40.24N 17.38E
Mandya India 28 12.33N 76.54E
Måne *r.* Norway 17 59.55N 8.48E
Manerbio Italy 9 45.21N 10.08E
Manevichi Ukraine 15 51.19N 25.35E
Manfredonia Italy 12 41.38N 15.54E
Manfredonia, Golfo di *g.* Italy 12 41.35N 16.05E
Mangalia Romania 15 43.50N 28.35E
Mangalore India 28 12.54N 74.51E
Mangaweka New Zealand 48 38.49S175.48E
Mangnai China 24 37.52N 91.26E
Mango Togo 38 10.23N 0.30E
Mangochi Malaŵi 37 14.29S 35.15E
Mangoky *r.* Madagascar 36 21.29S 43.41E
Mangonui New Zealand 48 35.00S173.34E
Mangueira, L. Brazil 59 33.06S 52.48W
Mangyshlak, Poluostrov *pen.* Kazakhstan 19 44.00N 52.30E
Manhiça Mozambique 39 25.24S 32.49E
Manhuaçu Brazil 59 20.16S 42.01W
Manhumirim Brazil 59 20.22S 41.57W
Maniago Italy 9 46.10N 12.43E
Maniamba Mozambique 37 12.30S 35.05E
Manica Mozambique 39 19.00S 33.00E
Manica *d.* Mozambique 39 20.00S 34.00E
Manicoré Brazil 60 5.49S 61.17W
Manicouagan *r.* Canada 55 49.15N 68.20W
Manicouagan, Résr. Canada 51 51.20N 68.48W
Maniitsoq *see* Sukkertoppen Greenland 51
Manila Phil. 27 14.36N120.59E
Manila U.S.A. 54 40.59N109.43W
Manildra Australia 47 33.12S148.41E
Manilla Australia 47 30.45S150.45E
Manipur *d.* India 29 25.00N 93.40E
Manisa Turkey 13 38.37N 27.28E
Manistee U.S.A. 55 44.14N 86.20W
Manistee *r.* U.S.A. 55 44.14N 86.20W
Manistique U.S.A. 55 45.58N 86.17W
Manitoba *d.* Canada 51 54.00N 96.00W
Manitoba, L. Canada 51 51.35N 99.00W
Manitoulin I. Canada 55 45.45N 82.30W
Maniwaki Canada 55 46.22N 75.58W
Manizales Colombia 60 5.03N 75.32W
Mānjhand Pakistan 28 25.50N 68.10E
Manjil Iran 31 36.44N 49.29E
Manjimup Australia 43 34.14S116.06E
Mankato U.S.A. 53 44.10N 94.00W
Mankono Ivory Coast 38 8.01N 6.09W
Manly Australia 47 33.47S151.17E
Mann *r.* Australia 44 12.20S134.07E
Mann *r.* Australia 47 29.38S152.21E
Mân Na Burma 29 23.30N 97.13E
Manna Indonesia 26 4.27S102.55E
Mannahill Australia 46 32.26S139.59E
Mannar Sri Lanka 29 8.59N 79.54E
Mannar, G. of India / Sri Lanka 29 8.20N 79.00E
Mannheim Germany 14 49.30N 8.28E
Mannin B. Rep. of Ire. 7 53.28N 10.06W
Mannu *r.* Sardegna Italy 12 39.16N 9.00E
Mannum Australia 46 34.50S139.20E
Manokwari Indonesia 27 0.53S134.05E
Manono Zaïre 37 7.18S 27.24E
Manorhamilton Rep. of Ire. 7 54.18N 8.10W
Manosque France 11 43.50N 5.47E
Manouane *r.* Canada 55 49.29N 71.13W
Manouane, Lac *l.* Canada 55 50.40N 70.45W
Mānpur India 29 20.22N 80.44E
Manresa Spain 10 41.43N 1.50E
Mansa Zambia 37 11.10S 28.52E
Mansel I. Canada 51 62.00N 80.00W
Mansfield U.K. 4 53.08N 1.12W
Mansfield Mass. U.S.A. 55 42.02N 71.13W
Mansfield Ohio U.S.A. 55 40.46N 82.31W
Manso *r.* Brazil 62 11.59S 50.25W
Manta Ecuador 60 0.59S 80.44W
Mantaro *r.* Peru 60 12.00S 74.00W
Manteca U.S.A. 54 37.48N121.13W
Mantes France 9 49.00N 1.41E
Mantiqueira, Serra da *mts.* Brazil 59 22.25S 45.00W
Mantova Italy 9 45.09N 10.47E
Mänttä Finland 17 62.02N 24.38E
Manturovo Russian Fed. 18 58.20N 44.42E
Mäntyluoto Finland 17 61.35N 21.29E
Manú Peru 60 12.14S 70.51W
Manui *i.* Indonesia 27 3.35S123.08E
Manukau New Zealand 48 36.59S174.53E
Manukau Harbour *est.* New Zealand 48 37.10S174.00E
Manunda Creek *r.* Australia 46 32.50S138.58E
Manus *i.* P.N.G. 27 2.00S147.00E
Manyane Botswana 39 23.23S 21.44E
Manyara, L. Tanzania 37 3.40S 35.50E
Manych *r.* Russian Fed. 19 47.14N 40.20E
Manych Gudilo, Ozero *l.* Russian Fed. 19 46.20N 42.45E
Manyoni Tanzania 37 5.46S 34.50E
Manzanares Spain 10 39.00N 3.23W
Manzanillo Cuba 57 20.21N 77.21W
Manzhouli China 25 49.36N117.28E
Manzilah, Buḩayrat al *l.* Egypt 32 31.20N 32.00E
Manzini Swaziland 39 26.29S 31.24E
Mao Chad 38 14.06N 15.11E
Maoke, Pegunungan *mts.* Indonesia 27 4.00S137.30E
Maoming China 25 21.50N110.56E
Mapai Mozambique 39 22.51S 32.00E
Mapi Indonesia 27 7.06S139.23E
Mapia, Kepulauan *is.* Indonesia 27 1.00N134.15E
Mapinhane Mozambique 39 22.19S 35.03E
Mapire Venezuela 60 7.46N 64.41W
Maple Creek *town* Canada 50 49.55N109.27W
Maprik P.N.G. 27 3.38S143.02E
Mapuera *r.* Brazil 61 2.00S 55.40W
Maputo Mozambique 39 25.58S 32.35E
Maputo *d.* Mozambique 39 26.00S 32.30E
Maqnā Saudi Arabia 32 28.26N 34.44E
Maqu China 29 34.05N102.15E
Maquela do Zombo Angola 36 6.06S 15.12E
Maquinchao Argentina 63 41.15S 68.44W
Mar, Serra do *mts.* Brazil 59 23.00S 44.40W
Mara Tanzania 37 1.30S 34.31E
Mara *d.* Tanzania 37 1.45S 34.30E
Mara *r.* Tanzania 37 1.30S 33.52E
Maraã Brazil 60 1.50S 65.22W
Marabá Brazil 61 5.23S 49.10W
Marabastad R.S.A. 39 23.58S 29.21E
Maracaibo Venezuela 60 10.44N 71.37W
Maracaibo, Lago de *l.* Venezuela 60 9.50N 71.30W
Maracaju, Serra de *mts.* Brazil 59 21.38S 55.10W
Maracay Venezuela 60 10.20N 67.28W
Maradi Niger 38 13.29N 7.10E
Maradi *d.* Niger 38 14.00N 8.10E
Marāgheh Iran 31 37.25N 46.13E
Maragogipe Brazil 61 12.48S 38.59W
Marahuaca, Cerro *mtn.* Venezuela 60 3.37N 65.25W
Marajó, Ilha de *i.* Brazil 61 1.00S 49.40W
Maralal Kenya 37 1.15N 36.48E
Maralinga Australia 43 30.13S131.32E
Maramba Zambia 39 17.52S 25.52E
Marana U.S.A. 54 32.27N111.13W
Marand Iran 31 38.25N 45.50E
Maranhão *d.* Brazil 61 6.00S 45.30W
Maranoa *r.* Australia 45 27.55S148.30E
Marañón *r.* Peru 60 4.40S 73.20W
Marão Mozambique 39 24.21S 34.07E
Marapi *mtn.* Indonesia 26 0.20S100.45E
Mărășești Romania 15 45.52N 27.14E
Marathón Greece 13 38.10N 23.59E
Maratua *i.* Indonesia 26 2.10N118.35E
Marāveh Tappeh Iran 31 37.55N 55.57E
Marawī Sudan 35 18.30N 31.49E
Marbella Spain 10 36.31N 4.53W
Marble Bar Australia 42 21.16S119.45E
Marburg Germany 14 50.49N 8.36E
Marcaria Italy 9 45.07N 10.32E
March U.K. 5 52.33N 0.05E
Marche Belgium 8 50.13N 5.21E
Marche *d.* Italy 12 43.35N 13.00E
Marchena Spain 10 37.20N 5.24W
Mar Chiquita *l.* Argentina 62 30.42S 62.36W
Marcos Paz Argentina 63 34.49S 58.51W
Marcq-en-Baroeul France 8 50.40N 3.01E
Mardān Pakistan 28 34.14N 72.05E
Mar del Plata Argentina 63 38.00S 57.32W
Marden U.K. 5 51.11N 0.30E
Mardie Australia 42 21.14S115.57E
Mardin Turkey 30 37.19N 40.43E
Maree, Loch U.K. 6 57.41N 5.28W
Mareeba Australia 44 17.00S145.26E
Marettimo *i.* Italy 12 37.58N 12.05E
Margai Caka *l.* China 29 35.11N 86.57E
Margaret *r.* Australia 46 29.26S137.00E
Margaret River *town* W. Aust. Australia 43 33.57S115.04E
Margaret River *town* W. Aust. Australia 42 18.38S126.52E
Margarita, Isla de *i.* Venezuela 60 11.00N 64.00W
Margate R.S.A. 39 30.51S 30.22E
Margate U.K. 5 51.23N 1.24E
Margow, Dasht-e *des.* Afghan. 28 30.45N 63.00E
Maria Elena Chile 62 22.21S 69.40W
María Grande Argentina 63 31.40S 59.55W
Maria I. Australia 44 14.52S135.40E

Mariana Brazil 59 20.23S 43.23W
Marianao Cuba 57 23.03N 82.29W
Mariánské Lázně Czech Republic 14 49.59N 12.43E
Marias *r.* U.S.A. 54 47.56N110.30W
Maribo Denmark 17 54.46N 11.31E
Maribor Slovenia 14 46.35N 15.40E
Marico *r.* R.S.A. 39 24.12S 26.57E
Maricopa U.S.A. 54 35.03N119.24W
Marié *r.* Brazil 60 0.27S 66.26W
Marieburg Belgium 8 50.07N 4.30E
Marie-Galante *i.* Guadeloupe 57 15.54N 61.11W
Mariehamn *see* Maarianhamina Finland 17
Mariemberg Neth. 8 52.32N 6.35E
Mariental Namibia 39 24.38S 17.58E
Mariestad Sweden 17 58.43N 13.51E
Marietta Ohio U.S.A. 55 39.26N 81.27W
Mariga *r.* Nigeria 38 9.37N 5.55E
Marijampolė Lithuania 17 54.33N 23.21E
Marília Brazil 59 22.13S 50.20W
Marín Spain 10 42.23N 8.42W
Marina di Ravenna Italy 9 44.29N 12.17E
Maringá Brazil 59 23.36S 52.02W
Maringue Mozambique 39 17.55S 34.24E
Marinha Grande Portugal 10 39.45N 8.55W
Marion Ind. U.S.A. 55 40.33N 85.40W
Marion Ohio U.S.A. 55 40.35N 83.08W
Marion Bay *town* Australia 46 35.13S137.00E
Marion Reef Australia 44 19.10S152.17E
Mariposa U.S.A. 54 37.29N119.58W
Mariscal Estigarribia Paraguay 59 22.03S 60.35W
Maritsa *r.* Turkey 13 41.00N 26.15E
Mariupol' Ukraine 19 47.05N 37.34E
Marka Somali Rep. 37 1.42N 44.47E
Markaryd Sweden 17 56.26N 13.36E
Marken *i.* Neth. 8 52.28N 5.03E
Markerwaard *f.* Neth. 8 52.30N 5.15E
Market Drayton U.K. 4 52.55N 2.30W
Market Harborough U.K. 5 52.29N 0.55W
Market Rasen U.K. 4 53.24N 0.20W
Market Weighton U.K. 4 53.52N 0.04W
Markha *r.* Russian Fed. 21 63.37N119.00E
Markham, Mt. Antarctica 64 83.00S164.00E
Marks Russian Fed. 19 51.43N 46.45E
Marl Germany 8 51.39N 7.03E
Marla Australia 45 27.22S133.48E
Marla Australia 44 27.22S133.48E
Marlborough Australia 44 22.51S149.50E
Marlborough U.K. 5 51.26N 1.44W
Marle France 9 49.44N 3.46E
Marlette U.S.A. 55 43.20N 83.04W
Marlo Australia 47 37.50S148.35E
Marmara *i.* Turkey 13 40.38N 27.37E
Marmara, Sea of *see* Marmara Denizi *sea* Turkey 13
Marmara Denizi *sea* Turkey 13 40.45N 28.15E
Marmaris Turkey 13 36.50N 28.17E
Marmolada *mtn.* Italy 9 46.26N 11.51E
Marne *d.* France 9 48.55N 4.10E
Marne *r.* France 9 48.50N 2.25E
Marnoo Australia 46 36.40S142.55E
Maromme France 9 49.28N 1.02E
Marondera Zimbabwe 39 18.11S 31.31E
Maroni *r.* Guiana 61 5.30N 54.00W
Maroochydore Australia 45 26.40S153.07E
Maroua Cameroon 38 10.35N 14.20E
Marquard R.S.A. 39 28.39S 27.25E
Marquette U.S.A. 55 46.33N 87.23W
Marra Australia 46 31.11S144.03E
Marra *r.* Australia 47 30.05S147.05E
Marracuene Mozambique 39 25.44S 32.41E
Marradi Italy 9 44.04N 11.37E
Marrah, Jabal *mtn.* Sudan 35 14.04N 24.21E
Marrakech Morocco 34 31.49N 8.00W
Marrawah Australia 45 40.55S144.42E
Marree Australia 46 29.40S138.04E
Marrupa Mozambique 37 13.10S 37.30E
Marsabit Kenya 37 2.20N 37.59E
Marsala Italy 12 37.48N 12.27E
Marsá Maṭrūḩ Egypt 30 31.21N 27.14E
Marsden Australia 47 33.46S147.35E
Marseille France 11 43.18N 5.22E
Marseille-en-Beauvaisis France 9 49.35N 1.57E
Marsfjället *mtn.* Sweden 16 65.05N 15.28E
Marshall Tex. U.S.A. 53 32.33N 94.22W
Martaban Burma 29 16.30N 97.35E
Martaban, G. of Burma 29 15.10N 96.30E
Martapura Indonesia 26 3.22S114.56E
Marte Nigeria 38 12.23N 13.46E
Martelange Belgium 8 49.50N 5.44E
Martés, Sierra *mts.* Spain 10 39.10N 1.00W
Marthaguy Creek *r.* Australia 47 30.16S147.35E
Martha's Vineyard *i.* U.S.A. 55 41.25N 70.40W
Martigny Switz. 14 46.07N 7.05E
Martin Slovakia 15 49.05N 18.55E
Martina Franca Italy 13 40.42N 17.21E
Martinique *i.* Windward Is. 57 14.40N 61.00W
Martin Pt. U.S.A. 50 70.10N143.50W
Martinsburg W.Va. U.S.A. 55 39.27N 77.58W
Martins Ferry *town* U.S.A. 55 40.07N 80.45W
Martinsville Ind. U.S.A. 55 39.25N 86.25W
Marton New Zealand 48 40.04S175.25E
Martos Spain 10 37.44N 3.58W
Martre, Lac la *l.* Canada 50 63.15N116.55W
Martti Finland 16 67.28N 28.28E
Marudi Malaysia 26 4.15N114.19E
Marula Zimbabwe 39 20.26S 28.06E
Marum Neth. 8 53.06N 6.16E
Marvejols France 11 44.33N 3.18E
Marvel Loch *town* Australia 43 31.31S119.30E
Mārwār India 28 25.44N 73.36E
Mary Turkmenistan 20 37.42N 61.54E
Maryborough Qld. Australia 44 25.32S152.36E
Maryborough Vic. Australia 46 37.05S143.47E
Marydale R.S.A. 39 29.24S 22.06E
Maryland *d.* U.S.A. 55 39.00N 76.45W
Maryport U.K. 4 54.43N 3.30W
Marysvale U.S.A. 54 38.27N112.11W
Maryvale Australia 44 24.41S134.04E
Marzūq Libya 34 25.56N 13.57E
Marzūq, Ṣaḩrā' *des.* Libya 34 24.30N 13.00E
Masāhim, Kūh-e *mtn.* Iran 31 30.26N 55.08E
Masai Steppe *f.* Tanzania 37 4.30S 37.00E
Masaka Uganda 37 0.20S 31.46E
Masan S. Korea 25 35.10N128.35E
Masasi Tanzania 37 10.43S 38.48E
Masba Nigeria 38 10.35N 13.01E
Masbate *i.* Phil. 27 12.00N123.30E
Maseru Lesotho 39 29.18S 27.28E
Mashhad Iran 31 36.16N 59.34E
Mashki Chāh Pakistan 28 29.01N 62.27E
Mashonaland *f.* Zimbabwe 39 18.20S 32.00E
Masi Norway 16 69.26N 23.40E
Masindi Uganda 37 1.41N 31.45E
Maṣīrah *i.* Oman 28 20.30N 58.50E
Masjed Soleymān Iran 31 31.59N 49.18E
Mask, Lough Rep. of Ire. 7 53.38N 9.22W
Mason City U.S.A. 53 43.10N 93.10W
Masqaṭ Oman 31 23.36N 58.37E
Massa Italy 9 44.02N 10.09E
Massachusetts *d.* U.S.A. 55 42.15N 71.50W
Massakory Chad 38 13.02N 15.43E
Massa Marittima Italy 12 43.03N 10.53E
Massangena Mozambique 39 21.31S 33.03E
Massangulo Mozambique 37 13.54S 35.24E
Massarosa Italy 9 43.52N 10.20E
Massena U.S.A. 55 44.56N 74.54W
Massif Central *mts.* France 11 45.00N 3.30E
Massillon U.S.A. 55 40.48N 81.32W
Massinga Mozambique 39 23.20S 35.25E
Massingir Mozambique 39 23.49S 32.04E
Masterton New Zealand 48 40.57S175.39E
Mastūrah Saudi Arabia 30 23.06N 38.50E
Masvingo Zimbabwe 39 20.10S 30.49E
Maşyāf Syria 32 35.03N 36.21E
Matabeleland *f.* Zimbabwe 39 19.50S 28.15E
Matachewan Canada 55 47.56N 80.39W
Matadi Zaïre 36 5.50S 13.32E
Matagami Canada 55 49.40N 77.41W
Matagami, L. Canada 55 49.42N 77.39W
Matagorda B. U.S.A. 53 28.30N 96.20W
Matakana Australia 47 32.59S145.53E
Matakana I. New Zealand 48 37.35S176.15E
Matam Senegal 34 15.40N 13.18W
Matamata New Zealand 48 37.49S175.46E
Matameye Niger 38 13.26N 8.28E
Matamoros Coahuila Mexico 56 25.33N103.15W
Matamoros Tamaulipas Mexico 56 25.50N 97.31W
Matandu *r.* Tanzania 37 8.44S 39.22E
Matane Canada 55 48.50N 67.31W
Matankari Niger 38 13.47N 4.00E
Matanzas Cuba 57 23.04N 81.35W
Mataram Indonesia 26 8.36S116.07E
Matarani Peru 62 16.58S 72.07W
Mataranka Australia 42 14.56S133.07E
Mataró Spain 10 41.32N 2.27E
Matatiele R.S.A. 39 30.19S 28.48E
Mataura *r.* New Zealand 48 46.34S168.45E
Matawai New Zealand 48 38.21S177.32E
Maṭāy Egypt 32 28.25N 30.46E
Matehuala Mexico 56 23.40N100.40W
Mateke Hills Zimbabwe 39 21.48S 31.00E
Matera Italy 13 40.41N 16.36E
Matetsi Zimbabwe 39 18.17S 25.57E
Matfors Sweden 17 62.21N 17.02E
Mathews Peak *mtn.* Kenya 37 1.18N 37.20E
Mathoura Australia 47 35.49S144.54E
Mathura India 28 27.30N 77.42E
Mati Phil. 27 6.55N126.15E
Matias Barbosa Brazil 59 21.52S 43.21W
Matipó Brazil 59 20.16S 42.17W
Matlock U.K. 4 53.09N 1.32W
Matochkin Shar Russian Fed. 20 73.15N 56.35E
Mato Grosso *d.* Brazil 62 13.00S 55.00W
Mato Grosso *town* Brazil 62 15.05S 59.57W
Mato Grosso, Planalto do *f.* Brazil 62 16.00S 54.00W
Mato Grosso do Sul *d.* Brazil 62 20.00S 54.30W
Matope Malaŵi 37 15.20S 34.57E
Matopo Hills Zimbabwe 39 20.45S 28.30E
Matosinhos Portugal 10 41.11N 8.42W
Maṭraḩ Oman 31 23.37N 58.33E
Matsena Nigeria 38 13.13N 10.04E
Matsubara Japan 23 34.34N135.33E
Matsudo Japan 23 35.47N139.54E
Matsue Japan 25 35.29N133.00E
Matsusaka Japan 23 34.34N136.32E
Matsuyama Japan 25 33.50N132.47E
Mattagami *r.* Canada 55 50.43N 81.29W
Mattawa Canada 55 46.19N 78.42W
Mattawamkeag U.S.A. 55 45.31N 68.21W
Matterhorn *mtn.* Italy / Switz. 9 45.58N 7.38E
Matterhorn *mtn.* U.S.A. 54 41.49N115.23W
Matthews Ridge *town* Guyana 60 7.30N 60.10W
Matthew Town Bahamas 57 20.57N 73.40W
Mattice Canada 55 49.36N 83.16W
Mattmar Sweden 16 63.19N 13.45E
Matua Indonesia 26 2.58S110.52E
Maturín Venezuela 60 9.45N 63.10W
Maua Mozambique 37 13.53S 37.10E
Maubeuge France 8 50.17N 3.58E
Maude Australia 46 34.27S144.21E
Maués Brazil 61 3.24S 57.42W
Maui *i.* Hawaii U.S.A. 52 20.45N156.15W
Maumee U.S.A. 55 41.34N 83.41W
Maumee *r.* U.S.A. 55 41.40N 83.35W
Maumere Indonesia 27 8.35S122.13E
Maun Botswana 39 19.52S 23.40E
Maurice, L. Australia 45 29.28S130.58E
Mauritania Africa 34 20.00N 10.00W
Mawjib, Wādī al *r.* Jordan 32 31.28N 35.34E
Mawlaik Burma 29 23.40N 94.26E
Mawlamyine *see* Moulmein Burma 29
Maxcanú Mexico 56 20.35N 89.59W
May, C. U.S.A. 55 38.58N 74.55W
Maya Spain 10 43.12N 1.29W
Mayaguana I. Bahamas 57 22.30N 73.00W
Mayagüez Puerto Rico 57 18.13N 67.09W
Mayāmey Iran 31 36.27N 55.40E
Maya Mts. Belize 57 16.30N 89.00W
Maybole U.K. 6 55.21N 4.41W
Maydena Australia 45 42.45S146.38E
Mayen Germany 8 50.19N 7.14E
Mayenne France 9 48.18N 0.37W
Mayenne *d.* France 9 48.05N 0.40W
Mayenne *r.* France 9 47.30N 0.37W
Maykop Russian Fed. 19 44.37N 40.48E
Maymyo Burma 29 22.05N 96.33E
Maynooth Rep. of Ire. 7 53.23N 6.37W
Mayo *d.* Rep. of Ire. 7 53.47N 9.07W
Mayo, Plains of *f.* Rep. of Ire. 7 53.46N 9.05W
Mayo Daga Nigeria 38 6.59N 11.25E
Mayo Landing Canada 50 63.45N135.45W
Mayor I. New Zealand 48 37.15S176.15E
Mayotte, Île *i.* Comoros 37 12.50S 45.10E
May Pen Jamaica 57 17.58N 77.14W
Maysville U.S.A. 55 38.38N 83.46W
Mazagão Brazil 61 0.07S 51.17W
Mazamba Mozambique 39 18.32S 34.50E
Mazamet France 11 43.30N 2.24E
Mazán Peru 60 3.15S 73.00W
Mazarredo Argentina 63 47.00S 66.45W
Mazarrón Spain 10 37.38N 1.19W
Mazatenango Guatemala 56 14.31N 91.30W
Mazatlán Mexico 56 23.13N106.25W
Mažeikiai Lithuania 17 56.19N 22.20E
Mazirbe Latvia 17 57.41N 22.21E
Mazowe *r.* Mozambique 37 16.32S 33.25E
Mazowe Zimbabwe 39 17.30S 30.58E
Mazu Liedao *is.* China 25 26.12N120.00E
Mazunga Zimbabwe 39 21.45S 29.52E
Mazurski, Pojezierze *lakes* Poland 15 53.50N 21.00E
Mbabane Swaziland 39 26.19S 31.08E
Mbala Zambia 37 8.50S 31.24E
Mbale Uganda 37 1.04N 34.12E
Mbalmayo Cameroon 38 3.35N 11.31E
Mbamba Bay *town* Tanzania 37 11.18S 34.50E
Mbandaka Zaïre 34 0.03N 18.28E
Mbarara Uganda 37 0.36S 30.40E
Mbeya Tanzania 37 8.54S 33.29E
Mbeya *d.* Tanzania 37 8.30S 32.30E
Mbinda Congo 36 2.11S 12.55E
Mbogo Tanzania 37 7.26S 33.26E
Mbomou *r.* C.A.R. 35 4.08N 22.25E
Mbuji Mayi Zaïre 36 6.10S 23.39E
Mbulamuti Uganda 37 0.50N 33.05E
Mbura Tanzania 37 11.14S 35.25E
Mbuzi Zambia 37 12.20S 32.17E
McAlester U.S.A. 53 34.56N 95.46W
McArthur *r.* Australia 44 15.54S136.40E
McClintock Channel Canada 51 71.20N102.00W
McClure Str. Canada 50 74.30N116.00W
McConaughy, L. U.S.A. 52 41.20N102.00W
McCook U.S.A 52 40.15N100.45W
McDermitt U.S.A. 54 41.59N117.36W
McDouall Peak Australia 46 29.51S134.55E
McGrath U.S.A. 50 62.58N155.40W
Mchinja Tanzania 37 9.44S 39.45E
Mchinji Malaŵi 37 13.48S 32.55E
McIlwraith Range *mts.* Australia 44 14.00S143.10E
McKeesport U.S.A. 55 40.21N 79.52W
McKinley, Mt. U.S.A. 50 63.00N151.00W
McKittrick U.S.A. 54 35.18N119.37W
McLennan Canada 50 55.42N116.54W
McLeod Lake *town* Canada 50 54.59N123.02W
McMinnville Oreg. U.S.A. 54 45.13N123.12W
McNary U.S.A. 54 34.04N109.51W
McPherson Range *mts.* Australia 47 28.15S153.00E
Mdantsane R.S.A. 39 32.54S 27.24E
Mead, L. U.S.A. 54 36.05N114.25W
Meadville U.S.A. 55 41.38N 80.09W
Mealhada Portugal 10 40.22N 8.27W
Meander River *town* Canada 50 59.02N117.42W
Mearim *r.* Brazil 61 3.20S 44.20W
Meath *d.* Rep. of Ire. 7 53.32N 6.40W
Meaux France 9 48.58N 2.54E
Mecca *see* Makkah Saudi Arabia 35
Mecca U.S.A. 54 33.35N116.03W
Mechelen Belgium 8 51.01N 4.28E
Mecklenburger Bucht *b.* Germany 14 54.05N 11.00E
Mecklenburg-Vorpommern *d.* Germany 14 53.30N 13.15E
Meconta Mozambique 37 15.00S 39.50E
Mecufi Mozambique 37 13.20S 40.32E
Meda Portugal 10 40.58N 7.16W
Medan Indonesia 26 3.35N 98.39E
Mede Italy 9 45.06N 8.44E
Mededsiz *mtn.* Turkey 30 37.33N 34.38E
Medellín Colombia 60 6.15N 75.36W
Medemblik Neth. 8 52.48N 5.06E
Médenine Tunisia 34 33.24N 10.25E
Mederdra Mauritania 34 17.02N 15.41W
Medford Oreg. U.S.A. 54 42.19N122.52W
Medgidia Romania 15 44.15N 28.16E
Mediaș Romania 15 46.10N 24.21E
Medicina Italy 9 44.28N 11.38E
Medicine Bow Peak *mtn.* U.S.A. 54 41.21N106.19W
Medicine Hat Canada 50 50.03N110.41W
Medina *see* Al Madīnah Saudi Arabia 30
Medina N.Y. U.S.A. 55 43.14N 78.23W
Medina del Campo Spain 10 41.20N 4.55W
Medina de Rioseco Spain 10 41.53N 5.03W
Mediterranean Sea 34 37.00N 15.00E
Mêdog China 24 29.19N 95.19E
Medveditsa *r.* Russian Fed. 19 49.35N 42.45E
Medvezhyegorsk Russian Fed. 18 62.56N 34.28E
Medvin Ukraine 15 49.25N 30.48E
Medway *r.* U.K. 5 51.24N 0.31E
Medzhibozh Ukraine 15 49.29N 27.28E
Meeberrie Australia 42 26.58S115.51E
Meekatharra Australia 42 26.35S118.30E
Meeker U.S.A. 54 40.02N107.55W
Meer Belgium 8 51.27N 4.46E
Meerhusener Moor *f.* Germany 8 53.36N 7.33E
Meerut India 28 29.00N 77.42E
Mēga Ethiopia 35 4.07N 38.16E
Mégara Greece 13 38.00N 23.21E
Meghalaya *d.* India 29 25.30N 91.00E
Mégiscane *r.* Canada 55 48.36N 76.00W
Mehadia Romania 15 44.55N 22.22E
Meiktila Burma 29 20.53N 95.54E
Meiningen Germany 14 50.34N 10.25E
Meissen Germany 14 51.10N 13.28E
Meizhou China 25 24.19N116.13E
Mekatina Canada 55 46.58N 84.05W
Mek'elē Ethiopia 35 13.33N 39.30E
Meknès Morocco 34 33.53N 5.37W
Mekong *r.* Asia 26 10.00N106.20E
Mekong Delta Vietnam 26 10.00N106.20E
Mekongga *mtn.* Indonesia 27 3.39S121.15E
Mékrou *r.* Benin 38 12.20N 2.47E
Melaka Malaysia 26 2.11N102.16E
Melanesia *is.* Pacific Oc. 40 5.00N165.00E
Melbourne Australia 47 37.45S144.58E
Melegnano Italy 9 45.21N 9.19E
Meleuz Russian Fed. 18 52.58N 55.56E
Mélèzes, Rivière aux *r.* Canada 51 57.40N 69.30W
Melfi Chad 34 11.04N 18.03E
Melfi Italy 12 40.59N 15.39E
Melfort Canada 50 52.52N104.36W
Melilla Spain 10 35.17N 2.57W
Melipilla Chile 63 33.42S 71.13W
Melitopol Ukraine 19 46.51N 35.22E
Melk Austria 14 48.14N 15.20E
Mellerud Sweden 17 58.42N 12.28E
Melmore Pt. Rep. of Ire. 7 55.15N 7.49W
Melnik Bulgaria 13 41.30N 23.22E
Mělník Czech Republic 14 50.20N 14.29E
Melo Uruguay 59 32.22S 54.10W
Melrose U.K. 6 55.36N 2.43W
Melrose Mont. U.S.A. 54 45.37N112.41W
Melstone U.S.A. 54 46.36N107.52W
Meltaus Finland 16 66.54N 25.22E
Melton Australia 47 37.41S144.36E
Melton Mowbray U.K. 4 52.46N 0.53W
Melun France 9 48.32N 2.40E
Melvich U.K. 6 58.33N 3.55W
Melville, C. Australia 44 14.11S144.30E
Melville B. Australia 44 12.10S136.32E
Melville Hills Canada 50 69.20N122.00W
Melville I. Australia 44 11.30S131.00E
Melville I. Canada 50 75.30N110.00W
Melville Pen. Canada 51 68.00N 84.00W
Melvin, Lough Rep. of Ire. / U.K. 7 54.26N 8.12W
Melzo Italy 9 45.30N 9.25E
Memba Mozambique 37 14.16S 40.30E
Memboro Indonesia 26 9.22S119.32E
Memmingen Germany 14 47.59N 10.11E
Memphis *ruins* Egypt 32 29.52N 31.12E
Memphis Tenn. U.S.A. 53 35.05N 90.00W
Mena Ukraine 15 51.30N 32.15E
Menai Str. U.K. 4 53.17N 4.20W
Ménaka Mali 38 15.55N 2.24E
Mendawai *r.* Indonesia 26 3.17S113.20E
Mende France 11 44.32N 3.30E
Mendi P.N.G. 27 6.13S143.39E
Mendip Hills U.K. 5 51.15N 2.40W
Mendocino, C. U.S.A. 54 40.25N124.25W
Mendooran Australia 47 31.48S149.08E
Mendoza Argentina 63 32.54S 68.50W
Mendoza *d.* Argentina 63 34.30S 68.00W
Mendung Indonesia 26 0.31N103.12E
Mene Grande Venezuela 60 9.51N 70.57W
Menemen Turkey 30 38.34N 27.03E
Menen Belgium 8 50.48N 3.07E
Menfi Italy 12 37.36N 12.59E
Mengzi China 29 23.20N103.21E
Menindee Australia 46 32.23S142.30E
Menindee L. Australia 46 32.21S142.20E
Menongue Angola 36 14.36S 17.48E
Menorca *i.* Spain 10 40.00N 4.00E
Mentawai, Kepulauan *is.* Indonesia 26 2.50S 99.00E
Mentekab Malaysia 26 3.29N102.21E
Mentok Indonesia 26 2.04S105.12E
Menton France 11 43.47N 7.30E
Menyapa, Gunung *mtn.* Indonesia 26 1.00N116.20E
Menzies Australia 43 29.41S121.02E
Menzies, Mt. Antarctica 64 71.50S 61.00E
Meppel Neth. 8 52.42N 6.12E
Meppen Germany 8 52.42N 7.17E
Mer France 9 47.42N 1.30E
Merano Italy 12 46.41N 11.10E
Merauke Indonesia 44 8.30S140.22E
Merbein Australia 46 34.11S142.04E
Mercato Saraceno Italy 9 43.57N 12.12E
Merced U.S.A. 54 37.18N120.29W
Mercedes Buenos Aires Argentina 63 34.40S 59.25W
Mercedes Corrientes Argentina 62 29.15S 58.05W
Mercedes San Luis Argentina 63 33.40S 65.30W
Mercedes Uruguay 63 33.16S 58.01W
Mercy, C. Canada 51 65.00N 63.30W
Mere U.K. 5 51.05N 2.16W
Meredith Australia 46 37.50S144.05E
Mereeg Somali Rep. 35 3.47N 47.18E
Merefa Ukraine 19 49.49N 36.05E
Mergenevo Kazakhstan 19 49.59N 51.19E
Mergui Burma 29 12.26N 98.34E
Mergui Archipelago *is.* Burma 29 11.30N 98.15E
Meribah Australia 46 34.42S140.53E
Meriç *r.* Turkey 13 40.52N 26.12E
Mérida Mexico 57 20.59N 89.39W
Mérida Spain 10 38.55N 6.20W
Mérida Venezuela 60 8.24N 71.08W
Mérida, Cordillera de *mts.* Venezuela 60 8.30N 71.00W
Meridian U.S.A. 53 32.21N 88.42W
Mérignac France 11 44.50N 0.42W
Merigur Australia 46 34.21S141.23E
Merikarvia Finland 17 61.51N 21.30E
Merimbula Australia 47 36.52S149.55E
Merino Australia 46 37.45S141.35E
Merir *i.* Pacific Ocean 27 4.19N132.18E
Merirumã Brazil 61 1.15N 54.50W
Merksem Belgium 8 51.14N 4.25E
Merlo Argentina 63 34.40S 58.45W
Merredin Australia 43 31.29S118.16E
Merrick *mtn.* U.K. 6 55.08N 4.29W
Merrill Oreg. U.S.A. 54 42.01N121.36W
Merrill Wisc. U.S.A. 53 45.12N 89.43W
Merriwa Australia 47 32.08S150.20E
Mersch Lux. 8 49.44N 6.05E
Mersea I. U.K. 5 51.47N 0.58E
Merseburg Germany 14 51.22N 12.00E
Mersey *r.* U.K. 4 53.22N 2.37W
Merseyside *d.* U.K. 4 53.28N 3.00W
Mersin Turkey 30 36.47N 34.37E
Mersing Malaysia 26 2.25N103.50E
Merthyr Tydfil U.K. 5 51.45N 3.23W
Mértola Portugal 10 37.38N 7.40W
Merton U.K. 5 51.25N 0.12W
Méru France 9 49.14N 2.08E
Meru *mtn.* Tanzania 37 3.15S 36.44E
Méry France 9 48.30N 3.53E
Merzifon Turkey 30 40.52N 35.28E
Merzig Germany 8 49.26N 6.39E
Mesa U.S.A. 54 33.25N111.50W
Mesagne Italy 13 40.33N 17.49E
Meslay-du-Maine France 9 47.57N 0.33W
Mesocco Switz. 9 46.23N 9.14E
Mesolóngion Greece 13 38.23N 21.23E
Mesopotamia *f.* Iraq 31 33.30N 44.30E
Messalo *r.* Mozambique 37 11.38S 40.27E
Messina Italy 12 38.13N 15.34E
Messina R.S.A. 39 22.20S 30.03E
Messina, Stretto di *str.* Italy 12 38.10N 15.35E
Messini Greece 13 37.03N 22.00E
Messiniakós, Kólpos *g.* Greece 13 36.50N 22.05E
Mesta *r.* Bulgaria *see* Néstos *r.* Greece 13
Mestre Italy 9 45.29N 12.15E
Meta *r.* Venezuela 60 6.10N 67.30W
Metán Argentina 62 25.30S 65.00W
Metangula Mozambique 37 12.41S 34.51E
Metković Yugo. 13 43.03N 17.38E
Métsovon Greece 13 39.46N 21.11E
Metz France 11 49.07N 6.11E
Meulaboh Indonesia 26 4.10N 96.09E
Meulan France 9 49.01N 1.54E
Meuse *r.* Belgium *see* Maas *r.* Neth. 8
Mexian *see* Meizhou China 25
Mexicali Mexico 54 32.40N115.29W
Mexico C. America 56 20.00N100.00W
México *d.* Mexico 56 19.45N 99.30W
Mexico, G. of N. America 56 25.00N 90.00W
Mexico City *see* Ciudad de México Mexico 56
Meymaneh Afghan. 28 35.54N 64.43E
Mezen Russian Fed. 18 65.50N 44.20E
Mezen *r.* Russian Fed. 18 65.50N 44.18E
Mézenc, Mont *mtn.* France 11 44.54N 4.11E
Mezenskaya Guba *g.* Russian Fed. 18 66.30N 44.00E
Mezőkövesd Hungary 15 47.50N 20.34E
Mezzolombardo Italy 9 46.13N 11.05E
Miahuatlán Mexico 56 16.20N 96.36W
Miami Fla. U.S.A. 53 25.45N 80.10W
Mīāndow Āb Iran 31 36.57N 46.06E
Mīāneh Iran 31 37.23N 47.45E
Miānwāli Pakistan 28 32.32N 71.33E
Mianyang Sichuan China 24 31.28N104.46E
Miass Russian Fed. 20 55.00N 60.00E
Mibu *r.* Japan 23 35.49N137.57E
Mica R.S.A. 39 24.09S 30.49E
Michalovce Slovakia 15 48.45N 21.55E
Michelson, Mt. U.S.A. 50 69.19N144.17W
Michigan *d.* U.S.A. 55 44.00N 85.00W
Michigan, L. U.S.A. 55 44.00N 87.00W
Michigan City U.S.A. 55 41.43N 86.54W
Michipicoten Canada 55 47.57N 84.55W
Michipicoten I. Canada 55 47.40N 85.48W
Michoacán *d.* Mexico 56 19.20N101.00W
Michurin Bulgaria 13 42.09N 27.51E
Michurinsk Russian Fed. 18 52.54N 40.30E
Micronesia *is.* Pacific Oc. 40 8.00N160.00E
Middelburg Neth. 8 51.30N 3.36E
Middelburg C.P. R.S.A. 39 31.29S 25.00E
Middelburg Trans. R.S.A. 39 25.45S 29.27E
Middelharnis Neth. 8 51.46N 4.09E
Middenmeer Neth. 8 52.51N 4.59E
Middlebury U.S.A. 55 44.01N 73.10W
Middle I. Australia 43 34.07S123.12E
Middlesboro U.S.A. 53 36.37N 83.43W
Middlesbrough U.K. 4 54.34N 1.13W
Middletown Ind. U.S.A. 55 39.31N 84.13W
Mid Glamorgan *d.* U.K. 5 51.38N 3.25W
Midi-Pyrénées *d.* France 11 44.10N 2.00E
Midland Canada 55 44.45N 79.53W
Midland Mich. U.S.A. 55 43.38N 84.14W
Midland Tex. U.S.A. 52 32.00N102.09W
Midland Junction Australia 43 31.54S115.57E
Midleton Rep. of Ire. 7 51.55N 8.10W
Midwest U.S.A. 54 43.25N106.16W
Midyan *f.* Saudi Arabia 32 27.50N 35.30E
Midye Turkey 13 41.37N 28.07E
Midžor *mtn.* Yugo. 13 43.23N 22.42E
Mie *d.* Japan 23 34.42N136.08E
Miechów Poland 15 50.23N 20.01E
Miedzychód Poland 14 52.36N 15.55E
Mielec Poland 15 50.18N 21.25E
Mienga Angola 39 17.16S 19.50E
Mieres Spain 10 43.15N 5.46W
Mijares *r.* Spain 10 39.58N 0.01W
Mikhaylov Russian Fed. 18 54.14N 39.00E

Mikhaylovgrad Bulgaria **13** 43.25N 23.11E
Mikhaylovka Russian Fed. **19** 50.05N 43.15E
Miki Japan **23** 34.48N134.59E
Mikínai Greece **13** 37.44N 22.45E
Mikindani Tanzania **37** 10.16S 40.05E
Mikkeli Finland **18** 61.44N 27.15E
Míkonos *i.* Greece **13** 37.29N 25.25E
Mikumi Tanzania **37** 7.22S 37.00E
Mikun Russian Fed. **18** 62.20N 50.01E
Milagro Ecuador **60** 2.11S 79.36W
Milan *see* Milano Italy **9**
Milange Mozambique **37** 16.09S 35.44E
Milano Italy **9** 45.28N 9.10E
Milâs Turkey **13** 37.18N 27.48E
Mildenhall U.K. **5** 52.20N 0.30E
Mildura Australia **46** 34.14S142.13E
Miles Australia **44** 26.40S150.11E
Miles City U.S.A. **54** 46.25N105.51W
Milford Utah U.S.A. **54** 38.24N113.01W
Milford Haven *town* U.K. **5** 51.43N 5.02W
Milford Sound *town* New Zealand **48** 44.41S167.56E
Miliana Algeria **34** 36.15N 2.15E
Miling Australia **43** 30.27S116.20E
Milk *r.* U.S.A. **52** 48.05N106.15W
Millau France **11** 44.06N 3.05E
Mille Lacs, Lac des *l.* Canada **55** 48.48N 90.34W
Mille Lacs L. U.S.A. **53** 46.15N 93.40W
Miller *r.* Australia **46** 30.05S136.07E
Millerovo Russian Fed. **19** 48.55N 40.25E
Millersburg Mich. U.S.A. **55** 45.21N 84.02W
Milleur Pt. U.K. **6** 55.01N 5.07W
Millicent Australia **46** 37.36S140.22E
Millinocket U.S.A. **55** 45.39N 68.43W
Millmerran Australia **45** 27.51S151.17E
Millom U.K. **4** 54.13N 3.16W
Milne Inlet *town* Canada **51** 72.30N 80.59W
Mílos Greece **13** 36.45N 24.27E
Mílos *i.* Greece **13** 36.40N 24.26E
Milparinka Australia **46** 29.45S141.55E
Milton Australia **47** 35.19S150.24E
Milton Keynes U.K. **5** 52.03N 0.42W
Milwaukee U.S.A. **53** 43.03N 87.56W
Milwaukie U.S.A. **54** 45.27N122.38W
Milyatino Russian Fed. **18** 54.30N 34.20E
Mim Ghana **38** 6.55N 2.34W
Mina U.S.A. **54** 38.24N118.07W
Mīnā 'al Aḥmadī Kuwait **28** 29.04N 48.08E
Mīnāb Iran **31** 27.07N 57.05E
Minas Uruguay **63** 34.23S 55.14W
Minas de Corrales Uruguay **63** 31.35S 55.28W
Minas de Ríotinto Spain **10** 37.41N 6.37W
Minas Gerais *d.* Brazil **59** 18.00S 45.00W
Minatitlán Mexico **56** 17.59N 94.32W
Mindanao *i.* Phil. **27** 7.30N125.00E
Mindanao Sea Phil. **27** 9.10N124.25E
Mindarie Australia **46** 34.51S140.12E
Minden Germany **14** 52.18N 8.54E
Mindif Cameroon **38** 10.25N 14.23E
Mindiptana Indonesia **27** 5.45S140.22E
Mindona L. Australia **46** 33.09S142.09E
Mindoro *i.* Phil. **27** 13.00N121.00E
Mindoro Str. Pacific Oc. **27** 12.30N120.10E
Mindra *mtn.* Romania **15** 45.20N 23.32E
Minehead U.K. **5** 51.12N 3.29W
Minerva Australia **44** 24.00S148.05E
Mingan Canada **51** 50.18N 64.02W
Mingary Australia **46** 32.09S140.46E
Mingela Australia **44** 19.53S146.40E
Mingenew Australia **43** 29.11S115.26E
Mingin Burma **29** 22.52N 94.39E
Minhe China **24** 36.20N102.50E
Minidoka U.S.A. **54** 42.46N113.30W
Minigwal, L. Australia **43** 29.35S123.12E
Minlaton Australia **46** 34.46S137.37E
Minna Nigeria **38** 9.39N 6.32E
Minneapolis U.S.A. **53** 45.00N 93.15W
Minnedosa Canada **51** 50.14N 99.51W
Minnesota *d.* U.S.A. **53** 46.00N 95.00W
Minnipa Australia **46** 32.51S135.09E
Mino Japan **23** 35.34N136.56E
Miño *r.* Spain **10** 41.50N 8.52W
Minobu-sanchi *mts.* Japan **23** 35.05N138.15E
Mino-kamo Japan **23** 35.26N137.01E
Mino-mikawa-kōgen *mts.* Japan **23** 35.16N137.10E
Minorca *i.* *see* Menorca *i.* Spain **10**
Minot U.S.A. **52** 48.14N101.18W
Minsen Germany **8** 53.44N 7.59E
Minsk Belorussia **15** 53.51N 27.30E
Minta Cameroon **38** 4.37N 12.47E
Minto, L. Canada **51** 51.00N 73.37W
Minturno Italy **12** 41.15N 13.45E
Minūf Egypt **32** 30.28N 30.56E
Minyā al Qamḥ Egypt **32** 30.31N 31.21E
Minyar Russian Fed. **18** 55.06N 57.29E
Miquelon Canada **55** 49.24N 76.29W
Mira Italy **9** 45.26N 12.08E
Mīrābād Afghan. **31** 30.32N 61.52E
Miracema Brazil **59** 21.22S 42.09W
Mīrah, Wādī al *r.* Iraq **30** 32.27N 41.21E
Miraj India **28** 16.51N 74.42E
Miranda de Ebro Spain **10** 42.41N 2.57W
Miranda do Douro Portugal **10** 41.30N 6.16W
Mirande France **11** 43.31N 0.25E
Mirandela Portugal **10** 41.28N 7.10W
Mirandola Italy **9** 44.53N 11.04E
Mirbāṭ Oman **28** 17.00N 54.45E
Mirecourt France **11** 48.18N 6.08E
Miri Malaysia **26** 4.28N114.00E
Miriam Vale Australia **44** 24.20S151.34E
Mirim, L. Brazil **59** 33.10S 53.30W
Mirintu Creek *r.* Australia **46** 28.58S143.18E
Mironovka Ukraine **15** 49.40N 30.59E
Miroşi Romania **15** 44.25N 24.58E
Mīrpur Khās Pakistan **28** 25.33N 69.05E
Miryeny Moldavia **15** 47.00N 29.06E
Mirzāpur India **29** 25.09N 82.34E
Mishawaka U.S.A. **55** 41.38N 86.10W
Mishima Japan **23** 35.07N138.55E
Mishkino Russian Fed. **18** 55.34N 56.00E
Misima I. P.N.G. **44** 10.40S152.45E
Misiones *d.* Argentina **62** 27.00S 54.40W
Miskolc Hungary **15** 48.07N 20.47E
Misool *i.* Indonesia **27** 1.50S130.10E
Mişr al Jadīdah Egypt **32** 30.06N 31.20E
Mişrātah Libya **34** 32.24N 15.04E
Mişr Baḥrī *f.* Egypt **32** 30.30N 31.00E
Missinaibi *r.* Canada **55** 50.44N 81.29W
Mississippi *d.* U.S.A. **53** 33.00N 90.00W
Mississippi *r.* U.S.A. **53** 28.55N 89.05W
Mississippi Delta U.S.A. **53** 29.00N 89.10W
Missoula U.S.A. **54** 46.52N114.01W
Missouri *d.* U.S.A. **53** 39.00N 93.00W
Missouri *r.* U.S.A. **53** 38.40N 90.20W
Mistake Creek *town* Australia **42** 17.06S129.04E
Mistassini Canada **55** 48.54N 72.13W
Mistassini *r.* Canada **55** 48.54N 72.13W
Mistassini, Lac *l.* Canada **55** 51.15N 73.10W
Mistretta Italy **12** 37.56N 14.22E
Mitchell Australia **44** 26.29S147.58E
Mitchell *r.* Qld. Australia **44** 15.12S141.35E
Mitchell *r.* Vic. Australia **47** 37.53S147.41E
Mitchell Oreg. U.S.A. **54** 44.34N120.09W
Mitchell S.Dak. U.S.A. **52** 43.40N 98.01W
Mitchell, Mt. U.S.A. **53** 35.57N 82.16W
Mitchelstown Rep. of Ire. **7** 52.16N 8.17W
Mīt Ghamr Egypt **32** 30.43N 31.16E
Mitilíni Greece **13** 39.06N 26.34E
Mitla, Mamarr *pass* Egypt **32** 30.00N 32.53E
Mitla Pass *see* Mitla, Mamarr *pass* Egypt **32**
Mitrovica Yugo. **13** 42.54N 20.51E
Mits'iwa Eritrea **35** 15.36N 39.29E
Mittagong Australia **47** 34.27S150.25E
Mittelandkanal Germany **8** 52.24N 7.52E
Mitú Colombia **60** 1.08N 70.03W
Mitumba, Monts *mts.* Zaïre **37** 3.00S 28.30E
Mitzic Gabon **36** 0.48N 11.30E
Miura Japan **23** 35.08N139.37E
Miya *r.* Japan **23** 34.32N136.44E
Miyako jima *i.* Japan **25** 24.45N125.25E
Miyakonojō Japan **25** 31.43N131.02E
Miyazaki Japan **25** 31.58N131.50E
Mizen Head Rep. of Ire. **7** 51.27N 9.50W
Mizil Romania **15** 45.00N 26.26E
Mizoch Ukraine **15** 50.30N 25.50E
Mizoram *d.* India **29** 23.40N 92.40E
Mizpe Ramon Israel **32** 30.36N 34.48E
Mizukaidō Japan **23** 36.01N139.59E
Mizunami Japan **23** 35.22N137.15E
Mjölby Sweden **17** 58.19N 15.08E
Mjösa *l.* Norway **17** 60.40N 11.00E
Mkata Tanga Tanzania **37** 5.47S 38.18E
Mkushi Zambia **37** 13.40S 29.26E
Mkuze R.S.A. **39** 27.10S 32.00E
Mkwaja Tanzania **37** 5.46S 38.51E
Mkwiti Tanzania **37** 10.27S 39.18E
Mladá Boleslav Czech Republic **14** 50.26N 14.55E
Mława Poland **15** 53.06N 20.23E
Mljet *i.* Croatia **13** 42.45N 17.30E
Mneni Zimbabwe **39** 20.38S 30.03E
Moab U.S.A. **54** 38.35N109.33W
Moa I. Australia **44** 10.12S142.16E
Moama Australia **47** 36.05S144.50E
Moamba Mozambique **39** 25.35S 32.13E
Moapa U.S.A. **54** 36.40N114.39W
Moatize Mozambique **37** 16.10S 33.40E
Moba Zaïre **37** 7.03S 29.42E
Mobara Japan **23** 35.25N140.18E
Mobert Canada **55** 48.41N 85.40W
Mobile U.S.A. **53** 30.40N 88.05W
Mobile B. U.S.A. **53** 30.30N 87.50W
Mobridge U.S.A. **52** 45.31N100.25W
Mobutu Sese Seko, L. *see* Albert, L. Uganda / Zaïre **37**
Moçambique *town* Mozambique **37** 15.00S 40.47E
Mocimboa da Praia Mozambique **37** 11.19S 40.19E
Mocimboa do Ruvuma Mozambique **37** 11.05S 39.15E
Moclips U.S.A. **54** 47.14N124.13W
Mococa Brazil **59** 21.28S 47.00W
Moctezuma Mexico **56** 30.10N106.28W
Mocuba Mozambique **37** 16.52S 37.02E
Modane France **11** 45.12N 6.40E
Modder *r.* R.S.A. **39** 29.03S 23.56E
Modena Italy **9** 44.39N 10.55E
Modena U.S.A. **54** 37.48N113.57W
Modesto U.S.A. **54** 37.39N121.00W
Modica Italy **12** 36.51N 14.51E
Moe Australia **47** 38.10S146.15E
Moebase Mozambique **37** 17.04S 38.41E
Moelv Norway **17** 60.56N 10.42E
Moffat U.K. **6** 55.20N 3.27W
Mogadishu *see* Muqdisho Somali Rep. **37**
Mogaung Burma **29** 25.20N 97.00E
Mogi das Cruzes Brazil **59** 23.33S 46.14W
Mogi-Guaçu Brazil **59** 20.55S 48.06W
Mogilev Belorussia **15** 53.54N 30.20E
Mogilev Podolskiy Ukraine **15** 48.29N 27.49E
Mogilno Poland **15** 52.40N 17.58E
Mogi-Mirim Brazil **59** 22.29S 46.55W
Mogincual Mozambique **37** 15.33S 40.29E
Mogliano Veneto Italy **9** 45.33N 12.14E
Mogok Burma **29** 23.00N 96.40E
Mogollon Rim *f.* U.S.A. **54** 32.30N111.00W
Mogumber Australia **43** 31.01S116.02E
Mohács Hungary **15** 45.59N 18.42E
Mohawk Ariz. U.S.A. **54** 32.41N113.47W
Mohéli *i.* Comoros **37** 12.22S 43.45E
Mohon France **9** 49.45N 4.44E
Mohoro Tanzania **37** 8.09S 39.07E
Mohoru Kenya **37** 1.01S 34.07E
Moi Norway **17** 58.28N 6.32E
Mointy Kazakhstan **20** 47.10N 73.18E
Mo-i-Rana Norway **16** 66.19N 14.10E
Mõisaküla Estonia **17** 58.06N 25.11E
Moisdon France **9** 47.37N 1.22W
Moisie *r.* Canada **51** 50.13N 66.02W
Moissac France **11** 44.07N 1.05E
Mojave U.S.A. **54** 35.03N118.10W
Mojave Desert U.S.A. **54** 35.00N117.00W
Mokau New Zealand **48** 38.41S174.37E
Mokmer Indonesia **27** 1.13S136.13E
Mokpo S. Korea **25** 34.50N126.25E
Mol Belgium **8** 51.11N 5.09E
Molchanovo Russian Fed. **20** 57.39N 83.45E
Mold U.K. **4** 53.10N 3.08W
Moldavia Europe **15** 47.30N 28.30E
Molde Norway **16** 62.44N 7.08E
Molepolole Botswana **39** 24.26S 25.34E
Molfetta Italy **13** 41.12N 16.36E
Molina de Aragón Spain **10** 40.50N 1.54W
Moline U.S.A. **53** 41.31N 90.26W
Molinella Italy **9** 44.37N 11.40E
Moliro Zaïre **37** 8.11S 30.29E
Molise *d.* Italy **12** 41.40N 15.00E
Mollendo Peru **62** 17.02S 72.01W
Mölndal Sweden **17** 57.39N 12.01E
Molodechno Belorussia **15** 54.16N 26.50E
Molokai *i.* Hawaii U.S.A. **52** 21.20N157.00W
Molong Australia **47** 33.08S148.53E
Molopo *r.* R.S.A. **39** 28.30S 20.22E
Moloundou Cameroon **38** 2.03N 15.14E
Molteno R.S.A. **39** 31.23S 26.21E
Moluccas *is.* Indonesia **27** 4.00S128.00E
Molucca Sea *see* Maluku, Laut *sea* Pacific Oc. **27**
Moma Mozambique **37** 16.40S 39.10E
Mombasa Kenya **37** 4.04S 39.40E
Mommark Denmark **14** 54.55N 10.03E
Mompós Colombia **60** 9.15N 74.29W
Mön *i.* Denmark **17** 55.00N 12.20E
Mona *i.* Puerto Rico **57** 18.06N 67.54W
Monaco Europe **11** 43.40N 7.25E
Monadhliath Mts. U.K. **6** 57.09N 4.08W
Monaghan Rep. of Ire. **7** 54.15N 6.58W
Monaghan *d.* Rep. of Ire. **7** 54.10N 7.00W
Moncalieri Italy **9** 45.00N 7.40E
Monchegorsk Russian Fed. **18** 67.55N 33.01E
Mönchen-Gladbach Germany **8** 51.12N 6.25E
Monchique Portugal **10** 37.19N 8.33W
Monclova Mexico **56** 26.55N101.20W
Moncton Canada **51** 46.06N 64.50W
Mondo Tanzania **37** 5.00S 35.54E
Mondoubleau France **9** 47.59N 0.54E
Mondovì Italy **9** 44.24N 7.50E
Mondrain I. Australia **43** 34.08S122.15E
Monessen U.S.A. **55** 40.08N 79.54W
Monet Canada **55** 48.10N 75.40W
Monfalcone Italy **12** 45.49N 13.32E
Monforte Spain **10** 42.32N 7.30W
Monga Zaïre **35** 4.05N 22.56E
Mong Cai Vietnam **26** 21.36N107.55E
Mongers L. Australia **43** 29.15S117.05E
Monghyr India **29** 25.24N 86.29E
Mongo Chad **34** 12.14N 18.45E
Mongolia Asia **24** 46.30N104.00E
Mongoro Chad **35** 12.22N 22.26E
Mongu Zambia **36** 15.17S 23.06E
Monifieth U.K. **6** 56.29N 2.50W
Monitor Range *mts.* U.S.A. **54** 38.45N116.30W
Monmouth U.K. **5** 51.48N 2.43W
Monmouth Oreg. U.S.A. **54** 44.51N123.14W
Mono L. U.S.A. **54** 38.00N119.00W
Monopoli Italy **13** 40.56N 17.19E
Monor Hungary **15** 47.21N 19.27E
Monreal del Campo Spain **10** 40.47N 1.20W
Monroe La. U.S.A. **53** 32.31N 92.06W
Monroe Mich. U.S.A. **55** 41.56N 83.21W
Monrovia Liberia **34** 6.20N 10.46W
Mons Belgium **8** 50.27N 3.57E
Monselice Italy **9** 45.14N 11.45E
Mönsterås Sweden **17** 57.02N 16.26E
Montabaur Germany **8** 50.27N 7.51E
Montagnana Italy **9** 45.14N 11.28E
Montalbán Spain **10** 40.50N 0.48W
Montalto di Castro Italy **12** 42.21N 11.37E
Montana Switz. **9** 46.18N 7.29E
Montana *d.* U.S.A. **52** 47.14N109.26W
Montargis France **9** 48.00N 2.44E
Montauban France **11** 44.01N 1.20E
Montbard France **9** 47.37N 4.20E
Montbéliard France **11** 47.31N 6.48E
Montbrison France **11** 45.37N 4.04E
Montceau-les-Mines France **11** 46.40N 4.22E
Mont Cenis, Col du *pass* France **11** 45.15N 6.55E
Montcornet France **9** 49.41N 4.01E
Mont de Marsan *town* France **11** 43.54N 0.30W
Montdidier France **9** 49.39N 2.34E
Monte Alegre *town* Brazil **61** 2.01S 54.04W
Monte Azul *town* Brazil **59** 15.53S 42.53W
Monte Carlo Monaco **11** 43.44N 7.25E
Monte Caseros Argentina **63** 30.15S 57.38W
Montecatini Terme Italy **9** 43.53N 10.46E
Montecristo *i.* Italy **12** 42.20N 10.19E
Montego Bay *town* Jamaica **57** 18.27N 77.56W
Montélimar France **11** 44.33N 4.45E
Montemor-o-Velho Portugal **10** 40.10N 8.41W
Montenegro *see* Crna Gora *d.* Yugo. **13**
Montepuez Mozambique **37** 13.09S 39.33E
Montereau France **9** 48.22N 2.57E
Monterey Calif. U.S.A. **54** 36.37N121.55W
Monterey B. U.S.A. **54** 36.45N121.55W
Montería Colombia **60** 8.45N 75.54W
Montero Bolivia **62** 17.20S 63.15W
Monteros Argentina **62** 27.10S 65.30W
Monterrey Mexico **56** 25.40N100.20W
Monte Santu, Capo di *c.* Italy **12** 40.05N 9.44E
Montes Claros Brazil **59** 16.45S 43.52W
Montevideo Uruguay **63** 34.53S 56.11W
Montfort-sur-Meu France **9** 48.08N 1.57W
Montgomery U.K. **5** 52.34N 3.09W
Montgomery Ala. U.S.A. **53** 32.22N 86.20W
Montguyon France **11** 45.13N 0.11W
Monthey Switz. **9** 46.15N 6.57E
Monthois France **9** 49.19N 4.43E
Monticello Utah U.S.A. **54** 37.52N109.21W
Montichiari Italy **9** 45.25N 10.23E
Montiel, Campo de *f.* Spain **10** 38.46N 2.44W
Montigny-le-Roi France **11** 48.00N 5.30E
Montijo Portugal **10** 38.42N 8.59W
Montijo Dam Spain **10** 38.52N 6.20W
Montilla Spain **10** 37.36N 4.40W
Montivilliers France **9** 49.33N 0.12E
Mont Joli *town* Canada **55** 48.36N 68.14W
Mont Laurier *town* Canada **55** 46.33N 75.31W
Mont Louis *town* Canada **55** 49.15N 65.46W
Montluçon France **11** 46.20N 2.36E
Montmagny Canada **55** 46.56N 70.28W
Montmédy France **8** 49.31N 5.21E
Montmirail France **9** 48.52N 3.32E
Montmorillon France **11** 46.26N 0.52E
Montmort France **9** 48.55N 3.49E
Monto Australia **44** 24.52S151.07E
Montoro Spain **10** 38.02N 4.23W
Montpelier Idaho U.S.A. **54** 42.20N111.20W
Montpelier Vt. U.S.A. **55** 44.16N 72.35W
Montpellier France **11** 43.36N 3.53E
Montreal Canada **55** 45.30N 73.36W
Montreal *r.* Canada **55** 47.14N 84.39W
Montrejeau France **11** 43.05N 0.33E
Montreuil France **11** 50.28N 1.46E
Montreux Switz. **14** 46.27N 6.55E
Montrichard France **9** 47.21N 1.11E
Montrose U.K. **6** 56.43N 2.29W
Montrose Colo. U.S.A. **54** 38.29N107.53W
Montserrat *i.* Leeward Is. **57** 16.45N 62.14W
Montserrat, Serra de *mts.* Spain **10** 41.20N 1.00E
Mont Tremblant Prov. Park Canada **55** 46.30N 74.35W
Monument Valley *f.* U.S.A. **54** 36.50N110.20W
Monveda Zaïre **36** 2.57N 21.27E
Monywa Burma **29** 22.07N 95.11E
Monza Italy **9** 45.35N 9.16E
Monze Zambia **36** 16.16S 27.28E
Monzón Spain **10** 41.52N 0.10E
Moolawatana Australia **46** 29.55S139.43E
Mooloogool Australia **42** 26.06S119.05E
Moomba Australia **45** 28.08S140.16E
Moomin Creek *r.* Australia **47** 29.35S148.45E
Moonbi Range *mts.* Australia **47** 31.00S151.10E
Moonie Australia **45** 27.40S150.19E
Moonie *r.* Australia **45** 29.30S148.40E
Moonta Australia **46** 34.04S137.37E
Moora Australia **43** 30.40S116.01E
Moorarie Australia **42** 25.56S117.35E
Moore *r.* Australia **43** 31.22S115.29E
Moore, L. Australia **43** 29.30S117.30E
Moorfoot Hills U.K. **6** 55.43N 3.03W
Moorhead U.S.A. **53** 46.51N 96.44W
Moornanyah L. Australia **46** 33.02S143.58E
Mooroopna Australia **47** 36.24S145.22E
Moosehead L. U.S.A. **55** 45.40N 69.40W
Moose Jaw Canada **50** 50.23N105.35W
Moosonee Canada **55** 51.18N 80.40W
Mootwingee Australia **46** 31.52S141.14E
Mopti Mali **38** 14.29N 4.10W
Mopti *d.* Mali **38** 15.20N 3.35W
Moquegua Peru **62** 17.20S 70.55W
Mora Cameroon **38** 11.02N 14.07E
Mora Spain **10** 39.41N 3.46W
Mora Sweden **17** 61.00N 14.33E
Morādābād India **29** 28.50N 78.45E
Moralana Australia **46** 31.42S138.12E
Moramanga Madagascar **36** 18.56S 48.12E
Morar, Loch U.K. **6** 56.56N 4.00W
Morava *r.* Czech Republic **15** 48.10N 16.59E
Morava *r.* Yugo. **15** 44.43N 21.02E
Moravské Budějovice Czech Republic **14** 49.03N 15.49E
Morawhanna Guyana **60** 8.17N 59.44W
Moray Firth *est.* U.K. **6** 57.35N 5.15W
Morbach Germany **8** 49.49N 7.05E
Morbegno Italy **9** 46.08N 9.34E
Morcenx France **11** 44.02N 0.55W
Morden Australia **46** 30.30S142.23E
Morden Canada **51** 49.15N 98.10W
Mordovo Russian Fed. **19** 52.06N 40.45E
Moreau *r.* U.S.A. **52** 45.18N100.43W
Morecambe U.K. **4** 54.03N 2.52W
Morecambe B. U.K. **4** 54.05N 3.00W
Moree Australia **47** 29.29S149.53E
Morée France **9** 47.55N 1.15E
Morehead U.S.A. **55** 38.11N 83.27W
Morelia Mexico **56** 19.40N101.11W
Morella Spain **10** 40.37N 0.06W
Morelos *d.* Mexico **56** 18.40N 99.00W
Morena, Sierra *mts.* Spain **10** 38.10N 5.00W
Morenci U.S.A. **54** 33.05N109.22W
Möre og Romsdal *d.* Norway **16** 63.00N 9.00E
Moreton I. Australia **45** 27.10S153.25E
Morez France **11** 46.31N 6.02E
Mórfou Cyprus **32** 35.12N 33.00E
Mórfou, Kólpos *b.* Cyprus **32** 35.15N 32.50E
Morgan Australia **46** 34.02S139.40E
Morgan City U.S.A. **53** 29.41N 91.13W
Morgantown U.S.A. **55** 39.38N 79.57W
Morghāb *r.* Afghan. **28** 36.50N 63.00E
Moriki Nigeria **38** 12.55N 6.30E
Morioka Japan **25** 39.43N141.08E
Morisset Australia **47** 33.06S151.29E
Moriyama Japan **23** 35.04N135.59E
Morlaix France **11** 48.35N 3.50W
Mormon Range *mts.* U.S.A. **54** 37.08N114.20W
Mornington I. Australia **44** 16.33S139.24E
Mornington Mission Australia **44** 16.40S139.10E
Morobe P.N.G. **27** 7.45S147.35E
Morocco Africa **34** 31.00N 5.00W
Moro G. Phil. **27** 6.30N123.20E
Morogoro Tanzania **37** 6.47S 37.40E
Morogoro *d.* Tanzania **37** 8.30S 37.00E
Moroleón Mexico **56** 20.08N101.12W
Morón Argentina **63** 34.39S 58.37W
Morón Cuba **57** 22.08N 78.39W
Mörön Mongolia **24** 49.36N100.08E
Morón Spain **10** 37.06N 5.28W
Moroni Comoros **37** 11.40S 43.19E
Morotai *i.* Indonesia **27** 2.10N128.30E
Moroto Uganda **37** 2.32N 34.41E
Moroto, Mt. Uganda **37** 2.30N 34.46E
Morpeth U.K. **4** 55.10N 1.40W
Morrinsville New Zealand **48** 37.39S175.32E
Morristown Ariz. U.S.A. **54** 33.51N112.37W
Morrumbene Mozambique **39** 23.41S 35.25E
Morsbach Germany **8** 50.52N 7.44E
Mortagne France **9** 48.32N 0.33E
Mortain France **9** 48.39N 0.56W
Mortara Italy **9** 45.15N 8.44E
Mortes *r.* *see* Manso *r.* Brazil **62**
Mortes *r.* Brazil **59** 21.09S 45.06W
Mortlake *town* Australia **46** 38.05S142.48E
Morundah Australia **47** 34.56S146.18E
Moruya Australia **47** 35.56S150.06E
Morven Australia **44** 26.25S147.05E
Morvern *f.* U.K. **6** 56.37N 5.45W
Morwell Australia **47** 38.14S146.25E
Morzhovets *i.* Russian Fed. **18** 66.45N 42.30E
Mosby Norway **17** 58.14N 7.54E
Moscow *see* Moskva Russian Fed. **18**
Moscow U.S.A. **54** 46.44N117.00W
Mosel *r.* Germany **8** 50.23N 7.37E
Moselle *r.* *see* Mosel *r.* France / Lux. **8**
Moses Lake *town* U.S.A. **54** 47.08N119.17W
Mosgiel New Zealand **48** 45.53S170.22E
Moshi Tanzania **37** 3.20S 37.21E
Mosjöen Norway **16** 65.50N 13.10E
Moskenes Norway **16** 67.55N 13.00E
Moskenesöy *i.* Norway **16** 67.55N 13.00E
Moskva Russian Fed. **18** 55.45N 37.42E
Moskva *r.* Russian Fed. **18** 55.08N 38.50E
Mosquera Colombia **60** 2.30N 78.29W
Mosquitia Plain Honduras **57** 15.00N 84.00W
Mosquitos, Costa de *f.* Nicaragua **57** 13.00N 84.00W
Mosquitos, Golfo de los *g.* Panama **57** 9.00N 81.00W
Moss Norway **17** 59.26N 10.42E
Mossburn New Zealand **48** 45.41S168.15E
Mosselbaai R.S.A. **39** 34.11S 22.08E
Mossgiel Australia **47** 33.18S144.05E
Mossman Australia **44** 16.28S145.22E
Mossoró Brazil **61** 5.10S 37.18W
Mossuril Mozambique **37** 14.58S 40.42E
Moss Vale *town* Australia **47** 34.33S150.24E
Most Czech Republic **14** 50.31N 13.39E
Mostar Bosnia-Herzegovina **13** 43.20N 17.50E
Mösting, Kap *c.* Greenland **51** 64.00N 41.00W
Mostiska Ukraine **15** 49.48N 23.05E
Mosul *see* Al Mawşil Iraq **30**
Motagua *r.* Guatemala **57** 15.56N 87.45W
Motala Sweden **17** 58.33N 15.03E
Motherwell U.K. **6** 55.48N 4.00W
Motīhāri India **29** 26.39N 84.55E
Motloutse *r.* Botswana **39** 22.15S 29.00E
Motol Belorussia **15** 52.25N 25.05E
Motril Spain **10** 36.44N 3.37W
Motueka New Zealand **48** 41.08S173.01E
Moúdhros Greece **13** 39.52N 25.16E
Mouhoun *r.* Burkina *see* Black Volta *r.* Ghana **38**
Mouka C.A.R. **35** 7.16N 21.52E
Moulamein Australia **46** 35.03S144.05E
Moulins France **11** 46.34N 3.20E
Moulins-la-Marche France **9** 48.39N 0.29E
Moulmein Burma **29** 16.30N 97.40E
Moundou Chad **34** 8.36N 16.02E
Moundsville U.S.A. **55** 39.54N 80.44W
Mountain Ash U.K. **5** 51.42N 3.24W
Mountain City U.S.A. **54** 41.50N115.58W
Mountain Home Idaho U.S.A. **54** 43.08N115.41W
Mountain Village U.S.A. **50** 62.05N163.44W
Mount Barker *town* S.A. Australia **46** 35.06S138.52E
Mount Barker *town* W.A. Australia **43** 34.36S117.37E
Mount Beauty *town* Australia **47** 36.43S147.11E
Mount Bellew *town* Rep. of Ire. **7** 53.28N 8.30W
Mount Darwin *town* Zimbabwe **37** 16.46S 31.36E
Mount Drysdale *town* Australia **47** 31.11S145.51E
Mount Eba *town* Australia **46** 30.12S135.33E
Mount Fletcher *town* R.S.A. **39** 30.41S 28.30E
Mount Gambier *town* Australia **46** 37.51S140.50E
Mount Hagen *town* P.N.G. **27** 5.54S144.13E
Mount Hope *town* N.S.W. Australia **47** 32.49S145.48E
Mount Hope *town* S.A. Australia **46** 34.07S135.23E
Mount Hopeless *town* Australia **46** 29.42S139.41E
Mount Isa *town* Australia **44** 20.50S139.29E
Mount Lofty Range *mts.* Australia **46** 34.40S139.03E
Mount Magnet *town* Australia **43** 28.06S117.50E
Mount Manara *town* Australia **46** 32.28S143.59E
Mountmellick Rep. of Ire. **7** 53.08N 7.21W
Mount Morgan *town* Australia **44** 23.39S150.23E
Mount Murchison *town* Australia **46** 31.23S143.42E
Mount Pleasant *town* Mich. U.S.A. **55** 43.36N 84.46W
Mount's B. U.K. **5** 50.05N 5.25W
Mount Vernon *town* Australia **42** 24.09S118.10E
Mount Vernon *town* Wash. U.S.A. **54** 48.25N122.20W
Mount Walker *town* Australia **43** 27.47S152.32E
Mount Willoughby Australia **46** 27.58S134.08E
Moura Australia **44** 24.33S149.58E
Moura Brazil **60** 1.27S 61.38W
Mourdi, Dépression de *f.* Chad **35** 18.10N 23.00E

Netanya Israel **32** 32.20N 34.51E
Netherlands Europe **8** 52.00N 5.30E
Netherlands Antilles S. America **57** 12.30N 69.00W
Neto *r.* Italy **13** 39.12N 17.08E
Nettilling L. Canada **51** 66.30N 70.40W
Neubrandenburg Germany **14** 53.33N 13.16E
Neuchâtel Switz. **14** 47.00N 6.56E
Neuchâtel, Lac de *l.* Switz. **14** 46.55N 6.55E
Neuenhaus Germany **8** 52.30N 6.58E
Neufchâteau Belgium **8** 49.51N 5.26E
Neufchâtel France **9** 49.44N 1.26E
Neuillé-Pont-Pierre France **9** 47.33N 0.33E
Neumarkt Germany **14** 49.16N 11.28E
Neumünster Germany **14** 54.06N 9.59E
Neuquén Argentina **63** 39.00S 68.05W
Neuquén *d.* Argentina **63** 38.30S 70.00W
Neuquén *r.* Argentina **63** 39.02S 68.07W
Neuruppin Germany **14** 52.55N 12.48E
Neuse *r.* U.S.A. **53** 35.04N 77.04W
Neusiedler See *l.* Austria **14** 47.52N 16.45E
Neuss Germany **8** 51.12N 6.42E
Neustadt Bayern Germany **14** 49.44N 12.11E
Neustrelitz Germany **14** 53.22N 13.05E
Neuvic France **11** 45.23N 2.16E
Neuwied Germany **8** 50.26N 7.28E
Nevada *d.* U.S.A. **54** 39.50N116.10W
Nevada, Sierra *mts.* Spain **10** 37.04N 3.20W
Nevada, Sierra *mts.* U.S.A. **52** 37.30N119.00W
Nevanka Russian Fed. **21** 56.31N 98.57E
Nevel Russian Fed. **18** 56.00N 29.59E
Nevers France **11** 47.00N 3.09E
Nevertire Australia **47** 31.52S147.47E
Nevinnomyssk Russian Fed. **19** 44.38N 41.59E
Nevşehir Turkey **30** 38.38N 34.43E
Newala Tanzania **37** 10.56S 39.15E
New Albany Ind. U.S.A. **55** 38.17N 85.50W
New Amsterdam Guyana **61** 6.18N 57.30W
New Angledool Australia **47** 29.06S147.57E
Newark N.J. U.S.A. **55** 40.44N 74.11W
Newark N.Y. U.S.A. **55** 43.03N 77.06W
Newark Ohio U.S.A. **55** 40.03N 82.25W
Newark-on-Trent U.K. **4** 53.06N 0.48E
New Bedford U.S.A. **55** 41.38N 70.56W
Newberg U.S.A. **54** 45.18N122.58W
New Bern U.S.A. **53** 35.05N 77.04W
Newberry Mich. U.S.A. **55** 46.22N 85.30W
Newbiggin-by-the-Sea U.K. **4** 55.11N 1.30W
New Braunfels U.S.A. **52** 29.43N 98.09W
New Britain *i.* P.N.G. **41** 6.00S150.00E
New Brunswick *d.* Canada **55** 46.30N 66.15W
New Brunswick U.S.A. **55** 40.29N 74.27W
Newburgh U.S.A. **55** 41.30N 74.00W
Newbury U.K. **5** 51.24N 1.19W
New Bussa Nigeria **38** 9.53N 4.29E
Newcastle Australia **47** 32.55S151.46E
Newcastle N.B. Canada **55** 47.01N 65.36W
Newcastle Ont. Canada **55** 43.55N 78.35W
Newcastle R.S.A. **39** 27.44S 29.55E
Newcastle U.K. **7** 54.13N 5.53W
New Castle Penn. U.S.A. **55** 41.00N 80.22W
Newcastle Wyo. U.S.A. **52** 43.50N104.11W
Newcastle B. Australia **44** 10.50S142.37E
Newcastle Emlyn U.K. **5** 52.02N 4.29W
Newcastle-under-Lyme U.K. **4** 53.02N 2.15W
Newcastle upon Tyne U.K. **4** 54.58N 1.36W
Newcastle Waters *town* Australia **44** 17.24S133.24E
Newcastle West Rep. of Ire. **7** 52.26N 9.04W
Newdegate Australia **43** 33.06S119.01E
New Delhi India **28** 28.37N 77.13E
New England Range *mts.* Australia **47** 30.30S151.50E
Newenham, C. U.S.A. **50** 58.37N162.12W
Newent U.K. **5** 51.56N 2.24W
New Forest *f.* U.K. **5** 50.50N 1.35W
Newfoundland *d.* Canada **51** 55.00N 60.00W
Newfoundland *i.* Canada **51** 48.30N 56.00W
New Galloway U.K. **6** 55.05N 4.09W
New Guinea *i.* Austa. **27** 5.00S140.00E
New Hampshire *d.* U.S.A. **55** 43.35N 71.40W
New Hanover *i.* Pacific Oc. **41** 2.00S150.00E
Newhaven U.K. **5** 50.47N 0.04E
New Haven U.S.A. **55** 41.18N 72.55W
New Ireland *i.* P.N.G. **41** 2.30S151.30E
New Jersey *d.* U.S.A. **55** 40.15N 74.30W
New Liskeard Canada **55** 47.30N 79.40W
New London Conn. U.S.A. **55** 41.21N 72.06W
Newman Australia **42** 23.22S119.43E
Newman, Mt. Australia **42** 23.15S119.33E
Newmarket Rep. of Ire. **7** 52.13N 9.00W
Newmarket U.K. **5** 52.15N 0.23E
Newmarket on Fergus Rep. of Ire. **7** 52.46N 8.55W
New Martinsville U.S.A. **55** 39.39N 80.52W
New Meadows U.S.A. **54** 44.58N116.32W
New Mexico *d.* U.S.A. **52** 33.30N106.00W
New Norcia Australia **43** 30.58S116.15E
New Norfolk Australia **45** 42.46S147.02E
New Orleans U.S.A. **53** 30.00N 90.03W
New Philadelphia U.S.A. **55** 40.31N 81.28W
New Plymouth New Zealand **48** 39.03S174.04E
Newport Mayo Rep. of Ire. **7** 53.53N 9.34W
Newport Tipperary Rep. of Ire. **7** 52.42N 8.25W
Newport Dyfed U.K. **5** 52.01N 4.51W
Newport Essex U.K. **5** 51.58N 0.13E
Newport Gwent U.K. **5** 51.34N 2.59W
Newport Hants. U.K. **5** 50.43N 1.18W
Newport Ark. U.S.A. **53** 35.35N 91.16W
Newport Maine U.S.A. **55** 44.50N 69.17W
Newport N.H. U.S.A. **55** 43.21N 72.09W
Newport Oreg. U.S.A. **54** 44.38N124.03W
Newport R.I. U.S.A. **55** 41.13N 71.18W
Newport News U.S.A. **53** 36.59N 76.26W
New Providence *i.* Bahamas **57** 25.03N 77.25W
Newquay U.K. **5** 50.24N 5.06W
New Quay U.K. **5** 52.13N 4.22W
New Radnor U.K. **5** 52.15N 3.10W
New Romney U.K. **5** 50.59N 0.58E
New Ross Rep. of Ire. **7** 52.24N 6.57W
Newry U.K. **7** 54.11N 6.21W
New Scone U.K. **6** 56.25N 3.25W
New South Wales *d.* Australia **47** 32.40S147.40E
Newton Kans. U.S.A. **53** 38.02N 97.22W
Newton Abbot U.K. **5** 50.32N 3.37W
Newton Aycliffe U.K. **4** 54.36N 1.34W
Newtonmore U.K. **6** 57.04N 4.08W
Newton Stewart U.K. **6** 54.57N 4.29W
Newtown U.K. **5** 52.31N 3.19W
Newtownabbey U.K. **7** 54.39N 5.57W
Newtownards U.K. **7** 54.35N 5.41W
Newtown Butler U.K. **7** 54.12N 7.22W
Newtown St. Boswells U.K. **6** 55.35N 2.40W
Newtownstewart U.K. **7** 54.43N 7.25W
New Westminster Canada **50** 49.12N122.55W
New York U.S.A. **55** 40.40N 73.50W
New York *d.* U.S.A. **55** 43.00N 75.00W
New Zealand Austa. **48** 41.00S175.00E
Neya Russian Fed. **18** 58.18N 43.40E
Neyagawa Japan **23** 34.46N135.38E
Neyrīz Iran **31** 29.12N 54.17E
Neyshābūr Iran **31** 36.13N 58.49E
Nezhin Ukraine **15** 51.03N 31.54E
Ngala Nigeria **38** 12.21N 14.10E
Ngami, L. Botswana **39** 20.32S 22.38E
Ngamiland *d.* Botswana **39** 19.40S 22.00E
Ngamiland *f.* Botswana **39** 20.00S 22.30E
Ngangla Ringco *l.* China **29** 31.40N 83.00E
Nganglong Kangri *mtn.* China **24** 32.45N 81.12E
N'Gao Congo **36** 2.28S 15.40E
Ngaoundéré Cameroon **38** 7.20N 13.35E
Ngaruawahia New Zealand **48** 37.40S175.09E
Ngaruroro *r.* New Zealand **48** 39.34S176.54E
Ngauruhoe *mtn.* New Zealand **48** 39.10S175.35E
Ng'iro, Mt. Kenya **37** 2.06N 36.44E
N'Giva Angola **39** 17.03S 15.47E
Ngomba Tanzania **37** 8.16S 32.51E
Ngomeni Kenya **37** 3.00S 40.11E
Ngong Kenya **37** 1.22S 36.40E
Ngorongoro Crater *f.* Tanzania **37** 3.13S 35.32E
Ngozi Burundi **37** 2.52S 29.50E
Nguigmi Niger **38** 14.00N 13.11E
Nguru Nigeria **38** 12.53N 10.30E
Nguruka Tanzania **37** 5.08S 30.58E
Ngwaketse *d.* Botswana **39** 25.10S 25.00E
Ngwerere Zambia **37** 15.18S 28.20E
Nhaccongo Mozambique **39** 24.18S 35.14E
Nhachengue Mozambique **39** 22.52S 35.10E
Nhandugue *r.* Mozambique **39** 18.47S 34.30E
Nha Trang Vietnam **26** 12.15N 109.10E
Nhill Australia **46** 36.20S141.40E
Nhulunbuy Australia **44** 12.11S136.46E
Niafounké Mali **38** 15.56N 4.00W
Niagara Falls *town* U.S.A. **55** 43.06N 79.02W
Niah Malaysia **26** 3.52N113.44E
Niamey Niger **38** 13.32N 2.05E
Niamey *d.* Niger **38** 14.00N 1.40E
Nia-Nia Zaïre **37** 1.30N 27.41E
Niapa, Gunung *mtn.* Indonesia **26** 1.45N117.30E
Nias *i.* Indonesia **26** 1.05N 97.30E
Niassa *d.* Mozambique **37** 13.00S 36.30E
Nicaragua C. America **57** 13.00N 85.00W
Nicaragua, Lago de *l.* Nicaragua **57** 11.30N 85.30W
Nicastro Italy **12** 38.58N 16.16E
Nice France **11** 43.42N 7.16E
Nichelino Italy **9** 44.59N 7.38E
Nicholson Australia **42** 18.02S128.54E
Nicholson *r.* Australia **44** 17.31S139.36E
Nicobar Is. India **29** 8.00N 94.00E
Nicolls Town Bahamas **57** 25.08N 78.00W
Nicosia *see* Levkosía Cyprus **32**
Nicoya, Golfo de *g.* Costa Rica **57** 9.30N 85.00W
Nicoya, Península de *pen.* Costa Rica **57** 10.30N 85.30W
Nid *r.* Norway **17** 58.24N 8.48E
Nida *r.* Poland **15** 50.18N 20.52E
Nidzica Poland **15** 53.22N 20.26E
Niederösterreich *d.* Austria **14** 48.20N 15.50E
Niedersachsen *d.* Germany **8** 52.55N 7.40E
Niekerkshoop R.S.A. **39** 29.19S 22.48E
Niéllé Ivory Coast **38** 10.05N 5.28W
Nienburg Germany **14** 52.38N 9.13E
Niers *r.* Neth. **8** 51.43N 5.56E
Nieuw Nickerie Surinam **61** 5.57N 56.59W
Nieuwpoort Belgium **8** 51.08N 2.45E
Nigde Turkey **30** 37.58N 34.42E
Niger Africa **34** 17.00N 9.30E
Niger *d.* Nigeria **38** 9.50N 6.00E
Niger *r.* Nigeria **38** 4.15N 6.05E
Niger Delta Nigeria **38** 4.00N 6.10E
Nigeria Africa **38** 9.00N 9.00E
Nightcaps New Zealand **48** 45.58S168.02E
Niigata Japan **25** 37.58N139.02E
Niiza Japan **23** 35.48N139.34E
Nijmegen Neth. **8** 51.50N 5.52E
Nikel Russian Fed. **16** 69.20N 30.00E
Nikiniki Indonesia **42** 9.49S124.29E
Nikki Benin **38** 9.55N 3.18E
Nikolayev Ukraine **19** 46.57N 32.00E
Nikolayevskiy Russian Fed. **19** 50.05N 45.32E
Nikolayevsk-na-Amure Russian Fed. **21** 53.20N140.44E
Nikolsk Russian Fed. **18** 59.33N 45.30E
Nikopol Ukraine **19** 47.34N 34.25E
Niksar Turkey **30** 40.35N 36.59E
Nīkshahr Iran **31** 26.14N 60.15E
Nikšić Yugo. **13** 42.48N 18.56E
Nīl, An *r.* Egypt **32** 31.30N 30.25E
Nila *i.* Indonesia **27** 6.45S129.30E
Nile *r. see* Nīl, An *r.* Egypt **32**
Nile Delta Egypt **32** 31.00N 31.00E
Niles Mich. U.S.A. **55** 41.51N 86.15W
Nilgiri Hills India **28** 11.30N 77.30E
Nimbin Australia **47** 28.35S153.12E
Nîmes France **11** 43.50N 4.21E
Nindigully Australia **47** 28.20S148.47E
Ninety Mile Beach *f.* Australia **47** 38.07S147.30E
Ninety Mile Beach *f.* New Zealand **48** 34.45S173.00E
Nineveh *ruins* Iraq **30** 36.24N 43.08E
Ningbo China **25** 29.54N121.33E
Ningde China **25** 26.41N119.32E
Ningnan China **24** 27.03N102.46E
Ningwu China **25** 39.00N112.19E
Ningxia Huizu *d.* China **24** 37.00N106.00E
Ninh Binh Vietnam **26** 20.14N106.00E
Ninove Belgium **8** 50.50N 4.02E
Niobrara *r.* U.S.A. **52** 42.45N 98.10W
Nioro Mali **34** 15.12N 9.35W
Niort France **11** 46.19N 0.27W
Nipāni India **28** 16.24N 74.23E
Nipigon Canada **55** 49.00N 88.17W
Nipigon, L. Canada **55** 49.50N 88.30W
Nipigon B. Canada **55** 48.53N 87.50W
Nipissing, L. Canada **55** 46.17N 80.00W
Niquelândia Brazil **59** 14.27S 48.27W
Nirasaki Japan **23** 35.42N138.27E
Niš Yugo. **13** 43.20N 21.54E
Nisa Portugal **10** 39.31N 7.39W
Nishinomiya Japan **23** 34.43N135.20E
Nisko Poland **15** 50.35N 22.07E
Nissedal Norway **17** 59.10N 8.30E
Nisser *l.* Norway **17** 59.10N 8.30E
Niṭā' Saudi Arabia **31** 27.13N 48.25E
Niterói Brazil **59** 22.54S 43.06W
Nith *r.* U.K. **6** 55.00N 3.35W
Nitra Slovakia **15** 48.20N 18.05E
Niue *i.* Cook Is. **40** 19.02S169.52W
Niut, Gunung *mtn.* Indonesia **26** 1.00N110.00E
Nivala Finland **16** 63.55N 24.58E
Nivelles Belgium **8** 50.36N 4.20E
Nizāmābād India **29** 18.40N 78.05E
Nizhneangarsk Russian Fed. **21** 55.48N109.35E
Nizhnekamskoye Vodokhranilishche Russian Fed. **18** 55.45N 53.50E
Nizhne Kolymsk Russian Fed. **21** 68.34N160.58E
Nizhneudinsk Russian Fed. **21** 54.55N 99.00E
Nizhnevartovsk Russian Fed. **20** 60.57N 76.40E
Nizhniy Novgorod Russian Fed. **18** 56.20N 44.00E
Nizhniy Tagil Russian Fed. **18** 58.00N 60.00E
Nizhnyaya Tunguska *r.* Russian Fed. **21** 65.50N 88.00E
Nizhnyaya Tura Russian Fed. **18** 58.40N 59.48E
Nizke Tatry *mts.* Slovakia **15** 48.54N 19.40E
Nizza Monferrato Italy **9** 44.46N 8.21E
Njazídja *see* Grande Comore *i.* Comoros **37**
Njombe Tanzania **37** 9.20S 34.47E
Njombe *r.* Tanzania **37** 7.02S 35.55E
Njoro Tanzania **37** 5.16S 36.30E
Nkalagu Nigeria **38** 6.28N 7.46E
Nkawkaw Ghana **38** 6.35N 0.47W
Nkayi Zimbabwe **39** 19.00S 28.54E
Nkhata Bay *town* Malaŵi **37** 11.37S 34.20E
Nkhotakota Malaŵi **37** 12.55S 34.19E
Nkongsamba Cameroon **38** 4.59N 9.53E
Nkungwe Mt. Tanzania **37** 6.15S 29.54E
Noatak U.S.A. **50** 67.34N162.59W
Noce *r.* Italy **9** 46.09N 11.04E
Nogales Mexico **56** 31.20N110.56W
Nogara Italy **9** 45.11N 11.04E
Nogayskiye Step *f.* Russian Fed. **19** 44.25N 45.30E
Nogent-le-Rotrou France **9** 48.19N 0.50E
Nogent-sur-Seine France **9** 48.29N 3.30E
Nogoyá Argentina **63** 32.22S 59.49W
Noguera Ribagorçana *r.* Spain **10** 41.27N 0.25E
Noirmoutier, Île de *i.* France **11** 47.00N 2.15W
Nojima-zaki *c.* Japan **23** 34.56N139.53E
Nokia Finland **17** 61.28N 23.30E
Nok Kundi Pakistan **28** 28.48N 62.46E
Nokomis Canada **50** 51.30N105.00W
Nokou Chad **38** 14.35N 14.47E
Nolinsk Russian Fed. **18** 57.38N 49.52E
Noma Omuramba *r.* Botswana **39** 19.14S 22.15E
Nome U.S.A. **50** 64.30N165.30W
Nomgon Mongolia **24** 42.50N105.13E
Nonancourt France **9** 48.47N 1.11E
Nonburg Russian Fed. **18** 65.32N 50.37E
Nong Khai Thailand **29** 17.50N102.46E
Nongoma R.S.A. **39** 27.58S 31.35E
Nonning Australia **46** 32.30S136.30E
Nonthaburi Thailand **26** 13.48N100.31E
Noojee Australia **47** 37.57S146.00E
Noonamah Australia **42** 12.35S131.03E
Noongaar Australia **43** 31.21S118.55E
Noonkanbah Australia **42** 18.30S124.50E
Noonthorangee Range *mts.* Australia **46** 31.00S142.20E
Noorama Creek *r.* Australia **47** 28.05S145.55E
Noord Beveland *f.* Neth. **8** 51.35N 3.45E
Noord Brabant *d.* Neth. **8** 51.37N 5.00E
Noord Holland *d.* Neth. **8** 52.37N 4.50E
Noordoost-Polder *f.* Neth. **8** 52.45N 5.45E
Noordwijk Neth. **8** 52.16N 4.29E
Noorvik U.S.A. **50** 66.50N161.14W
Noosa Heads *town* Australia **44** 26.23S153.07E
Nora Sweden **17** 59.31N 15.02E
Noranda Canada **55** 48.18N 79.01W
Nord *d.* Burkina **38** 13.50N 2.20W
Nord *d.* France **8** 50.17N 3.14E
Nordaustlandet *i.* Arctic Oc. **64** 79.55N 23.00E
Norddeich Germany **8** 53.35N 7.10E
Norden Germany **8** 53.34N 7.13E
Nordenham Germany **14** 53.30N 8.29E
Norderney Germany **8** 53.43N 7.09E
Norderney *i.* Germany **8** 53.45N 7.15E
Nordfjord *est.* Norway **17** 61.54N 5.12E
Nordfjordeid Norway **17** 61.54N 6.00E
Nordfold Norway **16** 67.48N 15.20E
Nordfriesische Inseln *is.* Germany **14** 54.30N 8.00E
Nordhausen Germany **14** 51.31N 10.48E
Nordhorn Germany **8** 52.27N 7.05E
Nordkapp *c.* Norway **16** 71.11N 25.48E
Nordkinnhalvöya *pen.* Norway **16** 70.55N 27.45E
Nordland *d.* Norway **16** 66.50N 14.50E
Nord-Ostsee-Kanal Germany **14** 53.54N 9.12E
Nordreisa Norway **16** 69.46N 21.00E
Nordrhein-Westfalen *d.* Germany **8** 51.18N 6.32E
Nord Tröndelag *d.* Norway **16** 64.20N 12.00E
Nordvik Russian Fed. **21** 73.40N110.50E
Nore Norway **17** 60.10N 9.01E
Nore *r.* Rep. of Ire. **7** 52.25N 6.58W
Norfolk *d.* U.K. **5** 52.39N 1.00E
Norfolk Va. U.S.A. **53** 36.54N 76.18W
Norfolk Broads *f.* U.K. **4** 52.43N 1.35E
Norheimsund Norway **17** 60.22N 6.08E
Norilsk Russian Fed. **21** 69.21N 88.02E
Norman *r.* Australia **44** 17.28S140.49E
Normanby *r.* Australia **44** 14.25S144.08E
Normanby New Zealand **48** 39.32S174.16E
Normanby I. P.N.G. **44** 10.05S151.05E
Normandie, Collines de *hills* France **9** 48.50N 0.40W
Normanton Australia **44** 17.40S141.05E
Norman Wells Canada **50** 65.19N126.46W
Nornalup Australia **43** 34.58S116.49E
Ñorquinco Argentina **63** 41.50S 70.55W
Norrahammar Sweden **17** 57.42N 14.06E
Norra Kvarken *str.* Sweden / Finland **16** 63.36N 20.43E
Norra Storfjället *mtn.* Sweden **16** 65.52N 15.18E
Norrbotten *d.* Sweden **16** 67.00N 19.50E
Nörresundby Denmark **17** 57.04N 9.56E
Norris L. U.S.A. **53** 36.20N 83.55W
Norristown U.S.A. **55** 40.07N 75.20W
Norrköping Sweden **17** 58.36N 16.11E
Norrsundet Sweden **17** 60.56N 17.08E
Norrtälje Sweden **17** 59.46N 18.42E
Norseman Australia **43** 32.15S121.47E
Norsk Russian Fed. **21** 52.22N129.57E
Norte, C. Brazil **61** 1.40N 49.55W
Norte, Punta *c.* Argentina **63** 36.17S 56.46W
Northallerton U.K. **4** 54.20N 1.26W
Northam Australia **43** 31.41S116.40E
Northampton Australia **43** 28.21S114.37E
Northampton U.K. **5** 52.14N 0.54W
Northamptonshire *d.* U.K. **5** 52.18N 0.55W
North Battleford Canada **50** 52.47N108.19W
North Bay *town* Canada **55** 46.20N 79.28W
North Bend Oreg. U.S.A. **54** 43.24N124.14W
North Berwick U.K. **6** 56.04N 2.43W
North Bourke Australia **47** 30.01S145.59E
North C. Antarctica **64** 71.00S166.00E
North C. New Zealand **48** 34.28S173.00E
North Canadian *r.* U.S.A. **53** 35.30N 95.45W
North Carolina *d.* U.S.A. **53** 35.30N 79.00W
North Channel *str.* Canada **55** 46.02N 82.50W
North Channel U.K. **7** 55.15N 5.52W
North China Plain *f. see* Huabei Pingyuan *f.* China **25**
Northcliffe Australia **43** 34.36S116.04E
North Dakota *d.* U.S.A. **52** 47.00N100.00W
North Dorset Downs *hills* U.K. **5** 50.46N 2.25W
North Downs *hills* U.K. **5** 51.18N 0.40E
North East *d.* Botswana **39** 20.45S 27.05E
North Eastern *d.* Kenya **37** 1.00N 40.00E
Northern *d.* Ghana **38** 9.00N 1.30W
Northern Ireland *d.* U.K. **7** 54.40N 6.45W
Northern Marianas *is.* Pacific Oc. **40** 15.00N145.00E
Northern Territory *d.* Australia **44** 20.00S133.00E
North Esk *r.* U.K. **6** 56.45N 2.25W
North Foreland *c.* U.K. **5** 51.23N 1.26E
North French *r.* Canada **55** 51.03N 80.52W
North Frisian Is. *see* Nordfriesische Inseln *is.* Germany **14**
North Horr Kenya **37** 3.19N 37.00E
North I. New Zealand **48** 39.00S175.00E
Northiam U.K. **5** 50.59N 0.39E
North Korea Asia **25** 40.00N128.00E
Northland *d.* New Zealand **48** 35.25S174.00E
North Las Vegas U.S.A. **54** 36.12N115.07W
North Ogden U.S.A. **54** 41.18N112.00W
North Platte U.S.A. **52** 41.09N100.45W
North Platte *r.* U.S.A. **52** 41.09N100.55W
North Powder U.S.A. **54** 45.13N117.55W
North Ronaldsay *i.* U.K. **6** 59.23N 2.26W
North Sea Europe **3** 56.00N 5.00E
North Sporades *see* Voríai Sporádhes *is.* Greece **13**
North Taranaki Bight *b.* New Zealand **48** 38.45S174.15E
North Tawton U.K. **5** 50.48N 3.55W
North Tonawanda U.S.A. **55** 43.02N 78.54W
North Uist *i.* U.K. **6** 57.35N 7.20W
Northumberland *d.* U.K. **4** 55.12N 2.00W
Northumberland, C. Australia **46** 38.04S140.40E
Northumberland Is. Australia **44** 21.40S150.00E
North Walsham U.K. **4** 52.49N 1.22E
Northway U.S.A. **50** 62.58N142.00W
North West C. Australia **42** 21.48S114.10E
North West Highlands U.K. **6** 57.30N 5.15W
North West River *town* Canada **51** 53.30N 60.10W
Northwest Territories *d.* Canada **51** 66.00N 95.00W
Northwich U.K. **4** 53.16N 2.30W
North York Moors *hills* U.K. **4** 54.21N 0.50W
North Yorkshire *d.* U.K. **4** 54.14N 1.14W
Norton Sound *b.* U.S.A. **50** 63.50N164.00W
Nort-sur-Erdre France **9** 47.26N 1.30W
Norwalk Conn. U.S.A. **55** 41.07N 73.25W
Norwalk Ohio U.S.A. **55** 41.14N 82.37W
Norway Europe **16** 65.00N 13.00E
Norway House *town* Canada **51** 53.59N 97.50W
Norwegian Dependency Antarctica **64** 77.00S 10.00E
Norwegian Sea Europe **64** 65.00N 5.00E
Norwich U.K. **5** 52.38N 1.17E
Norwood Ohio U.S.A. **55** 39.12N 84.21W
Noshul Russian Fed. **18** 60.04N 49.30E
Nosovka Ukraine **15** 50.55N 31.37E
Noşratābād Iran **31** 29.54N 59.58E
Noss Head U.K. **6** 58.28N 3.03W
Nossob *r.* R.S.A. / Botswana **36** 26.54S 20.39E
Noteć *r.* Poland **14** 52.44N 15.26E
Noto Italy **12** 36.53N 15.05E
Notodden Norway **17** 59.34N 9.17E
Notre Dame, Monts *mts.* Canada **55** 48.00N 69.00W
Nottawasaga B. Canada **55** 44.40N 80.30W
Nottaway *r.* Canada **55** 51.25N 78.50W
Nottingham U.K. **4** 52.57N 1.10W
Nottinghamshire *d.* U.K. **4** 53.10N 1.00W
Notwani *r.* Botswana **39** 23.46S 26.57E
Nouadhibou Mauritania **34** 20.54N 17.01W
Nouakchott Mauritania **34** 18.09N 15.58W
Nouméa New Caledonia **40** 22.16S166.27E
Nouna Burkina **38** 12.44N 3.54W
Noupoort R.S.A. **39** 31.11S 24.56E
Nouvelle Calédonia *is.* Pacific Oc. **40** 21.30S165.30E
Nouzonville France **9** 49.49N 4.45E
Novafeltria Bagnodi Romagna Italy **9** 43.53N 12.17E
Nova Friburgo Brazil **59** 22.16S 42.32W
Nova Iguaçu Brazil **59** 22.45S 43.27W
Nova Lima Brazil **59** 19.59S 43.51W
Novara Italy **9** 45.27N 8.37E
Nova Scotia *d.* Canada **51** 45.00N 64.00W
Nova Sofala Mozambique **39** 20.09S 34.24E
Novato U.S.A. **54** 38.06N122.34W
Novaya Ladoga Russian Fed. **18** 60.09N 32.15E
Novaya Lyalya Russian Fed. **20** 59.02N 60.38E
Novaya Sibir, Ostrov *i.* Russian Fed. **21** 75.20N148.00E
Novaya Ushitsa Ukraine **15** 48.50N 27.12E
Novaya Zemlya *i.* Russian Fed. **20** 74.00N 56.00E
Novelda Spain **10** 38.24N 0.45W
Nové Zámky Slovakia **15** 47.59N 18.11E
Novgorod Russian Fed. **18** 58.30N 31.20E
Novgorod Severskiy Belorussia **18** 52.00N 33.15E
Novi di Modena Italy **9** 44.54N 10.54E
Novigrad Croatia **14** 45.19N 13.34E
Novi Ligure Italy **9** 44.46N 8.47E
Novi Pazar Yugo. **13** 43.08N 20.28E
Novi Sad Yugo. **15** 45.16N 19.52E
Novoalekseyevka Ukraine **19** 46.14N 34.36E
Novoanninskiy Russian Fed. **19** 50.32N 42.42E
Novo Arkhangel'sk Ukraine **15** 48.34N 30.50E
Novocherkassk Russian Fed. **19** 47.25N 40.05E
Novofedorovka Ukraine **19** 47.04N 35.18E
Novograd Volynskiy Ukraine **15** 50.34N 27.32E
Novogrudok Belorussia **15** 53.35N 25.50E
Novo Hamburgo Brazil **59** 29.37S 51.07W
Novokazalinsk Kazakhstan **20** 45.48N 62.06E
Novokuznetsk Russian Fed. **20** 53.45N 87.12E
Novomoskovsk Russian Fed. **18** 54.06N 38.15E
Novomoskovsk Ukraine **19** 48.38N 35.15E
Novorossiysk Russian Fed. **19** 44.44N 37.46E
Novoshakhtinsk Russian Fed. **19** 47.46N 39.55E
Novosibirsk Russian Fed. **20** 55.04N 82.55E
Novosibirskiye Ostrova *is.* Russian Fed. **21** 76.00N144.00E
Novouzensk Russian Fed. **19** 50.29N 48.08E
Novo-Vyatsk Russian Fed. **18** 58.30N 49.40E
Novozybkov Russian Fed. **15** 52.31N 31.58E
Novska Croatia **14** 45.21N 16.59E
Nový Jičín Czech Republic **15** 49.36N 18.00E
Novyy Bykhov Belorussia **15** 53.20N 30.21E
Novyy Port Russian Fed. **20** 67.38N 72.33E
Nowa Ruda Poland **14** 50.34N 16.30E
Nowa Sól Poland **14** 51.49N 15.41E
Nowendoc Australia **47** 31.35S151.45E
Nowgong Assam India **29** 26.20N 92.41E
Nowingi Australia **46** 34.36S142.15E
Nowra Australia **47** 35.54S150.36E
Nowy Dwór Mazowiecki Poland **15** 52.26N 20.43E
Nowy Korczyn Poland **15** 50.19N 20.48E
Nowy Sacz Poland **15** 49.39N 20.40E
Nowy Targ Poland **15** 49.29N 20.02E
Nowy Tomśyl Poland **14** 52.20N 16.07E
Noxon U.S.A. **54** 48.01N115.47W
Noyant France **9** 47.31N 0.08E
Noyon France **9** 49.35N 3.00E
Nozay France **9** 47.34N 1.38W
Nsanje Malaŵi **37** 16.55S 35.12E
Nsawam Ghana **38** 5.49N 0.20W
Nsombo Zambia **37** 10.50S 29.56E
Nsukka Nigeria **38** 6.51N 7.29E
Nuatja Togo **38** 6.59N 1.11E
Nubian Desert Sudan **35** 21.00N 34.00E
Nueces *r.* U.S.A. **53** 27.55N 97.30W
Nueltin L. Canada **51** 60.20N 99.50W
Nueva Gerona Cuba **57** 21.53N 82.49W
Nueva Helvecia Uruguay **63** 34.19S 57.13W
Nueva Palmira Uruguay **63** 33.53S 58.25W
Nueva Rosita Mexico **56** 27.57N101.13W
Nueve de Julio Argentina **63** 35.30S 60.50W
Nuevitas Cuba **57** 21.34N 77.18W
Nuevo, Golfo *g.* Argentina **63** 42.42S 64.35W
Nuevo Berlín Uruguay **63** 32.59S 58.03W
Nuevo Laredo Mexico **56** 27.30N 99.30W
Nuevo León *d.* Mexico **56** 26.00N 99.00W
Nuevo Rocafuerte Ecuador **60** 0.56S 75.24W
Nu Jiang *r.* China *see* Salween *r.* Burma **29**
Nukha Azerbaijan **31** 41.12N 47.10E
Nuku'alofa Tonga **40** 21.07S175.12W
Nulato U.S.A. **50** 64.43N158.06W
Nullagine Australia **42** 21.56S120.06E
Nullarbor Australia **43** 31.26S130.55E
Nullarbor Plain *f.* Australia **43** 31.30S128.00E
Numalla, L. Australia **46** 28.45S144.21E
Numan Nigeria **38** 9.30N 12.01E
Numazu Japan **23** 35.06N138.52E
Numedal *f.* Norway **17** 60.06N 9.06E
Numurkah Australia **47** 36.05S145.26E

Nundle Australia **47** 31.28S151.08E
Nuneaton U.K. **5** 52.32N 1.29W
Nungo Mozambique **37** 13.25S 37.45E
Nunivak I. U.S.A. **50** 60.00N166.30W
Nuoro Italy **12** 40.19N 9.20E
Nuqūb Yemen **35** 14.59N 45.48E
Nürburg Germany **8** 50.20N 6.59E
Nure *r.* Italy **9** 45.03N 9.49E
Nuriootpa Australia **46** 34.27S139.02E
Nürnberg Germany **14** 49.27N 11.05E
Nurri, Mt. Australia **47** 31.44S146.04E
Nusa Tenggara *is.* Indonesia **26** 8.30S118.00E
Nusa Tenggara Barat *d.* Indonesia **26** 8.50S117.30E
Nusa Tenggara Timur *d.* Indonesia **27** 9.30S122.00E
Nusaybin Turkey **30** 37.05N 41.11E
Nutak Canada **51** 57.30N 61.59W
Nuuk *see* Godthåb Greenland **51**
Nuwaybi'al Muzayyinah Egypt **32** 28.58N 34.38E
Nuweveldberge *mts.* R.S.A. **39** 32.15S 21.50E
Nuyts, Pt. Australia **43** 35.02S116.32E
Nuyts Archipelago *is.* Australia **45** 32.35S133.17E
Nxaunxau Botswana **39** 18.19S 21.04E
Nyabing Australia **43** 33.32S118.09E
Nyahua Tanzania **37** 5.25S 33.16E
Nyahururu Falls *town* Kenya **37** 0.04N 36.22E
Nyah West Australia **46** 35.11S143.21E
Nyainqêntanglha Shan *mts.* China **24** 30.10N 91.00E
Nyakanazi Tanzania **37** 3.05S 31.16E
Nyaksimvol Russian Fed. **18** 62.30N 60.52E
Nyala Sudan **35** 12.01N 24.50E
Nyamandhlovu Zimbabwe **39** 19.50S 28.15E
Nyamapanda Zimbabwe **39** 16.59S 32.50E
Nyamtukusa Tanzania **37** 3.03S 32.44E
Nyandoma Russian Fed. **18** 61.33N 40.05E
Nyanza *d.* Kenya **37** 0.30S 34.30E
Nyanza Rwanda **37** 2.20S 29.42E
Nyashabozh Russian Fed. **18** 65.28N 53.42E
Nyaunglebin Burma **29** 17.57N 96.44E
Nyborg Denmark **17** 55.19N 10.48E
Nybro Sweden **17** 56.45N 15.54E
Nyda Russian Fed. **20** 66.35N 72.58E
Nyeri Kenya **37** 0.22S 36.56E
Nyhammar Sweden **17** 60.17N 14.58E
Nyika Plateau *f.* Malaŵi **37** 10.25S 33.50E
Nyimba Zambia **37** 14.33S 30.49E
Nyíregyháza Hungary **15** 47.59N 21.43E
Nyköbing Falster Denmark **17** 54.46N 11.53E
Nyköbing Jylland Denmark **17** 56.48N 8.52E
Nyköbing Sjaelland Denmark **17** 55.55N 11.41E
Nyköping Sweden **17** 58.45N 17.00E
Nylstroom R.S.A. **39** 24.42S 28.24E
Nymagee Australia **47** 32.05S146.20E
Nymboida Australia **47** 29.57S152.32E
Nymboida *r.* Australia **47** 29.39S152.30E
Nymburk Czech Republic **14** 50.11N 15.03E
Nynäshamn Sweden **17** 58.54N 17.57E
Nyngan Australia **47** 31.34S147.14E
Nyngynderry Australia **46** 32.16S143.22E
Nyong *r.* Cameroon **38** 3.15N 9.55E
Nyons France **11** 44.22N 5.08E
Nysa Poland **15** 50.29N 17.20E
Nysa Kłodzka *r.* Poland **15** 50.49N 17.50E
Nyssa U.S.A. **54** 43.53N117.00W
Nyuksenitsa Russian Fed. **18** 60.24N 44.08E
Nyunzu Zaïre **37** 5.55S 28.00E
Nyurba Russian Fed. **21** 63.18N118.28E
Nzega Tanzania **37** 4.13S 33.09E
N'zérékoré Guinea **34** 7.49N 8.48W
N'zeto Angola **36** 7.13S 12.56E
Nzwani *see* Anjouan *i.* Comoros **37**

O

Oahe Resr. U.S.A. **52** 45.45N100.20W
Oahu *i.* Hawaii U.S.A. **52** 21.30N158.00W
Oakbank Australia **46** 33.07S140.33E
Oakesdale U.S.A. **54** 47.08N117.15W
Oakey Australia **45** 27.26S151.43E
Oak Harbour U.S.A. **54** 48.18N122.39W
Oakland Calif. U.S.A. **54** 37.47N122.13W
Oakland Oreg. U.S.A. **54** 43.25N123.18W
Oaklands Australia **47** 35.25S146.15E
Oakley U.S.A. **54** 42.15N113.53W
Oakover *r.* Australia **42** 20.49S120.40E
Oakridge U.S.A. **54** 43.45N122.28W
Oak Ridge *town* U.S.A. **53** 36.02N 84.12W
Oakvale Australia **46** 33.01S140.41E
Oakville Canada **55** 43.27N 79.41W
Oamaru New Zealand **48** 45.07S170.58E
Oates Land *f.* Antarctica **64** 70.00S155.00E
Oaxaca Mexico **56** 17.05N 96.41W
Oaxaca *d.* Mexico **56** 17.30N 97.00W
Ob *r.* Russian Fed. **18** 66.50N 69.00E
Oba Canada **55** 49.04N 84.07W
Oban U.K. **6** 56.26N 5.28W
Oberá Argentina **62** 27.30S 55.07W
Oberhausen Germany **8** 51.28N 6.51E
Oberon Australia **47** 33.41S149.52E
Oberösterreich *d.* Austria **14** 48.15N 14.00E
Obi *i.* Indonesia **27** 1.45S127.30E
Obidos Brazil **61** 1.55S 55.31W
Obitsu *r.* Japan **23** 35.24N139.54E
Obo C.A.R. **35** 5.18N 26.28E
Obodovka Ukraine **15** 48.28N 29.10E
Oboyan Russian Fed. **19** 51.13N 36.17E
Obozerskiy Russian Fed. **18** 63.28N 40.29E
Obruk Platosu *f.* Turkey **30** 38.00N 33.30E
Obskaya Guba *g.* Russian Fed. **20** 68.30N 74.00E
Ōbu Japan **23** 35.00N136.58E
Obuasi Ghana **38** 6.15N 1.36W
Obudu Nigeria **38** 6.42N 9.07E
Ocala U.S.A. **53** 29.11N 82.09W
Ocaña Colombia **60** 8.16N 73.21W
Ocaña Spain **10** 39.57N 3.30W
Occidental, Cordillera *mts.* Colombia **60** 5.00N 76.15W
Occidental, Cordillera *mts.* S. America **62** 17.00S 69.00W
Oceanside Calif. U.S.A. **54** 33.12N117.23W
Oceanside N.Y. U.S.A. **55** 40.38N 73.38W
Ochamchire Georgia **19** 42.44N 41.30E
Ochil Hills U.K. **6** 56.16N 3.25W
Ochsenfurt Germany **14** 49.40N 10.03E
Ockelbo Sweden **17** 60.53N 16.43E
Ocotal Nicaragua **57** 13.37N 86.31W
Ocotlán Mexico **56** 20.21N102.42W
Octeville France **9** 49.37N 1.39W
Ocua Mozambique **37** 13.40S 39.46E
Oda Ghana **38** 5.55N 0.56W
Ódádhahraun *mts.* Iceland **16** 65.00N 17.30W
Odawara Japan **23** 35.15N139.10E
Odda Norway **17** 60.04N 6.33E
Ödeborg Sweden **17** 58.33N 12.00E
Odemira Portugal **10** 37.36N 8.38W
Ödemiş Turkey **13** 38.12N 28.00E
Odense Denmark **17** 55.24N 10.23E
Odenwald *mts.* Germany **14** 49.40N 9.20E
Oder *r.* Germany *see* Odra *r.* Poland **14**
Oderzo Italy **9** 45.47N 12.29E
Odessa Ukraine **15** 46.30N 30.46E
Odessa Tex. U.S.A. **52** 31.50N102.23W
Odorhei Romania **15** 46.18N 25.18E
Odra *r.* Poland **14** 53.30N 14.36E
Odžak Bosnia-Herzegovina **15** 45.03N 18.18E
Odzi *r.* Zimbabwe **39** 19.46S 32.22E
Oegstgeest Neth. **8** 52.12N 4.31E
Oeiras Brazil **61** 7.00S 42.07W
Ofanto *r.* Italy **12** 41.22N 16.12E
Ofaqim Israel **32** 31.19N 34.37E
Offa Nigeria **38** 8.09N 4.44E
Offaly *d.* Rep. of Ire. **7** 53.15N 7.30W
Offenbach Germany **14** 50.06N 8.46E
Offenburg Germany **14** 48.29N 7.57E
Offerdal Sweden **16** 63.28N 14.03E
Offranville France **9** 49.52N 1.03E
Ofir Portugal **10** 41.31N 8.47W
Ofotfjorden *est.* Norway **16** 68.25N 17.00E
Ōgaki Japan **23** 35.21N136.37E
Ogbomosho Nigeria **38** 8.05N 4.11E
Ogden Utah U.S.A. **54** 41.14N111.58W
Ogeechee *r.* U.S.A. **53** 32.54N 81.05W
Ogilvie Mts. Canada **50** 65.00N139.30W
Oginskiy, Kanal *canal* Belorussia **15** 52.25N 25.55E
Oglio *r.* Italy **9** 45.02N 10.39E
Ognon *r.* France **11** 47.20N 5.37E
Ogoja Nigeria **38** 6.40N 8.45E
Ogoki *r.* Canada **55** 51.38N 85.57W
Ogoki Resr. Canada **55** 50.50N 88.26W
Ogooué *r.* Gabon **36** 1.00S 9.05E
Ogosta *r.* Bulgaria **13** 43.44N 23.51E
Ogulin Croatia **14** 45.17N 15.14E
Ogun *d.* Nigeria **38** 6.50N 3.20E
Ohai New Zealand **48** 45.56S167.57E
Ohanet Algeria **34** 28.45N 8.55E
Ohey Belgium **8** 50.26N 5.06E
O'Higgins, L. Chile **63** 48.03S 73.10W
Ohio *d.* U.S.A. **55** 40.15N 82.45W
Ohio *r.* U.S.A. **55** 36.59N 89.08W
Ōhito Japan **23** 34.59N138.56E
Ohře *r.* Czech Republic **14** 50.32N 14.08E
Ohrid Macedonia **13** 41.06N 20.48E
Ohrid, L. Albania / Macedonia **13** 41.00N 20.43E
Ōi *r.* Japan **23** 34.45N138.18E
Oil City U.S.A. **55** 41.26N 79.42W
Oise *d.* France **9** 49.30N 2.30E
Oise *r.* France **9** 49.00N 2.10E
Oisterwijk Neth. **8** 51.34N 5.10E
Ojai U.S.A. **54** 34.27N119.15W
Ojocaliente Mexico **56** 22.35N102.18W
Ojo de Agua Argentina **62** 29.30S 63.44W
Ojos del Salado *mtn.* Argentina / Chile **62** 27.05S 68.05W
Oka Nigeria **38** 7.28N 5.48E
Oka *r.* Russian Fed. **18** 56.09N 43.00E
Okaba Indonesia **27** 8.06S139.46E
Okahandja Namibia **39** 21.58S 16.44E
Okanogan U.S.A. **54** 48.39N120.41W
Okanogan *r.* U.S.A. **54** 48.22N119.35W
Okaputa Namibia **39** 20.08S 16.58E
Okarito New Zealand **48** 43.14S 170.07
Okaukuejo Namibia **39** 19.12S 15.56E
Okavango *r.* Botswana **39** 18.30S 22.04E
Okavango Basin *f.* Botswana **39** 19.30S 22.30E
Okayama Japan **25** 34.40N133.54E
Okazaki Japan **23** 34.57N137.10E
Okeechobee, L. U.S.A. **53** 27.00N 80.45W
Okefenokee Swamp *f.* U.S.A. **53** 30.40N 82.40W
Okehampton U.K. **5** 50.44N 4.01W
Okene Nigeria **38** 7.31N 6.15E
Okere *r.* Uganda **37** 1.37N 33.53E
Okha Russian Fed. **21** 53.35N142.50E
Okhansk Russian Fed. **18** 57.42N 55.20E
Okhotsk Russian Fed. **21** 59.20N143.15E
Okhotsk, Sea of Russian Fed. **21** 55.00N150.00E
Okhotskiy Perevoz Russian Fed. **21** 61.55N135.40E
Okiep R.S.A. **39** 29.36S 17.49E
Oki guntō *is.* Japan **25** 36.30N133.20E
Okinawa jima *i.* Japan **25** 26.30N128.00E
Okipoko *r.* Namibia **39** 18.40S 16.03E
Okitipupa Nigeria **38** 6.31N 4.50E
Oklahoma *d.* U.S.A. **53** 35.00N 97.00W
Oklahoma City U.S.A. **53** 35.28N 97.33W
Oknitsa Moldavia **15** 48.22N 27.30E
Okola Cameroon **38** 4.03N 11.23E
Oksskolten *mtn.* Norway **16** 65.59N 14.15E
Oktyabr'sk Kazakhstan **19** 49.30N 57.22E
Oktyabrskiy Belorussia **15** 52.35N 28.45E
Oktyabrskiy Russian Fed. **18** 54.30N 53.30E
Oktyabr'skoy Revolyutsii, Ostrov *i.* Russian Fed. **21** 79.30N 96.00E
Okuru New Zealand **48** 43.56S168.55E
Okuta Nigeria **38** 9.13N 3.12E
Ólafsvík Iceland **16** 64.53N 23.44W
Olancha U.S.A. **54** 36.17N118.01W
Öland *i.* Sweden **17** 56.45N 16.38E
Olary Australia **46** 32.18S140.19E
Olascoaga Argentina **63** 35.14S 60.37W
Olavarría Argentina **63** 36.57S 60.20W
Oława Poland **15** 50.57N 17.17E
Olbia Italy **12** 40.55N 9.29E
Old Bar Australia **47** 31.59S152.35E
Old Crow Canada **50** 67.34N139.43W
Oldenburg Nschn. Germany **8** 53.08N 8.13E
Oldenburg Sch.-Hol. Germany **14** 54.17N 10.52E
Oldenzaal Neth. **8** 52.19N 6.55E
Old Forge Penn. U.S.A. **55** 41.22N 75.44W
Old Gumbiro Tanzania **37** 10.00S 35.24E
Oldham U.K. **4** 53.33N 2.08W
Old Head of Kinsale *c.* Rep. of Ire. **7** 51.37N 8.33W
Old Moolawatana Australia **46** 30.04S140.02E
Old Town U.S.A. **55** 44.56N 68.39W
Olean U.S.A. **55** 42.05N 78.26W
Olecko Poland **15** 54.03N 22.30E
Olekma *r.* Russian Fed. **21** 60.20N120.30E
Olekminsk Russian Fed. **21** 60.25N120.00E
Olema Russian Fed. **18** 64.25N 40.15E
Olenëk Russian Fed. **21** 68.38N112.15E
Olenëk *r.* Russian Fed. **21** 73.00N120.00E
Olenëkskiy Zaliv *g.* Russian Fed. **21** 74.00N120.00E
Oléron, Île d' *i.* France **11** 45.55N 1.16W
Oleśnica Poland **15** 51.13N 17.23E
Olevsk Ukraine **15** 51.12N 27.35E
Olga Russian Fed. **25** 43.46N135.14E
Olga, Mt. Australia **44** 25.18S130.44E
Olga L. Canada **55** 49.37N 77.26W
Ölgiy Mongolia **24** 48.54N 90.00E
Olgopol Ukraine **15** 48.10N 29.30E
Olhão Portugal **10** 37.01N 7.50W
Olifants *r.* Namibia **39** 25.28S 19.23E
Olifants *r.* C.P. R.S.A. **39** 31.42S 18.10E
Olifants *r.* Trans. R.S.A. **39** 24.08S 32.39E
Ólimbos *mtn.* Cyprus **32** 34.55N 32.52E
Ólimbos Greece **13** 35.44N 27.11E
Ólimbos *mtn.* Greece **13** 40.04N 22.20E
Olinda Brazil **61** 8.00S 34.51W
Oliva Argentina **62** 32.05S 63.35W
Oliva Spain **10** 38.58N 0.15W
Olivares Spain **10** 39.45N 2.21W
Oliveira Brazil **59** 20.39S 44.47W
Olivenza Spain **10** 38.41N 7.09W
Olney U.K. **5** 52.09N 0.42W
Olofström Sweden **17** 56.16N 14.30E
Olomouc Czech Republic **15** 49.36N 17.16E
Olonets Russian Fed. **18** 61.00N 32.59E
Oloron France **11** 43.12N 0.35W
Olot Spain **10** 42.11N 2.30E
Olovyannaya Russian Fed. **25** 50.58N115.35E
Olpe Germany **8** 51.02N 7.52E
Olsztyn Poland **15** 53.48N 20.29E
Olsztynek Poland **15** 53.36N 20.17E
Olt *r.* Romania **15** 43.43N 24.51E
Oltenița Romania **15** 44.05N 26.31E
Olteț *r.* Romania **15** 44.13N 24.28E
Olympia U.S.A. **54** 47.03N122.53W
Olympic Mts. U.S.A. **54** 47.50N123.45W
Olympic Nat. Park U.S.A. **54** 47.48N123.30W
Olympus *mtn. see* Ólimbos *mtn.* Greece **13**
Olympus, Mt. U.S.A. **54** 47.48N123.43W
Omae-zaki *c.* Japan **23** 34.36N138.14E
Omagh U.K. **7** 54.36N 7.20W
Omaha U.S.A. **53** 41.15N 96.00W
Oman Asia **28** 22.30N 57.30E
Oman, G. of Asia **31** 25.00N 58.00E
Omarama New Zealand **48** 44.29S169.58E
Omaruru Namibia **39** 21.25S 15.57E
Omate Peru **62** 16.40S 70.58W
Ombrone *r.* Italy **12** 42.40N 11.00E
Omdurman *see* Umm Durmān Sudan **35**
Omegna Italy **9** 45.53N 8.24E
Omeo Australia **47** 37.05S147.37E
Ometepec Mexico **56** 16.41N 98.25W
Ōmi-hachiman Japan **23** 35.08N136.06E
Omitara Namibia **39** 22.18S 18.01E
Ōmiya Japan **23** 35.54N139.38E
Ommen Neth. **8** 52.32N 6.25E
Omolon *r.* Russian Fed. **21** 68.50N158.30E
Omsk Russian Fed. **20** 55.00N 73.22E
Omulew *r.* Poland **15** 53.05N 21.32E
Omuramba Omatako *r.* Namibia **39** 18.19S 19.52E
Omuta Japan **25** 33.02N130.26E
Oña Spain **10** 42.44N 3.25W
Onda Spain **10** 39.58N 0.16W
Ondangua Namibia **39** 17.59S 16.02E
Ondo *d.* Nigeria **38** 7.10N 5.20E
Onega Russian Fed. **18** 63.57N 38.11E
Onega *r.* Russian Fed. **18** 63.59N 38.11E
Oneida U.S.A. **55** 43.06N 75.39W
Onezhskaya Guba *b.* Russian Fed. **18** 63.55N 37.30E
Onezhskoye Ozero *l.* Russian Fed. **18** 62.00N 35.30E
Ongerup Australia **43** 33.58S118.29E
Ongole India **29** 15.31N 80.04E
Onitsha Nigeria **38** 6.10N 6.47E
Onjiva Angola **36** 17.03S 15.41E
Onslow Australia **42** 21.41S115.12E
Onstwedde Neth. **8** 53.04N 7.02E
Ontario *d.* Canada **51** 52.00N 86.00W
Ontario Calif. U.S.A. **54** 34.04N117.39W
Ontario Oreg. U.S.A. **54** 44.02N116.58W
Ontario, L. Canada / U.S.A. **55** 43.45N 78.00W
Ontonagon U.S.A. **55** 46.52N 89.18W
Oodnadatta Australia **45** 27.30S135.27E
Ooldea Australia **45** 30.27S131.50E
Oostelijk-Flevoland *f.* Neth. **8** 52.30N 5.40E
Oostende Belgium **8** 51.13N 2.55E
Oosterhout Neth. **8** 51.38N 4.50E
Oosterschelde *est.* Neth. **8** 51.35N 3.57E
Oosthuizen Neth. **8** 52.33N 5.00E
Oostmalle Belgium **8** 51.18N 4.45E
Oost Vlaanderen *d.* Belgium **8** 51.00N 3.45E
Oost Vlieland Neth. **8** 53.18N 5.04E
Opaka Bulgaria **13** 43.28N 26.10E
Opala Russian Fed. **21** 51.58N156.30E
Oparino Russian Fed. **18** 59.53N 48.10E
Opasatika Canada **55** 49.32N 82.53W
Opasatika *r.* Canada **55** 50.23N 82.26W
Opava Czech Republic **15** 49.56N 17.54E
Opochka Russian Fed. **18** 56.41N 28.42E
Opole Poland **15** 50.40N 17.56E
Oporto *see* Porto Portugal **10**
Opotiki New Zealand **48** 38.00S177.18E
Oppdal Norway **16** 62.36N 9.41E
Oppland *d.* Norway **17** 61.30N 9.00E
Opportunity U.S.A. **54** 47.39N117.15W
Opunake New Zealand **48** 39.27S173.51E
Ora Italy **9** 46.21N 11.18E
Ora Banda Australia **43** 30.27S121.04E
Oradea Romania **15** 47.03N 21.55E
Öraefajökull *mtn.* Iceland **16** 64.02N 16.39W
Orai India **29** 26.00N 79.26E
Oran Algeria **34** 35.45N 0.38W
Orán Argentina **62** 23.07S 64.16W
Orange Australia **47** 33.19S149.10E
Orange France **11** 44.08N 4.48E
Orange *r.* R.S.A. **39** 28.38S 16.38E
Orange Tex. U.S.A. **53** 30.05N 93.43W
Orange, C. Brazil **61** 4.25N 51.32W
Orangeburg U.S.A. **53** 33.28N 80.53W
Orange Free State *d.* R.S.A. **39** 28.00S 28.00E
Orangevale U.S.A. **54** 38.41N121.13W
Oranienburg Germany **14** 52.45N 13.14E
Oranjefontein R.S.A. **39** 23.27S 27.40E
Oranjemund Namibia **39** 28.35S 16.26E
Oras Phil. **27** 12.09N125.22E
Orbetello Italy **12** 42.27N 11.13E
Orbost Australia **47** 37.42S148.30E
Örbyhus Sweden **17** 60.14N 17.42E
Orchies France **8** 50.28N 3.15E
Orchila *i.* Venezuela **57** 11.52N 66.10W
Orco *r.* Italy **9** 45.10N 7.52E
Ord *r.* Australia **42** 15.30S128.30E
Ordu Turkey **30** 41.00N 37.52E
Orduña Spain **10** 43.00N 3.00W
Örebro Sweden **17** 59.17N 15.13E
Örebro *d.* Sweden **17** 59.30N 15.00E
Oregon *d.* U.S.A. **54** 43.49N120.36W
Oregon City U.S.A. **54** 45.21N122.36W
Öregrund Sweden **17** 60.20N 18.26E
Orekhovo-Zuyevo Russian Fed. **18** 55.47N 39.00E
Orel Russian Fed. **18** 52.58N 36.04E
Orem U.S.A. **54** 40.19N111.42W
Orenburg Russian Fed. **18** 51.50N 55.00E
Orense Spain **10** 42.20N 7.52W
Oressa *r.* Belorussia **15** 52.33N 28.45E
Orestiás Greece **13** 41.30N 26.33E
Orfanoú, Kólpos *g.* Greece **13** 40.40N 24.00E
Orford U.S.A. **55** 43.54N 72.10W
Orford Ness *c.* Australia **44** 11.22S142.50E
Orford Ness *c.* U.K. **5** 52.05N 1.36E
Orgeyev Moldavia **15** 47.24N 28.50E
Orick U.S.A. **54** 41.17N124.04W
Oriental, Cordillera *mts.* Bolivia **62** 17.00S 65.00W
Oriental, Cordillera *mts.* Colombia **60** 5.00N 74.30W
Origny France **9** 49.54N 3.30E
Orihuela Spain **10** 38.05N 0.56W
Orillia Canada **55** 44.37N 79.25W
Orimattila Finland **17** 60.48N 25.45E
Orinduik Guyana **60** 4.42N 60.01W
Orinoco *r.* Venezuela **60** 9.00N 61.30W
Orinoco, Delta del *f.* Venezuela **60** 9.00N 61.00W
Orissa *d.* India **29** 20.15N 84.00E
Oristano Italy **12** 39.53N 8.36E
Oristano, Golfo di *g.* Italy **12** 39.50N 8.30E
Orizaba Mexico **56** 18.51N 97.08W
Orkanger Norway **16** 63.17N 9.52E
Orkney Is. *d.* U.K. **6** 59.00N 3.00W
Orlândia Brazil **59** 20.55S 47.54W
Orlando U.S.A. **53** 28.33N 81.21W
Orléans France **9** 47.54N 1.54E
Orléans, Canal d' France **9** 47.54N 1.55E
Ormāra Pakistan **28** 25.12N 64.38E
Ormoc Phil. **27** 11.00N124.37E
Ormond New Zealand **48** 38.35S177.58E
Ormskirk U.K. **4** 53.35N 2.53W
Orne *d.* France **9** 48.40N 0.05E
Orne *r.* France **9** 49.17N 0.10W
Örnsköldsvik Sweden **16** 63.17N 18.50E
Orobie, Alpi *mts.* Italy **9** 46.03N 10.00E
Orocué Colombia **60** 4.48N 71.20W
Orodara Burkina **38** 11.00N 4.54W
Oromocto Canada **55** 45.50N 66.28W
Oron Israel **32** 30.55N 35.01E
Oron Nigeria **38** 4.49N 8.15E
Orono U.S.A. **55** 44.53N 68.40W
Orosei Italy **12** 40.23N 9.40E
Orosei, Golfo di *g.* Italy **12** 40.15N 9.45E
Orosháza Hungary **15** 46.34N 20.40E
Orotukan Russian Fed. **21** 62.16N151.43E
Oroville Calif. U.S.A. **54** 39.31N121.33W
Oroville Wash. U.S.A. **54** 48.56N119.26W
Orroroo Australia **46** 32.46S138.39E
Orsa Sweden **17** 61.07N 14.37E
Orsha Belorussia **18** 54.30N 30.23E
Orsières Switz. **9** 46.02N 7.09E
Orsk Russian Fed. **18** 51.13N 58.35E
Orşova Romania **15** 44.42N 22.22E
Orta Nova Italy **12** 41.19N 15.42E
Orthez France **11** 43.29N 0.46W
Ortigueira Spain **10** 43.41N 7.51W
Ortona Italy **12** 42.21N 14.24E
Orūmīyeh Iran **31** 37.32N 45.02E
Oruro Bolivia **62** 17.59S 67.09W
Oruro *d.* Bolivia **62** 18.00S 72.30W
Oryakhovo Bulgaria **13** 43.42N 23.58E
Orzinuovi Italy **9** 45.24N 9.55E
Os Norway **16** 62.31N 11.11E
Osa, Península de *pen.* Costa Rica **57** 8.20N 83.30W
Osage *r.* U.S.A. **53** 38.35N 91.57W
Ōsaka Japan **23** 34.40N135.30E
Ōsaka *d.* Japan **23** 34.24N135.25E
Ōsaka-wan *b.* Japan **23** 34.30N135.18E
Osby Sweden **17** 56.22N 13.59E
Osen Norway **16** 64.18N 10.32E
Osh Kyrgyzstan **20** 40.37N 72.49E
Oshawa Canada **55** 43.54N 78.51W
Ō shima *i.* Tosan Japan **23** 34.43N139.24E
Oshmyany Belorussia **15** 54.22N 25.52E
Oshnovīyeh Iran **31** 37.03N 45.05E
Oshogbo Nigeria **38** 7.50N 4.35E
Oshtorān, Kūh *mtn.* Iran **31** 33.18N 49.15E
Oshvor Russian Fed. **18** 66.59N 62.59E
Osijek Croatia **13** 45.35N 18.43E
Osipovichi Belorussia **15** 53.19N 28.36E
Oskarshamn Sweden **17** 57.16N 16.26E
Oskol *r.* Ukraine **19** 49.08N 37.10E
Oslo Norway **17** 59.56N 10.45E
Oslofjorden *est.* Norway **17** 59.20N 10.35E
Osmancik Turkey **30** 40.58N 34.50E
Osmaniye Turkey **30** 37.04N 36.15E
Osnabrück Germany **8** 52.17N 8.03E
Osorno Chile **63** 40.35S 73.14W
Osorno Spain **10** 42.24N 4.22W
Osöyra Norway **17** 60.11N 5.30E
Osprey Reef Australia **44** 13.55S146.38E
Oss Neth. **8** 51.46N 5.31E
Ossa *mtn.* Greece **13** 39.47N 22.41E
Ossa, Mt. Australia **45** 41.52S146.04E
Osse *r.* Nigeria **38** 5.55N 5.15E
Ostashkov Russian Fed. **18** 57.09N 33.10E
Ostend *see* Oostende Belgium **8**
Oster Ukraine **15** 50.55N 30.53E
Oster *r.* Ukraine **15** 53.47N 31.46E
Österdal *r.* Sweden **17** 61.03N 14.30E
Österdalen *f.* Norway **17** 61.15N 11.10E
Östergötland *d.* Sweden **17** 58.25N 15.35E
Österö *i.* Faroe Is. **16** 62.10N 7.00W
Osteröy *i.* Norway **17** 60.33N 5.35E
Östersund Sweden **16** 63.10N 14.40E
Östfold *d.* Norway **17** 59.20N 11.10E
Ostfriesische Inseln *is.* Germany **8** 53.45N 7.00E
Östhammar Sweden **17** 60.16N 18.22E
Ostrava Czech Republic **15** 49.50N 18.15E
Ostróda Poland **15** 53.43N 19.59E
Ostrog Ukraine **15** 50.20N 26.29E
Ostrołeka Poland **15** 53.06N 21.34E
Ostrov Russian Fed. **18** 57.22N 28.22E
Ostrowiec-Świetokrzyski Poland **15** 50.57N 21.23E
Ostrów Mazowiecka Poland **15** 52.50N 21.51E
Ostrów Wielkopolski Poland **15** 51.39N 17.49E
Ostuni Italy **13** 40.44N 17.35E
Osŭm *r.* Bulgaria **13** 43.41N 24.51E
Ōsumi shotō *is.* Japan **25** 30.30N131.00E
Osun *d.* Nigeria **38** 7.15N 4.30E
Osuna Spain **10** 37.14N 5.06W
Oswego U.S.A. **55** 43.27N 76.31W
Oswestry U.K. **4** 52.52N 3.03W
Otago *d.* New Zealand **48** 45.10S169.20E
Otago Pen. New Zealand **48** 45.48S170.45E
Otaki New Zealand **48** 40.45S175.08E
Otaru Japan **25** 43.14N140.59E
Otavalo Ecuador **60** 0.14N 78.16W
Otavi Namibia **39** 19.37S 17.21E
Otelec Romania **15** 45.36N 20.50E
Otematata New Zealand **48** 44.37S170.11E
Oti *r.* Ghana **38** 8.43N 0.10E
Otira New Zealand **48** 42.51S171.33E
Otiwarongo Namibia **39** 20.30S 16.39E
Otjiwarongo Namibia **36** 20.29S 16.36E
Otjiwero Namibia **39** 17.59S 13.22E
Otju Namibia **39** 18.15S 13.18E
Otočac Croatia **14** 44.52N 15.14E
Otra *r.* Norway **17** 58.09N 8.00E
Otradnyy Russian Fed. **18** 53.26N 51.30E
Otranto Italy **13** 40.09N 18.30E
Otranto, Str. of Med. Sea **13** 40.10N 19.00E
Otrokovice Czech Republic **15** 49.13N 17.31E
Otsego U.S.A. **55** 42.26N 85.42W
Otsego Lake *town* U.S.A. **55** 44.55N 84.41W
Ōtsu Japan **23** 35.02N135.52E
Ōtsuki Japan **23** 35.36N138.57E
Otta Norway **17** 61.46N 9.32E
Ottawa Canada **55** 45.25N 75.43W
Ottawa *r.* Canada **55** 45.20N 73.58W
Ottawa Kans. U.S.A. **53** 38.35N 95.16W
Ottawa Is. Canada **51** 59.50N 80.00W
Otter *r.* U.K. **5** 50.38N 3.19W
Otterbäcken Sweden **17** 58.57N 14.02E
Otterburn U.K. **4** 55.14N 2.10W
Otterndorf Germany **14** 53.48N 8.53E
Otteröy *i.* Norway **16** 62.45N 6.50E
Ottosdal R.S.A. **39** 26.48S 26.00E
Ottumwa U.S.A. **53** 41.02N 92.26W
Oturkpo Nigeria **38** 7.13N 8.10E
Otway, C. Australia **46** 38.51S143.34E
Ouachita *r.* U.S.A. **53** 33.10N 92.10W
Ouachita Mts. U.S.A. **53** 34.40N 94.30W
Ouadda C.A.R. **35** 8.04N 22.24E
Ouagadougou Burkina **38** 12.20N 1.40W
Ouahigouya Burkina **38** 13.31N 2.21W
Ouallam Niger **38** 14.23N 2.09E
Ouallene Algeria **34** 24.37N 1.14E
Ouargla Algeria **34** 32.00N 5.16E
Ouarzazate Morocco **34** 30.57N 6.50W
Ouassouas *well* Mali **38** 16.01N 1.26E
Ouddorp Neth. **8** 51.49N 3.57E
Oudenaarde Belgium **8** 50.50N 3.37E
Oudenbosch Neth. **8** 51.35N 4.30E
Oude Rijn *r.* Neth. **8** 52.14N 4.26E
Oudon *r.* France **9** 47.47N 1.02W
Oudtshoorn R.S.A. **39** 33.35S 22.11E

Ouellé Ivory Coast **38** 7.26N 4.01W
Ouessant, Île d' *i.* France **11** 48.28N 5.05W
Ouezzane Morocco **34** 34.52N 5.35W
Oughter, Lough Rep. of Ire. **7** 54.01N 7.28W
Ouimet Canada **55** 48.43N 88.35W
Ouistreham France **9** 49.17N 0.15W
Oujda Morocco **34** 34.41N 1.45W
Oulu Finland **16** 65.01N 25.28E
Oulu *d.* Finland **16** 65.00N 27.00E
Oulu *r.* Finland **16** 65.01N 25.25E
Oulujärvi *l.* Finland **16** 64.20N 27.15E
Oum Chalouba Chad **35** 15.48N 20.46E
Oumé Ivory Coast **38** 6.25N 5.23W
Ounas *r.* Finland **16** 66.30N 25.45E
Oundle U.K. **5** 52.28N 0.28W
Our *r.* Lux. **8** 49.53N 6.16E
Ouray U.S.A. **54** 40.06N109.40W
Ourcq *r.* France **9** 49.01N 3.01E
Ourense *see* Orense Spain **10**
Ourinhos Brazil **59** 23.00S 49.54W
Ouro Fino Brazil **59** 22.16S 46.25W
Ouro Prêto Brazil **59** 20.54S 43.30W
Ourthe *r.* Belgium **8** 50.38N 5.36E
Ouse *r.* Humber. U.K. **4** 53.41N 0.42W
Outardes, Rivière aux *r.* Canada **55** 49.04N 68.25W
Outer Hebrides *is.* U.K. **6** 57.40N 7.35W
Outjo Namibia **39** 20.07S 16.10E
Ouyen Australia **46** 35.06S142.22E
Ouzouer-le-Marché France **9** 47.55N 1.32E
Ovalle Chile **62** 30.36S 71.12W
Ovamboland *f.* Namibia **39** 17.45S 16.00E
Ovar Portugal **10** 40.52N 8.38W
Ovens *r.* Australia **47** 36.20S146.18E
Overath Germany **8** 50.56N 7.18E
Overflakkee *i.* Neth. **8** 51.45N 4.08E
Overijssel *d.* Neth. **8** 52.25N 6.30E
Överkalix Sweden **16** 66.21N 22.56E
Overton U.S.A. **54** 36.33N114.27W
Övertorneå Sweden **16** 66.23N 23.40E
Ovidiopol Ukraine **15** 46.18N 30.28E
Oviedo Spain **10** 43.21N 5.50W
Ovinishche Russian Fed. **18** 58.20N 37.00E
Ovruch Ukraine **15** 51.20N 28.50E
Owaka New Zealand **48** 46.27S169.40E
Owando Congo **36** 0.30S 15.48E
Owel, Lough Rep. of Ire. **7** 53.34N 7.24W
Owen Falls Dam Uganda **37** 0.30N 33.07E
Owensboro U.S.A. **53** 37.45N 87.05W
Owens L. U.S.A. **54** 36.25N117.56W
Owen Sound *town* Canada **55** 44.34N 80.56W
Owen Stanley Range *mts.* P.N.G. **44** 9.30S148.00E
Owerri Nigeria **38** 5.29N 7.02E
Owo Nigeria **38** 7.10N 5.39E
Owosso U.S.A. **55** 43.00N 84.11W
Owyhee *r.* U.S.A. **54** 43.46N117.02W
Oxelösund Sweden **17** 58.40N 17.06E
Oxford U.K. **5** 51.45N 1.15W
Oxfordshire *d.* U.K. **5** 51.46N 1.10W
Oxley Australia **46** 34.11S144.10E
Oxnard U.S.A. **54** 34.12N119.11W
Oyapock *r.* Guiana **61** 4.10N 51.40W
Oyem Gabon **36** 1.34N 11.31E
Öyer Norway **17** 61.12N 10.22E
Öyeren *l.* Norway **17** 59.48N 11.14E
Oykel *r.* U.K. **6** 57.53N 4.21W
Oymyakon Russian Fed. **21** 63.30N142.44E
Oyo Nigeria **38** 7.50N 3.55E
Oyo *d.* Nigeria **38** 8.10N 3.40E
Oyonnax France **11** 46.15N 5.40E
Ozamiz Phil. **27** 8.09N123.59E
Ozarichi Belorussia **15** 52.28N 29.12E
Ozark Plateau U.S.A. **53** 36.00N 93.35W
Ózd Hungary **15** 48.14N 20.18E
Ozernoye Russian Fed. **18** 51.45N 51.29E
Ozersk Russian Fed. **15** 54.26N 22.00E
Ozinki Russian Fed. **19** 51.11N 49.43E

P

Paamiut *see* Frederikshåb Greenland **51**
Paarl R.S.A. **39** 33.44S 18.58E
Pabianice Poland **15** 51.40N 19.22E
Pābna Bangla. **29** 24.00N 89.15E
Pacaraima, Sierra *mts.* Venezuela **60** 4.00N 62.30W
Pacasmayo Peru **60** 7.27S 79.33W
Pachuca Mexico **56** 20.10N 98.44W
Packsaddle Australia **46** 30.28S141.28E
Packwood U.S.A. **54** 46.36N121.40W
Pacy-sur-Eure France **9** 49.01N 1.23E
Padang Indonesia **26** 0.55S100.21E
Padangpanjang Indonesia **26** 0.30S100.26E
Padangsidempuan Indonesia **26** 1.20N 99.11E
Padany Russian Fed. **18** 63.12N 33.20E
Padauari *r.* Brazil **60** 0.15S 64.05W
Paderborn Germany **14** 51.43N 8.44E
Padilla Bolivia **62** 19.19S 64.20W
Padlei Canada **51** 62.00N 96.50W
Padloping Island *town* Canada **51** 67.00N 62.50W
Padova Italy **9** 45.27N 11.52E
Padre I. U.S.A. **53** 27.00N 97.20W
Padstow U.K. **5** 50.33N 4.57W
Padthaway Australia **46** 36.37S140.28E
Padua *see* Padova Italy **9**
Paducah U.S.A. **53** 37.03N 88.36W
Paeroa New Zealand **48** 37.23S175.41E
Pafúri Mozambique **39** 22.27S 31.21E
Pag *i.* Croatia **14** 44.28N 15.00E
Pagadian Phil. **27** 7.50N123.30E
Pagai Selatan *i.* Indonesia **26** 3.00S100.18E
Pagai Utara *i.* Indonesia **26** 2.42S100.05E
Page U.S.A. **54** 36.57N111.27W
Pager *r.* Uganda **37** 3.05N 32.28E
Pagwa River *town* Canada **55** 50.02N 85.14W
Pahala Hawaii U.S.A. **52** 19.12N155.28W
Pahiatua New Zealand **48** 40.26S175.49E
Paible U.K. **6** 57.35N 7.27W
Paide Estonia **17** 58.54N 25.33E
Paihia New Zealand **48** 35.16S174.05E
Päijänne *l.* Finland **17** 61.35N 25.30E
Paimboeuf France **11** 47.14N 2.01W
Painan Indonesia **26** 1.21S100.34E
Painesville U.S.A. **55** 41.43N 81.15W
Pains Brazil **59** 20.23S 45.38W
Paisley U.K. **6** 55.50N 4.26W
País Vasco *d.* Spain **10** 43.00N 2.30W
Pajala Sweden **16** 67.11N 23.22E
Pajule Uganda **37** 2.58N 32.53E
Pakaraima Mts. Guyana **60** 5.00N 60.00W
Paki Nigeria **38** 11.33N 8.08E
Pakistan Asia **28** 30.00N 70.00E
Paks Hungary **15** 46.39N 18.53E
Pakwach Uganda **37** 2.27N 31.18E
Pakxé Laos **26** 15.05N105.50E
Pala Chad **38** 9.25N 15.05E
Palaiokhóra Greece **13** 35.14N 23.41E
Palaiseau France **9** 48.43N 2.15E
Palamós Spain **10** 41.51N 3.08E
Palana Russian Fed. **21** 59.05N159.59E
Palangkaraya Indonesia **26** 2.16S113.56E
Palanguinos Spain **10** 42.27N 5.31W
Pālanpur India **28** 24.10N 72.26E
Palapye Botswana **39** 22.33S 27.07E
Palau *is.* Pacific Oc. **27** 7.00N134.25E
Palawan *i.* Phil. **26** 9.30N118.30E
Paldiski Estonia **17** 59.20N 24.06E
Paleleh Indonesia **27** 1.04N121.57E
Palembang Indonesia **26** 2.59S104.50E
Palencia Spain **10** 42.01N 4.34W
Palenque Mexico **56** 17.32N 91.59W
Palermo Italy **12** 38.09N 13.22E
Palimé Togo **38** 6.55N 0.38E
Palisades Resr. U.S.A. **54** 43.15N111.05W
Palizada Mexico **56** 18.15N 92.05W
Palk Str. India/Sri Lanka **29** 10.00N 79.40E
Pallës, Bishti i *c.* Albania **13** 41.24N 19.23E
Pallinup *r.* Australia **43** 34.29S118.54E
Palliser, C. New Zealand **48** 41.35S175.15E
Palma Mozambique **37** 10.48S 40.25E
Palma Spain **10** 39.36N 2.39E
Palma, Bahía de *b.* Spain **10** 39.30N 2.40E
Palma del Río Spain **10** 37.43N 5.17W
Palmanova Italy **9** 45.54N 13.19E
Palmares Brazil **61** 8.41S 35.36W
Palmas, C. Liberia **34** 4.30N 7.55W
Palmas, Golfo di *g.* Italy **12** 39.00N 8.30E
Palmeira dos Indios Brazil **61** 9.25S 36.38W
Palmer *r.* Australia **42** 24.46S133.25E
Palmer U.S.A. **50** 61.36N149.07W
Palmer Land Antarctica **64** 74.00S 61.00W
Palmerston New Zealand **48** 45.29S170.43E
Palmerston, C. Australia **44** 21.32S149.29E
Palmerston North New Zealand **48** 40.20S175.39E
Palmi Italy **12** 38.22N 15.50E
Palmira Colombia **60** 3.33N 76.17W
Palm Is. Australia **44** 18.48S146.37E
Palms U.S.A. **55** 43.37N 82.46W
Palm Springs *town* U.S.A. **54** 33.50N116.33W
Palmyras Pt. India **29** 20.40N 87.00E
Paloh Indonesia **26** 1.46N109.17E
Palojoensuu Finland **16** 68.17N 23.05E
Palomani *mtn.* Bolivia **62** 14.38S 69.14W
Palopo Indonesia **27** 3.01S120.12E
Palu Turkey **30** 38.43N 39.56E
Pama Burkina **38** 11.15N 0.44E
Pamekasan Indonesia **26** 7.11S113.50E
Pamiers France **11** 43.07N 1.36E
Pamir *mts.* Tajikistan **24** 37.50N 73.30E
Pampa U.S.A. **52** 35.32N100.58W
Pampas *f.* Argentina **63** 34.00S 64.00W
Pamplona Colombia **60** 7.24N 72.38W
Pamplona Spain **10** 42.49N 1.39W
Panaca U.S.A. **54** 37.47N114.23W
Panaji India **28** 15.29N 73.50E
Panama C. America **57** 9.00N 80.00W
Panamá *town* Panama **57** 8.57N 79.30W
Panama Sri Lanka **29** 6.46N 81.47E
Panamá, Golfo de *g.* Panama **57** 8.30N 79.00W
Panama City U.S.A. **53** 30.10N 85.41W
Panamint Range *mts.* U.S.A. **54** 36.30N117.20W
Panaro *r.* Italy **9** 44.55N 11.25E
Panay *i.* Phil. **27** 11.10N122.30E
Pandan Phil. **27** 11.45N122.10E
Pando *d.* Bolivia **62** 11.20S 67.40W
Pando Uruguay **63** 34.43S 55.57W
Panevežys Lithuania **17** 55.44N 24.21E
Panfilov Kazakhstan **24** 44.10N 80.01E
Panga Zaïre **36** 1.51N 26.25E
Pangani Tanga Tanzania **37** 5.21S 39.00E
Pangkalpinang Indonesia **26** 2.05S106.09E
Pang Long Burma **29** 23.11N 98.45E
Pangnirtung Canada **51** 66.05N 65.45W
Pankshin Nigeria **38** 9.22N 9.25E
Pannawonica Australia **42** 21.42S116.22E
Páno Lévkara Cyprus **32** 34.55N 33.10E
Páno Plátres Cyprus **32** 34.53N 32.52E
Pantano del Esla *l.* Spain **10** 41.40N 5.50W
Pantelleria *i.* Italy **12** 36.48N 12.00E
Panton *r.* Australia **42** 17.05S128.46E
Pánuco Mexico **56** 22.03N 98.10W
Paola Italy **12** 39.21N 16.03E
Pápa Hungary **15** 47.19N 17.28E
Papeete Tahiti **40** 17.32S149.34W
Papenburg Germany **8** 53.05N 7.25E
Paphos *see* Néa Páfos Cyprus **32**
Papua, G. of P.N.G. **44** 8.30S145.00E
Papua New Guinea Austa. **41** 6.00S144.00E
Papun Burma **29** 18.05N 97.26E
Papunya Australia **44** 23.15S131.53E
Para *d.* Brazil **61** 4.00S 53.00W
Paraburdoo Australia **42** 23.12S117.40E
Paracatu Brazil **59** 17.14S 46.52W
Paracatu *r.* Brazil **59** 16.30S 45.10W
Paracel Is. S. China Sea **26** 16.20N112.00E
Parachilna Australia **46** 31.09S138.24E
Paraćin Yugo. **15** 43.52N 21.24E
Pará de Minas Brazil **59** 19.53S 44.35W
Paradise Calif. U.S.A. **54** 39.46N121.37W
Paradise Nev. U.S.A. **54** 36.09N115.10W
Paragonah U.S.A. **54** 37.53N112.46W
Paragua *r.* Venezuela **60** 6.55N 62.55W
Paraguaçu *r.* Brazil **61** 12.35S 38.59W
Paraguaná, Península de *pen.* Venezuela **60** 11.50N 69.59W
Paraguarí Paraguay **59** 25.36S 57.06W
Paraguay *r.* Argentina **59** 27.30S 58.50W
Paraguay S. America **59** 23.00S 57.00W
Paraíba *d.* Brazil **61** 7.30S 36.30W
Paraíba *r.* Brazil **59** 21.45S 41.10W
Paraibuna Brazil **59** 23.29S 45.32W
Paraisópolis Brazil **59** 22.33S 45.48W
Parakou Benin **38** 9.23N 2.40E
Paramagudi India **29** 9.33N 78.36E
Paramaribo Surinam **61** 5.52N 55.14W
Paramonga Peru **60** 10.42S 77.50W
Paraná Argentina **63** 31.45S 60.30W
Paraná *r.* Argentina **63** 34.00S 58.30W
Paranã Brazil **61** 12.33S 47.48W
Paraná *d.* Brazil **59** 24.30S 52.00W
Paranã *r.* Brazil **61** 12.30S 48.10W
Paranaguá Brazil **59** 25.32S 48.36W
Paranaíba Brazil **59** 19.44S 51.12W
Paranaíba *r.* Brazil **59** 20.00S 51.00W
Paranapanema *r.* Brazil **59** 22.30S 53.03W
Paranapiacaba, Serra *mts.* Brazil **59** 24.30S 49.15W
Paranavaí Brazil **59** 23.02S 52.36W
Parangaba Brazil **61** 3.45S 38.33W
Paraparaumu New Zealand **48** 40.55S175.00E
Paratoo Australia **46** 32.46S139.40E
Paray-le-Monial France **11** 46.27N 4.07E
Parchim Germany **14** 53.25N 11.51E
Parczew Poland **15** 51.39N 22.54E
Pardo *r.* Bahia Brazil **59** 15.40S 39.38W
Pardo *r.* Mato Grosso Brazil **59** 21.56S 52.07W
Pardo *r.* São Paulo Brazil **59** 20.10S 48.36W
Pardubice Czech Republic **14** 50.03N 15.45E
Parecis, Serra dos *mts.* Brazil **60** 13.30S 58.30W
Parent Canada **55** 47.55N 74.36W
Parent, Lac *l.* Canada **55** 48.40N 77.00W
Parepare Indonesia **26** 4.03S119.40E
Párga Greece **13** 39.17N 20.23E
Pargas Finland **17** 60.18N 22.18E
Paria, Golfo de *g.* Venezuela **60** 10.30S 62.00W
Paria, Península de *pen.* Venezuela **60** 10.45N 62.30W
Pariaguán Venezuela **60** 8.51N 64.43W
Pariaman Indonesia **26** 0.36S100.09E
Parichi Belorussia **15** 52.48N 29.25E
Parigi Indonesia **27** 0.49S120.10E
Parika Guyana **60** 6.51N 58.25W
Parima, Sierra *mts.* Venezuela **60** 2.30N 64.00W
Parinari Peru **60** 4.35S 74.25W
Paringa Australia **46** 34.10S140.49E
Parintins Brazil **61** 2.36S 56.44W
Paris France **9** 48.52N 2.20E
Paris Ky. U.S.A. **55** 38.13N 84.15W
Paris Tex. U.S.A. **53** 33.41N 95.33W
Parisienne *d.* France **9** 48.50N 2.20E
Parkano Finland **17** 62.01N 23.01E
Parker Ariz. U.S.A. **54** 34.09N114.17W
Parker, C. Canada **51** 75.04N 79.40W
Parker Dam U.S.A. **54** 34.18N114.10W
Parkersburg U.S.A. **55** 39.17N 81.33W
Parkes Australia **47** 33.10S148.13E
Parkland U.S.A. **54** 47.09N122.26W
Parlākimidi India **29** 18.46N 84.05E
Parma Italy **9** 44.48N 10.18E
Parma *r.* Italy **9** 44.56N 10.26E
Parma U.S.A. **55** 41.24N 81.44W
Parnaguá Brazil **61** 10.17S 44.39W
Parnaíba Brazil **61** 2.58S 41.46W
Parnaíba *r.* Brazil **61** 2.58S 41.47W
Parnassós *mtn.* Greece **13** 38.33N 22.35E
Parndana Australia **46** 35.44S137.14E
Pärnu Estonia **17** 58.24N 24.32E
Pärnu *r.* Estonia **17** 58.23N 24.29E
Paroo *r.* Australia **46** 31.30S143.34E
Páros *i.* Greece **13** 37.04N 25.11E
Parrakie Australia **46** 35.18S140.12E
Parral Chile **63** 36.09S 71.50W
Parramatta Australia **47** 33.50S150.57E
Parras Mexico **56** 25.25N102.11W
Parrett *r.* U.K. **5** 51.10N 3.00W
Parry, Kap *c.* Greenland **51** 76.50N 71.00W
Parry Is. Canada **51** 76.00N102.00W
Parry Sound *town* Canada **55** 45.21N 80.02W
Parsęta *r.* Poland **14** 54.12N 15.33E
Parsons Kans. U.S.A. **53** 37.20N 95.17W
Parthenay France **11** 46.39N 0.14W
Partille Sweden **17** 57.44N 12.07E
Partinico Italy **12** 38.03N 13.07E
Partry Mts. Rep. of Ire. **7** 53.40N 9.30W
Paru *r.* Brazil **61** 1.33S 52.38W
Parys R.S.A. **39** 26.54S 27.26E
Pasadena Calif. U.S.A. **54** 34.09N118.09W
Pasadena Tex. U.S.A. **53** 29.42N 95.14W
Pasaje Ecuador **60** 3.23S 79.50W
Pasay Phil. **27** 14.33N121.00E
Paşcani Romania **15** 47.15N 26.44E
Pasco U.S.A. **54** 46.14N119.06W
Pasewalk Germany **14** 53.30N 14.00E
Pasinler Turkey **30** 39.59N 41.41E
Pasir Puteh Malaysia **26** 5.50N102.24E
Påskallavik Sweden **17** 57.10N 16.27E
Pasley, C. Australia **43** 33.55S123.30E
Pasmore *r.* Australia **46** 31.07S139.48E
Paso de los Libres *town* Argentina **63** 29.45S 57.05W
Paso de los Toros *town* Uruguay **63** 32.49S 56.31W
Paso Robles U.S.A. **54** 35.38N120.41W
Paspébiac Canada **55** 48.03N 65.17W
Passau Germany **14** 48.35N 13.28E
Passero, C. Italy **12** 36.40N 15.08E
Passo Fundo Brazil **59** 28.16S 52.20W
Passos Brazil **59** 20.45S 46.38W
Pastaza *r.* Peru **60** 4.50S 76.25W
Pasto Colombia **60** 1.12N 77.17W
Pasuruan Indonesia **26** 7.38S112.44E
Patagonia *f.* Argentina **63** 42.20S 67.00W
Patchewollock Australia **46** 35.25S142.14E
Patea New Zealand **48** 39.46S174.29E
Pategi Nigeria **38** 8.44N 5.47E
Pate I. Kenya **37** 2.08S 41.02E
Paternò Italy **12** 37.34N 14.54E
Paterson U.S.A. **55** 40.55N 74.10W
Pathānkot India **28** 32.17N 75.39E
Pathein *see* Bassein Burma **29**
Pathfinder Resr. U.S.A. **54** 42.30N106.50W
Patía *r.* Colombia **60** 1.54N 78.30W
Patiāla India **28** 30.21N 76.27E
Patkai Hills Burma **29** 26.30N 95.40E
Pátmos *i.* Greece **13** 37.20N 26.33E
Patna India **29** 25.37N 85.12E
Patos Brazil **61** 6.55S 37.15W
Patos, Lagoa dos *l.* Brazil **59** 31.00S 51.10W
Patos de Minas Brazil **59** 18.35S 46.32W
Patquía Argentina **62** 30.02S 66.55W
Pátrai Greece **13** 38.15N 21.45E
Patraïkós Kólpos *g.* Greece **13** 38.15N 21.35E
Patrasuy Russian Fed. **18** 63.35N 61.50E
Patrickswell Rep. of Ire. **7** 52.36N 8.43W
Pattani Thailand **29** 6.53N101.16E
Patuca *r.* Honduras **57** 15.50N 84.18W
Pau France **11** 43.18N 0.22W
Pauillac France **11** 45.12N 0.44W
Paulina U.S.A. **54** 44.09N119.58W
Paulistana Brazil **61** 8.09S 41.09W
Paulo Afonso Brazil **61** 9.25S 38.15W
Pavia Italy **9** 45.10N 9.10E
Pavilly France **9** 49.34N 0.58E
Pavlodar Kazakhstan **20** 52.21N 76.59E
Pavlograd Ukraine **19** 48.34N 35.50E
Pavlovo Russian Fed. **18** 55.58N 43.05E
Pavlovsk Russian Fed. **19** 50.28N 40.07E
Pavlovskaya Russian Fed. **19** 46.18N 39.48E
Pavullo nel Frignano Italy **9** 44.20N 10.50E
Paxoí *i.* Greece **13** 39.12N 20.12E
Payette U.S.A. **54** 44.05N116.56W
Payne, L. Canada **51** 59.25N 74.00W
Paynes Find Australia **43** 29.15S117.41E
Paysandú Uruguay **63** 32.19S 58.05W
Pays de Caux *f.* France **9** 49.40N 0.40E
Pays de la Loire *d.* France **11** 47.30N 1.00W
Pazardzhik Bulgaria **13** 42.10N 24.22E
Peace *r.* Canada **50** 59.00N111.26W
Peace River *town* Canada **50** 56.15N117.18W
Peach Springs *town* U.S.A. **54** 35.32N113.25W
Peacock Hills Canada **50** 66.05N110.45W
Peake Creek *r.* Australia **46** 28.05S136.07E
Peak Hill *town* N.S.W. Australia **47** 32.47S148.13E
Peak Range *mts.* Australia **44** 23.18S148.30E
Peale, Mt. U.S.A. **54** 38.26N109.14W
Pearl *r.* U.S.A. **53** 30.15N 89.25W
Peary Land *f.* Greenland **64** 82.00N 35.00W
Pebane Mozambique **37** 17.14S 38.10E
Pebas Peru **60** 3.17S 71.55W
Peć Yugo. **13** 42.40N 20.17E
Pechenga Russian Fed. **16** 69.28N 31.04E
Pechora Russian Fed. **18** 65.14N 57.18E
Pechora *r.* Russian Fed. **18** 68.10N 54.00E
Pechorskaya Guba *g.* Russian Fed. **18** 69.00N 56.00E
Pechorskoye More *sea* Russian Fed. **18** 69.00N 55.00E
Pecos U.S.A. **52** 31.25N103.30W
Pecos *r.* U.S.A. **52** 29.45N101.25W
Pécs Hungary **15** 46.05N 18.14E
Peddie R.S.A. **39** 33.12S 27.07E
Pedregulho Brazil **59** 20.15S 47.29W
Pedreiras Brazil **61** 4.32S 44.40W
Pedrinhas Brazil **61** 11.12S 37.41W
Pedro Afonso Brazil **61** 8.59S 48.11W
Pedro de Valdivia Chile **62** 22.36S 69.40W
Pedro Juan Caballero Paraguay **59** 22.30S 55.44W
Peebinga Australia **46** 34.55S140.57E
Peebles U.K. **6** 55.39N 3.12W
Peebles U.S.A. **55** 38.57N 83.14W
Peel *r.* Canada **50** 68.13N135.00W
Peel I.o.M Europe **4** 54.14N 4.42W
Peel Inlet Australia **43** 32.35S115.44E
Peel Pt. Canada **50** 73.22N114.35W
Peene *r.* Germany **14** 53.53N 13.49E
Peera Peera Poolanna L. Australia **44** 26.43S137.42E
Pegasus B. New Zealand **48** 43.15S173.00E
Pegu Burma **29** 17.18N 96.31E
Pegunungan Van Rees *mts.* Indonesia **27** 2.35S138.15E
Pegu Yoma *mts.* Burma **29** 18.40N 96.00E
Pehuajó Argentina **63** 35.50S 61.50W
Peipus, L. Estonia/Russian Fed. **18** 58.30N 27.30E
Peixe Brazil **61** 12.03S 48.32W
Pekalongan Indonesia **26** 6.54S109.37E
Pekanbaru Indonesia **26** 0.33N101.20E
Peking *see* Beijing China **25**
Pelat, Mont *mtn.* France **11** 44.17N 6.41E
Peleaga *mtn.* Romania **15** 45.22N 22.54E
Peleng *i.* Indonesia **27** 1.30S123.10E
Peleniya Moldavia **15** 47.58N 27.48E
Pelkum Germany **8** 51.38N 7.44E
Pello Finland **16** 66.47N 24.00E
Pelly *r.* Canada **50** 62.50N137.35W
Pelly Bay *town* Canada **51** 68.38N 89.45W
Pelly L. Canada **51** 65.59N101.12W
Pelotas Brazil **59** 31.45S 52.20W
Pematangsiantar Indonesia **26** 2.59N 99.01E
Pemba Mozambique **37** 13.02S 40.30E
Pemba I. Tanzania **37** 5.10S 39.45E
Pemberton Australia **43** 34.28S116.01E
Pembroke Canada **55** 45.49N 77.07W
Pembroke U.K. **5** 51.41N 4.57W
Penang *see* Pinang, Pulau *i.* Malaysia **26**
Peñaranda de Bracamonte Spain **10** 40.54N 5.13W
Penarth U.K. **5** 51.26N 3.11W
Peñas, Cabo de *c.* Spain **10** 43.42N 5.52W
Penas, Golfo de *g.* Chile **63** 47.20S 75.00W
Pendine U.K. **5** 51.44N 4.33W
Pendleton U.S.A. **54** 45.40N118.47W
Penedo Brazil **61** 10.16S 36.33W
Penetanguishene Canada **55** 44.47N 79.55W
Penganga *r.* India **29** 18.52N 79.56E
Pengshui China **25** 29.17N108.13E
Penicuik U.K. **6** 55.49N 3.13W
Peninsular Malaysia *d.* Malaysia **26** 5.00N102.00E
Penneshaw Australia **46** 35.42S137.55E
Pennines, Alpes *mts.* Switz. **9** 46.08N 7.34E
Pennsylvania *d.* U.S.A. **55** 40.45N 77.30W
Penn Yan U.S.A. **55** 42.41N 77.03W
Penny Highland *mtn.* Canada **51** 67.10N 66.50W
Penobscot *r.* U.S.A. **55** 44.30N 68.50W
Penola Australia **46** 37.23S140.21E
Penong Australia **43** 31.55S133.01E
Penonomé Panama **57** 8.30N 80.20W
Penrith Australia **47** 33.47S150.44E
Penrith U.K. **4** 54.40N 2.45W
Penryn U.K. **5** 50.10N 5.07W
Pensacola U.S.A. **53** 30.30N 87.12W
Pensacola Mts. Antarctica **64** 84.00S 45.00W
Penshurst Australia **46** 37.52S142.20E
Penticton Canada **50** 49.29N119.38W
Pentland Australia **44** 20.32S145.24E
Pentland Firth *str.* U.K. **6** 58.40N 3.00W
Pentland Hills U.K. **6** 55.50N 3.20W
Penza Russian Fed. **18** 53.11N 45.00E
Penzance U.K. **5** 50.07N 5.32W
Penzhinskaya Guba *g.* Russian Fed. **21** 61.00N163.00E
Peoria Ariz. U.S.A. **54** 33.35N112.14W
Peoria Ill. U.S.A. **53** 40.43N 89.38W
Perabumulih Indonesia **26** 3.29S104.14E
Perche, Collines du *hills* France **9** 48.30N 0.40E
Percival Lakes Australia **42** 21.25S125.00E
Pereira Colombia **60** 4.47N 75.46W
Perekop Ukraine **19** 46.10N 33.42E
Perené *r.* Peru **62** 11.02S 74.19W
Perevolotskiy Russian Fed. **18** 51.10N 54.15E
Pereyaslav-Khmelnitskiy Ukraine **15** 50.05N 31.28E
Pergamino Argentina **63** 33.53S 60.35W
Pergine Valsugana Italy **9** 46.04N 11.14E
Péribonca *r.* Canada **55** 48.45N 72.05W
Périers France **9** 49.11N 1.25W
Périgueux France **11** 45.12N 0.44E
Perija, Sierra de *mts.* Venezuela **60** 10.30N 72.30W
Peri L. Australia **46** 30.44S143.34E
Perm Russian Fed. **18** 58.01N 56.10E
Pernambuco *d.* Brazil **61** 8.00S 39.00W
Pernatty L. Australia **46** 31.31S137.14E
Pernik Bulgaria **13** 42.35N 23.03E
Perniö Finland **17** 60.12N 23.08E
Péronne France **8** 49.56N 2.57E
Perosa Argentina Italy **9** 44.58N 7.10E
Perpendicular, Pt. Australia **47** 35.03S150.50E
Perpignan France **11** 42.42N 2.54E
Perranporth U.K. **5** 50.21N 5.09W
Perryton U.S.A. **52** 36.23N100.48W
Persepolis *ruins* Iran **31** 29.55N 53.00E
Perth Australia **43** 31.58S115.49E
Perth Canada **55** 44.54N 76.15W
Perth U.K. **6** 56.24N 3.28W
Perth Amboy U.S.A. **55** 40.32N 74.17W
Peru S. America **60** 10.00S 75.00W
Perugia Italy **12** 43.06N 12.24E
Péruwelz Belgium **8** 50.32N 3.36E
Pervomaysk Ukraine **15** 48.03N 30.50E
Pervouralsk Russian Fed. **18** 56.59N 59.58E
Pesaro Italy **9** 43.54N 12.54E
Pescara Italy **12** 42.27N 14.13E
Pescara *r.* Italy **12** 42.28N 14.13E
Pescia Italy **9** 43.54N 10.41E
Peshāwar Pakistan **28** 34.01N 71.40E
Pesqueira Brazil **61** 8.24S 36.38W
Pessac France **11** 44.48N 0.38W
Peşteana Jiu Romania **15** 44.50N 23.15E
Pestovo Russian Fed. **18** 58.32N 35.42E
Petah Tiqwa Israel **32** 32.05N 34.53E
Petaluma U.S.A. **54** 38.14N122.39W
Pétange Lux. **8** 49.32N 5.56E
Petare Venezuela **60** 10.31N 66.50W
Petatlán Mexico **56** 17.31N101.16W
Petauke Zambia **37** 14.16S 31.21E
Petawawa Canada **55** 45.54N 77.17W
Peterborough S.A. Australia **46** 33.00S138.51E
Peterborough Vic. Australia **46** 38.36S142.55E
Peterborough Canada **55** 44.18N 78.19W
Peterborough U.K. **5** 52.35N 0.14W
Peterhead U.K. **6** 57.30N 1.46W
Peterlee U.K. **4** 54.45N 1.18W
Petermann Ranges *mts.* Australia **42** 25.00S129.46E
Petersburg W.Va. U.S.A. **55** 39.00N 79.07W
Petersfield U.K. **5** 51.00N 0.56W
Petitot *r.* Canada **50** 60.14N123.29W
Petit St. Bernard, Col du *pass* France/Italy **9** 45.40N 6.53E
Petoskey U.S.A. **55** 45.22N 84.59W
Petra *ruins* Jordan **32** 30.19N 35.26E
Petrich Bulgaria **13** 41.25N 23.13E
Petrikov Belorussia **15** 52.09N 28.30E
Petrodvorets Russian Fed. **18** 59.50N 29.57E
Petrolina Brazil **61** 9.22S 40.30W
Petropavlovsk Kazakhstan **20** 54.53N 69.13E

Petropavlovsk Kamchatskiy Russian Fed. **21** 53.03N158.43E
Petrópolis Brazil **59** 22.30S 43.06W
Petroşani Romania **15** 45.25N 23.22E
Petrovaradin Yugo. **15** 45.16N 19.55E
Petrovsk Russian Fed. **18** 52.20N 45.24E
Petrovsk Zabaykal'skiy Russian Fed. **21** 51.20N108.55E
Petrozavodsk Russian Fed. **18** 61.46N 34.19E
Petrus Steyn R.S.A. **39** 27.38S 28.08E
Peureulak Indonesia **26** 4.48N 97.45E
Pevek Russian Fed. **21** 69.41N170.19E
Pézenas France **11** 43.28N 3.25E
Pezinok Slovakia **15** 48.18N 17.17E
Pezmog Russian Fed. **18** 61.50N 51.45E
Pfaffenhofen Germany **14** 48.31N 11.30E
Pfalzel Germany **8** 49.47N 6.41E
Pforzheim Germany **14** 48.53N 8.41E
Phangan, Ko *i.* Thailand **26** 9.50N100.00E
Phangnga Thailand **29** 8.29N 98.31E
Phan Rang Vietnam **26** 11.35N109.00E
Pharenda India **29** 27.06N 83.17E
Phenix City U.S.A. **53** 32.28N 85.01W
Phet Buri Thailand **29** 13.01N 99.55E
Philadelphia Penn. U.S.A. **55** 39.57N 75.07W
Philippeville Belgium **8** 50.12N 4.32E
Philippines Asia **27** 13.00N123.00E
Philippine Sea Pacific Oc. **40** 18.00N135.00E
Philippine Trench Pacific Oc. **27** 8.45N127.20E
Philipstown R.S.A. **39** 30.25S 24.26E
Phillip I. Australia **47** 38.29S145.14E
Phillips *r.* Australia **43** 33.55S120.01E
Phillips Maine U.S.A. **55** 44.49N 70.21W
Phillipson, L. Australia **46** 29.28S134.28E
Phnom Penh Cambodia **26** 11.35N104.55E
Phoenix Ariz. U.S.A. **54** 33.27N112.05W
Phoenix I. Kiribati **40** 4.00S172.00W
Phôngsali Laos **29** 21.40N102.06E
Phukao Miang *mtn.* Thailand **29** 16.50N101.00E
Phuket Thailand **29** 8.00N 98.28E
Phuket, Ko *i.* Thailand **29** 8.10N 98.20E
Phumi Sâmraông Cambodia **26** 14.12N103.31E
Phu Quoc *i.* Cambodia **26** 10.10N104.00E
Phu Tho Vietnam **26** 21.23N105.13E
Piacá Brazil **61** 7.42S 47.18W
Piacenza Italy **9** 45.03N 9.42E
Pialba Australia **44** 25.13S152.55E
Pian *r.* Australia **47** 30.03S148.18E
Piana France **11** 42.14N 8.38E
Piangil Australia **45** 35.04S143.20E
Pianoro Italy **9** 44.22N 11.20E
Pianosa *i.* Italy **12** 42.35N 10.05E
Piatra-Neamţ Romania **15** 46.56N 26.22E
Piauí *d.* Brazil **61** 7.45S 42.30W
Piauí *r.* Brazil **61** 6.14S 42.51W
Piave *r.* Italy **9** 45.33N 12.45E
Piawaning Australia **43** 30.51S116.22E
Pic *r.* Canada **55** 48.36N 86.28W
Picardie *d.* France **8** 49.47N 3.12E
Pickering U.K. **4** 54.15N 0.46W
Pickle Crow Canada **51** 51.30N 90.04W
Pickwick L. *resr.* U.S.A. **53** 35.00N 88.10W
Picos Brazil **61** 7.05S 41.28W
Picquigny France **9** 49.57N 2.09E
Picton Australia **47** 34.12S150.35E
Picton Canada **55** 44.01N 77.09W
Picton New Zealand **48** 41.17S174.02E
Picún Leufú Argentina **63** 39.30S 69.15W
Pidálion, Akrotírion *c.* Cyprus **32** 34.56N 34.05E
Piedecuesta Colombia **60** 6.59N 73.03W
Piedras *r.* Peru **60** 12.30S 69.10W
Piedras, Punta *c.* Argentina **63** 35.25S 57.07W
Piedras Negras Mexico **56** 28.40N100.32W
Piedra Sola Uruguay **63** 32.04S 56.21W
Pielavesi Finland **16** 63.14N 26.45E
Pielinen *l.* Finland **18** 63.20N 29.50E
Piemonte *d.* Italy **9** 44.45N 8.00E
Pierce U.S.A. **54** 46.29N115.48W
Pierre U.S.A. **52** 44.23N100.20W
Piesseville Australia **43** 33.11S117.12E
Piešt'any Slovakia **15** 48.36N 17.50E
Pietarsaari Finland **16** 63.40N 22.42E
Pietermaritzburg R.S.A. **39** 29.36S 30.23E
Pietersburg R.S.A. **39** 23.54S 29.27E
Pietrasanta Italy **9** 43.57N 10.14E
Piet Retief R.S.A. **39** 27.00S 30.49E
Pietrosu *mtn.* Romania **15** 47.36N 24.38E
Pietrosul *mtn.* Romania **15** 47.08N 25.11E
Pieve di Cadore Italy **9** 46.26N 12.22E
Pigailoe *i.* Federated States of Micronesia **27** 8.08N146.40E
Pigna Italy **9** 43.56N 7.40E
Pihtipudas Finland **16** 63.23N 25.34E
Pikalevo Russian Fed. **18** 59.35N 34.07E
Pikes Peak *mtn.* U.S.A. **52** 38.51N105.03W
Piketberg R.S.A. **39** 32.54S 18.43E
Piketon U.S.A. **55** 39.03N 83.01W
Pila Argentina **63** 36.00S 58.10W
Piła Poland **14** 53.09N 16.44E
Pilar Paraguay **59** 26.52S 58.23W
Pilar do Sul Brazil **59** 23.48S 47.45W
Pilcomayo *r.* Argentina / Paraguay **62** 25.15S 57.43W
Pilica *r.* Poland **15** 51.52N 21.17E
Pilliga Australia **47** 30.23S148.55E
Pílos Greece **13** 36.55N 21.40E
Pilsum Germany **8** 53.29N 7.06E
Pimba Australia **46** 31.18S136.47E
Pimenta Bueno Brazil **60** 11.40S 61.14W
Pinang, Pulau *i.* Malaysia **26** 5.30N100.10E
Pinarbaşi Turkey **30** 38.43N 36.23E
Pinar del Río Cuba **57** 22.24N 83.42W
Píndhos Óros *mts.* Albania / Greece **13** 39.40N 21.00E
Pindiga Nigeria **38** 9.58N 10.53E
Pine Bluff *town* U.S.A. **53** 34.13N 92.00W
Pine Creek *town* Australia **42** 13.51S131.50E
Pinega Russian Fed. **18** 64.42N 43.28E
Pinega *r.* Russian Fed. **18** 63.51N 41.48E
Pinerolo Italy **9** 44.53N 7.21E
Pinetown R.S.A. **39** 29.49S 30.52E
Piney France **9** 48.22N 4.20E
Ping *r.* Thailand **29** 15.45N100.10E
Pingaring Australia **43** 34.45S118.34E
Pingdingshan Liaoning China **25** 41.26N124.46E
Pingdong Taiwan **25** 22.40N120.30E
Pingelly Australia **43** 32.34S117.04E
Pingliang China **24** 35.25N107.14E
Pingrup Australia **43** 33.33S118.30E
Pingxiang Guang. Zhuang. China **24** 22.05N106.46E
Pinhal Brazil **59** 22.10S 46.46W
Pinhel Portugal **10** 40.46N 7.04W
Pini *i.* Indonesia **26** 0.10N 98.30E
Piniós *r.* Greece **13** 39.51N 22.37E
Pinjarra Australia **43** 32.37S115.53E
Pinnaroo Australia **46** 35.18S140.54E
Pinos, Isla de *i.* Cuba **57** 21.40N 82.40W
Pinrang Indonesia **26** 3.48S119.41E
Pinsk Belorussia **15** 52.08N 26.01E
Pinto Argentina **62** 29.09S 62.38W
Pinyug Russian Fed. **18** 60.10N 47.43E
Piombino Italy **12** 42.56N 10.30E
Piorini, L. Brazil **60** 3.34S 63.15W
Piotrków Trybunalski Poland **15** 51.25N 19.42E
Piove di Sacco Italy **9** 45.18N 12.02E
Pipinas Argentina **63** 35.30S 57.19W
Pipmouacane, Résr. Canada **55** 49.35N 70.30W
Piqua U.S.A. **55** 40.08N 84.14W
Piracicaba Brazil **59** 22.45S 47.40W
Piracicaba *r.* Brazil **59** 22.35S 48.14W
Piracuruca Brazil **61** 3.56S 41.42W
Piraeus *see* Piraiévs Greece **13**
Piraiévs Greece **13** 37.56N 23.38E
Pirassununga Brazil **59** 21.59S 47.25W
Pírgos Greece **13** 37.42N 21.27E
Pirna Germany **14** 50.58N 13.58E
Pirot Yugo. **13** 43.10N 22.32E
Piryatin Ukraine **19** 50.14N 32.31E
Pisa Italy **12** 43.43N 10.24E
Pisciotta Italy **12** 40.08N 15.12E
Pisco Peru **60** 13.46S 76.12W
Písek Czech Republic **14** 49.19N 14.10E
Pishan China **24** 37.30N 78.20E
Pistoia Italy **9** 43.55N 10.54E
Pisuerga *r.* Spain **10** 41.35N 5.40W
Pisz Poland **15** 53.38N 21.49E
Pita Guinea **34** 11.05N 12.15W
Pitalito Colombia **60** 1.51N 76.01W
Pitarpunga, L. Australia **46** 34.23S143.32E
Pite *r.* Sweden **16** 65.14N 21.32E
Piteå Sweden **16** 65.20N 21.30E
Piteşti Romania **15** 44.52N 24.51E
Pithāpuram India **29** 17.07N 82.16E
Pithiviers France **9** 48.10N 2.15E
Pitlochry U.K. **6** 56.43N 3.45W
Pittsburg N.H. U.S.A. **55** 45.03N 71.26W
Pittsburgh U.S.A. **55** 40.26N 80.00W
Pittsfield U.S.A. **55** 42.27N 73.15W
Pittston U.S.A. **55** 41.19N 75.47W
Pittville U.S.A. **54** 41.03N121.20W
Piũí Brazil **59** 20.28S 45.58W
Piura Peru **60** 5.15S 80.38W
Placentia Canada **51** 47.14N 53.58W
Plains U.S.A. **54** 47.27N114.53W
Plainview U.S.A. **52** 34.12N101.43W
Plampang Indonesia **26** 8.48S117.48E
Planá Czech Republic **14** 49.52N 12.44E
Plana Cays *is.* Bahamas **57** 21.31N 72.14W
Plasencia Spain **10** 40.02N 6.05W
Plassen Norway **17** 61.08N 12.31E
Plaster Rock *town* Canada **55** 46.55N 67.24W
Platani *r.* Italy **12** 37.24N 13.15E
Plate, R. *est. see* La Plata, Río de Argentina / Uruguay **63**
Plateau *d.* Nigeria **38** 8.50N 9.00E
Platí, Ákra *c.* Greece **13** 40.26N 23.59E
Platinum U.S.A. **50** 59.00N161.50W
Plato Colombia **60** 9.54N 74.46W
Platte *r.* U.S.A. **53** 41.05N 96.50W
Plattling Germany **14** 48.47N 12.53E
Plattsburgh U.S.A. **55** 44.42N 73.28W
Plauen Germany **14** 50.29N 12.08E
Plavsk Russian Fed. **18** 53.40N 37.20E
Pleasantville U.S.A. **55** 39.23N 74.32W
Pleiku Vietnam **26** 13.57N108.01E
Plenty, B. of New Zealand **48** 37.40S176.50E
Plesetsk Russian Fed. **18** 62.42N 40.21E
Pleshchenitsy Belorussia **15** 54.24N 27.52E
Pleszew Poland **15** 51.54N 17.48E
Pleven Bulgaria **13** 43.25N 24.39E
Pljevlja Yugo. **13** 43.22N 19.22E
Płock Poland **15** 52.33N 19.43E
Ploieşti Romania **15** 44.57N 26.02E
Plomb du Cantal *mtn.* France **11** 45.04N 2.45E
Plombières France **11** 47.58N 6.28E
Plön Germany **14** 54.09N 10.25E
Płońsk Poland **15** 52.38N 20.23E
Ploudalmézeau France **11** 48.33N 4.39W
Plovdiv Bulgaria **13** 42.09N 24.45E
Plumtree Zimbabwe **39** 20.30S 27.50E
Plymouth U.K. **5** 50.23N 4.09W
Plymouth Ind. U.S.A. **55** 41.20N 86.19W
Plzeň Czech Republic **14** 49.45N 13.22E
Pô Burkina **38** 11.11N 1.10W
Po *r.* Italy **9** 44.51N 12.30E
Pobé Benin **38** 7.00N 2.56E
Pobeda, Gora *mtn.* Russian Fed. **21** 65.20N145.50E
Pobla de Segur Spain **10** 42.15N 0.58E
Pocatello U.S.A. **54** 42.52N112.27W
Pocklington U.K. **4** 53.56N 0.48W
Poços de Caldas Brazil **59** 21.48S 46.33W
Poděbrady Czech Republic **14** 50.08N 15.07E
Podgaytsy Ukraine **15** 49.19N 25.10E
Podgorica Yugo. **13** 42.30N 19.16E
Podkamennaya Tunguska Russian Fed. **21** 61.45N 90.13E
Podkamennaya Tunguska *r.* Russian Fed. **21** 61.40N 90.00E
Podolsk Russian Fed. **18** 55.23N 37.32E
Podor Senegal **34** 16.35N 15.02W
Podporozhye Russian Fed. **18** 60.55N 34.02E
Pofadder R.S.A. **39** 29.08S 19.22E
Pogrebishche Ukraine **15** 49.30N 29.15E
Poh Indonesia **27** 1.00S122.50E
P'ohang S. Korea **25** 36.00N129.26E
Poinsett, C. Antarctica **64** 65.35S113.00E
Point Arena *f.* U.S.A. **54** 38.55N123.41W
Pointe-à-Pitre Guadeloupe **57** 16.14N 61.32W
Pointe aux Anglais *town* Canada **55** 49.38N 67.11W
Pointe-aux-Trembles *town* Canada **55** 45.40N 73.30W
Pointe Noire *town* Congo **36** 4.46S 11.53E
Point Hope *town* U.S.A. **50** 68.21N166.41W
Point Lookout *town* Australia **47** 30.33S152.20E
Point Pleasant *town* W.Va. U.S.A. **55** 38.53N 82.07W
Point Samson *town* Australia **42** 20.46S117.10E
Poissy France **9** 48.56N 2.03E
Poitiers France **11** 46.35N 0.20E
Poitou-Charentes *d.* France **11** 46.00N 0.00
Poix France **9** 49.47N 2.00E
Poix-Terron France **9** 49.39N 4.39E
Pokhara Nepal **29** 28.14N 83.58E
Polacca U.S.A. **54** 35.50N110.23W
Pola de Lena Spain **10** 43.10N 5.49W
Polān Iran **31** 25.29N 61.15E
Poland Europe **15** 52.30N 19.00E
Polatli Turkey **30** 39.34N 32.08E
Polch Germany **8** 50.18N 7.19E
Polda Australia **46** 33.30S135.10E
Polesye *f.* Belorussia **15** 52.15N 28.00E
Poli Cameroon **38** 8.30N 13.15E
Policastro, Golfo di *g.* Italy **12** 40.00N 15.35E
Poligny France **11** 46.50N 5.42E
Pólis Cyprus **32** 35.02N 32.26E
Políyiros Greece **13** 40.23N 23.27E
Pollino *mtn.* Italy **12** 39.53N 16.11E
Pollock Reef Australia **43** 34.28S123.40E
Polnovat Russian Fed. **20** 63.47N 65.54E
Polonnoye Ukraine **15** 50.10N 27.30E
Polotsk Russian Fed. **18** 55.30N 28.43E
Polperro U.K. **5** 50.19N 4.31W
Polson U.S.A. **54** 47.41N114.09W
Poltava Ukraine **19** 49.35N 34.35E
Polunochnoye Russian Fed. **18** 60.52N 60.28E
Polyarnyy Russian Fed. **18** 69.14N 33.30E
Polynesia *is.* Pacific Oc. **40** 4.00S165.00W
Pomarkku Finland **17** 61.42N 22.00E
Pombal Brazil **61** 6.45S 37.45W
Pombal Portugal **10** 39.55N 8.38W
Pomene Mozambique **39** 22.53S 35.33E
Pomeroy Wash. U.S.A. **54** 46.28N117.36W
Pomona Namibia **39** 27.09S 15.18E
Pomona U.S.A. **54** 34.04N117.45W
Pompey's Pillar *town* U.S.A. **54** 45.59N107.56W
Ponca City U.S.A. **53** 36.41N 97.04W
Ponce Puerto Rico **57** 18.00N 66.40W
Pondicherry India **29** 11.59N 79.50E
Pond Inlet *str.* Canada **51** 72.30N 75.00W
Ponferrada Spain **10** 42.32N 6.31W
Pongani P.N.G. **44** 9.05S148.35E
Pongola *r.* Mozambique **39** 26.13S 32.38E
Ponnāni India **28** 10.46N 75.54E
Ponoy Russian Fed. **18** 67.02N 41.03E
Ponoy *r.* Russian Fed. **18** 67.00N 41.10E
Ponta Grossa Brazil **59** 25.00S 50.09W
Pont-à-Mousson France **11** 48.55N 6.03E
Ponta Porã Brazil **59** 22.27S 55.39W
Pont-Audemer France **9** 49.21N 0.31E
Pont Canavese Italy **9** 45.25N 7.36E
Pontchartrain, L. U.S.A. **53** 30.50N 90.00W
Pont-d'Ain France **11** 46.03N 5.20E
Pontedera Italy **12** 43.40N 10.38E
Pontefract U.K. **4** 53.42N 1.19W
Ponte Nova Brazil **59** 20.25S 42.54W
Pontevedra Spain **10** 42.25N 8.39W
Pontiac Mich. U.S.A. **55** 42.39N 83.18W
Pontianak Indonesia **26** 0.05S109.16E
Pontivy France **11** 48.05N 3.00W
Pont l'Évêque France **9** 49.18N 0.11E
Pontoise France **9** 49.03N 2.05E
Pontorson France **9** 48.33N 1.31W
Pontremoli Italy **9** 44.22N 9.53E
Pontresina Switz. **9** 46.28N 9.53E
Pontrilas U.K. **5** 51.56N 2.53W
Pont-sur-Yonne France **9** 48.17N 3.12E
Pontypool U.K. **5** 51.42N 3.01W
Pontypridd U.K. **5** 51.36N 3.21W
Ponziane, Isole *is.* Italy **12** 40.56N 12.58E
Poochera Australia **46** 32.42S134.52E
Poole U.K. **5** 50.42N 2.02W
Pooncarie Australia **46** 33.23S142.34E
Poopelloe L. Australia **46** 31.39S144.00E
Poopó, Lago de *l.* Bolivia **62** 19.00S 67.00W
Popayán Colombia **60** 2.27N 76.32W
Poperinge Belgium **8** 50.51N 2.44E
Popilta L. Australia **46** 33.09S141.45E
Poplar Bluff *town* U.S.A. **53** 36.40N 90.25W
Popocatépetl *mtn.* Mexico **56** 19.02N 98.38W
Popondetta P.N.G. **44** 8.45S148.15E
Poprad Slovakia **15** 49.03N 20.18E
Popricani Romania **15** 47.18N 27.31E
Porbandar India **28** 21.40N 69.40E
Porcupine *r.* U.S.A. **50** 66.25N145.20W
Pordenone Italy **9** 45.57N 12.39E
Pori Finland **17** 61.29N 21.47E
Porirua New Zealand **48** 41.08S174.50E
Porjus Sweden **16** 66.57N 19.50E
Porkhov Russian Fed. **18** 57.43N 29.31E
Porkkala Finland **17** 59.59N 24.26E
Porlamar Venezuela **60** 11.01N 63.54W
Pornic France **11** 47.07N 2.05W
Porog Russian Fed. **18** 63.50N 38.32E
Poronaysk Russian Fed. **21** 49.13N142.55E
Porosozero Russian Fed. **18** 62.45N 32.48E
Porretta Terme Italy **9** 44.09N 10.59E
Porsangen *est.* Norway **16** 70.58N 25.30E
Porsangerhalvöya *pen.* Norway **16** 70.50N 25.00E
Porsgrunn Norway **17** 59.09N 9.40E
Porsuk *r.* Turkey **30** 39.41N 31.56E
Portachuela Bolivia **62** 17.21S 63.24W
Portadown U.K. **7** 54.25N 6.27W
Portaferry U.K. **7** 54.23N 5.33W
Portage la Prairie *town* Canada **51** 49.58N 98.20W
Port Albert Australia **47** 38.09S146.40E
Portalegre Portugal **10** 39.17N 7.25W
Port Alfred R.S.A. **39** 33.36S 26.52E
Port Alice Canada **50** 50.23N127.27W
Port Angeles U.S.A. **54** 48.07N123.27W
Port Antonio Jamaica **57** 18.10N 76.27W
Port Arthur Australia **45** 43.08S147.50E
Port Arthur U.S.A. **53** 29.55N 93.56W
Port Augusta Australia **46** 32.30S137.46E
Port-au-Prince Haiti **57** 18.33N 72.20W
Port Austin U.S.A. **55** 44.04N 82.59W
Port Blair India **29** 11.40N 92.30E
Portbou Spain **10** 42.25N 3.09E
Port Bouet Ivory Coast **38** 5.14N 3.58W
Port Bradshaw *b.* Australia **44** 12.30S136.42E
Port Broughton Australia **46** 33.36S137.56E
Port Campbell Australia **46** 38.37S143.04E
Port Cartier Canada **55** 50.01N 66.53W
Port Chalmers New Zealand **48** 45.49S170.37E
Port Curtis Australia **44** 23.50S151.13E
Port-de-Paix Haiti **57** 19.57N 72.50W
Port Edward R.S.A. **39** 31.03S 30.13E
Portela Brazil **59** 21.38S 41.59W
Port Elizabeth R.S.A. **39** 33.57S 25.34E
Port Ellen U.K. **6** 55.38N 6.12W
Port-en-Bessin France **9** 49.21N 0.45W
Port Erin I.o.M Europe **4** 54.05N 4.45W
Porterville R.S.A. **39** 33.01S 19.00E
Porterville U.S.A. **54** 36.04N119.01W
Port Fairy Australia **46** 38.23S142.17E
Port Germein Australia **46** 33.01S138.00E
Portglenone U.K. **7** 54.52N 6.30W
Port Harcourt Nigeria **38** 4.43N 7.05E
Port Harrison *see* Inukjuak Canada **51**
Port Hawkesbury Canada **51** 45.37N 61.21W
Porthcawl U.K. **5** 51.28N 3.42W
Port Hedland Australia **42** 20.24S118.36E
Port Henry U.S.A. **55** 44.03N 73.28W
Porthmadog U.K. **4** 52.55N 4.08W
Port Huron U.S.A. **55** 42.59N 82.28W
Portimão Portugal **10** 37.08N 8.32W
Port Isaac B. U.K. **5** 50.36N 4.50W
Portiţei, Gura *f.* Romania **13** 44.40N 29.00E
Port Jervis U.S.A. **55** 41.22N 74.40W
Port Keats Australia **42** 14.15S129.35E
Port Kembla Australia **47** 34.28S150.54E
Port Kenny Australia **46** 33.09S134.42E
Portland N.S.W. Australia **47** 33.20S150.00E
Portland Vic. Australia **46** 38.21S141.38E
Portland Maine U.S.A. **55** 43.39N 70.17W
Portland Oreg. U.S.A. **54** 45.33N122.36W
Port-la-Nouvelle France **11** 43.01N 3.03E
Port Laoise Rep. of Ire. **7** 53.03N 7.20W
Port Lavaca U.S.A. **53** 28.36N 96.39W
Port Lincoln Australia **46** 34.43S135.49E
Port MacDonnell Australia **46** 38.03S140.46E
Port Macquarie Australia **47** 31.28S152.25E
Port Maitland N.S. Canada **55** 43.59N 66.04W
Portmarnock Rep. of Ire. **7** 53.25N 6.09W
Port Moresby P.N.G. **44** 9.30S147.07E
Port Musgrave *b.* Australia **44** 11.59S142.00E
Portnaguiran U.K. **6** 58.15N 6.10W
Port Neill Australia **46** 34.07S136.20E
Port Nelson Canada **51** 57.10N 92.35W
Port Nolloth R.S.A. **39** 29.16S 16.54E
Porto Portugal **10** 41.09N 8.37W
Pôrto Alegre Brazil **59** 30.03S 51.10W
Porto Amboim Angola **36** 10.45S 13.43E
Pôrto de Moz Brazil **61** 1.45S 52.13W
Porto Esperança Brazil **59** 19.36S 57.24W
Pôrto Feliz Brazil **59** 23.11S 47.32W
Portoferraio Italy **12** 42.49N 10.19E
Port of Ness U.K. **6** 58.30N 6.13W
Pôrto Franco Brazil **61** 6.21S 47.25W
Port of Spain Trinidad **57** 10.38N 61.31W
Porto Grande Brazil **61** 0.42N 51.24W
Portogruaro Italy **9** 45.47N 12.50E
Pörtom Finland **16** 62.42N 21.37E
Portomaggiore Italy **9** 44.42N 11.48E
Pôrto Murtinho Brazil **59** 21.42S 57.52W
Porton U.K. **5** 51.08N 1.44W
Pôrto Nacional Brazil **61** 10.42S 48.25W
Porto-Novo Benin **38** 6.30N 2.47E
Pôrto Primavera, Represa *resr.* Brazil **59** 21.50S 52.00W
Porto San Giorgio Italy **12** 43.11N 13.48E
Porto Tolle Italy **9** 44.56N 12.22E
Porto Torres Italy **12** 40.49N 8.24E
Pôrto Valter Brazil **60** 8.15S 72.45W
Porto Vecchio France **11** 41.35N 9.16E
Pôrto Velho Brazil **60** 8.45S 63.54W
Portoviejo Ecuador **60** 1.07S 80.28W
Portpatrick U.K. **6** 54.51N 5.07W
Port Phillip B. Australia **47** 38.05S144.50E
Port Pirie Australia **46** 33.11S138.01E
Port Radium Canada **50** 66.05N118.02W
Portree U.K. **6** 57.24N 6.12W
Port Renfrew Canada **54** 48.30N124.20W
Portrush U.K. **7** 55.12N 6.40W
Port Said *see* Būr Sa'īd Egypt **32**
Portsea Australia **47** 38.19S144.43E
Port Shepstone R.S.A. **39** 30.44S 30.27E
Portsmouth U.K. **5** 50.48N 1.06W
Portsmouth N.H. U.S.A. **55** 43.04N 70.46W
Portsmouth Ohio U.S.A. **55** 38.45N 82.59W
Portsoy U.K. **6** 57.41N 2.41W
Port Stanley Canada **55** 42.40N 81.13W
Portstewart U.K. **7** 55.11N 6.43W
Port St. Louis France **11** 43.25N 4.40E
Port Sudan *see* Būr Sūdān Sudan **35**
Port Talbot U.K. **5** 51.35N 3.48W
Porttipahdan tekojärvi *resr.* Finland **16** 68.08N 26.40E
Port Townsend U.S.A. **54** 48.07N122.46W
Portugal Europe **10** 39.30N 8.05W
Port Vendres France **11** 42.31N 3.06E
Port Victoria Australia **46** 34.30S137.30E
Port Wakefield Australia **46** 34.12S138.11E
Port Warrender Australia **42** 14.30S125.50E
Porvenir Chile **63** 53.18S 70.22W
Porz Germany **8** 50.53N 7.05E
Posada Italy **12** 40.38N 9.43E
Posadas Argentina **62** 27.25S 55.48W
Poschiavo Switz. **9** 46.18N 10.04E
Posht *r.* Iran **31** 29.09N 58.09E
Poso Indonesia **27** 1.23S120.45E
Posse Brazil **59** 14.05S 46.22W
Postavy Lithuania **18** 55.07N 26.50E
Poste Maurice Cortier Algeria **34** 22.18N 1.05E
Postmasburg R.S.A. **39** 28.19S 23.03E
Postojna Slovenia **14** 45.47N 14.13E
Postoli Belorussia **15** 52.30N 28.00E
Potchefstroom R.S.A. **39** 26.42S 27.05E
Potenza Italy **12** 40.40N 15.47E
Potgietersrus R.S.A. **39** 24.11S 29.00E
Poti *r.* Brazil **61** 5.01S 42.48W
Poti Georgia **19** 42.11N 41.41E
Potiskum Nigeria **38** 11.40N 11.03E
Potosí Bolivia **62** 19.35S 65.45W
Potosí *d.* Bolivia **62** 21.00S 67.00W
Pototan Phil. **27** 10.54N122.38E
Potsdam Germany **14** 52.24N 13.04E
Potsdam U.S.A. **55** 44.40N 74.59W
Pottstown U.S.A. **55** 40.15N 75.38W
Pouancé France **9** 47.47N 1.11W
Poughkeepsie U.S.A. **55** 41.43N 73.56W
Pouso Alegre Brazil **59** 22.13S 45.49W
Poŭthisăt Cambodia **26** 12.33N103.55E
Povenets Russian Fed. **18** 62.52N 34.05E
Póvoa de Varzim Portugal **10** 41.22N 8.46W
Povorino Russian Fed. **19** 51.12N 42.15E
Powder *r.* U.S.A. **54** 46.44N105.26W
Powder River *town* U.S.A. **54** 43.03N106.58W
Powell U.S.A. **54** 44.45N108.46W
Powell, L. U.S.A. **54** 37.25N110.45W
Powers U.S.A. **55** 45.42N 87.31W
Powys *d.* U.K. **5** 52.26N 3.26W
Poyang Hu *l.* China **25** 29.05N116.20E
Požarevac Yugo. **15** 44.38N 21.12E
Poza Rica de Hidalgo Mexico **56** 20.34N 97.26W
Poznań Poland **14** 52.25N 16.53E
Pozoblanco Spain **10** 38.23N 4.51W
Prachuap Khiri Khan Thailand **29** 11.50N 99.49E
Pradera Colombia **60** 3.23N 76.11W
Prades France **11** 42.38N 2.25E
Praestö Denmark **17** 55.07N 12.03E
Prague *see* Praha Czech Republic **14**
Praha Czech Republic **14** 50.05N 14.25E
Prainha Amazonas Brazil **60** 7.16S 60.23W
Prainha Para Brazil **61** 1.48S 53.29W
Prairie City U.S.A. **54** 44.28N118.43W
Prang Ghana **38** 8.02N 0.58W
Prato Italy **9** 43.52N 11.06E
Pravia Spain **10** 43.30N 6.12W
Predazzo Italy **9** 46.19N 11.36E
Pré-en-Pail France **9** 48.27N 0.12W
Preesall U.K. **4** 53.55N 2.58W
Pregel *r.* Russian Fed. **15** 54.41N 20.22E
Premer Australia **47** 31.26S149.54E
Prenzlau Germany **14** 53.19N 13.52E
Preparis *i.* Burma **29** 14.40N 93.40E
Přerov Czech Republic **15** 49.27N 17.27E
Prescott Ariz. U.S.A. **54** 34.33N112.28W
Presidencia Roque Sáenz Peña Argentina **62** 26.50S 60.30W
Presidente Epitácio Brazil **59** 21.56S 52.07W
Presidente Hermes Brazil **62** 11.17S 61.55W
Presidente Prudente Brazil **59** 22.09S 51.24W
Presidio U.S.A. **52** 29.34N104.23W
Prešov Slovakia **15** 49.00N 21.15E
Prespa, L. Albania / Greece / Macedonia **13** 40.53N 21.02E
Presque Isle *town* Maine U.S.A. **55** 46.41N 68.01W
Prestea Ghana **38** 5.26N 2.07W
Presteigne U.K. **5** 52.17N 3.00W
Preston U.K. **4** 53.46N 2.42W
Preston Idaho U.S.A. **54** 42.06N111.53W
Prestonpans U.K. **6** 55.57N 3.00W
Prestwick U.K. **6** 55.30N 4.36W
Prêto *r.* Brazil **59** 22.00S 43.21W
Pretoria R.S.A. **39** 25.43S 28.11E
Préveza Greece **13** 38.58N 20.43E
Prey Vêng Cambodia **26** 11.29N105.19E
Priboj Yugo. **13** 43.35N 19.31E
Příbram Czech Republic **14** 49.42N 14.00E
Price Utah U.S.A. **54** 39.36N110.48W
Prieska R.S.A. **39** 29.40S 22.43E
Prijedor Bosnia-Herzegovina **13** 44.59N 16.43E
Prikaspiyskaya Nizmennost *see* Caspian Depression Kazakhstan / Russian Fed. **19**
Prilep Macedonia **13** 41.20N 21.32E
Priluki Russian Fed **18** 63.05N 42.05E
Priluki Ukraine **19** 50.35N 32.24E
Primorsk Russian Fed **18** 60.18N 28.35E
Primstal Germany **8** 49.33N 6.59E
Prince Albert Canada **50** 53.13N105.45W
Prince Albert R.S.A. **39** 33.14S 22.02E
Prince Albert Sd. Canada **50** 70.25N115.00W
Prince Alfred C. Canada **50** 74.30N125.00W
Prince Charles I. Canada **51** 67.50N 76.00W
Prince Edward Island *d.* Canada **51** 46.15N 63.10W
Prince George Canada **50** 53.55N122.49W
Prince of Wales, C. U.S.A. **50** 66.00N168.30W
Prince of Wales I. Australia **44** 10.40S142.10E

Prince of Wales I. Canada 51 73.00N 99.00W
Prince of Wales I. U.S.A. 50 55.00N 132.30W
Prince Patrick I. Canada 50 77.00N 120.00W
Prince Regent Inlet str. Canada 51 73.00N 90.30W
Prince Rupert Canada 50 54.09N 130.20W
Princess Charlotte B. Australia 44 14.25S 144.00E
Princeton Ind. U.S.A. 55 38.21N 87.33W
Príncipe i. São Tomé & Príncipe 38 1.37N 7.27E
Príncipe da Beira Brazil 60 12.23S 64.28W
Prinzapolca Nicaragua 57 13.19N 83.35W
Priozersk Russian Fed. 18 61.01N 30.08E
Pripet see Pripyat r. Europe/Belorussia 15
Pripet Marshes see Polesye f. Belorussia 15
Pripyat r. Belorussia 15 51.08N 30.30E
Priština Yugo. 13 42.39N 21.10E
Pritzwalk Germany 14 53.09N 12.10E
Privas France 14 44.44N 4.36E
Privolzhskaya Vozvyshennost f. Russian Fed. 18 53.15N 45.45E
Prizren Yugo. 13 42.13N 20.42E
Proddatūr India 29 14.44N 78.33E
Progreso Mexico 57 21.20N 89.40W
Prokopyevsk Russian Fed. 20 53.55N 86.45E
Prome see Pyè Burma 29
Propriá Brazil 61 10.15S 36.51W
Proserpine Australia 44 20.24S 148.34E
Prostějov Czech Republic 15 49.29N 17.07E
Provence-Côte d'Azur d. France 11 43.45N 6.00E
Providence U.S.A. 55 41.50N 71.25W
Providence Mts. U.S.A. 54 34.55N 115.35W
Providencia, Isla de i. Colombia 57 13.21N 81.22W
Provins France 9 48.34N 3.18E
Provo U.S.A. 54 40.14N 111.39W
Prozor Bosnia-Herzegovina 15 43.49N 17.37E
Prudhoe Bay town U.S.A. 50 70.20N 148.25W
Prüm Germany 8 50.12N 6.25E
Prüm r. Germany 8 49.50N 6.29E
Pruszcz Gdański Poland 15 54.17N 18.40E
Pruszków Poland 15 52.11N 20.48E
Prut r. Romania/Ukraine 15 45.29N 28.14E
Pruzhany Belorussia 15 52.23N 24.28E
Prydz B. Antarctica 64 68.30S 74.00E
Przemyśl Poland 15 49.48N 22.48E
Przeworsk Poland 15 50.05N 22.29E
Przhevalsk Kyrgyzstan 24 42.31N 78.22E
Psará i. Greece 13 38.34N 25.35E
Psel Ukraine 19 49.00N 33.30E
Pskov Russian Fed. 18 57.48N 28.00E
Pskovskoye, Ozero l. Russian Fed. 18 58.00N 27.55E
Ptich Belorussia 15 52.15N 28.49E
Ptich r. Belorussia 15 52.09N 28.52E
Ptolemaís Greece 13 40.31N 21.41E
Puán Argentina 63 37.30S 62.45W
Pucallpa Peru 60 8.21S 74.33W
Pucarani Bolivia 62 16.23S 68.30W
Pucheng China 25 27.55N 118.31E
Pudasjärvi Finland 16 65.25N 26.50E
Pudozh Russian Fed. 18 61.50N 36.32E
Pudozhgora Russian Fed. 18 62.18N 35.54E
Puebla Mexico 56 19.03N 98.10W
Puebla d. Mexico 56 18.30N 98.00W
Pueblo U.S.A. 52 38.16N 104.37W
Pueblo Hundido Chile 62 26.23S 70.03W
Puelches Argentina 63 38.09S 65.58W
Puelén Argentina 63 37.32S 67.38W
Puente Alta Chile 63 33.37S 70.35W
Puente-Genil Spain 10 37.24N 4.46W
Puerto Aisén Chile 63 45.27S 72.58W
Puerto Ángel Mexico 56 15.40N 96.29W
Puerto Armuelles Panama 57 8.19N 82.15W
Puerto Ayacucho Venezuela 60 5.39N 67.32W
Puerto Barrios Guatemala 57 15.41N 88.32W
Puerto Bermúdez Peru 60 10.20S 75.00W
Puerto Berrío Colombia 60 6.28N 74.28W
Puerto Cabello Venezuela 60 10.29N 68.02W
Puerto Cabezas Nicaragua 57 14.02N 83.24W
Puerto Carreño Colombia 60 6.08N 67.27W
Puerto Casado Paraguay 62 22.20S 57.55W
Puerto Coig Argentina 63 50.54S 69.15W
Puerto Cortés Costa Rica 57 8.58N 83.32W
Puerto Cortés Honduras 57 15.50N 87.55W
Puerto de Nutrias Venezuela 60 8.07N 69.18W
Puerto de Santa Maria Spain 10 36.36N 6.14W
Puerto Heath Bolivia 60 12.30S 68.40W
Puerto Juárez Mexico 57 21.26N 86.51W
Puerto La Cruz Venezuela 60 10.14N 64.40W
Puerto Leguízamo Colombia 60 0.12S 74.46W
Puertollano Spain 10 38.41N 4.07W
Puerto Lobos Argentina 63 42.01S 65.04W
Puerto Madryn Argentina 63 42.46S 65.02W
Puerto Maldonado Peru 60 12.37S 69.11W
Puerto Melendez Peru 60 4.30S 77.30W
Puerto Montt Chile 63 41.28S 73.00W
Puerto Natales Chile 63 51.44S 72.31W
Puerto Páez Venezuela 60 6.13N 67.28W
Puerto Peñasco Mexico 56 31.20N 113.33W
Puerto Pinasco Paraguay 59 22.36S 57.53W
Puerto Plata Dom. Rep. 57 19.48N 70.41W
Puerto Princesa Phil. 26 9.46N 118.45E
Puerto Quepos Costa Rica 57 9.28N 84.10W
Puerto Rey Colombia 60 8.48N 76.34W
Puerto Rico C. America 57 18.20N 66.30W
Puerto Rico Trench Atlantic Oc. 57 19.50N 66.00W
Puerto Saavedra Chile 63 38.47S 73.24W
Puerto Santa Cruz Argentina 63 50.03S 68.35W
Puerto Sastre Paraguay 59 22.02S 58.00W
Puerto Siles Bolivia 62 12.48S 65.05W
Puerto Tejado Colombia 60 3.16N 76.22W
Puerto Vallarta Mexico 56
Puerto Varas Chile 63 41.20S 73.00W
Pugachev Russian Fed. 18 52.02N 48.49E
Puglia d. Italy 13 41.00N 16.40E
Puisaye, Collines de la hills France 9 47.34N 3.28E
Pukaki, L. New Zealand 48 44.00S 170.10E
Pukekohe New Zealand 48 37.12S 174.56E
Pukeuri New Zealand 48 45.02S 171.02E
Pukhovichi Belorussia 15 53.28N 28.18E
Pula Croatia 14 44.52N 13.53E
Pulacayo Bolivia 62 20.25S 66.41W
Puławy Poland 15 51.25N 21.57E
Pulkkila Finland 16 64.16N 25.52E
Pullman U.S.A. 54 46.44N 117.10W
Pulog mtn. Phil. 27 16.50N 120.50E
Pulozero Russian Fed. 18 68.22N 33.15E
Pułtusk Poland 15 52.42N 21.02E
Puma Tanzania 37 5.02S 34.46E
Puncak Jaya mtn. Indonesia 27 4.00S 137.15E
Pune India 28 18.34N 73.58E
Punjab d. India 28 30.30N 75.15E
Puno Peru 60 15.53S 70.03W
Punta Alta town Argentina 63 38.50S 62.00W
Punta Arenas town Chile 63 53.10S 70.56W
Puntabie Australia 46 32.15S 134.13E
Punta Delgada town Argentina 63 42.43S 63.38W
Punta Gorda town Belize 57 16.10N 88.45W
Puntarenas Costa Rica 57 10.00N 84.50W
Punto Fijo Venezuela 60 11.50N 70.16W
Puolanka Finland 16 64.52N 27.40E
Puquio Peru 60 14.44S 74.07W
Pur r. Russian Fed. 20 67.30N 75.30E
Purari r. P.N.G. 27 7.49S 145.10E
Puri India 29 19.49N 85.54E
Purnea India 29 25.47N 87.28E
Purros Namibia 39 18.38S 12.59E
Purūlia India 29 23.20N 86.24E
Purus r. Brazil 60 3.58S 61.25W
Pusan S. Korea 25 35.05N 129.02E
Pushkin Russian Fed. 18 59.43N 30.22E
Pushkino Russian Fed. 19 51.16N 47.09E
Püspökladány Hungary 15 47.19N 21.07E
Pustoshka Russian Fed. 18 56.20N 29.20E
Putao Burma 29 27.22N 97.27E
Putaruru New Zealand 48 38.03S 175.47E
Putian China 25 25.32N 119.02E
Puting, Tanjung c. Indonesia 26 3.35S 111.52E
Putorana, Gory mts. Russian Fed. 21 68.30N 96.00E
Putsonderwater R.S.A. 39 29.14S 21.50E
Puttalam Sri Lanka 29 8.02N 79.50E
Puttgarden Germany 14 54.30N 11.13E
Putumayo r. Brazil 60 3.05S 68.10W
Puulavesi l. Finland 17 61.50N 26.42E
Puyallup U.S.A. 54 47.11N 122.18W
Puy de Dôme mtn. France 11 45.46N 2.56E
Puysegur Pt. New Zealand 48 46.10S 166.35E
Pwani d. Tanzania 37 7.00S 39.00E
Pweto Zaïre 37 8.27S 28.52E
Pwllheli U.K. 4 52.53N 4.25W
Pyaozero, Ozero l. Russian Fed. 18 66.00N 31.00E
Pyapon Burma 29 16.15N 95.40E
Pyasina r. Russian Fed. 21 73.10N 84.55E
Pyatigorsk Russian Fed. 19 44.04N 43.06E
Pyè Burma 29 18.50N 95.14E
Pyhä r. Finland 16 64.28N 24.13E
Pyhäjärvi l. Oulu Finland 16 63.35N 25.57E
Pyhäjärvi l. Turku-Pori Finland 17 61.00N 22.20E
Pyhäjoki Finland 16 64.28N 24.14E
Pyinmana Burma 29 19.45N 96.12E
Pyongyang N. Korea 25 39.00N 125.47E
Pyramid U.S.A. 54 40.05N 119.43W
Pyramid Hill town Australia 46 36.03S 144.24E
Pyramid L. U.S.A. 54 40.00N 119.35W
Pyrénées mts. France/Spain 11 42.40N 0.30E
Pyrzyce Poland 14 53.10N 14.55E
Pytteggja mtn. Norway 17 62.13N 7.42E

Q

Qaanaaq see Thule Greenland 51
Qā'emshahr Iran 31 36.28N 52.53E
Qagcaka China 29 32.32N 81.49E
Qahā Egypt 32 30.17N 31.12E
Qalāt Afghan. 28 32.07N 66.54E
Qal'eh-ye Now Afghan 31 34.58N 63.04E
Qalyūb Egypt 32 30.11N 31.12E
Qamdo China 24 31.11N 97.18E
Qanâtir Muhammad 'Alī Egypt 32 30.12N 31.08E
Qandahār Afghan. 28 31.36N 65.47E
Qandala Somali Rep. 35 11.23N 49.53E
Qaquortoq see Julianehab Greenland 51
Qārah Egypt 30 27.37N 26.30E
Qareh Sū Iran 31 34.52N 51.25E
Qareh Sū r. Iran 31 35.58N 56.25E
Qarqan He r. China 24 40.56N 86.27E
Qārūn, Birkat l. Egypt 32 29.30N 30.40E
Qasigiannguit see Christianshab Greenland 51
Qaşr al Farāfirah Egypt 30 27.15N 28.10E
Qaşr-e Qand Iran 31 26.13N 60.37E
Qatanā Syria 32 33.27N 36.04E
Qatar Asia 31 25.20N 51.10E
Qattara Depression see Qaţţārah, Munkhafaḑ al f. Egypt 30
Qaţţārah, Munkhafaḑ al f. Egypt 30 29.40N 27.30E
Qāyen Iran 31 33.44N 59.07E
Qazvīn Iran 31 36.16N 50.00E
Qeqertarsuaq see Godhavn Greenland 51
Qeqertarsuatsiaat see Fiskenaesset Greenland 51
Qeshm Iran 31 26.58N 57.17E
Qeshm i. Iran 31 26.48N 55.48E
Qezel Owzan r. Iran 31 36.44N 49.27E
Qezi'ot Israel 32 30.52N 34.28E
Qianjiang China 25 29.31N 108.46E
Qiemo China 24 38.08N 85.33E
Qilian Shan mts. China 24 38.30N 99.20E
Qimantag mts. China 24 37.45N 89.40E
Qinā Egypt 30 26.10N 32.43E
Qinā, Wādī r. Egypt 30 26.07N 32.42E
Qingdao China 25 36.04N 120.22E
Qinghai d. China 24 36.15N 96.00E
Qinghai Hu l. China 24 36.40N 100.00E
Qingjiang China 25 28.02N 115.23E
Qingxu China 25 37.36N 112.21E
Qingyang China 24 36.06N 107.49E
Qing Zang Gaoyuan f. China 24 34.00N 84.30E
Qinhuangdao China 25 39.55N 119.37E
Qin Ling mts. China 25 33.40N 109.00E
Qinzhou China 25 21.57N 108.37E
Qiqihar China 25 47.23N 124.00E
Qira China 24 37.02N 80.53E
Qiryat Ata Israel 32 32.48N 35.06E
Qiryat Gat Israel 32 31.37N 34.47E
Qiryat Shemona Israel 32 33.13N 35.35E
Qishn Yemen 28 15.25N 51.40E
Qom Iran 31 34.40N 50.57E
Qornet'es Sauda mtn. Lebanon 32 34.17N 36.04E
Qoţūr Iran 31 38.28N 44.25E
Quairading Australia 43 32.00S 117.22E
Quakenbrück Germany 8 52.41N 7.59E
Quambatook Australia 46 35.52S 143.36E
Quambone Australia 47 30.54S 147.55E
Quang Ngai Vietnam 26 15.09N 108.50E
Quang Tri Vietnam 26 16.46N 107.11E
Quan Long Vietnam 26 9.11N 105.09E
Quanzhou Fujian China 25 24.57N 118.36E
Qu'Appelle r. Canada 51 51.13N 98.05W
Quaqtaq Canada 51 61.05N 69.36W
Quaraí Brazil 63 30.23S 56.27W
Quaraí r. Brazil 63 30.12S 57.36W
Quartu Sant'Elena Italy 12 39.14N 9.11E
Quartzsite U.S.A. 54 33.40N 114.13W
Qūchān Iran 31 37.04N 58.29E
Queanbeyan Australia 47 35.24S 149.17E
Québec Canada 55 46.50N 71.15W
Québec d. Canada 51 52.00N 72.00W
Quebracho Uruguay 63 31.57S 57.53W
Quedlinburg Germany 14 51.48N 11.09E
Queen Charlotte Is. Canada 50 53.00N 132.30W
Queen Charlotte Str. Canada 50 51.00N 129.00W
Queen Elizabeth Is. Canada 51 78.30N 99.00W
Queen Maud G. Canada 51 68.30N 99.00W
Queen Maud Range mts. Antarctica 64 86.20S 165.00W
Queens Channel Australia 42 14.46S 129.24E
Queenscliff Australia 47 38.17S 144.42E
Queensland d. Australia 44 23.30S 144.00E
Queenstown Australia 45 42.07S 145.33E
Queenstown New Zealand 48 45.03S 168.41E
Queenstown R.S.A. 39 31.52S 26.51E
Queguay Grande r. Uruguay 63 32.09S 58.09W
Queimadas Brazil 61 10.58S 39.38W
Quela Angola 36 9.18S 17.05E
Quelimane Mozambique 37 17.53S 36.57E
Quemado U.S.A. 54 34.20N 108.30W
Quequén Argentina 63 38.34S 58.42W
Querétaro Mexico 56 20.38N 100.23W
Querétaro d. Mexico 56 21.03N 100.00W
Quesnel Canada 50 53.03N 122.31W
Quetta Pakistan 28 30.15N 67.00E
Quettehou France 9 49.36N 1.18W
Quevedo Ecuador 60 0.59S 79.27W
Quezaltenango Guatemala 56 14.50N 91.30W
Quezon City Phil. 27 14.39N 121.01E
Quibdo Colombia 60 5.40N 76.38W
Quiberon France 11 47.29N 3.07W
Quilán, C. Chile 63 43.16S 74.27W
Quilengues Angola 36 14.09S 14.04E
Quillabamba Peru 60 12.50S 72.50W
Quillacollo Bolivia 62 17.26S 66.17W
Quillota Chile 63 32.53S 71.16W
Quilpie Australia 44 26.37S 144.15E
Quilpué Chile 63 33.03S 71.27W
Quimilí Argentina 62 27.35S 62.25W
Quimper France 11 48.00N 4.06W
Quimperlé France 11 47.52N 3.33W
Quincy Ill. U.S.A. 53 39.55N 91.22W
Quincy Wash. U.S.A. 54 47.14N 119.51W
Qui Nhon Vietnam 26 13.47N 109.11E
Quintanar de la Orden Spain 10 39.36N 3.05W
Quintana Roo d. Mexico 57 19.00N 88.00W
Quinto Spain 10 41.25N 0.30W
Quionga Mozambique 37 10.37S 40.31E
Quirigua ruins Guatemala 57 15.20N 89.25W
Quirindi Australia 47 31.30S 150.42E
Quissanga Mozambique 37 12.24S 40.33E
Quissico Mozambique 39 24.42S 34.44E
Quiterajo Mozambique 37 11.46S 40.25E
Quito Ecuador 60 0.14S 78.30W
Quorn Australia 46 32.20S 138.02E
Qurayyah, Wādī r. Egypt 32 30.26N 34.01E
Qurdud Sudan 35 10.17N 29.56E
Qurlurtuuq Canada 50 67.49N 115.12W
Qu Xian China 25 28.57N 118.52E

R

Raahe Finland 16 64.41N 24.29E
Raalte Neth. 8 52.22N 6.17E
Raasay i. U.K. 6 57.25N 6.05W
Raas Caseyr c. Somali Rep. 35 12.00N 51.30E
Rába r. Hungary 15 47.42N 17.38E
Raba Indonesia 26 8.27S 118.45E
Rabat Morocco 34 34.02N 6.51W
Rabbit Flat town Australia 42 20.10S 129.53E
Rābor Iran 31 29.18N 56.56E
Racconigi Italy 9 44.46N 9.46E
Race, C. Canada 51 46.40N 53.10W
Rach Gia Vietnam 26 10.02N 105.05E
Racibórz Poland 15 50.06N 18.13E
Racine U.S.A. 53 42.42N 87.50W
Rădăuţi Romania 15 47.51N 25.55E
Radebeul Germany 14 51.06N 13.41E
Radekhov Ukraine 15 50.18N 24.35E
Radium Hill town Australia 46 32.30S 140.32E
Radom Poland 15 51.26N 21.10E
Radomir Bulgaria 13 42.32N 22.56E
Radomsko Poland 15 51.05N 19.25E
Radomyshl Ukraine 15 50.30N 29.14E
Radöy i. Norway 17 60.38N 5.05E
Radstock U.K. 5 51.17N 2.25W
Radstock, C. Australia 46 33.11S 134.21E
Raḑwá, Jabal mtn. Saudi Arabia 30 24.36N 38.18E
Rae Canada 50 62.50N 116.03W
Raeren Germany 8 50.41N 6.07E
Raeside, L. Australia 43 29.30S 122.00E
Rafaela Argentina 62 31.16S 61.44W
Rafaḩ Egypt 32 31.18N 34.15E
Rafaï C.A.R. 35 4.56N 23.55E
Rafsanjān Iran 28 30.24N 56.00E
Rafsanjān Iran 31 30.24N 56.00E
Ragged, Mt. Australia 43 33.27S 123.27E
Ragunda Sweden 16 63.06N 16.23E
Ragusa Italy 12 36.56N 14.44E
Raha Indonesia 27 4.50S 122.43E
Raḩā, Ḩarrat ar f. Saudi Arabia 32 28.00N 36.35E
Rāichūr India 28 16.15N 77.20E
Raiganj India 29 25.38N 88.11E
Raigarh India 29 21.53N 83.28E
Rainbow Australia 46 35.56S 142.01E
Rainier, Mt. U.S.A. 54 46.52N 121.46W
Raipur India 29 21.16N 81.42E
Ra's Saudi Arabia 30 23.35N 38.36E
Rājahmundry India 29 17.01N 81.52E
Rajang r. Malaysia 26 2.10N 112.45E
Rājapālaiyam India 28 9.26N 77.36E
Rājasthān d. India 28 27.00N 74.00E
Rājgarh Madhya P. India 28 23.56N 76.58E
Rājkot India 28 22.18N 70.53E
Rakaia New Zealand 48 43.45S 172.01E
Rakaia r. New Zealand 48 43.52S 172.13E
Rakhov Ukraine 15 48.02N 24.10E
Rakitnoye Ukraine 15 51.18N 27.10E
Rakops Botswana 39 21.00S 24.32E
Rakov Belorussia 15 53.58N 26.59E
Rakulka Russian Fed. 18 62.19N 46.52E
Råkvåg Norway 16 63.47N 10.10E
Rakvere Estonia 18 59.22N 26.28E
Raleigh U.S.A. 53 35.46N 78.39W
Rama Nicaragua 57 12.09N 84.15W
Rāmah Saudi Arabia 31 25.33N 47.08E
Rām Allāh Jordan 32 31.55N 35.12E
Ramallo Argentina 63 33.28S 60.02W
Ramat Gan Israel 32 32.05N 34.48E
Rambouillet France 9 48.39N 1.50E
Rame Head Australia 47 37.50S 149.25E
Rame Head U.K. 5 50.18N 4.13W
Ramelton Rep. of Ire. 7 55.02N 7.40W
Rāmhormoz Iran 31 31.14N 49.37E
Ramillies Belgium 8 50.39N 4.56E
Ramingstein Austria 14 47.04N 13.50E
Ramla Israel 32 31.56N 34.52E
Ramlu mtn. Eritrea 35 13.20N 41.45E
Ramona Calif. U.S.A. 54 33.08N 116.52W
Ramore Canada 55 48.27N 80.20W
Ramos Arizpe Mexico 56 25.35N 100.59W
Rāmpur Uttar P. India 29 28.48N 79.03E
Ramree I. Burma 29 19.10N 93.40E
Ramsey I.o.M. Europe 4 54.19N 4.23W
Ramsey England U.K. 5 52.27N 0.06W
Ramsey L. Canada 55 47.15N 82.16W
Ramsgate U.K. 5 51.20N 1.25E
Rāmshīr Iran 31 30.54N 49.24E
Ramsjö Sweden 17 62.11N 15.39E
Ramu r. P.N.G. 27 4.00S 144.40E
Ranau Malaysia 26 5.58N 116.41E
Rancagua Chile 63 34.10S 70.45W
Rānchī India 29 23.22N 85.20E
Rand Australia 47 35.34S 146.35E
Randalstown U.K. 7 54.45N 6.20W
Randburg R.S.A. 30 26.07S 28.02E
Randers Denmark 17 56.28N 10.03E
Randsburg U.S.A. 54 35.22N 117.39W
Randsfjorden l. Norway 17 60.25N 10.24E
Råne r. Sweden 16 65.52N 22.19E
Råneå Sweden 16 65.52N 22.18E
Ranfurly New Zealand 48 45.08S 170.08E
Rangely U.S.A. 54 40.05N 108.48W
Rangia India 29 26.28N 91.38E
Rangiora New Zealand 48 43.18S 172.38E
Rangitaiki r. New Zealand 48 37.55S 176.50E
Rangoon see Yangon Burma 29
Rankin Inlet town Canada 51 62.52N 92.00W
Rankins Springs town Australia 47 33.52S 146.18E
Rannoch, Loch U.K. 6 56.41N 4.20W
Rann of Kachchh f. India 28 23.50N 69.50E
Ranong Thailand 29 9.59N 98.40E
Rantauprapat Indonesia 26 2.05N 99.46E
Rantekombola mtn. Indonesia 26 3.30S 119.58E
Rapallo Italy 9 44.20N 9.14E
Rapid Bay town Australia 46 35.33S 138.09E
Rapid City U.S.A. 52 44.05N 103.14W
Raquette Lake town U.S.A. 55 43.49N 74.41W
Ra's al Ḩadd c. Oman 28 22.32N 59.49E
Ra's al Khaymah U.A.E. 31 25.48N 55.56E
Ra's an Naqb town Egypt 32 29.36N 34.51E
Ra's an Naqb town Jordan 32 30.30N 35.29E
Ra's Banās c. Egypt 35 23.54N 35.48E
Ras Dashen mtn. Ethiopia 35 13.20N 38.10E
Râs Ghârib Egypt 32 28.22N 33.04E
Rashīd Egypt 32 31.25N 30.25E
Rasht Iran 31 37.18N 49.38E
Raška Yugo. 13 43.17N 20.37E
Rason L. Australia 43 28.46S 124.20E
Ratangarh India 28 28.05N 74.36E
Rat Buri Thailand 26 13.30N 99.50E
Ratcatchers L. Australia 46 32.40S 143.13E
Rathcormack Rep. of Ire. 7 52.05N 8.18W
Rathdrum Rep. of Ire. 7 52.56N 6.15W
Rathenow Germany 14 52.37N 12.21E
Rathlin I. U.K. 7 55.17N 6.15W
Rath Luirc Rep. of Ire. 7 52.21N 8.41W
Rathmullen Rep. of Ire. 7 55.06N 7.32W
Ratlām India 28 23.18N 75.06E
Ratnāgiri India 28 16.59N 73.18E
Ratno Ukraine 15 51.40N 24.32E
Raton U.S.A. 52 36.54N 104.24W
Rattlesnake Range mts. U.S.A. 54 42.45N 107.10W
Rattray Head U.K. 6 57.37N 1.50W
Rättvik Sweden 17 60.53N 15.06E
Rauch Argentina 63 36.47S 59.05W
Raufoss Norway 17 60.43N 10.37E
Raul Soares Brazil 59 20.04S 42.27W
Rauma Finland 17 61.08N 21.30E
Rauma r. Norway 16 62.32N 7.43E
Raurkela India 29 22.16N 85.01E
Rautas Sweden 16 68.00N 19.55E
Rāvar Iran 31 31.14N 56.51E
Rava-Russkaya Ukraine 15 50.15N 23.36E
Ravena U.S.A. 55 42.29N 73.49W
Ravenna Italy 9 44.25N 12.12E
Ravensburg Germany 14 47.47N 9.37E
Ravenshoe Australia 44 17.37S 145.29E
Ravensthorpe Australia 43 33.35S 120.02E
Ravī r. Pakistan 28 30.30N 72.13E
Rāwalpindi Pakistan 28 33.40N 73.08E
Rawāndūz Iraq 31 36.38N 44.32E
Rawene New Zealand 48 35.24S 173.30E
Rawicz Poland 14 51.37N 16.52E
Rawlinna Australia 43 31.00S 125.21E
Rawlins U.S.A. 54 41.47N 107.14W
Rawson Argentina 63 34.40S 60.02W
Raya mtn. Indonesia 26 0.45S 112.45E
Rāyen Iran 31 29.34N 57.26E
Raymond U.S.A. 54 46.41N 123.44W
Raymond Terrace Australia 47 32.47S 151.45E
Razan Iran 31 35.22N 49.02E
Razdelnaya Ukraine 15 46.50N 30.02E
Razgrad Bulgaria 15 43.32N 26.30E
Ré, Île de i. France 11 46.10N 1.26W
Reading U.K. 5 51.27N 0.57W
Reading U.S.A. 55 40.20N 75.56W
Realicó Argentina 63 35.02S 64.14W
Reay Forest f. U.K. 6 58.17N 4.48W
Rebecca, L. Australia 43 30.07S 122.32E
Rebi Indonesia 27 6.24S 134.07E
Reboly Russian Fed. 18 63.50N 30.49E
Recalde Argentina 63 36.39S 61.05W
Recherche, Archipelago of the is. Australia 43 34.05S 122.45E
Rechitsa Belorussia 15 52.21N 30.24E
Recife Brazil 61 8.06S 34.53W
Recklinghausen Germany 8 51.36N 7.11E
Reconquista Argentina 62 29.08S 59.38W
Recreo Argentina 62 29.20S 65.04W
Red r. Canada 51 50.30N 96.50W
Red r. U.S.A. 53 31.10N 92.00W
Red r. see Hong Hà r. Vietnam 26
Red Bluff U.S.A. 54 40.11N 122.15W
Redcar U.K. 4 54.37N 1.04W
Red Cliffs town Australia 46 34.22S 142.13E
Red Deer Canada 50 52.15N 113.48W
Redding U.S.A. 54 40.35N 122.24W
Redditch U.K. 5 52.18N 1.57W
Rede r. U.K. 4 55.08N 2.13W
Redhill town Australia 46 33.34S 138.12E
Red L. U.S.A. 53 48.00N 95.00W
Red Lake town Canada 51 50.59N 93.40W
Redlands U.S.A. 54 34.03N 117.11W
Red Lodge U.S.A. 54 45.11N 109.15W
Redmond U.S.A. 54 44.17N 121.11W
Red Oak U.S.A. 53 41.01N 95.15W
Redondela Spain 10 42.15N 8.38W
Redondo Portugal 10 38.39N 7.33W
Redondo Beach town U.S.A. 54 33.51N 118.23W
Redrock U.S.A. 54 32.35N 111.19W
Redruth U.K. 5 50.14N 5.14W
Red Sea Africa/Asia 35 20.00N 39.00E
Red Volta r. Ghana 38 10.32N 0.31W
Redwood City U.S.A. 54 37.29N 122.13W
Ree, Lough Rep. of Ire. 7 53.31N 7.58W
Reed City U.S.A. 55 43.54N 85.31W
Reedsport U.S.A. 54 43.42N 124.06W
Reefton New Zealand 48 42.07S 171.52E
Reese r. U.S.A. 54 40.39N 116.54W
Reftele Sweden 17 57.11N 13.35E
Rega r. Poland 14 54.10N 15.18E
Regensburg Germany 14 49.01N 12.07E
Reggane Algeria 34 26.30N 0.30E
Reggio Calabria Italy 12 38.07N 15.38E
Reggio Emilia-Romagna Italy 9 44.40N 10.37E
Reghin Romania 15 46.47N 24.42E
Regina Canada 50 50.30N 104.38W
Regnéville France 9 49.01N 1.33W
Rehoboth Namibia 39 23.19S 17.10E
Rehovot Israel 32 31.54N 34.46E
Reigate U.K. 5 51.14N 0.13W
Reims France 9 49.15N 4.02E
Reindeer L. Canada 50 57.00N 102.20W
Reinosa Spain 10 43.01N 4.09W
Remanso Brazil 61 9.41S 42.04W
Remarkable, Mt. Australia 46 32.48S 138.10E
Rembang Indonesia 26 6.45S 111.22E
Remeshk Iran 31 26.52N 58.46E
Remich Lux. 8 49.34N 6.23E
Remiremont France 11 48.01N 6.35E
Remscheid Germany 8 51.10N 7.11E
Rena Norway 17 61.08N 11.22E
Rendsburg Germany 14 54.19N 9.39E
Renfrew Canada 55 45.28N 76.41W
Rengat Indonesia 26 0.26S 102.35E
Rengo Chile 63 34.25S 70.52W
Renheji China 25 31.56N 115.07E
Reni Ukraine 15 45.28N 28.17E
Renkum Neth. 8 51.59N 5.46E
Renmark Australia 46 34.10S 140.45E
Renner Springs town Australia 44 18.20S 133.48E

Rennes France 9 48.06N 1.40W
Reno *r.* Italy 9 44.36N 12.17E
Reno U.S.A. 54 39.31N119.48W
Renton U.S.A. 54 47.30N122.11W
Réo Burkina 38 12.20N 2.27W
Repki Ukraine 15 51.47N 31.06E
Republic Wash. U.S.A. 54 48.39N118.44W
Republican *r.* U.S.A. 53 39.05N 94.50W
Republic of Ireland Europe 7 53.00N 8.00W
Republic of South Africa Africa 39 28.30S 24.50E
Repulse B. Australia 44 20.36S148.43E
Repulse Bay *town* Canada 51 66.35N 86.20W
Requa U.S.A. 54 41.34N124.05W
Requena Peru 60 5.05S 73.52W
Requena Spain 10 39.29N 1.08W
Resistencia Argentina 62 27.28S 59.00W
Reşiţa Romania 15 45.17N 21.53E
Resolute Canada 51 74.40N 95.00W
Resolution I. Canada 51 61.30N 65.00W
Resolution I. New Zealand 48 45.40S166.30E
Restigouche *r.* Canada 55 48.02N 66.22W
Rethel France 9 49.31N 4.22E
Réthimnon Greece 13 35.22N 24.29E
Reus Spain 10 41.10N 1.06E
Reusel Neth. 8 51.21N 5.09E
Reutlingen Germany 14 48.30N 9.13E
Reutte Austria 14 47.29N 10.43E
Revda Russian Fed. 18 56.49N 59.58E
Revelstoke Canada 50 51.02N118.12W
Revilla Gigedo, Islas de *is.* Mexico 56 19.00N111.00W
Revin France 8 49.58N 4.40E
Revue *r.* Mozambique 39 19.58S 34.40E
Rexburg U.S.A. 54 43.49N111.47W
Rexford U.S.A. 54 48.53N115.13W
Rey Iran 31 35.35N 51.27E
Reykjavík Iceland 16 64.09N 21.58W
Reynosa Mexico 56 26.09N 97.10W
Rezé France 11 47.12N 1.34W
Rēzekne Latvia 18 56.30N 27.22E
Rhayader U.K. 5 52.19N 3.30W
Rheden Neth. 8 52.01N 6.02E
Rhein *r.* Europe 8 51.53N 6.03E
Rheinbach Germany 8 50.39N 6.59E
Rheine Germany 8 52.17N 7.26E
Rheinland-Pfalz *d.* Germany 8 50.05N 7.09E
Rhenen Neth. 8 51.58N 5.34E
Rheydt Germany 8 51.10N 6.25E
Rhine *see* Rhein *r.* Europe 8
Rhinelander U.S.A. 53 45.39N 89.23W
Rhino Camp *town* Uganda 37 2.58N 31.20E
Rho Italy 9 45.32N 9.02E
Rhode Island *d.* U.S.A. 55 41.40N 71.30W
Rhodes *i. see* Ródhos *i.* Greece 13
Rhodopi Planina *mts.* Bulgaria 13 41.35N 24.35E
Rhondda U.K. 5 51.39N 3.30W
Rhône *r.* France 11 43.25N 4.45E
Rhône-Alpes *d.* France 11 45.20N 5.45E
Rhosneigr U.K. 4 53.14N 4.31W
Rhyl U.K. 4 53.19N 3.29W
Riachão Brazil 61 7.22S 46.37W
Riau *d.* Indonesia 26 0.00 102.35E
Riau, Kepulauan *is.* Indonesia 26 0.50N104.00E
Ribadeo Spain 10 43.32N 7.04W
Ribarroja, Embalse de *resr.* Spain 10 41.12N 0.20E
Ribauè Mozambique 37 14.57S 38.27E
Ribble *r.* U.K. 4 53.45N 2.44W
Ribe Denmark 17 55.21N 8.46E
Ribeauvillé France 11 48.12N 7.19E
Ribécourt France 8 49.31N 2.52E
Ribécourt France 9 49.31N 2.55E
Ribeirão Prêto Brazil 59 21.09S 47.48W
Ribérac France 11 45.14N 0.22E
Riberalta Bolivia 62 10.59S 66.06W
Ribnitz-Damgarten Germany 14 54.15N 12.28E
Riccione Italy 9 43.59N 12.39E
Rice U.S.A. 54 34.06N114.50W
Richard's Bay *town* R.S.A. 39 28.47S 32.06E
Richfield Idaho U.S.A. 54 43.03N114.09W
Richfield Utah U.S.A. 54 38.46N112.05W
Richland U.S.A. 54 46.17N119.18W
Richmond Qld. Australia 44 20.44S143.08E
Richmond New Zealand 48 41.20S173.10E
Richmond C.P. R.S.A. 39 31.24S 23.56E
Richmond U.K. 4 54.24N 1.43W
Richmond Ind. U.S.A. 55 39.50N 84.51W
Richmond Utah U.S.A. 54 41.55N111.48W
Richmond Va. U.S.A. 53 37.34N 77.27W
Richmond Hill *town* Canada 55 43.53N 79.26W
Richmond Range *mts.* Australia 47 29.00S152.48E
Ricobayo, Embalse de *resr.* Spain 10 41.40N 5.50W
Ridderkerk Neth. 8 51.53N 4.39E
Rideau Lakes Canada 55 44.45N 76.14W
Ridgway U.S.A. 55 41.26N 78.44W
Ried Austria 14 48.13N 13.30E
Riemst Belgium 8 50.49N 5.38E
Riesa Germany 14 51.18N 13.18E
Rieti Italy 12 42.24N 12.53E
Rifle U.S.A. 54 39.32N107.47W
Rift Valley *d.* Kenya 37 1.00N 36.00E
Riga Latvia 17 56.53N 24.08E
Riga, G of Latvia / Estonia 17 57.30N 23.35E
Rīgān Iran 31 28.40N 58.58E
Rigas Jūras Licis *see* Riga, G. of *g.* Latvia 17
Rīgestān *f.* Afghan. 28 31.00N 65.00E
Riggins U.S.A. 54 45.25N116.19W
Rig Matī Iran 31 27.40N 58.11E
Rigo P.N.G. 44 9.50S147.35E
Rigolet Canada 51 54.10N 58.30W
Riia Laht *see* Riga, G of Estonia 17
Riihimäki Finland 17 60.45N 24.46E
Riiser-Larsenhalvöya *pen.* Antarctica 64 68.00S 35.00E
Rijeka Croatia 12 45.20N 14.25E
Rijssen Neth. 8 52.19N 6.31E
Rijswijk Neth. 8 52.03N 4.22E
Riley U.S.A. 54 43.31N119.28W
Rimah, Wādī ar *r.* Saudi Arabia 30 26.10N 44.00E
Rimavská Sobota Slovakia 15 48.23N 20.02E
Rimbo Sweden 17 59.45N 18.22E
Rimini Italy 9 44.01N 12.34E
Rîmnicu-Sărat Romania 15 45.24N 27.06E
Rîmnicu-Vîlcea Romania 15 45.06N 24.22E
Rimouski Canada 55 48.27N 68.32W
Rinconada Argentina 62 22.26S 66.10W
Rindal Norway 16 63.04N 9.13E
Ringebu Norway 17 61.31N 10.10E
Ringerike Norway 17 60.10N 10.12E
Ringim Nigeria 38 12.09N 9.08E
Ringköbing Denmark 17 56.05N 8.15E
Ringling U.S.A. 54 46.16N110.49W
Ringsted Denmark 17 55.27N 11.49E
Ringvassöy *i.* Norway 16 69.55N 19.10E
Ringwood U.K. 5 50.50N 1.48W
Riobamba Ecuador 60 1.44S 78.40W
Rio Branco Brazil 60 9.59S 67.49W
Río Bueno Chile 63 40.20S 72.55W
Rio Casca Brazil 59 20.13S 42.38W
Rio Claro Brazil 59 22.19S 47.35W
Río Cuarto Argentina 63 33.08S 64.20W
Rio de Janeiro Brazil 59 22.53S 43.17W
Rio de Janeiro *d.* Brazil 59 22.00S 42.30W
Río Gallegos Argentina 63 51.37S 69.10W
Río Grande *town* Argentina 63 53.50S 67.40W
Rio Grande *town* Brazil 59 32.03S 52.08W
Rio Grande *r.* Mexico / U.S.A. 56 25.55N 97.08W
Río Grande *r.* Nicaragua 57 12.48N 83.30W
Rio Grande do Norte *d.* Brazil 61 6.00S 36.30W
Rio Grande do Sul *d.* Brazil 59 30.15S 53.30W
Riohacha Colombia 60 11.34N 72.58W
Rio Largo Brazil 61 9.28S 35.50W
Río Negro *d.* Argentina 63 40.00S 67.00W
Rio Negro Brazil 59 26.06S 49.48W
Río Negro, Embalse del *resr.* Uruguay 63 32.45S 56.00W
Rio Novo Brazil 59 21.15S 43.09W
Rio Piracicaba Brazil 59 19.54S 43.10W
Rio Pomba Brazil 59 21.15S 43.12W
Rio Prêto Brazil 59 22.06S 43.52W
Ríosucio Colombia 60 7.27N 77.07W
Río Tercero Argentina 62 32.10S 64.05W
Rio Verde *town* Brazil 62 17.50S 50.55W
Ripley N.Y. U.S.A. 55 42.16N 79.43W
Ripon U.K. 4 54.08N 1.31W
Rirapora Brazil 59 17.20S 45.02W
Risbäck Sweden 16 64.42N 15.32E
Riscle France 11 43.40N 0.05W
Rishā, Wādī ar *r.* Saudi Arabia 31 25.40N 44.08E
Rishon LeZiyyon Israel 32 31.57N 34.48E
Risle *r.* France 9 49.26N 0.23E
Risör Norway 17 58.43N 9.14E
Riti Nigeria 38 7.57N 9.41E
Ritzville U.S.A. 54 47.08N118.23W
Riva Italy 9 45.53N 10.50E
Rivadavia Argentina 62 24.11S 62.53W
Rivarolo Canavese Italy 9 45.25N 7.36E
Rivas Nicaragua 57 11.26N 85.50W
Rivera Uruguay 63 30.54S 55.31W
River Cess *town* Liberia 34 5.28N 9.32W
Rivergaro Italy 9 44.55N 9.36E
Riverhead U.S.A. 55 40.55N 72.40W
Riverina *f.* Australia 47 34.30S145.20E
Rivers *d.* Nigeria 38 4.45N 6.35E
Riversdale R.S.A. 39 34.05S 21.15E
Riverside U.S.A. 54 33.59N117.22W
Riverton Australia 46 34.08S138.24E
Riverton Canada 51 50.59N 96.59W
Riverton New Zealand 48 46.21S168.01E
Riverton U.S.A. 54 43.02N108.23W
Riviera di Levante *f.* Italy 9 44.00N 9.40E
Riviera di Ponente *f.* Italy 9 43.40N 8.00E
Rivière-du-Loup *town* Canada 55 47.49N 69.32W
Rivière Pentecôte *town* Canada 55 49.46N 67.12W
Rivoli Italy 9 45.04N 7.31E
Riyadh *see* Ar Riyāḍ Saudi Arabia 31
Rize Turkey 30 41.03N 40.31E
Rizokárpason Cyprus 32 35.35N 34.24E
Rizzuto, Capo *c.* Italy 13 38.54N 17.06E
Rjukan Norway 17 59.52N 8.34E
Roa Norway 17 60.17N 10.37E
Roag, Loch U.K. 6 58.14N 6.50W
Roanne France 11 46.02N 4.05E
Roanoke *r.* U.S.A. 53 36.00N 76.35W
Roanoke Va. U.S.A. 53 37.15N 79.58W
Robāṭ Iran 31 30.04N 54.49E
Robe Australia 46 37.11S139.45E
Robe, Mt. Australia 46 31.39S141.16E
Robertson R.S.A. 39 33.48S 19.52E
Robertsport Liberia 34 6.45N 11.22W
Robertstown Australia 46 33.59S139.03E
Roberval Canada 55 48.31N 72.16W
Robin Hood's Bay *town* U.K. 4 54.26N 0.31W
Robinson *r.* Australia 44 16.03S137.16E
Robinson Range *mts.* Australia 42 25.45S119.00E
Robinvale Australia 46 34.37S142.50E
Robledo Spain 10 38.46N 2.26W
Roboré Bolivia 62 18.20S 59.45W
Robson, Mt. Canada 50 53.00N119.09W
Roccella Italy 13 38.19N 16.24E
Rocciamelone *mtn.* Italy 9 45.12N 7.05E
Rocha Uruguay 59 34.30S 54.22W
Rocha da Gale, Barragem *resr.* Portugal 10 38.20N 7.35W
Rochdale U.K. 4 53.36N 2.10W
Rochechouart France 11 45.49N 0.50E
Rochefort Belgium 8 50.10N 5.13E
Rochefort France 11 45.57N 0.58W
Rochester Australia 47 36.22S144.42E
Rochester Kent U.K. 5 51.22N 0.30E
Rochester Minn. U.S.A. 53 44.01N 92.27W
Rochester N.Y. U.S.A. 55 43.12N 77.37W
Rochfort Bridge Rep. of Ire. 7 53.25N 7.19W
Rock U.S.A. 55 46.03N 87.10W
Rockefeller Plateau Antarctica 64 80.00S140.00W
Rockford U.S.A. 53 42.16N 89.06W
Rockhampton Australia 44 23.22S150.32E
Rockingham Australia 43 32.16S115.21E
Rock Island *town* U.S.A. 53 41.30N 90.34W
Rockland Idaho U.S.A. 54 42.34N112.53W
Rockland Maine U.S.A. 55 44.06N 69.06W
Rockland Mich. U.S.A. 55 46.44N 89.12W
Rocklands Resr. Australia 46 37.13S141.52E
Rockport U.S.A. 54 39.45N123.47W
Rock Sound *town* Bahamas 57 24.54N 76.11W
Rock Springs Wyo. U.S.A. 54 41.35N109.13W
Rockville U.S.A. 55 39.05N 77.09W
Rocky Ford U.S.A. 52 38.03N103.44W
Rocky Gully *town* Australia 43 34.31S117.01E
Rocky Island L. Canada 55 46.56N 82.55W
Rocky Mts. N. America 52 43.21N109.50W
Rocroi France 8 49.56N 4.31E
Rod Pakistan 28 28.10N 63.05E
Rödby Denmark 17 54.42N 11.24E
Rodel U.K. 6 57.44N 6.58W
Rodez France 11 44.21N 2.34E
Ródhos *i.* Greece 13 36.12N 28.00E
Ródhos *town* Greece 13 36.24N 28.15E
Rodonit, Kep-i- *c.* Albania 13 41.34N 19.25E
Roe, L. Australia 43 30.40S122.10E
Roebourne Australia 42 20.45S117.08E
Roebuck B. Australia 42 19.04S122.17E
Roermond Neth. 8 51.12N 6.00E
Roeselare Belgium 8 50.57N 3.06E
Rogachev Belorussia 15 53.05N 30.02E
Rogaland *d.* Norway 17 59.00N 6.15E
Rogerson U.S.A. 54 42.14N114.47W
Rogliano France 11 42.57N 9.25E
Rogue *r.* U.S.A. 54 42.26N124.25W
Rohtak India 28 28.54N 76.35E
Rojas Argentina 63 34.15S 60.44W
Rokan *r.* Indonesia 26 2.00N101.00E
Rola Co *l.* China 29 35.26N 88.24E
Röldal Norway 17 59.49N 6.48E
Rolla Mo. U.S.A. 53 37.56N 91.55W
Rolleston Australia 44 24.25S148.35E
Rolleville Bahamas 57 23.41N 76.00W
Rolvsöya *i.* Norway 16 70.58N 24.00E
Roma Australia 44 26.35S148.47E
Roma Italy 12 41.54N 12.29E
Roma Sweden 17 57.32N 18.28E
Romain, C. U.S.A. 53 33.01N 79.23W
Romaine *r.* Canada 51 50.20N 63.45W
Roman Romania 15 46.55N 26.56E
Romang *i.* Indonesia 27 7.45S127.20E
Romania Europe 15 46.30N 24.00E
Romano, C. U.S.A. 53 25.50N 81.42W
Romans France 11 45.03N 5.03E
Rome *see* Roma Italy 12
Rome Ga. U.S.A. 53 34.01N 85.02W
Rome N.Y. U.S.A. 55 43.13N 75.27W
Romeo U.S.A. 55 42.47N 83.01W
Romilly France 9 48.31N 3.44E
Romney Marsh *f.* U.K. 5 51.03N 0.55E
Romorantin France 9 47.22N 1.44E
Rona *i.* U.K. 6 57.33N 5.58W
Ronan U.S.A. 54 47.32N114.06W
Roncesvalles Spain 10 43.01N 1.19W
Ronda Spain 10 36.45N 5.10W
Rondane *mtn.* Norway 17 61.55N 9.45E
Rondônia *d.* Brazil 60 12.10S 62.30W
Rondonópolis Brazil 61 16.29S 54.37W
Rongcheng China 25 37.09N122.23E
Rönne Denmark 17 55.06N 14.42E
Ronneby Sweden 17 56.12N 15.18E
Ronse Belgium 8 50.45N 3.36E
Ronuro *r.* Brazil 61 11.56S 53.33W
Roof Butte *mtn.* U.S.A. 54 36.28N109.05W
Roosendaal Neth. 8 51.32N 4.28E
Roosevelt *r.* Brazil 60 7.35S 60.20W
Roosevelt U.S.A. 54 40.18N109.59W
Roosevelt I. Antarctica 64 79.00S161.00W
Ropcha Russian Fed. 18 62.50N 51.55E
Roper *r.* Australia 44 14.40S135.30E
Roque Pérez Argentina 63 35.23S 59.22W
Roraima *d.* Brazil 60 2.00N 62.00W
Roraima, Mt. Guyana 60 5.14N 60.44W
Röros Norway 16 62.35N 11.23E
Rosa, Monte *mtn.* Italy / Switz. 9 45.56N 7.51E
Rosamond U.S.A. 54 34.52N118.10W
Rosario Argentina 63 32.57S 60.40W
Rosário Brazil 61 3.00S 44.15W
Rosario Uruguay 63 34.19S 57.21W
Rosario de la Frontera Argentina 62 25.50S 64.55W
Rosario del Tala Argentina 63 32.20S 59.10W
Rosário do Sul Brazil 59 30.15S 54.55W
Roscoff France 11 48.44N 4.00W
Roscommon Rep. of Ire. 7 53.38N 8.13W
Roscommon *d.* Rep. of Ire. 7 53.38N 8.11W
Roscrea Rep. of Ire. 7 52.57N 7.49W
Roseau Dominica 57 15.18N 61.23W
Rosebud Australia 47 38.21S144.54E
Roseburg U.S.A. 54 43.13N123.20W
Rosenheim Germany 14 47.51N 12.09E
Roses Spain 10 42.19N 3.10E
Rosetown Canada 50 51.34N107.59W
Rosetta R.S.A. 39 29.18S 29.58E
Roseville Calif. U.S.A. 54 38.45N121.17W
Rosières France 9 49.49N 2.43E
Rosignano Marittimo Italy 12 43.24N 10.28E
Roşiori-de-Vede Romania 15 44.07N 25.00E
Rositsa Bulgaria 15 43.57N 27.57E
Roska *r.* Ukraine 15 49.27N 29.45E
Roskilde Denmark 17 55.39N 12.05E
Roslags-Näsby Sweden 17 59.26N 18.04E
Roslavl Russian Fed. 18 53.55N 32.53E
Ross New Zealand 48 42.54S170.49E
Rossano Italy 13 39.35N 16.39E
Ross Dependency Antarctica 64 75.00S170.00W
Rossing Namibia 39 22.31S 14.52E
Rosslare Rep. of Ire. 7 52.17N 6.23W
Ross-on-Wye U.K. 5 51.55N 2.36W
Rossosh Russian Fed. 19 50.12N 39.35E
Rössvatnet *l.* Norway 16 65.45N 14.00E
Rosta Norway 16 68.59N 19.40E
Rosthern Canada 50 52.40N106.17W
Rostock Germany 14 54.06N 12.09E
Rostov Russian Fed 18 57.11N 39.23E
Rostov Russian Fed. 19 47.15N 39.45E
Rotem Belgium 8 51.04N 5.44E
Rothbury U.K. 4 55.19N 1.54W
Rotherham U.K. 4 53.26N 1.21W
Rothes U.K. 6 57.31N 3.13W
Rothesay Canada 55 45.23N 66.00W
Rothesay U.K. 6 55.50N 5.03W
Roti *i.* Indonesia 42 10.30S123.10E
Roto Australia 47 33.04S145.27E
Rotondella Italy 13 40.10N 16.32E
Rotorua New Zealand 48 38.07S176.17E
Rotorua, L. New Zealand 48 38.00S176.00E
Rotterdam Neth. 8 51.55N 4.29E
Rottnest I. Australia 43 32.01S115.28E
Rottweil Germany 14 48.10N 8.37E
Roubaix France 8 50.42N 3.10E
Rouen France 9 49.26N 1.05E
Rougé France 9 47.47N 1.26W
Rouku P.N.G. 44 8.40S141.35E
Round Mt. Australia 47 30.26S152.15E
Roundup U.S.A. 54 46.27N108.33W
Rousay *i.* U.K. 6 59.10N 3.02W
Rouyn Canada 55 48.20N 79.00W
Rovaniemi Finland 16 66.30N 25.40E
Rovato Italy 9 45.34N 10.00E
Rovereto Italy 9 45.53N 11.02E
Rovigo Italy 9 45.04N 11.47E
Rovinj Croatia 14 45.06N 13.39E
Rovno Ukraine 15 50.39N 26.10E
Rowena Australia 47 29.49S148.54E
Rowley Shoals *f.* Australia 42 17.30S119.00E
Roxburgh New Zealand 48 45.33S169.19E
Roxby Downs *town* Australia 46 30.42S136.46E
Roxen *l.* Sweden 17 58.30N 15.41E
Royale, Isle *i.* U.S.A. 55 48.00N 89.00W
Royal Leamington Spa U.K. 5 52.18N 1.32W
Royal Tunbridge Wells U.K. 5 51.07N 0.16E
Royan France 11 45.37N 1.02W
Roye France 9 49.42N 2.48E
Royston U.K. 5 52.03N 0.01W
Rozhishche Ukraine 15 50.58N 25.15E
Rožňava Slovakia 15 48.40N 20.32E
Rtishchevo Russian Fed. 18 52.16N 43.45E
Ruahine Range *mts.* New Zealand 48 40.00S176.00E
Ruapehu *mtn.* New Zealand 48 39.20S175.30E
Ruapuke I. New Zealand 48 46.45S168.30E
Rub 'al Khali *des. see* Ar Rub 'al Khālī *des.* Saudi Arabia 28
Rubino Ivory Coast 38 6.04N 4.18W
Rubio Colombia 60 7.42N 72.23W
Rubryn Belorussia 15 51.52N 27.30E
Rubtsovsk Russian Fed. 20 51.29N 81.10E
Ruby Mts. U.S.A. 54 40.25N115.35W
Rūdān *r.* Iran 31 27.02N 56.53E
Rūdbār Afghan. 31 30.10N 62.38E
Rudewa Tanzania 37 6.40S 37.08E
Rudki Ukraine 15 49.40N 23.28E
Rudnaya Pristan Russian Fed. 25 44.18N135.51E
Rudnichnyy Russian Fed. 18 59.10N 52.28E
Rudnik Poland 15 50.28N 22.15E
Rudnyy Kazakhstan 20 53.00N 63.05E
Rudolstadt Germany 14 50.44N 11.20E
Rue France 11 50.15N 1.40E
Ruffec France 11 46.02N 0.12E
Rufiji *r.* Tanzania 37 8.02S 39.19E
Rufino Argentina 63 34.16S 62.45W
Rufunsa Zambia 37 15.02S 29.35E
Rugao China 25 32.27N120.35E
Rugby U.K. 5 52.23N 1.16W
Rugby U.S.A. 52 48.24N 99.59W
Rügen *i.* Germany 14 54.30N 13.30E
Ruhr *f.* Germany 8 51.22N 7.26E
Ruhr *r.* Germany 8 51.27N 6.41E
Ruinen Neth. 8 52.47N 6.21E
Rukwa *d.* Tanzania 37 7.05S 31.25E
Rukwa, L. Tanzania 37 8.00S 32.20E
Rum *i.* U.K. 6 57.00N 6.20W
Ruma Yugo. 15 44.59N 19.51E
Rum Cay *i.* Bahamas 57 23.41N 74.53W
Rumford U.S.A. 55 44.33N 70.33W
Rummānah Egypt 32 31.01N 32.40E
Runcorn U.K. 4 53.20N 2.44W
Runde *r.* Zimbabwe 39 21.20S 32.23E
Rundvik Sweden 16 63.30N 19.24E
Rungwa *r.* Tanzania 37 7.38S 31.55E
Rungwa Singida Tanzania 37 6.57S 33.35E
Rungwe Mt. Tanzania 37 9.10S 33.40E
Runka Nigeria 38 12.28N 7.20E
Ruoqiang China 24 39.00N 88.00E
Ruo Shui *r.* China 24 42.15N101.03E
Rupert *r.* Canada 55 51.30N 78.45W
Rupununi *r.* Guyana 60 4.00N 58.30W
Rur *r.* Neth. 8 51.12N 5.58E
Rusape Zimbabwe 39 18.30S 32.08E
Ruse Bulgaria 13 43.50N 25.59E
Rushden U.K. 5 52.17N 0.37W
Rushworth Australia 47 36.38S145.02E
Russell Pt. Canada 50 73.30N115.00W
Russell Range *mts.* Australia 43 33.15S123.30E
Russian Federation Europe / Asia 20 62.00N 80.00E
Russkaya Polyana Russian Fed. 20 53.48N 73.54E
Rustavi Georgia 19 41.34N 45.03E
Rustenburg R.S.A. 39 25.39S 27.13E
Rutana Burundi 37 3.58S 30.00E
Rutanzige, L. *see* Edward, L. Uganda / Zaïre 37
Rütenbrock Germany 8 52.51N 7.06E
Ruteng Indonesia 27 8.35S120.28E
Rutenga Zimbabwe 39 21.15S 30.46E
Ruth U.S.A. 54 39.17N114.59W
Ruthin U.K. 4 53.07N 3.18W
Rutland U.S.A. 55 43.36N 72.59W
Rutog China 29 33.30N 79.40E
Rutshuru Zaïre 37 1.10S 29.26E
Ruvu Coast Tanzania 37 6.50S 38.42E
Ruvuma *r.* Mozambique / Tanzania 37 10.30S 40.30E
Ruvuma *d.* Tanzania 37 10.45S 36.15E
Ruwenzori Range *mts.* Uganda / Zaïre 37 0.30N 30.00E
Ruyigi Burundi 37 3.26S 30.14E
Ruzayevka Russian Fed. 18 54.04N 44.55E
Ruzitgort Russian Fed. 18 62.51N 64.52E
Ružomberok Slovakia 15 49.06N 19.18E
Rwanda Africa 37 2.00S 30.00E
Ryan, Loch U.K. 6 54.56N 5.02W
Ryasna Belorussia 15 54.00N 31.14E
Ryazan Russian Fed. 18 54.37N 39.43E
Ryazhsk Russian Fed. 18 53.40N 40.07E
Rybachiy, Poluostrov *pen.* Russian Fed. 18 69.45N 32.30E
Rybachye Kazakhstan 24 46.27N 81.30E
Rybinsk Russian Fed. 18 58.01N 38.52E
Rybinskoye Vodokhranilishche *resr.* Russian Fed. 18 58.30N 38.25E
Rybnik Poland 15 50.06N 18.32E
Rybnitsa Moldavia 15 47.42N 29.00E
Ryd Sweden 17 56.28N 14.41E
Rye U.K. 5 50.57N 0.46E
Rye *r.* U.K. 4 54.10N 0.44W
Ryki Poland 15 51.39N 21.56E
Rylstone Australia 47 32.48S149.58E
Ryūgasaki Japan 23 35.54N140.11E
Ryukyu Is. *see* Nansei shotō *is.* Japan 25
Rzeszów Poland 15 50.04N 22.00E
Rzhev Russian Fed. 18 56.15N 34.18E

S

Saa Cameroon 38 4.24N 11.25E
Saale *r.* Germany 14 51.58N 11.53E
Saanich Canada 54 48.28N123.22W
Saar *r.* Germany 8 49.43N 6.34E
Saarbrücken Germany 14 49.15N 6.58E
Saarburg Germany 8 49.36N 6.33E
Saaremaa *i.* Estonia 17 58.25N 22.30E
Saarijärvi Finland 16 62.43N 25.16E
Saariselkä *mts.* Finland 16 68.15N 28.30E
Saarland *d.* Germany 8 49.30N 6.50E
Saba *i.* Leeward Is. 57 17.42N 63.26W
Šabac Yugo. 15 44.45N 19.41E
Sabadell Spain 10 41.33N 2.07E
Sabah *d.* Malaysia 26 5.30N117.00E
Sabalān, Kūhhā-ye *mts.* Iran 31 38.15N 47.50E
Sabana, Archipiélago de Cuba 57 23.30N 80.00W
Sabanalarga Colombia 60 10.38N 75.00W
Sab'atayn, Ramlat as *f.* Yemen 35 15.30N 46.10E
Sabaudia Italy 12 41.18N 13.01E
Sabbioneta Italy 9 45.00N 10.39E
Sabhā Libya 34 27.04N 14.25E
Sabinas Mexico 56 26.33N101.10W
Sabinas Hidalgo Mexico 56 26.33N100.10W
Sabine *r.* U.S.A. 53 29.40N 93.50W
Sabkhat al Bardawīl *l.* Egypt 32 31.10N 33.15E
Sablayan Phil. 27 12.50N120.50E
Sable, C. Canada 51 43.30N 65.50W
Sable I. Canada 51 44.00N 60.00W
Sablé-sur-Sarthe France 9 47.50N 0.20W
Sabon Birni Nigeria 38 13.37N 6.15E
Sabongidda Nigeria 38 6.54N 5.56E
Sabrina Coast *f.* Antarctica 64 67.00S120.00E
Sabzevār Iran 31 36.13N 57.38E
Sacaca Bolivia 62 18.05S 66.25W
Sacajawea *mtn.* U.S.A. 54 45.15N117.17W
Sacedón Spain 10 40.29N 2.44W
Sachigo *r.* Canada 51 55.06N 88.58W
Sachsen *d.* Germany 14 51.10N 13.15E
Sachsen-Anhalt *d.* Germany 14 52.05N 11.30E
Saco U.S.A. 55 43.29N 70.28W
Sacramento Brazil 59 19.51S 26.47W
Sacramento U.S.A. 54 38.35N121.30W
Sacramento *r.* U.S.A. 54 38.03N121.56W
Sacramento Valley *f.* U.S.A. 54 39.15N122.00W
Sádaba Spain 10 42.19N 1.10W
Sadani Tanzania 37 6.00S 38.40E
Sadiya India 29 27.49N 95.38E
Şafājah *des.* Saudi Arabia 30 26.30N 39.30E
Şafāniyah Egypt 32 28.49N 30.48E
Şafarābād Iran 31 38.59N 47.25E
Säffle Sweden 17 59.08N 12.56E
Saffron Walden U.K. 5 52.02N 0.15E
Safi Morocco 34 32.20N 9.17W
Safid *r.* Iran 31 37.23N 50.11E
Safonovo Russian Fed. 18 55.08N 33.16E
Safonovo Russian Fed. 18 65.40N 48.10E
Sagaing Burma 29 22.00N 96.00E
Sagala Mali 38 14.09N 6.38W
Sagami *r.* Japan 23 35.14N139.23E
Sagamihara Japan 23 35.32N139.23E
Sagami-nada *b.* Japan 23 34.55N139.30E
Sāgar India 29 23.50N 78.44E
Sagara Japan 23 34.41N138.12E
Sage U.S.A. 54 41.49N110.59W
Saginaw U.S.A. 55 43.25N 83.54W
Saginaw B. U.S.A. 55 43.56N 83.40W
Sagiz Kazakhstan 19 47.31N 54.55E
Sagres Portugal 10 37.00N 8.56W
Sagua la Grande Cuba 57 22.55N 80.05W
Saguenay *r.* Canada 55 48.10N 69.45W
Sagunto Spain 10 39.40N 0.17W
Sahagún Spain 10 42.23N 5.02W
Sahand, Kūh-e *mtn.* Iran 31 37.37N 46.27E

Sahara *des.* Africa **34** 18.00N 12.00E
Sahāranpur India **28** 29.58N 77.33E
Sahbā, Wādī as *r.* Saudi Arabia **31** 23.48N 49.50E
Sahel *d.* Burkina **38** 14.00N 0.50W
Sāhīwāl Punjab Pakistan **28** 31.57N 72.22E
Saibai *i.* Australia **44** 9.24S142.40E
Sa'īdābād Iran **31** 29.28N 55.43E
Saidpur Bangla. **29** 25.48N 89.00E
Saigon *see* Ho Chi Minh Vietnam **26**
Saimaa *l.* Finland **18** 61.20N 28.00E
Saimbeyli Turkey **30** 38.07N 36.08E
St. Abb's Head U.K. **6** 55.54N 2.07W
St. Agapit Canada **55** 46.34N 71.26W
St. Albans U.K. **5** 51.46N 0.21W
St. Albans Vt. U.S.A. **55** 44.49N 73.05W
St. Amand France **8** 50.27N 3.26E
St. Amand-Mont-Rond *town* France **11** 46.43N 2.29E
St. Andrews U.K. **6** 56.20N 2.48W
St. Andries Belgium **8** 51.12N 3.10E
St. Ann's Bay *town* Jamaica **57** 18.26N 77.12W
St. Anthony Canada **51** 51.24N 55.37W
St. Anthony U.S.A. **52** 43.59N 111.40W
St. Arnaud Australia **46** 36.40S143.20E
St. Augustine U.S.A. **53** 29.54N 81.19W
St. Augustin Saguenay Canada **51** 51.14N 58.39W
St. Austell U.K. **5** 50.20N 4.48W
St. Barthélemy *i.* Leeward Is. **57** 17.55N 62.50W
St. Bees Head U.K. **4** 54.31N 3.39W
St. Boniface Canada **51** 49.54N 97.07W
St. Brides B. U.K. **5** 51.48N 5.03W
St. Brieuc France **11** 48.31N 2.45W
St. Calais France **9** 47.55N 0.45E
St. Catharines Canada **55** 43.10N 79.15W
St. Catherine's Pt. U.K. **5** 50.34N 1.18W
St. Céré France **11** 44.52N 1.53E
St. Cloud U.S.A. **53** 45.34N 94.10W
St. Croix *i.* U.S.V.Is. **57** 17.45N 64.35W
St. David's U.K. **5** 51.54N 5.16W
St. David's Head U.K. **5** 51.55N 5.19W
St. Denis France **9** 48.56N 2.21E
St. Dié France **11** 48.17N 6.57E
St. Dizier France **9** 48.38N 4.58E
Sainte-Agathe-des-Monts Canada **55** 46.03N 74.19W
Sainte Anne de Beaupré Canada **55** 47.02N 70.58W
St. Elias, Mt. U.S.A. **50** 60.20N139.00W
St. Éloi Canada **55** 48.03N 69.14W
Sainte Menehould France **9** 49.05N 4.54E
Sainte Menehould France **14** 49.05N 4.54E
Sainte Mère-Église France **9** 49.24N 1.19W
Saintes France **11** 45.44N 0.38W
Sainte-Thérèse-de-Blainville Canada **55** 45.38N 73.50W
St. Étienne France **11** 45.26N 4.26E
St. Fargeau France **9** 47.38N 3.04E
Saintfield U.K. **7** 54.28N 5.50W
St. Florent France **11** 42.41N 9.18E
St. Florentin France **9** 48.00N 3.44E
St. Flour France **11** 45.02N 3.05E
St. Gallen Switz. **14** 47.25N 9.23E
St. Gaudens France **11** 43.07N 0.44E
St. George Australia **45** 28.03S148.30E
St. George N.B. Canada **55** 45.08N 66.56W
St. George U.S.A. **54** 37.06N113.35W
St. Georges Belgium **8** 50.37N 5.20E
St. George's Grenada **57** 12.04N 61.44W
St. Georges Guiana **61** 3.54N 51.48W
St. George's Channel Rep. of Ire. /U.K. **7** 51.30N 6.20W
St. Germain France **9** 48.53N 2.04E
St. Gheorghe's Mouth *est.* Romania **13** 44.51N 29.37E
St. Gilles-Croix-de-Vie France **11** 46.42N 1.56W
St. Girons France **11** 42.59N 1.08E
St. Gotthard Pass Switz. **11** 46.30N 8.55E
St. Govan's Head U.K. **5** 51.36N 4.55W
St. Helena B. R.S.A. **39** 32.35S 18.05E
St. Helens U.K. **4** 53.28N 2.43W
St. Helens U.S.A. **54** 45.52N122.48W
St. Helier U.K. **5** 49.12N 2.07W
St. Hilaire-du-Harcouët France **9** 48.35N 1.06W
St. Hubert Belgium **8** 50.02N 5.22E
St. Hyacinthe Canada **55** 45.38N 72.57W
St. Ignace U.S.A. **55** 45.53N 84.44W
St. Ives U.K. **5** 50.13N 5.29W
St. Jean Canada **55** 45.18N 73.16W
St. Jean France **11** 45.17N 6.21E
St. Jean, Lac *l.* Canada **55** 48.35N 72.00W
St. Jean de Matha Canada **55** 46.14N 73.33W
St. Jean Pied-de-Port France **11** 43.10N 1.14W
St. Jérôme Canada **55** 45.47N 74.01W
St. John Canada **55** 45.16N 66.03W
St. John *r.* Canada **55** 45.15N 66.04W
St. John's Antigua **57** 17.07N 61.51W
St. John's Canada **51** 47.34N 52.41W
St. Johns U.S.A. **54** 34.30N109.22W
St. Johnsbury U.S.A. **55** 44.25N 72.01W
St. John's Pt. U.K. **7** 54.14N 5.39W
St. Jordi, Golf de *g.* Spain **10** 40.50N 1.10E
St. Joseph Mich. U.S.A. **55** 42.05N 86.30W
St. Joseph Mo. U.S.A. **53** 39.45N 94.51W
St. Joseph, L. Canada **51** 51.05N 90.35W
St. Junien France **11** 45.53N 0.55E
St. Just-en-Chaussée France **9** 49.30N 2.26E
St. Kitts-Nevis Leeward Is. **57** 17.20N 62.45W
St. Laurent Que. Canada **55** 45.31N 73.42W
St. Laurent du Maroni Guiana **61** 5.30N 54.02W
St. Lawrence *r.* Canada **55** 48.45N 68.30W
St. Lawrence, G. of Canada **51** 48.00N 62.00W
St. Lawrence I. U.S.A. **50** 63.00N170.00W
St. Lô France **9** 49.07N 1.05W
St. Louis Senegal **34** 16.01N 16.30W
St. Louis U.S.A. **53** 38.40N 90.15W
St. Lucia Windward Is. **57** 14.05N 61.00W
St. Lucia, L. R.S.A. **39** 28.05S 32.26E
St. Maixent France **11** 46.25N 0.12W
St. Malo France **9** 48.39N 2.00W
St. Malo, Golfe de *g.* France **11** 49.20N 2.00W
St.-Marc Haiti **57** 19.08N 72.41W
St. Margaret's Hope U.K. **6** 58.49N 2.57W
St. Maries U.S.A. **54** 47.19N116.35W
St. Martin *i.* Leeward Is. **57** 18.05N 63.05W
St. Martin U.K. **5** 49.27N 2.34W
St. Martin's *i.* U.K. **5** 49.57N 6.16W
St. Mary U.K. **5** 49.14N 2.10W
St.Mary Peak Australia **46** 31.30S138.35E
St. Marys Australia **45** 41.33S148.12E
St. Mary's *i.* U.K. **5** 49.55N 6.16W
St. Matthew I. U.S.A. **50** 60.30N172.45W
St. Maur France **9** 48.48N 2.30E
St. Maurice *r.* Canada **55** 46.21N 72.31W
St. Moritz Switz. **14** 46.30N 9.51E
St. Nazaire France **11** 47.17N 2.12W
St. Neots U.K. **5** 52.14N 0.16W
St. Niklaas Belgium **8** 51.10N 4.09E
St. Omer France **11** 50.45N 2.15E
St. Pacôme Canada **55** 47.24N 69.58W
St. Pascal Canada **55** 47.32N 69.48W
St. Paul Pyr. Or. France **11** 42.49N 2.29E
St. Paul Minn. U.S.A. **53** 45.00N 93.10W
St. Paul du Nord Canada **55** 48.27N 69.16W
St. Peter Port U.K. **5** 49.27N 2.32W
St. Petersburg U.S.A. **53** 27.45N 82.40W
St. Pierre Char. Mar. France **11** 45.57N 1.19W
St. Pierre S. Mar. France **9** 49.48N 0.29E
St. Pierre and Miquelon *is.* N. America **51** 47.00N 56.15W
St. Pierre-Église France **9** 49.40N 1.24W
St. Pölten Austria **14** 48.13N 15.37E
St. Quentin France **9** 49.51N 3.17E
St. Seine-l'Abbaye France **9** 47.26N 4.47E
St. Siméon Canada **55** 47.56N 69.58W
St. Stephen Canada **55** 45.12N 67.18W
St. Thomas Canada **55** 42.47N 81.12W
St. Thomas *i.* U.S.V.Is. **57** 18.22N 64.57W
St. Tropez France **11** 43.16N 6.39E
St. Truiden Belgium **8** 50.49N 5.11E
St. Valéry France **9** 49.52N 0.43E
St. Vallier France **11** 45.11N 4.49E
St. Vincent, G. Australia **46** 35.00S138.05E
St. Vincent and the Grenadines Windward Is. **57** 13.00N 61.15W
St. Vith Belgium **8** 50.15N 6.08E
St. Wendel Germany **8** 49.27N 7.10E
St. Yrieix France **11** 45.31N 1.12E
Saitama *d.* Japan **23** 35.55N139.00E
Sajama *mtn.* Bolivia **62** 18.06S 69.00W
Saka Kenya **37** 0.09S 39.18E
Sakai Japan **23** 34.35N135.28E
Sakākah Saudi Arabia **30** 29.59N 40.12E
Sakania Zaïre **37** 12.44S 28.34E
Sakarya *r.* Turkey **30** 41.08N 30.36E
Sakété Benin **38** 6.45N 2.45E
Sakhalin *i.* Russian Fed. **25** 50.00N143.00E
Sakht-Sar Iran **31** 36.54N 50.41E
Sakivier R.S.A. **36** 30.50S 20.26E
Sakrivier R.S.A. **39** 30.53S 20.24E
Sakuma Japan **23** 35.05N137.48E
Sal *r.* Russian Fed. **19** 47.33N 40.40E
Sala Sweden **17** 59.55N 16.36E
Salaca *r.* Latvia **17** 57.45N 24.21E
Salacgriva Latvia **17** 57.45N 24.21E
Salado *r.* Buenos Aires Argentina **63** 35.44S 57.22W
Salado *r.* Santa Fé Argentina **63** 31.40S 60.41W
Salado *r.* La Pampa Argentina **63** 36.15S 66.55W
Salado *r.* Mexico **56** 26.46N 98.55W
Salaga Ghana **38** 8.36N 0.32W
Salālah Oman **28** 17.00N 54.04E
Salamanca Spain **10** 40.58N 5.40W
Salamina Colombia **60** 5.24N 75.31W
Salatiga Indonesia **26** 7.15S110.34E
Salbris France **9** 47.26N 2.03E
Salcombe U.K. **5** 50.14N 3.47W
Saldaña Spain **10** 42.32N 4.48W
Saldanha R.S.A. **39** 33.00S 17.56E
Saldanha B. R.S.A. **39** 33.05S 17.50E
Saldus Latvia **17** 56.40N 22.30E
Sale Australia **47** 38.06S147.06E
Salekhard Russian Fed. **18** 66.33N 66.35E
Salem India **29** 11.38N 78.08E
Salem Ind. U.S.A. **55** 38.38N 86.06W
Salem Oreg. U.S.A. **54** 44.57N123.01W
Sälen Sweden **17** 61.10N 13.16E
Salerno Italy **12** 40.41N 14.45E
Salerno, Golfo di *g.* Italy **12** 40.30N 14.45E
Salford U.K. **4** 53.30N 2.17W
Salgótarján Hungary **15** 48.07N 19.48E
Salgueiro Brazil **61** 8.04S 39.05W
Salima Malaŵi **37** 13.45S 34.29E
Salim's Tanzania **37** 10.37S 36.33E
Salina Cruz Mexico **56** 16.11N 95.12W
Salinas Ecuador **60** 2.13S 80.58W
Salinas U.S.A. **54** 36.40N121.38W
Salinas *r.* U.S.A. **52** 36.45N121.48W
Salinópolis Brazil **61** 0.37S 47.20W
Salins France **11** 46.56N 5.53E
Salisbury U.K. **5** 51.04N 1.48W
Salisbury Md. U.S.A. **55** 38.22N 75.36W
Salisbury Plain *f.* U.K. **5** 51.15N 1.55W
Şalkhad Syria **32** 32.29N 36.42E
Salluit Canada **51** 62.10N 75.40W
Salmās Iran **31** 38.13N 44.50E
Salmi Russian Fed. **18** 61.19N 31.46E
Salmon U.S.A. **54** 45.11N113.55W
Salmon *r.* U.S.A. **54** 45.51N116.46W
Salmon Gums Australia **43** 32.59S121.39E
Salmon River Mts. U.S.A. **54** 44.45N115.30W
Salo Finland **17** 60.23N 23.08E
Salò Italy **9** 45.36N 10.31E
Salobreña Spain **10** 36.45N 3.35W
Salome U.S.A. **54** 33.47N113.37W
Salon France **11** 43.38N 5.06E
Salonta Romania **15** 46.48N 21.40E
Salsk Russian Fed. **19** 46.30N 41.33E
Salso *r.* Italy **12** 37.07N 13.57E
Salsomaggiore Terme Italy **9** 44.49N 9.59E
Salt *r.* U.S.A. **54** 33.23N112.18W
Salta Argentina **62** 24.47S 65.24W
Salta *d.* Argentina **62** 25.00S 65.00W
Saltdal Norway **16** 67.06N 15.25E
Saltee Is. Rep. of Ire. **7** 52.08N 6.36W
Saltfjorden *est.* Norway **16** 67.15N 14.10E
Saltfleet U.K. **4** 53.25N 0.11E
Salt Fork *r.* U.S.A. **53** 36.41N 97.05W
Saltillo Mexico **56** 25.30N101.00W
Salt Lake City U.S.A. **54** 40.46N111.53W
Salto Argentina **63** 34.17S 60.15W
Salto Brazil **59** 23.10S 47.16W
Salto *r.* Italy **12** 42.23N 12.54E
Salto Uruguay **63** 31.23S 57.58W
Salto da Divisa Brazil **61** 16.04S 40.00W
Salto Grande, Embalse de *resr.* Argentina / Uruguay **63** 31.00S 57.50W
Salton Sea *l.* U.S.A. **54** 33.19N115.50W
Saluzzo Italy **9** 44.39N 7.29E
Salvador Brazil **61** 12.58S 38.29W
Salween *r.* Burma **29** 16.30N 97.33E
Salyany Azerbaijan **31** 39.36N 48.59E
Salzbrunn Namibia **39** 24.23S 18.00E
Salzburg Austria **14** 47.54N 13.03E
Salzburg *d.* Austria **14** 47.25N 13.15E
Salzgitter Germany **14** 52.02N 10.22E
Salzwedel Germany **14** 52.51N 11.09E
Samālūt Egypt **32** 28.18N 30.43E
Samaná Dom. Rep. **57** 19.14N 69.20W
Samana Cay *i.* Bahamas **57** 23.05N 73.45W
Samanga Tanzania **37** 8.24S 39.18E
Samannūd Egypt **32** 30.58N 31.14E
Samar *i.* Phil. **27** 11.45N125.15E
Samara Russian Fed. **18** 53.10N 50.15E
Samara *r.* Russian Fed. **18** 53.17N 50.42E
Samarai P.N.G. **44** 10.37S150.40E
Samarinda Indonesia **26** 0.30S117.09E
Samarkand Uzbekistan **20** 39.40N 66.57E
Sāmarrā Iraq **31** 34.13N 43.52E
Sambalpur India **29** 21.28N 84.04E
Sambor Ukraine **15** 49.31N 23.10E
Samborombón, Bahía *b.* Argentina **63** 36.00S 57.00W
Sambre *r.* Belgium **8** 50.29N 4.52E
Samburu Kenya **37** 3.46S 39.17E
Samch'ŏk S. Korea **25** 37.30N129.10E
Same Tanzania **37** 4.10S 37.43E
Samobor Slovenia **14** 45.48N 15.43E
Samorogouan Burkina **38** 11.21N 4.57W
Sámos *i.* Greece **13** 37.44N 26.45E
Samothráki *i.* Greece **13** 40.26N 25.35E
Sampit Indonesia **26** 2.34S112.59E
Samsang China **29** 30.22N 82.50E
Samsun Turkey **30** 41.17N 36.22E
Samtredia Georgia **19** 42.10N 42.22E
Samui, Ko *i.* Thailand **29** 9.30N100.00E
Samur *r.* Russian Fed. **19** 42.00N 48.20E
Samut Sakhon Thailand **29** 13.32N100.17E
San Mali **38** 13.21N 4.57W
San *r.* Poland **15** 50.25N 22.20E
Şan'ā' Yemen **35** 15.23N 44.14E
Sanaba Burkina **38** 12.25N 3.47W
Sanaga *r.* Cameroon **38** 3.35N 9.40E
Sanandaj Iran **31** 35.18N 47.01E
San Andreas U.S.A. **54** 38.12N120.41W
San Andrés, Isla de *i.* Colombia **57** 12.33N 81.42W
San Andrés Tuxtla Mexico **56** 18.27N 95.13W
San Angelo U.S.A. **52** 31.28N100.28W
San Antonio Chile **63** 33.35S 71.38W
San Antonio Tex. U.S.A. **52** 29.25N 98.30W
San Antonio, C. Cuba **57** 21.50N 84.57W
San Antonio, Cabo *c.* Argentina **63** 36.40S 56.42W
San Antonio, Punta *c.* Mexico **56** 29.45N115.41W
San Antonio Abad Spain **10** 38.58N 1.18E
San Antonio de Areco Argentina **63** 34.16S 59.30W
San Antonio Oeste Argentina **63** 40.44S 64.57W
San Benedetto Italy **12** 42.57N 13.53E
San Benedetto Po Italy **9** 45.02N 10.55E
San Benito Guatemala **57** 16.55N 89.54W
San Bernardino U.S.A. **54** 34.06N117.17W
San Bernardo Chile **63** 33.36S 70.43W
San Blas, C. U.S.A. **53** 29.40N 85.25W
San Bonifacio Italy **9** 45.24N 11.16E
San Carlos Chile **63** 36.25S 71.58W
San Carlos Mexico **56** 29.01N100.51W
San Carlos Nicaragua **57** 11.07N 84.47W
San Carlos Phil. **27** 15.59N120.22E
San Carlos Venezuela **60** 9.39N 68.35W
San Carlos Venezuela **60** 1.55N 67.04W
San Carlos de Bariloche Argentina **63** 41.08S 71.15W
San Carlos del Zulia Venezuela **60** 9.01N 71.55W
Sancerre France **9** 47.20N 2.51E
Sancerrois, Collines du *hills* France **9** 47.25N 2.45E
San Clemente U.S.A. **54** 33.26N117.37W
San Clemente *i.* U.S.A. **54** 32.54N118.29W
San Cristóbal Argentina **62** 30.20S 61.41W
San Cristóbal Dom. Rep. **57** 18.27N 70.07W
San Cristóbal Venezuela **60** 7.46N 72.15W
Sancti Spíritus Cuba **57** 21.55N 79.28W
Sand Norway **17** 59.29N 6.15E
Sanda *i.* U.K. **6** 55.17N 5.34W
Sandakan Malaysia **26** 5.52N118.04E
Sanday *i.* U.K. **6** 59.15N 2.33W
Sandbach U.K. **4** 53.09N 2.23W
Sandefjord Norway **17** 59.08N 10.14E
Sanders U.S.A. **54** 35.13N109.20W
Sandgate Australia **47** 27.18S153.00E
Sandhornöy *i.* Norway **16** 67.05N 14.10E
Sandia Peru **60** 14.14S 69.25W
San Diego U.S.A. **54** 32.43N117.09W
San Diego, C. Argentina **63** 54.38S 65.05W
Sand Lake *town* Canada **55** 47.46N 84.31W
Sandnes Norway **17** 58.51N 5.44E
Sandness U.K. **6** 60.18N 1.38W
Sandö *i.* Faroe Is. **16** 61.50N 6.45W
Sandoa Zaïre **36** 9.41S 22.56E
Sandomierz Poland **15** 50.41N 21.45E
San Donà di Piave Italy **9** 45.38N 12.34E
Sandover *r.* Australia **44** 21.43S136.32E
Sandoway Burma **29** 18.28N 94.20E
Sandown U.K. **5** 50.39N 1.09W
Sandpoint *town* U.S.A. **54** 48.17N116.34W
Sandringham U.K. **4** 52.50N 0.30E
Sandstone Australia **43** 27.59S119.17E
Sandusky Ohio U.S.A. **55** 41.27N 82.42W
Sandveld *f.* Namibia **39** 21.25S 20.00E
Sandviken Sweden **17** 60.37N 16.46E
Sandy U.S.A. **54** 40.35N111.53W
Sandy Bight *b.* Australia **43** 33.53S123.25E
Sandy C. Australia **44** 24.42S153.17E
Sandy Creek *town* U.S.A. **55** 43.39N 76.05W
Sandy L. Ont. Canada **51** 53.00N 93.07W
San Enrique Argentina **63** 35.47S 60.22W
San Felipe Chile **63** 32.45S 70.44W
San Felipe Colombia **60** 1.55N 67.06W
San Felipe Mexico **56** 31.00N114.52W
San Felipe Venezuela **60** 10.25N 68.40W
San Fernando Argentina **63** 34.26S 58.34W
San Fernando Chile **63** 34.35S 71.00W
San Fernando Phil. **27** 16.39N120.19E
San Fernando Spain **10** 36.28N 6.12W
San Fernando Trinidad **60** 10.16N 61.28W
San Fernando de Apure Venezuela **60** 7.35N 67.15W
San Fernando de Atabapo Venezuela **60** 4.03N 67.45W
Sanford *r.* Australia **42** 27.22S115.53E
Sanford Fla. U.S.A. **53** 28.49N 81.17W
San Francisco Argentina **62** 31.29S 62.06W
San Francisco U.S.A. **54** 37.48N122.24W
San Francisco *r.* U.S.A. **54** 32.59N109.22W
San Francisco, C. Ecuador **60** 0.50N 80.05W
San Francisco de Macorís Dom. Rep. **57** 19.19N 70.15W
Sanga-Tolon Russian Fed. **21** 61.44N149.30E
Sanggan He *r.* China **25** 40.23N115.18E
Sangha *r.* Congo **36** 1.10S 16.47E
Sangihe *i.* Indonesia **27** 3.30N125.30E
Sangihe, Kepulauan *is.* Indonesia **27** 2.45N125.20E
San Gil Colombia **60** 6.35N 73.08W
San Giovanni in Persiceto Italy **9** 44.38N 11.11E
Sangkulirang Indonesia **26** 1.00N117.58E
Sāngli India **28** 16.55N 74.37E
Sangmélima Cameroon **38** 2.55N 12.01E
Sangonera *r.* Spain **10** 37.58N 1.04W
San Gottardo, Passo del *pass* Switz. **14** 46.30N 8.55E
San Gregorio Uruguay **63** 32.37S 55.40W
Sangri China **24** 29.18N 92.05E
San Ignacio Bolivia **62** 16.23S 60.59W
San Ignacio Paraguay **62** 26.52S 57.03W
San Isidro Argentina **63** 34.29S 58.31W
Saniyah, Hawr as *l.* Iraq **31** 31.52N 46.50E
San Javier Argentina **63** 30.40S 59.55W
San Javier Bolivia **62** 16.22S 62.38W
San Javier Chile **63** 35.35S 71.45W
San Joaquin *r.* U.S.A. **54** 38.03N121.50W
San Jorge, Golfo *g.* Argentina **63** 46.00S 66.00W
San José Costa Rica **57** 9.59N 84.04W
San José Guatemala **56** 13.58N 90.50W
San Jose U.S.A. **54** 37.20N121.53W
San José de Chiquitos Bolivia **62** 17.53S 60.45W
San José de Feliciano Argentina **63** 30.25S 58.45W
San José de Guanipa Venezuela **60** 8.54N 64.09W
San José del Guaviare Colombia **60** 2.35N 72.38W
San José de Mayo Uruguay **63** 34.20S 56.42W
San José de Ocuné Colombia **60** 4.15N 70.20W
San Juan Argentina **62** 31.30S 68.30W
San Juan *d.* Argentina **62** 31.00S 68.30W
San Juan *r.* Costa Rica **57** 10.50N 83.40W
San Juan Dom. Rep. **57** 18.40N 71.05W
San Juan Peru **62** 15.20S 75.09W
San Juan Phil. **27** 8.25N126.22E
San Juan Puerto Rico **57** 18.29N 66.08W
San Juan *r.* U.S.A. **54** 37.18N110 28W
San Juan, C. Argentina **63** 54.45S 63.50W
San Juan Bautista Spain **10** 39.05N 1.30E
San Juan del Norte Nicaragua **57** 10.58N 83.40W
San Juan de los Morros Venezuela **60** 9.53N 67.23W
San Juan del Río Querétaro Mexico **56** 20.23N100.00W
San Juan Mts. U.S.A. **54** 37.35N107.10W
San Julián Argentina **63** 49.19S 67.40W
San Justo Argentina **63** 30.47S 60.35W
Sankt Niklaus Switz. **9** 46.11N 7.48E
Sankt-Peterburg Russian Fed. **18** 59.55N 30.25E
San Lázaro, Cabo *c.* Mexico **56** 24.50N112.18W
San Leonardo Spain **10** 41.49N 3.04W
Şanlıurfa Turkey **30** 37.08N 38.45E
San Lorenzo Argentina **63** 32.45S 60.44W
San Lorenzo *mtn.* Chile **63** 47.37S 72.19W
San Lorenzo Ecuador **60** 1.17N 78.50W
San Lorenzo de El Escorial Spain **10** 40.34N 4.08W
Sanlúcar de Barrameda Spain **10** 36.46N 6.21W
Sanlúcar la Mayor Spain **10** 37.26N 6.18W
San Lucas Bolivia **62** 20.06S 65.07W
San Lucas, Cabo *c.* Mexico **56** 22.50N109.55W
San Luis Argentina **63** 33.20S 66.20W
San Luis *d.* Argentina **63** 34.00S 66.00W
San Luis Cuba **57** 20.13N 75.50W
San Luis Obispo U.S.A. **54** 35.17N120.40W
San Luis Potosí Mexico **56** 22.10N101.00W
San Luis Potosí *d.* Mexico **56** 23.00N100.00W
San Marcos U.S.A. **52** 29.54N 97.57W
San Marino Europe **9** 43.55N 12.27E
San Marino *town* San Marino **9** 43.55N 12.27E
San Martín *r.* Bolivia **62** 12.25S 64.25W
San Mateo U.S.A. **54** 37.35N122.19W
San Matías Bolivia **60** 16.22S 58.24W
San Matías, Golfo *g.* Argentina **63** 41.30S 64.00W
Sanmenxia China **25** 34.46N111.17E
San Miguel *r.* Bolivia **60** 13.52S 63.56W
San Miguel *r.* Bolivia **62** 12.25S 64.25W
San Miguel El Salvador **57** 13.28N 88.10W
San Miguel del Monte Argentina **63** 35.25S 58.49W
San Miguel de Tucumán Argentina **62** 26.49S 65.13W
San Miguelito Panama **57** 9.02N 79.30W
Sannār Sudan **35** 13.31N 33.38E
Sannicandro Italy **12** 41.50N 15.34E
San Nicolás Argentina **63** 33.20S 60.13W
Sanok Poland **15** 49.35N 22.10E
San Pablo Phil. **27** 13.58N121.10E
San Pedro Buenos Aires Argentina **63** 33.40S 59.41W
San Pedro Jujuy Argentina **62** 24.14S 64.50W
San Pedro Dom. Rep. **57** 18.30N 69.18W
San Pedro Paraguay **59** 24.08S 57.08W
San Pedro, Punta *c.* Costa Rica **57** 8.38N 83.45W
San Pedro, Sierra de *mts.* Spain **10** 39.20N 6.20W
San Pedro de las Colonias Mexico **56** 25.50N102.59W
San Pedro Sula Honduras **57** 15.26N 88.01W
San Pellegrino Terme Italy **9** 45.50N 9.40E
San Pietro *i.* Italy **12** 39.09N 8.16E
Sanquhar U.K. **6** 55.22N 3.56W
San Quintín Mexico **56** 30.28N115.58W
San Rafael U.S.A. **54** 37.59N122.31W
San Raphael Argentina **63** 34.40S 68.21W
San Remo Italy **9** 43.48N 7.46E
San Salvador Argentina **63** 31.37S 58.30W
San Salvador *i.* Bahamas **57** 24.00N 74.32W
San Salvador El Salvador **57** 13.40N 89.10W
San Salvador de Jujuy Argentina **62** 24.10S 65.20W
San Sebastián Argentina **63** 53.15S 68.30W
San Sebastián Spain **10** 43.19N 1.59W
San Severo Italy **12** 41.40N 15.24E
Santa *r.* Peru **60** 9.00S 78.35W
Santa Ana Argentina **62** 27.20S 65.35W
Santa Ana Bolivia **62** 13.45S 65.35W
Santa Ana El Salvador **57** 14.00N 89.31W
Santa Ana U.S.A. **54** 33.44N117.54W
Santa Bárbara Mexico **56** 26.48N105.49W
Santa Barbara U.S.A. **54** 34.25N119.42W
Santa Catarina *d.* Brazil **59** 27.00S 52.00W
Santa Clara Cuba **57** 22.25N 79.58W
Santa Clara Calif. U.S.A. **54** 37.21N121.57W
Santa Clara Utah U.S.A. **54** 37.08N113.39W
Santa Clotilde Peru **60** 2.25S 73.35W
Santa Comba Dão Portugal **10** 40.24N 8.08W
Santa Cruz *d.* Argentina **63** 48.00S 69.30W
Santa Cruz *r.* Argentina **63** 50.03S 68.35W
Santa Cruz Bolivia **62** 17.45S 63.14W
Santa Cruz *d.* Bolivia **62** 17.45S 62.00W
Santa Cruz Canary Is. **34** 28.27N 16.14W
Santa Cruz U.S.A. **54** 36.58N122.08W
Santa Cruz *i.* U.S.A. **54** 34.01N119.45W
Santa Cruz Is. Solomon Is. **40** 10.30S166.00E
Santa Domingo Mexico **54** 25.32N112.02W
Santa Elena Argentina **63** 31.00S 59.50W
Santa Elena, C. Costa Rica **57** 10.54N 85.56W
Santa Fé Argentina **63** 31.40S 60.40W
Santa Fé *d.* Argentina **62** 30.00S 61.00W
Santa Fe U.S.A. **52** 35.42N106.57W
Santa Filomena Brazil **61** 9.07S 45.56W
Santa Inés, Isla *i.* Chile **63** 53.40S 73.00W
Santa Isabel Argentina **63** 36.15S 66.55W
Santa Isabel do Morro Brazil **61** 11.36S 50.37W
Santa Lucía Uruguay **63** 34.27S 56.24W
Santa Lucía *r.* Uruguay **63** 34.48S 56.22W
Santa Lucia Range *mts.* U.S.A. **54** 36.00N121.20W
Santa Margherita Ligure Italy **9** 44.20N 9.12E
Santa María Brazil **59** 29.40S 53.47W
Santa Maria U.S.A. **54** 34.57N120.26W
Santa Maria di Leuca, Capo *c.* Italy **13** 39.47N 18.24E
Santa Maria Madalena Brazil **59** 21.58S 42.02W
Santa Marta Colombia **60** 11.18N 74.10W
Santa Marta, Sierra Nevada de *mts.* Colombia **60** 11.20N 73.00W
Santa Monica U.S.A. **54** 34.01N118.30W
Santana do Livramento Brazil **63** 30.53S 55.31W
Santander Colombia **60** 3.00N 76.25W
Santander Spain **10** 43.28N 3.48W
Santañy Spain **10** 39.20N 3.07E
Santarém Brazil **61** 2.26S 54.41W
Santarém Portugal **10** 39.14N 8.40W
Santa Rosa Argentina **63** 36.00S 64.40W
Santa Rosa Bolivia **60** 10.36S 67.25W
Santa Rosa Brazil **59** 27.52S 54.29W
Santa Rosa Honduras **57** 14.47N 88.46W
Santa Rosa Calif. U.S.A. **54** 38.26N122.34W
Santa Rosa *i.* U.S.A. **54** 33.58N120.06W
Santa Rosa de Cabal Colombia **60** 4.52N 75.37W
Santa Rosalía Mexico **56** 27.19N112.17W
Santa Rosa Range *mts.* U.S.A. **54** 41.00N117.40W
Santa Vitória do Palmar Brazil **59** 33.3[illegible] 53.21W
Sant Feliu de Guíxols Spain **10** [illegible]
Santhià Italy **9** 45.22N 8.10E

Santiago Chile 63 33.27S 70.40W
Santiago Dom. Rep. 57 19.30N 70.42W
Santiago Panama 57 8.08N 80.59W
Santiago r. Peru 60 4.30S 77.48W
Santiago de Compostela Spain 10 42.52N 8.33W
Santiago de Cuba Cuba 57 20.00N 75.49W
Santiago del Estero Argentina 62 27.50S 64.15W
Santiago del Estero d. Argentina 62 27.40S 63.30W
Santiago Vázquez Uruguay 63 34.48S 56.21W
Santo Amaro Brazil 61 12.35S 38.41W
Santo André Brazil 59 23.39S 46.29W
Santo Angelo Brazil 59 28.18S 54.16W
Santo Antônio do Içá Brazil 60 3.05S 67.57W
Santo Domingo Dom. Rep. 57 18.30N 69.57W
Santoña Spain 10 43.27N 3.26W
Santos Brazil 59 23.56S 46.22W
Santos Dumont Brazil 59 21.30S 43.34W
Santo Tomás Peru 60 14.34S 72.30W
Santo Tomé Argentina 62 28.31S 56.03W
Santpoort Neth. 8 52.27N 4.38E
San Valentín, Cerro mtn. Chile 63 46.40S 73.25W
San Vicente El Salvador 57 13.38N 88.42W
San Vito al Tagliamento Italy 9 45.54N 12.52E
Sanya China 25 18.20N 109.31E
São Borja Brazil 59 28.35S 56.01W
São Caetano do Sul Brazil 59 23.36S 46.34W
São Carlos Brazil 59 22.01S 47.54W
São Francisco r. Brazil 61 10.20S 36.20W
São Francisco do Sol Brazil 59 26.17S 48.39W
São Gabriel Brazil 59 30.20S 54.19W
São Gonçalo do Sapucaí Brazil 59 21.54S 45.35W
Sao Hill town Tanzania 37 8.21S 35.10E
São João da Boa Vista Brazil 59 21.59S 46.45W
São João da Madeira Portugal 10 40.54N 8.30W
São João del Rei Brazil 59 21.08S 44.15W
São João do Piauí Brazil 61 8.21S 42.15W
São Joaquim da Barra Brazil 59 20.36S 47.51W
São José do Calçado Brazil 59 21.01S 41.37W
São José do Rio Prêto Brazil 59 20.50S 49.20W
São José dos Campos Brazil 59 23.07S 45.52W
São Leopoldo Brazil 59 29.46S 51.09W
São Lourenço Brazil 59 22.08S 45.05W
São Luís Brazil 61 2.34S 44.16W
São Manuel Brazil 59 22.40S 48.35W
São Manuel r. see Teles Pires r. Brazil 61
São Miguel d'Oeste Brazil 59 26.45S 53.34W
Saona i. Dom. Rep. 57 18.09N 68.42W
Saône r. France 14 45.46N 4.52E
São Paulo Brazil 59 23.33S 46.39W
São Paulo d. Brazil 59 22.05S 48.00W
São Paulo de Olivença Brazil 60 3.34S 68.55W
São Roque Brazil 59 23.31S 47.09W
São Sebastião Brazil 59 23.48S 45.26W
São Sebastião, Ilha de i. Brazil 59 23.53S 45.17W
São Sebastião do Paraíso Brazil 59 20.54S 46.59W
São Tiago Brazil 59 20.54S 44.30W
São Tomé i. São Tomé & Príncipe 34 0.19N 6.43E
São Tomé & Príncipe Africa 34 1.00N 7.00E
São Vicente Brazil 59 23.57S 46.23W
São Vicente, Cabo de c. Portugal 10 37.01N 8.59W
São Vicente de Minas Brazil 59 21.40S 44.26W
Sapé Brazil 61 7.06S 35.13W
Sapele Nigeria 38 5.53N 5.41E
Sapporo Japan 25 43.05N 141.21E
Sapri Italy 12 40.04N 15.38E
Saqqârah Egypt 32 29.51N 31.13E
Saqqez Iran 31 36.14N 46.15E
Sarāb Iran 31 37.56N 47.35E
Sarābiyūm Egypt 32 30.23N 32.17E
Sara Buri Thailand 29 14.32N 100.53E
Sarajevo Bosnia-Herzegovina 15 43.52N 18.26E
Saranac Lake town U.S.A. 55 44.20N 74.08W
Sarandí del Yi Uruguay 63 33.21S 55.38W
Sarandí Grande Uruguay 63 33.44S 56.20W
Sārangarh India 29 21.38N 83.09E
Saranley Somali Rep. 37 2.19N 42.15E
Saranpaul Russian Fed. 18 64.15N 60.58E
Saransk Russian Fed. 18 54.12N 45.10E
Sarapul Russian Fed. 18 56.30N 53.49E
Sarasota U.S.A. 53 27.20N 82.32W
Sarata Ukraine 15 46.00N 29.40E
Saratoga U.S.A. 54 37.16N 122.02W
Saratoga Springs U.S.A. 55 43.05N 73.47W
Saratov Russian Fed. 19 51.30N 45.55E
Sarawak d. Malaysia 26 2.00N 113.00E
Saraychik Kazakhstan 19 47.29N 51.42E
Sarbāz Iran 31 26.39N 61.20E
Sarcelles France 9 49.00N 2.23E
Sardegna d. Italy 12 40.05N 9.00E
Sardegna i. Italy 12 40.00N 9.00E
Sardinia i. see Sardegna i. Italy 12
Sarek mtn. Sweden 16 67.25N 17.46E
Sareks Nat. Park Sweden 16 67.15N 17.30E
Sargodha Pakistan 28 32.01N 72.40E
Sarh Chad 34 9.08N 18.22E
Sārī Iran 31 36.33N 53.06E
Sarikamiş Turkey 30 40.19N 42.35E
Sarikei Malaysia 26 2.07N 111.31E
Sarina Australia 44 21.26S 149.13E
Sark i. U.K. 5 49.26N 2.22W
Sarlat France 11 44.53N 1.13E
Sărmasu Romania 15 46.46N 24.11E
Sarmi Indonesia 27 1.51S 138.45E
Sarmiento Argentina 63 45.35S 69.05W
Särna Sweden 17 61.41N 13.08E
Sarnia Canada 55 42.58N 82.23W
Sarny Ukraine 15 51.21N 26.31E
Saronno Italy 9 45.38N 9.02E
Saros Körfezi g. Turkey 13 40.32N 26.25E
Sárospatak Hungary 15 48.19N 21.34E
Sarpsborg Norway 17 59.17N 11.07E
Sarrebourg France 11 48.43N 7.03E
Sarreguemines France 11 49.06N 7.03E
Sarria Spain 10 42.47N 7.25W
Sarro Mali 38 13.40N 5.05W
Sartène France 11 41.36N 8.59E
Sarthe d. France 9 48.00N 0.05E
Sarthe r. France 9 47.29N 0.30W
Sartilly France 9 48.45N 1.27W
Sartynya Russian Fed. 20 63.22N 63.11E
Şarūr Oman 31 23.25N 58.10E
Sárvár Hungary 14 47.15N 16.57E
Saryshagan Kazakhstan 24 46.08N 73.32E
Sarzana Italy 9 44.07N 9.58E
Sasebo Japan 25 33.10N 129.42E
Saser mtn. Jammu & Kashmir 28 34.50N 77.50E
Saskatchewan d. Canada 50 55.00N 105.00W
Saskatchewan r. Canada 51 53.25N 100.15W
Saskatoon Canada 50 52.10N 106.40W
Sasovo Russian Fed. 18 54.21N 41.58E
Sassandra Ivory Coast 38 4.58N 6.08W
Sassari Italy 12 40.43N 8.33E
Sassnitz Germany 14 54.32N 13.40E
Sasso Marconi Italy 9 44.24N 11.15E
Sassuolo Italy 9 44.33N 10.47E
Sasyk, Ozero l. Ukraine 15 45.38N 29.38E
Sātāra India 28 17.43N 74.05E
Satna India 29 24.33N 80.50E
Sátoraljaújhely Hungary 15 48.24N 21.39E
Sātpura Range mts. India 28 21.50N 76.00E
Satu Mare Romania 15 47.48N 22.52E
Sauce Argentina 63 30.05S 58.45W
Sauda Norway 17 59.39N 6.20E
Saudi Arabia Asia 30 26.00N 44.00E
Saulieu France 9 47.17N 4.14E
Sault Sainte Marie Canada 55 46.31N 84.20W
Sault Sainte Marie U.S.A. 55 46.29N 84.22W
Saumarez Reef Australia 44 21.50S 153.40E
Saumlaki Indonesia 44 7.59S 131.22E
Saumur France 9 47.16N 0.05W
Saurimo Angola 36 9.38S 20.20E
Sava r. Bosnia-Herzegovina 15 44.50N 20.26E
Sava r. Croatia 14 45.03N 16.23E
Savalou Benin 38 7.55N 1.59E
Savannah Ga. U.S.A. 53 32.09N 81.01W
Savannah r. U.S.A. 53 32.10N 81.00W
Savannakhét Laos 26 16.34N 104.55E
Savant L. Canada 55 50.48N 90.20W
Savant Lake town Canada 55 50.20N 90.40W
Savé Benin 38 8.04N 2.37E
Save r. Mozambique 39 20.59S 35.02E
Save r. Zimbabwe 39 21.16S 32.20E
Sāveh Iran 31 35.00N 50.25E
Savelugu Ghana 38 9.39N 0.48W
Saverdun France 11 43.14N 1.35E
Savigliano Italy 9 44.38N 7.40E
Savigny-sur-Braye France 9 47.53N 0.49E
Savona Italy 9 44.18N 8.28E
Savonlinna Finland 18 61.52N 28.51E
Savoonga U.S.A. 50 63.42N 170.27W
Savu Sea see Sawu, Laut sea Pacific Oc. 27
Sawākin Sudan 35 19.04N 37.19E
Sawbridgeworth U.K. 5 51.50N 0.09W
Sawdā', Qurnat as mtn. Lebanon 32 34.17N 36.04E
Sawhāj Egypt 30 26.33N 31.42E
Sawston U.K. 5 52.07N 0.11E
Sawtell Australia 47 30.21S 153.05E
Sawtooth Mts. U.S.A. 54 44.03N 114.35W
Sawu i. Indonesia 27 10.30S 121.50E
Sawu, Laut sea Pacific Oc. 27 9.30S 122.30E
Saxmundham U.K. 5 52.13N 1.29E
Saxon Switz. 9 46.09N 7.11E
Say Mali 38 13.50N 4.57W
Say Niger 38 13.08N 2.22E
Sayama Japan 23 35.51N 139.24E
Şaydā Lebanon 32 33.32N 35.22E
Sayers Lake town Australia 46 32.46S 143.20E
Saynshand Mongolia 25 44.58N 110.10E
Saynshand Mongolia 24 43.33N 106.13E
Sayula Mexico 56 19.52N 103.36W
Sázava r. Czech Republic 14 49.53N 14.21E
Scafell Pike mtn. U.K. 4 54.27N 3.12W
Scalea Italy 12 39.49N 15.48E
Scalloway U.K. 6 60.08N 1.17W
Scammon Bay town U.S.A. 50 61.50N 165.35W
Scapa Flow str. U.K. 6 58.53N 3.05W
Scarborough Tobago 60 11.11N 60.45W
Scarborough U.K. 4 54.17N 0.24W
Schaerbeek Belgium 8 50.54N 4.20E
Schaffhausen Switz. 14 47.42N 8.38E
Schagen Neth. 8 52.47N 4.47E
Schefferville Canada 51 54.50N 67.00W
Schelde r. Belgium 8 51.13N 4.25E
Schell Creek Range mts. U.S.A. 54 39.10N 114.40W
Schenectady U.S.A. 55 42.47N 73.53W
Scheveningen Neth. 8 52.07N 4.16E
Schiedam Neth. 8 51.55N 4.25E
Schiermonnikoog i. Neth. 8 53.28N 6.15E
Schio Italy 9 45.43N 11.21E
Schleiden Germany 8 50.32N 6.29E
Schleswig Germany 14 54.32N 9.34E
Schleswig-Holstein d. Germany 14 54.00N 10.30E
Schouten, Kepulauan is. Indonesia 27 0.45S 135.50E
Schouwen i. Neth. 8 51.42N 3.45E
Schreiber Canada 55 48.48N 87.17W
Schwandorf Germany 14 49.20N 12.08E
Schwaner, Pegunungan mts. Indonesia 26 0.45S 113.20E
Schwarzrand mts. Namibia 39 25.40S 16.53E
Schwarzwald f. Germany 14 48.00N 7.45E
Schwedt Germany 14 53.04N 14.17E
Schweich Germany 8 49.50N 6.47E
Schweinfurt Germany 14 50.03N 10.16E
Schwelm Germany 8 51.17N 7.18E
Schwerin Germany 14 53.38N 11.25E
Schwyz Switz. 14 47.02N 8.40E
Sciacca Italy 12 37.31N 13.05E
Scilla Italy 12 38.15N 15.44E
Scilly, Isles of U.K. 5 49.55N 6.20W
Scone Australia 47 32.01S 150.53E
Scotia Calif. U.S.A. 54 40.26N 123.31W
Scotland U.K. 6 55.30N 4.00W
Scottburgh R.S.A. 39 30.17S 30.45E
Scott Reef Australia 42 14.00S 121.50E
Scottsbluff U.S.A. 52 41.52N 103.40W
Scottsdale Australia 45 41.09S 147.31E
Scottsdale U.S.A. 54 33.30N 111.56W
Scranton U.S.A. 55 41.24N 75.40W
Scugog, L. Canada 55 44.10N 78.51W
Scunthorpe U.K. 4 53.35N 0.38W
Scutari, L. Yugo. / Albania 13 42.10N 19.18E
Seabrook, L. Australia 43 30.56S 119.40E
Seaford U.S.A. 55 38.39N 75.37W
Seahouses U.K. 4 55.35N 1.38W
Sea Isle City U.S.A. 55 39.09N 74.42W
Seal r. Canada 51 59.00N 95.00W
Sea Lake town Australia 46 35.31S 142.54E
Searchlight U.S.A. 54 35.28N 114.55W
Seascale U.K. 4 54.24N 3.29W
Seaside Calif. U.S.A. 54 36.37N 121.50W
Seaside Oreg. U.S.A. 54 46.02N 123.55W
Seaton U.K. 5 50.43N 3.05W
Seattle U.S.A. 54 47.36N 122.20W
Seaview Range mts. Australia 44 18.56S 146.00E
Sebastián Vizcaíno, Bahía b. Mexico 56 28.00N 114.30W
Sebba Burkina 38 13.27N 0.33E
Sebeş Romania 15 45.58N 23.34E
Sebidiro P.N.G. 27 9.00S 142.15E
Sebinkarahisar Turkey 30 40.19N 38.25E
Sechura, Desierto de des. Peru 60 6.00S 80.30W
Seclin France 8 50.34N 3.01E
Sêda r. Portugal 10 38.55N 7.30W
Sedalia U.S.A. 53 38.42N 93.15W
Sedan France 9 49.42N 4.57E
Seddon New Zealand 48 41.40S 174.04E
Sédhiou Senegal 34 12.44N 15.30W
Sedom Israel 32 31.04N 35.23E
Seeheim Namibia 39 26.50S 17.45E
Sées France 9 48.38N 0.10E
Ségou Mali 38 13.28N 6.18W
Ségou d. Mali 38 13.55N 6.20W
Segovia Spain 10 40.57N 4.07W
Segozero, Ozero l. Russian Fed. 18 63.15N 33.40E
Segré France 9 47.41N 0.53W
Segre r. Spain 10 41.25N 0.21E
Séguédine Niger 34 20.12N 12.59E
Segura Portugal 10 39.50N 6.59W
Segura r. Spain 10 38.07N 0.14W
Segura, Sierra de mts. Spain 10 38.00N 2.50W
Seiches-sur-le-Loir France 9 47.35N 0.22W
Seiland i. Norway 16 70.25N 23.10E
Seinäjoki Finland 16 62.47N 22.50E
Seine r. France 9 49.28N 0.25E
Seine, Baie de la b. France 9 49.25N 0.15E
Seine-et-Marne d. France 9 48.30N 3.00E
Seine-Maritime d. France 9 49.45N 1.00E
Sekayu Indonesia 26 2.58S 103.58E
Seki Japan 23 35.29N 136.55E
Sekoma Botswana 39 24.41S 23.50E
Sekondi-Takoradi Ghana 38 4.57N 1.44W
Sekūheh Iran 31 30.45N 61.29E
Selaru i. Indonesia 44 8.09S 131.00E
Selatan, Tanjung c. Indonesia 26 4.20S 114.45E
Selayar i. Indonesia 27 6.07S 120.28E
Selbu Norway 16 63.14N 11.03E
Selby U.K. 4 53.47N 1.05W
Seldovia U.S.A. 50 59.27N 151.43W
Sele r. Italy 12 40.30N 14.50E
Selebi-Pikwe Botswana 36 22.01S 27.50E
Selenga r. Russian Fed. 24 52.20N 106.20E
Selenge Mörön r. see Selenga Mongolia 24
Sélestat France 14 48.16N 7.28E
Seligman U.S.A. 54 35.20N 112.53W
Seljord Norway 17 59.29N 8.37E
Selkirk U.K. 6 55.33N 2.51W
Selkirk Mts. Canada / U.S.A. 50 49.00N 116.00W
Selles-sur-Cher France 9 47.16N 1.33E
Selma Calif. U.S.A. 54 36.34N 119.37W
Selseleh ye Safid Kūh mts. Afghan 31 34.30N 63.30E
Selsey Bill c. U.K. 5 50.44N 0.47W
Selty Russian Fed. 18 57.19N 52.12E
Sélune r. France 9 48.35N 1.15W
Selva Argentina 59 29.50S 62.02W
Selvas f. Brazil 60 6.00S 65.00W
Selwyn Mts. Canada 50 63.00N 130.00W
Selwyn Range mts. Australia 44 21.35S 140.35E
Seman r. Albania 13 40.53N 19.25E
Semara W. Sahara 34 26.44N 11.41W
Semarang Indonesia 26 6.58S 110.29E
Sembabule Uganda 37 0.08S 31.27E
Seminoe Resr. U.S.A. 54 42.00N 106.50W
Semiozernoye Kazakhstan 20 52.22N 64.06E
Semipalatinsk Kazakhstan 20 50.26N 80.16E
Semīrom Iran 31 31.31N 52.10E
Semiyarka Kazakhstan 20 50.52N 78.23E
Semliki r. Zaïre 37 1.12N 30.27E
Semmering Pass Austria 14 47.40N 16.00E
Semnān Iran 31 35.31N 53.24E
Semois r. France 8 49.53N 4.45E
Semporna Malaysia 26 4.27N 118.36E
Semu r. Tanzania 37 3.57S 34.20E
Semur-en-Auxois France 9 47.29N 4.20E
Sena Mozambique 37 17.36S 35.00E
Senador Pompeu Brazil 61 5.30S 39.25W
Senaja Malaysia 26 6.49N 117.02E
Sena Madureira Brazil 60 9.04S 68.40W
Sendai Tofuku Japan 25 38.16N 140.52E
Sendenhorst Germany 8 51.52N 7.50E
Seneca Oreg. U.S.A. 54 44.08N 118.58W
Senegal Africa 34 14.30N 14.30W
Sénégal r. Senegal / Mauritania 34 16.00N 16.28W
Senekal R.S.A. 39 28.18S 27.37E
Senhor do Bonfim Brazil 61 10.28S 40.11W
Senica Slovakia 15 48.41N 17.22E
Senigallia Italy 14 43.42N 13.14E
Senise Italy 12 40.09N 16.18E
Senj Croatia 14 45.00N 14.58E
Senja i. Norway 16 69.15N 17.20E
Senlis France 9 49.12N 2.35E
Sennan Japan 23 34.22N 135.17E
Sennen U.K. 5 50.04N 5.42W
Senneterre Canada 55 48.24N 77.14W
Sens France 9 48.12N 3.18E
Senta Yugo. 15 45.56N 20.04E
Sentinel U.S.A. 54 32.53N 113.12W
Seoni India 29 22.05N 79.32E
Seoul see Sŏul S. Korea 25
Sepik r. P.N.G. 27 3.54S 144.30E
Sepopa Botswana 39 18.45S 22.11E
Sept Îles town Canada 55 50.13N 66.22W
Sepúlveda Spain 10 41.18N 3.45W
Seraing Belgium 8 50.37N 5.33E
Seram i. Indonesia 27 3.10S 129.30E
Seram, Laut sea Pacific Oc. 27 2.50S 128.00E
Serang Indonesia 26 6.07S 106.09E
Serbia d. see Srbija d. Yugo. 15
Seremban Malaysia 26 2.42N 101.54E
Serengeti Nat. Park Tanzania 37 2.30S 35.00E
Serengeti Plain f. Tanzania 37 3.00S 35.00E
Serenje Zambia 37 13.12S 30.50E
Sergach Russian Fed. 18 55.32N 45.27E
Sergipe d. Brazil 61 11.00S 37.00W
Sergiyev Posad Russian Fed. 18 56.20N 38.10E
Sergiyevsk Russian Fed. 18 53.56N 50.01E
Seria Brunei 26 4.39N 114.23E
Serian Malaysia 26 1.10N 110.35E
Sericho Kenya 37 1.13N 39.06E
Sérifos i. Greece 13 37.11N 24.31E
Serle, Mt Australia 46 30.34S 138.55E
Sermata i. Indonesia 27 8.30S 129.00E
Serodino Argentina 63 32.37S 60.57W
Serov Russian Fed. 18 59.42N 60.32E
Serowe Botswana 39 22.22S 26.42E
Serpa Portugal 10 37.56N 7.36W
Serpentine r. Australia 43 32.33S 115.46E
Serpent's Mouth str. Venezuela 60 9.50N 61.00W
Serpukhov Russian Fed. 18 54.53N 37.25E
Serra do Navio Brazil 61 0.59N 52.03W
Sérrai Greece 13 41.04N 23.32E
Serra Talhada Brazil 61 8.01S 38.17W
Serravalle Scrivia Italy 9 44.43N 8.51E
Serre r. France 8 49.40N 3.22E
Serrinha Brazil 61 11.38S 38.56W
Serui Indonesia 27 1.53S 136.15E
Serule Botswana 39 21.54S 27.17E
Serviceton Australia 46 36.22S 141.02E
Şes, Munţii mts. Romania 15 47.05N 22.30E
Seseganaga L. Canada 55 50.02N 90.08W
Sese Is. Uganda 37 0.20S 32.30E
Sesepe Indonesia 27 1.30S 127.59E
Sesheke Zambia 39 17.27S 24.19E
Sesia r. Italy 9 45.05N 8.37E
Sesimbra Portugal 10 38.26N 9.06W
Sestao Spain 10 43.18N 3.00W
Sestri Levante Italy 9 44.16N 9.24E
Sète France 11 43.25N 3.43E
Sete Lagoas Brazil 59 19.29S 44.15W
Sétif Algeria 34 36.09N 5.26E
Seto Japan 23 35.14N 137.06E
Settat Morocco 34 33.04N 7.37W
Setté Cama Gabon 36 2.32S 9.46E
Settimo Torinese Italy 9 45.09N 7.46E
Settle U.K. 4 54.05N 2.18W
Setúbal Portugal 10 38.31N 8.54W
Setúbal, Baia de b. Portugal 10 38.20N 9.00W
Sevan, Ozero l. Armenia 31 40.22N 45.20E
Sevastopol' Ukraine 19 44.36N 33.31E
Sevenoaks U.K. 5 51.16N 0.12E
Sévérac France 11 44.20N 3.05E
Severn r. Australia 47 29.08S 150.50E
Severn r. Canada 51 56.00N 87.40W
Severn r. U.K. 5 51.50N 2.21W
Severnaya Zemlya is. Russian Fed. 21 80.00N 96.00E
Severnyy Russian Fed. 18 69.55N 49.01E
Severnyy Donets r. Ukraine 19 49.08N 37.28E
Severnyy Dvina r. Russian Fed. 18 57.03N 24.00E
Severodvinsk Russian Fed. 18 64.35N 39.50E
Severomorsk Russian Fed. 18 69.05N 33.30E
Sevier r. U.S.A. 54 39.04N 113.06W
Sevier L. U.S.A. 54 38.55N 113.09W
Sevilla Spain 10 37.24N 5.59W
Sèvre-Nantaise r. France 11 47.12N 1.35W
Sèvre Niortaise r. France 11 46.35N 1.05W
Seward U.S.A. 50 60.05N 149.34W
Seward Pen. U.S.A. 50 65.00N 164.10W
Seydhisfjördhur town Iceland 16 65.16N 14.02W
Seylac Somali Rep. 35 11.21N 43.30E
Seym r. Ukraine 19 51.30N 32.30E
Seymour Australia 47 37.01S 145.10E
Sézanne France 9 48.44N 3.44E
Sfax Tunisia 34 34.45N 10.43E
Sfîntu-Gheorghe Romania 15 45.52N 25.50E
's-Gravenhage Neth. 8 52.05N 4.16E
Shaanxi d. China 25 35.00N 109.00E
Shaba d. Zaïre 37 8.00S 27.00E
Shabeelle r. Somali Rep. 37 0.30N 43.10E
Shache China 24 38.27N 77.16E
Shafter U.S.A. 54 35.30N 119.16W
Shaftesbury U.K. 5 51.00N 2.12W
Shahbā' Syria 32 32.51N 36.37E
Shahdād Iran 31 30.27N 57.44E
Shāh Jahān, Kūh-e mts. Iran 31 37.00N 58.00E
Shāhjahānpur India 29 27.53N 79.55E
Shāh Kūh mtn. Iran 31 31.38N 59.16E
Shahr-e Bābak Iran 31 30.08N 55.04E
Shahrezā Iran 31 32.00N 51.52E
Shahr Kord Iran 31 32.40N 50.52E
Shahsavār Iran 31 36.49N 50.54E
Sha'īb Abā al Qūr wadi Saudi Arabia 30 31.02N 42.00E
Shakawe Botswana 39 18.22S 21.50E
Shaker Heights town U.S.A. 55 41.29N 81.36W
Shakhty Russian Fed. 19 47.43N 40.16E
Shakhunya Russian Fed. 18 57.41N 46.46E
Shaki Nigeria 38 8.41N 3.24E
Shakshūk Egypt 32 29.28N 30.42E
Shala Hāyk' l. Ethiopia 35 7.25N 38.30E
Shām, Jabal ash mtn. Oman 31 23.14N 57.17E
Shāmat al Akbād des. Saudi Arabia 30 28.15N 43.05E
Shamokin U.S.A. 55 40.47N 76.34W
Shamva Zimbabwe 37 17.20S 31.38E
Shandong d. China 25 35.45N 117.30E
Shandong Bandao pen. China 25 37.00N 121.30E
Shanghai China 25 31.13N 121.25E
Shanghai d. China 25 31.14N 121.28E
Shangrao China 25 28.28N 117.54E
Shangshui China 25 33.33N 114.38E
Shannon r. Rep. of Ire. 7 52.39N 8.43W
Shannon, Mouth of the est. Rep. of Ire. 7 52.29N 9.57W
Shanshan China 24 42.52N 90.10E
Shantarskiy Ostrova is. Russian Fed. 21 55.00N 138.00E
Shantou China 25 23.23N 116.39E
Shanwa Tanzania 37 3.09S 33.48E
Shanxi d. China 25 36.45N 112.00E
Shaoguan China 25 24.54N 113.33E
Shaoxing China 25 30.02N 120.35E
Shaoyang China 25 27.43N 111.24E
Shap U.K. 4 54.32N 2.40W
Shapinsay i. U.K. 6 59.03N 2.51W
Shapur ruins Iran 31 29.42N 51.30E
Shaqrā' Saudi Arabia 31 25.17N 45.14E
Shaqrā' Yemen 35 13.21N 45.42E
Shark B. Australia 42 25.30S 113.30E
Sharlyk Russian Fed. 18 52.58N 54.46E
Sharm ash Shaykh Egypt 32 27.51N 34.16E
Sharon U.S.A. 55 41.16N 80.30W
Sharqī, Al Jabal ash mts. Lebanon 32 34.00N 36.25E
Sharqīyah, Aş Şaḩrā' ash des. Egypt 32 27.40N 32.00E
Sharya Russian Fed. 18 58.22N 45.50E
Shashi r. Botswana / Zimbabwe 39 22.10S 29.15E
Shashi China 25 30.16N 112.20E
Shasta, Mt. U.S.A. 54 41.20N 122.20W
Shatt al Arab r. Iraq 31 30.00N 48.30E
Shaunavon Canada 50 49.40N 108.25W
Shaw I. Australia 44 20.29S 149.05E
Shawinigan Canada 55 46.33N 72.45W
Shay Gap town Australia 42 20.28S 120.05E
Shaykh, Jabal ash mtn. Lebanon 32 33.24N 35.52E
Shchara r. Belorussia 15 53.27N 24.45E
Shchelyayur Russian Fed. 18 65.16N 53.17E
Shchors Ukraine 15 51.50N 31.59E
Sheboygan U.S.A. 53 43.46N 87.44W
Shebshi Mts. Nigeria 38 8.30N 11.45E
Sheeffry Hills Rep. of Ire. 7 53.41N 9.42W
Sheelin, Lough Rep. of Ire. 7 53.48N 7.20W
Sheep Range mts. U.S.A. 54 36.45N 115.05W
Sheffield U.K. 4 53.23N 1.28W
Shefford U.K. 5 52.02N 0.20W
Sheki Azerbaijan 19 41.12N 47.10E
Sheksna r. Russian Fed. 18 60.00N 37.49E
Shelburne N.S. Canada 51 43.46N 65.19W
Shelburne B. Australia 44 11.49S 143.00E
Shelby Mich. U.S.A. 55 43.36N 86.22W
Shelby Mont. U.S.A. 54 48.30N 111.51W
Shelbyville Ind. U.S.A. 55 39.31N 85.46W
Sheldrake Canada 55 50.18N 64.54W
Shelikof Str. U.S.A. 50 58.00N 153.45W
Shelley U.S.A. 54 43.23N 112.07W
Shellharbour Australia 47 34.35S 150.52E
Shelton U.S.A. 54 47.13N 123.06W
Shenandoah r. U.S.A. 55 39.19N 78.12W
Shenandoah Va. U.S.A. 55 38.29N 78.37W
Shëngjin Albania 13 41.49N 19.33E
Shengze China 25 30.55N 120.39E
Shenkursk Russian Fed. 18 62.05N 42.58E
Shenyang China 25 41.50N 123.26E
Shepetovka Ukraine 15 50.12N 27.01E
Shepparton Australia 47 36.25S 145.26E
Sheppey, Isle of U.K. 5 51.24N 0.50E
Sherborne U.K. 5 50.56N 2.31W
Sherbrooke Canada 55 45.24N 71.54W
Sherburne U.S.A. 55 42.41N 75.30W
Sheridan U.S.A. 54 44.48N 106.58W
Sheringa Australia 46 33.51S 135.15E
Sheringham U.K. 4 52.56N 1.11E
Sherkin I. Rep. of Ire. 7 51.28N 9.25W
Sherman Tex. U.S.A. 53 33.39N 96.35W
Sherman Mills U.S.A. 55 45.52N 68.23W
Sherridon Canada 51 57.07N 101.05W
's-Hertogenbosch Neth. 8 51.42N 5.19E
Shetland Is. d. U.K. 6 60.20N 1.15W
Shetpe Kazakhstan 19 44.09N 52.06E
Shevchenko Kazakhstan 19 43.37N 51.11E
Shibīn al Kawm Egypt 32 30.33N 31.00E
Shibīn al Qanāţir Egypt 32 30.19N 31.19E
Shiel, Loch U.K. 6 56.48N 5.33W
Shiga d. Japan 23 34.55N 136.00E
Shijiazhuang China 25 38.04N 114.28E
Shikārpur Pakistan 28 27.58N 68.42E
Shikoku i. Japan 25 33.30N 133.30E
Shilka Russian Fed. 25 51.55N 116.01E
Shilka r. Russian Fed. 25 53.20N 121.10E
Shillong India 29 25.34N 91.53E
Shima Japan 23 34.13N 136.51E
Shimada Japan 23 34.49N 138.11E
Shima-hantō pen. Japan 23 34.25N 136.45E
Shimizu Japan 23 35.01N 138.29E
Shimoda Japan 23 34.40N 138.57E

Shimoga India 28 13.56N 75.31E
Shimonoseki Japan 25 33.59N130.58E
Shimpek Kazakhstan 24 44.50N 74.10E
Shin, Loch U.K. 6 58.06N 4.32W
Shindand Afghan. 28 33.18N 62.08E
Shingleton U.S.A. 55 46.21N 86.28W
Shinshār Syria 32 34.36N 36.45E
Shinshiro Japan 23 34.54N137.30E
Shinyanga Tanzania 37 3.40S 33.20E
Shinyanga d. Tanzania 37 3.30S 33.00E
Shipka Pass Bulgaria 13 42.45N 25.25E
Shippensburg U.S.A. 55 40.03N 77.31W
Shiprock U.S.A. 54 36.47N108.41W
Shipston on Stour U.K. 5 52.04N 1.38W
Shiqian China 25 27.30N108.20E
Shirakskaya Step f. Georgia 31 41.40N 46.20E
Shirane san mtn. Japan 23 35.40N138.15E
Shirāz Iran 31 29.36N 52.33E
Shirbin Egypt 32 31.13N 31.31E
Shire r. Mozambique 37 17.46S 35.20E
Shīr Kūh mtn. Iran 31 31.38N 54.07E
Shirvān Iran 31 37.24N 57.55E
Shivpuri India 28 25.26N 77.39E
Shiyan Hubei China 25 32.34N110.47E
Shizuishan China 24 39.17N106.52E
Shizuoka Japan 23 34.58N138.23E
Shizuoka d. Japan 23 35.00N138.00E
Shklov Belorussia 15 54.16N 30.16E
Shkodër Albania 13 42.03N 19.30E
Shkumbin r. Albania 13 41.01N 19.26E
Shoal C. Australia 43 33.51S121.10E
Shoalhaven r. Australia 47 34.51S150.40E
Sholāpur India 28 17.43N 75.56E
Shonai r. Japan 23 35.04N136.50E
Shoshone Calif. U.S.A. 54 35.58N116.17W
Shoshone Idaho U.S.A. 54 42.57N114.25W
Shoshone Mts. U.S.A. 54 39.25N117.15W
Shoshoni U.S.A. 54 43.14N108.07W
Shostka Belorussia 18 51.53N 33.30E
Show Low U.S.A. 54 34.15N110.02W
Shpola Ukraine 15 49.00N 31.25E
Shreveport U.S.A. 53 32.30N 93.46W
Shrewsbury U.K. 5 52.42N 2.45W
Shropshire d. U.K. 5 52.35N 2.40W
Shuangliao China 25 43.30N123.29E
Shuangyashan China 25 46.37N131.22E
Shubrā al Khaymah Egypt 32 30.06N 31.15E
Shuksan U.S.A. 54 48.55N121.43W
Shule China 24 39.25N 76.06E
Shumagin Is. U.S.A. 50 55.00N160.00W
Shumerlya Russian Fed. 18 55.30N 46.25E
Shumikha Russian Fed. 20 55.15N 63.14E
Shumyachi Russian Fed. 15 53.52N 32.25E
Shunde China 25 22.50N113.16E
Shūr r. Khorāsān Iran 31 34.11N 60.07E
Shūr r. Kermān Iran 31 31.14N 55.29E
Shūr r. Kermān Iran 31 30.45N 57.55E
Shūrāb Iran 31 28.09N 60.18E
Shūrāb r. Iran 31 31.30N 55.18E
Shurugwi Zimbabwe 39 19.40S 30.00E
Shūshtar Iran 31 32.04N 48.53E
Shuwak Sudan 35 14.23N 35.52E
Shuya Russian Fed. 18 56.49N 41.23E
Shwebo Burma 29 22.35N 95.42E
Shyok Jammu & Kashmir 29 34.11N 78.08E
Siāhān Range mts. Pakistan 28 27.25N 64.30E
Siālkot Pakistan 28 32.29N 74.35E
Sian see Xi'an China 25
Siargao i. Phil. 27 9.55N126.05E
Siau i. Indonesia 27 2.42N125.24E
Siauliai Lithuania 17 55.56N 23.19E
Sibasa R.S.A. 39 22.56S 30.28E
Šibenik Croatia 12 43.45N 15.55E
Siberut i. Indonesia 26 1.30S 99.00E
Sibi Pakistan 28 29.31N 67.54E
Sibiti r. Tanzania 37 3.47S 34.45E
Sibiu Romania 13 45.47N 24.09E
Sibolga Indonesia 26 1.42N 98.48E
Sibu Malaysia 26 2.18N111.49E
Sibut C.A.R. 36 5.46N 19.06E
Sicasica Bolivia 62 17.22S 67.45W
Siccus r. Australia 46 31.26S139.30E
Sichuan d. China 24 30.30N103.00E
Sicilia d. Italy 12 37.30N 14.00E
Sicilia i. Italy 12 37.30N 14.00E
Sicily i. see Sicilia i. Italy 12
Sicuani Peru 60 14.21S 71.13W
Sidaouet Niger 38 18.34N 8.03E
Sīdī Barrānī Egypt 30 31.38N 25.58E
Sidi bel Abbès Algeria 34 35.15N 0.39W
Sidi Ifni Morocco 34 29.24N 10.12W
Sīdī Sālim Egypt 32 31.16N 30.47E
Sidlaw Hills U.K. 6 56.31N 3.10W
Sidley, Mt. Antarctica 64 77.30S125.00W
Sidmouth U.K. 5 50.40N 3.13W
Sidney Canada 54 48.39N123.24W
Sidney Nebr. U.S.A. 52 41.09N102.59W
Sidney Ohio U.S.A. 55 40.16N 84.10W
Sidon see Şaydā Lebanon 32
Sidra, G. of see Surt, Khalīj g. Libya 34
Siedlce Poland 15 52.10N 22.18E
Sieg r. Germany 8 50.49N 7.11E
Siegburg Germany 8 50.48N 7.13E
Siegen Germany 8 50.52N 8.02E
Siemiatycze Poland 15 52.26N 22.53E
Siena Italy 12 43.19N 11.20E
Sieradz Poland 15 51.36N 18.45E
Sierck-les-Bains France 8 49.28N 6.20E
Sierpc Poland 15 52.52N 19.41E
Sierra Colorada Argentina 63 40.35S 67.50W
Sierra Leone Africa 34 9.00N 12.00W
Sierra Mojada town Mexico 56 27.17N103.42W
Sierra Nevada mts. U.S.A. 54 37.45N119.30W
Sierre Switz. 9 46.18N 7.32E
Sífnos i. Greece 13 36.59N 24.60E
Sig Russian Fed. 18 65.31N 34.16E
Sighetul Marmaţiei Romania 15 47.56N 23.54E
Sighişoara Romania 15 46.13N 24.49E
Sigli Indonesia 26 5.23N 95.57E
Siglufjördhur Iceland 16 66.12N 18.55W
Signy France 9 49.42N 4.25E
Sigüenza Spain 10 41.04N 2.38W
Siguiri Guinea 34 11.28N 9.07W
Siika r. Finland 16 64.50N 24.44E
Siirt Turkey 30 37.56N 41.56E
Sīkar India 28 27.33N 75.12E
Sikasso Mali 38 11.18N 5.38W
Sikasso d. Mali 38 11.20N 6.05W
Sikhote Alin mts. Russian Fed. 25 44.00N135.00E
Síkinos i. Greece 13 36.39N 25.06E
Sikkim d. India 29 27.30N 88.30E
Sil r. Spain 10 42.24N 7.15W
Silchar India 29 24.49N 92.47E
Silgarhi-Doti Nepal 29 29.14N 80.58E
Silifke Turkey 30 36.22N 33.57E
Silīguri India 29 26.42N 88.30E
Siling Co l. China 29 31.40N 88.30E
Silistra Bulgaria 13 44.07N 27.17E
Siljan l. Sweden 17 60.50N 14.45E
Silkeborg Denmark 17 56.10N 9.34E
Sille-le-Guillaume France 9 48.12N 0.08E
Silloth U.K. 4 54.53N 3.25W
Silogui Indonesia 26 1.10S 98.46E
Silver Bow U.S.A. 54 46.00N112.40W
Silver City U.S.A. 54 32.46N108.17W
Silver Lake town U.S.A. 54 43.08N120.56W
Silverstone U.K. 5 52.05N 1.03W
Silverton Australia 46 31.53S141.13E
Silverton U.S.A. 54 45.01N122.47W
Silvi Italy 12 42.34N 14.05E
Simanggang Malaysia 26 1.10N111.32E
Simàrd, Lac l. Canada 55 47.38N 78.40W
Simav r. Turkey 13 40.24N 28.31E
Simba Kenya 37 2.10S 37.37E
Simcoe Canada 55 42.50N 80.18W
Simcoe, L. Canada 55 44.20N 79.20W
Simenga Russian Fed. 21 62.42N108.25E
Simeria Romania 13 45.51N 23.01E
Simeulue i. Indonesia 26 2.30N 96.00E
Simferopol' Ukraine 19 44.57N 34.05E
Simitli Bulgaria 13 41.51N 23.09E
Simiyu r. Tanzania 37 2.32S 33.25E
Simla India 28 31.07N 77.09E
Simleul Silvaniei Romania 15 47.14N 22.48E
Simmern Germany 8 49.59N 7.32E
Simo r. Finland 16 65.37N 25.03E
Simojärvo l. Finland 16 66.06N 27.03E
Simon's Town R.S.A. 39 34.12S 18.26E
Simoom Sound town Canada 50 50.45N126.45W
Simplon Pass Switz. 11 46.15N 8.03E
Simplon Tunnel Italy / Switz. 12 46.20N 8.05E
Simpson Desert Australia 44 25.00S136.50E
Simrishamn Sweden 17 55.33N 14.20E
Simuco Mozambique 37 14.00S 40.35E
Sīnā', Shibh Jazīrat pen. Egypt 32 29.00N 34.00E
Sinai see Sīnā', Shibh Jazīrat pen. Egypt 32
Sinaloa d. Mexico 56 25.00N107.30W
Sinan China 25 27.56N108.22E
Sincelejo Colombia 60 9.17N 75.23W
Sinclair U.S.A. 54 41.47N107.07W
Sines Portugal 10 37.58N 8.52W
Sinfra Ivory Coast 38 6.35N 5.56W
Singapore Asia 26 1.20N103.45E
Singapore town Singapore 26 1.20N103.45E
Singaraja Indonesia 26 8.06S115.07E
Singida Tanzania 37 4.45S 34.42E
Singida d. Tanzania 37 6.00S 34.30E
Singing India 29 28.53N 94.47E
Singitikós Kólpos g. Greece 13 40.12N 24.00E
Singkaling Hkāmti Burma 29 26.00N 95.42E
Singkang Indonesia 27 4.09S120.02E
Singkawang Indonesia 26 0.57N108.57E
Singkep i. Indonesia 26 0.30S104.20E
Singleton Australia 47 32.33S151.11E
Singosan N. Korea 25 38.50N127.27E
Sinj Croatia 13 43.42N 16.38E
Sinkiang see Xinjiang Uygur Zizhiqu 24
Sînnicolau Mare Romania 13 46.05N 20.38E
Sinnūris Egypt 32 29.25N 30.52E
Sinop Turkey 30 42.02N 35.09E
Sinsheim Germany 14 49.15N 8.53E
Sintang Indonesia 26 0.03N111.31E
Sint Eustatius i. Leeward Is. 57 17.33N 63.00W
Sint Maarten i. see St. Martin i. Leeward Is. 57
Sinŭiju N. Korea 25 40.04N124.25E
Sinyavka Belorussia 15 52.58N 26.30E
Sinyukha r. Ukraine 15 48.03N 30.51E
Siocon Phil. 27 7.42N122.08E
Siófok Hungary 15 46.54N 18.04E
Sion Switz. 9 46.14N 7.21E
Sioux City U.S.A. 53 42.30N 96.28W
Sioux Falls town U.S.A. 53 43.34N 96.42W
Sioux Lookout town Canada 51 50.07N 91.54W
Siphaqeni R.S.A. 39 31.05S 29.29E
Siping Jilin China 25 43.15N124.25E
Sipura i. Indonesia 26 2.10S 99.40E
Sira r. Norway 17 58.17N 6.24E
Siracusa Italy 12 37.05N 15.17E
Sirasso Ivory Coast 38 9.16N 6.06W
Sir Edward Pellew Group is. Australia 44 15.40S136.48E
Siret r. Romania 13 45.28N 27.56E
Sirḩān, Wādī as f. Saudi Arabia 30 31.00N 37.30E
Sir James MacBrien, Mt. Canada 50 62.07N127.41W
Sir Joseph Banks Group is. Australia 46 34.35S136.12E
Síros i. Greece 13 37.26N 24.56E
Sirrah, Wādī as r. Saudi Arabia 31 23.10N 44.22E
Sisak Croatia 12 45.30N 16.21E
Sishen R.S.A. 39 27.46S 22.59E
Sisimiut see Holsteinsborg Greenland 51
Sisŏphŏn Cambodia 26 13.37N102.58E
Sissonne France 9 49.34N 3.54E
Sisteron France 11 44.16N 5.56E
Sitka U.S.A. 50 57.05N135.20W
Sittang r. Burma 29 17.30N 96.53E
Sittard Neth. 8 51.00N 5.52E
Sittwe Burma 29 20.09N 92.55E
Siuruan r. Finland 16 65.20N 25.55E
Sīvan r. Iran 31 29.50N 52.47E
Sivas Turkey 30 39.44N 37.01E
Sivomaskinskiy Russian Fed. 18 66.45N 62.44E
Sivrihisar Turkey 30 39.29N 31.32E
Sīwah Egypt 30 29.12N 25.31E
Sīwah, Wāḩat oasis Egypt 30 29.10N 25.40E
Siwa Oasis see Sīwah, Wāḩat oasis Egypt 30
Siximilecross U.K. 7 54.34N 7.08W
Siya Russian Fed. 18 63.38N 41.40E
Sjaelland i. Denmark 17 55.30N 11.45E
Sjötorp Sweden 17 58.50N 13.59E
Skagafjördhur est. Iceland 16 65.55N 19.35W
Skagen Denmark 17 57.44N 10.36E
Skagerrak str. Denmark / Norway 17 57.45N 8.55E
Skagway U.S.A. 50 59.23N135.20W
Skaill U.K. 6 58.56N 2.43W
Skála Oropoú Greece 13 38.20N 23.46E
Skala Podolskaya Ukraine 15 48.51N 26.11E
Skalat Ukraine 15 49.20N 25.59E
Skanderborg Denmark 17 56.02N 9.56E
Skånevik Norway 17 59.44N 5.59E
Skara Sweden 17 58.22N 13.25E
Skaraborg d. Sweden 17 58.20N 13.30E
Skarnes Norway 17 60.15N 11.41E
Skarżysko-Kamienna Poland 15 51.08N 20.53E
Skeena r. Canada 50 54.10N129.08W
Skegness U.K. 4 53.09N 0.20E
Skellefte r. Sweden 16 64.42N 21.06E
Skellefteå Sweden 16 64.46N 20.57E
Skelleftehamn Sweden 16 64.41N 21.14E
Skelmersdale U.K. 4 53.34N 2.49W
Skene Sweden 17 57.29N 12.38E
Skerries Rep. of Ire. 7 53.35N 6.07W
Skhíza i. Greece 13 36.42N 21.45E
Ski Norway 17 59.43N 10.50E
Skiddaw mtn. U.K. 4 54.40N 3.09W
Skidel Belorussia 15 53.37N 24.19E
Skien Norway 17 59.12N 9.36E
Skierniewice Poland 15 51.58N 20.08E
Skikda Algeria 34 36.50N 6.58E
Skipness U.K. 6 56.45N 5.22W
Skipton U.K. 4 53.57N 2.01W
Skíros Greece 13 38.53N 24.33E
Skíros i. Greece 13 38.50N 24.33E
Skive Denmark 17 56.34N 9.02E
Skjálfanda Fljót r. Iceland 16 65.55N 17.30W
Skjálfandi est. Iceland 16 66.08N 17.38W
Skjönsta Norway 16 67.12N 15.45E
Skoghall Sweden 17 59.19N 13.26E
Skole Ukraine 15 49.00N 23.30E
Skopje Macedonia 13 41.58N 21.27E
Skotterud Norway 17 59.59N 12.07E
Skövde Sweden 17 58.24N 13.50E
Skovorodino Russian Fed. 21 54.00N123.53E
Skreia Norway 17 60.39N 10.56E
Skull Rep. of Ire. 7 51.32N 9.33W
Skuodas Lithuania 17 56.16N 21.32E
Skutskär Sweden 17 60.38N 17.25E
Skvira Ukraine 15 49.42N 29.40E
Skye i. U.K. 6 57.20N 6.15W
Slagelse Denmark 17 55.24N 11.22E
Slalowa Wola Poland 15 50.40N 22.05E
Slamet mtn. Indonesia 26 7.10S109.10E
Slaney r. Rep. of Ire. 7 52.21N 6.30W
Slantsy Russian Fed. 18 59.09N 28.09E
Slatina Romania 13 44.26N 24.23E
Slave r. Canada 50 61.10N113.30W
Slavgorod Belorussia 15 53.25N 31.00E
Slavgorod Russian Fed. 20 53.01N 78.37E
Slavuta Ukraine 15 50.20N 26.58E
Slavyansk Ukraine 19 48.51N 37.36E
Slawno Poland 14 54.22N 16.40E
Sleaford U.K. 4 53.00N 0.22W
Sleaford B. Australia 46 35.00S136.50E
Sleat, Sd. of str. U.K. 6 57.05N 5.48W
Sledmere U.K. 4 54.04N 0.35W
Sleetmute U.S.A. 50 61.40N157.11W
Sliedrecht Neth. 8 51.48N 4.46E
Slieve Aughty Mts. Rep. of Ire. 7 53.05N 8.31W
Slieve Bloom Mts. Rep. of Ire. 7 53.03N 7.35W
Slieve Callan mtn. Rep. of Ire. 7 52.51N 9.18W
Slieve Donard mtn. U.K. 7 54.11N 5.56W
Slieve Gamph mts. Rep. of Ire. 7 54.06N 8.52W
Slievekimalta mtn. Rep. of Ire. 7 52.45N 8.17W
Slieve Mish mts. Rep. of Ire. 7 52.48N 9.48W
Slieve Miskish mts. Rep. of Ire. 7 51.41N 9.56W
Slievenamon mtn. Rep. of Ire. 7 52.25N 7.34W
Slieve Snaght mtn. Donegal Rep. of Ire. 7 55.12N 7.20W
Sligo Rep. of Ire. 7 54.17N 8.28W
Sligo d. Rep. of Ire. 7 54.10N 8.35W
Sligo B. Rep. of Ire. 7 54.18N 8.40W
Slite Sweden 17 57.43N 18.48E
Sliven Bulgaria 13 42.41N 26.19E
Slobodka Ukraine 15 47.56N 29.18E
Slobodskoy Russian Fed. 18 58.42N 50.10E
Slonim Belorussia 15 53.05N 25.21E
Slough U.K. 5 51.30N 0.35W
Slovakia Europe 15 48.50N 19.00E
Slovechna r. Belorussia 15 51.41N 29.41E
Slovechno Ukraine 15 51.23N 28.20E
Slovenia Europe 12 46.10N 14.45E
Slovenjgradec Slovenia 12 46.31N 15.05E
Slubice Poland 14 52.20N 14.32E
Sluch r. Belorussia 15 52.08N 27.31E
Sluis Neth. 8 51.18N 3.23E
Slunj Croatia 14 45.07N 15.35E
Slupsk Poland 15 54.28N 17.01E
Slurry R.S.A. 39 25.48S 25.49E
Slutsk Belorussia 15 53.02N 27.31E
Slyne Head Rep. of Ire. 7 53.25N 10.12W
Slyudyanka Russian Fed. 24 51.40N103.40E
Smallwood Resr. Canada 51 54.00N 64.00W
Smederevo Yugo. 13 44.40N 20.56E
Smela Ukraine 19 49.15N 31.54E
Smilde Neth. 8 52.58N 6.28E
Smilovichi Belorussia 15 53.45N 28.00E
Smith Arm b. Canada 50 66.15N124.00W
Smithfield R.S.A. 39 30.11S 26.31E
Smiths Falls town Canada 55 44.54N 76.01W
Smithton Australia 45 40.52S145.07E
Smithtown Australia 47 31.03S152.53E
Smoky Bay town Australia 46 32.22S133.56E
Smoky C. Australia 47 30.55S153.05E
Smoky Hill r. U.S.A. 52 39.03N 96.48W
Smöla i. Norway 16 63.20N 8.00E
Smolensk Russian Fed. 18 54.49N 32.04E
Smolevichi Belorussia 15 54.00N 28.01E
Smólikas mtn. Greece 13 40.06N 20.55E
Smolyan Bulgaria 13 41.34N 24.45E
Smorgon Belorussia 15 54.28N 26.20E
Snaefell mtn. I.o.M. Europe 4 54.16N 4.28W
Snaefell mtn. Iceland 16 64.48N 15.34W
Snake r. Idaho U.S.A. 52 43.50N117.05W
Snake r. Wash. U.S.A. 54 46.12N119.02W
Snake Range mts. U.S.A. 54 39.00N114.15W
Snake River town U.S.A. 54 44.10N110.40W
Snake River Plain f. U.S.A. 54 43.00N113.00W
Snåsa Norway 16 64.15N 12.23E
Snåsavatn l. Norway 16 64.05N 12.00E
Sneek Neth. 8 53.03N 5.40E
Sneem Rep. of Ire. 7 51.50N 9.54W
Sneeuwberg mtn. R.S.A. 39 32.30S 19.09E
Śniardwy, Jezioro l. Poland 15 53.46N 21.44E
Snina Slovakia 15 48.59N 22.07E
Snizort, Loch U.K. 6 57.35N 6.30W
Snöhetta mtn. Norway 17 62.20N 9.17E
Snov r. Ukraine 15 51.45N 31.45E
Snowdon mtn. U.K. 4 53.05N 4.05W
Snowdrift Canada 50 62.23N110.47W
Snowflake U.S.A. 54 34.30N110.05W
Snowtown Australia 46 33.47S138.13E
Snowy r. Australia 47 37.49S148.30E
Snowy Mts. Australia 47 36.30S148.20E
Snyatyn Ukraine 15 48.30N 25.50E
Soacha Colombia 60 4.35N 74.13W
Soalala Madagascar 37 16.06S 45.20E
Soasiu Indonesia 27 0.40N127.25E
Sob r. Ukraine 15 48.42N 29.17E
Sobat r. Sudan / Ethiopia 35 9.30N 31.30E
Sobernheim Germany 8 49.47N 7.40E
Sobradinho, Représa de resr. Brazil 61 10.00S 42.30W
Sobral Brazil 61 3.45S 40.20W
Sochi Russian Fed. 19 43.35N 39.46E
Socorro Colombia 60 6.30N 73.16W
Socorro, Isla i. Mexico 56 18.45N110.58W
Socotra i. see Suquṭrá i. Indian Oc. 35
Socuéllamos Spain 10 39.16N 2.47W
Sodankylä Finland 16 67.29N 26.32E
Söderhamn Sweden 17 61.18N 17.03E
Söderköping Sweden 17 58.29N 16.18E
Södermanland d. Sweden 17 59.10N 16.35E
Södertälje Sweden 17 59.12N 17.37E
Sodium R.S.A. 39 30.10S 23.08E
Sodo Ethiopia 35 6.52N 37.47E
Södra Vi Sweden 17 57.45N 15.48E
Soest Germany 8 51.34N 8.06E
Sofala Australia 47 33.05S149.42E
Sofala d. Mozambique 39 19.00S 34.39E
Sofia see Sofiya Bulgaria 13
Sofiya Bulgaria 13 42.41N 23.19E
Sofiysk Russian Fed. 21 52.19N133.55E
Soforog Russian Fed. 18 65.47N 31.30E
Sogamoso Colombia 60 5.43N 72.56W
Sögel Germany 8 52.51N 7.31E
Sognefjorden est. Norway 17 61.06N 5.10E
Sogn og Fjordane d. Norway 17 61.30N 6.50E
Söğüt Turkey 30 40.02N 30.10E
Soignies Belgium 8 50.35N 4.04E
Soissons France 9 49.23N 3.20E
Sokal Ukraine 15 50.30N 24.10E
Söke Turkey 13 37.46N 27.26E
Sokodé Togo 38 8.59N 1.11E
Sokol Russian Fed. 18 59.28N 40.04E
Sokólka Poland 15 53.25N 23.31E
Sokolo Mali 38 14.53N 6.11W
Sokolov Czech Republic 14 50.09N 12.40E
Sokoto Nigeria 38 13.02N 5.15E
Sokoto d. Nigeria 38 11.50N 5.05E
Sokoto r. Nigeria 38 13.05N 5.13E
Solbad Hall Austria 14 47.17N 11.31E
Solec Kujawski Poland 15 53.06N 18.14E
Soledad Venezuela 60 8.10N 63.34W
Solesmes France 8 50.12N 3.32E
Solginskiy Russian Fed. 18 61.07N 41.30E
Solheim Norway 17 60.53N 5.27E
Soligalich Russian Fed. 18 59.02N 42.15E
Solikamsk Russian Fed. 18 59.40N 56.45E
Sol-Iletsk Russian Fed. 18 51.09N 55.00E
Solingen Germany 8 51.10N 7.05E
Sollefteå Sweden 16 63.12N 17.20E
Sollentuna Sweden 17 59.28N 17.54E
Sóller Spain 10 39.47N 2.41E
Sollia Norway 17 61.47N 10.24E
Solola Somali Rep. 37 0.08N 41.30E
Solomon Is. Pacific Oc. 40 8.00S160.00E
Solomon Sea Pacific Oc. 41 7.00S150.00E
Solon U.S.A. 55 44.57N 69.52W
Solothurn Switz. 14 47.13N 7.32E
Solovetskiye, Ostrova is. Russian Fed. 18 65.05N 35.30E
Šolta i. Croatia 12 43.23N 16.17E
Solṭānābād Iran 31 36.25N 58.02E
Soltau Germany 14 52.59N 9.49E
Sölvesborg Sweden 17 56.03N 14.33E
Solway Firth est. U.K. 4 54.50N 3.30W
Solzach r. Austria 14 48.35N 13.30E
Soma Turkey 13 39.11N 27.36E
Somabhula Zimbabwe 39 19.40S 29.38E
Somali Republic Africa 35 5.30N 47.00E
Sombor Yugo. 13 45.48N 19.08E
Sombrerete Mexico 56 23.38N103.39W
Somerset d. U.K. 5 51.09N 3.00W
Somerset East R.S.A. 39 32.43S 25.33E
Somerset I. Canada 51 73.00N 93.30W
Somes r. Hungary 15 48.40N 22.30E
Somme r. France 11 50.01N 1.40E
Sommen l. Sweden 17 58.01N 15.15E
Sompuis France 9 48.41N 4.23E
Son r. India 29 25.55N 84.55E
Sonbong N. Korea 25 42.19N130.24E
Sönderborg Denmark 17 54.55N 9.47E
Sondershausen Germany 14 51.22N 10.52E
Söndreströmfjord Greenland 51 66.30N 50.52W
Sondrio Italy 9 46.10N 9.52E
Songa r. Norway 17 59.45N 7.59E
Songea Tanzania 37 10.42S 35.39E
Songhua Jiang r. China 25 47.46N132.30E
Songkhla Thailand 29 7.13N100.37E
Song Xian China 25 34.02N111.48E
Son La Vietnam 26 21.20N103.55E
Sonneberg Germany 14 50.22N 11.10E
Sonora d. Mexico 56 29.30N110.40W
Sonora r. Mexico 56 28.50N111.33W
Sonsorol i. Pacific Ocean 27 5.20N132.13E
Son Tay Vietnam 26 21.06N105.32E
Sopi Indonesia 27 2.40N128.28E
Sopot Poland 15 54.28N 18.34E
Sopotskin Belorussia 15 53.49N 23.42E
Soppero Sweden 16 68.07N 21.40E
Sopron Hungary 14 47.41N 16.36E
Sorel Canada 55 46.03N 73.06W
Sörfjorden Norway 16 66.29N 13.20E
Sörfold Norway 16 67.30N 15.30E
Sorgono Italy 12 40.01N 9.06E
Soria Spain 10 41.46N 2.28W
Soriano Uruguay 63 33.24S 58.19W
Sor Kvalöy i. Norway 16 69.40N 18.30E
Sörli Norway 16 64.15N 13.50E
Sor Mertvyy Kultuk f. Kazakhstan 19 45.30N 54.00E
Sorocaba Brazil 59 23.29S 47.27W
Sorochinsk Russian Fed. 18 52.29N 53.15E
Soroki Moldavia 15 48.08N 28.12E
Sorol i. Federated States of Micronesia 27 8.09N140.25E
Sorong Indonesia 27 0.50S131.17E
Soroti Uganda 37 1.40N 33.37E
Söröya i. Norway 16 70.35N 22.30E
Sorraia r. Portugal 10 39.00N 8.51W
Sorrento Italy 12 40.37N 14.22E
Sör-Rondane mts. Antarctica 64 72.30S 22.00E
Sorsele Sweden 16 65.30N 17.30E
Sortavala Russian Fed. 18 61.40N 30.40E
Sortland Norway 16 68.44N 15.25E
Sör Tröndelag d. Norway 16 63.00N 10.20E
Sosnogorsk Russian Fed. 18 63.32N 53.55E
Sosnovo Russian Fed. 18 60.33N 30.11E
Sosnovyy Russian Fed. 18 66.01N 32.40E
Sosnowiec Poland 15 50.18N 19.08E
Sosva Russian Fed. 18 59.10N 61.50E
Sosyka Russian Fed. 19 46.11N 38.49E
Sotik Kenya 37 0.40S 35.08E
Sotra i. Norway 17 60.15N 5.10E
Sotteville France 9 49.25N 1.06E
Souflíon Greece 13 41.12N 26.18E
Sŏul S. Korea 25 37.30N127.00E
Sources, Mont-aux- mtn. Lesotho 39 28.44S 28.52E
Soure Portugal 10 40.04N 8.38W
Souris r. Canada 52 49.38N 99.35W
Sousa Brazil 61 6.41S 38.14W
Sousse Tunisia 34 35.48N 10.38E
Soustons France 11 43.45N 1.19W
South Alligator r. Australia 44 12.53S132.29E
Southampton Canada 55 44.29N 81.23W
Southampton U.K. 5 50.54N 1.23W
Southampton I. Canada 51 64.30N 84.00W
South Australia d. Australia 46 30.00S137.00E
South Bend Ind. U.S.A. 55 41.40N 86.15W
South Bend Wash. U.S.A. 54 46.40N123.48W
South Branch U.S.A. 55 44.29N 83.36W
South Carolina d. U.S.A. 53 34.00N 81.00W
South Cerney U.K. 5 51.40N 1.55W
South China Sea Asia 26 12.30N115.00E
South Dakota d. U.S.A. 52 44.30N100.00W
South Dorset Downs hills U.K. 5 50.40N 2.25W
South Downs hills U.K. 5 50.04N 0.34W
South East d. Botswana 39 25.00S 25.45E
South East C. Australia 45 43.38S146.48E
South East Is. Australia 43 34.23S123.30E
Southend-on-Sea U.K. 5 51.32N 0.43E
Southern Alps mts. New Zealand 48 43.20S170.45E
Southern Cross Australia 43 31.14S119.16E
Southern Indian L. Canada 51 57.10N 98.40W
Southern Ocean Pacific Oc. 40 50.00S135.00E
Southern Uplands hills U.K. 6 55.30N 3.30W
South Esk r. U.K. 6 56.43N 2.32W
South Esk Tablelands f. Australia 42 20.50S126.40E
South Glamorgan d. U.K. 5 51.27N 3.22W
South-haa U.K. 6 60.34N 1.17W
South Haven U.S.A. 55 42.25N 86.16W
South Horr Kenya 37 2.10N 36.45E
South I. Kenya 37 2.36N 36.38E
South I. New Zealand 48 43.00S171.00E
South Korea Asia 25 36.00N128.00E
South Lake Tahoe town U.S.A. 54 38.57N119.57W
Southland d. New Zealand 48 45.40S168.00E
South Molton U.K. 5 51.01N 3.50W
South Nahanni r. Canada 50 61.00N123.20W
Southport Qld. Australia 47 27.58S153.20E
Southport Tas. Australia 45 43.25S146.59E
Southport U.K. 4 53.38N 3.01W
South Ronaldsay i. U.K. 6 58.47N 2.56W
South Shields U.K. 4 55.00N 1.24W
South Tyne r. U.K. 6 54.59N 2.08W

South Uist *i.* U.K. **6** 57.15N 7.20W
Southwest C. New Zealand **48** 47.15S167.30E
South Windham U.S.A. **55** 43.44N 70.26W
Southwold U.K. **5** 52.19N 1.41E
South Yorkshire *d.* U.K. **4** 53.28N 1.25W
Soutpansberg *mts.* R.S.A. **39** 22.58S 29.50E
Sovetsk Lithuania **17** 55.05N 21.53E
Sovetsk Russian Fed. **18** 57.39N 48.59E
Sovetskaya Gavan Russian Fed. **21** 48.57N140.16E
Soweto R.S.A. **39** 26.16S 27.51E
Soyo Angola **36** 6.12S 12.25E
Sozh *r.* Belorussia **15** 51.57N 30.48E
Spa Belgium **8** 50.29N 5.52E
Spain Europe **10** 40.00N 4.00W
Spalding Australia **46** 33.29S138.40E
Spalding U.K. **4** 52.47N 0.09W
Spandau Germany **14** 52.32N 13.13E
Spanish Fork U.S.A. **54** 40.07N111.39W
Sparks U.S.A. **54** 39.32N119.45W
Spartanburg U.S.A. **53** 34.56N 81.57W
Spárti Greece **13** 37.04N 22.28E
Spartivento, Capo *c.* Calabria Italy **12** 37.55N 16.04E
Spartivento, Capo *c.* Sardegna Italy **12** 38.53N 8.50E
Spátha, Ákra *c.* Greece **13** 35.42N 23.43E
Speculator U.S.A. **55** 43.30N 74.17W
Speke G. Tanzania **37** 2.20S 33.30E
Spence Bay *town* Canada **51** 69.30N 93.20W
Spencer Idaho U.S.A. **54** 44.21N112.11W
Spencer Iowa U.S.A. **53** 43.08N 95.08W
Spencer, C. Australia **46** 35.18S136.53E
Spencer G. Australia **46** 34.00S137.00E
Sperrin Mts. U.K. **7** 54.49N 7.06W
Spétsai *i.* Greece **13** 37.15N 23.10E
Spey *r.* U.K. **6** 57.40N 3.06W
Speyer Germany **14** 49.18N 8.26E
Spiekeroog *i.* Germany **8** 53.48N 7.45E
Spilimbergo Italy **9** 46.07N 12.54E
Spilsby U.K. **4** 53.10N 0.06E
Spina *ruins* Italy **9** 44.42N 12.08E
Spinazzola Italy **12** 40.58N 16.06E
Spišská Nova Ves Slovakia **15** 48.57N 20.34E
Spithead *str.* U.K. **5** 50.45N 1.05W
Spitsbergen *is.* Arctic Oc. **64** 78.00N 17.00E
Spittal an der Drau Austria **14** 46.48N 13.30E
Split Croatia **13** 43.32N 16.27E
Spokane U.S.A. **54** 47.40N117.23W
Spokane *r.* U.S.A. **54** 47.44N118.20W
Spratly *i.* S. China Sea **26** 8.45N111.54E
Spray U.S.A. **54** 44.50N119.48W
Spree *r.* Germany **14** 52.32N 13.15E
Springbok R.S.A. **39** 29.40S 17.50E
Springerville U.S.A. **54** 34.08N109.17W
Springfield New Zealand **48** 43.20S171.56E
Springfield Ill. U.S.A. **53** 39.49N 89.39W
Springfield Mass. U.S.A. **55** 42.07N 72.35W
Springfield Miss. U.S.A. **53** 37.11N 93.19W
Springfield Ohio U.S.A. **55** 39.55N 83.48W
Springfield Oreg. U.S.A. **54** 44.03N123.01W
Springfield Vt. U.S.A. **55** 43.18N 72.29W
Springfontein R.S.A. **39** 30.15S 25.41E
Springs *town* R.S.A. **39** 26.16S 28.27E
Springsure Australia **44** 24.07S148.05E
Springville Utah U.S.A. **54** 40.10N111.37W
Spry U.S.A. **54** 37.55N112.28W
Spurn Head U.K. **4** 53.35N 0.08E
Squamish Canada **50** 49.42N123.09W
Squillace Italy **13** 38.46N 16.31E
Srbija *d.* Yugo. **13** 44.30N 20.30E
Srednekolymsk Russian Fed. **21** 67.27N153.35E
Sredne Russkaya Vozvyshennost *f.* Russian Fed. **18** 53.00N 37.00E
Sredne Sibirskoye Ploskogor'ye *f.* Russian Fed. **21** 66.00N108.00E
Sretensk Russian Fed. **25** 52.15N117.52E
Srīkākulam India **29** 18.18N 83.54E
Sri Lanka Asia **29** 7.30N 80.50E
Srīnagar Jammu & Kashmir **28** 34.08N 74.50E
Srnetica Bosnia-Herzegovina **13** 44.26N 16.40E
Staaten *r.* Australia **44** 16.24S141.17E
Stadskanaal Neth. **8** 53.02N 6.55E
Stadtkyll Germany **8** 50.21N 6.32E
Stadtlohn Germany **8** 52.00N 6.58E
Staffa *i.* U.K. **6** 56.26N 6.21W
Stafford U.K. **4** 52.49N 2.09W
Staffordshire *d.* U.K. **4** 52.40N 1.57W
Staines U.K. **5** 51.26N 0.31W
Stainforth U.K. **4** 53.37N 1.01W
Stakhanov Ukraine **19** 48.34N 38.40E
Stalina Kanal *canal* Russian Fed. **18** 64.33N 34.48E
Stamford U.K. **5** 52.39N 0.28W
Stamford Conn. U.S.A. **55** 41.03N 73.32W
Stamford N.Y. U.S.A. **55** 42.25N 74.37W
Standerton R.S.A. **39** 26.57S 29.14E
Stanger R.S.A. **39** 29.20S 31.17E
Stanley Canada **50** 55.45N104.55W
Stanley Falkland Is. **63** 51.42W 57.51W
Stanley U.K. **4** 54.53N 1.42W
Stanley Idaho U.S.A. **54** 44.13N114.35W
Stanovoy Khrebet *mts.* Russian Fed. **21** 56.00N125.40E
Stanthorpe Australia **47** 28.37S151.52E
Starachowice Poland **15** 51.03N 21.04E
Stara Dorogi Belorussia **15** 53.02N 28.18E
Stara Planina *mts.* Bulgaria **13** 42.50N 24.30E
Staraya Russa Russian Fed. **18** 58.00N 31.22E
Staraya Sinyava Ukraine **15** 49.38N 27.39E
Stara Zagora Bulgaria **13** 42.26N 25.37E
Stargard Szczeciński Poland **14** 53.21N 15.01E
Staritsa Russian Fed. **18** 56.29N 34.59E
Starnberg Germany **14** 48.00N 11.20E
Starobin Belorussia **15** 52.40N 27.29E
Starogard Gdański Poland **15** 53.59N 18.33E
Starokonstantinov Ukraine **15** 49.48N 27.10E
Start Pt. U.K. **5** 50.13N 3.38W
Staryy Oskol Russian Fed. **19** 51.20N 37.50E
State College U.S.A. **55** 40.48N 77.52W
Staten I. *see* Estados, Isla de los *i.* Argentina **63**
Staunton U.S.A. **53** 38.10N 79.05W
Stavanger Norway **17** 58.58N 5.45E
Stavelot Belgium **8** 50.23N 5.54E
Staveren Neth. **8** 52.53N 5.21E
Stavropol' Russian Fed. **19** 45.03N 41.59E
Stavropolskaya Vozvyshennost *mts.* Russian Fed. **19** 45.00N 42.30E
Stawell Australia **46** 37.06S142.52E
Stawiski Poland **15** 53.23N 22.09E
Steamboat Springs *town* U.S.A. **54** 40.29N106.50W
Steelpoort R.S.A. **39** 24.44S 30.13E
Steelton U.S.A. **55** 40.14N 76.49W
Steenbergen Neth. **8** 51.36N 4.19E
Steenvoorde France **8** 50.49N 2.35E
Steenwijk Neth. **8** 52.47N 6.07E
Steep Rock Lake *town* Canada **51** 48.50N 91.38W
Steiermark *d.* Austria **14** 47.10N 15.10E
Steilloopbrug R.S.A. **39** 23.26S 28.37E
Steinkjer Norway **16** 64.00N 11.30E
Steinkopf R.S.A. **39** 29.16S 17.41E
Stella R.S.A. **39** 26.32S 24.51E
Stellenbosch R.S.A. **39** 33.56S 18.51E
Stenay France **9** 49.29N 5.11E
Stendal Germany **14** 52.36N 11.52E
Stensträsk Sweden **16** 66.20N 19.50E
Stepan Ukraine **15** 51.09N 26.18E
Stepanakert Azerbaijan **31** 39.48N 46.45E
Stepnyak Kazakhstan **20** 52.52N 70.49E
Sterkstroom R.S.A. **39** 31.32S 26.31E
Sterling Colo. U.S.A. **52** 40.37N103.13W
Sterling Mich. U.S.A. **55** 44.02N 84.02W
Sterlitamak Russian Fed. **18** 53.40N 55.59E
Šternberk Czech Republic **15** 49.44N 17.18E
Stettler Canada **50** 52.21N112.40W
Steuben U.S.A. **55** 46.12N 86.27W
Steubenville U.S.A. **55** 40.22N 80.39W
Stevenage U.K. **5** 51.54N 0.11W
Stevenston U.K. **6** 55.39N 4.45W
Stewart Canada **50** 55.56N130.01W
Stewart I. New Zealand **48** 47.00S168.00E
Stewart River *town* Canada **50** 63.19N139.26W
Steynsburg R.S.A. **39** 31.17S 25.48E
Steyr Austria **14** 48.04N 14.25E
Stikine *r.* Canada **50** 56.45N132.30W
Stikine Mts. Canada **50** 59.00N129.00W
Stiklestad Norway **16** 63.48N 11.22E
Stilbaai R.S.A. **39** 34.22S 21.22E
Stillwater Range *mts.* U.S.A. **54** 39.50N118.15W
Stilton U.K. **5** 52.29N 0.17W
Stimson Canada **55** 48.58N 80.37W
Stinchar *r.* U.K. **6** 55.06N 5.00W
Stînisoara, Munţii *mts.* Romania **15** 47.10N 26.00E
Štip Macedonia **13** 41.44N 22.12E
Stirling U.K. **6** 56.07N 3.57W
Stirling Range *mts.* Australia **43** 34.23S117.50E
Stjernöya *i.* Norway **16** 70.17N 22.40E
Stjördalshalsen Norway **16** 63.29N 10.51E
Stockaryd Sweden **17** 57.18N 14.35E
Stockbridge U.K. **5** 51.07N 1.30W
Stockerau Austria **14** 48.23N 16.13E
Stockett U.S.A. **54** 47.21N111.10W
Stockholm Sweden **17** 59.20N 18.03E
Stockholm *d.* Sweden **17** 59.40N 18.10E
Stockinbingal Australia **47** 34.03S147.53E
Stockport U.K. **4** 53.25N 2.11W
Stocksbridge U.K. **4** 53.30N 1.36W
Stockton Calif. U.S.A. **54** 37.57N121.17W
Stockton-on-Tees U.K. **4** 54.34N 1.20W
Stoeng Trêng Cambodia **26** 13.31N105.58E
Stoffberg R.S.A. **39** 25.25S 29.49E
Stoke-on-Trent U.K. **4** 53.01N 2.11W
Stokes Bay *town* Canada **55** 44.55N 81.21W
Stokhod *r.* Ukraine **15** 51.52N 25.38E
Stokksund Norway **16** 64.03N 10.05E
Stolac Bosnia-Herzegovina **13** 43.05N 17.58E
Stolberg Germany **8** 50.47N 6.12E
Stolbtsy Belorussia **15** 53.30N 26.44E
Stolin Belorussia **15** 51.52N 26.51E
Stone U.K. **4** 52.55N 2.10W
Stonehaven U.K. **6** 56.58N 2.13W
Stooping *r.* Canada **55** 52.08N 82.00W
Stora Lulevatten *l.* Sweden **16** 67.10N 19.16E
Stora Sjöfallets Nat. Park Sweden **16** 67.44N 18.16E
Storavan *l.* Sweden **16** 65.40N 18.15E
Storby Finland **17** 60.13N 19.34E
Stord *i.* Norway **17** 59.53N 5.25E
Store Baelt *str.* Denmark **17** 55.30N 11.00E
Stor Elvdal Norway **17** 61.32N 11.02E
Stören Norway **16** 63.03N 10.18E
Storlien Sweden **16** 63.20N 12.05E
Stornoway U.K. **6** 58.12N 6.23W
Storozhevsk Russian Fed. **18** 62.00N 52.20E
Storozhinets Ukraine **15** 48.11N 25.40E
Storsjön *l.* Sweden **16** 63.10N 14.20E
Storuman Sweden **16** 65.06N 17.06E
Storuman *l.* Sweden **16** 65.10N 16.40E
Stour *r.* Dorset U.K. **5** 50.43N 1.47W
Stour *r.* Kent U.K. **5** 51.19N 1.22E
Stour *r.* Suffolk U.K. **5** 51.56N 1.03E
Stourport-on-Severn U.K. **5** 52.21N 2.16W
Stowmarket U.K. **5** 52.11N 1.00E
Stow on the Wold U.K. **5** 51.55N 1.42W
Strabane U.K. **7** 54.50N 7.30W
Stradbally Laois Rep. of Ire. **7** 53.01N 7.09W
Stradbroke I. Australia **45** 27.38S153.45E
Stradella Italy **9** 45.05N 9.18E
Straelen Germany **8** 51.27N 6.14E
Strahan Australia **45** 42.08S145.21E
Strakonice Czech Republic **14** 49.16N 13.55E
Stralsund Germany **14** 54.18N 13.06E
Strand R.S.A. **39** 34.07S 18.50E
Stranda Norway **16** 62.19N 6.58E
Strangford Lough U.K. **7** 54.28N 5.35W
Strangways Australia **46** 29.08S136.35E
Stranraer U.K. **6** 54.54N 5.02W
Strasbourg France **11** 48.35N 7.45E
Stratford Australia **47** 37.57S147.05E
Stratford Canada **55** 43.22N 80.57W
Stratford New Zealand **48** 39.20S174.18E
Stratford-upon-Avon U.K. **5** 52.12N 1.42W
Strathalbyn Australia **46** 35.16S138.54E
Strathclyde *d.* U.K. **6** 55.45N 4.45W
Strathmore *f.* Tayside U.K. **6** 56.44N 2.45W
Strathspey *f.* U.K. **6** 57.25N 3.25W
Straubing Germany **14** 48.53N 12.35E
Straumnes *c.* Iceland **16** 66.30N 23.05W
Streaky B. Australia **46** 32.36S134.08E
Streaky Bay *town* Australia **46** 32.48S134.13E
Street U.K. **5** 51.07N 2.43W
Stresa Italy **9** 45.53N 8.32E
Stretton Australia **43** 32.30S117.42E
Strimon *r.* Greece **13** 40.47N 23.51E
Stromboli *i.* Italy **12** 38.48N 15.14E
Stromeferry U.K. **6** 57.21N 5.34W
Stromness U.K. **6** 58.57N 3.18W
Strömö *i.* Faroe Is. **16** 62.08N 7.00W
Strömsbruk Sweden **17** 61.53N 17.19E
Strömstad Sweden **17** 58.56N 11.10E
Strömsund Sweden **16** 63.51N 15.35E
Strömsvattudal *f.* Sweden **16** 64.15N 15.00E
Stronsay *i.* U.K. **6** 59.07N 2.36W
Stroud Australia **47** 32.25S151.58E
Stroud U.K. **5** 51.44N 2.12W
Struan Australia **46** 37.08S140.49E
Struer Denmark **17** 56.29N 8.37E
Struga Macedonia **13** 41.10N 20.41E
Struma *r.* Bulgaria *see* Strimon *r.* Greece **13**
Strumica Macedonia **13** 41.26N 22.39E
Strydenburg R.S.A. **39** 29.56S 23.39E
Stryker U.S.A. **54** 48.40N114.44W
Stryy Ukraine **15** 49.16N 23.51E
Strzelecki Creek *r.* Australia **46** 29.37S139.59E
Strzelno Poland **15** 52.38N 18.11E
Stuart Creek *town* Australia **46** 29.43S137.01E
Stuart L. Canada **50** 54.32N124.35W
Stuart Range *mts.* Australia **46** 29.10S134.56E
Stuart Town Australia **47** 32.51S149.08E
Sturgeon Falls *town* Canada **55** 46.22N 79.55W
Sturgeon L. Ont. Canada **55** 49.47N 90.40W
Sturminster Newton U.K. **5** 50.56N 2.18W
Sturt B. Australia **46** 35.24S137.32E
Sturt Creek *r.* Australia **42** 20.08S127.24E
Sturt Desert Australia **46** 28.30S141.12E
Sturt Plain *f.* Australia **44** 17.00S132.48E
Stutterheim R.S.A. **39** 32.32S 27.25E
Stuttgart Germany **14** 48.47N 9.12E
Stviga *r.* Belorussia **15** 52.04N 27.54E
Stykkishólmur Iceland **16** 65.06N 22.48W
Styr *r.* Belorussia **15** 52.07N 26.35E
Subotica Yugo. **13** 46.04N 19.41E
Suceava Romania **15** 47.39N 26.19E
Suck *r.* Rep. of Ire. **7** 53.16N 8.04W
Suckling, Mt. P.N.G. **44** 9.45S148.55E
Sucre Bolivia **62** 19.02S 65.17W
Sucuriu *r.* Brazil **59** 20.44S 51.40W
Sudan Africa **35** 14.00N 30.00E
Sudbury Canada **55** 46.30N 81.00W
Sudbury U.K. **5** 52.03N 0.45E
Sudety *mts.* Czech Republic / Poland **14** 50.30N 16.30E
Sudirman, Pegunungan *mts.* Indonesia **27** 3.50S136.30E
Sud Ouest *d.* Burkina **38** 10.45N 3.10W
Sueca Spain **10** 39.12N 0.21W
Suez *see* As Suways Egypt **32**
Suez, G. of *see* Suways, Khalīj as *g.* Egypt **32**
Suez Canal *see* Suways, Qanāt as *canal* Egypt **32**
Şufaynah Saudi Arabia **30** 23.09N 40.32E
Suffolk *d.* U.K. **5** 52.16N 1.00E
Şuhār Oman **31** 24.23N 56.43E
Suhl Germany **14** 50.37N 10.43E
Suibin China **25** 47.19N131.49E
Suide China **25** 37.32N110.12E
Suihua China **25** 46.39N126.59E
Suileng China **25** 47.15N127.05E
Suipacha Argentina **63** 34.47S 59.40W
Suiping China **25** 33.09N113.59E
Suippes France **9** 49.08N 4.32E
Suir *r.* Rep. of Ire. **7** 52.17N 7.00W
Suita Japan **23** 34.45N135.32E
Sui Xian Hubei China **25** 31.43N113.22E
Sukabumi Indonesia **26** 6.55S106.50E
Sukadana Indonesia **26** 1.15S110.00E
Sukaraja Indonesia **26** 2.23S110.35E
Sukhinichi Russian Fed. **18** 54.07N 35.21E
Sukhona *r.* Russian Fed. **18** 61.30N 46.28E
Sukhumi Georgia **19** 43.01N 41.01E
Sukkertoppen Greenland **51** 65.40N 53.00W
Sukkur Pakistan **28** 27.42N 68.54E
Sula *i.* Norway **17** 61.08N 4.55E
Sula, Kepulauan *is.* Indonesia **27** 1.50S125.10E
Sulaimān Range *mts.* Pakistan **28** 30.50N 70.20E
Sulak *r.* Russian Fed. **19** 43.18N 47.35E
Sulawesi *i.* Indonesia **27** 2.00S120.30E
Sulawesi Selatan *d.* Indonesia **27** 3.45S120.30E
Sulawesi Utara *d.* Indonesia **27** 1.45S120.30E
Sulechów Poland **14** 52.06N 15.37E
Sulejów Poland **15** 51.22N 19.53E
Sulina Romania **13** 45.08N 29.40E
Sulitjelma Norway **16** 67.10N 16.05E
Sullana Peru **60** 4.52S 80.39W
Sully France **9** 47.46N 2.22E
Sulmona Italy **12** 42.04N 13.57E
Sultan Canada **55** 47.36N 82.47W
Sultan Hamud Kenya **37** 2.02S 37.20E
Sulu Archipelago Phil. **27** 5.30N121.00E
Sulu Sea Pacific Oc. **27** 8.00N120.00E
Sumatera *i.* Indonesia **26** 2.00S102.00E
Sumatera Barat *d.* Indonesia **26** 1.00S100.00E
Sumatera Selatan *d.* Indonesia **26** 3.00S104.00E
Sumatera Utara *d.* Indonesia **26** 2.00N 99.00E
Sumatra *see* Sumatera *i.* Indonesia **26**
Sumatra U.S.A. **54** 46.38N107.31W
Sumba *i.* Indonesia **26** 9.30S119.55E
Sumbar *r.* Turkmenistan **31** 38.00N 55.20E
Sumbawa *i.* Indonesia **26** 8.45S117.50E
Sumbawanga Tanzania **37** 7.58S 31.36E
Sumbe Angola **36** 11.11S 13.52E
Sumburgh Head U.K. **6** 59.51N 1.16W
Šumen Bulgaria **13** 43.15N 26.55E
Sumgait Azerbaijan **31** 40.35N 49.38E
Šumperk Czech Republic **14** 49.58N 16.58E
Sumusţā al Waqf Egypt **32** 28.55N 30.51E
Sumy Ukraine **19** 50.55N 34.49E
Sunart, Loch U.K. **6** 56.43N 5.45W
Sunbury Australia **47** 37.36S144.45E
Sunda, Selat *str.* Indonesia **26** 6.00S105.50E
Sundarbans *f.* India / Bangla. **29** 22.00N 89.00E
Sundays *r.* R.S.A. **39** 33.43S 25.50E
Sunderland U.K. **4** 54.55N 1.22W
Sundsvall Sweden **17** 62.23N 17.18E
Sungaipakning Indonesia **26** 1.19N102.00E
Sungaipenuh Indonesia **26** 2.00S101.28E
Sungguminasa Indonesia **26** 5.14S119.27E
Sungurlu Turkey **30** 40.10N 34.23E
Sunne Sweden **17** 59.50N 13.09E
Sunnyside U.S.A. **54** 46.20N120.00W
Suntar Russian Fed. **21** 62.10N117.35E
Sun Valley *town* U.S.A. **52** 43.42N114.21W
Sunwu China **25** 49.40N127.10E
Sunyani Ghana **38** 7.22N 2.18W
Suoyarvi Russian Fed. **18** 62.02N 32.20E
Superior Mont. U.S.A. **54** 47.12N114.53W
Superior Wisc. U.S.A. **53** 46.42N 92.05W
Superior Wyo. U.S.A. **54** 41.46N108.58W
Superior, L. Canada / U.S.A. **55** 48.00N 88.00W
Süphan Dagi *mtn.* Turkey **19** 38.55N 42.55E
Süphan Dağlari *mtn.* Turkey **30** 38.55N 42.55E
Suquţrá *i.* Indian Oc. **35** 12.30N 54.00E
Şūr Lebanon **32** 33.16N 35.12E
Şūr Oman **31** 22.23N 59.32E
Sur, Punta *c.* Argentina **63** 36.53S 56.41W
Sura Russian Fed. **18** 53.52N 45.45E
Surabaya Indonesia **26** 7.14S112.45E
Surakarta Indonesia **26** 7.32S110.50E
Şūrān Syria **32** 35.18N 36.44E
Surany Slovakia **15** 48.06N 18.14E
Surat Australia **45** 27.09S149.05E
Surat India **28** 21.10N 72.54E
Sūratgarh India **28** 29.19N 73.54E
Surat Thani Thailand **29** 9.03N 99.28E
Surazh Russian Fed. **15** 53.00N 32.22E
Sûre *r.* Lux. **8** 49.43N 6.31E
Surfer's Paradise Australia **47** 27.58S153.26E
Surgut Russian Fed. **20** 61.13N 73.20E
Surigao Phil. **27** 9.47N125.29E
Surin Thailand **29** 14.50N103.34E
Surinam S. America **61** 4.00N 56.00W
Suriname *r.* Surinam **61** 5.52N 55.14W
Surrey *d.* U.K. **5** 51.16N 0.30W
Surt Libya **34** 31.10N 16.39E
Surt, Khalīj *g.* Libya **34** 31.45N 17.50E
Surtsey *i.* Iceland **16** 63.18N 20.30W
Surud Ad *mtn.* Somali Rep. **35** 10.41N 47.18E
Suruga-wan *b.* Japan **23** 34.45N138.30E
Susa Italy **9** 45.08N 7.03E
Susanino Russian Fed. **21** 52.46N140.09E
Susanville U.S.A. **54** 40.25N120.39W
Susquehanna *r.* U.S.A. **55** 39.33N 76.05W
Sussex Wyo. U.S.A. **54** 43.42N106.19W
Sutherland Australia **47** 34.02S151.04E
Sutherland R.S.A. **39** 32.23S 20.38E
Sutherlin U.S.A. **54** 43.25N123.19W
Sutlej *r.* Pakistan **28** 29.26N 71.09E
Sutton England U.K. **5** 51.22N 0.12W
Sutton W. Va. U.S.A. **55** 38.41N 80.43W
Sutton in Ashfield U.K. **4** 53.08N 1.16W
Suva Fiji **40** 18.08S178.25E
Suwałki Poland **15** 54.07N 22.56E
Suwanee *r.* U.S.A. **53** 29.15N 82.50W
Suways, Khalīj as *g.* Egypt **32** 28.48N 33.00E
Suways, Qanāt as *canal* Egypt **32** 30.40N 32.20E
Suwon S. Korea **25** 37.16N126.59E
Suzhou China **25** 31.21N120.40E
Suzuka Japan **23** 34.51N136.35E
Suzuka *r.* Japan **23** 34.54N136.39E
Suzuka-sammyaku *mts.* Japan **23** 35.00N136.20E
Suzzara Italy **9** 45.00N 10.45E
Svalyava Ukraine **15** 48.33N 23.00E
Svanvik Norway **16** 69.25N 30.00E
Svappavaara Sweden **16** 67.39N 21.04E
Svarhofthalvöya Norway **16** 70.35N 26.00E
Svartenhuk Halvo *c.* Greenland **51** 71.55N 55.00W
Svartisen *mtn.* Norway **16** 66.40N 13.56E
Svatovo Ukraine **19** 49.24N 38.11E
Svedala Sweden **17** 55.30N 13.14E
Sveg Sweden **17** 62.02N 14.21E
Svelgen Norway **17** 61.47N 5.15E
Svendborg Denmark **17** 55.03N 10.37E
Svenstrup Denmark **17** 56.59N 9.52E
Sverdlovsk *see* Yekaterinburg Russian Fed. **18**
Svetlograd Russian Fed. **19** 45.25N 42.58E
Svetogorsk Russian Fed. **18** 61.07N 28.50E
Svetozarevo Yugo. **13** 43.58N 21.16E
Svinö *i.* Faroe Is. **16** 62.17N 6.18W
Svir *r.* Russian Fed. **18** 60.09N 32.15E
Svishtov Bulgaria **13** 43.36N 25.23E
Svisloch Belorussia **15** 53.28N 29.00E
Svitavy Czech Republic **14** 49.45N 16.27E
Svobodnyy Russian Fed. **25** 51.24N128.05E
Svolvaer Norway **16** 68.15N 14.40E
Swaffham U.K. **5** 52.38N 0.42E
Swain Reefs Australia **44** 21.40S152.15E
Swakop *r.* Namibia **39** 22.38S 14.32E
Swakopmund Namibia **39** 22.40S 14.34E
Swale *r.* U.K. **4** 54.05N 1.20W
Swan *r.* Australia **43** 32.03S115.45E
Swanage U.K. **5** 50.36N 1.59W
Swan Hill *town* Australia **46** 35.23S143.37E
Swansea Australia **45** 42.08S148.00E
Swansea U.K. **5** 51.37N 3.57W
Swastika Canada **55** 48.07N 80.06W
Swatow *see* Shantou China **25**
Swaziland Africa **39** 26.30S 32.00E
Sweden Europe **16** 63.00N 16.00E
Swedru Ghana **38** 5.31N 0.42W
Sweetwater U.S.A. **52** 32.37N100.25W
Swidnica Poland **14** 50.51N 16.29E
Swiebodzin Poland **14** 52.15N 15.32E
Świetokrzyskie, Góry *mts.* Poland **15** 51.00N 20.30E
Swift Current *town* Canada **50** 50.17N107.49W
Swilly, Lough Rep. of Ire. **7** 55.10N 7.32W
Swindon U.K. **5** 51.33N 1.47W
Świnoujście Poland **14** 53.55N 14.18E
Switzerland Europe **11** 47.00N 8.00E
Syderö *i.* Faroe Is. **16** 61.30N 6.50W
Sydney Australia **47** 33.55S151.10E
Sydney Canada **51** 46.10N 60.10W
Sydpröven Greenland **51** 60.30N 45.35W
Syktyvkar Russian Fed. **18** 61.42N 50.45E
Sylhet Bangla. **29** 24.53N 91.51E
Sylt *i.* Germany **14** 54.50N 8.20E
Sylte Norway **16** 62.31N 7.07E
Syracuse N.Y. U.S.A. **55** 43.03N 76.09W
Syr Darya *r.* Kazakhstan **20** 46.00N 61.12E
Syria Asia **30** 35.00N 38.00E
Syriam Burma **26** 16.45N 96.17E
Syrian Desert *see* Bādiyat ash Shām *des.* Asia **30**
Syzran Russian Fed. **18** 53.10N 48.29E
Szarvas Hungary **15** 46.52N 20.34E
Szczecin Poland **14** 53.25N 14.32E
Szczecinek Poland **14** 53.42N 16.41E
Szczytno Poland **15** 53.34N 21.00E
Szécsény Hungary **15** 48.06N 19.31E
Szeged Hungary **13** 46.16N 20.08E
Székesfehérvár Hungary **15** 47.12N 18.25E
Szekszárd Hungary **13** 46.22N 18.44E
Szentes Hungary **15** 46.39N 20.16E
Szolnok Hungary **15** 47.10N 20.12E
Szombathely Hungary **14** 47.12N 16.38E
Sztutowo Poland **15** 54.20N 19.15E

T

Tabagne Ivory Coast **38** 7.59N 3.04W
Ţābah Saudi Arabia **30** 27.02N 42.10E
Ţabas Khorāsān Iran **31** 33.36N 56.55E
Ţabas Khorāsān Iran **31** 32.48N 60.14E
Tabasco *d.* Mexico **56** 18.30N 93.00W
Tābask, Kūh-e *mtn.* Iran **31** 29.51N 51.52E
Tabili Zaïre **37** 0.04N 28.01E
Table B. R.S.A. **39** 33.52S 18.26E
Tábor Czech Republic **14** 49.25N 14.41E
Tabora Tanzania **37** 5.02S 32.50E
Tabora *d.* Tanzania **37** 5.30S 32.50E
Tabou Ivory Coast **34** 4.28N 7.20W
Tabrīz Iran **31** 38.05N 46.18E
Tabūk Saudi Arabia **32** 28.23N 36.36E
Tabulam Australia **47** 28.50S152.35E
Tachikawa Japan **23** 35.42N139.25E
Tacloban Phil. **27** 11.15N124.59E
Tacna Peru **62** 18.01S 70.15W
Tacoma U.S.A. **54** 47.15N122.27W
Tacora *mtn.* Chile **62** 17.40S 69.45W
Tacuarembó Uruguay **63** 31.44S 55.59W
Tademaït, Plateau du *f.* Algeria **34** 28.45N 2.10E
Tadmor New Zealand **48** 41.26S172.47E
Tadmur Syria **30** 34.36N 38.15E
Tadoussac Canada **55** 48.09N 69.43W
Taegu S. Korea **25** 35.52N128.36E
Taejŏn S. Korea **25** 36.20N127.26E
Tafalla Spain **10** 42.31N 1.40W
Tafí Viejo Argentina **62** 26.45S 65.15W
Taftān, Kūh-e *mtn.* Iran **31** 28.38N 61.08E
Taganrog Russian Fed. **19** 47.14N 38.55E
Taganrogskiy Zaliv *g.* Ukraine / Russian Fed. **19** 47.00N 38.30E
Tagaytay City Phil. **27** 14.07N120.58E
Tagbilaran Phil. **27** 9.38N123.53E
Tagish Canada **50** 60.18N134.16W
Tagliamento *r.* Italy **9** 45.38N 13.06E
Taglio di Po Italy **9** 45.00N 12.12E
Tagula I. P.N.G. **44** 11.30S153.30E
Tagum Phil. **27** 7.33N125.53E
Tagus *r.* Portugal / Spain *see* Tejo *r.* Portugal **10**
Tahara Japan **23** 34.40N137.16E
Tahat *mtn.* Algeria **34** 23.20N 5.40E
Tahe China **25** 52.35N124.48E
Tahiti *i.* Is. de la Société **40** 17.37S149.27W
Tahoe, L. U.S.A. **54** 39.07N120.03W
Tahoua Niger **38** 14.57N 5.16E
Tahoua *d.* Niger **38** 15.38N 4.50E
Ţahţā Egypt **30** 26.46N 31.30E
Tahuna Indonesia **27** 3.37N125.29E
Taibai Shan *mtn.* China **29** 34.00N107.40E
Taidong Taiwan **25** 22.49N121.10E
Taihape New Zealand **48** 39.40S175.48E
Tailai China **25** 46.23N123.24E
Tailem Bend *town* Australia **46** 35.14S139.29E
Tain U.K. **6** 57.48N 4.04W
Tainan Taiwan **25** 23.01N120.14E
Taínaron, Ákra *c.* Greece **13** 36.22N 22.28E
Taipei Taiwan **25** 25.05N121.32E
Taiping Malaysia **26** 4.54N100.42E
Taito, Peninsula de *pen.* Chile **63** 46.30S 74.25W
Taivalkoski Finland **16** 65.34N 28.15E
Taiwan Asia **25** 23.30N121.00E
Taiwan Str. China / Taiwan **25** 25.00N120.00E
Taiyuan China **25** 37.50N112.30E
Taizhong Taiwan **25** 24.09N120.40E
Taizhou China **25** 32.30N119.50E
Ta'izz Yemen **35** 13.35N 44.02E
Tajikistan Asia **24** 39.00N 70.30E
Tajimi Japan **23** 35.19N137.08E
Tajo *r.* Spain *see* Tejo *r.* Portugal **10**
Tajrīsh Iran **31** 35.48N 51.20E

Tajuna r. Spain 10 40.10N 3.35W
Tak Thailand 29 16.47N 99.10E
Takaka New Zealand 48 40.51S172.48E
Takalar Indonesia 26 5.29S119.26E
Takamatsu Japan 25 34.20N134.01E
Takapuna New Zealand 48 36.48S174.47E
Takarazuka Japan 23 34.49N135.21E
Takatsuki Japan 23 34.51N135.37E
Tākestān Iran 31 36.02N 49.40E
Takhādīd well Iraq 31 29.59N 44.30E
Taklimakan Shamo des. China 24 38.10N 82.00E
Talā Egypt 32 30.41N 30.56E
Tala Uruguay 63 34.21S 55.46W
Talagante Chile 63 33.40S 70.56W
Talangbetutu Indonesia 26 2.48S104.42E
Talara Peru 60 4.38S 81.18W
Talasskiy Alatau mts. Kyrgyzstan 24 42.20N 73.20E
Talata Mafara Nigeria 38 12.37N 6.05E
Talaud, Kepulauan is. Indonesia 27 4.20N126.50E
Talavera de la Reina Spain 10 39.58N 4.50W
Talbragar r. Australia 47 32.12S148.37E
Talca Chile 63 35.26S 71.40W
Talcahuano Chile 63 36.43S 73.07W
Taldom Russian Fed. 18 56.49N 37.30E
Taldy Kurgan Kazakhstan 24 45.02N 78.23E
Talia Australia 46 33.16S134.53E
Taliabu i. Indonesia 27 1.50S124.55E
Talkeetna U.S.A. 50 62.20N150.09W
Ṭalkhā Egypt 32 31.04N 31.22E
Tallahassee U.S.A. 53 30.28N 84.19W
Tallangatta Australia 47 36.14S147.19E
Tallard France 11 44.28N 6.03E
Tallinn Estonia 17 59.22N 24.48E
Tall Kalakh Syria 32 34.40N 36.18E
Tall Kūshik Syria 30 36.48N 42.04E
Tall Salḩab Syria 32 35.15N 36.22E
Talmont France 11 46.28N 1.36W
Talnoye Ukraine 15 48.55N 30.40E
Talsi Latvia 17 57.15N 22.36E
Taltal Chile 62 25.24S 70.29W
Talvik Norway 16 70.05N 22.52E
Talwood Australia 47 28.29S149.25E
Talyawalka r. Australia 46 31.49S143.25E
Tama r. Japan 23 35.32N139.47E
Tamala Australia 42 26.42S113.47E
Tamale Ghana 38 9.26N 0.49W
Tamanrasset Algeria 34 22.50N 5.31E
Tamar r. U.K. 5 50.28N 4.13W
Tamaské Niger 38 14.55N 5.55E
Tamaulipas d. Mexico 56 24.00N 98.20W
Tamazunchale Mexico 56 21.16N 98.47W
Tambacounda Senegal 34 13.45N 13.40W
Tambara Mozambique 37 16.42S 34.17E
Tambar Springs town Australia 47 31.20S149.50E
Tambellup Australia 43 34.03S117.36E
Tambo Australia 44 24.53S146.15E
Tambo r. Australia 47 37.51S147.48E
Tambohorano Madagascar 37 17.30S 43.58E
Tambov Russian Fed. 18 52.44N 41.28E
Tambre r. Spain 10 42.50N 8.55W
Tambura Sudan 35 5.36N 27.28E
Tamchaket Mauritania 34 17.25N 10.40W
Tâmega r. Portugal 10 41.04N 8.17W
Tamil Nadu d. India 29 11.15N 79.00E
Ṭāmiyah Egypt 32 29.29N 30.58E
Tam Ky Vietnam 26 15.34N108.29E
Tammisaari Finland 17 59.58N 23.26E
Tampa U.S.A. 53 27.58N 82.38W
Tampa B. U.S.A. 53 27.48N 82.15W
Tampere Finland 17 61.30N 23.45E
Tampico Mexico 56 22.18N 97.52W
Tamsagbulag Mongolia 25 47.10N117.21E
Tamworth Australia 47 31.07S150.57E
Tamworth U.K. 5 52.38N 1.42W
Tana r. Kenya 37 2.32S 40.32E
Tana Norway 16 70.26N 28.14E
Tana r. Norway 16 69.45N 28.15E
Tanacross U.S.A. 50 63.12N143.30W
Tanafjorden Norway 16 70.54N 28.40E
T'ana Hāyk' l. Ethiopia 35 12.00N 37.20E
Tanahgrogot Indonesia 26 1.55S116.12E
Tanahmerah Indonesia 27 6.08S140.18E
Tanami Desert Australia 42 19.50S130.50E
Tanana U.S.A. 50 65.11N152.10W
Tanana r. U.S.A. 50 65.09N151.55W
Tananarive see Antananarivo Madagascar 36
Tanaro r. Italy 9 45.01N 8.46E
Tanda Ivory Coast 38 7.48N 3.10W
Tăndărei Romania 15 44.38N 27.40E
Tandil Argentina 63 37.18S 59.10W
Tandou L. Australia 46 32.38S142.05E
Tanezrouft f. Algeria 34 22.50N 1.05E
Tanga Tanzania 37 5.07S 39.05E
Tanga d. Tanzania 37 5.20S 38.30E
Tangalla Sri Lanka 29 6.02N 80.47E
Tanganyika, L. Africa 37 6.00S 29.30E
Tanger Morocco 34 35.48N 5.45W
Tanggula Shan mts. China 29 32.40N 92.30E
Tangier see Tanger Morocco 34
Tangra Yumco l. China 24 31.00N 86.22E
Tangshan China 25 39.37N118.05E
Tanguiéta Benin 38 10.37N 1.18E
Tanimbar, Kepulauan is. Indonesia 27 7.50S131.30E
Tanjay Phil. 27 9.31N123.10E
Tanjona Bobaomby c. Madagascar 36 11.57S 49.17E
Tanjona Vilanandro c. Madagascar 37 16.11S 44.27E
Tanjona Vohimena c. Madagascar 36 25.36S 45.08E
Tanjung Indonesia 26 2.10S115.25E
Tanjungbalai Indonesia 26 2.59N 99.46E
Tanjungkarang Indonesia 26 5.28S105.16E
Tanjungpandan Indonesia 26 2.44S107.36E
Tanjungredeb Indonesia 26 2.09N117.29E
Tankapirtti Finland 16 68.16N 27.20E
Tännäs Sweden 17 62.27N 12.40E
Tannin Canada 55 49.40N 91.00W
Tannu Ola mts. Russian Fed. 21 51.00N 93.30E
Tannūrah, Ra's c. Saudi Arabia 31 26.40N 50.10E
Tano r. Ghana 38 5.07N 2.54W
Tanout Niger 38 14.55N 8.49E
Ṭanṭā Egypt 32 30.48N 31.00E
Tanzania Africa 37 5.00S 35.00E
Tao'an China 25 45.25N122.46E
Taoudenni Mali 34 22.45N 4.00W
Tapachula Mexico 56 14.54N 92.15W
Tapajós r. Brazil 61 2.25S 54.40W
Tapaktuan Indonesia 26 3.30N 97.10E
Tapalquén Argentina 63 36.20S 60.02W
Tapanahoni r. Surinam 61 4.20N 54.25W
Tapanui New Zealand 48 45.57S169.16E
Tapauá r. Brazil 60 5.40S 64.20W
Tapirapecó, Serra mts. Venezuela / Brazil 60 1.00N 64.30W
Tapolca Hungary 15 46.53N 17.27E
Tāpti r. India 28 21.05N 72.45E
Tapurucuara Brazil 60 0.24S 65.02W
Taquari r. Brazil 59 19.00S 57.27W
Taquaritinga Brazil 59 21.23S 48.33W
Tara Russian Fed. 20 56.55N 74.24E
Tara r. Russian Fed. 20 56.30N 74.40E
Tara r. Yugo. 13 43.23N 18.47E
Taraba Nigeria 38 8.15N 11.00E
Tarabuco Bolivia 62 19.10S 64.57W
Ṭarābulus Lebanon 32 34.27N 35.50E
Ṭarābulus Libya 34 32.58N 13.12E
Ṭarābulus f. Libya 34 29.45N 14.30E
Tarago Australia 47 35.05S149.10E
Tarakan Indonesia 26 3.20N117.38E
Taranaki d. New Zealand 48 39.00S174.30E
Tarancón Spain 10 40.01N 3.01W
Taranto Italy 13 40.28N 17.14E
Taranto, Golfo di g. Italy 13 40.00N 17.20E
Tarapacá Colombia 60 2.52S 69.44W
Tarapoto Peru 60 6.31S 76.23W
Tarashcha Ukraine 15 49.35N 30.20E
Tarasovo Russian Fed. 18 66.14N 46.43E
Tarauacá Brazil 60 8.10S 70.46W
Tarauacá r. Brazil 60 6.42S 69.48W
Tarawera New Zealand 48 39.02S176.36E
Tarbagatay, Khrebet mts. Kazakhstan 24 47.00N 83.00E
Tarbat Ness c. U.K. 6 57.52N 3.46W
Tarbert Rep. of Ire. 7 52.34N 9.24W
Tarbert Strath. U.K. 6 55.51N 5.25W
Tarbert W. Isles U.K. 6 57.54N 6.49W
Tarbes France 11 43.14N 0.05E
Tarcento Italy 9 46.13N 13.13E
Tarcoola S.A. Australia 46 30.41S134.33E
Tarcoon Australia 47 30.19S146.43E
Tarcutta Australia 47 35.17S147.45E
Taree Australia 47 31.54S152.26E
Tarella Australia 46 30.55S143.06E
Tärendö Sweden 16 67.10N 22.38E
Ṭarfā, Wādī aṭ r. Egypt 32 28.36N 30.50E
Tarfaya Morocco 34 27.58N 12.55W
Tarifa Spain 10 36.01N 5.36W
Tarija Bolivia 62 21.31S 64.45W
Tarija d. Bolivia 62 21.40S 64.20W
Tarim He r. China 24 41.00N 83.30E
Taritatu r. Indonesia 27 2.54S138.27E
Tarkwa Ghana 38 5.16N 1.59W
Tarlac Phil. 27 15.29N120.35E
Tarm Denmark 17 55.55N 8.32E
Tarma Peru 60 11.28S 75.41W
Tarn r. France 11 44.15N 1.15E
Tärnaby Sweden 16 65.43N 15.16E
Tarnica mtn. Poland 15 49.05N 22.44E
Tarnobrzeg Poland 15 50.35N 21.41E
Tarnów Poland 15 50.01N 20.59E
Taro r. Italy 9 45.00N 10.15E
Taroom Australia 44 25.39S149.49E
Tarragona Spain 10 41.07N 1.15E
Tarran Hills Australia 47 32.27S146.27E
Tarrasa Spain 10 41.34N 2.00E
Tarsus Turkey 30 36.52N 34.52E
Tartagal Argentina 62 22.32S 63.50W
Tartu Estonia 18 58.20N 26.44E
Ṭarṭūs Syria 32 34.55N 35.52E
Tarutino Ukraine 15 46.09N 29.04E
Tarutung Indonesia 26 2.01N 98.54E
Tashauz Uzbekistan 20 41.49N 59.58E
Tashkent Uzbekistan 24 41.16N 69.13E
Tasiilaq see Ammassalik Greenland 51
Tasikmalaya Indonesia 26 7.20S108.16E
Tåsjön Sweden 16 64.15N 15.47E
Tasman B. New Zealand 48 41.00S173.15E
Tasmania d. Australia 45 42.00S147.00E
Tasman Mts. New Zealand 48 41.00S172.40E
Tasman Pen. Australia 45 43.08S147.51E
Tatabánya Hungary 15 47.34N 18.26E
Tatarsk Russian Fed. 20 55.14N 76.00E
Tatarskiy Proliv g. Russian Fed. 21 47.40N141.00E
Tateyama Japan 23 34.59N139.52E
Tathra Australia 47 36.44S149.58E
Tatnam, C. Canada 51 57.00N 91.00W
Tatong Australia 47 36.46S146.03E
Tatvan Turkey 30 38.31N 42.15E
Taubaté Brazil 59 23.00S 45.36W
Taumarunui New Zealand 48 38.53S175.16E
Taumaturgo Brazil 60 8.57S 72.48W
Taung R.S.A. 39 27.32S 24.46E
Taung-gyi Burma 29 20.49N 97.01E
Taunton U.K. 5 51.01N 3.07W
Taunus mts. Germany 14 50.07N 7.48E
Taupo New Zealand 48 38.42S176.06E
Taupo, L. New Zealand 48 38.45S175.30E
Taurage Lithuania 17 55.15N 22.17E
Tauranga New Zealand 48 37.42S176.11E
Taureau, Résr. Canada 55 46.43N 73.54W
Taurianova Italy 12 38.21N 16.01E
Taurus Mts. see Toros Dağlari mts. Turkey 30
Tavani Canada 51 62.00N 93.20W
Tavda Russian Fed. 20 58.04N 65.12E
Tavda r. Russian Fed. 20 57.40N 67.00E
Taveta Kenya 37 3.23S 37.42E
Tavira Portugal 10 37.07N 7.39W
Tavistock U.K. 5 50.33N 4.09W
Tavoy Burma 29 14.07N 98.18E
Taw r. U.K. 5 51.05N 4.05W
Tawas City U.S.A. 55 44.16N 83.33W
Tawau Malaysia 26 4.16N117.54E
Tawitawi i. Phil. 27 5.10N120.05E
Ṭawkar Sudan 35 18.26N 37.44E
Tay r. U.K. 6 56.21N 3.18W
Tay, L. Australia 43 33.00S120.52E
Tay, Loch U.K. 6 56.32N 4.08W
Tayabamba Peru 60 8.15S 77.15W
Tayan Indonesia 26 0.02S110.05E
Taylor, Mt. U.S.A. 54 35.14N107.37W
Taymā' Saudi Arabia 30 27.37N 38.30E
Taymyr, Ozero l. Russian Fed. 21 74.20N101.00E
Taymyr, Poluostrov Russian Fed. Russian Fed. 21 75.30N 99.00E
Tayport U.K. 6 56.27N 2.53W
Tayshet Russian Fed. 21 55.56N 98.01E
Tayside d. U.K. 6 56.35N 3.28W
Taytay Phil. 26 10.47N119.32E
Taz r. Russian Fed. 20 67.30N 78.50E
Taza Morocco 34 34.16N 4.01W
Tazovskiy Russian Fed. 20 67.28N 78.43E
Tbilisi Georgia 31 41.43N 44.48E
Tchad, Lac see Chad, L. Africa 38
Tchamba Togo 38 9.05N 1.27E
Tcholliré Cameroon 38 8.25N 14.10E
Tczew Poland 15 54.06N 18.47E
Te Anau New Zealand 48 45.25S167.43E
Te Anau, L. New Zealand 48 45.10S167.15E
Teapa Mexico 56 17.33N 92.57W
Te Araroa New Zealand 48 37.38S178.25E
Tebingtinggi Sumatera Selatan Indonesia 26 3.37S103.09E
Tebingtinggi Sumatera Utara Indonesia 26 3.20N 99.08E
Tebulos Mta mtn. Georgia 19 42.34N 45.17E
Techiman Ghana 38 7.36N 1.55W
Tecuci Romania 15 45.49N 27.27E
Tees r. U.K. 4 54.35N 1.11W
Tefé Brazil 60 3.24S 64.45W
Tefé r. Brazil 60 3.35S 64.47W
Tegal Indonesia 26 6.52S109.07E
Tegelen Neth. 8 51.20N 6.08E
Tegina Nigeria 38 10.06N 6.11E
Tego Australia 47 28.48S146.47E
Tegouma well Niger 38 15.33N 9.19E
Tegucigalpa Honduras 57 14.05N 87.14W
Teguidda I-n-Tessoum Niger 38 17.21N 6.32E
Tehamiyam Sudan 35 18.20N 36.32E
Téhini Ivory Coast 38 9.39N 3.32W
Tehrān Iran 31 35.40N 51.26E
Tehuacán Mexico 56 18.30N 97.26W
Tehuantepec Mexico 56 16.21N 95.13W
Tehuantepec, Golfo de g. Mexico 56 16.00N 95.00W
Tehuantepec, Istmo de f. Mexico 56 17.00N 94.30W
Teifi r. U.K. 5 52.05N 4.41W
Teignmouth U.K. 5 50.33N 3.30W
Teixeiras Brazil 59 20.37S 42.52W
Tejo r. Portugal 10 39.00N 8.57W
Te Kaha New Zealand 48 37.44S177.52E
Tekapo, L. New Zealand 48 43.35S170.30E
Tekax Mexico 57 20.12N 89.17W
Tekirdağ Turkey 13 40.59N 27.30E
Te Kuiti New Zealand 48 38.20S175.10E
Tela Honduras 57 15.56N 87.25W
Telavi Georgia 31 41.56N 45.30E
Tel Aviv-Yafo Israel 32 32.05N 34.46E
Telegraph Creek town Canada 50 57.56N131.10W
Telemark d. Norway 17 59.40N 8.30E
Teleneshty Moldavia 15 47.35N 28.17E
Teles Pires r. Brazil 61 7.20S 57.30W
Telfer Australia 42 21.42S122.13E
Telford U.K. 5 52.42N 2.30W
Telfs Austria 14 47.19N 11.04E
Telgte Germany 8 51.59N 7.46E
Tell Atlas mts. Algeria 34 36.10N 4.00E
Tell City U.S.A. 55 37.56N 86.46W
Teller U.S.A. 50 65.16N166.22N
Telpos-Iz mtn. Russian Fed. 18 63.56N 59.02E
Telsen Argentina 63 42.25S 67.00W
Telšiai Lithuania 17 55.59N 22.15E
Telukbetung Indonesia 26 5.28S105.16E
Teluk Intan Malaysia 26 4.00N101.00E
Tema Ghana 38 5.41N 0.01W
Temagami, L. Canada 55 47.00N 80.05W
Tembo Aluma Angola 36 7.42S 17.15E
Teme r. U.K. 5 52.10N 2.13W
Temir Kazakhstan 19 49.09N 57.06E
Temirtau Kazakhstan 20 50.05N 72.55E
Témiscaming Canada 55 46.44N 79.06W
Temora Australia 47 34.27S147.35E
Tempe U.S.A. 54 33.25N111.56W
Tempino Indonesia 26 1.55S103.23E
Tempio Italy 12 40.54N 9.06E
Temple U.S.A. 53 31.06N 97.22W
Temple B. Australia 44 12.10S143.04E
Templemore Rep. of Ire. 7 52.48N 7.51W
Templin Germany 14 53.07N 13.30E
Temuco Chile 63 38.44S 72.36W
Tenabo Mexico 56 20.03N 90.14W
Tenasserim Burma 29 12.05N 99.00E
Tenby U.K. 5 51.40N 4.42W
Tende France 11 44.05N 7.36E
Tende, Col de pass France / Italy 9 44.09N 7.34E
Ten Degree Channel Indian Oc. 29 10.00N 92.30E
Tenenkou Mali 38 14.25N 4.58W
Tenerife i. Canary Is. 34 28.10N 16.30W
Tengchong China 29 25.02N 98.28E
Tengiz, Ozero l. Kazakhstan 20 50.30N 69.00E
Teng Xian China 25 35.10N117.14E
Tenke Zaïre 36 10.34S 26.12E
Tenkodogo Burkina 38 11.47N 0.19W
Tennant Creek town Australia 44 19.31S134.15E
Tennessee d. U.S.A. 53 36.00N 86.00W
Tennessee r. U.S.A. 53 37.10N 88.25W
Tenosique Mexico 56 17.29N 91.26W
Tenryū Japan 23 34.52N137.49E
Tenryū r. Japan 23 34.39N137.47E
Tenterfield Australia 47 29.01S152.04E
Teófilo Otoni Brazil 59 17.52S 41.31W
Tepa Indonesia 27 7.52S129.31E
Tepelenë Albania 13 40.18N 20.01E
Tepic Mexico 56 21.30N104.51W
Teplice Czech Republic 14 50.40N 13.50E
Ter r. Spain 10 42.02N 3.10E
Téra Niger 38 14.01N 0.45E
Tera r. Portugal 10 38.55N 8.01W
Teramo Italy 12 42.40N 13.43E
Terang Australia 46 38.13S142.56E
Tercan Turkey 30 39.47N 40.23E
Terebovlya Ukraine 15 49.18N 25.44E
Terekhova Belorussia 15 52.13N 31.28E
Teresina Brazil 61 5.09S 42.46W
Teresópolis Brazil 59 22.26S 42.59W
Tergnier France 9 49.39N 3.18E
Termez Uzbekistan 20 37.15N 67.15E
Termination I. Australia 43 34.25S121.53E
Termini Italy 12 37.59N 13.42E
Términos, Laguna de b. Mexico 56 18.30N 91.30W
Termoli Italy 12 41.58N 14.59E
Ternate Indonesia 27 0.48N127.23E
Terneuzen Neth. 8 51.20N 3.50E
Terni Italy 12 42.34N 12.44E
Ternopol Ukraine 15 49.35N 25.39E
Terra Bella U.S.A. 54 35.58N119.03W
Terracina Italy 12 41.17N 13.15E
Terralba Italy 12 39.43N 8.38E
Terrassa see Tarrasa Spain 10
Terre Adélie f. Antarctica 64 80.00S140.00E
Terre Haute U.S.A. 55 39.27N 87.24W
Terschelling i. Neth. 8 53.25N 5.25E
Teruel Spain 10 40.21N 1.06W
Tervola Finland 16 66.05N 24.48E
Tešanj Bosnia-Herzegovina 15 44.37N 18.00E
Teslin Canada 50 60.10N132.42W
Teslin r. Canada 50 62.00N135.00W
Tessaoua Niger 38 13.46N 7.55E
Tessy-sur-Vire France 9 48.58N 1.04W
Test r. U.K. 5 50.55N 1.29W
Têt r. France 11 42.43N 3.00E
Tete Mozambique 37 16.10S 33.30E
Tete d. Mozambique 37 15.30S 33.00E
Teterev r. Ukraine 15 51.03N 30.30E
Teterow Germany 14 53.46N 12.34E
Teteven Bulgaria 13 42.55N 24.16E
Tetiyev Ukraine 15 49.22N 29.40E
Tétouan Morocco 34 35.34N 5.22W
Tetovo Macedonia 13 42.01N 20.58E
Teulada Italy 12 38.58N 8.46E
Teun i. Indonesia 27 6.59S129.08E
Teuva Finland 16 62.29N 21.44E
Tevere r. Italy 12 41.45N 12.16E
Teverya Israel 32 32.48N 35.32E
Teviot r. U.K. 6 55.36N 2.27W
Teviotdale f. U.K. 4 55.26N 2.46W
Teviothead U.K. 6 55.20N 2.56W
Tewkesbury U.K. 5 51.59N 2.09W
Texarkana Ark. U.S.A. 53 33.28N 94.02W
Texas Australia 47 28.50S151.09E
Texas d. U.S.A. 52 32.00N100.00W
Texel i. Neth. 8 53.05N 4.47E
Texoma, L. U.S.A. 53 34.00N 96.40W
Tezpur India 29 26.38N 92.49E
Thabana Ntlenyana mtn. Lesotho 39 29.28S 29.17E
Thabazimbi R.S.A. 39 24.36S 27.23E
Thādiq Saudi Arabia 31 25.18N 45.52E
Thailand Asia 29 16.00N102.00E
Thailand, G. of Asia 29 10.30N101.00E
Thai Nguyen Vietnam 26 21.31N105.55E
Thal Pakistan 28 33.22N 70.33E
Thale Luang l. Thailand 29 7.30N100.20E
Thallon Australia 47 28.39S148.49E
Thamarīt Oman 28 17.39N 54.02E
Thames r. Canada 55 42.19N 82.28W
Thames New Zealand 48 37.08S175.35E
Thames r. U.K. 5 51.30N 0.05E
Thāna India 28 19.14N 73.02E
Thanh Hóa Vietnam 26 19.50N105.48E
Thanjāvūr India 29 10.46N 79.09E
Thar Desert India 28 28.00N 72.00E
Thargomindah Australia 45 27.59S143.45E
Tharrawaddy Burma 29 17.37N 95.48E
Tharthār, Wādī ath r. Iraq 30 34.18N 43.07E
Thásos Greece 13 40.47N 24.42E
Thásos i. Greece 13 40.40N 24.39E
Thatcher U.S.A. 54 32.51N109.56W
Thaton Burma 29 17.00N 97.39E
Thaungdut Burma 29 24.26N 94.45E
Thayetmyo Burma 29 19.20N 95.18E
Thazi Burma 29 20.51N 96.05E
Thebes ruins Egypt 30 25.41N 32.40E
The Bight town Bahamas 57 24.19N 75.24W
The Cherokees, L. O' U.S.A. 53 36.45N 94.50W
The Cheviot mtn. U.K. 4 55.29N 2.10W
The Cheviot Hills U.K. 4 55.22N 2.24W
The Coorong g. Australia 46 36.00S139.30E
The Dalles town U.S.A. 54 45.36N121.10W
The Everglades f. U.S.A. 53 26.00N 80.30W
The Fens f. U.K. 5 55.10N 4.13W
The Gulf Asia 31 27.00N 50.00E
The Hague see 'sGravenhage Neth. 8
The Little Minch str. U.K. 6 57.40N 6.45W
Thelon r. Canada 51 64.23N 96.15W
The Machers f. U.K. 6 54.45N 4.28W
The Minch str. U.K. 6 58.10N 5.50W
The Needles c. U.K. 5 50.39N 1.35W
Theodore Australia 44 24.57S150.05E
Theodore Roosevelt L. U.S.A. 54 33.30N110.57W
The Pas Canada 51 53.50N101.15W
The Pennines hills U.K. 4 55.40N 2.20W
Thérain r. France 9 49.15N 2.27E
Theresa U.S.A. 55 44.13N 75.48W
The Rhinns f. U.K. 6 54.50N 5.02W
Thermaïkós Kólpos g. Greece 13 40.10N 23.00E
Thermopolis U.S.A. 54 43.39N108.13W
Thermopylae, Pass of Greece 13 38.47N 22.34E
The Rock town Australia 47 35.16S147.07E
The Salt L. Australia 46 30.05S142.10E
The Solent str. U.K. 5 50.45N 1.20W
The Sound str. Denmark / Sweden 17 55.35N 12.40E
Thessalon Canada 55 46.20N 83.34W
Thessaloníki Greece 13 40.38N 22.56E
Thetford U.K. 5 52.25N 0.44E
Thetford Mines town Canada 55 46.06N 71.18W
The Twins town Australia 46 30.00S135.16E
The Wash b. U.K. 4 52.55N 0.15E
The Weald f. U.K. 5 51.05N 0.20E
Thiene Italy 9 45.42N 11.29E
Thiers France 11 45.51N 3.33E
Thika Kenya 37 1.04S 37.04E
Thimbu Bhutan 29 27.29N 89.40E
Thingvallavatn l. Iceland 16 64.10N 21.10W
Thionville France 11 49.22N 6.11E
Thíra i. Greece 13 36.24N 25.27E
Thirsk U.K. 4 54.15N 1.20W
Thiruvananthapuram India 28 8.41N 76.57E
Thisted Denmark 17 56.57N 8.42E
Thistilfjördhur b. Iceland 16 66.11N 15.20W
Thistle I. Australia 46 35.00S136.09E
Thívai Greece 13 38.21N 23.19E
Thjórsá r. Iceland 16 63.53N 20.38W
Tholen i. Neth. 8 51.34N 4.07E
Thomas U.S.A. 55 39.09N 79.30W
Thomasville Fla. U.S.A. 53 30.50N 83.59W
Thompson Canada 51 55.45N 97.45W
Thompson Utah U.S.A. 54 38.58N109.43W
Thompsonville U.S.A. 55 44.32N 85.57W
Thomson r. Australia 44 25.11S142.53E
Thonburi Thailand 29 13.43N100.27E
Thórisvatn l. Iceland 16 64.15N 18.50W
Thorshavn Faroe Is. 16 62.02N 6.47W
Thorshöfn Iceland 16 66.12N 15.17W
Thouars France 11 46.59N 0.13W
Thrapston U.K. 5 52.24N 0.32W
Three Forks U.S.A. 54 45.54N111.33W
Three Rivers town Australia 42 25.07S119.09E
Three Sisters Mt. U.S.A. 54 44.10N121.46W
Thuin Belgium 8 50.21N 4.20E
Thule Greenland 51 77.30N 69.29W
Thun Switz. 14 46.46N 7.38E
Thunder Bay town Canada 55 48.25N 89.14W
Thunkar Bhutan 29 27.55N 91.00E
Thuringen d. Germany 14 50.50N 11.35E
Thüringer Wald mts. Germany 14 50.40N 10.50E
Thurles Rep. of Ire. 7 52.41N 7.50W
Thurloo Downs town Australia 46 29.18S143.30E
Thursday I. Australia 27 10.45S142.00E
Thursday Island town Australia 44 10.34S142.14E
Thurso U.K. 6 58.35N 3.32W
Thury-Harcourt France 9 48.59N 0.29W
Tianjin China 25 39.08N117.12E
Tianjin d. China 25 39.08N117.12E
Tianjun China 24 37.16N 98.52E
Tian Shan mts. Asia 24 42.00N 80.30E
Tianshui China 24 34.25N105.58E
Tibati Cameroon 38 6.25N 12.33E
Tiber r. see Tevere r. Italy 12
Tiberias see Teverya Israel 32
Tiberias, L. see Yam Kinneret l. Israel 32
Tibesti mts. Chad 34 21.00N 17.30E
Tibet d. see Xizang d. China 24
Tibetan Plateau see Qing Zang Gaoyuan f. China 24
Tibooburra Australia 46 29.28S142.04E
Tiburón, Isla Mexico 56 29.00N112.20W
Tîchît Mauritania 34 18.28N 9.30W
Ticino r. Italy 9 45.09N 9.12E
Ticonderoga U.S.A. 55 43.51N 73.26W
Tidaholm Sweden 17 58.11N 13.57E
Tidjikdja Mauritania 34 18.29N 11.31W
Tiel Neth. 8 51.53N 5.26E
Tieling China 25 42.18N123.49E
Tielt Belgium 8 51.00N 3.20E
Tienen Belgium 8 50.49N 4.56E
Tiénigbé Ivory Coast 38 8.11N 5.43W
Tientsin see Tianjin China 25
Tierp Sweden 17 60.20N 17.30E
Tierra Blanca Mexico 56 18.28N 96.12W
Tierra del Fuego d. Argentina 63 54.30S 67.00W
Tierra del Fuego i. Argentina / Chile 63 54.00S 69.00W
Tietar r. Spain 10 39.50N 6.00W
Tietê Brazil 59 23.04S 47.41W
Tiger U.S.A. 54 48.42N117.24W
Tigil Russian Fed. 21 57.49N158.40E
Tignère Cameroon 38 7.23N 12.37E
Tigre r. Venezuela 60 9.20N 62.30W
Tigris r. see Dijlah r. Asia 31
Tīh, Jabal at f. Egypt 32 28.50N 34.00E
Tihāmah f. Saudi Arabia 35 20.30N 40.30E
Tijuana Mexico 56 32.32N117.01W
Tikaré Burkina 38 13.16N 1.44W
Tikhoretsk Russian Fed. 19 45.52N 40.07E
Tikhvin Russian Fed. 18 59.35N 33.29E
Tikitiki New Zealand 48 37.47S178.25E
Tiksha Russian Fed. 18 64.04N 32.35E
Tiksi Russian Fed. 21 71.40N128.45E
Tilburg Neth. 8 51.34N 5.05E

Turon r. Australia 47 33.03S149.33E
Turov Belorussia 15 52.04N 27.40E
Turpan China 24 42.55N 89.06E
Turpan Pendi f. China 24 43.40N 89.00E
Turquino mtn. Cuba 57 20.05N 76.50W
Turriff U.K. 6 57.32N 2.28W
Turtkul Uzbekistan 31 41.30N 61.00E
Turukhansk Russian Fed. 21 65.21N 88.05E
Turya r. Ukraine 15 51.48N 24.52E
Tuscaloosa U.S.A. 53 33.12N 87.33W
Tuscarora U.S.A. 54 41.19N116.14W
Tutera see Tudela Spain 10
Tuticorin India 29 8.48N 78.10E
Tutóia Brazil 61 2.45S 42.16W
Tutrakan Bulgaria 13 44.02N 26.40E
Tuttlingen Germany 14 47.59N 8.49E
Tutuala Indonesia 27 8.24S127.15E
Tutubu Tanzania 37 5.28S 32.43E
Tuţūn Egypt 32 29.09N 30.46E
Tuul Gol r. Mongolia 24 48.53N104.35E
Tuvalu Pacific Oc. 40 8.00S178.00E
Tuxpan Mexico 56 21.00N 97.23W
Tuxtla Gutiérrez Mexico 56 16.45N 93.09W
Túy Spain 10 42.03N 8.39W
Tuz Gölü l. Turkey 30 38.45N 33.24E
Ţūz Khurmātū Iraq 31 34.53N 44.38E
Tuzla Bosnia-Herzegovina 13 44.33N 18.41E
Tvedestrand Norway 17 58.37N 8.55E
Tveitsund Norway 17 59.01N 8.32E
Tver' Russian Fed. 18 56.47N 35.57E
Tweed r. U.K. 6 55.46N 2.00W
Tweed Heads town Australia 47 28.13S153.33E
Twentynine Palms U.S.A. 54 34.08N116.03W
Twin Bridges town U.S.A. 54 45.33N112.20W
Twin Falls town U.S.A. 54 42.34N114.28W
Twins Creek r. Australia 46 29.10S139.27E
Twizel New Zealand 48 44.15S170.06E
Twofold B. Australia 47 37.06S149.55E
Twyford U.K. 5 51.01N 1.19W
Tyler Tex. U.S.A. 53 32.22N 95.18W
Tyndinskiy Russian Fed. 21 55.11N124.34E
Tyne r. U.K. 4 55.00N 1.25W
Tyne and Wear d. U.K. 4 54.57N 1.35W
Tynemouth U.K. 4 55.01N 1.24W
Tynset Norway 17 62.17N 10.47E
Tyre see Şūr Lebanon 32
Tyrifjorden l. Norway 17 60.02N 10.08E
Tyrone d. U.K. 7 54.35N 7.15W
Tyrone U.S.A. 55 40.40N 78.14W
Tyrrell r. Australia 46 35.28S142.55E
Tyrrell, L. Australia 46 35.22S142.50E
Tyrrhenian Sea Med. Sea 12 40.00N 12.00E
Tysnesöy i. Norway 17 60.00N 5.35E
Tyumen Russian Fed. 20 57.11N 65.29E
Tywi r. U.K. 5 51.46N 4.22W
Tzaneen R.S.A. 39 23.49S 30.10E

U

Uatumã r. Brazil 61 2.30S 57.40W
Uaupés Brazil 60 0.07S 67.05W
Uaupés r. Brazil 60 0.00S 67.10W
Ubá Brazil 59 21.08S 42.59W
Ubangi r. Congo/Zaïre 36 0.25S 17.50E
Ubatuba Brazil 59 23.26S 45.05W
Ubayyiḍ, Wādī al r. Iraq 30 32.04N 42.17E
Ubeda Spain 10 38.01N 3.22W
Uberaba Brazil 59 19.47S 47.57W
Uberlândia Brazil 59 18.57S 48.17W
Ubombo R.S.A. 39 27.35S 32.05E
Ubort r. Belorussia 15 52.06N 28.28E
Ubundu Zaïre 35 0.24S 25.28E
Ucayali r. Peru 60 4.40S 73.20W
Udaipur India 28 24.36N 73.47E
Udaquiola Argentina 63 36.35S 58.30W
Uddevalla Sweden 17 58.21N 11.55E
Uddjaur l. Sweden 16 65.55N 17.49E
Udine Italy 9 46.03N 13.15E
Udipi India 28 13.21N 74.45E
Udon Thani Thailand 29 17.29N102.46E
Uele r. Zaïre 36 4.08N 22.25E
Uelzen Germany 14 52.58N 10.34E
Ueno Japan 23 34.45N136.08E
Ufa Russian Fed. 18 54.45N 55.58E
Ufa r. Russian Fed. 18 54.45N 56.00E
Uffculme U.K. 5 50.45N 3.19W
Ugab r. Namibia 39 21.12S 13.37E
Ugalla r. Tanzania 37 5.43S 31.10E
Uganda Africa 37 2.00N 33.00E
Ugep Nigeria 38 5.48N 8.05E
Ughelli Nigeria 38 5.33N 6.00E
Uglegorsk Russian Fed. 21 49.01N142.04E
Uglovka Russian Fed. 18 58.13N 33.30E
Ugoma mtn. Zaïre 37 4.00S 28.45E
Ugra r. Russian Fed. 18 54.30N 36.10E
Uherske Hradiště Czech Republic 15 49.05N 17.28E
Uig U.K. 6 57.35N 6.22W
Uíge Angola 36 7.40S 15.09E
Uil Kazakhstan 19 49.08N 54.43E
Uil r. Kazakhstan 19 48.33N 52.25E
Uinta Mts. U.S.A. 54 40.45N110.05W
Uitenhage R.S.A. 39 33.46S 25.23E
Uithuizen Neth. 8 53.24N 6.41E
Uivlleq see Nanortalik Greenland 51
Uji r. Japan 23 34.53N135.48E
Ujiji Tanzania 37 4.55S 29.39E
Ujjain India 28 23.11N 75.50E
Ujpest Hungary 15 47.33N 19.05E
Ujście Poland 14 53.04N 16.43E
Ujung Pandang Indonesia 26 5.09S119.28E
Uka Russian Fed. 21 57.50N162.02E
Ukerewe I. Tanzania 37 2.00S 33.00E
Ukhta Russian Fed. 18 63.33N 53.44E
Ukiah U.S.A. 54 39.09N123.13W
Ukmerge Lithuania 18 55.14N 24.49E
Ukraine Europe 15 49.45N 27.00E
Ukwi Botswana 39 23.22S 20.30E
Ulaanbaatar Mongolia 24 47.54N106.52E
Ulaangom Mongolia 24 49.59N 92.00E
Ulan Bator see Ulaanbaatar Mongolia 24
Ulan-Ude Russian Fed. 24 51.55N107.40E
Ulan Ul Hu l. China 29 34.45N 90.25E
Ulcinj Yugo. 13 41.55N 19.11E
Ulenia, L. Australia 46 29.57S142.24E
Ulhāsnagar India 28 19.13N 73.07E
Uliastay Mongolia 24 47.42N 96.52E
Ulla r. Spain 10 42.38N 8.45W
Ulladulla Australia 47 35.21S150.25E
Ullånger Sweden 16 62.58N 18.16E
Ullapool U.K. 6 57.54N 5.10W
Ullswater l. U.K. 4 54.34N 2.52W
Ulm Germany 14 48.24N 10.00E
Ulongwé Mozambique 37 14.34S 34.21E
Ulricehamn Sweden 17 57.47N 13.25E
Ulsan S. Korea 25 35.32N129.21E
Ulsberg Norway 16 62.45N 9.59E
Ultima Australia 46 35.30S143.20E
Ulúa r. Honduras 57 15.50N 87.38W
Uluguru Mts. Tanzania 37 7.05S 37.40E
Uluru mtn. Australia 44 25.20S131.01E
Ulverston U.K. 4 54.13N 3.07W
Ulverstone Australia 45 41.09S146.10E
Ul'yanovsk Russian Fed. 18 54.19N 48.22E
Umaisha Nigeria 38 8.01N 7.12E
Umala Bolivia 62 17.21S 68.00W
Uman Ukraine 15 48.45N 30.10E
Umbria d. Italy 12 42.55N 12.10E
Ume r. Sweden 16 63.47N 20.16E
Ume r. Zimbabwe 39 17.00S 28.22E
Umeå Sweden 16 63.45N 20.20E
Umfors Sweden 16 65.56N 15.00E
Umfuli r. Zimbabwe 39 17.32S 29.23E
Umiat U.S.A. 50 69.25N152.20W
Umm-al-Qaywayn U.A.E. 31 25.32N 55.34E
Umm Durmān Sudan 35 15.37N 32.59E
Umm el Faḥm Israel 32 32.31N 35.09E
Umm Lajj Saudi Arabia 30 25.03N 37.17E
Umniati Zimbabwe 39 18.41S 29.45E
Umtata R.S.A. 39 31.35S 28.47E
Umuahia Nigeria 38 5.31N 7.26E
Umzimkulu R.S.A. 39 30.15S 29.56E
Umzimvubu R.S.A. 39 31.37S 29.32E
Una r. Bosnia-Herzegovina 13 45.16N 16.55E
Unalakleet U.S.A. 50 63.53N160.47W
'Unayzah Jordan 32 30.29N 35.48E
'Unayzah Saudi Arabia 31 26.05N 43.57E
'Unayzah, Jabal mtn. Iraq 30 32.15N 39.19E
Uncia Bolivia 62 18.27S 66.37W
Uncompahgre Peak U.S.A. 54 38.04N107.28W
Uncompahgre Plateau f. U.S.A. 54 38.30N108.25W
Underberg R.S.A. 39 29.46S 29.26E
Underbool Australia 46 35.10S141.50E
Unecha Russian Fed. 15 52.52N 32.42E
Ungarie Australia 47 33.38S147.00E
Ungava, Péninsule d' pen. Canada 51 60.00N 74.00W
Ungava B. Canada 51 59.00N 67.30W
União Brazil 61 4.35S 42.52W
União da Vitória Brazil 59 26.13S 51.05W
Unimak I. U.S.A. 50 54.50N164.00W
Unini Peru 60 10.41S 73.59W
Uniondale R.S.A. 39 33.39S 23.07E
Union Gap U.S.A. 54 46.34N120.34W
Uniontown U.S.A. 55 39.54N 79.44W
United Arab Emirates Asia 31 24.00N 54.00E
United Kingdom Europe 3 54.00N 2.00W
United States of America N. America 52 39.00N100.00W
Unna Germany 8 51.32N 7.41E
Unst i. U.K. 6 60.45N 0.55W
Ünye Turkey 30 41.09N 37.15E
Upata Venezuela 60 8.02N 62.25W
Upernavik Greenland 51 72.50N 56.00W
Upington R.S.A. 39 28.26S 21.12E
Upper East d. Ghana 38 10.40N 0.20W
Upper Egypt see Aş Şa'īd f. Egypt 30
Upper Hutt New Zealand 48 41.07S175.04E
Upper Klamath L. U.S.A. 54 42.23N122.55W
Upper Lough Erne U.K 7 54.13N 7.32W
Upper Tean U.K. 4 52.57N 1.59W
Upper Volta see Burkina Africa 38
Upper West d. Ghana 38 10.25N 2.00W
Upper Yarra Resr. Australia 47 37.43S145.56E
Uppsala Sweden 17 59.52N 17.38E
Uppsala d. Sweden 17 60.10N 17.50E
Uqlat aş Şuqūr Saudi Arabia 30 25.50N 42.12E
Ur ruins Iraq 31 30.55N 46.07E
Uracoa Venezuela 60 9.03N 62.27W
Uraga-suido str. Japan 23 35.10N139.42E
Ural r. Kazakhstan 19 47.00N 52.00E
Uralla Australia 47 30.40S151.31E
Ural Mts. see Ural'skiye Gory mts. Russian Fed. 18
Ural'sk Kazakhstan 19 51.19N 51.20E
Ural'skiye Gory mts. Russian Fed. 18 60.00N 59.00E
Urana Australia 47 35.21S146.19E
Urana, L. Australia 47 35.21S146.19E
Urandangi Australia 44 21.36S138.18E
Uranium City Canada 50 59.32N108.43W
Urapunga Australia 44 14.41S134.34E
Uraricoera r. Brazil 60 3.10N 60.30W
Urawa Japan 23 35.51N139.39E
Uray Russian Fed. 20 60.11N 65.00E
Urbino Italy 12 43.43N 12.38E
Urcos Peru 60 13.40S 71.38W
Urda Kazakhstan 19 48.44N 47.30E
Urdzhar Kazakhstan 20 47.06N 81.33E
Ure r. U.K. 4 54.05N 1.20W
Urechye Belorussia 15 52.59N 27.50E
Uren Russian Fed. 18 57.30N 45.50E
Urengoy Russian Fed. 20 65.59N 78.30E
Ures Mexico 56 29.26N110.24W
Ürgüp Turkey 30 38.39N 34.55E
Uribia Colombia 60 11.43N 72.16W
Urisino Australia 46 29.44S143.49E
Urjala Finland 17 61.05N 23.32E
Urk Neth. 8 52.40N 5.36E
Urlingford Rep. of Ire. 7 52.44N 7.35W
Urmia, L. see Daryācheh-ye Orūmīyeh l. Iran 31
Ursus Poland 15 52.12N 20.53E
Uruaçu Brazil 61 14.30S 49.10W
Uruapan Mexico 56 19.26N102.04W
Urubamba Peru 60 13.20S 72.07W
Urubamba r. Peru 60 10.43S 73.55W
Urucará Brazil 61 2.32S 57.45W
Uruçui Brazil 61 7.14S 44.33W
Uruguaiana Brazil 63 29.45S 57.05W
Uruguay r. Argentina/Uruguay 63 34.00S 58.30W
Uruguay S. America 59 33.15S 56.00W
Ürümqi China 24 43.43N 87.38E
Urun P.N.G. 44 8.36S147.15E
Urunga Australia 47 30.30S152.28E
Urup r. Russian Fed. 19 44.59N 41.12E
Urzhum Russian Fed. 18 57.08N 50.00E
Urziceni Romania 13 44.43N 26.38E
Usa r. Russian Fed. 18 65.58N 56.35E
Uşak Turkey 30 38.42N 29.25E
Usakos Namibia 39 22.02S 15.35E
Usambara Mts. Tanzania 37 4.45S 38.25E
Ushant i. see Ouessant, Île d' i. France 11
Ush-Tobe Kazakhstan 24 45.15N 77.59E
Ushuaia Argentina 63 54.47S 68.20W
Ushumun Russian Fed. 21 52.48N126.27E
Usisya Malaŵi 37 11.10S 34.12E
Usk r. U.K. 5 51.34N 2.59W
Uskedal Norway 17 59.56N 5.52E
Üsküdar Turkey 13 41.00N 29.03E
Usman Russian Fed. 19 52.02N 39.43E
Usovo Ukraine 15 51.20N 28.01E
Uspenskiy Kazakhstan 20 48.41N 72.43E
Ussuriysk Russian Fed. 25 43.48N131.59E
Ustaoset Norway 17 60.30N 8.04E
Ustica i. Italy 12 38.42N 13.11E
Ust'-Ilga Russian Fed. 21 54.59N105.00E
Ústí nad Labem Czech Republic 14 50.41N 14.00E
Ust Ishim Russian Fed. 20 57.45N 71.05E
Ustka Poland 14 54.35N 16.50E
Ust'kamchatsk Russian Fed. 21 56.14N162.28E
Ust-Kamenogorsk Kazakhstan 20 50.00N 82.40E
Ust Kulom Russian Fed. 18 61.34N 53.40E
Ust Kut Russian Fed. 21 56.40N105.50E
Ust Lyzha Russian Fed. 18 65.45N 56.38E
Ust'Maya Russian Fed. 21 60.25N134.28E
Ust Nem Russian Fed. 18 61.38N 54.50E
Ust Olenëk Russian Fed. 21 72.59N120.00E
Ust-Omchug Russian Fed. 21 61.08N149.38E
Ust Port Russian Fed. 20 69.44N 84.23E
Ust Tapsuy Russian Fed. 18 62.25N 61.42E
Ust'Tsilma Russian Fed. 18 65.28N 53.09E
Ust-Tungir Russian Fed. 21 55.25N120.15E
Ust Ura Russian Fed. 18 63.06N 44.41E
Ust Vaga Russian Fed. 18 62.42N 42.45E
Ust Vym Russian Fed. 18 62.15N 50.25E
Ustyurt, Plato f. Kazakhstan 19 43.30N 55.00E
Usu China 24 44.27N 84.37E
Usumacinta r. Mexico 56 18.22N 92.40W
U.S. Virgin Is. C. America 57 18.30N 65.00W
Ut Belorussia 15 52.18N 31.10E
Utah d. U.S.A. 54 39.37N112.28W
Utah L. U.S.A. 54 40.13N111.49W
'Utaybah, Buḥayrat al l. Syria 32 33.31N 36.37E
Utengule Tanzania 37 8.55S 35.43E
Utete Tanzania 37 8.00S 38.49E
Utiariti Brazil 60 13.02S 58.17W
Utica N.Y. U.S.A. 55 43.05N 75.14W
Utiel Spain 10 39.33N 1.13W
Utopia Australia 44 22.14S134.33E
Utrecht Neth. 8 52.04N 5.07E
Utrecht d. Neth. 8 52.04N 5.10E
Utrecht R.S.A. 39 27.38S 30.19E
Utrera Spain 10 37.10N 5.47W
Utsjoki Finland 16 69.53N 27.00E
Utsunomiya Japan 25 36.33N139.52E
Utta Russian Fed. 19 46.24N 46.01E
Uttaradit Thailand 29 17.38N100.05E
Uttar Pradesh d. India 29 27.40N 80.00E
Uummannarsuaq see Farvel, Kap c. Greenland 51
Uusikaupunki Finland 17 60.48N 21.25E
Uusimaa d. Finland 17 60.30N 25.00E
Uvalde U.S.A. 52 29.14N 99.49W
Uvarovichi Belorussia 15 52.35N 30.44E
Uvat Russian Fed. 20 59.10N 68.49E
Uvinza Tanzania 37 5.08S 30.23E
Uvira Zaïre 37 3.22S 29.06E
Uvs Nuur l. Mongolia 24 50.30N 92.30E
Uwajima Japan 25 33.13N132.32E
Uwayl Sudan 35 8.46N 27.24E
Uyo Nigeria 38 5.01N 7.56E
Uyuni Bolivia 62 20.28S 66.50W
Uyuni, Salar de f. Bolivia 62 20.20S 67.42W
Uzbekistan Asia 20 42.00N 63.00E
Uzda Belorussia 15 53.28N 27.11E
Uzh r. Ukraine 15 51.15N 30.12E
Uzhgorod Ukraine 15 48.38N 22.15E
Užice Yugo. 15 43.52N 19.51E
Užice Yugo. 15 43.52N 19.51E

V

Vaagö i. Faroe Is. 16 62.03N 7.14W
Vaal r. R.S.A. 39 29.04S 23.37E
Vaala Finland 16 64.26N 26.48E
Vaal Dam R.S.A. 39 26.51S 28.08E
Vaasa Finland 16 63.06N 21.36E
Vaasa d. Finland 16 62.50N 22.50E
Vác Hungary 15 47.49N 19.10E
Vadodara India 28 22.19N 73.14E
Vado Ligure Italy 9 44.17N 8.27E
Vadsö Norway 16 70.05N 29.46E
Vaduz Liech. 14 47.08N 9.32E
Vaeröy i. Norway 16 67.40N 12.40E
Vaga r. Russian Fed. 18 62.45N 42.48E
Vågåmo Norway 17 61.53N 9.06E
Vaggeryd Sweden 17 57.30N 14.07E
Váh r. Slovakia 15 47.40N 17.50E
Vahsel B. Antarctica 64 77.00S 38.00W
Vailly-sur-Aisne France 9 49.25N 3.31E
Vakarai Sri Lanka 29 8.08N 81.26E
Vålådalen Sweden 16 63.09N 13.00E
Valavsk Belorussia 15 51.40N 28.38E
Valcheta Argentina 63 40.40S 66.10W
Valdagno Italy 9 45.39N 11.18E
Valday Russian Fed. 18 57.59N 33.10E
Valdayskaya Vozvyshennost mts. Russian Fed. 18 57.10N 33.00E
Valdemārpils Latvia 17 57.22N 22.35E
Valdemarsvik Sweden 17 58.12N 16.36E
Valdepeñas Spain 10 38.46N 3.24W
Valdés, Pen. Argentina 63 42.30S 64.00W
Valdez U.S.A. 50 61.07N146.17W
Val d'Isère France 9 45.27N 6.59E
Valdivia Chile 63 39.46S 73.15W
Val d'Oise d. France 9 49.10N 2.10E
Val d'Or town Canada 55 48.07N 77.47W
Valença Bahia Brazil 61 13.22S 39.06W
Valença R. de Janeiro Brazil 59 22.14S 43.45W
Valença Portugal 10 42.02N 8.38W
Valence France 11 44.56N 4.54E
Valencia Spain 10 39.29N 0.24W
Valencia d. Spain 10 39.30N 0.40W
Valencia Venezuela 60 10.14N 67.59W
Valencia, Golfo de g. Spain 10 39.38N 0.20W
Valencia de Alcántara Spain 10 39.25N 7.14
Valenciennes France 8 50.22N 3.32E
Vale of Evesham f. U.K. 5 52.05N 1.55W
Vale of Pewsey f. U.K. 5 51.21N 1.45W
Vale of York f. U.K. 4 54.12N 1.25W
Valera Venezuela 60 9.21N 70.38W
Valga Estonia 18 57.44N 26.00E
Valinco, Golfe de g. France 11 41.40N 8.50E
Valjevo Yugo. 15 44.16N 19.56E
Valkeakoski Finland 17 61.16N 24.02E
Valkenswaard Neth. 8 51.21N 5.27E
Valladolid Mexico 57 20.41N 88.12W
Valladolid Spain 10 41.39N 4.45W
Vall de Uxó town Spain 10 39.49N 0.15W
Valle Norway 17 59.12N 7.32E
Valle d'Aosta d. Italy 9 45.45N 7.25E
Valle de la Pascua Venezuela 60 9.15N 66.00W
Valledupar Colombia 60 10.31N 73.16W
Valle Edén Uruguay 63 31.50S 56.09W
Vallegrande Bolivia 62 18.29S 64.06W
Vallenar Chile 62 28.35S 70.46W
Valletta Malta 12 35.53N 14.31E
Valley City U.S.A. 52 46.57N 97.58W
Valley Falls town U.S.A. 54 42.29N120.16W
Valleyfield Canada 55 45.15N 74.08W
Vallgrund i. Finland 16 63.12N 21.14E
Valls Spain 10 41.18N 1.15E
Valmiera Latvia 18 57.32N 25.29E
Valnera mtn. Spain 10 43.10N 3.40W
Valognes France 9 49.31N 1.28W
Valparaíso Chile 63 33.02S 71.38W
Valparaíso Mexico 56 22.46N103.34W
Vals, Tanjung c. Indonesia 27 8.30S137.30E
Valverde Dom. Rep. 57 19.37N 71.04W
Valverde del Camino Spain 10 37.35N 6.45W
Vammala Finland 17 61.20N 22.54E
Van Turkey 30 38.28N 43.20E
Van Blommestein Meer, W.J. resr. Surinam 61 4.45N 55.05W
Vancouver Canada 50 49.13N123.06W
Vancouver U.S.A. 54 45.39N122.40W
Vancouver I. Canada 50 50.00N126.00W
Vanderbilt U.S.A. 55 45.09N 84.39W
Vanderlin I. Australia 44 15.44S137.02E
Van Diemen, C. Australia 44 16.31S139.41E
Van Diemen G. Australia 44 11.50S132.00E
Vandry Canada 55 47.50N 73.34W
Vänern l. Sweden 17 59.00N 13.15E
Vänersborg Sweden 17 58.22N 12.19E
Vang Norway 17 61.10N 8.40E
Vanga Kenya 37 4.37S 39.13E
Van Gölü l. Turkey 30 38.35N 42.52E
Vanimo P.N.G. 27 2.40S141.17E
Vankarem Russian Fed. 21 67.50N175.51E
Vanna i. Norway 16 70.10N 19.40E
Vännäs Sweden 16 63.58N 19.48E
Vannes France 11 47.40N 2.44W
Vanrhynsdorp R.S.A. 39 31.37S 18.42E
Vansbro Sweden 17 60.31N 14.13E
Vantaa Finland 17 60.13N 25.01E
Vanua Levu i. Fiji 40 16.33S179.15E
Vanuatu Pacific Oc. 40 16.00S167.00E
Van Wert U.S.A. 55 40.53N 84.36W
Vanzylsrus R.S.A. 39 26.51S 22.03E
Vapnyarka Ukraine 15 48.31N 28.44E
Var r. France 14 43.39N 7.11E
Varades France 9 47.23N 1.02W
Varallo Italy 9 45.49N 8.15E
Varāmīn Iran 31 35.20N 51.39E
Vārānasi India 29 25.20N 83.00E
Varangerfjorden est. Norway 16 70.00N 30.00E
Varangerhalvöya pen. Norway 16 70.25N 29.30E
Varaždin Croatia 12 46.18N 16.20E
Varazze Italy 9 44.22N 8.34E
Varberg Sweden 17 57.06N 12.15E
Vardar r. Macedonia see Axiós r. Greece 13
Varde Denmark 17 55.38N 8.29E
Varel Germany 8 53.24N 8.08E
Varennes France 11 46.19N 3.24E
Varese Italy 9 45.48N 8.48E
Varese Ligure Italy 9 44.22N 9.37E
Varginha Brazil 59 21.33S 45.25W
Varley Australia 43 32.48S119.31E
Värmland d. Sweden 17 59.55N 13.00E
Varna Bulgaria 15 43.13N 27.57E
Värnamo Sweden 17 57.11N 14.02E
Várpalota Hungary 15 47.12N 18.09E
Vartofta Sweden 17 58.06N 13.40E
Varzo Italy 9 46.12N 8.15E
Varzy France 9 47.21N 3.23E
Vasa see Vaasa Finland 16
Vashka r. Russian Fed. 18 64.55N 45.50E
Vasilkov Ukraine 15 50.12N 30.15E
Vaslui Romania 15 46.38N 27.44E
Västerås Sweden 17 59.37N 16.33E
Västerbotten d. Sweden 16 64.50N 18.10E
Västerdal r. Sweden 17 60.33N 15.08E
Västernorrland d. Sweden 16 63.20N 17.30E
Västervik Sweden 17 57.45N 16.38E
Västmanland d. Sweden 17 59.50N 16.15E
Vasto Italy 12 42.07N 14.42E
Vatan France 11 47.05N 1.48E
Vatican City Italy 12 41.54N 12.27E
Vatiua Mozambique 37 14.15S 37.22E
Vatnajökull mts. Iceland 16 64.20N 17.00W
Vatneyri Iceland 16 65.36N 23.59W
Vatra Dornei Romania 15 47.21N 25.21E
Vättern l. Sweden 17 58.30N 14.30E
Vaughn Mont. U.S.A. 54 47.35N111.34W
Vaughn N.Mex. U.S.A. 52 34.36N105.13W
Vaupés r. Colombia 60 0.20N 69.00W
Vavuniya Sri Lanka 29 8.45N 80.30E
Växjö Sweden 17 56.52N 14.49E
Vaygach Russian Fed. 20 70.28N 58.59E
Vaygach, Ostrov i. Russian Fed. 18 70.00N 59.00E
Vecht r. Neth. 8 52.39N 6.01E
Vecsés Hungary 15 47.26N 19.19E
Veddige Sweden 17 57.16N 12.19E
Veendam Neth. 8 53.08N 6.52E
Veenendaal Neth. 8 52.03N 5.32E
Vega i. Norway 16 65.39N 11.50E
Veghel Neth. 8 51.37N 5.35E
Vegreville Canada 50 53.30N112.02W
Veinticinco de Mayo Argentina 63 35.25S 60.11W
Vejen Denmark 17 55.29N 9.09E
Vejer Spain 10 36.15N 5.59W
Vejle Denmark 17 55.42N 9.32E
Velddrif R.S.A. 39 32.47S 18.09E
Vélez Málaga Spain 10 36.48N 4.05W
Vélez Rubio Spain 10 37.41N 2.05W
Velhas r. Brazil 59 17.20S 44.55W
Velikiye-Luki Russian Fed. 18 56.19N 30.31E
Velikiy Ustyug Russian Fed. 18 60.48N 45.15E
Veliko Tŭrnovo Bulgaria 13 43.04N 25.39E
Velizh Russian Fed. 18 55.36N 31.13E
Velletri Italy 12 41.41N 12.47E
Vellore India 29 12.56N 79.09E
Velsen Neth. 8 52.28N 4.39E
Velsk Russian Fed. 18 61.05N 42.06E
Veluwe f. Neth. 8 52.17N 5.45E
Vemdalen Sweden 16 62.29N 13.55E
Venado Tuerto Argentina 63 33.45S 61.56W
Venaria Italy 9 45.08N 7.38E
Vence France 9 43.43N 7.07E
Venda Africa 39 22.40S 30.40E
Vendas Novas Portugal 10 38.41N 8.27W
Vendeuvre-sur-Barse France 9 48.14N 4.28E
Vendôme France 9 47.48N 1.04E
Veneto d. Italy 9 45.25N 11.50E
Venev Russian Fed. 18 54.22N 38.15E
Venezia Italy 9 45.26N 12.20E
Venezuela S. America 60 7.00N 65.20W
Venezuela, Golfo de g. Venezuela 60 11.30N 71.00W
Vengurla India 28 15.52N 73.38E
Veniaminof Mtn. U.S.A. 50 56.05N159.20W
Venice see Venezia Italy 9
Venice, G. of Med. Sea 14 45.20N 13.00E
Venlo Neth. 8 51.22N 6.10E
Venraij Neth. 8 51.32N 5.58E
Venta r. Latvia 17 57.24N 21.33E
Ventersdorp R.S.A. 39 26.19S 26.48E
Ventimiglia Italy 9 43.47N 7.36E
Ventnor U.K. 5 50.35N 1.12W
Ventspils Latvia 17 57.24N 21.36E
Ventuari r. Venezuela 60 4.00N 67.35W
Venus B. Australia 47 38.40S145.43E
Vera Argentina 59 29.31S 60.30W
Vera Spain 10 37.15N 1.51W
Veracruz Mexico 56 19.11N 96.10W
Veracruz d. Mexico 56 18.00N 95.00W
Verāval India 28 20.53N 70.28E
Verbania Italy 9 45.56N 8.33E
Vercelli Italy 9 45.19N 8.26E
Verde r. Argentina 63 42.10S 65.03W
Verde r. Brazil 62 19.11S 50.44W
Verden Germany 14 52.55N 9.13E
Verdon r. France 11 43.42N 5.39E
Verdun Canada 55 45.28N 73.35W
Verdun Meuse France 11 49.10N 5.24E
Vereeniging R.S.A. 39 26.40S 27.55E
Vergelee R.S.A. 39 25.46S 24.09E
Verín Spain 10 41.55N 7.26W
Verkhniy Baskunchak Russian Fed. 19 48.14N 46.44E
Verkhniy Lyulyukary Russian Fed. 18 65.45N 64.28E
Verkhniy Shar Russian Fed. 18 68.21N 50.45E
Verkhniy Ufaley Russian Fed. 18 56.05N 60.14E
Verkhnyaya Taymyra r. Russian Fed. 21 74.10N 99.50E
Verkhnyaya Tura Russian Fed. 18 58.22N 59.50E
Verkhovye Russian Fed. 18 52.49N 37.14E
Verkhoyansk Russian Fed. 21 67.25N133.25E
Verkhoyanskiy Khrebet mts. Russian Fed. 21 66.00N130.00E
Vermenton France 9 47.40N 3.42E
Vermilion Canada 50 53.21N110.52W
Vermilion U.S.A. 55 41.24N 82.21W
Vermont d. U.S.A. 55 43.50N 72.45W
Vernal U.S.A. 54 40.27N109.32W
Verneuil France 9 48.44N 0.56E
Vernon Canada 50 50.16N119.16W
Vernon France 9 49.05N 1.29E
Véroia Greece 13 40.31N 22.12E

Verona Italy **9** 45.27N 10.59E
Verónica Argentina **63** 35.24S 57.22W
Verrès Italy **9** 45.40N 7.42E
Versailles France **9** 48.48N 2.08E
Vert, Cap *c.* Senegal **34** 14.45N 17.25W
Vertou France **11** 47.10N 1.28W
Vertus France **9** 48.54N 4.00E
Verviers Belgium **8** 50.36N 5.52E
Vervins France **9** 49.50N 3.54E
Vesanto Finland **16** 62.56N 26.25E
Veselí nad Lužnicí Czech Republic **14** 49.11N 14.43E
Vesle *r.* France **9** 49.23N 3.38E
Vesoul France **14** 47.38N 6.09E
Vest-Agder *d.* Norway **17** 58.30N 7.10E
Vestfjorden *est.* Norway **16** 68.10N 15.00E
Vestfold *d.* Norway **17** 59.20N 10.10E
Vestmanhavn Faroe Is. **16** 62.09N 7.11W
Vestmannaeyjar *is.* Iceland **16** 63.30N 20.20W
Vestvågöy *i.* Norway **16** 68.10N 13.50E
Vesuvio *mtn.* Italy **12** 40.48N 14.25E
Vesyegonsk Russian Fed. **18** 58.38N 37.19E
Veszprém Hungary **15** 47.06N 17.55E
Vésztö Hungary **15** 46.55N 21.16E
Vetka Belorussia **15** 52.35N 31.13E
Vetlanda Sweden **17** 57.26N 15.04E
Vetluga Russian Fed. **18** 57.50N 45.42E
Vetluga *r.* Russian Fed. **18** 56.18N 46.19E
Vettore, Monte *mtn.* Italy **12** 42.50N 13.18E
Veurne Belgium **8** 51.04N 2.40E
Vevelstad Norway **16** 65.43N 12.30E
Vézelise France **11** 48.29N 6.05E
Vézère *r.* France **11** 44.53N 0.55E
Vezhen *mtn.* Bulgaria **13** 42.45N 24.22E
Viacha Bolivia **60** 16.40S 68.17W
Viadana Italy **9** 44.56N 10.31E
Viana Brazil **61** 3.13S 45.00W
Viana Portugal **10** 38.20N 8.00W
Viana do Castelo Portugal **10** 41.41N 8.50W
Viangchan *see* Vientiane Laos **29**
Viar *r.* Spain **10** 37.45N 5.54W
Viareggio Italy **9** 43.52N 10.14E
Viborg Denmark **17** 56.26N 9.24E
Vibo Valentia Italy **12** 38.40N 16.06E
Vibraye France **9** 48.03N 0.44E
Vic *see* Vich Spain **10**
Vicente López Argentina **63** 34.32S 58.29W
Vicenza Italy **9** 45.33N 11.32E
Vich Spain **10** 41.56N 2.16E
Vichada *r.* Colombia **60** 4.58N 67.35W
Vichuga Russian Fed. **18** 57.12N 41.50E
Vichy France **11** 46.07N 3.25E
Vicksburg U.S.A. **53** 32.21N 90.51W
Viçosa Alagoas Brazil **61** 9.22S 36.10W
Viçosa Minas Gerais Brazil **59** 20.45S 42.53W
Victor Harbor Australia **46** 35.36S138.35E
Victoria Argentina **63** 32.40S 60.10W
Victoria *d.* Australia **47** 37.20S145.00E
Victoria *r.* Australia **42** 15.12S129.43E
Victoria Canada **50** 48.26N123.20W
Victoria Chile **63** 38.13S 72.20W
Victoria U.S.A. **53** 28.49N 97.01W
Victoria, L. Africa **37** 1.00S 33.00E
Victoria, L. Australia **46** 34.00S141.15E
Victoria, Mt. P.N.G. **44** 8.55S147.35E
Victoria Beach *town* Canada **51** 50.43N 96.33W
Victoria Falls *f.* Zimbabwe/Zambia **39** 17.58S 25.45E
Victoria I. Cañada **50** 71.00N110.00W
Victoria L. Australia **46** 32.29S143.22E
Victoria Nile *r.* Uganda **37** 2.14N 31.20E
Victoria River *town* Australia **42** 15.36S131.06E
Victoria River Downs *town* Australia **44** 16.24S131.00E
Victoriaville Canada **55** 46.04N 71.57W
Victoria West R.S.A. **39** 31.24S 23.07E
Victorica Argentina **63** 36.15S 65.25W
Videle Romania **15** 44.16N 25.31E
Viderö *i.* Faroe Is. **16** 62.20N 6.30W
Vidin Bulgaria **15** 43.58N 22.51E
Viedma Argentina **63** 40.50S 63.00W
Viedma, L. Argentina **63** 49.40S 72.30W
Vienna *see* Wien Austria **14**
Vienne France **11** 45.32N 4.54E
Vienne *r.* France **11** 47.13N 0.05W
Vientiane Laos **29** 18.01N102.48E
Vieques *i.* Puerto Rico **57** 18.08N 65.30W
Viersen Germany **8** 51.16N 6.22E
Vierwaldstätter See *l.* Switz. **14** 47.10N 8.50E
Vierzon France **9** 47.14N 2.03E
Vietnam Asia **26** 15.00N108.00E
Vieux-Condé France **8** 50.29N 3.31E
Vigan Phil. **27** 17.35N120.23E
Vigevano Italy **9** 45.19N 8.51E
Vignemale, Pic de *mtn.* France **11** 42.46N 0.08W
Vigo Spain **10** 42.15N 8.44W
Vigrestad Norway **17** 58.34N 5.42E
Vijayawāda India **29** 16.34N 80.40E
Vik Norway **16** 65.19N 12.10E
Vikajärvi Finland **16** 66.37N 26.12E
Vikeke Indonesia **27** 8.42S126.30E
Vikersund Norway **17** 59.59N 10.02E
Vikna *i.* Norway **16** 64.52N 10.57E
Vikulovo Russian Fed. **20** 56.51N 70.30E
Vila Vanuatu **40** 17.44S168.19E
Vila da Maganja Mozambique **37** 17.25S 37.32E
Vila Franca Portugal **10** 38.57N 8.59W
Vilaine *r.* France **11** 47.30N 2.25W
Vilanculos Mozambique **39** 21.59S 35.16E
Vilanova i la Geltrú *see* Villanueva y Geltrú Spain **10**
Vila Real Portugal **10** 41.17N 7.45W
Vila Real de Santo António Portugal **10** 37.12N 7.25W
Vila Velha Brazil **59** 20.20S 40.17W
Vileyka Belorussia **15** 54.30N 26.50E
Vilhelmina Sweden **16** 64.37N 16.39E
Vilhena Brazil **60** 12.40S 60.08W
Viliga Kushka Russian Fed. **21** 61.35N156.55E
Viljandi Estonia **18** 58.22N 25.30E
Vilkavišhkis Lithuania **15** 54.39N 23.02E
Vil'kitskogo, Proliv *str.* Russian Fed. **21** 77.57N102.30E
Vilkovo Ukraine **15** 45.28N 29.32E
Villa Angela Argentina **62** 27.34S 60.45W
Villa Bella Bolivia **62** 10.23S 65.24W
Villablino Spain **10** 42.57N 6.19W
Villacañas Spain **10** 39.38N 3.20W
Villach Austria **14** 46.37N 13.51E
Villa Clara Argentina **63** 31.46S 58.50W
Villa Constitución Argentina **63** 33.14S 60.21W
Villa Dolores Argentina **62** 31.58S 65.12W
Villafranca di Verona Italy **9** 45.21N 10.50E
Villagarcía Spain **10** 42.35N 8.45W
Villaguay Argentina **63** 31.55S 59.00W
Villahermosa Mexico **56** 18.00N 92.53W
Villa Hernandarias Argentina **63** 31.15S 59.58W
Villa Huidobro Argentina **63** 34.50S 64.34W
Villaines-la-Juhel France **9** 48.21N 0.17W
Villajoyosa Spain **10** 38.31N 0.14W
Villalba Spain **10** 43.18N 7.41W
Villa María Argentina **62** 32.25S 63.15W
Villa Montes Bolivia **62** 21.15S 63.30W
Villanueva de la Serena Spain **10** 38.58N 5.48W
Villaputzu Italy **12** 39.28N 9.35E
Villarrica Chile **63** 39.15S 72.15W
Villarrica Paraguay **59** 25.45S 56.28W
Villarrobledo Spain **10** 39.16N 2.36W
Villa San José Argentina **63** 32.12S 58.15W
Villasayas Spain **10** 41.24N 2.39W
Villavicencio Colombia **60** 4.09N 73.38W
Villaviciosa Spain **10** 43.29N 5.26W
Villazón Bolivia **62** 22.06S 65.36W
Villedieu France **9** 48.50N 1.13W
Villefranche France **11** 46.00N 4.43E
Villena Spain **10** 38.39N 0.52W
Villenauxe-la-Grande France **9** 48.35N 3.33E
Villeneuve France **11** 44.25N 0.43E
Villeneuve d'Ascq France **8** 50.37N 3.10E
Villeneuve-St. Georges France **9** 48.44N 2.27E
Villeneuve-sur-Yonne France **9** 48.05N 3.18E
Villers-Bocage France **9** 49.05N 0.39W
Villers-Cotterêts France **9** 49.15N 3.04E
Villers-sur-Mer France **9** 49.21N 0.02W
Villeurbanne France **14** 45.46N 4.54E
Vilnius Lithuania **15** 54.40N 25.19E
Vilvoorde Belgium **8** 50.56N 4.25E
Vilyuy *r.* Russian Fed. **21** 64.20N126.55E
Vilyuysk Russian Fed. **21** 63.46N121.35E
Vimianzo Spain **10** 43.07N 9.02W
Vimmerby Sweden **17** 57.40N 15.51E
Vimoutiers France **9** 48.55N 0.12E
Vina *r.* Chad **38** 7.43N 15.30E
Viña del Mar Chile **63** 33.02S 71.34W
Vinaroz Spain **10** 40.30N 0.27E
Vincennes France **9** 48.51N 2.26E
Vincennes U.S.A. **55** 38.42N 87.30W
Vindel *r.* Sweden **16** 63.54N 19.52E
Vindeln Sweden **16** 64.12N 19.44E
Vinderup Denmark **17** 56.29N 8.47E
Vindhya Range *mts.* India **28** 22.55N 76.00E
Vineland U.S.A. **55** 39.29N 75.02W
Vingåker Sweden **17** 59.02N 15.52E
Vinh Vietnam **26** 18.42N105.41E
Vînju Mare Romania **15** 44.26N 22.52E
Vinkovci Croatia **13** 45.17N 18.38E
Vinnitsa Ukraine **15** 49.11N 28.30E
Vinson Massif Antarctica **64** 78.00S 85.00W
Vioolsdrif R.S.A. **39** 28.45S 17.33E
Vipava Slovenia **14** 45.51N 13.58E
Virac Phil. **27** 13.35N124.15E
Viranşehir Turkey **30** 37.13N 39.45E
Vire France **11** 48.50N 0.53W
Vire *r.* France **9** 49.20N 0.53W
Vírgenes, C. Argentina **63** 52.00S 68.50W
Virgin Gorda *i.* B.V.Is. **57** 18.30N 64.26W
Virginia U.S.A. **53** 47.30N 92.28W
Virginia *d.* U.S.A. **53** 37.30N 79.00W
Virginia City Mont. U.S.A. **54** 45.18N111.56W
Virginia City Nev. U.S.A. **54** 39.19N119.39W
Virovitica Croatia **15** 45.51N 17.23E
Virrat Finland **16** 62.14N 23.47E
Virserum Sweden **17** 57.19N 15.35E
Virton Belgium **8** 49.35N 5.32E
Virtsu Estonia **17** 58.34N 23.31E
Virunga Nat. Park Zaïre **37** 0.30S 29.15E
Vis Croatia **12** 43.03N 16.21E
Vis *i.* Croatia **12** 43.03N 16.10E
Visalia U.S.A. **54** 36.20N119.18W
Visayan Sea Phil. **27** 11.35N123.51E
Visby Sweden **17** 57.38N 18.18E
Visconde do Rio Branco Brazil **59** 21.00S 42.51W
Viscount Melville Sd. Canada **50** 74.30N104.00W
Visé Belgium **8** 50.44N 5.42E
Višegrad Bosnia-Herzegovina **13** 43.47N 19.20E
Viseu Brazil **61** 1.12S 46.07W
Viseu Portugal **10** 40.40N 7.55W
Viseu de Sus Romania **15** 47.44N 24.22E
Vishākhapatnam India **29** 17.42N 83.24E
Viso, Monte *mtn.* Italy **9** 44.38N 7.05E
Visp Switz. **9** 46.18N 7.53E
Vista U.S.A. **54** 33.12N117.15W
Vistula *r. see* Wisła *r.* Poland **15**
Vitarte Peru **60** 12.03S 76.51W
Vitebsk Belorussia **18** 55.10N 30.14E
Viterbo Italy **12** 42.26N 12.07E
Vitim Russian Fed. **21** 59.28N112.35E
Vitim *r.* Russian Fed. **21** 59.30N112.36E
Vitoria Spain **10** 42.51N 2.40W
Vitória da Conquista Brazil **61** 14.53S 40.52W
Vitória Espírito Santo Brazil **59** 20.19S 40.21W
Vitré France **9** 48.07N 1.12W
Vitry-le-François France **9** 48.44N 4.35E
Vitteaux France **9** 47.24N 4.30E
Vittoria Italy **12** 36.57N 14.21E
Vittorio Veneto Italy **9** 45.59N 12.18E
Viveiro *see* Vivero Spain **10**
Vivero Spain **10** 43.40N 7.24W
Vivonne Bay *town* Australia **46** 35.58S137.10E
Vizcaíno, Desierto de *des.* Mexico **56** 27.40N114.40W
Vizianagaram India **29** 18.07N 83.30E
Vizinga Russian Fed. **18** 61.06N 50.05E
Vjosë *r.* Albania **13** 40.39N 19.20E
Vlaardingen Neth. **8** 51.55N 4.20E
Vladikavkaz Russian Fed. **19** 43.02N 44.43E
Vladimir Russian Fed. **18** 56.08N 40.25E
Vladimirets Ukraine **15** 51.28N 26.03E
Vladimir Volynskiy Ukraine **15** 50.51N 24.19E
Vladivostok Russian Fed. **25** 43.09N131.53E
Vlasenica Bosnia-Herzegovina **15** 44.11N 18.56E
Vlieland *i.* Neth. **8** 53.15N 5.00E
Vlissingen Neth. **8** 51.27N 3.35E
Vlorë Albania **13** 40.28N 19.27E
Vltava *r.* Czech Republic **14** 50.22N 14.28E
Voerde Germany **8** 51.37N 6.39E
Vogelkop *f. see* Jazirah Doberai *f.* Indonesia **27**
Voghera Italy **9** 44.59N 9.01E
Voi Kenya **37** 3.23S 38.35E
Voiron France **11** 45.22N 5.35E
Volborg U.S.A. **54** 45.50N105.40W
Volda Norway **17** 62.09N 6.06E
Volga *r.* Russian Fed. **19** 45.45N 47.50E
Volgograd Russian Fed. **19** 48.45N 44.30E
Volgogradskoye Vodokhranilishche *resr.* Russian Fed. **19** 51.00N 46.05E
Volkhov Russian Fed. **18** 59.54N 32.47E
Volkhov *r.* Russian Fed. **18** 60.15N 32.15E
Völklingen Germany **14** 49.15N 6.50E
Volkovysk Belorussia **15** 53.10N 24.28E
Vollenhove Neth. **8** 52.41N 5.59E
Volnovakha Ukraine **19** 47.36N 37.32E
Volochanka Russian Fed. **21** 70.59N 94.18E
Volochisk Ukraine **15** 49.34N 26.10E
Volodarsk Russian Fed. **18** 56.14N 43.10E
Vologda Russian Fed. **18** 59.10N 39.55E
Volokolamsk Russian Fed. **18** 56.02N 35.56E
Vólos Greece **13** 39.22N 22.57E
Volovets Ukraine **15** 48.44N 23.14E
Volsk Russian Fed. **18** 52.04N 47.22E
Volta *d.* Ghana **38** 7.30N 0.25E
Volta *r.* Ghana **38** 5.50N 0.41E
Volta, L. Ghana **38** 7.00N 0.00
Volta-Noire *d.* Burkina **38** 12.30N 3.25W
Volta Redonda Brazil **59** 22.31S 44.05W
Volterra Italy **12** 43.24N 10.51E
Voltri Italy **9** 44.26N 8.45E
Volturno *r.* Italy **12** 41.02N 13.56E
Volzhskiy Russian Fed. **19** 48.48N 44.45E
Voorburg Neth. **8** 52.05N 4.22E
Vopnafjördhur *est.* Iceland **16** 65.50N 14.30W
Vopnafjördhur *town* Iceland **16** 65.46N 14.50W
Vorarlberg *d.* Austria **14** 47.15N 9.55E
Vordingborg Denmark **17** 55.01N 11.55E
Voríai Sporádhes *is.* Greece **13** 39.00N 24.00E
Vorkuta Russian Fed. **18** 67.27N 64.00E
Vormsi *i.* Estonia **17** 59.00N 23.20E
Voronezh Russian Fed. **19** 51.40N 39.13E
Voronovo Belorussia **15** 54.09N 25.19E
Vosges *mts.* France **14** 48.10N 7.00E
Voss Norway **17** 60.39N 6.26E
Vostochno Sibirskoye More *sea* Russian Fed. **21** 73.00N160.00E
Vostochnyy Sayan *mts.* Russian Fed. **24** 51.30N102.00E
Votkinsk Russian Fed. **18** 57.02N 53.59E
Votkinskoye Vodokhranilishche *resr.* Russian Fed. **18** 57.00N 55.00E
Votuporanga Brazil **62** 20.26S 49.53W
Vouga *r.* Portugal **10** 40.41N 8.38W
Vouillé France **11** 46.38N 0.10E
Vouziers France **9** 49.24N 4.42E
Voves France **9** 48.16N 1.37E
Voxna Sweden **17** 61.20N 15.30E
Voxna *r.* Sweden **17** 61.17N 16.26E
Voyvozh Russian Fed. **18** 64.19N 55.12E
Vozhega Russian Fed. **18** 60.25N 40.11E
Voznesensk Ukraine **19** 47.34N 31.21E
Vrangelya, Ostrov *i.* Russian Fed. **21** 71.00N180.00
Vranje Yugo. **13** 42.34N 21.52E
Vratsa Bulgaria **13** 43.12N 23.33E
Vrbas *r.* Bosnia-Herzegovina **13** 45.06N 17.29E
Vrede R.S.A. **39** 27.24S 29.09E
Vredendal R.S.A. **39** 31.40S 18.28E
Vresse Belgium **8** 49.53N 4.57E
Vries Neth. **8** 53.06N 6.35E
Vrnograč Bosnia-Herzegovina **12** 45.10N 15.56E
Vršac Yugo. **15** 45.08N 21.18E
Vryburg R.S.A. **39** 26.57S 24.42E
Vught Neth. **8** 51.39N 5.18E
Vukovar Croatia **15** 45.21N 19.00E
Vung Tau Vietnam **26** 10.21N107.04E
Vyatka *r.* Russian Fed. **20** 55.40N 51.40E
Vyatskiye Polyany Russian Fed. **18** 56.14N 51.08E
Vyazma Russian Fed. **18** 55.12N 34.17E
Vyazniki Russian Fed. **18** 56.14N 42.08E
Vyborg Russian Fed. **18** 60.45N 28.41E
Vychegda *r.* Russian Fed. **18** 61.15N 46.28E
Vychodné Beskydy *mts.* Europe **15** 49.30N 22.00E
Vygozero, Ozero *l.* Russian Fed. **18** 63.30N 34.30E
Vyrnwy, L. U.K. **4** 52.46N 3.30W
Vyshka Turkmenistan **31** 39.19N 54.10E
Vyshniy-Volochek Russian Fed. **18** 57.34N 34.23E
Vytegra Russian Fed. **18** 61.04N 36.27E

W

Wa Ghana **38** 10.07N 2.28W
Waal *r.* Neth. **8** 51.45N 4.40E
Waalwijk Neth. **8** 51.42N 5.04E
Wabag P.N.G. **27** 5.28S143.40E
Wabash U.S.A. **55** 40.47N 85.48W
Wabash *r.* U.S.A. **53** 38.25N 87.45W
Wabrzeźno Poland **15** 53.17N 18.57E
Wabush City Canada **51** 53.00N 66.50W
Waco U.S.A. **53** 31.33N 97.10W
Wad Pakistan **28** 27.21N 66.30E
Waddeneilanden *is.* Neth. **8** 53.20N 5.00E
Waddenzee *b.* Neth. **8** 53.15N 5.05E
Waddikee Australia **46** 33.18S136.12E
Waddington, Mt. Canada **50** 51.30N125.00W
Wadhurst U.K. **5** 51.03N 0.21E
Wādī Ḩalfā' Sudan **30** 21.56N 31.20E
Wādī Mūsá *town* Jordan **32** 30.19N 35.29E
Wad Madanī Sudan **35** 14.24N 33.30E
Wafrah Kuwait **31** 28.39N 47.56E
Wageningen Neth. **8** 51.58N 5.39E
Wager B. Canada **51** 65.26N 88.40W
Wager Bay *town* Canada **51** 65.55N 90.40W
Wagga Wagga Australia **47** 35.07S147.24E
Wagin Australia **43** 33.18S117.21E
Wāh Pakistan **28** 33.50N 72.44E
Wahai Indonesia **27** 2.48S129.30E
Wahiba Sands *des.* Oman **28** 21.56N 58.55E
Wahpeton U.S.A. **53** 46.16N 96.36W
Waiau New Zealand **48** 42.39S173.03E
Waidhofen Austria **14** 47.58N 14.47E
Waigeo *i.* Indonesia **27** 0.05S130.30E
Waihi New Zealand **48** 37.24S175.50E
Waikato *d.* New Zealand **48** 38.15S175.10E
Waikato *r.* New Zealand **48** 37.19S174.50E
Waikerie Australia **46** 34.11S139.59E
Waikokopu New Zealand **48** 39.05S177.50E
Waikouaiti New Zealand **48** 45.36S170.41E
Waimakariri *r.* New Zealand **48** 43.23S172.40E
Waimate New Zealand **48** 44.45S171.03E
Waingapu Indonesia **27** 9.30S120.10E
Wainwright U.S.A. **50** 70.39N160.00W
Waiouru New Zealand **48** 39.39S175.40E
Waipara New Zealand **48** 43.03S172.45E
Waipawa New Zealand **48** 39.56S176.35E
Waipiro New Zealand **48** 38.02S178.21E
Waipu New Zealand **48** 35.59S174.26E
Waipukurau New Zealand **48** 40.00S176.33E
Wairau *r.* New Zealand **48** 41.32S174.08E
Wairoa New Zealand **48** 39.03S177.25E
Waitaki *r.* New Zealand **48** 44.56S171.10E
Waitara New Zealand **48** 38.59S174.13E
Waiuku New Zealand **48** 37.15S174.44E
Wajir Kenya **37** 1.46N 40.05E
Wakatipu, L. New Zealand **48** 45.10S168.30E
Wakayama Japan **23** 34.13N135.11E
Wakefield U.K. **4** 53.41N 1.31W
Wakkanai Japan **25** 45.26N141.43E
Wakre Indonesia **27** 0.30S131.05E
Walamba Zambia **37** 13.27S 28.44E
Wałbrzych Poland **14** 50.48N 16.19E
Walcha Australia **47** 31.00S151.36E
Walcheren *f.* Neth. **8** 51.32N 3.35E
Wałcz Poland **14** 53.17N 16.28E
Waldbröl Germany **8** 50.52N 7.34E
Waldeck Germany **14** 51.12N 9.04E
Walden U.S.A. **54** 40.34N106.11W
Waldorf U.S.A. **55** 38.37N 76.54W
Waldport U.S.A. **54** 44.26N124.04W
Wales *d.* U.K. **5** 52.30N 3.45W
Walgett Australia **47** 30.03S148.10E
Walikale Zaïre **37** 1.29S 28.05E
Walker L. U.S.A. **54** 38.44N118.43W
Wallace Idaho U.S.A. **54** 47.28N115.55W
Wallaceburg Canada **55** 42.36N 82.23W
Wallachia *f.* Romania **15** 44.35N 25.00E
Wallambin, L. Australia **43** 30.58S117.30E
Wallangarra Australia **47** 28.51S151.52E
Wallaroo Australia **46** 33.57S137.36E
Walla Walla Australia **47** 35.48S146.52E
Walla Walla U.S.A. **54** 46.08N118.20W
Wallis, Îles *is.* Pacific Oc. **40** 13.16S176.15W
Wallowa U.S.A. **54** 45.34N117.32W
Wallowa Mts. U.S.A. **54** 45.10N117.30W
Wallsend Australia **47** 32.55S151.40E
Walpole Australia **43** 34.57S116.44E
Walsall U.K. **5** 52.36N 1.59W
Walsenburg U.S.A. **52** 37.37N104.47W
Walton on the Naze U.K. **5** 51.52N 1.17E
Walton on the Wolds U.K. **4** 52.49N 0.49W
Walvis B. R.S.A. **39** 22.55S 14.30E
Walvisbaai R.S.A. **39** 22.57S 14.30E
Walvis Bay *town see* Walvisbaai R.S.A. **39**
Walvis Bay *d.* R.S.A. **39** 22.56S 14.35E
Walvis Bay *town* R.S.A. **36** 22.50S 14.31E
Wamanfo Ghana **38** 7.16N 2.44W
Wamba Kenya **37** 0.58N 37.19E
Wamba Nigeria **38** 8.57N 8.42E
Wamba Zaïre **37** 2.10N 27.59E
Wami *r.* Tanzania **37** 6.10S 38.50E
Wamsasi Indonesia **27** 3.27S126.07E
Wan Indonesia **44** 8.23S137.55E
Wāna Pakistan **28** 32.20N 69.32E
Wanaaring Australia **46** 29.42S144.14E
Wanaka New Zealand **48** 44.42S169.08E
Wanaka, L. New Zealand **48** 44.30S169.10E
Wan'an China **25** 26.27N114.46E
Wanapiri Indonesia **27** 4.30S135.50E
Wanapitei *r.* Canada **55** 46.02N 80.51W
Wanapitei L. Canada **55** 46.45N 80.45W
Wanbi Australia **46** 34.46S140.19E
Wandana Australia **46** 32.04S133.45E
Wandoan Australia **44** 26.09S149.51E
Wanganella Australia **47** 35.13S144.53E
Wanganui New Zealand **48** 39.56S175.00E
Wangaratta Australia **47** 36.22S146.20E
Wangary Australia **46** 34.30S135.26E
Wangerooge *i.* Germany **8** 53.50N 7.50E
Wangianna Australia **46** 29.42S137.32E
Wantage U.K. **5** 51.35N 1.25W
Wanxian China **29** 30.52N108.20E
Wanyuan China **29** 32.04N108.02E
Warangal India **29** 18.00N 79.35E
Waranga Resr. Australia **47** 36.32S145.04E
Waratah B. Australia **45** 38.55S146.04E
Warburton *r.* Australia **45** 27.55S137.15E
Warburton Range *mts.* S.A. Australia **46** 30.30S134.32E
Warburton Range *mts.* W.A. Australia **42** 26.09S126.38E
Ward Rep. of Ire. **7** 53.26N 6.20W
Warden R.S.A. **39** 27.49S 28.57E
Wardenburg Germany **8** 53.04N 8.11E
Wardha India **29** 20.41N 78.40E
Waren Germany **14** 53.31N 12.40E
Warendorf Germany **8** 51.57N 8.00E
Warialda Australia **47** 29.33S150.36E
Wark Forest *hills* U.K. **4** 55.06N 2.24W
Warkopi Indonesia **27** 1.12S134.09E
Warkworth New Zealand **48** 36.24S174.40E
Warley U.K. **5** 52.29N 2.02W
Warmbad Namibia **39** 28.26S 18.41E
Warminster U.K. **5** 51.12N 2.11W
Warm Springs *town* U.S.A. **54** 39.39N114.49W
Waroona Australia **43** 32.51S115.50E
Warracknabeal Australia **46** 36.15S142.28E
Warragul Australia **47** 38.11S145.55E
Warrakalanna, L. Australia **46** 28.13S139.23E
Warrambool *r.* Australia **47** 30.04S147.38E
Warrego *r.* Australia **47** 30.25S145.18E
Warrego Range *mts.* Australia **44** 24.55S146.20E
Warren Australia **47** 31.44S147.53E
Warren Mich. U.S.A. **55** 42.28N 83.01W
Warren Ohio U.S.A. **55** 41.15N 80.49W
Warren Penn. U.S.A. **55** 41.51N 79.08W
Warrenpoint U.K. **7** 54.06N 6.15W
Warrenton R.S.A. **39** 28.07S 24.49E
Warri Nigeria **38** 5.36N 5.46E
Warrina Australia **46** 28.10S135.49E
Warriner Creek *r.* Australia **46** 29.15S137.03E
Warrington U.K. **4** 53.25N 2.38W
Warrnambool Australia **46** 38.23S142.03E
Warrumbungle Range *mts.* Australia **47** 31.20S149.00E
Warsaw *see* Warszawa Poland **15**
Warsaw Ind. U.S.A. **55** 41.13N 85.52W
Warszawa Poland **15** 52.15N 21.00E
Warta *r.* Poland **14** 52.45N 15.09E
Warwick Australia **47** 28.12S152.00E
Warwick U.K. **5** 52.17N 1.36W
Warwickshire *d.* U.K. **5** 52.13N 1.30W
Wasatch Plateau *f.* U.S.A. **54** 39.20N111.30W
Wasco Calif. U.S.A. **54** 35.36N119.20W
Wasco Oreg. U.S.A. **54** 45.35N120.42W
Washburn L. Canada **50** 70.03N106.50W
Washington U.K. **4** 54.55N 1.30W
Washington *d.* U.S.A. **54** 47.43N120.00W
Washington D.C. U.S.A. **55** 38.55N 77.00W
Washington Ind. U.S.A. **55** 38.40N 87.10W
Washington N.C. U.S.A. **53** 35.33N 77.04W
Washington Utah U.S.A. **54** 37.08N113.30W
Washington Va. U.S.A. **55** 38.43N 78.10W
Wasian Indonesia **27** 1.51S133.21E
Wasior Indonesia **27** 2.38S134.27E
Wasiri Indonesia **27** 7.30S126.30E
Waskaganish Canada **55** 51.29N 78.45W
Wassenaar Neth. **8** 52.10N 4.26E
Wassy France **9** 48.30N 4.59E
Waswanipi Lac *l.* Canada **55** 49.36N 76.39W
Watampone Indonesia **27** 4.33S120.20E
Watchet U.K. **5** 51.10N 3.20W
Waterbury U.S.A. **55** 41.33N 73.03W
Waterford Rep. of Ire. **7** 52.16N 7.08W
Waterford *d.* Rep. of Ire. **7** 52.10N 7.40W
Waterford Harbour *est.* Rep. of Ire. **7** 52.12N 6.56W
Waterloo Belgium **8** 50.44N 4.24E
Waterloo Canada **55** 43.28N 80.31W
Waterloo Iowa U.S.A. **53** 42.30N 92.20W
Watertown N.Y. U.S.A. **55** 43.59N 75.55W
Watertown S.Dak. U.S.A. **53** 44.54N 97.08W
Watervale Australia **46** 33.58S138.39E
Waterville Rep. of Ire. **7** 51.50N 10.11W
Waterville Maine U.S.A. **55** 44.33N 69.38W
Waterville Wash. U.S.A. **54** 47.39N120.04W
Watford U.K. **5** 51.40N 0.25W
Watrous Canada **50** 51.40N105.29W
Watsa Zaïre **37** 3.03N 29.29E
Watson Lake *town* Canada **50** 60.07N128.49W
Watsonville U.S.A. **54** 36.55N121.45W
Wattiwarriganna Creek *r.* Australia **46** 28.57S136.10E
Wau P.N.G. **27** 7.22S146.40E
Wauchope N.S.W. Australia **47** 31.27S152.43E
Wauchope N.T. Australia **44** 20.39S134.13E
Waukaringa Australia **46** 32.18S139.27E
Wausau U.S.A. **53** 44.58N 89.40W
Wave Hill *town* Australia **42** 17.29S130.57E
Waveney *r.* U.K. **5** 52.29N 1.46E
Wavre Belgium **8** 50.43N 4.37E
Wāw Sudan **35** 7.40N 28.04E
Waxweiler Germany **8** 50.08N 6.20E
Way, L. Australia **42** 26.47S120.21E
Waycross U.S.A. **53** 31.08N 82.22W
Waynesboro Penn. U.S.A. **55** 39.45N 77.35W
Waziers France **8** 50.24N 3.05E
Wear *r.* U.K. **4** 54.55N 1.21W
Weda Indonesia **27** 0.30N127.52E
Weddell Sea Antarctica **64** 70.00S 40.00W
Wedderburn Australia **46** 36.26S143.39E
Wedgeport Canada **55** 43.44N 66.00W
Wedmore U.K. **5** 51.14N 2.50W
Wedza Zimbabwe **39** 18.37S 31.33E
Weelde Belgium **8** 51.25N 5.00E
Weemelah Australia **47** 29.02S149.15E
Weert Neth. **8** 51.14N 5.40E
Wee Waa Australia **47** 30.34S149.27E
Wegorzyno Poland **14** 53.32N 15.33E
Wegrów Poland **15** 52.25N 22.01E
Weichang China **25** 41.56N117.34E

Weiden in der Oberpfalz Germany 14 49.40N 12.10E
Weifang China 25 36.44N119.10E
Weihai China 25 37.30N122.04E
Weilmoringle Australia 47 29.16S146.55E
Weimar Germany 14 50.59N 11.20E
Weipa Australia 44 12.41S141.52E
Weir r. Australia 47 29.10S149.06E
Weiser U.S.A. 54 44.37N116.58W
Weissenfels Germany 14 51.12N 11.58E
Weiya China 24 41.50N 94.24E
Wejherowo Poland 15 54.37N 18.15E
Weldon U.S.A. 54 35.40N118.20W
Welkom R.S.A. 39 27.59S 26.42E
Welland Canada 55 42.59N 79.14W
Welland r. U.K. 4 52.53N 0.00
Wellesley Is. Australia 44 16.42S139.30E
Wellin Belgium 8 50.05N 5.07E
Wellingborough U.K. 5 52.18N 0.41W
Wellington N.S.W. Australia 47 32.33S148.59E
Wellington S.A. Australia 46 35.21S139.23E
Wellington New Zealand 48 41.17S174.47E
Wellington d. New Zealand 48 40.00S175.30E
Wellington Shrops. U.K. 5 52.42N 2.31W
Wellington Somerset U.K. 5 50.58N 3.13W
Wellington Nev. U.S.A. 54 38.45N119.22W
Wellington, Isla i. Chile 63 49.30S 75.00W
Wells U.K. 5 51.12N 2.39W
Wells Nev. U.S.A. 54 41.07N114.58W
Wellsboro U.S.A. 55 41.45N 77.18W
Wells-next-the-Sea U.K. 4 52.57N 0.51E
Wellton U.S.A. 54 32.40N114.08W
Wels Austria 14 48.10N 14.02E
Welshpool U.K. 5 52.40N 3.09W
Welwyn Garden City U.K. 5 51.48N 0.13W
Wem U.K. 4 52.52N 2.45W
Wembere r. Tanzania 37 4.07S 34.15E
Wemindji Canada 51 53.00N 78.42W
Wenatchee U.S.A. 54 47.25N120.19W
Wenchi Ghana 38 7.40N 2.06W
Wendel U.S.A. 54 40.20N120.14W
Wendover U.S.A. 54 40.44N114.02W
Wenebegon L. Canada 55 47.24N 83.08W
Wenlock r. Australia 44 12.02S141.55E
Wenquan China 29 33.13N 91.50E
Wenshan China 29 23.25N104.15E
Wensleydale f. U.K. 4 54.19N 2.04W
Wentworth Australia 46 34.06S141.56E
Wenzhou China 25 28.02N120.40E
Weott U.S.A. 54 40.19N123.54W
Wepener R.S.A. 39 29.43S 27.01E
Werda Botswana 39 25.15S 23.16E
Werdohl Germany 8 51.16N 7.47E
Weri Indonesia 27 3.10S132.30E
Werne Germany 8 51.39N 7.36E
Werra r. Germany 14 51.26N 9.39E
Werribee Australia 47 37.54S144.40E
Werris Creek town Australia 47 31.20S150.41E
Wesel Germany 8 51.39N 6.37E
Weser r. Germany 14 53.15N 8.30E
Wessel, C. Australia 44 10.59S136.46E
Wessel Is. Australia 44 11.30S136.25E
West Bank Jordan 32 32.00N 35.25E
West Bengal d. India 29 23.00N 87.40E
West Bromwich U.K. 5 52.32N 2.01W
Westbrook U.S.A. 55 43.41N 70.21W
West Coast d. New Zealand 48 43.15S170.10E
Westende Belgium 8 51.10N 2.46E
Western d. Ghana 38 6.00N 2.40W
Western d. Kenya 37 0.30N 34.30E
Western Australia d. Australia 42 24.20S122.30E
Western Ghāts mts. India 28 15.30N 74.30E
Western Isles d. U.K. 6 57.40N 7.10W
Western Sahara Africa 34 25.00N 13.30W
Western Samoa Pacific Oc. 40 13.55S172.00W
Westerschelde est. Neth. 8 51.25N 3.40E
Westerstede Germany 8 53.15N 7.56E
Westerwald f. Germany 8 50.40N 8.00E
West Falkland i. Falkland Is. 63 51.40W 60.00W
West Felton U.K. 4 52.49N 2.58W
Westfield Mass. U.S.A. 55 42.07N 72.45W
Westfield Penn. U.S.A. 55 41.55N 77.32W
West Frisian Is. see Waddeneilanden Neth. 14
West Glamorgan d. U.K. 5 51.42N 3.47W
West Lafayette U.S.A. 55 40.26N 86.56W
West Linton U.K. 6 55.45N 3.21W
Westmeath d. Rep. of Ire. 7 53.30N 7.30W
West Midlands d. U.K. 5 52.28N 1.50W
Westmoreland Australia 44 17.18S138.12E
West Nicholson Zimbabwe 39 21.06S 29.25E
Weston Malaysia 26 5.14N115.35E
Weston-Super-Mare U.K. 5 51.20N 2.59W
West Palm Beach town U.S.A. 53 26.42N 80.05W
Westport New Zealand 48 41.46S171.38E
Westport Rep. of Ire. 7 53.48N 9.32W
Westport Wash. U.S.A. 54 46.53N124.06W
Westray i. U.K. 6 59.18N 2.58W
West Siberian Plain f. see Zapadno-Sibirskaya Ravnina Russian Fed. 20
West Sussex d. U.K. 5 50.58N 0.30W
West Terschelling Neth. 8 53.22N 5.13E
West Virginia d. U.S.A. 53 38.45N 80.30W
West Vlaanderen d. Belgium 8 51.00N 3.00E
West Wyalong Australia 47 33.54S147.12E
West Yellowstone U.S.A. 54 44.30N111.05W
West Yorkshire d. U.K. 4 53.45N 1.40W
Wetar i. Indonesia 27 7.45S126.00E
Wetaskiwin Canada 50 52.57N113.20W
Wetteren Belgium 8 51.00N 3.51E
Wetzlar Germany 14 50.33N 8.30E
Wewak P.N.G. 27 3.35S143.35E
Wexford Rep. of Ire. 7 52.20N 6.28W
Wexford d. Rep. of Ire. 7 52.20N 6.25W
Wexford B. Rep. of Ire. 7 52.27N 6.18W
Weyburn Canada 50 49.41N103.52W
Weymouth U.K. 5 50.36N 2.28W
Weymouth, C. Australia 44 12.32S143.36E
Whakatane New Zealand 48 37.56S177.00E
Whalan r. Australia 47 29.10S148.42E
Whale Cove town Canada 51 62.30N 93.00W
Whalsay i. U.K. 6 60.22N 0.59W
Whangarei New Zealand 48 35.43S174.20E
Wharfe r. U.K. 4 53.50N 1.07W
Wharfedale f. U.K. 4 54.00N 1.55W
Whataroa New Zealand 48 43.16S170.22E
Wheeler Peak mtn. Nev. U.S.A. 54 38.59N114.19W
Wheeler Peak mtn. N.Mex. U.S.A. 52 36.34N105.25W
Wheeler Ridge town U.S.A. 54 35.06N119.01W
Wheeler Springs town U.S.A. 54 34.30N119.18W
Wheeling U.S.A. 55 40.05N 80.43W
Whernside mtn. U.K. 4 54.14N 2.25W
Whidbey Is. Australia 46 34.50S135.00E
Whitburn U.K. 6 55.52N 3.41W
Whitby Canada 55 43.52N 78.56W
Whitby U.K. 4 54.29N 0.37W
Whitchurch Shrops. U.K. 4 52.58N 2.42W
White r. Ark. U.S.A. 53 33.53N 91.10W
White r. Ind. U.S.A. 55 38.29N 87.45W
White r. S.Dak. U.S.A. 52 43.40N 99.30W
White r. Utah U.S.A. 52 40.04N109.41W
White, L. Australia 42 21.05S129.00E
White Cliffs town Australia 46 30.51S143.05E
Whitefish U.S.A. 54 48.25N114.20W
Whitefish B. U.S.A. 55 46.32N 84.45W
Whitehall Mont. U.S.A. 54 45.52N112.06W
Whitehaven U.K. 4 54.33N 3.35W
Whitehorse Canada 50 60.41N135.08W
Whitemark Australia 45 40.07S148.00E
White Mountain Peak U.S.A. 54 37.38N118.15W
White Mts. Calif. U.S.A. 54 37.30N118.15W
White Plains town U.S.A. 55 41.02N 73.46W
White Sea see Beloye More sea Russian Fed. 18
White Volta r. Ghana 38 9.13N 1.15W
Whitewater Baldy mtn. U.S.A. 54 33.20N108.39W
Whitfield Australia 47 36.49S146.22E
Whithorn U.K. 6 54.44N 4.25W
Whitianga New Zealand 48 36.50S175.42E
Whitley Bay town U.K. 4 55.03N 1.25W
Whitney Canada 55 45.30N 78.14W
Whitney, Mt. U.S.A. 54 36.35N118.18W
Whitstable U.K. 5 51.21N 1.02E
Whitsunday I. Australia 44 20.17S148.59E
Whittier U.S.A. 50 60.46N148.41W
Whittlesea Australia 47 37.31S145.08E
Whitton U.K. 4 53.42N 0.39W
Wholdaia L. Canada 50 60.43N104.10W
Whyalla Australia 46 33.02S137.35E
Wichita U.S.A. 53 37.43N 97.20W
Wichita Falls town U.S.A. 52 33.55N 98.30W
Wick U.K. 6 58.26N 3.06W
Wickenburg U.S.A. 54 33.58N112.44W
Wickepin Australia 43 32.45S117.31E
Wicklow Rep. of Ire. 7 52.59N 6.03W
Wicklow d. Rep. of Ire. 7 52.59N 6.25W
Wicklow Head Rep. of Ire. 7 52.58N 6.00W
Wicklow Mts. Rep. of Ire. 7 53.06N 6.20W
Widgiemooltha Australia 43 31.30S121.34E
Widnes U.K. 4 53.22N 2.44W
Wiehl Germany 8 50.57N 7.32E
Wieluń Poland 15 51.14N 18.34E
Wien Austria 14 48.13N 16.22E
Wiener Neustadt Austria 14 47.49N 16.15E
Wieprz r. Poland 15 51.34N 21.49E
Wiesbaden Germany 14 50.05N 8.15E
Wigan U.K. 4 53.33N 2.38W
Wight, Isle of U.K. 3 50.40N 1.17W
Wigton U.K. 4 54.50N 3.09W
Wigtown U.K. 6 54.47N 4.26W
Wigtown B. U.K. 6 54.47N 4.15W
Wilcannia Australia 46 31.33S143.24E
Wildhorn mtn. Switz. 11 46.22N 7.22E
Wildon Austria 14 46.53N 15.31E
Wildspitze mtn. Austria 14 46.55N 10.55E
Wildwood U.S.A. 55 38.59N 74.49W
Wilgena Australia 46 30.46S134.44E
Wilhelm, Mt. P.N.G. 27 6.00S144.55E
Wilhelm II Land Antarctica 64 68.00S 89.00E
Wilhelmshaven Germany 8 53.32N 8.07E
Wilkes-Barre U.S.A. 55 41.15N 75.50W
Wilkes Land f. Antarctica 64 69.00S120.00E
Wilkie Canada 50 52.27N108.42W
Wilkinsburg U.S.A. 55 40.27N 79.53W
Wilkinson Lakes Australia 45 29.40S132.39E
Willandra Billabong r. Australia 46 33.08S144.06E
Willemstad Neth. Antilles 60 12.12N 68.56W
Willeroo Australia 42 15.17S131.35E
William, Mt. Australia 46 37.20S142.41E
William Creek town Australia 46 28.52S136.18E
Williams Australia 43 33.01S116.45E
Williams r. Australia 43 32.59S116.24E
Williams Lake town Canada 50 52.08N122.09W
Williamsport Penn. U.S.A. 55 41.14N 77.00W
Willis Group is. Australia 44 16.18S150.00E
Williston R.S.A. 39 31.21S 20.53E
Williston U.S.A. 52 48.09N103.37W
Williston L. Canada 50 55.00N126.00W
Willits U.S.A. 54 39.25N123.21W
Willmar U.S.A. 53 45.06N 95.00W
Willochra Australia 46 32.12S138.10E
Willochra r. Australia 46 31.57S137.52E
Willow U.S.A. 50 61.42N150.08W
Willowmore R.S.A. 39 33.18S 23.28E
Willow Ranch U.S.A. 54 41.55N120.21W
Willunga Australia 46 35.18S138.33E
Wilmington Del. U.S.A. 55 39.44N 75.33W
Wilmington N.C. U.S.A. 53 34.14N 77.55W
Wilmslow U.K. 4 53.19N 2.14W
Wilpena r. Australia 46 31.13S139.25E
Wilson's Promontory c. Australia 47 39.06S146.23E
Wilton r. Australia 44 14.45S134.33E
Wilton U.K. 5 51.05N 1.52W
Wiltshire d. U.K. 5 51.20N 0.34W
Wiltz Lux. 8 49.59N 5.53E
Wiluna Australia 42 26.36S120.13E
Wimmera r. Australia 46 36.05S141.56E
Winam b. Kenya 37 0.15S 34.30E
Winburg R.S.A. 39 28.30S 27.01E
Wincanton U.K. 5 51.03N 2.24W
Winchester U.K. 5 51.04N 1.19W
Winchester Va. U.S.A. 55 39.11N 78.10W
Winchester Wyo. U.S.A. 54 43.51N108.10W
Windermere l. U.K. 4 54.20N 2.56W
Windhoek Namibia 39 22.34S 17.06E
Windorah Australia 44 25.26S142.39E
Wind River Range mts. U.S.A. 54 43.05N109.25W
Windsor Australia 47 33.38S150.47E
Windsor Ont. Canada 55 42.18N 83.01W
Windsor Que. Canada 55 45.35N 72.01W
Windsor U.K. 5 51.29N 0.38W
Windward Is. C. America 57 13.00N 60.00W
Windward Passage str. Carib. Sea 57 20.00N 74.00W
Wingen Australia 47 31.43S150.54E
Wingham Australia 47 31.50S152.20E
Wingham Canada 55 43.53N 81.19W
Winifred U.S.A. 54 47.34N109.23W
Winisk Canada 51 55.15N 85.12W
Winisk r. Canada 51 55.20N 85.20W
Winisk L. Canada 51 52.55N 87.22W
Winneba Ghana 38 5.22N 0.38W
Winnebago, L. U.S.A. 53 44.00N 88.25W
Winnemucca U.S.A. 52 40.58N117.45W
Winnemucca L. U.S.A. 54 40.09N119.20W
Winnipeg Canada 51 49.53N 97.10W
Winnipeg, L. Canada 51 52.45N 98.00W
Winnipegosis, L. Canada 51 52.00N100.00W
Winona Minn. U.S.A. 53 44.02N 91.37W
Winooski U.S.A. 55 44.29N 73.11W
Winschoten Neth. 8 53.07N 7.02E
Winsford U.K. 4 53.12N 2.31W
Winslow Ariz. U.S.A. 54 35.01N110.42W
Winslow Maine U.S.A. 55 44.32N 69.38W
Winston U.S.A. 54 46.28N111.38W
Winston-Salem U.S.A. 53 36.05N 80.05W
Winsum Neth. 8 53.20N 6.31E
Winterswijk Neth. 8 51.58N 6.44E
Winterthur Switz. 14 47.30N 8.45E
Winthrop Wash. U.S.A. 54 48.29N120.11W
Winton Australia 44 22.22S143.00E
Winton New Zealand 48 46.10S168.20E
Winton U.S.A. 54 41.45N109.10W
Wirrabara Australia 46 33.03S138.18E
Wirraminna Australia 46 31.11S136.04E
Wirrappa Australia 46 31.28S137.00E
Wirrega Australia 46 36.11S140.37E
Wirrida, L. Australia 46 29.45S134.39E
Wirulla Australia 46 32.24S134.33E
Wisbech U.K. 5 52.39N 0.10E
Wisconsin d. U.S.A. 53 45.00N 90.00W
Wisconsin Rapids town U.S.A. 53 44.24N 89.55W
Wisdom U.S.A. 54 45.37N113.27W
Wisła r. Poland 15 54.23N 18.52E
Wismar Germany 14 53.54N 11.28E
Wisznice Poland 15 51.48N 23.12E
Witham r. U.K. 4 52.56N 0.04E
Withernsea U.K. 4 53.43N 0.02E
Witkowo Poland 15 52.27N 17.47E
Witney U.K. 5 51.47N 1.29W
Witsand R.S.A. 39 34.23S 20.49E
Witten Germany 8 51.26N 7.19E
Wittenberg Germany 14 51.53N 12.39E
Wittenberge Germany 14 52.59N 11.45E
Wittenoom Australia 42 22.19S118.21E
Wittlich Germany 8 49.59N 6.54E
Witu Kenya 37 2.22S 40.20E
Witvlei Namibia 39 22.25S 18.29E
Wiveliscombe U.K. 5 51.02N 3.20W
Wkra r. Poland 15 52.27N 20.44E
Władysławowo Poland 15 54.49N 18.25E
Włocławek Poland 15 52.39N 19.01E
Włodawa Poland 15 51.33N 23.31E
Wodonga Australia 47 36.08S146.09E
Woerden Neth. 8 52.07N 4.55E
Wokam i. Indonesia 27 5.45S134.30E
Woking U.K. 5 51.20N 0.34W
Wolf Creek town U.S.A. 54 46.50N112.20W
Wolfenbüttel Germany 14 52.10N 10.33E
Wolf Point town U.S.A. 54 48.05N105.39W
Wolfsberg Austria 14 46.51N 14.51E
Wolfsburg Germany 14 52.27N 10.49E
Wolin Poland 14 53.51N 14.38E
Wollaston L. Canada 50 58.15N103.30W
Wollaston Pen. Canada 50 70.00N115.00W
Wollongong Australia 47 34.25S150.52E
Wolmaransstad R.S.A. 39 27.11S 25.58E
Wołomin Poland 15 52.21N 21.14E
Wolseley Australia 46 36.21S140.55E
Wolvega Neth. 8 52.53N 6.00E
Wolverhampton U.K. 5 52.35N 2.06W
Wondai Australia 44 26.19S151.52E
Wongan Hills town Australia 43 30.55S116.41E
Wŏnsan N. Korea 25 39.07N127.26E
Wonthaggi Australia 47 38.38S145.37E
Woocalla Australia 46 31.44S137.10E
Woodbridge U.K. 5 52.06N 1.19E
Woodbridge U.S.A. 55 38.39N 77.15W
Woodburn Australia 47 29.04S153.21E
Wooded Bluff f. Australia 47 29.22S153.22E
Woodenbong Australia 47 28.28S152.35E
Woodland U.S.A. 54 38.41N121.46W
Woodlark I. P.N.G. 44 9.05S152.50E
Woodroffe, Mt. Australia 44 26.20S131.45E
Woods, L. Australia 44 17.50S133.30E
Woods, L. of the Canada/U.S.A. 51 49.15N 94.45W
Woodside Australia 47 38.31S146.52E
Woodstock Canada 55 43.08N 80.45W
Woodstock U.K. 5 51.51N 1.20W
Woodville New Zealand 48 40.20S175.52E
Wooler U.K. 4 55.33N 2.01W
Woolgoolga Australia 47 30.07S153.12E
Wooltana Australia 46 30.28S139.26E
Woomera Australia 46 31.11S136.54E
Woonsocket U.S.A. 55 42.00N 71.31W
Wooramel Australia 42 25.42S114.20E
Wooramel r. Australia 42 25.47S114.10E
Woorong, L. Australia 46 29.24S134.06E
Worcester R.S.A. 39 33.39S 19.25E
Worcester U.K. 5 52.12N 2.12W
Worcester U.S.A. 55 42.16N 71.48W
Workington U.K. 4 54.39N 3.34W
Worksop U.K. 4 53.19N 1.09W
Workum Neth. 8 53.00N 5.26E
Worland U.S.A. 54 44.01N107.57W
Worms Germany 14 49.38N 8.23E
Worthing U.K. 5 50.49N 0.21W
Worthington Minn. U.S.A. 53 43.37N 95.36W
Worthington Ohio U.S.A. 55 40.03N 83.03W
Worthville U.S.A. 55 38.38N 85.05W
Wosi Indonesia 27 0.15S128.00E
Woutchaba Cameroon 38 5.13N 13.05E
Wowoni i. Indonesia 27 4.10S123.10E
Wragby U.K. 4 53.17N 0.18E
Wrangel I. see Vrangelya, Ostrov i. Russian Fed. 21
Wrangell U.S.A. 50 56.28N132.23W
Wrangell Mts. U.S.A. 50 62.00N143.00W
Wrangle U.K. 4 53.03N 0.09E
Wrath, C. U.K. 6 58.37N 5.01W
Wrexham U.K. 4 53.05N 3.00W
Wrigley Canada 50 63.16N123.39W
Wrocław Poland 15 51.05N 17.00E
Wronki Poland 14 52.43N 16.23E
Września Poland 15 52.20N 17.34E
Wubin Australia 43 30.06S116.38E
Wuchang China 25 30.32N114.18E
Wudham 'Alwā' Oman 31 23.48N 57.33E
Wudinna Australia 46 33.03S135.28E
Wuhan China 25 30.35N114.19E
Wuhu China 25 31.23N118.25E
Wu Jiang r. China 24 30.10N107.26E
Wukari Nigeria 38 7.57N 9.42E
Wuliang Shan mts. China 24 24.27N100.43E
Wum Cameroon 38 6.25N 10.03E
Wumbulgal Australia 47 34.25S146.16E
Wuppertal Germany 8 51.15N 7.10E
Wuppertal R.S.A. 39 32.16S 19.12E
Wurno Nigeria 38 13.20N 5.28E
Würzburg Germany 14 49.48N 9.57E
Wutongqiao China 24 29.21N103.48E
Wuwei China 24 38.00N102.54E
Wuxi Jiangsu China 25 31.35N120.19E
Wuzhan China 25 50.14N125.18E
Wuzhou China 25 23.30N111.21E
Wyalkatchem Australia 43 31.21S117.22E
Wyalong Australia 47 33.55S147.17E
Wyandotte U.S.A. 55 42.11N 83.10W
Wyandra Australia 45 27.15S146.00E
Wyangala Resr. Australia 47 33.58S148.55E
Wyara, L. Australia 46 28.42S144.16E
Wycheproof Australia 46 36.04S143.14E
Wye U.K. 5 51.11N 0.56E
Wye r. U.K. 5 51.37N 2.40W
Wymondham U.K. 5 52.34N 1.07E
Wynbring Australia 45 30.33S133.32E
Wyndham Australia 42 15.29S128.05E
Wyoming d. U.S.A. 52 43.10N107.36W
Wyong Australia 47 33.17S151.25E
Wyszków Poland 15 52.36N 21.28E

X

Xainza China 24 30.56N 88.38E
Xai-Xai Mozambique 39 25.05S 33.38E
Xam Nua Laos 29 20.25N104.04E
Xangongo Angola 36 16.43S 15.01E
Xanten Germany 8 51.40N 6.29E
Xánthi Greece 13 41.07N 24.55E
Xau, L. Botswana 39 21.15S 24.50E
Xenia U.S.A. 55 39.41N 83.56W
Xhora R.S.A. 39 31.58S 28.40E
Xiaguan see Dali China 24
Xiamen China 25 24.26N118.07E
Xi'an China 25 34.16N108.54E
Xiangfan China 25 32.20N112.05E
Xiangkhoang Laos 29 19.11N103.23E
Xiangtan China 25 27.55N112.47E
Xiangyin China 25 28.40N112.53E
Xianyang China 25 34.23N108.40E
Xiao Hinggan Ling mts. China 25 48.40N128.30E
Xichang China 24 27.53N102.18E
Xigazê China 24 29.18N 88.50E
Xi Jiang r. China 25 22.23N113.20E
Xilin China 29 24.30N105.03E
Ximeng China 29 22.45N 99.29E
Xinfeng Jiangxi China 25 25.27N114.58E
Xing'an China 25 25.37N110.40E
Xingkai Hu l. see Khanka, Ozero China/Russian Fed. 25
Xingtai China 25 37.08N114.29E
Xingu r. Brazil 61 1.40S 52.15W
Xinhe Xin. Uygur China 24 41.34N 82.38E
Xining China 24 36.35N101.55E
Xinjiang Uygur Zizhiqu d. China 24 41.15N 87.00E
Xinjin Liaoning China 25 39.25N121.58E
Xin Xian China 25 38.24N112.47E
Xinxiang China 25 35.16N113.51E
Xinyu China 25 27.48N114.56E
Xinzhu Taiwan 25 24.48N120.59E
Xique Xique Brazil 61 10.47S 42.44W
Xixabangma Feng mtn. China 29 28.21N 85.47E
Xizang Zizhiqu d. China 29 32.20N 86.00E
Xorkol China 24 39.04N 91.05E
Xuanhua China 25 40.36N115.01E
Xuchang China 25 34.03N113.48E
Xueshuiwen China 25 49.15N129.39E
Xugou China 25 34.42N119.28E
Xuyong China 24 28.10N105.24E
Xuzhou China 25 34.17N117.18E

Y

Ya'an China 29 30.00N102.59E
Yaapeet Australia 46 35.48S142.07E
Yabassi Cameroon 38 4.30N 9.55E
Yablonovyy Khrebet mts. Russian Fed. 21 53.20N115.00E
Yabrūd Syria 32 33.58N 36.40E
Yacheng China 25 18.30N109.12E
Yacuiba Bolivia 62 22.00S 63.25W
Yādgīr India 28 16.46N 77.08E
Yagaba Ghana 38 10.13N 1.14W
Yagoua Cameroon 38 10.23N 15.13E
Yahagi r. Japan 23 34.50N136.59E
Yaizu Japan 23 34.52N138.20E
Yajua Nigeria 38 11.27N 12.49E
Yakima U.S.A. 54 46.36N120.31W
Yaksha Russian Fed. 18 61.51N 56.59E
Yakutat U.S.A. 50 59.33N139.44W
Yakutsk Russian Fed. 21 62.10N129.20E
Yala Thailand 29 6.32N101.19E
Yalgoo Australia 43 28.20S116.41E
Yalinga C.A.R. 35 6.31N 23.15E
Yallourn Australia 47 38.09S146.22E
Yalong Jiang r. China 24 26.35N101.44E
Yalta Ukraine 19 44.30N 34.09E
Yalutorovsk Russian Fed. 20 56.41N 66.12E
Yamal, Poluostrov pen. Russian Fed. 20 70.20N 70.00E
Yamanashi Japan 23 35.40N138.40E
Yamanashi d. Japan 23 35.30N138.35E
Yaman Tau mtn. Russian Fed. 19 54.20N 58.10E
Yamato Japan 23 35.29N139.29E
Yamato-takada Japan 23 34.31N135.45E
Yamba N.S.W. Australia 47 29.26S153.22E
Yamba S.A. Australia 46 34.15S140.54E
Yambio Sudan 35 4.34N 28.23E
Yambol Bulgaria 13 42.28N 26.30E
Yamdena i. Indonesia 27 7.30S131.00E
Yamethin Burma 29 20.24N 96.08E
Yam Kinneret l. Israel 32 32.49N 35.36E
Yamma Yamma, L. Australia 44 26.20S141.25E
Yamoussoukro Ivory Coast 38 6.51N 5.18W
Yampi Sound Australia 42 16.11S123.30E
Yampol Ukraine 15 48.13N 28.12E
Yamuna r. India 29 25.20N 81.49E
Yan Nigeria 38 10.05N 12.11E
Yana r. Russian Fed. 21 71.30N135.00E
Yanac Australia 46 36.09S141.29E
Yanbu'al Baḩr Saudi Arabia 30 24.07N 38.04E
Yancannia Australia 46 30.16S142.50E
Yancheng China 25 33.23N120.10E
Yanchep Australia 43 31.32S115.33E
Yanchuan China 25 36.55N110.04E
Yanco Australia 47 34.36S146.25E
Yanco Glen town Australia 46 31.43S141.39E
Yanda r. Australia 47 30.22S145.38E
Yangarey Russian Fed. 18 68.46N 61.29E
Yangjiang China 25 21.51N111.58E
Yangon Burma 29 16.45N 96.20E
Yangquan China 25 37.52N113.29E
Yangtze r. see Chang Jiang r. China 25
Yanji China 25 42.45N129.25E
Yanko Creek r. Australia 47 35.25S145.27E
Yanqi China 24 42.00N 86.30E
Yanshan China 29 23.36N104.20E
Yanskiy Zaliv g. Russian Fed. 21 72.00N136.10E
Yantabulla Australia 47 29.13S145.01E
Yantai China 25 37.30N121.22E
Yao Chad 34 12.52N 17.34E
Yao Japan 23 34.37N135.36E
Yaoundé Cameroon 38 3.51N 11.31E
Yap i. Federated States of Micronesia 27 9.30N138.09E
Yapen i. Indonesia 27 1.45S136.10E
Yaqui r. Mexico 56 27.37N110.39W
Yar Russian Fed. 18 58.13N 52.08E
Yaraka Australia 44 24.53S144.04E
Yaransk Russian Fed. 18 57.22N 47.49E
Yardea Australia 46 32.23S135.32E
Yare r. U.K. 5 52.34N 1.45E
Yaremcha Ukraine 15 48.26N 24.29E
Yarensk Russian Fed. 18 62.10N 49.07E
Yargora Moldavia 15 46.25N 28.20E
Yaritagua Venezuela 60 10.05N 69.07W
Yarkant He r. China 24 40.30N 80.55E
Yarlung Zangbo Jiang r. China see Brahmaputra r. Asia 29
Yarmouth Canada 55 43.50N 66.08W
Yaroslavl Russian Fed. 18 57.34N 39.52E
Yarra r. Australia 47 37.51S144.54E
Yarram Australia 47 38.30S146.41E
Yarrawonga Australia 47 36.02S145.59E
Yarrow r. U.K. 6 55.32N 2.51W
Yar Sale Russian Fed. 20 66.50N 70.48E
Yartsevo Russian Fed. 21 60.17N 90.02E
Yartsevo Russian Fed. 18 55.06N 32.43E
Yarumal Colombia 60 6.59N 75.25W
Yaselda r. Belorussia 15 52.07N 26.28E
Yasen Belorussia 15 53.10N 28.55E
Yashi Nigeria 38 12.23N 7.54E
Yashkul Russian Fed. 19 46.10N 45.20E
Yasinya Ukraine 15 48.12N 24.20E
Yasothon Thailand 29 15.46N104.12E
Yass Australia 47 34.51S148.55E
Yatakala Niger 38 14.52N 0.22E
Yaví, Cerro mtn. Venezuela 60 5.32N 65.59W
Yavorov Ukraine 15 49.59N 23.20E
Ya Xian see Sanya China 25
Yazd Iran 31 31.54N 54.22E
Ybbs Austria 14 48.11N 15.05E
Ye Burma 29 15.15N 97.50E
Yea Australia 47 37.12S145.25E
Yecla Spain 10 38.35N 1.05W

Yedintsy Moldavia 19 48.09N 27.18E
Yeeda Australia 42 17.36S123.39E
Yefremov Russian Fed. 18 53.08N 38.08E
Yegorlyk r. Russian Fed. 19 46.30N 41.52E
Yegoryevsk Russian Fed. 18 55.21N 39.01E
Yegros Paraguay 59 26.24S 56.25W
Yei Sudan 35 4.05N 30.40E
Yei r. Sudan 35 7.40N 30.13E
Yekaterinburg Russian Fed. 18 56.52N 60.35E
Yelets Russian Fed. 18 52.36N 38.30E
Yeletskiy Russian Fed. 18 67.04N 64.00E
Yell i. U.K. 6 60.35N 1.05W
Yellowdine Australia 43 31.19S119.06E
Yellowhead Pass Canada 50 52.53N118.28W
Yellowknife Canada 50 62.30N 114.29W
Yellow Mt. Australia 47 32.19S146.50E
Yellowstone r. U.S.A. 52 47.55N103.45W
Yellowstone r. U.S.A. 54 46.58N103.59W
Yellowstone L. U.S.A. 54 44.25N110.38W
Yellowstone Nat. Park U.S.A. 54
 44.30N110.35W
Yell Sd. U.K. 6 60.30N 1.11W
Yelma Australia 42 26.30S121.40E
Yelsk Belorussia 15 51.50N 29.10E
Yelwa Nigeria 38 10.48N 4.42E
Yemen Asia 35 14.20N 45.50E
Yemilchino Ukraine 15 50.58N 27.40E
Yenagoa Nigeria 38 4.59N 6.15E
Yenda Australia 47 34.15S146.13E
Yendi Ghana 38 9.29N 0.01W
Yenisey r. Russian Fed. 21 69.00N 86.00E
Yeniseysk Russian Fed. 21 58.27N 92.13E
Yeniseyskiy Zaliv g. Russian Fed. 20 73.00N
 79.00E
Yenyuka Russian Fed. 21 57.57N121.15E
Yeo L. Australia 43 28.04S124.23E
Yeoval Australia 47 32.44S148.39E
Yeovil U.K. 5 50.57N 2.38W
Yeppoon Australia 44 23.08S150.45E
Yerbent Turkmenistan 31 39.23N 58.35E
Yercha Russian Fed. 21 69.34N147.30E
Yerda Australia 46 31.05S135.04E
Yerepol Russian Fed. 21 65.15N168.43E
Yerevan Armenia 31 40.10N 44.31E
Yerington U.S.A. 54 38.59N119.10W
Yermak Kazakhstan 20 52.03N 76.55E
Yermitsa Russian Fed. 18 66.56N 52.20E
Yermo U.S.A. 54 34.54N116.50W
Yershov Russian Fed. 19 51.22N 48.16E
Yertom Russian Fed. 18 63.31N 47.51E
Yerushalayim Israel / Jordan 32 31.47N 35.13E
Yeşil r. Turkey 30 41.22N 36.37E
Yessey Russian Fed. 21 68.29N102.15E
Yetman Australia 47 28.55S150.49E
Yeu Burma 29 22.49N 95.26E
Yeu, Île d' i. France 11 46.43N 2.20W
Yevpatoriya Ukraine 19 45.12N 33.20E
Yevstratovskiy Russian Fed. 19 50.07N 39.45E
Yeysk Russian Fed. 19 46.43N 38.17E
Yi r. Uruguay 63 33.17S 58.08W
Yiannitsá Greece 13 40.48N 22.25E
Yibin China 24 28.50N104.35E
Yichang China 25 30.43N111.22E
Yilan China 25 46.22N129.31E
Yilehuli Shan mts. China 25 51.20N124.20E
Yilliminning Australia 43 32.54S117.22E
Yinchuan China 24 38.30N106.19E
Yindarlgooda, L. Australia 43 30.45S121.55E
Yingde China 25 24.20N113.20E
Yingkou China 25 40.40N122.17E
Yingtan China 25 28.14N117.00E
Yinkanie Australia 46 34.21S140.20E
Yinning China 24 43.57N 81.23E
Yíthion Greece 13 36.46N 22.34E
Yiyang Hunan China 25 28.36N112.20E
Ylitornio Finland 16 66.19N 23.40E

Ylivieska Finland 16 64.05N 24.33E
Yobe d. Nigeria 38 12.30N 11.45E
Yodo r. Japan 23 34.41N135.25E
Yogyakarta Indonesia 26 7.48S110.24E
Yokadouma Cameroon 38 3.26N 15.06E
Yokkaichi Japan 23 34.58N136.37E
Yoko Cameroon 38 5.29N 12.19E
Yokohama Japan 23 35.27N139.39E
Yokosuka Japan 23 35.18N139.40E
Yola Nigeria 38 9.14N 12.32E
Yongxiu China 25 29.03N115.49E
Yonkers U.S.A. 55 40.56N 73.54W
Yonne d. France 9 47.55N 3.45E
Yonne r. France 9 48.22N 2.57E
York Australia 43 31.55S 116.45E
York U.K. 4 53.58N 1.07W
York Penn. U.S.A. 55 39.58N 76.44W
York, C. Australia 44 10.42S142.31E
Yorke Pen. Australia 46 35.00S137.30E
Yorketown Australia 46 35.02S137.35E
York Factory town Canada 51 57.08N 92.25W
Yorkshire Wolds hills U.K. 4 54.00N 0.39W
Yorkton Canada 50 51.12N102.29W
Yoro Honduras 57 15.09N 87.07W
Yörö Japan 23 35.32N140.04E
Yosemite Nat. Park U.S.A. 54 37.45N119.35W
Yoshino r. Japan 23 34.22N135.40E
Yoshkar Ola Russian Fed. 18 56.38N 47.52E
Yos Sudarsa, Pulau i. Indonesia 27
 8.00S138.30E
Yŏsu S. Korea 25 34.46N127.45E
Youghal Rep. of Ire. 7 51.58N 7.51W
You Jiang r. Guang. Zhuang. China 25
 23.25N110.00E
Young r. Australia 47 34.19S148.20E
Young r. Australia 43 33.45S121.12E
Young Uruguay 63 32.41S 57.38W
Young U.S.A. 54 34.06N110.57W
Younghusband, L. Australia 46 30.51S136.05E
Younghusband Pen. Australia 46 36.00S139.15E
Youngstown U.S.A. 55 41.05N 80.40W
Yoxford U.K. 5 52.16N 1.30E
Yozgat Turkey 30 39.50N 34.48E
Yreka U.S.A. 54 41.44N122.38W
Ystad Sweden 17 55.25N 13.49E
Ythan r. U.K. 6 57.21N 2.01W
Yuba City U.S.A. 54 39.08N121.27W
Yucatán d. Mexico 57 19.30N 89.00W
Yucatan Channel Carib. Sea 57 21.30N 86.00W
Yucatan Pen. Mexico 56 19.00N 90.00W
Yucca U.S.A. 54 34.52N114.09W
Yuci China 25 37.40N112.44E
Yudino Russian Fed. 20 55.05N 67.55E
Yuendumu Australia 44 22.14S131.47E
Yuexi China 24 28.36N102.35E
Yugorskiy Poluostrov pen. Russian Fed. 18
 69.00N 62.30E
Yugoslavia Europe 13 44.00N 20.00E
Yukon r. U.S.A. 50 62.35N164.20W
Yukon Territory d. Canada 50 65.00N135.00W
Yulara Australia 44 25.14S131.02E
Yule r. Australia 42 20.19S118.08E
Yuleba Australia 44 26.37S149.20E
Yuma Ariz. U.S.A. 54 32.43N114.37W
Yumen China 24 40.19N 97.12E
Yungas f. Bolivia 62 16.20S 65.00W
Yungera Australia 46 34.48S143.10E
Yunnan d. China 24 24.30N101.30E
Yunta Australia 46 32.37S139.34E
Yuribey Russian Fed. 20 71.02N 77.02E
Yurimaguas Peru 60 5.54S 76.07W

Yuryuzan Russian Fed. 18 54.51N 58.25E
Yushkozero Russian Fed. 18 64.45N 32.03E
Yushu China 24 33.06N 96.48E
Yūto Japan 23 34.42N137.38E
Yuzhno Sakhalinsk Russian Fed. 25
 46.58N142.45E
Yuzhnyy Bug r. Ukraine 15 46.55N 31.59E
Yvelines d. France 9 48.50N 1.50E
Yvetot France 9 49.37N 0.45E

Z

Zaandam Neth. 8 52.27N 4.49E
Zábol Iran 31 31.00N 61.32E
Záboli Iran 31 27.08N 61.36E
Zabrze Poland 15 50.18N 18.47E
Zacapa Guatemala 57 15.00N 89.30W
Zacatecas Mexico 56 22.48N102.33W
Zacatecas d. Mexico 56 24.00N103.00W
Zadar Croatia 12 44.08N 15.14E
Zafra Spain 10 38.25N 6.25W
Zagreb Croatia 12 45.49N 15.58E
Zagros, Kûhhā-ye mts. Iran 31 32.00N 51.00E
Zagros Mts. see Zāgros, Kûhhā-ye mts. Iran 31
Záhedān Iran 31 29.32N 60.54E
Zahlah Lebanon 32 33.50N 35.55E
Zaindeh r. Iran 31 32.40N 52.50E
Zaïre Africa 36 2.00S 22.00E
Zaïre r. Zaïre 36 6.00S 12.30E
Zaječar Yugo. 13 43.55N 22.15E
Zakataly Azerbaijan 31 41.39N 46.40E
Zákinthos i. Greece 13 37.46N 20.46E
Zakopane Poland 15 49.19N 19.57E
Zalaegerszeg Hungary 14 46.51N 16.51E
Zalău Romania 15 47.11N 23.03E
Zaleshchiki Ukraine 15 48.39N 25.50E
Zalim Saudi Arabia 30 22.41N 42.11E
Zambezi r. Mozambique / Zambia 36 18.15S
 35.55E
Zambezi Zambia 36 13.33S 23.09E
Zambezia d. Mozambique 37 16.30S 37.30E
Zambia Africa 36 14.00S 28.00E
Zamboanga Phil. 27 6.55N122.05E
Zambrów Poland 15 53.00N 22.15E
Zambue Mozambique 37 15.09S 30.47E
Zamfara r. Nigeria 38 12.04N 4.00E
Zamora Mexico 56 20.00N102.18W
Zamora Spain 10 41.30N 5.45W
Zamość Poland 15 50.43N 23.15E
Zamtang China 29 32.26N101.06E
Zaña Peru 60 7.00S 79.30W
Záncara r. Spain 10 39.18N 3.18W
Zanda China 29 31.32N 79.50E
Zanesville U.S.A. 55 39.55N 82.02W
Zanjān Iran 31 36.40N 48.30E
Zanthus Australia 43 31.02S123.34E
Zanzibar Tanzania 37 6.10S 39.16E
Zanzibar I. Tanzania 37 6.00S 39.20E
Zaozhuang China 25 34.40N117.30E
Zapadno-Sibirskaya Ravnina f. Russian Fed. 20
 60.00N 75.00E
Zapadnyy Sayan mts. Russian Fed. 21 53.00N
 92.00E
Zapala Argentina 63 38.55S 70.05W
Zaporozhye Ukraine 19 47.50N 35.10E
Zara Turkey 30 39.55N 37.44E
Zaragoza Spain 10 41.39N 0.54W
Zarand Iran 31 30.50N 56.35E
Zárate Argentina 63 34.05S 59.02W
Zaraza Venezuela 60 9.23N 65.20W
Zard Kūh mtn. Iran 31 32.21N 50.04E
Zarghūn Shahr Afghan. 28 32.51N 68.25E
Zari Nigeria 38 13.03N 12.46E
Zaria Nigeria 38 11.01N 7.44E
Zaruma Ecuador 60 3.40S 79.30W
Zary Poland 14 51.40N 15.10E

Zarzal Colombia 60 4.24N 76.01W
Zaslavl Belorussia 15 54.00N 27.15E
Zatishye Ukraine 15 47.20N 29.58E
Zave Zimbabwe 37 17.14S 30.02E
Zavitinsk Russian Fed. 25 50.08N129.24E
Záwiyat al Amwât Egypt 32 28.04N 30.50E
Zäyandeh r. Iran 31 32.40N 52.50E
Zaysan Kazakhstan 24 47.30N 84.57E
Zaysan, Ozero l. Kazakhstan 24 48.00N 83.30E
Zbarazh Ukraine 15 49.40N 25.49E
Zborov Ukraine 15 49.40N 25.09E
Zdolbunov Ukraine 15 50.30N 26.10E
Zduńska Wola Poland 15 51.36N 18.57E
Zebediela R.S.A. 39 24.19S 29.17E
Zeebrugge Belgium 8 51.20N 3.13E
Zeehan Australia 45 41.55S145.21E
Zeeland d. Neth. 8 51.30N 3.45E
Zeerust R.S.A. 39 25.32S 26.04E
Zefa' Israel 32 31.07N 35.12E
Zefat Israel 32 32.57N 35.27E
Zeist Neth. 8 52.03N 5.16E
Zeitz Germany 14 51.03N 12.08E
Zelechów Poland 15 51.49N 21.54E
Zelenodolsk Russian Fed. 18 55.50N 48.30E
Zelenogorsk Russian Fed. 18 60.15N 29.31E
Zelenokumsk Russian Fed. 19 44.25N 43.54E
Zelentsovo Russian Fed. 18 59.51N 44.59E
Zell Germany 8 50.02N 7.11E
Zelts Ukraine 15 46.38N 30.00E
Zelzate Belgium 8 51.12N 3.49E
Zemio C.A.R. 35 5.00N 25.08E
Zemun Yugo. 13 44.51N 20.23E
Zenica Bosnia-Herzegovina 15 44.12N 17.55E
Zenne r. Belgium 8 51.04N 4.25E
Zetel Germany 8 53.28N 7.57E
Zeven Germany 14 53.18N 9.16E
Zevenaar Neth. 8 51.57N 6.04E
Zevenbergen Neth. 8 51.41N 4.42E
Zeya Russian Fed. 21 53.48N127.14E
Zeya r. Russian Fed. 21 50.20N127.30E
Zêzere r. Portugal 10 39.28N 8.20W
Zgierz Poland 15 51.52N 19.25E
Zgorzelec Poland 14 51.12N 15.01E
Zhailma Kazakhstan 20 51.37N 61.33E
Zhanatas Kazakhstan 24 43.11N 69.35E
Zhanghua Taiwan 24 24.05N120.31E
Zhangjiakou China 25 41.00N114.50E
Zhangye China 24 38.56N100.27E
Zhangzhou China 25 24.57N118.36E
Zhanjiang China 25 21.05N110.12E
Zhashkov Ukraine 15 49.12N 30.05E
Zhejiang d. China 25 29.15N120.00E
Zheleznodorozhnyy Russian Fed. 18 62.39N
 50.59E
Zheleznodorozhnyy Russian Fed. 18 67.59N
 64.47E
Zhengzhou China 25 34.35N113.38E
Zhenjiang China 25 32.05N119.30E
Zherdnoye Belorussia 15 51.40N 30.11E
Zhigansk Russian Fed. 21 66.48N123.27E
Zhitkovichi Belorussia 15 52.12N 27.49E
Zhitomir Ukraine 15 50.18N 28.40E
Zhlobin Belorussia 15 52.50N 30.00E
Zhmerinka Ukraine 15 49.00N 28.02E
Zhob r. Pakistan 28 31.40N 70.54E
Zhongba China 29 29.56N 84.20E
Zhongdian China 29 28.00N 99.30E
Zhupanovo Russian Fed. 21 53.40N159.52E
Zhuzhou China 25 27.53N113.07E
Ziar nad Hronom Slovakia 15 48.36N 18.52E
Zibo China 25 36.50N118.00E
Ziel, Mt. Australia 42 23.24S132.23E
Zielona Góra Poland 14 51.57N 15.30E
Ziftâ Egypt 32 30.43N 31.14E
Zigong China 29 29.18N104.45E

Zile Turkey 30 40.18N 35.52E
Žilina Slovakia 15 49.14N 18.46E
Zillah Libya 34 28.33N 17.35E
Zima Russian Fed. 21 53.58N102.02E
Zimatlán Mexico 56 16.52N 96.45W
Zimba Zambia 39 17.19S 26.12E
Zimbabwe Africa 36 18.55S 30.00E
Zimbor Romania 15 47.00N 23.16E
Zimnicea Romania 15 43.38N 25.22E
Zimniy Bereg f. Russian Fed. 18 65.50N 41.30E
Zinder Niger 38 13.46N 8.58E
Zinder d. Niger 38 14.20N 9.30E
Zinga Mtwara Tanzania 37 9.01S 38.47E
Ziniaré Burkina 38 12.34N 1.12W
Ziro India 29 27.38N 93.42E
Zitundo Mozambique 39 26.45S 32.49E
Ziway Hāyk' l. Ethiopia 35 8.00N 38.50E
Zlatograd Bulgaria 13 41.23N 25.06E
Zlatoust Russian Fed. 18 55.10N 59.38E
Zlín Czech Republic 15 49.13N 17.41E
Zloczew Poland 15 51.25N 18.36E
Złotów Poland 15 53.22N 17.02E
Zlynka Russian Fed. 15 52.24N 31.45E
Zmeinogorsk Russian Fed. 20 51.11N 82.14E
Zmiyevka Russian Fed. 18 52.40N 36.22E
Znamenka Ukraine 19 48.42N 32.40E
Znin Poland 15 52.52N 17.43E
Znojmo Czech Republic 14 48.52N 16.05E
Zobia Zaïre 36 3.07N 25.56E
Zobue Mozambique 37 15.35S 34.26E
Zoétélé Cameroon 38 3.17N 11.54E
Zogno Italy 9 45.48N 9.40E
Zohreh r. Iran 31 30.04N 49.32E
Zolochev Ukraine 15 49.48N 24.51E
Zolotonosha Ukraine 15 49.39N 32.05E
Zomba Malawi 37 15.22S 35.22E
Zonguldak Turkey 30 41.26N 31.47E
Zorritos Peru 60 3.50S 80.40W
Zouar Chad 34 20.27N 16.32E
Zoutkamp Neth. 8 53.21N 6.18E
Zrenjanin Yugo. 13 45.22N 20.23E
Zuénoula Ivory Coast 38 7.34N 6.03W
Zug Switz. 14 47.10N 8.31E
Zuid Beveland f. Neth. 8 51.30N 3.50E
Zuidelijk-Flevoland f. Neth. 8 52.22N 5.22E
Zuid Holland d. Neth. 8 52.00N 4.30E
Zuidhorn Neth. 8 53.16N 6.25E
Zújar r. Spain 10 38.58N 5.40W
Zújar, Embalse del resr. Spain 10 38.57N 5.30W
Zülpich Germany 8 50.42N 6.36E
Zululand see Kwa Zulu f. R.S.A. 39
Zumbo Mozambique 37 15.36S 30.24E
Zungeru Nigeria 38 9.48N 6.03E
Zunyi China 29 27.41N106.50E
Zurich Neth. 8 53.08N 5.25E
Zürich Switz. 14 47.23N 8.33E
Zuru Nigeria 38 11.26N 5.16E
Zushi Japan 23 35.18N139.35E
Zutphen Neth. 8 52.08N 6.12E
Zuwārah Libya 34 32.56N 12.06E
Zvenigorodka Ukraine 15 49.05N 30.58E
Zverinogolovskoye Kazakhstan 20 54.23N
 64.47E
Zvishavane Zimbabwe 39 20.20S 30.05E
Zvolen Slovakia 15 48.35N 19.08E
Zwettl Austria 14 48.37N 15.10E
Zwickau Germany 14 50.43N 12.30E
Zwischenahn Germany 8 53.13N 7.59E
Zwoleń Poland 15 51.22N 21.35E
Zwolle Neth. 8 52.31N 6.06E
Zyryanovsk Kazakhstan 20 49.45N 84.16E
Żywiec Poland 15 49.41N 19.12E

112